JAMES HALLIDAY

WINE ATLAS

OF AUSTRALIA
AND
NEW ZEALAND

JAMES HALLIDAY

WINE ATLAS

OF AUSTRALIA
AND
NEW ZEALAND

ANGUS
& ROBERTSON

An imprint of HarperCollins*Publishers*

First published in 1991 by
HarperCollins Publishers,
77-85 Fulham Palace Road,
Hammersmith, London W6 8JB

First published in Australia in 1991 by
CollinsAngus&Robertson Publishers Pty Limited (ACN 009 913 517)
A division of HarperCollins Publishers (Australia) Pty Limited
Unit 4, Eden Park, 31 Waterloo Road, North Ryde NSW 2113, Australia

William Collins Publishers Ltd
31 View Road, Glenfield, Auckland 10, New Zealand
9 8 7 6 5 4 3 2 1

British Library Cataloguing-in-Publication Data
A CIP catalogue record for this book
is available from the British Library

ISBN 0 207 16476 2.

Printed in Australia by Griffin Press

ACKNOWLEDGMENTS

This book would not have been possible were it not for the unfailing hospitality of the Australasian wine industry extended to me over the past 35 years. Since my first visit to the Hunter Valley in New South Wales in the second half of the 1950s I have been made welcome no matter how inconvenient the timing of my arrival may have been. Equally importantly, at the winery floor level there is a complete openness and frankness: ask a question, and you will be given an answer. (It is true that the large wine companies tend to be somewhat secretive about production and sales, but even here information is easier to come by than it once was.)

What is more, wine books continue to proliferate, and as the chief executive of a small winery, I know only too well how many requests for information, labels and forms each winery receives. This book gave rise to yet more requests, and I and my publisher are truly grateful for the tremendous co-operation we received from the winemakers of Australasia.

Many others helped. Dr Grahame Gregory, Peter Hayes, John Elliott, Dany Schuster, Geoff Kelly, the Wine Institute of New Zealand, the Australian Wine and Brandy Corporation and local vignerons' associations all provided essential statistical and other information willingly and cheerfully. Numerous friends and winemakers knowingly or unknowingly provided missing details: to them my thanks.

Two authors unknowingly helped: Michael Cooper and Bob Campbell. While I have visited New Zealand many times (and thrice in 1990), seen most of its wineries and tasted and retasted its wines on countless occasions, I found Cooper's *The Wines and Vineyards of New Zealand* (Hodder & Stoughton, 1988) an invaluable reference work and strongly recommend it to anyone wishing to know more about New Zealand wine. Bob Campbell is both author and friend, and more importantly New Zealand's second Master of Wine. He was principal author and editor of "New Zealand Wine 1990", an excellent magazine format guide to New Zealand wine published by *Cuisine,* a wine and food magazine distributed in both New Zealand and Australia.

But to Dr Richard Smart I owe an especial debt. He spent considerable time in reading that part of the manuscript which deals in detail with climate, viticulture and soils, and made numerous constructive suggestions. I am sure that he will not agree with everything I have finally written, and equally sure that he might well have placed a very different emphasis on some of the material. But his input was considerable, and in particular he collated the material in the table 'Climate — A Comparison of Regions in Australasia and France', which appears on page 30.

Next, my thanks to Oliver Strewe and George Seper, whose brilliantly evocative photography has contributed so much to what I believe is a beautiful book. Thanks, too, to Prudential-Bache Securities (Australia) Limited for giving their support to this project. And finally of course there has been the team at Collins/Angus and Robertson, led by Kim Anderson. The logistics in organising a work such as this — and above all else in getting the maps and graphs right — are extremely complicated. If there were an unlimited budget and unlimited time, it would not be so difficult: in fact there is never enough of either, and the team worked unremittingly and without complaint. Beyond all others, my thanks and gratitude to you.

CONTENTS

WINE REGIONS OF AUSTRALIA

NORTHERN

WESTERN AUSTRALIA

SOUTH

KEY TO REGIONS

1. Lower Hunter Valley
2. Upper Hunter Valley
3. Mudgee
4. Murrumbidgee Irrigation Area
5. Bendigo
6. Central Goulburn Valley
7. Geelong
8. Great Western
9. Macedon
10. Mornington Peninsula
11. Murray River
12. North Goulburn River
13. North-eastern Victoria
14. Pyrenees
15. Southern and Central Victoria
16. Yarra Valley
17. Adelaide Hills
18. Adelaide and Surrounds
19. Barossa Valley
20. Clare Valley
21. Coonawarra
22. Padthaway
23. Southern Vales
24. Lower Great Southern Region
25. Margaret River
26. Perth Hills
27. South-west Coastal Plain
28. Swan Valley
29. Canberra District
30. Granite Belt
31. Northern Tasmania
32. Southern Tasmania

Perth
28
26
27
25
24

TERRITORY

QUEENSLAND

AUSTRALIA

NEW SOUTH WALES

Brisbane •

30

Sydney •

2

3

1

20

19

18

18

17

Adelaide •

11

4

VICTORIA

ACT

29

12

5

14

13

8

6

22

9

16

21

7

Melbourne

15

10

TASMANIA

31 Launceston •

32 Hobart •

WINE REGIONS OF
NEW ZEALAND

Auckland • □ 1

NORTH ISLAND

□ 3

□ 2

□ 5
Wellington •
□ 6
□ 4

SOUTH ISLAND

• 7
Christchurch

□ 8

KEY TO REGIONS

1. Auckland Area
2. Hawke's Bay
3. Gisborne/Poverty Bay
4. Wairarapa/Martinborough
5. Nelson
6. Marlborough
7. Canterbury
8. Central Otago

HOW TO USE THIS BOOK

I have endeavoured to present as much new material as possible in this book, and to constantly remember that it is an atlas. But geography is not a narrow subject confined to mountains, plains, rivers and seas, it is also the study both of the physical world and of man's interaction with it, and of the evolution both of that world and that interaction. It therefore looks at the past, the present and the future: one of the major concerns of our time is land degradation and climatic change, and these are at the heart of the geographer's domain.

That geography is a dynamic and ever changing subject is reinforced by this book's most basic division, which is by geographical area. Twenty-two years ago a considerable number of these areas simply did not exist as wine regions, and in another 20 years the boundaries of many of these wine regions will be quite different, while others will have come into existence. As the introductions to each region indicate, many of the changes — in particular the emergence of 'new' regions — do no more than recreate the nineteenth century viticultural map. This is particularly true of the cooler areas of southern Australia which are enjoying a marked renaissance, and which point the way for the future.

The wine regions are grouped by State or Territory (for Australia) and by North or South Island (for New Zealand) and each State, Territory and Island has an introductory chapter. In reading each regional chapter you will find data on climate, soil, grape varieties, wine styles and wineries. All these subjects (except the wineries) are also discussed in the introductory chapters, and I strongly recommend you read those introductory chapters before moving on to the region-by-region, winery-by-winery discussion.

Inevitably, much attention will be focused on the winery ratings. Constructing these, and ascribing the individual ratings, caused me much concern. Other books published over the past few years have tended to be very conservative in their ratings, according no wineries a maximum rating (whether by stars, numbers or whatever system is used) and only a very few near-maximum ratings. I have taken the view that this is a book about actual Australian and New Zealand wineries, which are to be judged as they are, and not against either some abstract theory of perfection or against the first growth chateaux of Bordeaux or the great vineyards of Burgundy. So I have not hesitated to give maximum (A-A) ratings, and have quite deliberately erred on the side of generosity. Apart from stirring up controversy, what is the point of selecting, say, three out of 600 wineries for A-A status?

Further, in looking at the quality side of the rating, I have taken the view that where a winery produces a range of products from low to high price, I am entitled to look at the relative quality within each level and judge it against wines of similar status from other makers. If I did not do that, no large winery in the land would be entitled to an A rating for quality, only small wineries producing, say, three or four wines of equal (high) quality and price would be so entitled.

In the manner of wine shows — notwithstanding that the real difference between a gold and a silver medal can be one-third of a point (out of 20), with gold, silver or bronze medals commonly given at different shows to the same wine — all of the attention will be given to the gold medals, in other words, the A-A ratings. But I urge you to realise there is only the finest distinction between a BA-A rating (or an A-AB rating) and an A-A rating — and so on down the scale. And please remember, too, that a B-B rating indicates the winery is producing good wines offered at a fair price.

The ratings are as follows:

	QUALITY		PRICE
A	Very good to outstanding	A	Very well priced
B	Good	B	Fairly priced
C	Adequate commercial wine	C	Borderline value
D	Variable or poor	D	Over-priced for quality
NR	Not rated		

Therefore a B-A rating indicates good wines which are very well priced.

Two letters linked in a rating (eg, CA) means one of two things: either that there is some real variation in the quality or value from wine to wine (within the terms of reference of each, or simply that the average falls somewhere between the level ascribed to each single letter rating. To try to avoid this ambiguity would have led to an impossibly complex rating scheme, and at the end of the day one has to accept the ratings as subjective and arbitrary, and as an imprecise guide at best.

You will see that the majority (though by no means all) of the featured wineries are rated B-B or better. I make no apology for this: they are, after all, in the top half of the 700 plus wineries in Australasia, and these are all making wines which stand proud on the world stage. Cultural cringe is a debilitating and unnecessary disease.

The vintage ratings and vintage guides should be treated with even greater caution. To the extended they are valid, that validity will be proved by the exceptions — individual wineries or individual wines which are better or worse than the rating suggests.

Finally, unless specific reference is made to 1990, all the statistics are for the 1989 vintage or financial year (as the case may be). The collection and dissemination of statistics is a leisurely affair, particularly in Australia.

GRAPE VARIETIES

CHARDONNAY

PRINCIPAL SYNONYMS
Pinot Chardonnay; Beaunois (Chablis); Pinot Blanc
(incorrect).
PLANTINGS
Australia, 3742ha 6.48 per cent of total
New Zealand, 486 ha 11.1 per cent of total

AUSTRALIA
It is little more than a statement of self-evident fact to point
out that plantings of Chardonnay have increased over the past
20 years at a greater rate than any other variety, and that this
rate of increase is projected to continue for some years at least.
It is no less trite to observe that Chardonnay is now
Australia's premium white wine grape variety, and, although a
few myopic observers would have it otherwise, it will
continue to retain that status for as long as wine is made in
this country.

There are three reasons for this: first, in world terms it is
regarded as the premium white wine grape. Secondly, it is an
immensely adaptable variety, producing well and providing
wines of distinctive varietal character in almost any
combination of climate and *terroir*. Thirdly, it is a wonderfully
malleable variety in the hands of the winemaker, responding
well to a wide range of making techniques, and even putting
up a measure of defence against incompetent or lazy
winemaking.

There is no question there has been an extended honey-
moon between producers on the one hand and consumers on
the other: love has blinded all concerned, and Chardonnay
has assumed a quite illogical status in terms of price and
profile. It became accepted that Chardonnay would bring

two, three or four times the price of all other grapes, and that
the price of the wine on the retail shelf would reflect that
differential. With the rapidly increasing supply, Chardonnay
will assume a more rational role: it will appear in casks, in
low-priced bottles and in high-priced bottles, in much the
same way as Cabernet Sauvignon. The interaction of climate,
terroir and winemaking philosophy and practice results in
Chardonnays of extraordinarily diverse styles being made,
but with a common thread of pure fruit, that hallmark of
Australian white wine making. Those from the leading warm
areas (Hunter Valley, Mudgee, Cowra, Southern Vales,
Barossa Valley, Clare Valley and selected parts of the
Riverland) are unctuously rich, creamy, peachy, mouthfilling
wines with a warm afterglow. Those from the cooler areas
(Southern and Highland Victoria, Padthaway, Coonawarra,
Tasmania, Margaret River and the Lower Great Southern
area) are much more delicate and restrained, with
citric/grapefruit flavours and length to the finish which
augurs well for their longevity.

NEW ZEALAND
The rate of increase of Chardonnay in New Zealand has been
every bit as dramatic as that of Australia. The variety made
its appearance more recently than in Australia, but has found
similar acceptance. The greater spread of climatic conditions
in New Zealand has, if it were possible, resulted in an even
wider range of style, from the exceedingly delicate, Chablis-
like wines from Marlborough and further south in the South
Island, through to the super opulent and heavily botrytis
influenced wines of Hawke's Bay north to Auckland. By
default, many New Zealand wineries situated around
Auckland (which received machine harvested fruit from
Hawke's Bay) have been forced into acceptance of a
reasonably heavy degree of skin contact which, when allied
with some botrytis, can produce disconcerting and to me not
terribly pleasant results. However, other winemakers
confronted with the same handling problems have produced
gloriously pure Chardonnays, and the quality of New
Zealand Chardonnay is growing in leaps and bounds.

RHINE RIESLING

PRINCIPAL SYNONYMS
In fact properly called Riesling, but in many countries — as
in Australia and New Zealand — a geographical rider is
added; synonyms include Johannesberg Riesling and White
Riesling (United States); Weisser Riesling (South Africa).
PLANTINGS
Australia, 3606 ha   6.25 per cent of total
New Zealand, 265 ha   6.06 per cent of total

AUSTRALIA

Until very recently, there were still more 750 millilitre bottles of Rhine Riesling sold than any other variety, white or red. The mere fact that Chardonnay has surpassed it in popularity does not mean the end of Rhine Riesling: indeed, as the figures show, its production is projected to significantly increase over the next few years. What is more, the rise in popularity in Chardonnay should not be taken as evidence of any want of character or quality in Australian Rhine Riesling. The reality is that it is of a very high quality, even if the style is not duplicated elsewhere.

Just as South Australia was for many years the focal point of winemaking in Australia, so it was the home of Rhine Riesling. In turn, the greatest Rhine Rieslings are widely accepted as coming from the Clare and Eden valleys. Each can lay claim to primacy, although their styles are subtly different. That of the Eden Valley shows pronounced lime juice aroma and flavour which peaks after 3 or 4 years in bottle, before developing the more complex aromas and flavours of fully mature Rhine Riesling. That of the Clare Valley is initially less opulently fruity, with a steely structure which can mask the passionfruit and lime flavours of the young wine, and which develops a characteristic toasty aroma and flavour as it matures.

Traditionally, considerable quantities of Rhine Riesling were also grown on the floor of the Barossa Valley, but Yalumba pioneered the move to the Adelaide Hills with its progressive establishment of Pewsey Vale, Heggies Vineyard and Hill Smith Estate. Riesling of the Barossa Valley floor makes a full flavoured style, but seldom one of the quality of the Adelaide Hills or Clare Valley. Similarly, Southern Vales

Rhine Riesling tends to be heavy, and certainly to lack the extraordinary longevity of the best wines of the Clare and Eden valleys. Despite its statistical importance in Coonawarra, it has proved a difficult variety for most of the major companies: only Wynns Coonawarra Estate seems to have mastered the variety.

Padthaway has been a far happier hunting ground for Lindemans, Thomas Hardy and Seppelt. Lindemans releases its Padthaway Rhine Riesling, while Thomas Hardy now sources almost all of its Siegersdorf Rhine Riesling from Padthaway. These are delicately fruity wines, and not infrequently show the effects of a lesser or greater degree of botrytis. Not surprisingly, the great botrytised Rieslings of South Australia come from Padthaway, with Thomas Hardy and Seppelt to the fore.

New South Wales is simply not a producer of quality Rhine Riesling, either in the premium regions or in the irrigation areas along the Murrumbidgee and Murray rivers. The South Australian Riverlands does produce one or two wines of good value, thanks largely to the efforts of Berri Renmano and Angove's, but one has to travel to the Lower Great Southern Region of Western Australia to again find Rieslings of comparable style and quality to South Australia's best. They certainly do exist here: the Lower Great Southern Region produces what are arguably the slowest developing and most tightly structured examples of all.

NEW ZEALAND

Rhine Riesling is a Cinderella variety which has really only come into its own in New Zealand over the past 5 years. It was certainly grown and produced prior to that time, but the wines altogether lacked the quality which is now commonplace.

Its principal home is the South Island, with by far the greatest plantings to be found in the Marlborough region. Here it produces finely structured, delicately fruity wines, closest in style to those of Coonawarra in South Australia. It is also grown in Gisborne and Hawke's Bay in the North Island, but seldom produces a wine of note from these districts. Reverting to the South Island, there are increasing plantings of Rhine Riesling around Christchurch, and small but important vineyards of the grape in Nelson. Botrytised styles can be produced in almost all growing regions, and although the total market for such wines is small, the quality potential is unlimited.

SEMILLON

PRINCIPAL SYNONYMS

Hunter River Riesling (Australia); Green grape (South Africa).

PLANTINGS

Australia, 2713 ha	4.7 per cent of total	
New Zealand, 129 ha	2.95 per cent of total	

Tyrrell's Wines and the Rothbury Estate all produce significant quantities, and some of the smaller wineries lend support. The Rothbury wines of the early 1970s, made as they were from young vines, suggest I may be excessively pessimistic in suggesting we will not again see the likes of those old Lindemans' wines.

In most of the rest of Australia Semillon performs much as it does elsewhere in the world (outside of Bordeaux). In other words, it produces a pleasant wine, usually dry, of no great distinction either when it is young or when it is old. There are, however, two exceptions: one is the botrytised Semillon (made in a Sauternes-style). Pioneered by De Bortoli Wines (Griffith), it is now copied by an increasing number of makers. The De Bortoli Wines are still unequalled in their luscious intensity, and have a virtual mortgage on wine show gold medals and trophies for this class of wine. The other exception is (increasingly) the Barossa Valley: Semillon has existed there for many decades, but in the 1980s received increasing recognition as a worthy alternative to Chardonnay, particularly when oak matured. The leader of this renaissance has been Basedows, where Douglas Lehmann has shown an uncanny ability in the use of American oak to produce a wholly seductive wine. Others have watched and learned, and Semillon increasingly comes into its own.

AUSTRALIA
If South Australia has been the home of Rhine Riesling, so the Hunter Valley has been the home of Semillon. Here it has produced a wine which has no correlative anywhere else in the world, but which nonetheless has generally been recognised as being of world class. The greatest of all were Lindemans' wines, which died an abrupt death in 1970: the old, low yielding vines from which the fabulously honeyed, toasty, mouthfilling wines of the 1950s and '60s were abandoned as subeconomic, and the production base shifted to much higher yielding vines at Fordwich. The magic lay almost entirely in the vineyard: this was no-frills winemaking, with oak playing no role at all. This fact astonishes those who taste 20-year-old Lindemans' white wines for the first time, for the toasty/nutty/honeyed characters are disconcertingly similar to oak-derived flavours in other white wines (notably Chardonnay).

The downside was (and is) that wines made in this fashion tend to be austere and rather featureless when young. The obvious answer has been the use of new oak, and it has to be admitted that the synergy achieved is not significantly different to that between Chardonnay and new oak. But it does produce a different style, and certainly adds force to the already apparent trend to early consumption. There are, as yet, no 20-year-old barrel fermented Semillons around to tell the tale, but I have great doubt whether they will achieve the magnificence of those old traditional styles.

Unwooded Semillons are still made, however: McWilliam's,

NEW ZEALAND
Presumably as a result of climate (although this is not an altogether convincing explanation) most of New Zealand's Semillon tastes like, and is usually blended with, Sauvignon Blanc. Its plantings are concentrated in the Gisborne area, with lesser quantities at Marlborough and around Auckland. Plantings are increasing, but by no means increasing dramatically, and there is as yet no evidence to suggest that it will become an important variety in its own right.

SAUVIGNON BLANC

PRINCIPAL SYNONYMS
None, other than the meaningless Fumé Blanc label in Australia and the United States.

PLANTINGS
Australia, 891 ha	1.54 per cent of total	
New Zealand, 343 ha	7.85 per cent of total	

AUSTRALIA
Sauvignon Blanc first made its appearance in the statistical records in Australia in the mid-1970s: in the 1977 vintage, a total of 674 tonnes were crushed across Australia. It has since been established in almost all wine growing districts, but has by and large failed to capture the imagination of either winemakers or consumers. Part of the problem stems from a lack of distinctive varietal character in the first place,

compounded in the second place by the confusion regarding the names Fumé Blanc and Sauvignon Blanc. In fact the former label has no legal meaning whatsoever, it simply indicates a dry white wine which has probably received some oak treatment but which can be (and often is) made from any grape variety the winemaker chooses, and not necessarily from Sauvignon Blanc. There are, indeed, those for whom this anonymity is a blessing: winemakers and consumers in this group find the assertive herbal/gooseberry character of Sauvignon Blanc quite offensive, and usually describe it in unflattering terms such as 'cat's pee'.

For those who enjoy the pungent cut of varietal Sauvignon Blanc (and I am one) the best examples in Australia regularly come from the Southern Vales and Padthaway (in South Australia). Southern Victoria and the Lower Great Southern region of Western Australia wait in the wings, and Katnook Estate (in Coonawarra, South Australia) has performed well from time to time. However, its indifferent performance in most other regions of Australia explain why production is not expected to increase in the near future.

NEW ZEALAND
Sauvignon Blanc is the variety which has put New Zealand on the world map. It produces significantly more Chardonnay and infinitely more Müller-Thurgau, but it has achieved recognition through Sauvignon Blanc. The most important plantings, both in terms of size and quality, are those of the Marlborough region, but there are also significant plantings in Hawke's Bay, Gisborne and around Auckland.

Sauvignon Blanc was essentially the creation of Montana;

its first vintage of Marlborough Sauvignon Blanc was made in 1980 and the wine still stands as a landmark achievement, drinking superbly 10 years later. Montana has never sought to make Sauvignon Blanc into something it is not. It is content to make the wine as simply as possible, with no thought of oak, and to market the wine while it retains all its exuberant freshness of youth. (The performance of that 1980 vintage should not mislead anyone into thinking this is a classic cellaring wine style: it is not.)

What Montana started, first Selaks and then Cloudy Bay (with dramatic flair) continued. Cloudy Bay, in particular, has introduced an element of sophistication in the wine which Montana does not have, but on the other hand the consumer is rightly expected to pay for that sophistication. It comes in the form of barrel fermentation of a percentage of the finished wine, some delicately-judged winemaking decisions in terms of chemical composition and residual sugar, and in the form of some selected viticultural practices. But virtually every New Zealand winemaker has at least one Sauvignon Blanc in its stable, and very often two or more. The wines are now made in an immense diversity of style: involving wooded and non-wooded wines; those blended with a touch of Semillon; those in which the winemaker has sought to introduce complexity by the use of skin contact and/or malolactic fermentation; and those, deliberately or otherwise, influenced by botrytis. If one looks at the full spectrum of style, that of Montana stands at one extreme, and those of Morton Estate and Kumeu River (although different from each other) stand at the other extreme. Unless you are one of those who are implacably opposed to any hint of Sauvignon Blanc aroma or flavour, one or other maker of Sauvignon Blanc in New Zealand will produce wines at a relatively modest cost which you will find totally irresistible.

MUSCAT GORDO BLANCO (Australia)
MUSCAT DR HOGG (New Zealand)

PRINCIPAL SYNONYMS
Muscatel, Lexia (Australia); Moscatel (Europe, with various other words added); Hanepoot (South Africa).

PLANTINGS
Australia, 3846 ha   6.66 per cent of total
New Zealand, 224 ha   5.12 per cent of total

AUSTRALIA
Muscat Gordo Blanco, which is in fact more correctly named Muscat of Alexandria, is to Australia what Müller-Thurgau is to New Zealand. It provides the flavour in tens of millions of litres of cask white wine, the balance of which is made up with the far more neutral wines fashioned from the various forms of Sultana and Trebbiano. Its plantings are overwhelmingly concentrated in the Riverland areas of Australia,

but despite the resultant very high yields, it retains that distinctive spicy/grapey flavour which the uninitiated can confuse with Traminer. All in all, Australia seems to have done better with the variety than most other countries, and it is no doubt for this reason that its production is projected to increase, thereby going against world trends. The two distinctive Australian table wines produced from it are the late-picked (Spatlese) versions, exemplified by Brown Brothers (North-east Victoria) Spatlese Lexia, and by the lightly fortified wines made at D'Arenberg and Woodstock in the Southern Vales (South Australia) and labelled Muscat of Alexandria. Finally, it is used extensively in cheap sparkling wine to produce something with greater or lesser similarity to Asti Spumante.

NEW ZEALAND
The New Zealand Muscat is not in fact Muscat Gordo Blanco, but another member of the vast Muscat family which started life as a table grape in England's greenhouses. It performs as one expects it should, making wine with a strong grapey, aromatic scent and flavour; it is used in precisely the same way as in Australia — ie to add flavour to cask wines (in this case blended with Müller-Thurgau), to make limited quantities of semi-sweet varietal table wine, and in spumante-styled sparkling wine.

COLOMBARD

PRINCIPAL SYNONYMS
Colombier (France); French Colombard (California) and Colombar (South Africa).

PLANTINGS
Australia, 641 ha   1.11 per cent of total
New Zealand,   nil

Colombard has been the quiet achiever in Australia over the past decade, and its surprising rate of increase is expected to continue. As has happened so often before, we seem to be following California, where Colombard grew from virtual obscurity at the start of the 1970s to the most widely planted variety. In California, South Africa and Australia it has one highly desirable characteristic: it retains high levels of acidity in warm climates, providing a very fresh, crisp and fruity wine which does have a distinctive, slightly oily, acid finish. It is also high yielding, and these two characteristics make it ideal for cask and low priced bottle wine, the latter usually masquerading under the name Chablis in Australia. As has happened with many other varieties, Brown Brothers (North-east Victoria) was one of the early pioneers, and released a varietal Colombard early in the 1970s. However, since that time it has usually been relegated to the anonymity of generically labelled wines or (at best) blends. Its origin,

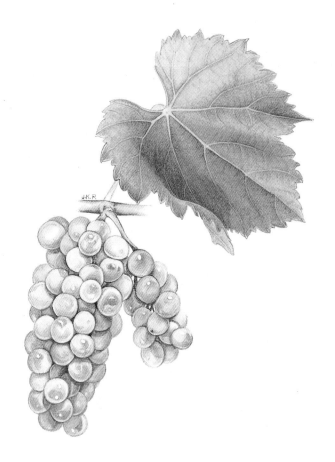

incidentally, was as the third ranked grape for making cognac and armagnac, coming after Ugni Blanc and Folle Blanche.

TREBBIANO

PRINCIPAL SYNONYMS
White Shiraz, White Hermitage (Australia); St Emilion (California, and Charente, France); in its native Italy there are a range of clones which add on the regional name — thus Trebbiano Toscano.

PLANTINGS
Australia, 1338 ha   2.32 per cent of total
New Zealand,   nil

AUSTRALIA
In terms of production, it is an important variety in Australia, but that importance is seldom obvious. As in Italy, it produces an essentially neutral, and rather hard wine, which does however have a certain toughness. It is used extensively in cask wine (particularly where a less aromatic style is required) and likewise as a blend component in cheap sparkling wine. Its chief viticultural, and for that matter, winemaking, advantage is that it is an extremely high yielding variety, producing just under 18 tonnes per hectare across Australia in 1989. Small plantings crop up in almost all regions, but (not surprisingly) it is most common in the Riverland region.

CHENIN BLANC

PRINCIPAL SYNONYMS
Pineau de la Loire (and other specified districts in France);
Steen (South Africa).
PLANTINGS
Australia, 562 ha   0.97 per cent of total
New Zealand, 204 ha   4.67 per cent of total

AUSTRALIA
Yet another of the army of white varieties to have made
substantial inroads in Australia since 1970. What is more, it
is very evident on wine labels: for some reason which I am
unable to discern, winemakers have decided that it is worthy
of being treated as a named white varietal, and the public has
seemingly accepted that this should be so. However, neither
in Australia nor California does it show more than a fleeting
glimpse of the wonderful flavour and character it achieves in
Vouvray and Anjou (in the Loire Valley, France). In Australia
it exhibits a soft, fruit salad flavour which I often describe as
tutti-frutti — a description intended to gently disparage the
variety. It is grown almost everywhere; the Swan Valley and
Gingin (Western Australia) can produce wines of superior
flavour, while in North-east Victoria, St Leonards has
produced one or two memorable late harvest versions.

NEW ZEALAND
Chenin Blanc rose from nowhere to a position of importance
in the New Zealand industry in a very short period of time.
However, its susceptibility to botrytis, and its failure to
produce a wine of distinctive character, has seen its growth
level off, and future predictions are that hectareage will not
increase. It is concentrated in the Hawke's Bay and Gisborne
areas, with smaller plantings at Marlborough and around
Auckland. It is used in New Zealand in much the same way
as Colombard is used in Australia; its high acid (under New
Zealand growing conditions) makes it useful for blending
with varieties such as Müller-Thurgau. That fastidious
winemaker Collards, in the Auckland area, is one of the few
companies to have produced Chenin Blancs with distinctive
character.

WHITE FRONTIGNAC

PRINCIPAL SYNONYMS
Muscat Blanc à Petits Grains, Muscat Blanc, Frontignan and
Brown Muscat (Australia); Muscat de Frontignan and Muscat
d'Alsace, Muscato (Italy); White Muscat and Muscat Canelli
(California).
PLANTINGS
Australia, 489 ha   0.84 per cent of total.
New Zealand,   nil

AUSTRALIA
To put it mildly, the statistics for the Muscat family in
Australia have been somewhat confused. The confusion
comes from the fact that almost all of the Muscats taste
superficially similar, but they can appear very different: just
to make matters worse, Frontignac is a genetically unstable
variety which can produce white, pink or brown grapes. The
final confusion has come from the fact that the variety is used
to make intensely fruity, light Spatlese styles (in precisely the
same style as Muscat Gordo Blanco) at the one extreme, and
at the other end of the spectrum it produces the magnificent
fortified Muscats of North-east Victoria. These
extraordinarily luscious and concentrated wines, with the
almost searing sweetness of the mid-palate giving way to a
cleansing, drying finish, are unchallenged as one of the great
wine styles of the world.

MÜLLER-THURGAU

PRINCIPAL SYNONYM
Riesling-Sylvaner (New Zealand and Switzerland).
PLANTINGS
Australia, almost nil
New Zealand, 1257 ha   28.77 per cent of total

AUSTRALIA

Tiny patches of the variety do exist, but they are too small to fall into the statistical net. Rare commercial releases have been made, but one wonders why.

NEW ZEALAND

Müller-Thurgau was the first *Vitis vinifera* grape to establish itself in New Zealand in effective competition with the *vinifera-labrusca* hybrid crosses which had dominated the scene for the first half of this century. Plantings grew at a phenomenal rate through the 1960s and 1970s; by 1975 it accounted for 50 per cent of all new vineyards, and in 1989 it represented just under 30 per cent of New Zealand's total plantings. This success tracked the explosion of the variety in plantings in Germany in the years following the Second World War: it is also the most commonly encountered variety in Germany, but not by the huge margin that one finds in New Zealand. Whereas Australians are prepared to accept its equivalents (Muscat Gordo Blanco and sultana) as common, if utilitarian, varieties which cannot and do not aspire to greatness, New Zealanders are very proud of their Müller-Thurgau, and are ever ready to leap to its defence. They say, perhaps with some justification, that it does better in New Zealand than anywhere else; the problem is that others may see that as merely damning by faint praise. I vividly remember judging at the 1983 Auckland Wine Show, and thinking to myself 'Müller, Müller everywhere,

and not a drop to drink'. There were endless classes of Müller-Thurgau, each containing 5 grams more residual sugar than the class before, with the fruit flavour never changing, and the sweetness simply building. Since that time I have become considerably more familiar with the variety, and encountered wines made from it which I could bear to drink. I cannot honestly say that I have ever encountered one which I would choose to drink in preference to, say, a reasonably well made Rhine Riesling. But then I could say precisely the same thing (if not worse) of any Muscat-based Australian cask or low-priced bottled wine. The prodigious yields of Müller-Thurgau mean that while its plantings are only 30 per cent of the surface area, it in fact produces around 40 per cent of the annual crop, a statistic which will no doubt keep it in the forefront of growers' minds for the foreseeable future.

SULTANA

PRINCIPAL SYNONYM
Thompson Seedless (California and Australia).
PLANTINGS
Australia, 15,855 ha   27.48 per cent of total
New Zealand,   nil

AUSTRALIA

Sultana is the table and dried grape with which everyone is familiar. Of the 320,000 tonnes produced in Australia in 1989, only 75,000 tonnes were used for winemaking, the balance going to drying and table grape purposes. In any given vintage the use to which the multipurpose grape is put will depend strictly on the relative balance of supply and demand on the winemaking and eating sides of the equation. From a winemaking viewpoint, it is one of the least exciting varieties, and it is technically quite difficult to handle because of the absence of seeds, which makes pressing difficult. Its chief attribute is a moderately high acidity, and its flavour is neutral but not coarse.

PALOMINO AND PEDRO XIMINEZ

PRINCIPAL SYNONYM
Palomino-Sweetwater (Australia).
PLANTINGS
Australia, 1372 ha   2.38 per cent of total
New Zealand, 135 ha   3.09 per cent of total

AUSTRALIA

The statistics have always unceremoniously lumped Palomino and Pedro Ximinez together. The pragmatic genesis of this practice is both the near identical use of the two varieties, and a certain degree of confusion with a third and lesser Spanish variety, Canocazo (which one suspects is still treated as being within this statistical group). Although the use of the two grapes may be identical, it is in fact multi-purpose: in years gone by, the principal use was in making sherry, but with the decline in sherry consumption, increasing quantities are diverted to cask wine. The vast bulk of the plantings are in South Australia spread between the Riverland region, the Barossa Valley and the Clare Valley. Given the decline in the fortified wine market, and the increasing availability of premium white varieties, it is not the least bit surprising to see that production has declined continuously and sharply since 1969.

NEW ZEALAND

The grape is used almost exclusively in the production of New Zealand's motley band of sherries; the plantings, concentrated around Auckland, with smaller plantings in Hawke's Bay, Gisborne and Marlborough, are not expected to increase. In New Zealand, as in Australia, the variety is popular because of its high yield.

DORADILLO

PRINCIPAL SYNONYM
Blancet (incorrectly, Australia).
PLANTINGS
Australia, 968 ha   1.67 per cent of total
New Zealand,   nil

AUSTRALIA

A fugitive from Spain (where it no longer exists) Doradillo is heading on a firm downward path in Australia. It was once a highly productive and popular variety in the Riverland region of South Australia, producing large yields of neutral wine with both table and fortified wine uses.

CABERNET SAUVIGNON

PRINCIPAL SYNONYMS
Bouchet, Vidure, Petite-Vidure (France).
PLANTINGS
Australia, 3886 ha   6.73 per cent of total
New Zealand, 351 ha   8.95 per cent of total

AUSTRALIA

There is no apparent challenger to the supremacy of Cabernet Sauvignon at the quality end of the market. Indeed, its dominance is likely to increase rather than decrease. This is an extraordinary performance for a grape which in 1958 barely existed, and it reflects its adaptability to varying

regimes of climate and *terroir* as well as its sturdiness in the winery. In both respects it is similar to Chardonnay, as is the largely unquestioning acceptance of its multitudinous faces by the wine-drinking public. It has one great advantage in the vineyard: the thick-skinned, small berries and loose clusters stand up almost indefinitely to rain — a characteristic which more than compensates for its moderate yield. In the winery, the winemaking techniques and options are fairly well known and understood.

In South Australia it finds its greatest expression in Coonawarra, although differing viticultural and winemaking practices lead to a greater diversity in style than the uniform *terroir* and climate of that region would suggest. Thus one moves from the almost thick, juicy opulence of Wynns John Riddoch through the scented, complex, oaky wines of Lindemans to the much more classic cassis/cigar box/herbaceous characters of Bowen Estate. In the Barossa Valley it produces a dark, fleshy wine, high in tannin and rich in body, while in the Southern Vales wines of somewhat tighter structure, often with a touch of dark chocolate, are produced. In Central Victoria its eucalypt/mint character is a hallmark, though this is best when it is not too pronounced; in Southern Victoria that mint character all but disappears to be replaced by more classic flavours of blackcurrant, a touch of green capsicum and softer tannins. The Margaret River in Western Australia imposes its particular qualities: a curious mixture of slightly gravelly astringency, and soft red berry fruit at the core. Further south, the Lower Great Southern Area provides truly great Cabernet Sauvignon, tight, reserved, and long-lived, but correct in every nuance of

aroma and flavour. The Hunter Valley emulates the Margaret River, and perhaps exceeds it, in placing its regional thumbprint on the variety, a thumbprint which tends to increase rather than decrease with age. Finally, there is the Cabernet Sauvignon of the Riverlands, which is usually consigned to cask but in the hands of makers such as Renmano and Angove's (both of the Riverland, South Australia), and Lindemans and Mildara (both of the Murray River, Victoria) is capable of much better things. Throughout all these regions shines the Australian expression of abundant, easily accessible fruit flavour.

NEW ZEALAND

The dominance of Cabernet Sauvignon is New Zealand even more complete than in Australia, for there is no other red variety to challenge it in terms of planting or production. While the largest plantings are to be found in Hawke's Bay and Marlborough, the best Cabernet Sauvignon wines are made from Hawke's Bay and Auckland grapes, with Hawke's Bay being to New Zealand what Coonawarra is to Australia. The Hawke's Bay climate is more reliable than that of Auckland, where growing season and vintage rainfall frequently causes problems. Of course, it is here that Cabernet's tough skin comes to the fore, and it is not surprising that the grape is Auckland's most successful variety. The large Marlborough plantings have tended to produce rather light-bodied wines lacking the extract and body which international markets expect to find in the variety, and it is significant that Montana has made its move into Hawke's Bay via the McDonald Winery.

Stonyridge, Matua Valley, Kumeu River and St Nesbit all produce top quality wines from Auckland-region fruit; Te Mata, Villa Maria and Vidal lead the formidable Hawke's Bay charge; while Cloudy Bay and Vavasour show just how dangerous it is to generalise about the Marlborough region (even if the Awatere Valley in which Vavasour is situated is a new and quite distinct subregion). All of the Cabernets of these makers, and all of their frequent Cabernet Merlot blends, have the flavour, structure and style to handsomely compete on world markets, yet are distinctively New Zealand in character: the tannins are softer, and the fruit more supple yet more herbaceous than their Australian counterparts. Perhaps the New Zealand wines do not have the same complexity, richness or longevity, but they cannot be ignored.

CABERNET FRANC

PRINCIPAL SYNONYMS
Carmenet, Bouchet, Grosse-Vidure (Bordeaux).
PLANTINGS
Australia, 311 ha   0.52 per cent of total
New Zealand, 33.7 ha   0.7 per cent of total

AUSTRALIA

A grape which so far makes a greater contribution to press releases and back labels than it does to wine in the bottle; very frequently, token percentages are grown simply to satisfy the Bordeaux model. It is strictly a blending proposition, providing a wine very similar to, but slightly softer and more aromatic than, Cabernet Sauvignon. Its plantings are increasing slowly but steadily, and will continue to do so for the forseeable future.

NEW ZEALAND

The grape fulfils almost exactly the same function as it does in Australia, being grown in small quantities purely as a blending variety.

SHIRAZ

PRINCIPAL SYNONYMS
Hermitage (Australia), Syrah, Sirah (France), Petite Syrah (France and the United States).
PLANTINGS
Australia, 4919 ha   8.52 per cent of total
New Zealand , 2.7 ha

AUSTRALIA

Shiraz remains Australia's most widely grown grape, and it will be a long time — if ever — before Cabernet Sauvignon takes over the volume lead. For the first 60 years of this century it was also regarded as the finest red grape, and its precipitous fall from grace as Cabernet Sauvignon blossomed is a classic case of the pendulum swinging too far — or so the majority of overseas experts say. It was the red grape upon which the reputations of the Hunter Valley, the Barossa Valley and Coonawarra were founded. It produced the incomparable wines of Maurice O'Shea at McWilliam's Mount Pleasant and of Lindemans (both in the lower Hunter Valley), the fabled Woodley Treasure Chest series from Coonawarra, and last but by no means least Max Schubert chose it in preference to Cabernet Sauvignon when he fashioned Penfolds Grange Hermitage (the Barossa Valley). More recently the wonderfully spicy, textured wines of Central and Southern Victoria have added another dimension.

The fact that Shiraz can produce wines of the highest quality is often forgotten. It is a versatile grape which can flourish in a wide range of climates and soil types. It is exceedingly useful for blending with Cabernet Sauvignon.

The variety has always been a favourite of the grape growers: it yields well, but reacts adversely to excessive rain (or irrigation). The berries continue to swell as the vine takes up moisture, and failure to ripen, coupled with berry split and rot, are the inevitable consequences of overcropping. In the winery it is handled in much the same way as Cabernet Sauvignon, with similar options to the winemaker (although with the honourable exception of Penfolds Grange Hermitage it is seldom allocated as much new oak as is Cabernet Sauvignon).

It is grown everywhere: initially the influence of region is very pronounced, but with 20 or 30 years bottle age that gently earthy, softly velvety and almost luminous sweet core of fruit takes over. At this stage a great Coonawarra Shiraz can resemble a Hunter, and a Hunter (such as Lindemans 1959 Bin 1590) may well be confused with a Jaboulet La Chapelle of the same age — and so on. Over a shorter time frame, there is certainly an Australian Shiraz to suit every palate and, indeed, every pocket.

NEW ZEALAND
The variety barely exists in New Zealand: in the North Island, rain is the enemy; in the South Island, it is lack of warmth.

PINOT NOIR

PRINCIPAL SYNONYMS
Pineau (France and archaic Australian), Spatburgunder (Germany), Klevner (Switzerland).
PLANTINGS
Australia, 930 ha   1.61 per cent of total
New Zealand, 138 ha   3.15 per cent of total

AUSTRALIA
Pinot Noir is still much the debutante, pretty but unsure of herself and of what dresses she should wear — and with a few adolescent spots on her complexion. Although plantings have soared over the past decade, most of the production is still used to make sparkling wine. Most of the early plantings were in regions which have proved unsuited to making table wine, and in any event demand for sparkling wine base has proved insatiable.

This classic grape of Burgundy is grown in practically every country in the world but is generally thought to produce wine of real quality in cool climates only. There are those who would say that these (warm) regions are little more suited to growing Pinot Noir for sparkling wine than they are for table wine, and such critics may be right — but then, carefully picked warm-grown Pinot Noir is surely better than no Pinot Noir at all.

Pinot Noir's real success as a table wine has come from the three areas around Melbourne (Geelong, Mornington Peninsula and Yarra Valley), all of which have achieved a consistency of style and quality unmatched by other regions. Elsewhere the successes are limited to individual wineries: Montara at Great Western in Victoria, Mountadam in the Adelaide Hills, South Australia, Pipers Brook and Moorilla Estate in Tasmania and Wignalls King River in the Lower Great Southern region of Western Australia. The Southern Adelaide Hills, Tumbarumba (in New South Wales) and (possibly) Coonawarra wait in the wings, promising to deliver a high quality product in due time. The demand for Pinot

MERLOT

PRINCIPAL SYNONYMS
Nil.
PLANTINGS

Australia, 383 ha	0.66 per cent of total
New Zealand, 89 ha	2.03 per cent of total

Noir to be used for sparkling wine is sure to encourage more wineries in these areas to give space to this variety.

It hardly needs be said that Pinot Noir is extraordinarily sensitive to climate (primarily) and *terroir* (secondly), and — in the areas in which it does succeed — to wind and rain during flowering. It is the most difficult variety to make well in the winery, demanding constant adjustments in winemaking technique from year to year and even from vat to vat within each year — and all this against an extremely complex range of fruit handling techniques, fermentation regimes, and oak selection and handling.

The top Australian Pinot Noirs have shown in international tastings and competitions in Paris, London, California and Australia that they rank with the best the world has to offer, but by and large the Australian wine media refuses to accept these verdicts in what is yet another well-developed example of cultural cringe.

NEW ZEALAND

While second only to Cabernet Sauvignon in terms of plantings, Pinot Noir has had an equally chequered career in New Zealand. Here, too, much of the annual crush goes to sparkling wine, though with considerably more justification than in Australia.

At this stage, the only Pinot Noir table wines of note have come from St Helena (near Christchurch) and Martinborough Vineyards (Wairarapa/Martinborough), although former St Helena winemaker Dany Schuster will presumably produce a top class Pinot Noir from his new vineyard, Omihi Hills.

AUSTRALIA

Very much a newcomer, Merlot is almost exclusively used for blending with Cabernet Sauvignon in the manner of the wines of Bordeaux. Poor fruiting caused some experimental plantings to be abandoned. However, others are persisting and plantings are now on the increase. In the generally warmer climate of Australia it produces wines with riper fruit flavours which lack the distinctive green tinge of the wines of St Emilion but which share the same softness — and hence make it the right variety to blend with the more angular and at times slightly hollow Cabernet Sauvignon.

NEW ZEALAND

Merlot is used in New Zealand in much the same way as it is used in Australia, although it is more a case of complementary use given the softer structure of the Cabernet Sauvignon with which it is blended. Clearly, New Zealand winemakers are pleased with the result, and plantings are steadily increasing. Cabernet Franc, incidentally, is also used in blends in both countries, but is relatively more important in New Zealand than it is in Australia.

GRENACHE

PRINCIPAL SYNONYMS
Garnacha, Tinto, Carignan Rosso (Spain), Alicante, Rousillon (France).
PLANTINGS

Australia, 2222 ha	3.85 per cent of total
New Zealand,	nil

AUSTRALIA
A high yielding workhorse but nonetheless declining in importance, which once provided the major part of Australia's cask wine, and before that its cheapest versions of so-called Burgundy. Its ability to satisfactorily ripen large yields under heavy irrigation has all but prevented any attention being given to it as a quality grape: only the tiny Charles Melton Wines in the Barossa Valley has shown with its Nine Popes just what a wonderful wine can be made from low-yielding, dryland vines.

MATARO

PRINCIPAL SYNONYMS
Mouvedre (France), Esparte (Australia).
PLANTINGS

Australia, 659ha	1.14 per cent of total
New Zealand,	nil

AUSTRALIA
An even more rapidly fading star than Grenache, producing wine which on its own is rather hard and graceless, but which can be useful in blends.

PINOTAGE

PRINCIPAL SYNONYMS
Nil.
PLANTINGS

Australia,	nil
New Zealand, 51.7 ha	1.18 per cent of total

NEW ZEALAND
Pinotage is a hybrid bred in South Africa which was originally thought to be a cross between Pinot Noir and Hermitage (or Shiraz), but which is in fact a Pinot Noir-Cinsaut cross. Both in South Africa and New Zealand it makes a wine of soft, velvety flavour and structure which can respond very well to bottle age. In both countries it has become unfashionable, and underrated in consequence. Its strengths lie in the vineyard: it yields generously, and its thick-skinned berries stand up well to humidity and rain.

AUSTRALIAN GRAPE VARIETIES

1	CHARDONNAY	
2	*RHINE RIESLING	
3	SEMILLON	
4	COLOMBARD	
5	MUSCAT GORDO BLANCO	
6	TREBBIANO	
7	SULTANA	
8	DORADILLO	
9	CHENIN BLANC	
10	SAUVIGNON BLANC	
11	MUSCAT BLANC	
12	PALOMINO & PEDRO XIMENEZ	
13	CABERNET SAUVIGNON	
14	SHIRAZ	
15	GRENACHE	
16	MATARO	
17	PINOT NOIR	
18	MERLOT	
19	MALBEC	

* Estimate: Statistics under the heading Riesling include several grape varieties which were not in fact Rhine Riesling at all.

VITICULTURE

Yield and quality have always been locked in battle with each other, and the lament has ever been, 'Wines aren't what they used to be'. Edward Hyams (Dionysus, *A Social History of Wine,* Sidgwick and Jackson, 1965) traces the demise of ancient Rome's most famous wine, Falernian (immortalised by Horace and Martial). 'The primacy of Falernian lasted three centuries, but under economic pressure, the owners were tempted to increase output at the expense of quality. . . not much later it was just one of a score of good, reliable wines.' The British winewriters of the early twentieth century, led by Professor George Saintsbury, were clearly convinced we would never again see wines of the longevity, the power and the quality of the golden years before phylloxera.

There is at once truth and mendacity in these laments; what many observers fail to recognise is that wine and wine style are dynamic and ever-changing commodities which necessarily have to be produced in the social and economic conditions of their time and equally necessarily must meet their economic and aesthetic expectations.

In Roman times vineyards were planted at a density of 50,000 vines per hectare and were tended by hand; by the middle of the nineteenth century, as horses became common-place, the density was 10,000 to 15,000, in modern European viticulture the density is usually 4000 to 8000; in Australasia it

is 1500 to 3000, allowing for large tractors, mechanical harvesters and so on (with a few hectares here and there at European density). Yet yields per hectare have increased rather than decreased, which means, of course, that the yield per vine has increased dramatically. This is a pattern strikingly evident in Australia over this century, and which has rapidly gathered momentum since 1950 (see the chart below).

It is a vivid indication of the massive changes in viticultural practice which have taken place in Australia (and New Zealand, where yields have always been much higher but where similar trends are evident). Before looking at the principal causes and implications of the changes, there are two lesser aspects which need to be recognised.

First, while nominal vine density per hectare has not changed greatly (if anything, it has decreased), improved selection of vine stock has largely eliminated the once-common occurrence of barren (non-fruiting) vines, and gaps, where vines have died and not been replaced. Secondly, extraction of juice from the grapes, recovery of lees, and general winery efficiency has increased the effective yield per tonne of grapes.

The trend to higher yields is very evident, and notwithstanding the theoretical constraints of appellation control on Europe's wine regions, the same trend is evident there. Indeed Germany has experienced yield increase on a scale similar to that of Australia, and many see this as one of the most important factors in the dramatic decline in the reputation (and marketability) of German wine.

The impetus in Germany came partly through the development of early-ripening higher yielding varieties (*Vitis vinifera* hybrid crosses), partly through the selection of vigorous rootstocks onto which the *vinifera* scions are grafted, partly through clonal selection within varieties, partly through improved disease and pest control, and partly through increased use of herbicides and fertilisers. Clonal selection and rootstock selection have played a similar role in Australasia over the past 20 years, and are going to continue to play an important role.

Next, irrigation has ceased to be the dirty word it once was. It has taken Australian vignerons and commentators (myself included) a long time to realise the fundamental difference between the climate of, for example, Bordeaux and Burgundy on the one hand, and the vast majority of Australian and New Zealand regions on the other. In France, not only does 45 to 55 per cent of the rainfall occur during the growing season, but it tends to be spread fairly evenly over this season. In Australasia, the rain most regions receive between the end of November and the end of March is inadequate to keep the vine in balance. A vine which is suffering from excessive moisture-stress (that is, lack of moisture) will produce fruit which is chemically out of balance (high pH and low acid) and almost certainly lacking in flavour.

HISTORY OF WINE IN AUSTRALIA

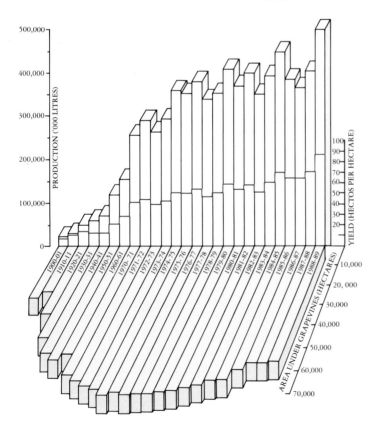

The flexibility which irrigation allows has meant larger vines with more vegetative growth. This in turn has led to the development of trellises and of canopy management systems as far removed from the traditional single-wire low trellis as a T-model Ford is from a Lamborghini. In Australasia most of the research and development has come from two academics: Peter Clingeleffer of the Commonwealth Scientific and Industrial Research Organisation (CSIRO) and Dr Richard Smart. Their paths have taken sharply divergent courses (Smart favouring highly complex trellis design and canopy manipulation, Clingeleffer allowing the vine to make all its own adjustments by eliminating pruning and canopy manipulation altogether), but the aim has been much the same. That aim has been to produce a vine with the appropriate balance between new growth (canes and leaves) and crop levels, and to ensure in so doing that the grapes and the buds which will produce next season's growth receive sufficient sunlight. Suffice it to say here that most of these developments have led (once again) to increased crop levels, even if there has been a concomitant increase in quality from improved trellis design and better canopy management techniques.

For the best part of a decade now it has been fashionable to talk about 'making wine in the vineyard' and to prophesy that the next quantum leap in improvement in wine quality will occur in the vineyard rather than in the winery. While there is no resiling from that view, there is a subtle groundswell of opinion across France, America and Australasia that we have become altogether too clever in our selection, breeding and manipulation of the vine, and that far more attention should be paid to limiting yield and to improving grape quality.

One of the most obvious ways of achieving this is to reverse the trend to bigger and more vigorous vines. Europe has a different regime (although similar concerns), but in Australasia one method of achieving this would be to select rootstocks which suppress vigour and yield, rather than enhance it. Another means would be to pay far more attention to the taste of the wine in clonal selection trials, rather than to select purely on the basis of yield and chemical composition, which is the traditional tendency. Some growers, too, are sharply cutting back the use of fertilisers and synthetic fungicides in a conscious endeavour to turn back the clock.

CONSUMER PRICE INDEX 1983–90
WINE VERSUS ALL GOODS

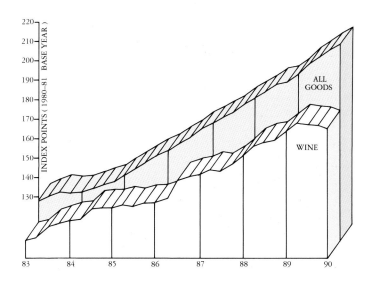

ABOVE: Stoneleigh Vineyard, Marlborough: here, as in all cool climate regions, there is an unending war against mildews.

SOIL

The French do not speak of soil, but of *terroir*, one of those wonderful words which encapsulates many different things. It expresses the coming together of climate, soil and landscape, thereby incorporating the influences of temperature, rainfall, sunlight; of soil depth and structure, pH, minerals and water retention capacity; of slope, aspect and drainage. To the French in particular, *terroir* assumes almost mystical importance. Says Peter Sichel (president of the Grand Crus de Bordeaux), '*Terroir* determines the character of a wine, man its quality'.

It lies at the heart of the French appellation system, built upon a thousand years of practical experience and observation which has led to a most precise and detailed delineation of quality, and to the identification of a limited number of grape varieties considered to be especially suited to the *terroir* and the climate, and to the exclusion by force of law of all others. It has led to the prescription of pruning methods, the specification of maximum yields (but with such a dose of pragmatism as to render the restraints largely meaningless) and of minimum alcoholic strengths (again largely emasculated by the rampant use of chaptalisation — the addition of sugar to the fermenting wine).

History shows that the vineyards were originally planted by default, ie in *terroir* which was too deficient to support other forms of horticulture or farming. In Bordeaux there is a saying, 'If these soils were not the best in the world, they would be the worst'. But that in no way diminishes the validity of the subsequent matching of grape and soil, nor of the identification of those microscopic dots on the face of the earth which produce wines of the ineffable majesty of Chateau Pétrus (Bordeaux), La Romanée-Conti and Montrachet (Burgundy) and their ilk.

Australasian vignerons may be denied the extraordinary prestige and marketing power of the top French producers, or even the reflected glory which shines on the lesser producers — even poor French wine finds a ready market in many parts of the world. But there are compensations: we are free of the rigidity and constraints of the appellation system, and can (and do) prove that fine wine can be made in a far wider range of circumstances than the French would ever admit.

It may well be that ignorance is bliss, but the average Australasian vigneron has made little or no attempt to correlate specific soil types with particular grape varieties and, outside of certain broad parameters, has made almost no attempt to link soil type and quality. (Such linkage as occurs is between climate, variety and quality.)

Those broad parameters define an ideal soil as a sandy loam, preferably interspersed with gravel or small, fragmented rock. It should be deep, free draining and of low to moderate fertility. Conversely, the most frequently encountered problems are excess clay and excess acidity. Heavy clay provides poor drainage, holding too much water after rain or irrigation, and is frequently associated with dense and hard subsoils which roots cannot penetrate.

Excessively acid subsoils are far more widespread than is commonly realised, and have a significantly adverse impact on vine health and vigour. The vine's roots cannot tolerate the aluminium toxicity which is associated with high acidity (and low pH), which forces them to remain in the shallow topsoils (which are usually less acid), making the vine much more susceptible to drought, even though the rainfall may in theory appear adequate.

Correct moisture supply is all-important, and apart from anchorage and nutrients, is the principal function of soil in determining growth. During early shoot growth up until flowering (early November to late December, depending on region and variety) vines should be well supplied with moisture. By the time the fruit starts to ripen (January to February) available water should tail off, causing vegetative growth to cease, and the vine to focus its attention on ripening the grapes by sugar accumulation. (The photo-synthetic activity of the vine's leaves causes carbohydrates stored in the system to be converted to sugar in the grapes.)

What is more, there are few Australasian regions which do not contain a wide range of soil types. Coonawarra (at least within the so called terra rosa boundaries), Eden Valley and Marlborough (at least in the existing vineyards) are regions in which a single (or few) soil type exists. In almost all others, soils vary widely: it is not uncommon to find three or four different soil types on a 15 hectare vineyard.

Next, a large proportion of grapes are grown by farmers who sell to the winemaker. That winemaker may have never

ABOVE: *Contrasting soil varieties from the Coonawarra region.*

visited the vineyard and certainly will lack any intimate knowledge of variation in vine growth within its confines. By contrast, the French winemaker will typically know every vine, every tiny variation in soil. Moreover, that observation will have been repeated over many centuries and handed down through generations. In Australasia, experience in winemaking is typically confined to a single generation, or perhaps two.

But it does exist in the small estate, and is very probably one of the reasons why the small winery can produce top quality wine to rank with the best the big winery can produce. All observers are agreed that the future of Australasian winemaking lies in the vineyard, and, as a consequence, perhaps more attention will in fact be paid to soil in the future.

So it is that the vineyards of Australasia are established on a wide range of soil types, and, just as with grape varieties, over the years local names for these soils have been used with little scientific basis and even less consistency from one region to the next. Dr K H Northcote, of the Common-wealth Scientific and Industrial Research Organisation (CSIRO) Division of Soils, was responsible for developing a co-ordinated classification of soil for Australia, and it is that system which has been used in this book. That for New Zealand is rather less precise, and has been taken from a number of sources.

Northcote ('Viticulture', *Resources in Australia* Vol 1, Australian Industrial Publishers Pty Ltd, 1988) has divided Australian soils into four primary groups denoted by the letters O, V, G and D. The O group soils are derived from organic matter (peat and the like) and are not used in grape growing. This leaves the three mineral groups, all of which are used.

By far the most widespread are the D group soils. These exhibit a sudden change from sandy or loamy surface soils to clay subsoils, with a pronounced contrast in texture. This group is the duplex soils, and is in turn broken down into four subgroups: red duplex soils (Dr soils), brown duplex (Db soils), yellow and yellow-grey duplex (Dy soils), and black duplex (Dd soils). Once again, two subgroups dominate: the Dr and Dy soils.

The colour classification is not as straightforward as might appear at first sight, for it essentially refers to the colour of the clay subsoil rather than the surface soil. The latter may vary from brown to reddish brown to black in the Dr group, those of the Dy group from light brownish grey through dark grey-brown to grey and finally to brown. This simply serves to underline the importance of the subsoil, which becomes progressively less permeable with the progression from Dr to Db to Dy to Dd and finally Dg (no vines can be grown on the last soil).

There are then further numeric subdivisions reflecting various degrees and combinations of friability and

permeability of both surface and subsoils: Dr1, 2, 3 and 4 groupings. Once again, the Dr2 group (hard red duplex soils) is by far the most important, and is in turn broken down into sub-subgroups Dr2.21, 2.22, 2.23, 2.32, 2.33, 2.41, 2.42, 2.43, 2.61 and 2.62. Dr2.22 is the most common vineyard soil in Forbes, Cowra, Mudgee, Glenrowan-Milawa-Rutherglen, and the Goulburn Valley, while the closely-related Dr2.23 (the only difference being a slightly more alkaline subsoil) dominates the Adelaide Plains, the Barossa Valley, Clare Valley, Padthaway and the Southern Vales.

The next most common group is the U (or Uniform) group, in which there is little change between surface soils and subsoils, hence Uniform. There are in turn four subgroups: Uc, sandy; Um, loamy; and Uf and Ug, clay soils. The most celebrated soil in Australia, the so-called terra rosa (or *rossa*) of Coonawarra, which at various times has had all sorts of descriptions (including volcanic) attached to it, is in fact of two types, Um 6.4 and Uf 5.31. Even more confusing, soil and subsoil in this situation are seldom more than 150 centimetres deep before one passes into the soft limestone subsolum. If this were not enough, these are some of the more obviously red coloured soils (hence *rossa*), yet this is not reflected in their names. Uf 5.31 is correctly non-cracking subplastic clay, a highly friable loam which only becomes clay-like if heavily compressed. Um 6.4 (6.41, 6.42 and 6.43) is technically known as shallow friable loam with smooth-ped fabric, and is of slightly finer and tighter structure than Uf 5.31.

Finally there is the G (or Gradational) group, in which there is a gradual increase in fine particles as the soil deepens, and so becomes more clay-like. There are three subgroups: calcareous earths (Gc group), sandy earths (Gn 1) and massive earths (Gn 2). The most frequently encountered the Gc 1.22 group — brown to red-brown loamy sand, with strongly calcareous clay loam subsoils.

ABOVE: Sandy alluvial soils promote vine growth and high crop levels,desirable for some but not for others.

CLIMATE

To the winemakers of the New World, and hence to Australia and New Zealand, climate is the most significant factor (outside their control) impinging on grape quality and wine style. For the winemakers of France, *terroir* (or soil) is equally important.

Indeed, if one looks at Bordeaux and Burgundy, France's two greatest wine districts, and then narrows down the microscope to their principal subregions, climatic variation has little relevance, and *terroir* becomes all-important in determining the character of the wines. For example, the Haut-Médoc, is a tiny area with an almost flat topography. To all intents and purposes the climate at Chateau Margaux at the southern end of the Haut-Médoc is the same as that at Chateau Lafite Rothschild, 25 kilometres to the north, and abutting St Estéphe. Similarly, if you consider the Côte de Nuits, the climate of Nuits-St Georges at the southern end is identical to that of Gevrey-Chambertin at the northern end.

It is true that spring frosts and summer hailstorms may hit one spot and miss another, and no less true that one chateau or grower may be more successful than his neighbour in one year but not in the next. Even more so is it true that climatic swings from one vintage to the next are of crucial importance in shaping the quality (and to a lesser degree the character) of the wines of each vintage. There is a fundamental distinction between climate and weather, and by their very nature these swings or changes cannot usefully be individually recorded; one inevitably has to take long term averages in ascribing temperature, rainfall, humidity, wind, frost and whatever other data one wishes to use in presenting an overall picture of the climate of a region. So it is understandable that the French tend to take climate for granted, and to look to the effect of *terroir* to explain and characterise their wines.

All of this in turn proceeds on patterns of classification and constraint which have been built up over many centuries, even if formal codification did not start until the middle of the nineteenth century and only gained legislative teeth in the twentieth century.

How different the position of the New World. There are effectively no constraints on which grape varieties you can plant, how you prune them or how you use and blend the wine you make from the grapes. Almost every one of the regions discussed in this book is of much larger scale and of more diverse topography than most of the regions of France: Coonawarra and Padthaway in South Australia are two exceptions on the Australian front, and (superficially) Marlborough might appear to fall into the same category in New Zealand.

If this were not enough, the New World's experience in matching *terroir*, climate and grape varieties is typically less than a century old, and frequently less than a decade old. As time goes by we may well see a greater extent of specialisation, although not to the degree found in France.

So with an impossibly complex matrix of grape variety, soil, aspect and topography within each Australasian region (and each subregion) we have had little option but to come back to climate as the most significant factor in determining wine character. But in doing so the experts in Australasia and the United States have encountered great difficulties in providing climatic indices which are on the one hand sufficiently succinct to be understood and to be of practical use, and on the other hand are meaningful and reasonably accurate.

Nonetheless, most attention has focused on temperature as being the most important aspect of climate in determining wine style. In 1944 the distinguished American oenologists Amerine and Winkler introduced a classification system which traces its roots back to 1735, and then to the mid-nineteenth century observation by de Candolle that there is little vegetative growth in the vine at temperatures below 10°C (50°F). Amerine and Winkler assumed a 7 month growing season (in Australasia, this means October to April) and calculated what is now called heat degree days or HDD by taking the difference between 50°F (or 10°C) and the mean temperature of the month, multiplying that difference by the number of days in the month, and then adding the resultant figures for each of the seven months. Having done that, they then divided California's wine regions into five, with 500 day degree increments, starting with Region I (the coldest) at less than 2500 HDD (expressed in degrees Fahrenheit).

The system has been refined, adapted and also roundly criticised, but remains the most widely used and understood system available, and in the regional summaries which appear throughout this book I have given the HDD figure. Nonetheless, it is interesting to look at the criticisms and refinements, and at the same time to recognise some decidedly curious statistical anomalies within the system.

The major Australian criticism has come from the leading viticulturists Dr Richard Smart and Peter Dry, and to a lesser degree from Dr John Kirk. It is Dr Kirk who has best summarised the shortcomings of the system as a one-dimensional blurring or obliteration of climatic dissimilarities. Dry and Smart make the same point, and developed a climatic index which measures the mean January temperature (MJT); the mean annual range (MAR) or continentality (MJT minus mean July temperature, with the highest figures denoting a continental climate; the lowest a maritime climate); mean sunshine hours per day in the growing season (SSH), aridity (the difference between rainfall and 50 per cent evaporation); and humidity (RH), calculated as the mean for January at 9 am. A variation of this system is

to take the mean temperature of the warmest month ie the MTWM (as opposed to January, which may or may not be the warmest month) as a single measure.

Most recently Gerard Bentryn of the United States presented a paper to the Second International Symposium for Cool Climate Viticulture and Oenology (New Zealand 1988) in which he reaffirmed the objections to the heat summation system and proposed instead a system which concentrates on the mean low temperature of the coldest month and the mean high temperature of the warmest month, but also takes into account the diurnal temperature range, the yearly rainfall and the warmest month rainfall. His argument is that a slow, even accumulation of a given heat summation is likely to be very much better than a rapid accumulation of the same summation due to extreme diurnal (and seasonal) temperature fluctuations. In fact Bentryn is simply emphasising the importance of the MAR or continentality index of Smart, and presenting it in a matrix form, but his point regarding the significance of temperature fluctuation (or lack of it) remains valid.

A further complication stems from inconsistent HDD figures ascribed by various authorities to the one region, despite claiming to use the same compilation method. Sometimes the discrepancy is small, sometimes large. In one or two instances different recording stations may have been used, and the period of time during which the data was collected may well be different. In others it is apparent there have been mathematical errors.

And in a sense it simply serves to underline an even greater problem: there frequently is enormous variation in the mesoclimates of Australian regions. To take one practical example, in the 1990 vintage at my winery in the Yarra Valley I received Pinot Noir grapes from 11 vineyards: the first were picked on 19 March, the last on 27 April, and the grapes picked first had the higher sugar levels. (Both vineyards were in excellent condition at the time of harvest.) Or to take another example, leading viticulturist Garry Crittenden calculates that the warmest vineyard on the Mornington Peninsula has an HDD of 1500, and the coldest as little as 1150 HDD. Similar examples abound in the Barossa Valley, the Southern Vales, the Clare Valley, the Lower Great Southern region, Mudgee, the Hunter Valley, Auckland, Hawke's Bay — indeed almost anywhere.

Confronted with all these difficulties, I have elected to use a composite table (see overleaf) kindly provided by Dr Richard Smart which incorporates figures collated by him (and others assisting him) over many years. His primary indices (MJT and HDD) are measures of temperature, and in the final analysis all commentators come back to this factor, simply using different numbers or expressions to measure the same thing. So in a sense it does not matter whether you look at HDD, MJT, MTWM, if mean numbers are high, you have a hot climate and an early vintage; if they are low, a cool climate and a late vintage.

On a broader view, there are climates within the Australasian wine growing regions which correspond to almost any European district you care to name, and some well known French regions have been included for the sake of comparison. But no two districts, no two subregions, will ever precisely mirror the combined climate and *terroir* of each other. It is for this reason that books such as this are written and (hopefully) read.

ABOVE: *Rosemount Estate: the beauty of vineyards at dusk.*

CLIMATE
A COMPARISON OF REGIONS IN AUSTRALASIA AND FRANCE

STATION	REGION	MJT (°C)	MAR (°C)	HDD (°C)	Annual RAIN (mm)	Oct-Apr Month RAIN (mm)	ARIDITY (mm)	RH per cent	SSH hours per day
VERY HOT >23.0°C									
Alice Springs	Central Australia	29.4	17.5	337.0	250	170	810	31	10
Roma	Queensland	27.3	15.2	3140	600	400	240	56	9.0
Swan Upper	Swan Valley	24.3	11.4	2340	740	145	530	47	9.7
Mildura	Sunraysia	23.9	13.7	2240	280	130	640	49	9.7
Griffith	Murrimbidgee Irrigation Area	23.8	15.3	2201	410	200	510	51	9.3
Montpellier*	Midi	23.8	17.4	1920	730	310	—	59	9.6
Swan Hill	Central Murray	23.6	14.3	2150	350	150	500	52	(9.3)
Cowra	Lachlan Valley	23.5	15.5	2070	660	370	(330)	51	(9.0)
Loxton	Riverland	23.0	13.2	2080	270	130	510	51	9.6
Roseworthy	Adelaide Plains	23.0	13.2	2081	270	130	510	51	9.6
HOT 21.0 — 22.9°C									
Mudgee	Mudgee	22.9	15.0	2050	670	360	300	63	8.0
Cessnock	Lower Hunter	22.7	12.8	2070	740	530	[50]	58	7.3
Wauchope	Hastings Valley	22.5	10.5	2310	1280	1080	[430]	67	(7.5)
Muswellbrook	Upper Hunter	22.3	12.7	2170	620	400	90	75	(7.5)
Rutherglen	North-east Victoria	22.3	15.4	1770	590	260	380	50	9.3
Clare	Clare Valley	21.9	13.6	1770	630	200	430	47	(8.8)
Southern Adelaide	Southern Vales	21.7	10.8	1910	660	180	420	49	(8.6)
Nuriootpa	Barossa Valley	21.4	12.6	1710	500	160	460	47	8.8
Seymour	Goulburn Valley	21.2	13.7	1680	600	250	310	52	9.0
WARM 20.9°C–19°C									
Avoca	Pyrenees	20.9	13.7	1530	540	220	—	57	—
Applethorpe	Granite Belt	20.5	13.1	1703	800	500	10	69	(8.1)
Margaret River	Margaret River	20.4	7.6	1690	1160	200	(400)	62	8.1
Mount Barker	Lower Great Southern	20.4	9.8	1620	750	230	350	61	(7.9)
Padthaway	Padthaway	20.4	11.4	1610	530	180	480	65	(8.2)
Stawell	Great Western	20.2	12.2	1460	590	240	(360)	59	8.3
Canberra	Canberra	20.2	14.9	1410	630	360	—	57	—

Milang	Langhorne Creek	19.9	10.3	1520	410	140	440	60	8.3
Mornington	Mornington Peninsula	19.9	9.8	1570	740	320	—	64	—
Coonawarra	Coonawarra	19.6	9.8	1430	650	220	350	(65)	7.8
Bordeaux*	Bordeaux	19.5	10.1	1352	890	380	—	74	7.6
Healesville	Yarra Valley	19.4	11.0	1490	910	400	50	63	7.4
Dijon*	Burgundy	19.5	18.1	1140	740	400	360	65	7.8
Stirling	Adelaide Hills	19.1	11.3	1270	1120	310	—	53	(8.5)
Strasbourg*	Alsace	19.1	18.5	1060	745	400	—	71	6.6
Geelong	Geelong	19.0	9.6	1470	540	250	270	62	7.8

COOL 17.0 – 18.9°C

Napier	Hawke's Bay	18.8	10.2	1460	780	340	160	64	7.4
Gisborne	Gisborne	18.6	9.4	1380	1030	420	120	64	7.3
Kyneton	Macedon	18.5	12.5	1030	750	290	170	64	(8.0)
Ballarat	Ballarat	18.5	11.9	1110	720	310	—	59	—
Reims*	Champagne	18.3	16.3	990	600	320	—	70	6.7
Auckland	Auckland	18.1	8.2	1350	1370	560	60	72	6.6
Heywood	Drumborg	17.7	8.4	1300	850	300	—	67	7.0
Blenheim	Marlborough	17.7	11.0	1152	740	300	160	63	7.8
Launceston	Tamar Valley	17.2	10.3	1020	790	310	220	65	7.3
Nelson	Nelson	17.0	10.6	997	1000	460	80	68	7.6

COLD 16.9°C

South Hobart	South Tasmania	16.8	9.0	1000	570	280	—	56	—
Canterbury/ Christchurch	Canterbury	16.4	10.9	910	660	280	170	68	6.4

( ) denotes estimate

[ ] denotes surplus of rainfall over vineyard water requirements.

* French data is all inverted by 6 months.

SOURCES OF DATA

(1) 'The Grape-growing Regions of Australia', Peter Dry and Richard Smart. In B Coombe and P Dry (eds),
'Viticulture', *Resources in Australia* Vol. 1, Australian Industrial Publishers, Adelaide (1988), pages 37–60.
(2) 'A Climatic Classification for Australian Viticultural Regions', by Richard Smart
and Peter Dry, in *Australian Grapevines and Winemakers* (April 1980), pages 8–16.
(3) *Climate Change and the New Zealand Wine Industry — Prospects for the Third Millennium*, Richard Smart.
(4) *Climatic Averages of Australia*, Australian Government Publishing Service, Canberra (1975).
(5) *Summaries of Climatological Observations to 1970*, Government Printer, Wellington (1973).

CLIMATIC CHANGE AND
THE GREENHOUSE EFFECT

The last Ice Age occurred 25,000 to 14,000 years ago. The earth then warmed rapidly, and in Australasia 8000 to 10,000 years ago reached temperatures 1°C to 2°C higher than those of today, before progressive waves of cooling and warming ultimately produced the regime of the late twentieth century.

On a shorter time scale, there is considerable evidence to suggest that the period from the late 1400s to the mid 1500s was exceptionally warm in Europe. In 1509 there were 139 vineyards recorded in England, of which 11 were owned by the monarch, Henry VIII, 67 by noblemen and 52 by the Church. In Germany there were a series of abundant and high quality vintages, culminating in the fabulous vintage of 1540. In that year the Rhine stopped flowing and could be crossed by foot: wine was cheaper than water. As in 1989 in France, there were two vintages: a 'normal' albeit early, vintage, followed by a second harvest four to six weeks later of the secondary bunches which usually failed to ripen.

The worm then turned in dramatic fashion. Between 1625 and 1715 the coldest weather recorded in the last 1000 years struck the vineyards of Europe. It put an end to English viticulture for centuries to come, but it was no less severe in France. The 1690s saw a catastrophic run of vintages: Chateau Latour sold no wine at all in the four vintages up to 1693, and 1694 and 1695 were terrible years. Then in the winter of 1709 the great freeze struck: even at Marseilles, in the warmest part of France, the temperature dropped to 17.5°C below zero. It caused near total destruction of the French vineyards, although the wisdom of hindsight tells us that the wholesale replanting which followed gave rise to Bordeaux as we know it today.

I recount these swings in fortune simply to put the events of today, and in particular the Greenhouse effect, into perspective. It is not to say we should not be concerned about our environment and the damage or change — the two words are in effect used interchangeably — mankind's occupation of earth causes to the environment. Perspective is also needed when we look at the causes. The Greenhouse gases, so-called because along with water vapour and clouds they trap heat energy which would otherwise be re-radiated into space, are carbon dioxide, methane and chlorofluorocarbons (CFCs).

All one hears about is CFCs, yet methane accumulation is increasing at 2 per cent a year — largely as a result of the internal combustion mechanics of the ever increasing herds of beef and dairy cattle. Carbon dioxide is increasing at the rate of 0.5 per cent per year, and its concentration is now 25 per cent higher than it was 200 years ago. And carbon dioxide is the base building block for all plant growth via the process of photosynthesis: increase the concentration of carbon dioxide

and you increase the rate of growth of the plant. Studies have predicted a 10 to 15 per cent increase in the growth rate of vines, while *Pinus radiata* (pine tree) seedlings have shown a 30 per cent increase. No one other than those directly profiting supports the destruction of the world's rainforests, but nature may outsmart us all yet by accelerating the growth of all other vegetation and hence pull the carbon dioxide levels back into balance.

All of this, of course, suggests that global warming is far from an unmitigated disaster for vignerons, and in particular for those in New Zealand. On the other hand, there is simply no way of knowing what effect accelerated growth will have on grape (and wine) quality. Dr Stuart Boag of Charles Sturt University, New South Wales, has pointed out that the chemical compounds which are key determinants of grape and wine flavour — principally monoterpenes and methoxy pyrazines — are not part of normal growth and development by the metabolic pathways common to all plants. In other words, these flavour determinants may be diluted in the wake of increased growth and yield.

What seems to be beyond dispute is that in Australasia we will see temperature increases of between 1.5°C and 4.5°C (depending on which rate of annual increase you accept) by the year 2030. This year is selected because it is well within the commercial life expectancy of a vineyard planted in 1990. And as Dr Richard Smart has pointed out, a 3°C increase in the mean January temperature would make Coonawarra (South Australia) almost as hot as the Hunter Valley (New South Wales), and the Barossa Valley (South Australia) hotter than the Riverland regions. On the other side of the ledger, Tasmania, the Macedon Ranges and the Dandenong Hills (Victoria), Otago and Christchurch on New Zealand's South Island (to name a few regions) would move from marginal to secure climates, while a host of high country or low latitude regions presently not under consideration in Australia and New Zealand would become viable.

Similarly in Europe, the axis for premium wine production would shift to the north, creating great wealth and opportunity for some, but causing immense problems for areas such as Bordeaux, Burgundy and Champagne. Established regions in the New World will cope: they will simply alter the balance of the varieties grown in the vineyard and happily create new styles in the winery. Appellation Controlée, and the investment of 1000 years, allows no such flexibility. Bordeaux may cope to a degree (Cabernet Sauvignon is a flexible variety), but Pinot Noir is very intolerant and exacting, so what is the future of red Burgundy? And what of Champagne? Only time will tell.

WINEMAKING IN AUSTRALIA
AND NEW ZEALAND

Thanks to a long history of distinguished research (principally through the Commonwealth Scientific and Industrial Research Organisation (CSIRO) and the Australian Wine Research Institute, but also through its teaching institutions, headed by Roseworthy Agricultural College in South Australia and Charles Sturt University in Western Australia) and no less to the imperatives of a warm to hot climate which is friendly to grapes but not to winemaking, Australia has developed formidable winemaking expertise. Its research scientists, its viticulturists and its winemakers are all highly regarded on the world stage. New Zealand, which has no specialist tertiary institution for winemakers, has drawn heavily on Australia's practical winemaking talents but has more than contributed its share in research.

For much of this century most of that effort went into building winery and winemaking skills, but over the last decade the focus has shifted to the vineyard, and it is likely to remain there for the remainder of this century. Winemaking is essentially a simple process — because wine is a natural product, and not a manufactured one — and it is exceedingly unlikely there will be any major technological innovations in the winery. Rather there will be more sophisticated use of the many options open to winemakers, the choice of which will become increasingly informed. For while there are limits on innovation, there are almost none on research into increasing the understanding of the interrelationship between the chemistry of grapes, wine and winemaking on the one hand, and what we taste on the other.

One small example of this is the research of Dr Malcolm Allen and others into methoxypyrazine, the flavour compound responsible for the distinctive herbaceous aroma and flavour of Cabernet Sauvignon and Sauvignon Blanc. Methoxypyrazines occur at levels of between 2 and 35 parts per trillion, and humans can detect their presence (in smell and/or taste) at the lower end of the scale. Dr Allen's techniques can detect concentrations at 0.1 or 0.2 parts per trillion, which is as one millimetre is to the circumference of the earth.

Techniques such as nuclear magnetic resonance, gas chromatography, mass photospectrometry, coupled to a computer, and ultra-violet spectrophotometry will take analysis of the components of wine into the next century, but they are not going to change the basic process of fermentation, which was first harnessed some time around 8000 BC, and which resulted in wine becoming one of the most important food commodities used and traded over the ensuing 10,000 years.

But it is true that Australasian winemakers have established distinctive wine styles by their selection of techniques, and it is to these techniques, philosophies and consequences that I now turn.

AROMATIC DRY WHITE WINE
(Rhine Riesling, Gewurztraminer in Australia; Müller-Thurgau, Rhine Riesling, Gewurztraminer, in New Zealand.)

The aim here is to produce a crisp, intensely fruity wine with residual sugar at or below the threshold level (5 to 7 grammes per litre) and with the lowest possible phenolic levels. (Phenols are the flavour and colour compounds present in the skins of grapes.) This is achieved by pressing the grapes immediately after they are crushed, and — in the manner of Champagne — separating the freely running and lightly pressed juice from the more heavily pressed material. The juice is then either cold settled or filtered to brilliant clarity, and the wine fermented in stainless steel (using carefully selected cultured yeasts) at temperatures below 13°C.

There are relatively few choices in a fairly narrow winemaking pathway. One occurs at the point of crushing: do you protect the must and juice with additions of sulphur dioxide and ascorbic acid or do you deliberately allow the juice to oxidise? The latter course is an example of winemakers opting to turn back the clock by a hundred years or more, the rationale being to remove (through that process of oxidation) unstable phenolics which, if protected pre-fermentation, may ultimately cause the wine to age more quickly in both colour and flavour. Most makers eschew juice oxidation, as it does lead to lower total flavour.

The next choice is of the temperature of the fermentation: some winemakers opt for extremely slow fermentation rates (achieved by chilling the fermenting must to lower than normal temperatures), others prefer a slightly faster rate which will see fermentation completed in 2 to 3 weeks. The ultra-cold and slow fermentation (taking up to 2 months) appears to be going out of favour, as it exacerbates reductive or 'armpit' aromas which tend to linger on in bottle.

The last choice is the level of residual sugar: the rule of thumb here is the higher the quality of the wine, the lower the residual sugar (down to the point of absolute dryness). In New Zealand, partly in deference to public taste, the residual sugar levels tend to be substantially higher than they do in Australia.

There are no direct equivalents to Australasian dry white aromatic wines in other countries.

MEDIUM BODIED NEUTRAL DRY WHITE WINES

(Chenin Blanc, Colombard, Muscat Gordo Blanco, Crouchen, Trebbiano in Australia; Müller-Thurgau, Muscat Dr Hogg, Chenin Blanc in New Zealand.)

These wines are basically headed towards cask, flagon and the very bottom end of the bottled wine market where they will typically appear under generic labels such as White Burgundy and Chablis. The making techniques are similar to those for aromatic dry white wines, although it is fair to assume that slightly less care will be taken to separate pressings, that fermentation temperatures may be a little higher, and that residual sugar levels will often be higher (particularly in New Zealand). Oak is seldom used, and the aim is to present a moderately fruity white wine which has limitations on its flavour deriving from the high cropping levels of the relevant vines.

MEDIUM TO FULL BODIED WHITE WINES, FREQUENTLY OAK FERMENTED OR MATURED

(Chardonnay, Semillon, Sauvignon Blanc, Verdelho in Australia; Chardonnay, Sauvignon Blanc, Semillon in New Zealand.)

It is with these wines that the winemaking options and techniques expand dramatically, so much so that it becomes impractical to fully explain the implications of the choices, nor indeed to even mention some of the less frequently encountered possibilities which are feasible in a small winery or specialist situation, but not in a normal commercial winery.

The first choice lies between the conventional approach of first crushing the grapes to remove the stalks and split the berries before taking the must to the press, and the alternative of placing the whole bunches directly into the press. The latter is a very ancient technique, but was commercialised in Champagne, France and has always been an essential part of the winemaking of that region. Whole-bunch pressing is a state-of-the-art approach, its supporters pointing to the much finer and crisper wines (with lower phenolic levels) which result. If the winemaker elects to crush the grapes, there are then two choices: to proceed direct to the press, which will leave more phenolics than if the whole bunch is placed in the press, or the juice can be left in contact with the skin. This is done by leaving the juice and crushed berries in contact with each other, usually in a stainless steel tank, but sometimes in the press itself (depending on press design and winery capacity) for periods of anything between 2 and 24 hours, with a sub-choice of temperature. This is precisely the opposite route to that of whole-bunch pressing, leading to sharply increased levels of extraction of phenolics.

The implicit tug of war between phenolic and non-phenolic winemaking is not, or should not be, waged in a vacuum. If the winemaker has ripe, high flavoured grapes which are high in phenols and which have been grown in a warm climate, whole-bunch pressing and/or oxidative handling may well be the appropriate pathway. Conversely, if the winemaker is dealing with delicately flavoured, cool-climate grapes with low phenolic levels, or with grapes which have come from high yielding vines which accordingly lack flavour concentration, the skin contact method may well be the appropriate choice.

The next option concerns juice clarification prior to fermentation. The choices here range between rough settling overnight through to brilliantly clear juice achieved either by prolonged settling in tank at low temperatures or by filtration or centrifugation. For a while in Australia, absolutely clear juice was considered the only proper option, but a feeling that greater complexity could be obtained from slightly cloudy juice have led to some winemakers opting for partial clarification.

Next comes the choice of fermentation temperature, coupled with the choice of fermentation vehicle. Chardonnay is typically fermented at slightly warmer temperatures than Rhine Riesling, one rule of thumb being the conversion of half a degree of sugar to alcohol per day, speeding up towards the end of fermentation by allowing the temperature to rise somewhat. However, either by choice or through lack of appropriate cooling mechanisms some Australasian winemakers and almost all French winemakers ferment at substantially higher temperatures, ranging from 15 to 28°C.

This lack of control occurs most commonly where the winemaker opts for fermentation in oak barrels. Unless there is a refrigerated cool room available to store the barrels, or the barrels are pumped out at least once a day and the wine is passed through a must chiller or heat exchanger, barrel fermentation necessarily involves temperatures above 20°C. Once again, the choices (and the implications of the choice) have to be viewed against the style and quality of the base

BOTTLED RED & WHITE TABLE WINE

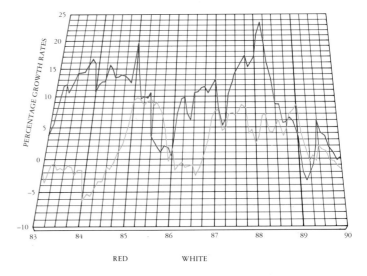

RED   WHITE

material. If the juice is high in sugar and high in flavour and concentration, temperature control is far less critical than it is with delicate juice. Likewise, if the juice has been totally clarified prior to fermentation, temperature control is again less critical.

Allied with barrel fermentation is the question of oak: what oak type, and what should be the degree of charring of the oak. The three main groups of oak are French, American and German, each giving radically different effects.

Then comes the question: should the wine be taken through the secondary malolactic fermentation or not — or more precisely, whether there should be total, partial or no malolactic fermentation. This is a bacterially-triggered fermentation causing malic acid to decompose and form lactic acid and carbon dioxide. It occurs in almost every red wine, and is sometimes artificially induced and sometimes naturally occurring; it normally has to be induced in white wines. Its effect is to soften the texture of the wine and to add complexity to its structure and flavour; the downside is a reduction in primary fruit flavour and varietal character. Almost all French White Burgundies undergo malolactic fermentation (usually without the necessity of inoculation) and most Californian Chardonnays undergo at least a partial malolactic fermentation. Practices vary widely in Australia: once again, the decision whether to use it or not should be dependent on the degree of available flavour in the base wine. If it is abundant, and if the acid levels are good, malolactic fermentation (in whole or in part) may well be the appropriate choice.

Whether or not the wine is in tank or in barrel, but especially in the latter situation, there is a choice between post fermentation clarification and filtration, or lees contact. At the end of fermentation all of the dead yeast cells form a thick creamy/muddy coating on the bottom of the barrel or tank. The French have always highly prized the lees, retaining them in the wine and indeed stirring them once or twice a week in the period of 4 to 6 months after fermentation. Traditional Australian winemaking regarded lees as unhealthy and undesirable by-products of fermentation, and got rid of them by racking and filtration as quickly as possible after fermentation. Now lees contact and stirring are extremely common; all those who practise it are unanimous that it protects the wine against oxidation and significantly enhances the structure and feel of the wine in the mouth, inducing a creamy texture which will not otherwise occur.

Finally, there is the question of length of time in barrel prior to bottling. This involves a judgment on the part of the winemaker about the desirable level of oak flavour. There is a strong move towards more subtle use of oak — a move fostered by the high cost of oak barrels. It is this cost, incidentally, which has led to the formal recognition and legalisation of the use of oak chips: the chips are placed in special inert food grade polythene netting bags and are suspended in the fermenting wine and/or the maturing wine. This process can partially or wholly bypass the need for oak barrels in imparting oak flavour. It is a technique which is very useful for low to mid-priced wines, and, properly handled, can have spectacularly successful results. It is not used at the top end of the market, for oak barrels do more than impart flavour: they play a very important role in shaping the texture and structure of high quality wines through gentle oxidation and other physical processes of change which cannot occur in tank.

Semillon and Sauvignon Blanc can both be treated in an identical fashion to Chardonnay, or they can be made in a manner much closer to that of aromatic dry white wines. New Zealand Sauvignon Blanc is the classic example: there are the intensely fruity and pungent steel fermented, early-bottled styles exemplified by Montana, the partially barrel fermented wines of Cloudy Bay, and the heavily oaked variants which are often labelled Fumé Blanc, from a wide range of producers.

BOTRYTISED SWEET WINES
(Rhine Riesling and Semillon.)

Clearly, there are two styles: the Germanic, non-wooded Rhine Rieslings, and the Sauternes-style oaked Semillons. There is in fact a third style, which is of declining importance: it is the Hunter Sauternes/porphyry type made by McWilliam's and Lindemans. Here, a very full bodied but otherwise undistinguished dry base white wine is sweetened by the addition of grape juice concentrate, and the resultant mix is given reasonably extended wood maturation and (in order to show its best) very extended bottle maturation. Botrytis plays no part in these wines, which are as close as any Australian table wine comes to being manufactured.

The handling of botrytised wines is (or can be) extremely difficult because of the viscosity and turgidity of the material, making it difficult to pump from the crusher to the press, and then extremely difficult to press once it arrives. The handling of the juice, too, can cause all sorts of problems, as it is extremely difficult to protect. Much higher sulphur levels are needed than in dry white wine making, but otherwise the same care and slow fermentation is required.

NOUVEAU AND CARBONIC MACERATION STYLES

The concept of carbonic maceration is as old as wine itself. It seems almost certain that the first wine was made when grapes stored in clay pots as a source of winter food spontaneously fermented. Two things happen under these conditions: the bunches cut from the vine are deprived of carbon dioxide through the plant's system, and so create their own carbon dioxide by converting sugar within the berry to alcohol. This is not a yeast-induced fermentation, and it is relatively short lived, for once 4 degrees baume of sugar has been so converted, the alcohol poisons and kills the grape, terminating this phase of chemical change. The other trigger is quite separate: juice leaks from damaged berries, or from undamaged berries at the bottom of the container owing to pressure from above. This juice then reacts with wild yeasts and commences to ferment. In an uncontrolled situation, there will be a gradual breakdown and a near-total fermentation may occur. This, at least, was the primitive and spontaneous form of fermentation which I postulate for the dawn of wine-time.

Modern winemaking obviously controls the whole process far better. Once the intra-cellular fermentation has been completed (usually in 7 to 12 days, depending on temperature — the higher the temperature, the quicker the fermentation), the grapes are removed from their container, crushed, and a normal fermentation then proceeds. In the meantime, any juice that has exuded will have been protected from oxidation by carbon dioxide gas introduced into the storage vessel; some winemakers add yeast to ensure this juice will ferment, while others deliberately suppress fermentation with the use of sulphur dioxide. After the grapes have been crushed and placed in a conventional fermenter, they are basically treated like any other red wine, although it is common practice for the must to be pressed before the end of primary fermentation. The aim of this style of winemaking is to provide a fresh and fruity wine, in which tannin plays no significant role.

LIGHT BODIED RED WINES
(Pinot Noir, Gamay (in New Zealand) and Shiraz in limited quantities.)

The options available to the maker of Pinot Noir are almost as diverse as those for the handling of Chardonnay. It is quite possible that three quite different fermentation techniques will be employed, and the wines made by those different fermentation techniques will then be blended together to provide the finished wine. Thus part of the wine may be made using the first method, ie the carbonic maceration process described above. In the second technique, part of the wine — usually the major part, and indeed frequently the whole — is made by filling an open-topped fermenter to one-third of its capacity with whole bunches of grapes. The remainder of the fermenter is filled with conventionally crushed grapes, and the fermentation is commenced by the addition of yeast in the usual manner. Conventional crushing may be a misnomer: many Pinot Noir makers use adjustable crushers which can be set so that the stalks are removed, but the berries themselves are left whole. In this scenario in particular the third method may

be preferred: namely, passing all of the grapes through a crusher with the rollers set wide, and filling the fermenter with largely intact berries.

There are then four alternatives for handling the fermenting must. If whole bunches have been used, rather than pass them through the crusher, one can use the traditional French pigeage method: standing in the vat and treading the grapes by foot. After several days of this process, there is so much juice that it then becomes possible to agitate the must by plunging, which is the method used from the start where one has two-thirds crushed grapes and one-third whole bunches. The winemaker stands on top of the vat (on a plank or board if it is open) with a stainless steel pole on the bottom end of which is fixed a small circular disc. This pushes down the surface of the must in 20 centimetre plate-sized pieces, allowing the juice underneath the cap (which forms on top of the must) to then circulate and pass over the top of the cap.

The next method is to use heavy wooden boards (fitted underneath lugs on the side of the fermenter) to keep the skins, which would otherwise rise to the surface and form a cap, submerged. The next method is to pump off fluid from the bottom of the vat and spray it over the cap until the cap is totally saturated and broken up. Pumping over may also be used in conjunction with header-boards.

Most makers of Pinot Noir wish the temperature of the ferment to reach 30°C, and will take no steps to cool it until it reaches this level.

There are three choices once the fermentation nears completion. One is to press the must with one or two degrees of sugar remaining, and to complete the fermentation in barrel (red wine barrel fermentation, which is quite different to white wine barrel fermentation). The next is to simply allow the fermentation to fully complete, press the wine and take it to tank, allow the heavy lees to settle, and then at some subsequent stage take clear wine to barrel. The third option is to allow extended maceration (contact between the skin and the by-now dry wine) at the end of primary fermentation. This extracts tannins of a different kind to those extracted during the primary fermentation.

A few brave makers then use lees contact in the same way as Chardonnay; some will inoculate the wine to initiate malolactic fermentation during the course of the primary fermentation, others will leave it until later, and yet others will rely on naturally-occurring malolactic fermentations. The choice of oak is extremely important: Pinot Noir is an exceedingly delicate wine, and can easily be overwhelmed by inappropriate oak. Accordingly, some prefer to use old oak, but the top Burgundy estates all use substantial new oak — some use 100 per cent new oak. The oak type should be restricted to French, with Troncais, Allier and Nevers the leading contenders.

Pinot Noir is usually bottled somewhere between 8 and 14 months after vintage — much earlier than full bodied dry reds. The techniques described here are basically those of Burgundy, although there one finds an amazing array of handling techniques including the controversial cold maceration pre-fermentation where the grapes are crushed but the onset of fermentation is delayed by very high sulphur additions; other controversial techniques include various forms of semi or total pasteurisation.

Small quantities of other red wines, notably Shiraz, are made using at least some of the techniques described above.

Unless the more conventional Burgundian-inspired techniques are used, 'normal' red wine making techniques (being those used for full bodied red wines) tend to produce very simple, one-dimensional wines which are deficient in colour and flavour and structure.

MEDIUM TO FULL BODIED DRY REDS
(Shiraz, Cabernet Sauvignon, Cabernet Franc, Merlot, and Malbec.)

The techniques here are less diverse, but as with all winemaking, the particular technique chosen should be consciously matched to the winemaker's perception of the quality and type of fruit he or she is dealing with, and to the style objective the winemaker has in mind. Making wine from a recipe book without an intuitive feeling for what one is doing is no more satisfactory than someone who has never cooked blindly following the recipe of a three star chef.

The grapes are crushed with the rollers set at a conventional distance, and there is no return of stalks to the fermenter. A few winemakers, such as Michael Brajkovich at Kumeu River in New Zealand, Philip Shaw at Rosemount Estate (in Coonawarra, South Australia, and the Upper Hunter Valley, New South Wales) and (sometimes) Murray Tyrrell (of Tyrrell's Wines in the Lower Hunter Valley, New South Wales) are content to rely upon natural yeasts to commence the ferment, and hope that the yeasts will not do their work for several days, and so allow a degree of pre-fermentation maceration. Most winemakers however, immediately initiate fermentation by the addition of cultured yeasts, and some add small quantities of sulphur dioxide at the time the grapes are crushed to make quite certain that wild yeasts do not play a role. Increasingly, however, where the grapes are free of mould or disease, winemakers do not add any sulphur dioxide before fermentation, nor indeed until the completion of malolactic fermentation.

The wine is then fermented in stainless steel (or possibly wax-lined concrete tanks) which are very often closed. If closed, either header boards or pumping over is used to agitate the must, this process being repeated two or three times a day. Some small wineries prefer to use open fermenters and to plunge the cap.

Fermentation temperatures may be checked by refrigeration and held to between 18 and 28°C, depending on the philosophy of the winemaker. The top end of the range is used in Bordeaux, France, and is believed by many to assist in the extraction of colour and tannins. Those who opt for fermentation temperatures at the lower end of the range say they are retaining more of the volatile flavour esters and compounds, thereby enhancing the fruitiness of the finished wine. With full bodied dry reds, many winemakers opt to leave the wine in contact with the skins for 7 to 14 days (or even longer) at the end of fermentation. If the grapes are low in tannin, this is an appropriate way to proceed. If they are naturally tannic, typically where they have been grown in a warm climate, it seems entirely illogical: it is the trap into which Californian winemakers fell throughout much of the 1970s and 1980s. The alternative, of course, is to run the wine off shortly before the end of fermentation — as is done in the case of Penfolds Grange Hermitage and many Wolf Blass wines (both of the Barossa Valley in South Australia), and an increasing number of other small maker red wines — extracting oak tannins in a way that cannot be achieved if inert wine is added to a barrel. There is a school of thought which says that if the malolactic fermentation takes place in barrel, the effect is not very different to that of completing the fermentation in barrel, but not all would agree.

The choice of oak type is very wide: American oak, which imparts a distinctive vanilla bean character, has always been widely used in Australia by companies such as Penfolds, and is also used to a degree in New Zealand. Interestingly, it is little used in the United States, even though it is extremely cheap compared to French oak. Although all types of French oak are used, as is Portuguese, Yugoslav and German, the conventional choice is Nevers or Allier .

The wine is usually bottled after spending at least a year in oak: in a big winery it may well have spent another 4 or 5 months in tank both before it goes into oak and after it comes out.

SALES BY WINE STYLE—MARKET SHARE
(JULY 1989 to JUNE 1990)

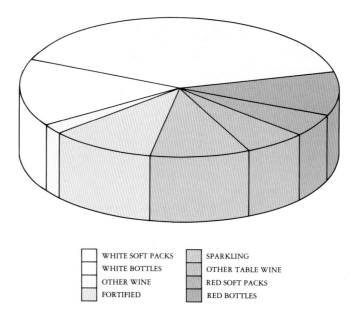

WHITE SOFT PACKS   SPARKLING
WHITE BOTTLES   OTHER TABLE WINE
OTHER WINE   RED SOFT PACKS
FORTIFIED   RED BOTTLES

REGION OF ORIGIN

Appellation Controllée (commonly abbreviated to AC or AOC) is such a fundamental part of French wine law that it is assumed that it grew up four, five or six centuries ago at the same time as the great estates and chateaux. In fact, it is strictly a creature of the twentieth century, born in the chaotic aftermath of phylloxera which had decimated France's vineyards in the last quarter of the nineteenth century. By devastating the vineyards, phylloxera destroyed the orderly wine market: there was an acute shortage of quality wine, and producers were in dire financial straits. It was a perfect environment for fraud, shortcuts and passing-off, all of which duly flourished. The French Government was forced to act, and between 1905 and 1935 the legislative framework we know today was put into place.

It did not end fraud, of course. Scandals have erupted regularly since 1935, the most famous being the Cruse prosecution of 1974. Anyone who is interested in this whole subject should read Nicholas Faith's *The Winemasters* (Hamish Hamilton, 1978), an immaculately researched and eminently readable history of the Bordeaux wine trade.

AOC, or guarantee of region of origin, is an extraordinarily badly understood concept. The basic misunderstanding is that it is a guarantee of quality, when in fact it is principally a guarantee of origin. It is true that many appellation schemes do provide for a tasting of the wine seeking appellation status, but this tasting is usually concerned with establishing that the wine has 'typicite' — in other words, it has the typical character of other wines of the same appellation of that year. In a poor vintage the hallmark of that 'typicite' may be greenness, bitterness or hardness, and it is an increasingly common occurrence for wines in a poor vintage which are too different (ie too good) to be denied appellation: this trend has emerged in the wake of the invasion of New World winemakers (principally Australasian and American) into the bastions of France.

Many of the French (and other European) AOC schemes rigidly prescribe those grape varieties which are permitted and those which are prohibited; pruning methods and maximum yields; and minimum alcoholic strengths. In France these were simply the codification of centuries of empirical experience and observation, formalised to combat the problems which had arisen in the wake of phylloxera.

The wholly inappropriate nature of such regulations for the New World can best be understood against the background of the Italian experience following the introduction of Denominazione d'Origine Controllata (DOC) in 1963. This took existing viticultural and production practices and enshrined them in all their imperfection. Within a decade Italian winemakers had discovered Chardonnay and Cabernet Sauvignon, and Antinori estate in the Chianti region in Tuscany had put Sassicaia and Tignanello onto the market, establishing once and for all that some of Italy's greatest wines could easily overcome the stigma of illegitimacy and thrive under the supposed denigration of 'Vino da Tavola'.

So it is that Australia has very sensibly limited the scope of its controls. By sheer coincidence, the initial piece of uniform legislation (adopted by all States) was passed in 1963, in the form of the Pure Foods Act Regulations. The effect and implications of these regulations, and of the recent Label Integrity Programme, are explained on page 39.

What was missing was a nationally agreed scheme defining the regions (and subregions). Victoria started the ball rolling with a comprehensive guarantee of origin scheme, which was so detailed that it listed every licensed vigneron and even a number of vineyards with no winery or label attached.

The Australian Wine and Brandy Corporation has now compiled a national list which is the basis of ongoing discussions with the EEC (European Economic Community) and with the BATF (the United States regulatory authority). Once again we can learn from Italy. The maze and complexity of Italian regions, grape varieties and wine names (frequently interchangeable) do not present any particular problem to the Italians; however for the rest of the world they are still a nightmare, and before the advent of DOC they made Italian wine all but impossible to market in other countries. Australian place names are familiar to us, but are unknown and incomprehensible in the United States or in Scandinavia, two of our largest overseas markets.

From a marketing viewpoint it is essential we start with an agreed area description which is consistently and uniformly applied. Only then can the long process of education begin. There is, however, a sting in the tail. There is no point in bringing the Australian region scheme into law unless it is agreed with by the EEC and BATF. For so long as Australia insists on using names stolen from the French (Champagne, Claret, Burgundy, Chablis, Beaujolais and so on), it seems very unlikely that EEC agreement will be forthcoming. At the moment we are held to an archaic, fragmented and illogical patchwork quilt built up in haphazard fashion over the years. By way of example, Yarra Valley (Victoria) wineries cannot use Yarra Valley as their region of origin: most have to use either 'Lilydale' or 'Victoria' — a manifestly unfair andstupid situation.

Finally, one common misconception should be laid to rest. The regions or origin schemes do not prevent winemakers from making and marketing regional blends. A wine made from a number of regions within, say, Victoria can be labelled 'Victoria', one made from South Australian and Victorian regions can be labelled 'South-east Australia' — and, wines are entitled to just such labelling.

UNDERSTANDING THE LABEL:
THE LABEL INTEGRITY PROGRAMME

Since 1963 Australia has had the legal framework designed to guarantee that the consumer gets what the label on the bottle says he or she is getting (apart from the all-important agreement on the geographic boundaries and names of Australia's regions of origin).

There have been two major flaws. First and foremost, there has been little effective enforcement of the law; and secondly, like most legislation of its kind, there are loopholes or shortcomings. The major problem of enforcement of the law has now been cured: as a result of resolutions passed at the 1988 and 1989 annual general meetings of the Australian Wine and Brandy Corporation, Australian winemakers by their own vote and initiative caused amendments to be made to the Australian Wine and Brandy Corporation Act which will result in effective enforcement of the law.

Indeed, the vignerons of Australia went one step further and imposed on themselves a levy to provide the funds necessary for enforcement. Previously, that duty had been left to the various State health departments; with a few exceptions, those departments hadn't the time, money or inclination to pursue the few winemakers who were prepared to put the reputation of the whole industry at stake.

The amendments to the Australian Wine and Brandy Corporation Act meant that all winemakers have to keep very detailed records of grape purchases, crushings, production and sales to support any claim made about the vintage, the variety or the region of origin of any of their wines. The key to this is the so-called 'label claim': this will catch 99 per cent of all wine sold in bottles, and an increasing percentage of wine sold in cask. In other words, wines marketed in this fashion will almost certainly stipulate one or more of the vintage, the variety or the region of origin. The only wines to escape the net are those which make no claim: they are non vintage wines sold under a brand name which makes no reference to the variety used or the region from which the grapes came.

The records which must be kept are sufficiently detailed for an auditor to trace the fate of every bunch of grapes which comes into the winery and which finishes up in the bottle or cask making a label claim.

This initiative did not, however, make any changes to the framework of the Pure Foods Act Regulations (first enacted in 1963 and now effectively embodied in the regulations of the Commonwealth Food Standards Code 1987). The five basic provisions of that legislation are as follows: if a wine is said to be made from a particular variety, it must contain at least 80 per cent of that variety. If it is said to be made from a blend of varieties, those varieties must be listed in descending order of volume. If the wine is claimed to come from a particular region, it must contain 80 per cent of wine from that region, while if it is said to be a blend of regions, they too must be listed in descending order. Finally, if a vintage is claimed, 95 per cent of the wine must be from that vintage.

There are several obvious shortcomings in the legislation. For a start, there is no requirement that the actual percentages be specified, so a 'Shiraz Cabernet' may contain 55 per cent Shiraz and 45 per cent Cabernet Sauvignon, but equally well may be 95 per cent Shiraz and 5 per cent Cabernet Sauvignon. Next, the 80 per cent rule has a 'double-up' effect: a wine labelled Coonawarra Cabernet Sauvignon will comply with the regulations if it contains 60 per cent Coonawarra Cabernet Sauvignon, 20 per cent Coonawarra Shiraz, and 20 per cent Southern Vales Cabernet Sauvignon.

But perhaps the greatest problem of all stems (completely inadvertently) from the legal requirement that the producer specify on the label either its full name and address, or provide a registered number under the Pure Foods Act. Most in fact opt for the name and address route. So 'Smith Vintners, Happy Dreams Road, Erewhon, New South Wales' can perfectly legally label a wine '1988 Chardonnay', and the unwary consumer will naturally assume the Chardonnay was grown in Erewhon — indeed grown at Smith's vineyard (which the consumer can see as he or she drives to the front door) in Happy Dreams Road — when in fact it came from a co-operative 600 kilometres away.

A modest start has been made on circumscribing the use of meaningless terms on labels, once again spurred on by the requirements of the EEC, which dictates that 'descriptive terms' may only be used if they are prescribed by the producing country and approved by the EEC. The committee of the Australian Wine and Brandy Corporation has recommended that some descriptive terms be supported (under strict conditions) and that others be not supported. Those terms considered meaningless include 'Vintage Reserve', 'Special Vintage', 'Specially Selected', 'Exceptional' and 'Superior'. The committee suggests 'Winemaker's Selection' can only be used when the specific reason for its selection is specified on the label; 'Traditional' can be used only when none of the modern techniques of winemaking have been used in making the wine; 'Estate' must connote wine grown and produced (though not necessarily bottled) on the property described; and 'Show Reserve' can be used only for specific parcels of wine actually held for shows and ultimately released for sale.

NEW SOUTH WALES

Given the population, size and diverse geography of New South Wales, one might expect it would play a far more important role in viticulture and winemaking than it in fact does. After all, more people (over 3,500,000) live in Sydney than in the whole of South Australia, Western Australia and Tasmania put together, yet its vineyards cover only 12,508 hectares out of a total of 57,766 hectares, producing around 28 per cent of the total Australian grape crush.

The reasons are partly historical, partly climatic and partly demographic. Not surprisingly, Australia's first vines were planted in New South Wales (on the Farm Cove foreshore, near the present-day Government House), the first commercial wine was made there, and the first wine exported to England — by Gregory Blaxland in 1823 — emanated from the banks of the Parramatta River near what is now the industrial suburb of Ermington.

The centre of viticultural activity soon shifted to the Hunter Valley, and it remained there for a century. But neither the Hunter nor any other part of New South Wales experienced a gold rush remotely like that of Victoria, nor did it receive a nineteenth century influx of Silesian settlers with grape-growing in their blood as did South Australia which enabled these States — first Victoria, then South Australia — to establish wine industries of far greater size and importance.

It took the advent of irrigation (in 1914) and two successive waves of Italian immigrants, one after the First World War, the next after the Second World War, to establish the Griffith and Sunraysia areas along the Murrumbidgee and Murray Rivers.

Griffith was to become the most prolific wine producing area in the State in the aftermath of the Second World War and the table wine boom of the 1960s. It is a highly efficient and economical producer of white wine in particular, much of it of good cask quality. Like any similar region, it aspires to greater things, but really only achieves this with its botrytis-infected Semillon.

The Hunter Valley has always depended on its proximity to the Sydney and Newcastle market; as tourism has flourished, the Hunter has blossomed, and its future is absolutely assured. But for the reasons I discuss on pages 45 to 47, it is by no means a natural winemaking region.

Indeed, outside of high-altitude havens on the slopes of the Great Dividing Range, most of New South Wales is too hot, too dry, too humid and/or too wet to be really suitable for grape growing. Modern fungicide sprays, an ever-increasing understanding of the physiology of the grapevine and modern winery technology (and in the case of the Riverland areas, irrigation) make grape growing and winemaking possible in almost any situation. But it is very much the case of the dog preaching: the wonder is not that it does it well, but that it does it at all.

Increasingly, wine regions will flourish if they have outstanding climatic and geographic (principally soil) advantages or if they are close to major markets or on high-volume tourist routes. Areas such as Tumbarumba in the Southern Alps fall into the former category, while McWilliam's clearly believes the Hilltops region around Young does likewise. The Canberra District falls into the latter category, even if its vignerons wish Canberra's population would grow faster than at present. The Hastings Valley, under the energetic — indeed visionary — direction of the Cassegrain family, likewise relies heavily on the tourist trade and the attractions of nearby Port Macquarie.

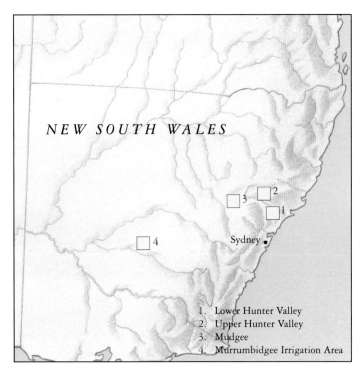

1. Lower Hunter Valley
2. Upper Hunter Valley
3. Mudgee
4. Murrumbidgee Irrigation Area

NEW SOUTH WALES WINE REGIONS
HECTAREAGE AND PRODUCTION

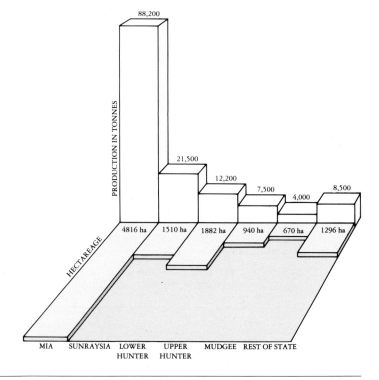

One can never be certain about the catalytic effect of success, but the mere fact of major wine company involvement in areas such as the Hilltops and Tumbarumba (the latter attracting both Seppelt and Rosemount) must give credibility and increase the chances of others big or small following the example. And vineyards are being established in (hopefully) frost-free sites up and down the Great Dividing Range: Inverell, Quirindi, Goulburn and Orange are but some of numerous locations being tried.

But I would be most surprised if a significant new wine-growing area were to emerge anywhere in New South Wales in the next 20 years — in other words, an area with 400 hectares of grapes and at least a dozen producing wineries within its confines. If that somewhat negative prediction is fulfilled, New South Wales will remain by far the most important wine market, but will increasingly lag behind South Australia in the production of all types of wine, as well as behind Victoria in the production of premium wine.

ABOVE: *Field induction of botrytis through water-spraying (Department of Agriculture trials at Lindemans).*

LOWER HUNTER VALLEY

If you were born and bred in Sydney, the Lower Hunter Valley is not only the greatest and the most important wine region in Australia, it is tantamount to the only region. If you come from overseas, and have an interest in wine, it is a fair bet it is one of the two wine districts (the Barossa Valley being the other) you will have heard of prior to your arrival and which you will propose to visit. For South Australians, it is an object of derision (with a generous dash of jealousy); for Victorians it is an area which arouses a mixture of curiosity and respect.

To a disinterested observer (if there is such a person), the most obvious characteristic of the region is the peculiar Australian beauty of the Valley. In no small measure this comes from the smoky blue of the Brokenback Range, rising threateningly above the nearest vineyards along Broke Road and distant though clearly etched as you look back from Allandale and Wilderness Road — but wherever you are, a significant part of the landscape. Apart from the Brokenback Range, the valley has only the most gentle undulations; the vineyards are concentrated on the southern side, and the Barrington Tops, on the northern side, are out of sight.

So there is that feeling of open, endless, timeless space so special to Australia. Under the pale blue summer sky, the dark, glistening green of the vines is in stark contrast to the patterns of straw, yellow and golden grass and the more olive tones of the gum trees. Attesting to the modest rainfall, which in any event tends to come in erratic heavy bursts, the grass is brown through much of the year, tenuously greening in autumn and spring.

The brown landscape hints at what the statistics say loud and clear: the Hunter Valley is an unlikely place in which to grow grapes. But when vineyards were tried across the State in the nineteenth century the situation was different. The coastal fringe (around Sydney) was too wet and too humid, and if one moved too far west, spring frosts could pose threats, even though some distinguished wines were made at

AUSTRALASIAN WINE REGIONS
1980 – 1990

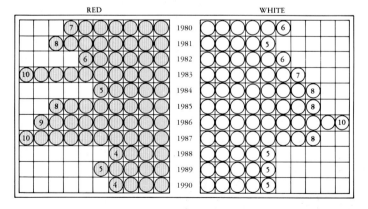

ABOVE: Chardonnay's progress: on the left, fermenting wine; in the middle, partially settled after five weeks in barrel; on the right, filter-bright finished wine.

THE REGION IN BRIEF

LOCATION AND ELEVATION
32°50'S 151°21'E
75 m

CLIMATE
The climate is undeniably hot, but there are a number of mitigating factors. Rainfall is 740 mm, of which 530 mm falls between October and April, and the summer humidity and afternoon cloud cover which comes in with the sea breeze means that evaporation is surprisingly low, and the vines' need of supplementary water is far less than the temperature summation would indicate. That summation is 2070 HDD, and is exceeded only by the Upper Hunter and Riverland irrigation areas.

SOIL
The soils vary widely, from friable red duplex soils (Dr2.23, 2.33 and 2.43), through to deep friable loam soils (Um6.11) such as one sees around the Tyrrell's winery, and at Lake's Folly and McWilliam's Rosehill. The painful lessons of 1968 to 1988 are that much of the poorer soil, with heavy clay subsoils and poor drainage, is simply not suited to viticulture. Acidity has recently been recognised as an additional significant problem in restricting yields.

HARVEST TIME
Mid-January — early March

PRINCIPAL GRAPE VARIETIES
Semillon, 436 ha	*Shiraz, 449 ha*
Chardonnay, 475 ha	*Cabernet Sauvignon, 163 ha*
Gewurztraminer, 28 ha	*Pinot Noir, 85 ha*
Verdelho, 28 ha	
Sauvignon Blanc, 24 ha	
TOTAL PLANTINGS 1882 ha	

FACING PAGE: Peterson's Vineyard at the aptly-named Mount View, near Pokolbin in the Lower Hunter Valley.

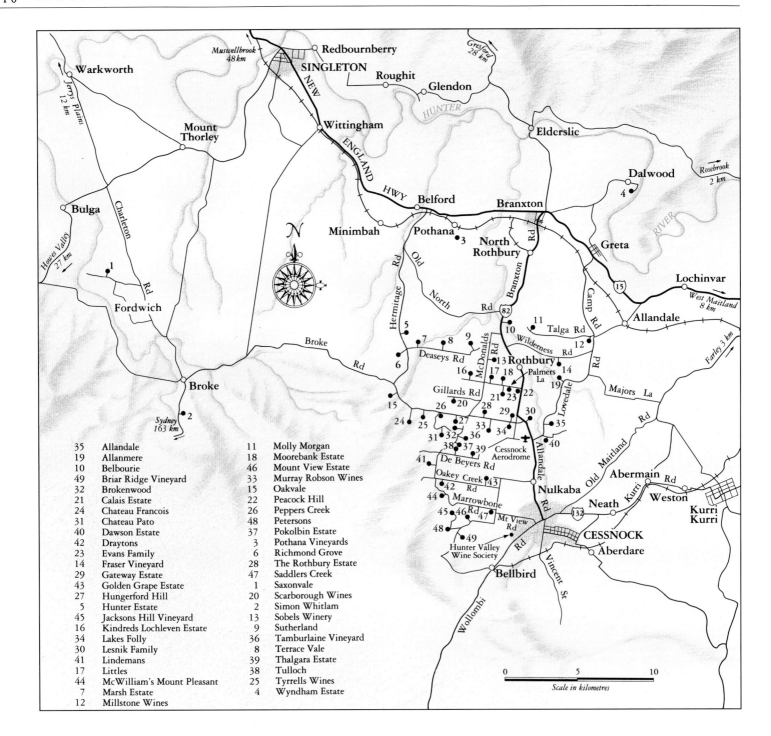

35	Allandale	11	Molly Morgan
19	Allanmere	18	Moorebank Estate
10	Belbourie	46	Mount View Estate
49	Briar Ridge Vineyard	33	Murray Robson Wines
32	Brokenwood	15	Oakvale
21	Calais Estate	22	Peacock Hill
24	Chateau Francois	26	Peppers Creek
31	Chateau Pato	48	Petersons
40	Dawson Estate	37	Pokolbin Estate
42	Draytons	3	Pothana Vineyards
23	Evans Family	6	Richmond Grove
14	Fraser Vineyard	28	The Rothbury Estate
29	Gateway Estate	47	Saddlers Creek
43	Golden Grape Estate	1	Saxonvale
27	Hungerford Hill	20	Scarborough Wines
5	Hunter Estate	2	Simon Whitlam
45	Jacksons Hill Vineyard	13	Sobels Winery
16	Kindreds Lochleven Estate	9	Sutherland
34	Lakes Folly	36	Tamburlaine Vineyard
30	Lesnik Family	8	Terrace Vale
41	Lindemans	39	Thalgara Estate
17	Littles	38	Tulloch
44	McWilliam's Mount Pleasant	25	Tyrrells Wines
7	Marsh Estate	4	Wyndham Estate
12	Millstone Wines		

HUNTER VALLEY (UPPER & LOWER) — HECTAREAGE

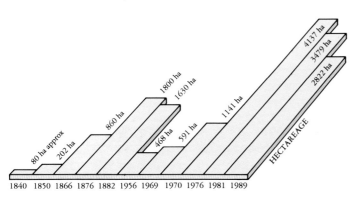

Rooty Hill and Smithfield until the 1950s and 1960s. More importantly, overall soil fertility in the previously unfarmed Hunter Valley was high, and the modern diseases of downy and powdery mildew were unknown. Also, the European experience suggested the more heat, the better: it did not occur to anyone that there might be too much warmth. Finally, there has been speculation that rainfall patterns then were different to those of today.

So it was that the Hunter Valley quickly came to dominate viticulture in New South Wales, although once again there are curious historical quirks. All the early vineyards were established well to the north-east of where they are to be

found now; it was not until the 1860s that the first vignerons came into the Cessnock/Pokolbin area, where almost all of the vineyards of today are to be found.

History also reveals that at the Paris Exhibition of 1855 (which led to the 1855 classification of the great Bordeaux wines which stands to this day) James King of Irrawang Vineyard had his sparkling wine — said by the judges to have 'a bouquet, body and flavour equal to the finest champagnes' — served at the table of Napoleon III during the closing ceremony. Another fascinating snippet is that although most of the wines were named by variety and vintage, H J Lindeman (the founder of Lindemans) produced what I can but guess to be Australia's only Lachryma Christi, far from the slopes of Mount Vesuvius.

The Hunter Valley has long since been supplanted by Griffith as the largest producer, but it remains in quality by far the most important region. Nonetheless, as the **chart below** reveals, it has been an area of cyclical prosperity and depression. One would be brave, indeed foolish, to deny the possibility of a future recession, but it is improbable.

The Hunter Valley wine industry of today is inextricably bound up with tourism. It was the wineries which brought the tourists in the first place — starting in the mid-1960s — but today more dollars are spent on tourism (meals, accommodation and so on) than on wine: the Lower Hunter Valley has no equal in Australia for the abundance of first class accommodation, restaurants and general tourist facilities. If even some of the developments planned as at 1990 go ahead, it will become one of Australia's prime tourist areas.

It is this ready-made market which sees the cellar door sales outlets of the wineries full from daybreak to dusk, and which provides that all-important cashflow for the small winery in particular. From the outside looking in, it is an ideal life-style (the reality is a little less perfect) and I am sure we will see more, rather than fewer, wineries in the future. So there is a mix of the big and the small, the new and the old, the professional and the amateur; all are geared to make the visitor welcome, and almost all succeed.

PRINCIPAL WINE STYLES

SEMILLON
When the dust settles down, Semillon will be regarded as the great wine of the Lower Hunter. It demands time in bottle, growing from an anaemic, thin and vaguely grassy youth to a crescendo of honeyed, nutty, buttery/toasty mouthfilling richness at 10 to 20 years of age. The old Lindeman Show wines from 1970 and before may never be repeated (the vineyards are gone) but the Rothbury Estate, Tyrrell's Wines, McWilliam's Mount Pleasant and (once again) Lindemans are the best of the major producers, and Allanmere, Brokenwood and Petersons are the best of the small wineries.

CHARDONNAY
Chardonnay started its Australia-wide reign of terror, ecstasy or whatever, when Murray Tyrrell produced the 1971 Vat 47 Pinot Chardonnay. Virtually every winery today produces a Chardonnay, some are richer or more complex, more oaky than others, but all with a peaches and cream cast to their makeup. Opinions differ sharply about the keeping qualities of these wines: if varietal character is unimportant to you, then the deep golden, buttery, viscous opulence of aged Hunter Chardonnay will be extremely satisfying.

SHIRAZ
Hermitage is to Cabernet Sauvignon what Semillon is to Chardonnay. The Hunter Valley imposes its regional stamp on both wines, and I think the inherent varietal character of Shiraz bends more compliantly than does Cabernet Sauvignon to that stamp. Given that France's Rhone Valley is very much warmer than is Bordeaux (home of Cabernet), that is as it should be. Moreover, Shiraz makes the same transformation in bottle as Semillon, moving from an astringent, angular and spiky youth into a velvety, almost luminous maturity at 20 or even 30 years of age. At this distance, many fine judges can confuse a Jaboulet La Chapelle with a Lindemans of similar age. Lindemans, Tyrrell's Wines, Brokenwood, Draytons, Marsh Estate and Tamburlaine Vineyard are among the foremost producers.

CABERNET SAUVIGNON
You would, however, never ever confuse an old Hunter Cabernet Sauvignon with an old Bordeaux. You might well think it was an old Hunter Shiraz, however. Max Lake reintroduced the variety to the valley (along with Petit Verdot and Malbec it was relatively common in the gold years of the nineteenth century) and Lake's Folly has always produced a highly regarded (and highly idiosyncratic) Cabernet Sauvignon. Almost all the wineries provide a Cabernet.

PINOT NOIR
Finally, some very great Hunter reds have been made wholly or partially from Pinot Noir — wines which say a great deal about the district and absolutely nothing about varietal Pinot Noir. Tyrrell's 1976 and 1981 Pinot Noirs are prime examples; those with long memories or great cellars will know that the legendary Maurice O'Shea made magnificent blends from Shiraz and Pinot Noir, but modern-day winemakers seem to have lost the art.

ABOVE: Semillon rootlings about to be planted.

THE ROTHBURY ESTATE: ONE MAN'S VISION

The Rothbury Estate is the most tangible contribution of Len Evans to the Australian wine industry, and — rightly perhaps — it will be the one for which he is best remembered. The main Rothbury winery and Cask Hall were very much his concept — elegantly realised by architect Keith Cottier — and will stand proud in the Hunter landscape for centuries to come. It is one of those timeless pieces of design which is accepted as classic even before the first coat of paint wears off.

And it is with Rothbury (and Evans' single-minded defence of it) that I am most concerned here. But it would be wrong not to give at least passing acknowledgment to the crucial role Evans has played in the education of generations of wine drinkers. For the better part of 30 years it has been his face, his voice and his pen which have brought wine into the minds and the houses of countless Australians who, were it not for Len, might never have raised a glass to their lips in the first place. Evans has always believed that life should be fun — wine likewise, and he is right.

It was indeed this belief, shared by a syndicate of ten Sydney businessmen and professionals, which led to the establishment of the Rothbury Estate (and a number of associated though then separately owned land-owning and grape growing syndicates) in 1968. The winery was erected just in time for the 1971 vintage, the worst in living memory in the Hunter. Perhaps it was an omen, for although Rothbury immediately commenced to make great white wine — its 1972 Semillon is a wonderful wine, still at the peak of its power — it entered a long period of financial difficulty. Len Evans, with typical honesty, summarised its problems this way: 'At the time of the red wine boom we planted too much Shiraz, not foreseeing the end to the demand for it; we planted too many vines on soils that could not sustain an appropriate yield; . . . we were the wrong size, being too big for a boutique and too small to compete with the major wineries; we suffered badly from the drought of 1980-83, the vineyards sometimes yielding less than a tonne per hectare . . .'.

It was for these and other reasons that Evans had to fight with such obstinacy to save Rothbury from the jaws of its lenders. He did so with the help of some loyal friends and financial backers, but truly it was his faith, his pride, his

vision which guided Rothbury through the dark years and into the sunlight.

Ironically, its present prosperity comes not from Semillon nor even Shiraz, but from a grape which barely figured in the initial plantings: Chardonnay. What is more, much of that Chardonnay is grown not in the Hunter Valley, but at Cowra. Having purchased Chardonnay from that region since 1981 (and having made a voluptuous Chardonnay that year which has aged superbly into a creamy, honeyed mouthful of nectar) Rothbury purchased 36 hectares of mature vineyard in 1982, and with grafting and further plantings, now has 44 hectares of Chardonnay.

Chardonnay, too, now occupies 40 hectares of the Hunter Valley plantings; Semillon claims 37 hectares, Shiraz 44 hectares, Cabernet Sauvignon 11 hectares and Pinot Noir 9 hectares. The Chardonnay is made in two styles: rich and super-rich. The latter wine, more respectfully called Chardonnay Reserve, was initially specifically created for markets in the United States of America and the United Kingdom. The ripest fruit was barrel-fermented in 100 per cent new oak (Vosges); a percentage was taken through malolactic fermentation and the wine was left in contact with its yeast lees for over 6 months. The result is a wine of enormous flavour, body and impact, variously described as a peaches and cream or a Dolly Parton style. It received rave reviews in both countries, and generated such interest that Rothbury was forced to release small quantities onto the Australian market.

Rothbury has also developed a very stylised Pinot Noir, made with heavy reliance on whole-bunch maceration and a diverse bag of other Burgundian winemaking tricks. Evans has had a significant personal input into the pinot noir — he normally vociferously disavows any winemaking expertise — and he is content with the results, particularly when the wine is given some bottle age. I wish I could share his enthusiasm, but others have no such difficulty, and the wine has a strong following.

The Hermitage and Cabernet Sauvignon-based wines are supremely honest: now that the vines are fully mature, and with only the best red vineyards retained, the wines have improved greatly over those of the early years and will richly repay cellaring for 10 years or more.

ABOVE: Leonard Paul Evans, OBE (by courtesy of Captain W E Johns).

But, perhaps obstinately, I believe it is the Semillons which are the greatest wines of Rothbury, and are those upon which its reputation should be judged. I therefore arranged a vertical tasting from my private cellar, and arranged for Evans to be present. The tasting notes and points are mine, but I have also given Evans' views of some of the wines, where those views differed from mine. The points given are out of 100, and in three instances two bottles were tasted because the first was either corked or out of condition — with 10 to 20 year old white wines, some bottle variation is inevitable. I am assuming good cellaring conditions, sound corks and no abnormal ullage.

TASTING NOTES

1972 WHITE LABEL [91]
Still incredibly youthful, with crisp fruit and acidity, and a markedly long finish. At its peak, but may be kept.

1973 WHITE LABEL [89]
Like the '72, a Peter Pan wine with relatively light colour, firm and crisp fresh fruit. At its peak and will not improve. Evans liked the wine less, finding it slightly phenolic.

1973 BLACK LABEL [93]
A golden-coloured, classic Hunter wine with enormous depth of complex, toasty/honeyed/buttery aroma and flavour. Good acidity and length. Holding superbly.

1974 BLACK LABEL INDIVIDUAL PADDOCK BROKENBACK [88]
A beautifully smooth, honeyed wine with some toasty characters, and considerable richness. At its peak.

1974 BLACK LABEL INDIVIDUAL PADDOCK ROTHBURY [90]
Yellow gold in colour with striking scented tropical/apricot aroma and flavour, showing botrytis influence. Not by any means classic, but given high points because of its flavour. Evans liked it less. Drink now.

1975 BLACK LABEL INDIVIDUAL PADDOCK WOOD MATURED [90]
The most extraordinary wine in the line-up, from a single 4500 litre new French (the back label incorrectly states American) upright vat, which has invested the wine with an exceptionally complex, Burgundian character, with life in front of it yet. One of Evans' top pointed wines.

1976 BLACK LABEL INDIVIDUAL PADDOCK ROTHBURY [86]
Full yellow in colour, with rich, tropical/pineapple/honeyed aroma and fruit, reminiscent of the '74, and with some sweetness on a strikingly-flavoured palate. The question is, will the flavours break up?

1977 BLACK LABEL INDIVIDUAL PADDOCK BROKENBACK [64]
A disappointing, rather plain and common wine with a broad and baggy bouquet. No point in cellaring. Evans found more to enjoy on the palate, but agreed with the criticisms of the bouquet.

1978 BLACK LABEL INDIVIDUAL PADDOCK BROKENBACK [88]
A wine with a definite lift of volatility in both bouquet and palate; however, it has abundant flavour, very good balance and quite surprising length.

1979 BLACK LABEL INDIVIDUAL PADDOCK SHAREHOLDERS RESERVE [90]
Medium to full yellow-green in colour, with a honeyed bouquet still showing some lemony/herbaceous varietal character; the palate is soft, rich and complex and the wine has developed (relatively speaking) quickly. Certainly at its peak, and should be drunk.

1979 BLACK LABEL INDIVIDUAL PADDOCK DIRECTOR'S RESERVE WOOD MATURED [94]
Two bottles tasted. One very slightly corked, the other with magnificently intense fruit, superb definition to the structure, and beautifully integrated oak. Will hold.

1979 WHITE LABEL HERLSTONE VINEYARD [82]
A stylish, tangy/lemony aroma leads on to a full flavoured lemon/toast palate, with good balance and length. Evans was less enthusiastic.

1980 BLACK LABEL WOOD MATURED [67]
Lemony American oak dominates the wine on both bouquet and palate; not classic. Age will not improve it.

1980 BLACK LABEL INDIVIDUAL PADDOCK ROTHBURY [78]
A complex bouquet with a touch of 'hot solids' fermentation character; the wine is much better on the palate with tangy fruit and a long finish. Evans forgave the bouquet and pointed the wine higher.

1981 BLACK LABEL WOOD MATURED [69]
Aggressive oak with a slight Plasticine edge tends to dominate the fruit. There is also some volatility evident. Drink now.

1982 BLACK LABEL INDIVIDUAL PADDOCK ROTHBURY/BROKENBACK [60]
A strong volatile lift on both bouquet and palate will worry some, but appeal to others. It worried me, though Evans was less critical and pointed the wine higher. Nonetheless, the wine has some time in front of it.

1983 BLACK LABEL INDIVIDUAL PADDOCK SHAREHOLDERS' RESERVE [79]
Once again, a touch of volatility evident, with a lemon-essence edge to the bouquet, and tangy-zesty flavour on the palate with a crisp finish. In some ways a traditional, early picked style. Will develop.

1983 BLACK LABEL INDIVIDUAL PADDOCK WOOD MATURED [75]
Lifted lemony/tangy American oak and fruit showing much better integration and balance than most in this series. Evans liked the length of the finish, noting a touch of sweetness.

1984 WHITE LABEL BROKENBACK [NP]
The wine was corked, and no replacement was available.

1985 BLACK LABEL INDIVIDUAL PADDOCK SHAREHOLDERS' RESERVE [60]
A very disappointing wine with smelly, hot solids, fermentation/kerosene characters. May improve marginally with further age.

1986 BLACK LABEL INDIVIDUAL PADDOCK [82]
The wine in which there was the greatest divergence of opinion: Evans selected it as one of his top wines; I found it less outstanding. It seems to lack the intensity one would expect from the excellent 1986 vintage, but it certainly does have potential, and may well end up justifying Evans' higher points.

1987 BLACK LABEL INDIVIDUAL PADDOCK [67]
Another very disappointing wine, with a rather closed, hard and thin bouquet, and common palate. Age may help, but not much.

1988 BLACK LABEL INDIVIDUAL PADDOCK [84]
A surprisingly forward wine with a honeyed, complex bouquet and smooth, honeyed fruit on the palate; will improve markedly over the short term, but will never be long lived.

1989 BLACK LABEL INDIVIDUAL PADDOCK [90]
A triumph for the vintage, with floral/lemony fruit on both bouquet and palate; crisp acidity gives balance, and the wine has the requisite weight and structure to benefit from up to 10 years cellaring.

WINERIES OF THE LOWER HUNTER VALLEY

ALLANDALE   C-CB
Lovedale Road
Pokolbin via
Maitland 2321   (049) 90 4526
Established   1977
Winemaker   Bill Sneddon
Production   12,000 cases
Principal Wines   Semillon, Sauvignon Blanc,
Chardonnay, Shiraz, Pinot Noir, and Cabernet
Sauvignon.
Best Vintages   W 1980, '84, '86, '87
                    R 1979, '80, '83, '86, '87
A winery which once produced an array of wines
which were never dull, and were sometimes very
good and sometimes rather bad, but which now
seems to be content to err on the side of safety,
producing adequate but not stimulating wines.

ALLANMERE   A-A
Allandale Road
Allandale via
Pokolbin 2321   (049) 30 7387
Established   1984
Winemakers   Newton Potter,
                    Geoff Broadfield
Production   3500 cases
Principal Wines   Semillon, Chardonnay,
Sauvignon Blanc, Trinity (a blend of the three
foregoing varieties), Cabernet Sauvignon, Shiraz
and Trilogy (a blend of Cabernet, Merlot and
Shiraz).
Best Vintages   W 1986, '88, '90
                    R 1985, '87, '88, '90
In the space of only five vintages, expatriate
English medical practitioner Newton Potter has
produced a startlingly good range of white and
red wines. Sensitively handled oak and mouthfilling fruit is a feature of the whites, with melon
and oak-spiced Chardonnay and smooth, honeyed
Semillon developing majestically over 3 to 5
years. The red wines are clean, deep flavoured
and well balanced, even if not quite in the class
of those lovely whites. Allanmere managed to
rise above the vicissitudes of the 1990 vintage to
(once again) produce lovely wines.

BROKENWOOD   A-A
McDonalds Road
Pokolbin 2321   (049) 98 7559
Established   1970
Winemaker   Iain Riggs
Production   12,500 cases
Principal Wines   Semillon, Chardonnay, Pinot
Noir, Hermitage, Cabernet Sauvignon. Special
'Graveyard' and 'Cricket Pitch' releases in small
quantities.
Best Vintages   W 1983, '85, '86, '87
                    R 1975, '79, '83, '85, '86,
                    '87, '88

Generally regarded as one of the foremost small
— these days not so small, indeed — Hunter
wineries which does not know how to produce a
bad wine. Its unwooded Semillon, crisp and
gently herbaceous, has a strong following, as
does its complex, nutty Chardonnay. Most
serious are the deep coloured, moderately tannic
reds which have the structure to last a lifetime.

CALAIS ESTATES CB-B
Palmers Lane
Pokolbin 2321   (049) 98 7654
Established   1971
Winemaker   Colin Peterson
Production   10,000 cases
Principal Wines   Semillon, Chardonnay,
Traminer, Pinot Noir, Shiraz Cabernet
Sauvignon, and Sauternes.
Best Vintages   W 1988, '89,
                    R 1988, '89
This is the reincarnation of Wollundry Wines,
acquired by Colin Peterson shortly prior to the
1987 vintage. The 24 ha of fully mature estate
vineyards should see first class wines appear
under the Calais label if teething problems in
the refurbished winery are resolved.

DRAYTONS   CA-BA
Oakey Creek Road
Cessnock 2321   (049) 98 7513
Established   1853
Winemaker   Trevor Drayton
Production   Not for publication

Principal Wines   Semillon, Chardonnay,
Rhine Riesling, Traminer, Shiraz, Cabernet
Sauvignon, some additionally identified by
vineyard names and others by bin number.
Best Vintages   W 1979, '80, '82, '83, '87, '88
                    R 1970, '73, '75, '79, '80, '81,
                    '85,'86, '87
A long-established family owned and run winery
which is not particularly fashionable but which
produces some very fine and modestly priced
wines, with the clean, cherry-flavoured and
softly tannic Bin 5555 Hermitage frequently
outstanding.

EVANS FAMILY   A-A
Palmers Lane
Pokolbin 2321   (049) 98 7604
Established   1979
Winemakers   David Lowe, Len Evans
Production   3000 cases
Principal Wines   Chardonnay
Best Vintages   W 1982, '84, '86, '87
This extremely rich and complex barrel fermented
Chardonnay is made at the Rothbury Estate from
a beautifully sited vineyard on Len Evans' family
property; a Pinot Noir and a Gamay are scheduled
for future release. The Chardonnay is a cameo
version of the Rothbury Reserve, but is strictly
(and 100 per cent) estate-grown.

HUNGERFORD HILL   CB-B
Cnr McDonalds and
Broke Roads
Pokolbin 2321   (049) 98 7666
Established   1967
Winemaker   Gerry Sissingh
Production   55,000 cases
Principal Wines   Hunter Valley Chardonnay,
Hunter Valley Pinot Noir, Hunter Valley
Semillon, Sauvignon Blanc and Hunter Valley
Cabernet Merlot. Cellar door releases under
Collection and Show Reserve range labels.
Best Vintages   W 1980, '81, '84, '86, '88
                    R 1982, '83, '84, '86, '89
A substantial operation which over the years has
produced some excellent wines from its Hunter
Valley and Coonawarra vineyards. Quality has
been extremely variable over the past few years;

---

*ABOVE LEFT: Iain Riggs, Brokenwood General Manager and
Winemaker.*

*ABOVE RIGHT: Evans Family Chardonnay in the courtyard at
'Loggerheads', the family home.*

changes in senior winemaking staff and sale rumours did not help. With stability returned, in the wake of its acquisition by Seppelt in August 1990, better things should be in store.

HUNTER ESTATE B-B

Hermitage Road
Pokolbin 2321   (049) 98 7521
Established   1972
Winemaker   Neil McGuigan
Production   20,000 cases
Principal Wines   Chardonnay, Fumé Blanc, Semillon, Semillon Verdelho, Traminer Riesling, White Burgundy, Pinot Noir, Shiraz, and Cabernet Sauvignon.
Best Vintages   W 1979, '83, '87, '89
                         R 1979, '83, '85, '87, '89

Part of the Wyndham Estate empire and part of the label and brand game-play much beloved of Wyndham. Wine snobs tend to sneer, but some remarkably good wines have appeared from time to time, full of fruit and flavour even if showing little or no regional characteristics.

LAKE'S FOLLY   A-A

Broke Road
Pokolbin 2321   (049) 98 7507
Established   1963
Winemaker   Stephen Lake
Production   3000 cases
Principal Wines   Cabernet Sauvignon and Chardonnay.
Best Vintages   W 1983, '85, '86, '87
                         R 1969, '72, '78, '81, '85, '87

The first and still the most famous of the 'weekend wineries', the inspiration of former Sydney surgeon Max Lake, producing complex, pungent Chardonnay and elegant, earthy/cedary, long-lived Cabernet Sauvignon which, when fully mature (at 10 to15 years) shows more regional than varietal character.

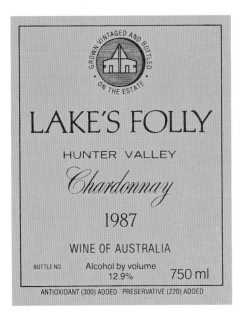

LINDEMANS   BA-A

McDonalds Road
Pokolbin 2321   (049) 98 7501
Established   1870
Winemaker   Patrick Auld
Production   Not stated, but approximately 60,000 cases.
Principal Wines   Hunter Valley Bin range (with annually changing bin numbers) of Semillon, Chablis, White Burgundy, Semillon/Chardonnay, Chardonnay and Verdelho. Burgundy and Steven Hermitage both made from Shiraz. Older vintages under the Classic release label.
Best Vintages   W 1966, '68, '70, '72, '75, '79, '86, '87
                         R 1965, '70, '73, '80 '83, '86, '87

The fabulous (and appropriately expensive) Classic releases of Show Reserves from the 1960s are, more or less, all but exhausted. It was in these wines (and their predecessors) that the exceptional reputation of Lindemans depended. Vineyard rationalisation (old, low yielding vineyards being discarded) and winemaker changes during the 1970s accompanied by a deliberate repositioning of the wines in the marketplace (with much reduced real prices) saw a sharp decline in quality. Gerry Sissingh's stewardship between 1986 and 1990 saw a significant return to form, but it is now less certain where Lindemans' Hunter Valley products will be positioned within the Penfolds' empire.

LITTLE'S   CB-CB

Lot 3, Palmers Lane
Pokolbin 2321   (049) 98 7626
Established   1983
Winemaker   Ian Little
Production   5000 cases
Principal Wines   Semillon, Chardonnay, Traminer, Shiraz, Pinot Noir, Cabernet Sauvignon and Vintage Port.

Best Vintages   W 1984, '85, '86, '89
                         R 1985, '86, '89

Ian Little is a fastidious winemaker, conducting a substantial part of the vintage operations in a cool room inside the winery proper. Highly aromatic, scented and fruity white wines (some oak matured, some not) are the result; the red wines are pleasant but not terribly distinctive, other than for the occasional first class Vintage Port, a testimony to Ian Little's apprenticeship at Chateau Reynella (South Australia).

McWILLIAM'S
MOUNT PLEASANT   CA-A

Marrowbone Road,
Pokolbin 2321   (049) 98 7505
Established   1880
Winemaker   Phillip Ryan
Production   Not stated, but in excess of 150,000 cases.
Principal Wines   Semillon, Chardonnay, Traminer, Pinot Noir, Hermitage and Cabernet Sauvignon. Releases include popular lines such as Elizabeth (Semillon) and Philip (Hermitage) to rarer releases like OP and OH Hermitage and Rosehill Hermitage. Special releases are offered in limited quantities through the 'Homestead' cellar door sales area.
Best Vintages   W 1979, '81, '82, '83, '85, '86, '87
                         R 1965, '66, '75, '79, '83 '85, '86, '87

No doubt purely by coincidence McWilliam's is experiencing a similar renaissance to Lindemans. The McWilliam's reputation was every bit as great as that of Lindemans — some would say greater still — thanks to the extraordinary skills of Maurice O'Shea who died in 1956. Most of the O'Shea reds are starting to fade, but the greatest (from the '30s, '40s and '50s) can still be sublime. After 1956 the red wines became ever more tiring, until finally they were a caricature of themselves. In 1968 the first Elizabeth Riesling was introduced, and passed

ABOVE: Shiraz vines planted by Charles King in 1880 on the Hunter's finest red soil (of volcanic origin); now McWilliams Mount Pleasant 'Old Hill' vineyard.

largely unnoticed in the shadow of producers such as Lindemans, Tyrrell's Wines and the Rothbury Estate; nor was it at a price and a volume calculated to set hearts aflutter. The installation of Phillip Ryan as chief winemaker, backed up by Jim Brayne as group chief winemaker in the Murrumbidgee Irrigation Area, has seen an invertible transformation in red wine styles since the mid-1980s (the best are yet to be released) while Elizabeth Semillon has assumed a dominant position not only as a brand, but as a Semillon of rare quality at an absolutely exceptional price, thanks to McWilliam's policy of not releasing it until it is 6 years old. It shows the miraculous transformation which occurs to unoaked Semillon in bottle.

MARSH ESTATE   BA-BA

Deasey Road
Pokolbin 2321   (049) 98 7587
Established   1971
Winemaker   Peter Marsh
Production   5000 cases
Principal Wines   Semillon, Chardonnay, Traminer, Champagne, Sauternes, Hermitage Vat S and Vat R, Private Bin Hermitage, CabernetShiraz and Cabernet Sauvignon Vat N.
Best Vintages   W 1979, '86, '87, '89
                       R 1979, '81, '85, '86, '89

Peter Marsh, a Sydney surburban pharmacist while not at the winery, and wife Robyn, have quietly built up both the quality and production of Marsh Estate over the past decade, culminating with the winning of the trophy for Most Successful Small Winemaker Exhibitor at the 1987 Hunter Valley Wine Show. The white wines are clean, solid and not flashy; oak is held in restraint, and time and bottle are needed to bring them to their best. The red wines are far more aggressive in terms of early flavour and complexity, but also more variable in quality.

MURRAY ROBSON WINES   B-B

Halls Road
Pokolbin 2321   (049) 98 7539
Established   1987
Winemaker   Murray Robson
Production   3000 cases
Principal Wines   Semillon Early Harvest, Semillon Traditional, Chardonnay, Traminer, Light Cabernet, Hermitage and Cabernet Sauvignon.
Best Vintages   Too early to assess.
If you have a feeling of deja vu when you look at the label of Murray Robson Wines, you are correct. It is strikingly similar to that of the Robson Vineyard which Murray Robson founded in 1972 but which owing to financial difficulties was taken from him in 1977 and renamed the Briar Ridge Vineyard. Murray Robson Wines now has an entirely different vineyard base, and is yet to determine the long term winery site. However, Murray Robson has always set his stamp on the style of wines he makes: all are fine, clean and elegant, the whites not infrequently rather too much so for my tastes, but others apparently enjoy the understated character.

OAKVALE   CB-CB

Broke Road
Pokolbin 2321   (049) 98 7520
Established   1893
Winemaker   Barry Shields
Production   5000 cases
Principal Wines   Semillon, Semillon Chardonnay, Chardonnay, Shiraz and Cabernet Sauvignon.
Best Vintages   W 1988, '89
                       R 1987
Oakvale, purchased by former Sydney solicitor Barry Shields in 1985, was the famous winery of Doug Elliott. Shields has done much to modernise the winery in the ensuing years, and with the aid of skilled consultancy advice, has sharply lifted wine quality, which had slipped disastrously over the preceding 10 or so years. Best are the white wines, based on Semillon and Chardonnay, sometimes oaked, and sometimes not; quite often I have preferred the unoaked to the oaked versions, and certainly all will repay cellaring as they move from the herbaceous flavours of youth to the honeyed richness of maturity.

PETERSONS   BA-BA

Mount View Road
Mount View 2325   (049) 90 1704
Established   1971
Winemaker   Gary Reed
Production   6000 cases
Principal Wines   Semillon, Chardonnay, Traminer, Pinot Noir, Malbec, Hermitage, Cabernet Sauvignon, Sauternes and Vintage Port.

Best Vintages   W 1983, '85, '86, '88, '89
                       R 1982, '83, '85, '88, '89
Newcastle pharmacist Ian Peterson and wife Shirley purchased their beautiful hillside vineyard property in 1964, savouring its rich, volcanic soil but never dreaming they would plant grapes. The wine boom of the late 1960s led to the first grapes being planted in 1971, and, as so often happens, contract grape growing led to winemaking. The first serious vintage was in 1982, and in 1983 and again in 1984, Petersons received the trophy for Most Successful Small Winemaker Exhibitor at the Hunter Valley Wine Show, following this success with a superb 1985 Semillon and equally good Chardonnays in both that year and 1986 — the latter won the prestigious Peaches Trophy for Best 1987 and older Chardonnay at the 1989 National Wine Show. Skilled consultancy was obviously very important, for quality slipped dramatically in 1987 when that consultancy ceased, but there are some indications of a return to the previous spectacular form.

RICHMOND GROVE   CB-B

Hermitage Road
Pokolbin 2321   (049) 98 7792
Established   1977
Winemaker   Ian Scarborough
Production   175,000 cases
Principal Wines   Oak Matured Chablis, French Cask Chardonnay, Fumé Blanc, Nouvelle Chardonnay, White Bordeaux, White Burgundy, Cabernet Merlot, Nouvelle Cabernet Merlot and Cabernet Sauvignon.
Best Vintages   W 1979, '87, '89
                       R 1978, '87, '89
The establishment date for Richmond Grove could equally read 1987, when the operational base of the winery was moved from the Upper Hunter to the Lower Hunter, and more particularly to a state of the art winery erected in Hermitage Road. It is believed that the change will also see a marked change in the quality and positioning of the brand, or at least of the best wines under the label. Given the great skills of winemaker Ian Scarborough such a change seems highly probable. It should be added that Richmond Grove is at

times a wayward part of the Wyndham group — wayward because of the idiosyncratic marketing approach of Mark Cashmore.

THE ROTHBURY ESTATE   CA-A
Broke Road
Pokolbin 2321   (049) 98 7555
Established   1968
Winemaker   David Lowe
Production   120,000 cases
Principal Wines   The Rothbury Estate has a complex and ever changing series of labels and brands, complicated further by the fact that the best wines have entirely different labels according to whether they are sold through the cellar door/mailing list side of the business or through conventional retail distribution. The label of the former is the Fred Williams' design adopted by Rothbury with its first vintage in 1971, the latter a striking silver abstract design introduced in the mid-1980s. The top wines are based on Semillon, Chardonnay, Pinot Noir and Hermitage grown in the Hunter Valley and Chardonnay grown in Cowra. Then there are ranges of cheaper, lesser quality branded wines under labels such as Dove Crag and Scribbly Bark, which are very often wines purchased in bulk or clean skin (ie unlabelled) from other producers. In much the same price range are the Denman Estate (Upper Hunter Valley) wines now owned by Rothbury.
Best Vintages   W 1972, '73, '74, '76, '79, '83, '86, '89
                 R 1973, '75, '79, '83 '86, '89

To my mind, truly great wines of Rothbury — wines which will grow majestically in bottle for 10 to 20 years — continue to be its Semillons, even though the market says its Cowra Chardonnay (and Hunter Reserve Chardonnay) are the ones to buy.

SAXONVALE   B-B
Fordwich Estate
Broke Road
Broke 2330   (065) 79 1009
Established   1969
Winemaker   John Baruzzi
Production   200,000 cases

Principal Wines   There are two distinct ranges of wines: first the Premium Bin range, consisting of Bin 1 Chardonnay, Bin 1 Semillon, Bin 1Hermitage and Bin 1 Cabernet Sauvignon; and second, thecheaper Spring Mountain Varietal range.
Best Vintages   W 1977, '79, '80, '83, '85, '86, '87
                 R 1981, '83, '86, '87
For the past few years yet another part of the Wyndham Estate empire; its acquisition has seen a change in the way the wines are marketed, with sales limited to restaurant distribution and (the major part) through the American Express/Cellarmasters direct mail operation. Contrary to what one might expect, wine quality has not suffered at all, indeed it is arguable it has significantly improved, with some abundantly fleshy/peachy early maturing Chardonnay, and chewy, chocolatey berry flavoured Cabernet Sauvignon leading the field.

SCARBOROUGH WINES   A-A
Gillards Road
Pokolbin 2321   (049) 98 7563
Established   1987
Winemaker   Ian Scarborough
Production   Limited.
Principal Wines   Presently only Chardonnay made; limited Pinot Noir releases and possibly Merlot and Verdelho may appear in the future.
Best Vintages   Too recent to assess.
Scarborough Wines is included simply because of Ian Scarborough's second-to-none track record as a winemaker and, more particularly, wine consultant. His is the brilliance which lies behind some of the more notable success stories among the small Hunter Valley wineries of the past few years. His consultancy activities were curtailed when he accepted a position with Richmond Grove, but his future direction is still uncertain, and may conceivably once again revolve around consultancy and his own operation. The brand is included as an article of faith on my part, as is the rating, but the one wine tasted (a 1987 Chardonnay) was all that one could expect.

SIMON WHITLAM   B-B
Wollombi Brook Vineyard
Broke 2330   (02) 387 8622
Established   1982
Winemaker   Simon Gilbert

Production   3500 cases
Principal Wines   Semillon, Show Reserve Semillon, Late Harvest Semillon, Chardonnay and Cabernet Sauvignon. The second label is Wollombi Brook.

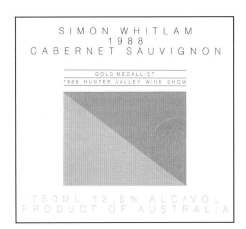

Best Vintages: W 1986, '87, '88
                 R 1985, '86, '88
Simon Whitlam was established as a plaything of leading wine retailer Andrew Simon and merchant banker Nick Whitlam (subsequently attracting merchant banker David Clarke), with the wines being made under contract by Simon Gilbert at Mountarrow (Upper Hunter Valley). The minnow has now swallowed the whale: the Simon Whitlam interests (with other investors and with Simon Gilbert also holding equity) acquired Mountarrow (then called Arrowfield) in 1989, and majority ownership of the group is now in Japanese hands. The white wines are particularly luscious and opulently oaked, and are made to be consumed within 2 or 3 years of vintage. The red wines are also full flavoured and quite precocious, reaching maturity at 3 to 5 years.

SUTHERLAND   CB-CB
Deasey's Road
Pokolbin 2321   (049) 98 7650
Established   1979
Winemaker   Neil Sutherland
Production   7000 cases
Principal Wines   Chenin Blanc, Semillon, Chardonnay, Shiraz, Pinot Noir and Cabernet Sauvignon.
Best Vintages   W 1983, '85, '86, '87
                 R 1983, '85, '87
The quite substantial Sutherland operation revolves around a 20 year old vineyard acquired by the Sutherlands in 1977 in a somewhat run down state, but since fully resuscitated. With wine consultancy assistance, Neil Sutherland put the quality of the fruit beyond doubt with rich, full flavoured Chardonnays in 1985 and 1987, also producing excellent ripe berry Shiraz in the latter year. Overall, however, quality has been somewhat variable in the past few years.

ABOVE: Barrel maturation, The Rothbury Estate.

TAMBURLAINE VINEYARD   **B-B**
McDonalds Road
Pokolbin 2321   (049) 98 7570
Established   1966
Winemakers   Mark Davidson,
                        Greg Silkman
Production   5000 cases
Principal Wines   Semillon, Late Harvest
Semillon, Chardonnay, Syrah and Cabernet
Sauvignon.
Best Vintages   **W** 1975, '79, '86, '87, '89,
                        R 1975, '79, '83, '86, '89
Dr Lance Allen followed in the footsteps of Max
Lake and Jim Roberts to establish the third
Hunter Valley weekend winery, taking time
from his very busy Cessnock medical practice to
do so. After 20 years, and with no member of his
family wishing to continue the tradition, he sold
the winery to a syndicate headed by Mark
Davidson and Greg Silkman at the end of 1985.
The fully mature vineyards produce low yields of
very concentrated and highly flavoured grapes

which inevitably shape the quality and style of
the resultant wines. Overall, these have been of
exemplary consistency and quality, and the
rating of the winery might have been higher still
were it not for one somewhat disappointing
tasting in 1989.

TERRACE VALE   **C-C**
Deasey's Lane
Pokolbin 2321 (049) 98 7517
Established   1971
Winemaker   Alain le Prince
Production   6000 cases
Principal Wines   Wines released under a
combination varietal/bin number system.
Semillon Bin 1, Semillon Bin 1A, Chardonnay
Bin 2, Gewurztraminer Bin 3, Semillon
Chardonnay Bin 12, HermitageBins 6 and 6A,
Cabernet/Hermitage Bin 76, Pinot Noir
andVintage Port.
Best Vintages   **W** 1979, '85, '87, '89
                        R 1979, '83, '85, '86

Terrace Vale is owned by a syndicate of Sydney-
based professional and businessmen, who have
derived much enjoyment from it over many
years. I have always found wine quality to be
variable, due in the main (for me) to
unacceptable levels of hydrogen sulphide
manifesting itself in gravelly/leathery/bitter
characters in the red wines. A magnificent 1979
Chardonnay shows what the vineyard can
produce, and overall the white wines have been
far more successful.

TULLOCH   **CA-BA**
De Beyers Road
Pokolbin 2321   (049) 98 7503
Established   1893
Winemakers   J Y (Jay) Tulloch,
                        Patrick Auld
Production   Not for publication.
Principal Wines   Selected Vintage varietals
(Chardonnay, Verdelho, Hermitage,Semillon
Chardonnay and Vintage Brut Champagne) head
thequality tree, made in small quantities; large
volume commercial releases are of Hunter River
Hermitage, Hunter River White Burgundy and
J Y Chablis.
Best Vintages   **W** 1974, '76, '83, '86, '87, '89
                        R 1965, '75, '83, '86, '87
Few with firsthand knowledge of the great
Hunter wines of bygone days will forget the
1953 Tulloch Hermitage which won first prize
in both the Claret and Burgundy classes at the
1956 Sydney Wine Show. Reds of equal stature
were made in 1958 and 1965, but with a
seemingly endless succession of ownership
changes triggered by the family sale of the
winery in 1969, the image slipped. Almost
unnoticed were some very fine white wines, none
better than three made in 1974, which drink
superbly to this day. In more recent times,
complex full-bodied buttery/peachy Chardonnay
has been the star performer, but the commercial
releases of Hermitage, White Burgundy and
Chablis are just that.

TYRRELLS WINES   **CA-BA**
Broke Road
Pokolbin 2321   (049) 98 7509
Established   1853
Winemaker   Murray Tyrrell
Production   350,000 cases
Principal Wines   A very large range, headed
by the 'Vat' wines: whites comprise Semillon
Vats 1 and 15; Chardonnay Vat 47 and
Chardonnay Semillon Vat 63; Red Vats 5, 7, 8,
9, 10 and 11, together with Pinot Noir and
Shiraz Merlot. Then follow the top commercial
varietal white and red releases under the Old
Winery label, HVD Label and Belford, and
finally the traditional range, including Long Flat
White and Long Flat Red. Also top-quality
Méthode Champenois wines from Pinot Noir,
Chardonnay and Semillon.

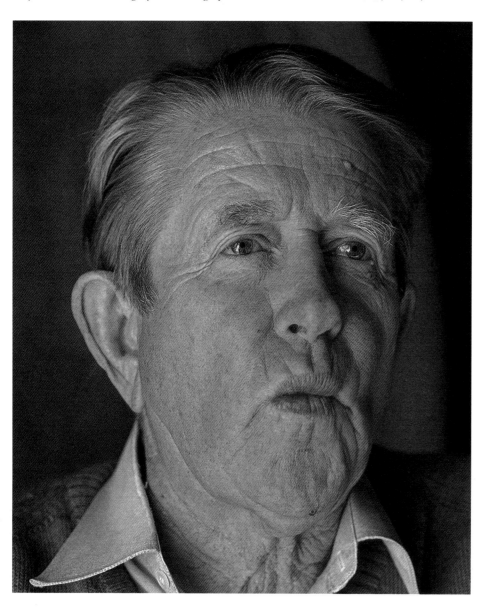

ABOVE: *Murray Tyrell, the voice of the Hunter, stilled for a moment by
a mouthful of young wine.*

Best Vintages W 1968, '70, '72, '76, '79, '83, '86, '89
R 1965, '73, '75, '79, '83, '85, '87

Murray Tyrrell has stood defiantly astride the Hunter Valley for the past 30 years, his foghorn voice frequently pouring scorn on new arrivals and extolling the virtues of the old ways. Behind the showmanship there is a highly intelligent and astute mind, and of course no one should forget that it was Murray Tyrrell who introduced Australia to Chardonnay with his inaugural vintage of Vat 47 in 1971. Vat 47 and Vat 1 Semillon remain the two great wines from Tyrrell's.

The red wines are stridently regional, but do achieve a silky patina with 20 or so years bottle age. At the bottom end of the market, Long Flat White and Long Flat Red do not aspire to greatness but can represent excellent value for money.

WYNDHAM ESTATE B-BA
Dalwood via Branxton
2335 (049) 38 1311
Established 1828
Winemaker Brian McGuigan
Production 500,000 cases
Principal Wines A substantial range of red and white table wines available in three distinct price categories. Benchmark Accredited wines, Bin 888 Cabernet Merlot, Hunter Chardonnay and the recently released Verdelho and Chardonnay Cuvée are the flagship wines. These are followed by Oak Cask Chardonnay, Bin 444 Cabernet Sauvignon, Limited Release Semillon, Pinot Noir and Bin 222 Chardonnay Semillon. There is a wide range of more popular styles available, including Chablis Superior, Bin 777 Graves Exceptional, Bin 555 Hermitage, TR2 Traminer and Riesling, GT Bin 6 Gewurz-traminer and White Burgundy.
Best Vintages W 1981, '85, '88, '89
R 1978, '79, '83, '86, '88, '89
Early in 1990 ownership of the Wyndham Estate empire passed to Orlando (South Australia), ending a quite remarkable 20 years of growth engineered by the unquestioned genius of Brian McGuigan. McGuigan never lost sight of the fact that wine, like any other product, has to be sold.

His unashamedly market-driven approach is paralleled by Wolf Blass and Mildara; for some reason, Wyndham has never been taken seriously by the wine media in Australia, but the quality of its products has been consistently good — something far more readily recognised in export markets, where Wyndham has enjoyed such great success. The best wines have been 444 Cabernet Sauvignon and various Chardonnays; the red wines show little or no regional character, reflecting the fact that many of them are multi-district blends.

OTHER WINERIES

BELBOURIE DC-C
Branxton Road
Rothbury 2330 (049) 38 1556

BRIAR RIDGE VINEYARD CB-B
Mount View Road
Mount View 2325 (049) 90 3670

CHATEAU FRANCOIS DB-CB
Off Broke Road
Pokolbin 2321 (049) 98 7548

CHATEAU PATO C-B
Thompson's Road
Pokolbin 2321 (049) 98 7634

DAWSON ESTATE CB-C
Londons Road
Lovedale 2325 (049) 90 2904

FRASER VINEYARD CA-B
Lot 5, Wilderness Road
Rothbury 2321 (049) 30 7594

GATEWAY ESTATE NR
Cnr Broke and Branxton Roads
Pokolbin 2321 (049) 98 7844

GOLDEN GRAPE ESTATE NR
Oakey Creek Road
Pokolbin 2321 (049) 89 7588

JACKSONS HILL VINEYARD NR
Mount View Road
Mount View 2325 (049) 90 1273

KINDRED'S LOCHLEVEN ESTATE CB-BA
Palmers Lane
Pokolbin 2321 (049) 98 7686

LESNIK FAMILY DC-C
Branxton Road
Pokolbin 2321 (049) 98 7755

MILLSTONE WINES C-C
Talga Road
Allandale 2321 (049) 30 7317

MOLLY MORGAN CB-B
Talga Road
Allandale via Pokolbin 2321 (049) 30 7695

MOOREBANK WINERY NR
Palmers Lane
Pokolbin 2321 (049) 98 7610

MOUNT VIEW ESTATE C-C
Mount View Road
Mount View 2325 (049) 90 3307

PEACOCK HILL B-B
Cnr Palmers Lane and Branxton Road
Pokolbin 2325

PEPPERS CREEK CB-C
Cnr Ekerts and Broke Roads
Pokolbin 2321 (049) 98 7532

POKOLBIN ESTATE C-CB
MacDonalds Road
Pokolbin 2321 (049) 938 7524

POTHANA VINEYARDS C-B
Carramar
Belford 2335 (065) 74 7164

SADDLERS CREEK NR
PO Box 390
Cessnock 2325 (049) 91 1770

SOBELS WINERY NR
McDonalds Road
Pokolbin 2321 (049) 98 7585

THALGARA ESTATE CB-C
DeBeyers Road
Pokolbin 2321 (049) 98 7717

ABOVE: Wyndham Estate: roses are more traditional but no prettier.

NEW SOUTH WALES

UPPER HUNTER VALLEY

When in 1960 Penfolds decided to sell its Dalwood vineyard and winery at Branxton in the Lower Hunter Valley and establish a new operation at Wybong in the Upper Hunter it was seen as a bold and adventurous move. The disappointment of the following 17 years, culminating in the sale of a by-then sharply reduced vineyard and under-utilised winery to Rosemount Estate, suggested the decision was not only brave, but foolish — particularly when one takes into account the spectacular success which the McGuigan family made with the vineyard at Dalwood, which became the starting point of the Wyndham Estate juggernaut.

With the wisdom of longer hindsight, the rationale behind the move can be seen as correct, even if some of the particular decisions were not. Viticulture ceased in the region around 1900 to 1910, so there was effectively no viticultural experience for Penfolds to draw on — notwithstanding that a young German settler named Carl Brecht had planted vines in 1860 at the junction of Wybong Creek and the Goulburn River, and had gone on to make wines which won gold medals at international shows throughout the 1870s.

It took much trial and error, not only by Penfolds but most notably by Arrowfield (now called Mountarrow) which did not come on the scene until 1969, to establish that this was white wine country first and foremost, and more particularly that the staple red variety of the Lower Hunter — Shiraz — was basically unsuited to the area. It also became apparent that not only was irrigation absolutely essential, but site (and soil) selection was as critical as it is in the Lower Hunter.

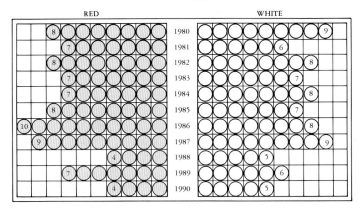

AUSTRALASIAN WINE REGIONS
1980 – 1990

RED		WHITE
8	1980	9
7	1981	6
8	1982	8
7	1983	7
7	1984	8
8	1985	7
10	1986	8
9	1987	9
4	1988	5
7	1989	6
4	1990	5

THE REGION IN BRIEF

LOCATION AND ELEVATION
32°15'S 150°53'E
150 –250 m

CLIMATE
The all-important difference from the Lower Hunter is the lower rainfall: 620 mm compared with 750 mm. As in the Lower Hunter, January and February are the 2 wettest months, with rain ever-likely to interfere with vintage. In this context, the lower total rainfall is an advantage, but it does mean that irrigation is absolutely essential. The heat summation (at Muswellbrook) is even greater than that of the Lower Hunter at 2170 HDD, reflecting the lack of the afternoon sea breezes which slightly temper the latter district.

SOIL
The majority of the vineyards, and certainly the most successful, are situated on the black silty loams (Um6.11) which are well drained and moderately fertile, overlying alkaline dark clay loam. These soils promote vigorous growth and substantial yields. The other main soil type is the red duplex soils (Dr2.23, 2.33 and 2.43), brown in colour, moderately acid to moderately alkaline, and also quite permeable and well drained.

HARVEST TIME
Mid-January — early March

PRINCIPAL GRAPE VARIETIES

Semillon, 244 ha	*Cabernet Sauvignon, 104 ha*
Chardonnay, 169 ha	*Shiraz, 76.4 ha*
Traminer, 117 ha	
Rhine Riesling, 88 ha	
Sauvignon Blanc, 32 ha	

TOTAL PLANTINGS *939 ha*

ABOVE: *Shaving deposits from the inside of four-year-old barrels gives them a new lease of life (two years or so).*

FACING PAGE: *Alluvial soils on the flood plain of the Goulburn River are a friendly home for the Rosemount Estate Vineyards.*

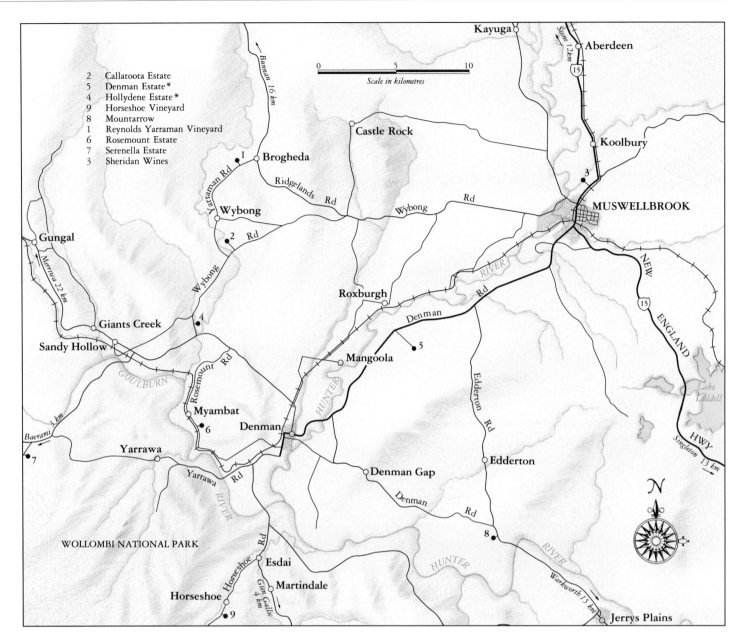

2　Callatoota Estate
5　Denman Estate*
4　Hollydene Estate*
9　Horseshoe Vineyard
8　Mountarrow
1　Reynolds Yarraman Vineyard
6　Rosemount Estate
7　Serenella Estate
3　Sheridan Wines

With appropriate management, site and varietal selection, grape-growing in the Upper Hunter is economically viable — more so, indeed, than in many Lower Hunter locations. This has resulted in the acquisition of major vineyards by leading winemakers: Mount Dangar (one of Adelaide Steamship Co Pty Ltd's (Adsteam) earliest wine ventures — it now owns Penfolds/Lindemans) by Rosemount Estate, Chateau Douglas by Tyrrell's Wines and — most recently — Denman Estate by the Rothbury Estate.

Overall, plantings seem to have stabilised after declining sharply from the peak of the second half of the 1970s. It remains a region of big wineries and vineyards, dominated by Rosemount Estate, with only four small makers, two long established (Callatoota Estate and Reynolds Yarraman, formerly Horderns Wybong Estate) and two much newer (Horseshoe Vineyard and Serenella Estate).

Scenically, it is every bit as beautiful as the Hunter: rocky outcrops and small hills rise abruptly from vineyards, while places such as Horderns Wybong Estate have wonderful vistas — as well as a striking, stone winery. The region is often ignored by the Lower Hunter wine tourist, but it shouldn't be.

ABOVE: *Rosemount Edinglassie.*

PRINCIPAL WINE STYLES

SEMILLON
Notwithstanding the decline in plantings from 323 ha in 1984 to 244 ha in 1989, Semillon remains the dominant variety — and hence wine — in the region. Most of the best wines, with Rosemount Estate to the fore, but with Mountarrow, Reynolds Yarraman, Serenella Estate and Horseshoe Vineyard lending support, are fleshy, soft and significantly oak-influenced. The often lemony/spicy oak flavour helps flesh out the young wines, but they develop more quickly than those of the Lower Hunter in any event. In the result, they tend to peak at 2 to 4 years of age, with soft buttery fruit and sometimes (particularly Mountarrow) slightly overplayed oak. The best (Rosemount Show Reserve) will continue on for another 3 or 4 years, but without further improvement.

CHARDONNAY
The rate of increase in plantings since 1984 (60 ha to 169 ha) seems to have slowed to a near stop, but this does not indicate any disillusionment with the variety. Rosemount Roxburgh is on one view Australia's greatest example of the style, incredibly rich and complex, toasty, textured and creamy, with a strong charred oak overlay. As with Semillon, the wines develop relatively quickly, reaching full maturity at

around 3 years: full bodied, soft and with honey/peach/butter flavours. Semillon-Chardonnay blends are quite common, too, but Chardonnay has to be regarded as the outstanding wine of the region, with all makers producing wines of real merit.

RHINE RIESLING AND TRAMINER
Once far more important than they are today, they are now being used to make commercial lime/apricot/passionfruit flavoured wines, with some residual sugar sweetness, aimed at the lower end of the mass market. Rosemount Estate and Verona Vineyard are the principal contributors and Rosemount makes no claim that the wines are Hunter-sourced.

CABERNET SAUVIGNON
This is often blended with wine from other regions (particularly Rosemount Estate) to produce a soft, chocolatey, dark berry-flavoured, low tannin style which is ready at around 3 to 4 years.

SHIRAZ AND PINOT NOIR
Likewise commonly blended with other regions to produce soft, pleasant, clean fruity wines with no outstanding characteristics, but equally no obvious vices.

ABOVE: *Rosemount Estate: the beauty of vineyards at dusk.*

ROSEMOUNT ESTATE: UNIVERSAL APPEAL

Rosemount Estate and Philip Shaw, its chief winemaker, have achieved quite remarkable synergy since Shaw joined the management team in early 1982. Right from the outset, Rosemount has shown exceptional skill and flair in marketing its products. It was well served by its first winemaker, John Ellis, who joined prior to the first on-site vintage in 1975, but it was the willingness and financial ability of owner Bob Oatley to invest relatively large sums in the marketing support of those early wines which was crucial. It was the right time: wine consumption was rising rapidly, and while the original choice of plantings of Shiraz and Traminer might now seem less than inspired, the wines won immediate acceptance.

Prolific show success in 1975 added fuel to the flames which Oatley's willingness to spend had ignited, and a national brand was established almost overnight. The early years rested upon Traminer and Rhine Riesling, but by 1980 Semillon had become a key wine, and Chardonnay was on the way. That year saw the first Chardonnay Show Reserve wine, and 1983 saw the first Roxburgh Chardonnay.

Success in the national marketplace created a rapidly increasing demand for grapes and wine which was satisfied in three ways: the acquisition of Penfolds, Wybong winery and vineyard in 1977, Roxburgh vineyard from Denman Estate in 1980, and the 400 hectare Mount Dangar property (with 113 hectares under vine) from Adsteam in 1983; the establishment of a series of new vineyards including Giants Creek and Whites Creek; and the purchase of substantial quantities of grapes, and sometimes wine, from other regions.

As volumes have increased, Rosemount has more frequently turned to regional blends, for pragmatic reasons of availability, and also because Philip Shaw and general manager Chris Hancock — the latter another key person in Rosemount's success, and who was stand-in winemaker between Ellis' departure and Shaw's arrival — believe that blended wines can be, and frequently are, superior.

Initially, these blends stayed within the 80 per cent content rule, so the wines could still be labelled as of Hunter Valley origin. Now the net is cast wider and the large volume Diamond Label series makes no claim of geographic origin. (By contrast, the Show Reserve series does claim to be and is of Hunter origin, while Roxburgh, Giants Creek and Whites Creek are of specific vineyard origin.) As if to prove

Rosemount's point, the Diamond Label wines are good enough to win gold medals at national shows.

They have also been a major force in Rosemount's spectacularly successful move into international markets. Having enjoyed such success in establishing its local market franchise, it is tempting to say that international success should have been a logical follow-on. In fact very different rules apply: far larger Australian wine companies started to seriously export wines around the same time as Rosemount (in the early 1980s) and some have not been nearly as successful. What is more, Rosemount's success has come in all four major markets: the United Kingdom, Sweden, New Zealand and the most difficult of all, the United States.

In the latter market, in particular, Rosemount captured the minds and hearts of the wine media: one rave review followed another and another. To a degree this success reflects painstaking research into the way the system worked (research ignored by many of the other Australian exporters), but to an even greater degree it reflects the enormous thought which Rosemount has given to the style of its wines: somehow it has managed to strike a balance between creative integrity on the one hand and sensitivity to the demands and tastes of the mass market on the other.

This balancing act has been the particular contribution of Philip Shaw, with input from Chris Hancock. If Rosemount had followed the path of the typical large Australian wine company, the Diamond label series would have been to a strict and largely predetermined formula, with only the final blend decisions involving any degree of choice or intuition.

Against all the odds, Shaw adopts a freewheel approach to making the wine right from the outset. Almost uniquely, natural yeasts (rather than cultured yeasts) are relied on for the fermentation; Shaw believes not only in making the wine as naturally as possible, but also in letting vintage variation have full play. The more conventional approach is to deliberately iron-out such variations so that each release of a given varietal or generic wine tastes as similar as possible to the preceding one.

Yet on the other hand, Shaw very deliberately and consciously designs and shapes the style of the wine. 'Elegance combined with complexity is what I am after in all wines' he says. Nebulous, perhaps, but then so is the subtlety of finding the balance which appeals to the greatest number

---

ABOVE: *Bob Oatley, Squire of Rosemount.*

of wine drinkers. At the level of the Diamond label series, the aim is not to challenge or to overwhelm consumers: that is the function of Roxburgh Chardonnay. Rather it is to construct wines which are soft, harmonious and which retain their fruit core without stridently proclaiming it.

It is an Australian version of the American philosophy of 'food wines', wines which blend easily with the everyday meal rather than challenging or overwhelming it. It is the easiest thing in the world to go too far, to strip the wine of all its individuality, all its fruit and to end up with a bland, meaningless fluid the only virtue of which is 12 degrees (or thereabouts) of alcohol. A significant number of Californian wines seem to have stepped over the edge, but Rosemount does not — and it is for this reason that it continues to attract such praise and enjoy such success in the marketplace.

As if conscious of the danger of lowest-common-denominator anonymity, Rosemount added Giants Creek and Whites Creek to its armoury in 1990, fitting them in below its flagship Roxburgh and catering to the strongly held belief among connoisseurs that mono-cru, estate made, grown and bottled wines are inherently superior to all others. From whichever viewpoint you perceive Rosemount, it looks good.

ABOVE: *The Upper Hunter has a quiet beauty all of its own — and room to spare for the ever-growing empire of Rosemount Estate.*

WINERIES OF THE UPPER HUNTER VALLEY

DENMAN ESTATE   C-B
Denman Road
Muswellbrook 2333   (065) 47 2473
Established   1969
Winemaker   David Lowe
Production   Not stated.

Principal Wines   Semillon, Chardonnay,
Sauvignon Blanc, Botrytis Semillon, Pinot Noir,
Shiraz and Cabernet Sauvignon.
Best Vintages   W 1979, '80, '84, '86, '89
                       R No significant vintages
Denman has had a shadowy existence,
principally acting as a grape grower and, to a
lesser degree, a seller of wine in bulk to other
Hunter Valley wineries. In 1987 and 1988, the
Rothbury Estate purchased all of the grapes; and
acquired the vineyard outright in June 1988. It
is now making and marketing the wines, aimed
fairly and squarely at the middle market.

HORSESHOE VINEYARD BA-B
Horseshoe Road
Horseshoe Valley via Denman
2328   (065) 47 3528
Established   1986
Winemaker   John Hordern
Production   1000 cases
Principal Wines   Shiraz Nouveau, Chardonnay
and Semillon.
Best Vintages   W 1987, '89
                       R Not applicable
John Hordern was for some years part of the
Horderns Wybong Estate (now called Reynolds
Yarraman Vineyard) operation, moving to set up
his own label in 1986. Thanks to a handsome
investment in new oak, he produced spectacular
wines in 1987, with an outstanding melon/
grapefruit Chardonnay with its icing of nutmeg/
clove/spice oak. Subsequent wines have followed
down a similar, though not quite so brilliant,
style path.

MOUNTARROW CB-B
Highway 213
Jerry's Plains 2330   (065) 76 4041
Established   1969
Winemaker   Simon Gilbert
Production   Not stated.
Principal Wines   The range of brands and
labels is increasing at an exponential rate; those
on sale in early 1990 included Simon Gilbert,
Arrowfield Premium, Arrowfield Reserve,
Arrowfield Circle Hill, Mountarrow Pro Hart
and Carisbrook Estate as well as thesatellite
labels of Simon Whitlam and Wollombi Brook.
These in turn variously include some or all of
Semillon, Chardonnay, Sauvignon Blanc,
Semillon Chardonnay, Pinot Noir, Shiraz,
Cabernet Sauvignon and Merlot.
Best Vintages   W 1982, '85, '87, '88, '89
                       R 1979, '85, '86, '88
With five different owners in less than a decade,
it is understandable that Mountarrow (formerly
Arrowfield) would be facing something of an
identity crisis. The most recent change which
took place in early 1990 (majority ownership by
Hokkuriku Coca-Cola of Japan) has kept the
fires burning as a plethora of new labels has
appeared. One must assume the marketing team,
led by part owner and former leading Sydney
wine retailer Andrew Simon, knows what it is
doing, but this has not always been obvious. As
against this, there has been remarkable stability
(and competence) on the winemaking side, with
first Gary Baldwin and then Simon Gilbert
consistently producing attractive, barrel
fermented and matured Semillon, Chardonnay
and Sauvignon Blanc (often drawing on grapes
from elsewhere in Australia or New Zealand)
and supple though less interesting red wines. In
recent years the oak handling has threatened to
become claustrophobic in its impact; a lighter
touch might lessen the load both on palate and
wallet.

REYNOLDS
YARRAMAN VINEYARD BA-BA
Yarraman Road, Wybong
Muswellbrook 2333 (065) 47 8127
Established   1965
Winemaker   Jon Reynolds
Production   4000 cases

*ABOVE: Richard Hordern installing drip irrigation in new plantings at
Horseshoe Vineyard.*

Principal Wines Chablis, Semillon, Chardonnay, Spatlese Rhine Riesling, Potters Shiraz, Shiraz and Cabernet Sauvignon.

Best Vintages **W** 1973, '74, '79, '82, '85, '86, '87, '90

R 1975, '79, '85, '86, '90

The winery is one of the most beautiful and unusual in Australia; the walls are made from a convict-hewn stone prison moved block by block from nearby Bengala, while the supports, bearers and joists came from a century old Dalgety wool store. Sydney orthopaedic surgeon Bob Smith and wife Theo gave their heart and soul to Horderns Wybong Estate for 20 years before selling it to Jon Reynolds (formerly chief winemaker at Houghton and then at Wyndham Estate in the Lower Hunter Valley) in mid-1989. The winery has had a chequered career, producing superb white wines in 1973 and 1974, but faltering badly thereafter until consultancy advice was obtained in the mid-1980s. Notwithstanding that advice, not all the wines have shone, but clearly Jon Reynolds must have great faith in the capacity of the vineyard to produce first class wines, and there seems every reason to suppose that an A-A rating is just around the corner.

ROSEMOUNT ESTATE **BA-A**
Rosemount Road
Denman 2328 (065) 47 2410
Established 1975
Winemaker Philip Shaw
Production Over 400,000 cases.
Principal Wines A wide range of sparkling, white and red table wines, variously identified by area (eg Hunter or Coonawarra in South Australia), by vineyard (eg Roxburgh, Giants

Creek), or variety (with special emphasis on Chardonnay). The commercial Diamond label range are area/State blends.

Best Vintages **W** 1983, '85, '86, '87

R 1983, '85, '86, '87

The Australian wine industry owes much to and can learn much from Rosemount Estate, which has handsomely demonstrated the synergy to be gained from expert winemaking and expert marketing, particularly when applied with dedication and a long term view to building up export markets. This is a thoroughly commercial operation, with profit its avowed objective, but that has not prevented the development of Roxburgh Chardonnay, Australia's white wine equivalent to Grange Hermitage, nor the success of the Show Reserve range and the ever increasing quality of the Diamond label wines. In Roxburgh Chardonnay you can discover every flavour and nuance possible in barrel fermented and oak matured fully ripened Chardonnay,

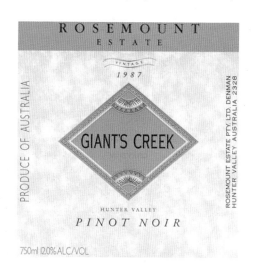

ranging from opulent butterscotch through to echoes of Burgundian cabbage.

SERENELLA ESTATE **B-B**
Mudgee Road Baerami
via Denman 2333 (065) 47 5126
Established 1981
Winemaker Letitia Cecchini
Production 6000 cases
Principal Wines Chardonnay, Semillon, Chablis, White Burgundy, Shiraz and Cabernet Sauvignon.
Best Vintages **W** 1988, '89,

R 1987, '88

The newest arrival in the Upper Hunter scene, although the vineyard operation has been on foot for some time. The white wines promise to be very good indeed, with both Chardonnay and Semillon showing rich peachy fruit and good oak. As with many of the wines of the district, they are probably best consumed within 2 or 3 years of vintage.

OTHER WINERIES

CALLATOOTA ESTATE **DC-C**
Wybong Road
Wybong 2333 (065) 47 8149

HOLLYDENE ESTATE **DB-CB**
Merriwa Road
Hollydene 2333 (065) 47 2316

SHERIDAN WINES **C-C**
New England Highway
Muswellbrook 2333 (065) 43 1055

ABOVE LEFT: Jon Reynolds and daughter Coco; a new career at Reynolds Yarraman.

ABOVE RIGHT: Grapegrowing is frequently part of a broader-based farming activity.

MUDGEE

Mudgee, or Nest in the Hills as the Aboriginals knew it, has always had to live in the shadow of the Hunter Valley — and more recently live with the knowledge that some of its grape production would be heading over the Great Dividing Range to wineries in that region. For, thanks to its more reliable summer weather and the strength and depth of its reds, it has always represented an insurance policy against a wet and thin Hunter vintage.

It has its own particular history. Three German families — Roth, Kurtz and Buchholz — were instrumental in establishing vines from 1858, with the descendants of the first two carrying on viticulture for a century and keeping the tradition alive when all others had abandoned it. The other event of importance was the discovery of gold in 1872. This was nowhere near on the scale of Victoria's gold rush, but was enough to bring people and prosperity to the district until the great bank crash of 1893.

Although the vineyard and winery of the celebrated Dr Thomas Fiaschi continued in production until his death in 1927, and Craigmoor, founded by Adam Roth in 1858, survived until the renaissance of the 1960s, from the 1920s until then the 55 vineyards which existed in 1893 slowly dwindled. Even when the renaissance came, it was essentially driven by a few energetic enthusiasts.

THE REGION IN BRIEF

LOCATION AND ELEVATION
32°36'S 149°36'E
450 — 600 m

CLIMATE
Because it is situated on the western slopes of the Great Dividing Range, Mudgee has a very different climate to that of its nearest and most illustrious neighbour, the Hunter Valley. Contrary to some wishful thinking in some quarters, it is not a cool area: while its HDD measurement of 2050 is slightly less than the Lower Hunter, its MJT is higher at 22.9°C. The nights are cold, spring frosts are a problem in some vineyards, but the summers are uncompromisingly hot. The saving grace is that they are relatively dry: the growing season rainfall is 360 mm (out of an annual total of 670 mm) compared with 530 mm in the Hunter (and an annual total of 740 mm).

SOIL
The most common soils (in the duplex group) are similar or identical to those found in many — indeed the majority of — Australian wine districts: slightly acidic loam or sandy loam topsoils over neutral clay subsoils (Dr2.22, 2.32, 2.42, Dy3.41 and 3.42). These brownish-coloured soils are quite friable and moderately fertile, and both surface and subsoils are relatively well drained. They are thus highly suited to viticulture, but yields have always been restricted because of insufficient surface or bore water to allow optimum irrigation, and one suspects that acidity may also play an inhibiting role.

HARVEST TIME
Late February — late March

PRINCIPAL GRAPE VARIETIES

Chardonnay, 155 ha	*Shiraz, 83 ha*
Semillon, 55.5 ha	*Cabernet Sauvignon, 130 ha*
Rhine Riesling, 18.5 ha	*Pinot Noir, 30 ha*

TOTAL PLANTINGS 668 ha
(including 156 ha coming into bearing)

AUSTRALASIAN WINE REGIONS
1980 – 1990

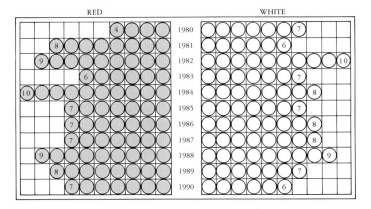

ABOVE: *Patterson's Curse (rather than thistles) makes a colourful foreground to Pinot Noir at Thistle Hill.*

FACING PAGE: *Spring budburst of lightly pruned vines.*

PRINCIPAL WINE STYLES

CABERNET SAUVIGNON
This variety makes Mudgee's best wines, usually as a 100 per cent varietal, but sometimes blended with Merlot (at Huntington Estate) or with Shiraz (by a number of producers). The wines have tremendous depth of colour, and hold their purple-red hues for longer than those of the Hunter, turning brick-red at 7 to 10 years of age. The generous flavours reflect the warm climate: a melange of tastes of red berry, dark chocolate and (sometimes) eucalypt/peppermint; the tannins are almost invariably pronounced, but are not excessively astringent and are balanced by the fruit generosity. Well made wines demand 5 years cellaring, and will usually profit from 10. Huntington Estate, Montrose and Thistle Hill have produced most of the best wines.

SHIRAZ
The wines can be somewhat schizophrenic; some are determined to out-Hunter the Hunter, with strong earthy/tarry/leathery characters which the makers swear are of regional origin rather than sulphide-derived. Other wines are much cleaner and closer to Cabernet Sauvignon, with lush red berry fruits and hints of chocolate. It is frequently blended with Cabernet Sauvignon, sometimes with Cabernet and Malbec — almost always to very good effect. Like Cabernet, it has a 5 to 10 year peak, but will fade a little more quickly thereafter. Over the years

Montrose has stood out from the rest, making some wines of unusual elegance, while Burnbrae has provided some richly fruity Cabernet Shiraz.

CHARDONNAY
This is by far the best-performing white wine from the region, consistently producing good, sometimes excellent, wine. The flavours are usually in the peach/melon/fig spectrum, but sometimes citric/grapefruit characters emerge, particularly where the maker (such as Miramar) employs barrel-ferment techniques. The wines show at their best varietal character in the second and third years, but do go on to develop into rich, regional honeyed white Burgundy styles over a much longer time frame, with those of Miramar often outstanding.

All other white varieties — with the heavily qualified exceptions of Semillon and Sauvignon Blanc — perform erratically at best.

FORTIFIED WINES
A miscellany of styles are made: rich, sweet and chocolatey vintage ports are the best; full bodied tawnies usually deprived of sufficient cask-age (and hence rancio complexity) are next; and some unusual 'Muscats' (made from the wrong grapes) have a local following.

ABOVE: *The annual miracle: a spur-pruned vine in the first days of budburst.*

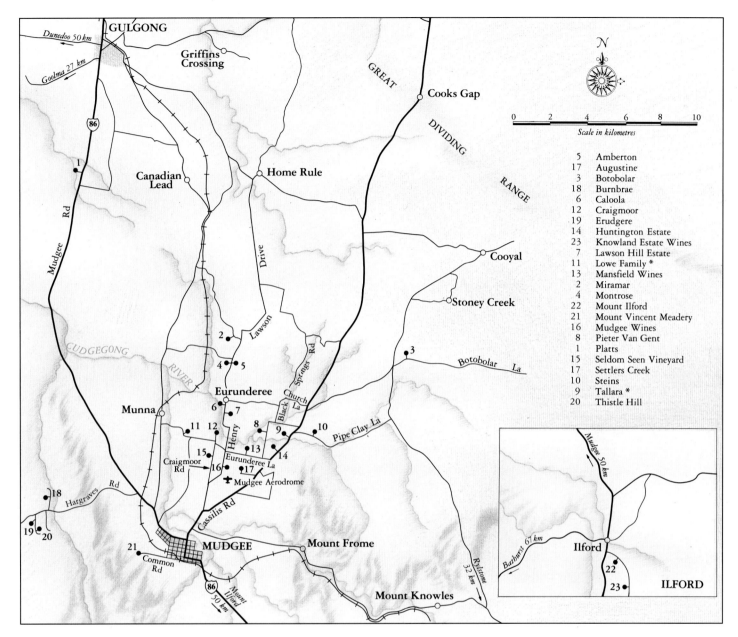

Both through the circumstance of relatively small scale winemaking and the softly beautiful and intimate nature of much of the scenery — the outer rim of hills providing a sense of security, and the smaller hills within the perimeter creating mini-vistas and valleys of their own — Mudgee has always seemed an especially friendly and welcoming place to its visitors.

Not all of those who have established wineries in this area over the past 20 years have succeeded: the fact that Mudgee is not overrun by weekend tourists has had its darker implications for some less well situated or less skilled wineries. Some have quietly faded away; others have been forced to merge into larger groupings.

The most spectacular of these was the Montrose acquisition of both Amberton and Craigmoor; the Montrose group then fell prey to Wyndham Estate (Lower Hunter Valley) in 1988, the latter in turn to Orlando (South Australia) in early 1990.

So after 132 years a large winery finally acquired a substantial stake in the district, and one can only suspect that the sense of identity which was so important (and which gave rise to the Appellation Scheme explained on page 68) will be severely tested.

On the other hand, district identities such as Bob Roberts have done and will continue to do much to support it. Roberts not only makes the best red wines in the region, but has turned the Huntington Estate classical music concerts into major events in the New South Wales musical calendar. There are others — such as Dave Robertson of Thistle Hill, who threatens to steal Roberts' red wine mantle and Ian MacRae of Miramar with lovely white wines —who are also most competent ambassadors, and the list certainly does not stop there.

If you live in Sydney, and want to get away from it all, Mudgee is the place to go.

APPELLATION CONTROL:
A MARKETING NECESSITY

The appellation debate is as old as wine. Wine jars recovered from King Tutankhamen's tomb prove beyond doubt the Egyptians had a sophisticated system, one which even grasped the nettle that most modern systems either ignore or address in a most perfunctory fashion — quality. It is true that some present day structures have a taste assessment as part of the qualifying process, but it is limited to ensuring the wine is reasonably true to its type and/or free from objectionable winemaking faults. The Egyptians went further, grading the wine: only South Africa, with its gold capsule indicating superior quality, presently attempts such differentiation.

I am in fact far from sure that the absence of any real quality assessment is a bad thing. It is better that appellation be seen as simply guaranteeing truth in labelling, and as fitting label claims into a coherent, consistent and logical framework — ensuring that, in the vernacular, what you see is what you get, leaving the consumer to make the more subjective assessment of quality.

There can no longer be any argument that Australia needs a single appellation system, with internationally recognised and agreed areas of origin and with suitable guarantees of accuracy in all label claims. It is rapidly moving to such a system, but it may well stop short of the very rigidly controlled and administered Mudgee system.

The Society for the Appellation of the Wines of Mudgee is a voluntary organisation of the winemakers of Mudgee. But it has an independent controller, a member of a firm of chartered accountants with whom full details of all vine plantings, grape yields and litres of wine produced must be registered. He has an absolute and unqualified right to inspect vineyards, winery and wine stocks at any time.

A winemaker desiring to use the Mudgee mark on a wine makes an application by sworn declaration after the wine has been bottled. The controller then visits the winery, checks the quantities in stock and selects random bottles for subsequent tasting by the Wine Assessment Committee.

The committee is made up of winemakers from the region, which may seem a cause for concern, but the reality is otherwise. All wines are tasted blind, and all those on the panel must be satisfied the wine is free from objectionable fault. If this prima facie test is satisfied, the essential details of the label claims (though not, of course, the identity of the maker) are communicated to the panel.

The next task is to assess the fidelity of the wine to its label. In other words, if it is labelled Chardonnay it must taste of Chardonnay; if it is said to be oak-matured, oak must

be detectable, and so on. This satisfied, the wine must also satisfy other criteria: to be labelled Chardonnay, it must contain 100 per cent Chardonnay, not merely 80 per cent as is the case nationally. It must be 100 per cent Mudgee sourced wine, and it must have been made and bottled in the district.

If it passes all these tests, each bottle will qualify for an individually numbered strip or mark — the total corresponding precisely with the number of bottles made. Despite its stringency, the system has worked well from a practical viewpoint and has certainly had the desired effect from a promotional and marketing standpoint.

What, then, is the national position? In 1989 the winemakers of Australia, through the Wine and Brandy Corporation of which all winemakers are members, resolved to implement a Label Integrity Programme, or LIP. Through amendments to the Commonwealth Australian Wine and Brandy Corporation Act, all winemakers are henceforth obliged to keep records which will enable auditors appointed by the corporation to establish the veracity of any label claim as to vintage, variety or region of origin.

The records do not have to be automatically provided to the corporation, and at least initially it is likely that audit inspections will concentrate on makers, varieties or producing areas which have given concern or in respect to which complaints have been received. But audits there will be, and a healthy budget has been allocated for this purpose.

There are two difficulties confronting LIP — one temporary, the other of wider import. The first is that nationwide region of origin definitions are still only in draft form. Each is to be agreed by the vignerons of the area concerned, and in regions such as Coonawarra in South Australia this may cause great difficulty: there is an animated, if not bitter, debate over the entitlement of adjacent black soil areas to be regarded as part of Coonawarra. Moreover, to be really worthwhile, the names adopted have to be recognised by the European Economic Community (EEC) and the BATF (the regulatory body in the United States).

The second difficulty lies in the shortcomings of the uniform Food Standards Regulations, which I explain in some detail at page 39. If Australia wishes to effectively participate in the EEC after 1992, it will need to address these shortcomings urgently. On all of the evidence to date, the wine producers of Europe will only too happily accept excuses — particularly excuses as obvious as these — to deny or restrict the entry of Australian wine into their own bailiwick.

WINERIES OF MUDGEE

AMBERTON B-B
Lowe's Peak Vineyard
Henry Lawson Drive
Mudgee 2850 (063) 73 3910
Established 1975
Winemaker Robert Paul
Production 20,000 cases
Principal Wines Varietal white and red table wines; labels include Semillon, Sauvignon Blanc, Traminer, Chardonnay, Shiraz and Cabernet Sauvignon.
Best Vintages W 1982, '84, '88, '89
R 1981, '84, '85, '88, '89
Yet another arm of the Wyndham Estate empire acquired when Wyndham purchased Montrose (which had previously taken Amberton and Craigmoor under its wing). Always known more as a white wine than red wine producer, it is also one of the few to achieve any success with the aromatic white varieties in Mudgee, notably Traminer. These days its wines are sold only through cellar door and through the American Express/Cellarmaster direct mail organisation.

AUGUSTINE CB-B
Airport Road
Mudgee 2850 (063) 72 3880
Established 1918
Winemaker Various contract winemakers, all situated outside the Mudgee region.
Production 1500 cases
Principal Wines Chablis, Trebbiano Semillon, Moselle, Chardonnay, Pinot Noir, Cabernet Shiraz and Cabernet Port.
Best Vintages Not relevant because of ownership changes.
The Augustine vineyards were originally planted by the famous Dr Fiaschi, the Italian-trained senior surgeon at Sydney Hospital who tried so manfully to overcome the indifference of the early twentieth century towards fine table wine in New South Wales with his vineyards at the Hawkesbury River and in Mudgee. It was largely abandoned by the late 1940s with only a small planting of aleatico surviving; after a modest revival in the 1970s, it wandered along until the syndicate headed by Dr Ray Healey, which also owns Settlers Creek, acquired it in 1988. The winery restaurant already shows the touch of the new owners, and much better things must be in store for its wines.

BOTOBOLAR B-BA
Botobolar Lane
Mudgee 2850 (063) 73 3840
Established 1970
Winemaker Gil Wahlquist
Production 4000 cases
Principal Wines Crouchen, Marsanne, Budgee Budgee, Chardonnay, Shiraz, St Gilbert,

Cabernet Sauvignon and Cooyal Port.
Best Vintages W 1979, '82, '84, '86, '87, '88
R 1976, '79, '80, '82, '86, '87, '88
Owners Gil and Vincie Wahlquist have been leaders in the development of organic viticulture in Australia, eschewing the use of herbicides and insecticides, and limiting fungicides almost exclusively to sulphur and copper sprays. They encourage a complicated life-chain system in the vineyard starting with ancient herbs and weeds from England, and culminating in predatory birds (predatory to things other than grapes, that is). Some of the red wines, notably a Shiraz, are likewise made without the use of chemicals, although the majority are conventionally made with the assistance of SO2 and added acid. Botobolar's strength undoubtedly lies with its reds, which age beautifully into supple, velvety warmth, with very soft tannins and flavours of dark red berries and dark chocolate.

BURNBRAE CB-B
The Hargraves Road
Erudgere via Mudgee 2850 (063) 73 3504
Established 1976
Winemaker Robert B Mace
Production 2000 cases
Principal Wines Semillon Chardonnay, Chardonnay, Semillon, Grenache Rosé, Cabernet Sauvignon, Shiraz, Shiraz Cabernet, Sauvignon Malbec, Pinot Noir, Vintage Port and Liqueur Muscat.
Best Vintages W 1984, '85, '88, '89
R 1979, '82, '84, '85, '87, '89
As I have commented elsewhere, the wines of Burnbrae are like the curate's egg: very good in parts. The red wines are the pick of the bunch, with the Shiraz Cabernet Malbec frequently leading the way with its rich, sweet, dark berry and dark chocolate flavours. Owners Robert and Pamela Mace are born of the old school, and always make visitors to the winery especially welcome.

CRAIGMOOR CB-B
Craigmoor Road
Mudgee 2850 (063) 72 2208
Established 1858
Winemaker Robert Paul
Production 15,000 cases
Principal Wines Chablis, Semillon Chardonnay, Chardonnay, Semillon, Spatlese Rhine Riesling, Late-picked Semillon, Shiraz, Cabernet Shiraz, Cabernet Sauvignon, Liqueur Muscat and Port.
Best Vintages: W 1979, '84, '86, '87, '88, '89
R 1973, '74, '78, '79, '84, '87, '88
One of the most historic wineries in New South Wales; indeed, the lower section (built by Adam Roth in 1860) is the oldest winery construction in Australia to have remained in continuous use other than Olive Farm on the outskirts of Perth. The winery remained in the Roth family's hands until 1969, but several changes of ownership since see it as part of the Wyndham group. It vies with Tyrrell's Wines (of the Lower Hunter Valley) for the honour of making the first Chardonnay after the Second World War. Chardonnay and Semillon, each with a great capacity for aging, are the mainstay of the Craigmoor winery.

ERUDGERE B-BA
Hargraves/Hill End Road
Erudgere via Mudgee 2850 (063) 72 1118
Established 1982
Winemakers Ian MacRae,
David Robertson (white wines);
Paul Tuminello (red wines).
Production Approximately 250 cases.
Principal Wines The wines on offer at any time represent a moveable feast, as in each vintage half or all of the grapes are sold to other

ABOVE: Botobolar's Gil Wahlquist practices organic viticulture with the help of a keen sense of humour.

producers and only part vinified. Typically, however, a Rhine Riesling, a Shiraz, a Cabernet Sauvignon and a Shiraz Cabernet will be available at any one time.

Best Vintages   W 1982, '84, '85, '86, '89
                    R 1980, '82, '83, '84, '86

Owner Keith Carew has some of the oldest and best vineyards in Mudgee under his control, but is content to run a very low key cellar door operation, with small batches of wine variously contract made by Ian MacRae and David Robertson (white wines) and the highly talented but shadowy figure of Paul Tuminello (red wines). It is the red wines which can be particularly impressive, with soft, dusty/velvety fruit; a touch of new oak would lift them into the highest class.

HUNTINGTON ESTATE   A-A
Cassilis Road
Mudgee 2850 (063) 73 3825
Established   1969
Winemaker   Bob Roberts
Production   12,000 cases
Principal Wines   White table wine labels include Semillon, Chardonnay, Sweet White blend; light reds include Pinot Noir, Dry Rosé and Rosé Medium Dry; red table wines labelled by variety and progressively changing bin number with FB (full bodied) or MB (medium bodied) prefix: they include Shiraz, Shiraz Cabernet Sauvignon, Cabernet Sauvignon and Cabernet Merlot.
Best Vintages   W 1979, '82, '85, '89
                    R 1974, '79, '81, '83, '84, '86, '88

Bob Roberts is one of my favourite Australian winemakers, a renaissance man transplanted to the twentieth century. When he became sufficiently interested in viticulture (and the Mudgee area) to commence the search for a vineyard and winery site in 1967, he had collected a Diploma in Agriculture from Wagga,

Law Degree from Sydney, and experience on his family's plantation in New Guinea. He then enrolled in a correspondence course run by the Oenological Research Institute in Surrey, England, and duly obtained his Diploma in Winemaking. As if all this were not enough, he and his vineyard manager designed and built the substantial winery in 1972. Since the early 1970s he has produced an almost endless stream of red wines with tremendous character and style, built for long aging in the bottle with

minty/red berry flavours when young, slowly taking on flavours of wild game and dark chocolate, but always retaining that core of sweet fruit.

MIRAMAR   BA-B
Henry Lawson Drive
Mudgee 2850   (063) 73 3874
Established   1977
Winemaker   Ian MacRae
Production   9000 cases
Principal Wines   Semillon, Semillon Chardonnay, Chardonnay, Sauvignon Blanc, Fumé Blanc, Doux Blanc, Traminer Rhine Riesling, Rhine Riesling, Rosé, Pinot Noir, Shiraz, Cabernet Sauvignon and Vintage Port.
Best Vintages   W 1979, '84, '87, '88
                    R 1978, '84, '85, '86, '88

Ian MacRae runs against the normal pattern of the small Mudgee winery in producing white wines which are every bit as good (if not better) than his red wines. Over the years, some outstanding barrel fermented Chardonnays have appeared under the Miramar label, with Semillon not far behind. Thanks to careful fermentation and exclusion of oxygen, the whites show very high-toned floral citric/tropical fruit when young, often with smoky overtones. Bottle age allows more conventional characters to manifest themselves, and it is really a question of choice whether one drinks the wines young or old.

ABOVE: *The annual concert season at Huntington Estate threatens to upstage its harvest season; the concerts are amazingly successful and taken very seriously by the music world of Sydney.*

TOP: *The lime green tips of vines in a peacock's tail display of colour.*

MONTROSE   BA-A
Henry Lawson Drive
Mudgee 2850   (063) 73 3853
Established   1973
Winemaker   Robert Paul
Production   50,000 cases
Principal Wines   Semillon, Chardonnay, Auslese Rhine Riesling, Sauvignon Blanc, Sauternes, Shiraz, Cabernet Sauvignon and Pinot Noir.
Best Vintages   W 1984, '86, '88, '89
                     R 1977, '80, '82, '84, '86, '87, '89

In terms of size, it is the senior winery of the Mudgee district, and is also capable of producing the best white wines and some of the best red wines. Where it and its associate wineries will ultimately fit into the scheme of things of the Orlando/Wyndham Estate group remains to be seen. Former winemaker Carlo Corino, much loved in Australia, has returned to his native Italy, but leaves a rich inheritance.

PLATT'S   CB-CB
Mudgee Road
Gulgong 2852   (063) 74 1700
Established   1983
Winemaker   Barry Platt
Production   4000 cases
Principal Wines   Semillon, Chardonnay, Sauvignon Blanc and Cabernet Sauvignon.
Best Vintages   W 1984, '86, '87, '89
                     R 1983, '84, '86, '87

Barry Platt has vast experience in winemaking. He trained and graduated at Geisenhein in Germany, and having helped plan and establish Richmond Grove (Lower Hunter Valley), moved to Mudgee to become winemaker at Craigmoor after the departure of Pieter Van Gent. His small winery is the furthest flung of all in the district, not far short of Gulgong. He is active as a consultant, and has made some

good white and red wines, although intermittent oak problems have taken the gloss off some.

STEIN'S   CB-CB
Sandal Park Estate
Pipeclay Lane
Mudgee 2850   (063) 73 3991
Established   1976
Winemaker   Robert S Stein
Production   2000 cases
Principal Wines   Semillon Riesling, Chardonnay, Shiraz, Quarry Port, Rum Cask Port and Liqueur Muscat.
Best Vintages   W 1986, '87, '89
                     R 1988, '89

One of the more remote wineries of the district, it sits at the head of a valley and has superb sweeping views. Bob Stein planned the winery as a retirement hobby, but in the manner of such things, it has now become a full time job. Wine quality overall has been adequate but not exciting, yet that does not represent any lack of commitment on the part of Stein, and better things may well be in store.

THISTLE HILL   A-A
McDonalds Road
Mudgee 2850   (063) 73 3546
Established   1976
Winemaker   David Robertson
Production   2500 cases
Principal Wines   Chardonnay, Rhine Riesling, Pinot Noir, Cabernet Sauvignon, Port and Liqueur Muscat.
Best Vintages   W 1984, '86, '87, '88, '89
                     R 1984, '86, '87, '88, '89

Arguably one of the most underrated wineries in the district, if not Australia. Owner David Robertson turned adversity into good fortune when he used the compensation monies gained as a result of losing a leg in a motor accident to establish Thistle Hill. Having done that, he has

not allowed the inconvenience of an artificial leg to in any way impede his progress in either vineyard or winery, and his wines seem to go from strength to strength. The Chardonnay is consistently good, often very complex in a Burgundian fashion, and sometimes showing tantalising lift. The Cabernets are better still, hitting a purple patch with the '85, '86 and '87 vintages. They show typical characteristics of deep fruit and dark chocolate, allied with soft, lingering tannins and will handsomely repay cellaring for a decade or more.

OTHER WINERIES

CALOOLA   D-DC
Henry Lawson Drive
Mudgee 2850 (063) 73 3954

KNOWLAND ESTATE WINES   NR
Mount Vincent Road
Ilford 2850

LAWSON HILL ESTATE   NR
Henry Lawson Drive
Mudgee 2850 (063) 733953

LOWE FAMILY   B-B
Ashbourne Vineyard
Tinja Lane,
Mudgee 2850

MANSFIELD WINES   DC-C
Eurunderee Lane
Mudgee 2850 (063) 73 3871

MOUNT ILFORD   NR
Mount Vincent Road
Ilford 2850 (063) 58 8544

MOUNT VINCENT MEADERY   CB-CB
Common Road
Mudgee 2850 (063) 72 3184

MUDGEE WINES   NR
Henry Lawson Drive
Mudgee 2850 (063) 72 2258

PIETER VAN GENT   DC-DC
Black Springs Road
Mudgee 2850 (063) 73 3807

SELDOM SEEN VINEYARD   CB-B
Craigmoor Road
Mudgee 2850 (063) 72 4482

SETTLERS CREEK   CB-B
C/O Augustine
Airport Road
Mudgee 2850 (063) 72 3880

TALLARA   B-BA
'Tallara' Cassilis Road
Mudgee 2850

ABOVE: David Robertson of Thistle Hill: a passionate love of wine, and a will to surmount all difficulties.

NEW SOUTH WALES

MURRUMBIDGEE
IRRIGATION AREA

The birth of the Murrumbidgee Irrigation Scheme Area in 1906 and 1912 stands as a lasting testament to the skills and the vision of a group of dedicated Australians fired by the imagination of Sir Samuel McCaughey. Its subsequent development as a major wine producing area is primarily due to the remarkable McWilliam family, even if two successive waves of Italian immigrants (after the First and Second World Wars) built on the opportunities created by McWilliam.

Until the second half of the 1950s production in the area was almost entirely of fortified wine. Just as John James McWilliam had led the way in 1912, so Glen McWilliam pioneered the move to table wine. Not only was he responsible for the trial of premium varieties previously unknown in the district, but he was also responsible for leading the way in developing the winery technology necessary to produce modern table wine in a fiercely hot summer climate. Glen McWilliam embraced the technology pioneered by Orlando and Yalumba in the mid-50s for the handling of white grapes, adapting it to the particular requirements of the region.

No one can have a perfect vision of the future, and the initial success with Cabernet Sauvignon (the '63 vintage still stands as a freakish landmark) and Rhine Riesling was a false dawn. The chart below traces the fluctuating fortunes of the key varieties.

MURRUMBIDGEE IRRIGATION AREA HECTAREAGE & GRAPE VARIETIES

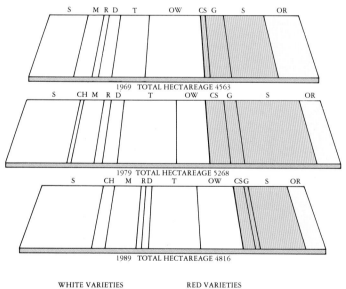

1969   TOTAL HECTAREAGE 4563

1979   TOTAL HECTAREAGE 5268

1989   TOTAL HECTAREAGE 4816

WHITE VARIETIES	RED VARIETIES
S – SEMILLON	CS – CABERNET SAUVIGNON
CH – CHARDONNAY	G –GRENACHE
M – MUSCAT GORDO BLANCO	S –SHIRAZ
R – RHINE RIESLING	OR – OTHER RED
D – DORADILLO	
T – TREBBIANO	
OW – OTHER WHITE	

As can be seen from the graph, this is increasingly recognised as white wine country, but without ambitions of greatness: there are few other regions in Australia in which

THE REGION IN BRIEF

LOCATION AND ELEVATION
34°S 146°E
140 m

CLIMATE
The climate is uncompromisingly hot and dry, and it hardly needs be said that grape growers are totally reliant upon irrigation. The HDD is 2201, the MJT 23.8 and the annual rainfall is 410 mm, with a surprisingly high 200 mm falling in the 7 month growing season. This summer rainfall, evenly spread over the months, helps promote the botrytis which comes in April (and even May) to produce the great sweet wines of the region.

SOIL
The soils are generally sandy loam overlying a sandy clay loam or clay subsoil; however, as they were deposited by ancient streams they are very variable. They range from red sandy earths (Gn1.13) through to red and brown massive earths (Gn2.13 and 2.46); the duplex soils in the Dr2.23 and 2.33 range found in so many Australian regions are also common. While free draining near the surface, subsoil water-logging has been a major problem, particularly with associated salinity build up.

HARVEST TIME
Early February — early May

PRINCIPAL GRAPE VARIETIES
Semillon, 1128 ha   *Shiraz, 721 ha*
Trebbiano, 828 ha   *Cabernet Sauvignon, 180 ha*
Muscat Gordo Blanco, 490 ha   *Mataro, 96 ha*
Chardonnay, 195 ha   *Grenache, 78 ha*
Colombard, 170 ha

TOTAL PLANTINGS *4816 ha*

FACING PAGE: Vines reaching for the sky — and for that all-important sunlight.

ABOVE: In large numbers galahs can be destructive, but are not normally regarded as a threat to vineyards.

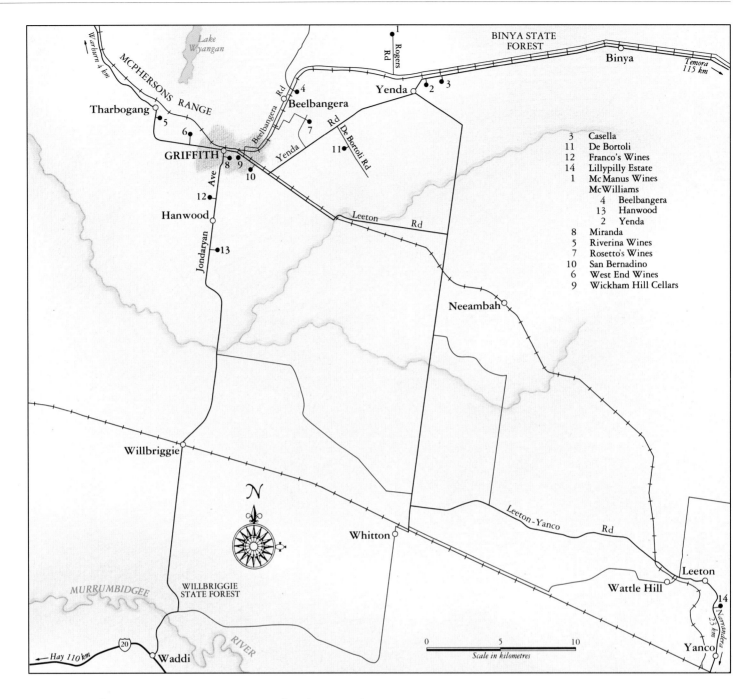

3   Casella
11   De Bortoli
12   Franco's Wines
14   Lillypilly Estate
1   McManus Wines
      McWilliams
4   Beelbangera
13   Hanwood
2   Yenda
8   Miranda
5   Riverina Wines
7   Rosetto's Wines
10   San Bernadino
6   West End Wines
9   Wickham Hill Cellars

plantings of varieties such as Muscat Gordo Blanco and Trebbiano have shown such healthy (and sustained) growth over the past two decades.

Its real strength lies in its efficiency: the 4816 hectares produced 88,290 tonnes of grapes in 1989 at an average of 18.33 tonnes per hectare. This compares with the average yield of 7.76 tonnes per hectare for the Upper and Lower Hunter Valley.

Consistent with this penchant for efficiency the Murrumbidgee is a scenically barren area: the vineyards are laser-flat, the wineries functional, and the cellar door sales areas a rococo blend of Australian-Italian do-it-yourself architecture. As a final deterrent to visitors, Griffith is a long way from anywhere.

AUSTRALASIAN WINE REGIONS
1980 – 1990

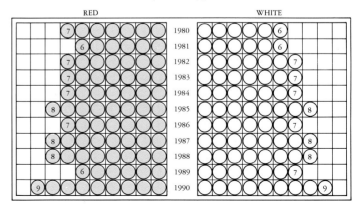

PRINCIPAL WINE STYLES

SEMILLON

Picked at normal maturity, Semillon provides a pleasant wine (which may be blended with other varieties) and is used in the making of generic styles such as Chablis and White Burgundy. When left on the vine for a full 2 months after normal maturity (and if the weather conditions are favourable) Botrytis cinerea, 'noble rot', may attack the grapes, concentrating both sugar and acid, and producing the luscious Sauternes-style dessert wine which is the district's one great table wine.

CHARDONNAY

Not surprisingly, Chardonnay is of increasing importance, and with the judicious use of oak (whether as oak chips or through oak barrels) it can produce a wine of fair varietal flavour, weight and style. Before long, it is probable that much of the Chardonnay made in the district will appear in casks. De Bortoli, Miranda (the Wyangan Estate range), Rossetto (the Mount Bingar range) and McWilliam's (particularly the latter two) have done best.

OTHER WHITE WINES

The substantial plantings of Trebbiano, Muscat Gordo Blanco and Colombard are principally used as a blend component in major wine company casks and flagons, with Orlando and McWilliam's the major users.

RED WINES

McWilliam's is the major producer of bottled red wine from the region, with its Cabernet Merlot offering a pleasant, leafy, light bodied, early-maturing (1 to 3 years) drink. As with the white wines, much of the annual crush disappears into the anonymity of casks.

FORTIFIED WINES

The region is also a major producer of fortified wines. While most are cheap (and of modest reputation and quality), McWilliam's in particular has some superb aged material which it uses in its much-gold medal winning Show Reserve series, with its Muscat, Amontillado Sherry and Oroloso Sherry the outstanding wines.

ABOVE: *Wasps feeding on botrytised grapes: pretty, but dangerous to both the wine and the winemaker.*

IRRIGATION: NOT A DIRTY WORD

Irrigation is an emotive and largely misunderstood subject. The feelings of antipathy stem from two sources: the French ban on its use in producing vineyards, and the old storyline that the vine will only give of its best quality when it is made to struggle.

The French ban is but another example of the pragmatism which underlies so many of their regulations: other than in freak vintages such as 1990, their growing season rainfall is more than sufficient to ensure the vine receives enough moisture, and in quality terms irrigation is simply not necessary. The shibboleth of the struggling vine has a grain of truth in it, but no more: just as with wine, the one essential for first class viticulture (and first class grapes) is that the vine must be in balance. The vine's balance is achieved through correct pruning and trellising and through correct nutrients being given to it: once any soil amelioration (lime, gypsum, manure, trace elements or whatever) has been attended to, the only ongoing nutrient routinely supplied is water.

It goes without saying that the Riverland areas of Australia (principally along the Murray River but also along the Murrumbidgee River) are entirely dependent on irrigation. The hot and dry climate, with its low humidity, means there is an enormous deficit (called the aridity index) in the naturally occurring water: for the Riverland areas this ranges between 497 and 637 millimetres in the growing season. It is this water which has to be provided through irrigation if the vine is to have sufficient vigour to produce its crop.

For a series of thoroughly understandable reasons — some historic, some climatic — the whole thrust of irrigation in the Riverland has not simply been to produce a crop, but to produce the largest possible crop without overmuch regard to the quality implications. Some research, notably by Dr Brian Freeman, has studied the effect of minimising water application rates in reducing yield and increasing quality. While that research has shown that it is definitely possible to

increase quality, the commercial reality is that the Riverland is best suited to the production of low cost grapes through maximum yields, and it is exceedingly unlikely there will be any change in this role.

Irrigation in other regions of Australia has — or may have — a very different role. Certainly it is possible to use it so as to increase production at the expense of quality, and even in the finest wine regions of Australia some grape growers use it in this fashion. But properly understood and properly used, its aim is merely to maximise the quality of the grapes up to a yield which the producer believes can be achieved without impairing resultant wine quality.

For the fact is that in almost all Australian grape growing districts summer rainfall is either insufficient or too unreliable to ensure that the vines will avoid undue stress. The problem is compounded where soils are very free draining (desirable, but only where there is sufficient water) or where compacted subsoils encourage surface root growth at the expense of deep roots.

Botanically, the vine is classed as a drought-tolerant species, and it can survive and produce small crops in extremely harsh, arid conditions. But there has been a great deal of research into the effect of stress on grape quality and chemical composition. Much of it is too technical for a book such as this, suffice it to say that too much water will swell the crop, reducing colour and flavour, reducing potential sugar and also decreasing acidity. Too little water may be no less damaging: in the ultimate, the vine will lose almost all its leaves and be unable to ripen the grapes. Even moderate water stress (water deficiency) can cause potassium uptake and increase pH: there may be a compensating concentration in colour, flavour and sugar, but there may not.

Irrigation is no more or less than a tool available to the vigneron. If used skilfully, it can be enormously beneficial; if abused, it can return short term profits and/or long term mediocrity. It is in no way an evil in itself.

ABOVE: *When water is in plentiful supply, and the climate is dry, spray irrigation is a highly efficient method.*

WINERIES OF MURRUMBIDGEE

DE BORTOLI WINES   CA-B
De Bortoli Road
Bilbul 2680   (069) 63 5344
Established   1928
Winemakers   Darren de Bortoli, Nick Gu
Production   The equivalent of over 1,000,000 cases.
Principal Wines   Increasing emphasis is being placed on varietal table wines, but the kaleidoscopic range of every conceivable type of table, fortified and flavoured wine in every container size and shape imaginable is still produced.
Best Vintages   Botrytised Sauternes 1982, '84, '85, '86, '87, '88
Since 1982, De Bortoli Wines has dominated the Sauternes-style white wine classes in Australian wine shows to an unprecedented and

never-likely-to-be repeated degree. De Bortoli was the pioneer, and others have now hopped on the bandwagon, so the competition grows day by day. The other De Bortoli wines are work-manlike and adequate for their purpose.

LILLYPILLY ESTATE   CB-B
Lillypilly Road
off Leeton-Yanco Road
Leeton 2705   (069) 53 4069
Established   1982
Winemaker   Robert Fiumara
Production   7000 cases
Principal Wines   Tramillon (a blend of Sem-illon and Traminer), Fumé Blanc, Chardonnay, Rhine Riesling, Novello, Spatlese Lexia, Noble Rhine Riesling, Noble Muscat of Alexandria, Hermitage, Cabernet Sauvignon, Vintage Port and Red Velvet.
Best Vintages   W 1984, '86, '87, '88
                      R 1984, '86, '87, '88
Robert Fiumara was a distinguished student at the Riverina College of Advanced Education in Western Australia (now the Charles Sturt University), receiving the Inaugural Ron Potter Scholarship and graduating Bachelor of Applied Science in Wine Science in 1980. However, neither he nor his family could have anticipated

the dream debut Lillypilly Estate had, when, as a completely unknown winery, it won the top gold medal and State Bank trophy for Best Small Maker White Wine at the 1983 Royal Sydney Show. The award went to Lillypilly's Tramillon, a clever and registered trademark for a blend of Semillon and Traminer. Since that time, the best wines have been the botrytised whites, with a memorable botrytised Muscat of Alexandria.

McWILLIAM'S   CB-A
Hanwood Winery, Winery Road
Hanwood 2680   (069) 62 1333
Yenda Winery, Winery Road
Yenda 2681   (069) 68 1001
Beelbangera Winery, Winery Road
Beelbangera 2680   (069) 63 5227
Established   1877
Winemakers   Chief Winemaker: J F BrayneYenda: G P McWilliam, G Quarisa, Beelbangera: J A Martin, L W McWilliam, Robinvale: Max McWilliam, Hanwood: B K McWilliam, S Crook
Production   Not for publication.
Principal Wines   The main brands are McWilliam's, Hanwood, Max, Markview, Bodega, and Inheritance Collection white and red table wines, and Hanwood Tawny Port. The Inheritance Collection was introduced in late 1989, providing bottled generic wines. Two-litre flagons and varietal casks are also made and sold in vast quantities. Recently introduced Show series fortified wines and brandy are of the highest quality.
Best Vintages   W 1966, '67, '71, '84, '86, '87, '88
                      R 1963, '72, '78, '84, '86, '87, '88
Jim Brayne is a hard-headed realist and knows that the Murrumbidgee Irrigation Area can only offer wines of modest quality (outside of botrytised Semillon). Accordingly, McWilliam's has embarked upon a policy of buying premium grapes from other regions, and we shall see more of wines such as Eden Valley Rhine Riesling and Coonawarra Cabernet Sauvignon alongside the traditional and more modestly priced Hanwood and Inheritance brands.

MIRANDA   CB-B
57 Jondaryan Avenue
Griffith 2680   (069) 62 4033
Established   1949
Winemakers   Lou Miranda plus two qual-ified winemakers.
Production   Over 1 million cases.
Principal Wines   The usual array running from Golden Gate Spumante through to Marsala. The best table wines are released under the new Wyangan Estate range.

Best Vintages   Not relevant.
Once again, the Wyangan Estate Botrytised Semillon Sauternes is the best wine to be found in the Miranda armoury. The other wines are workmanlike at best, or purpose-designed for a particular price or ethnic markets.

ROSSETTO   CB-B
Farm 576
Beelbangera 2686   (069) 63 5214
Established   1930
Winemaker   Ralph Graham
Production   80,000 cases
Principal Wines   Premium white varietals marketed under the Mount Bingar label, comprising French Colombard Chablis, Oak Matured Semillon, Sauvignon Blanc, Chardonnay, Traminer, Traminer Riesling, Rhine Riesling, Semillon Moselle, Hermitage and Cabernet Sauvignon. Apart from this, the usual array, including table and fortified wines under the Beelgara brand.
Best Vintages   W and R 1980, '87, '88, '89
The quality of the Mount Bingar range of table wines is good, equal to that of Lillypilly Estate and second only to McWilliam's. The oak matured Semillon, Semillon Chardonnay and Chardonnay have been particularly successful, needing only a final touch of fruit concentration to lift them into the highest category.

OTHER WINERIES

CASELLA   D-C
Farm 1471
Yenda 2681 (069) 68 1346

FRANCO'S WINES   D-C
Farm 161, Irrigation Way
Hanwood 2680 (069) 62 1675

McMANUS WINES   NR
Farm 1347
Yenda 2681 (069) 68 1064

RIVERINA WINES   DC-C
Farm 1, 305 Hillston Road
Tharbogang 2680 (069) 624 1222

SAN BERNADINO   NR
Farm 644, Leeton Road
Griffith 2680 (069) 62 4944

WEST END WINES   C-B
Farm 1283, Brayne Road
Griffith 2680 (069) 62 2868

WICKHAM HILL   CB-BA
Griffith 2680 (069) 62 2605

NEW SOUTH WALES

OTHER DISTRICTS

There is a little discussed (or understood) phenomenon which I call the isolation factor. It affects grape growing, winemaking and winemarketing more or less equally. In its most extreme form it engenders a kind of autism: there is no one else the vigneron can talk to so as to gauge whether his vines are growing well or badly; no one to help solve problems in the vineyard or winery, or to provide points of comparison to even identify the existence of those problems in the first place; no helping hand nor replacement piece of equipment to be borrowed in any emergency when his breaks down; and only the occasional wine enthusiast coming to the cellar door to discuss and buy the wine.

A few winemakers working in isolated areas have enough experience to overcome the difficulties — experience gained before they moved into their chosen area of isolation. John Cassegrain of Cassegrain winery in the Hastings Valley on the mid-north coast of New South Wales (just inland of Port Macquarie) is a prime example. Tony Murphy of Trentham Estate, near Mildura, is another, although it could hardly be said he is in an isolated viticultural area — quite the reverse.

The isolation factor does not mean one cannot succeed; people can and do, but it certainly significantly increases the odds against success, and in many instances limits the degree of success actually achieved. And it operates to a lesser or greater degree against every one of the wineries discussed in this chapter (arguably with the exception of Trentham Estate). In my introduction to New South Wales as a whole I somewhat arbitrarily nominated 400 hectares of vines and 12 producing wineries as the minimum criteria for a significant wine producing area, one in which the isolation factor will by definition no longer play a part.

The four districts with the greatest potential to reach that status are the Hilltops (centred around Young), the Hastings Valley, Cowra and the Tumbarumba district. The Hilltops and Cowra share similar soils (principally red duplex soils in the Dr2.22, 2.23, 2.33 and 2.42 groups), but due to its higher elevation, the Hilltops is distinctly cooler with an HDD of 1852 compared to 2071 for Cowra, and the vintage starts later.

Cowra has firmly established itself as a high quality producer of Chardonnay. The first Petaluma (South Australia) Chardonnays were sourced there, at the far extreme (in terms of climate) from the present base of the ultra-cool Adelaide Hills. Cowra Chardonnay provides a luscious wine, with a soft, creamy texture and peachy fruit flavour: with age, honeyed characters gradually take over, blurring the varietal definition but giving tremendous richness. At almost 10 years of age, the 1981 Rothbury Cowra Chardonnay was absolutely delicious, a mouthfilling wine of great flavour. The other good Cowra wines are white: Sauvignon Blanc and Traminer are the best, but are not up to the quality or style of the Chardonnay.

The Hilltops has a broader portfolio, here Semillon, Shiraz, Cabernet Sauvignon and a little Merlot and Cabernet Franc all do well. Semillon has been made in two styles: conventional dry wine without oak, and as a late harvested botrytised Sauternes-style. In 1989 McWilliam's (Murrumbidgee Irrigation Area), which purchased the long-established Barwang vineyard prior to the vintage, showed just how good the dry Semillon is with two batches of gold medal winning wine. The Semillon is tangy and gently herbaceous, but has all the body one could wish for. Peter Robertson at Barwang had long shown how good the botrytised style could be, his first class wines antedating those of De Bortoli Wines in Griffith.

McWilliam's also produced an excellent Shiraz, with cherry-flavoured fruit and just a hint of spice, the sophisticated use of new oak adding lustre to an undeniably high quality wine. In the same year Roger Harris of Brindabella Hills Winery in the Canberra District purchased Cabernet Sauvignon, Merlot and Cabernet Franc from the Hercynia and Nioka Ridge Vineyards to produce wines of exhilarating potential, far better than any previously produced by vignerons in the area although sadly not all the wines successfully made the transition from barrel to bottle.

FACING PAGE: *Spray irrigation at Camden Estate on the banks of the Nepean River.*

ABOVE: *Among the many methods of scaring birds, gas guns remain popular (though not with neighbours in semi-urban areas).*

The next district of potential is still in its earliest days: the Tumbarumba region of Southern New South Wales. The first vineyards were established by Ian Cowell a decade ago on red volcanic soil at an altitude of 750 to 850 metres with the specific aim of producing sparkling wine. Pinot Noir and Chardonnay are the main varieties, with 30 hectares under vine, but a second vineyard on a slightly lower (and hence warmer) site was planted in 1989 which included table wine varieties such as Cabernet Sauvignon.

The initial production was sold to Rosemount Estate (Upper Hunter Valley), and thereafter to Seppelt (based in South Australia). Although no wine made from Tumbarumba grapes has been sold by either company, Seppelt in particular has been very pleased with the quality. Seppelt has a second involvement with a joint-venture vineyard at Tooma, 25 kilometres south of Tumbarumba. Here 10 hectares of Pinot Noir and Chardonnay have been established on granitic sandy soils at an altitude of 540 metres.

While production to date has once again gone to sparkling wine, it is known that the grapes achieve high sugar levels in late April every year, and in 1990 Seppelt made an experimental batch of Pinot Noir table wine. Overall, Seppelt's chief winemaker Ian McKenzie believes the region has the greatest potential for sparkling wine of any site in Australia, and has a feeling in his bones that it may produce a great Pinot Noir. It will be fascinating to see what comes out of it in the years ahead.

Finally, there is the fascinating — and for those involved frequently frustrating — Hastings Valley, driven by the extraordinary vision and entrepreneurial skills of the Cassegrain family. Here one finds the only modern vineyards established on a large scale without irrigation: the growing season rainfall is an awesome 1080 millimetres,

ABOVE: Working with the soil is still practised in many New South Wales vineyards but is in decline elsewhere.

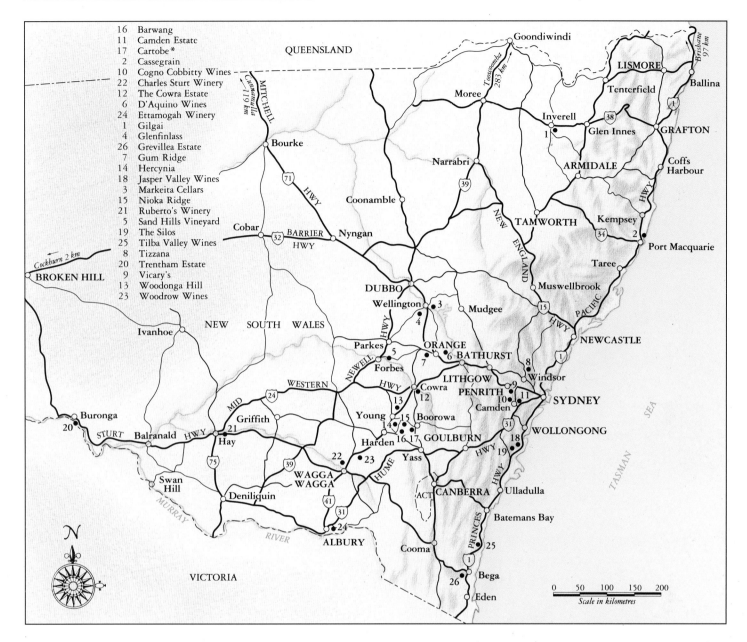

16 Barwang
11 Camden Estate
17 Cartobe *
2 Cassegrain
10 Cogno Cobbitty Wines
22 Charles Sturt Winery
12 The Cowra Estate
6 D'Aquino Wines
24 Ettamogah Winery
1 Gilgai
4 Glenfinlass
26 Grevillea Estate
7 Gum Ridge
14 Hercynia
18 Jasper Valley Wines
3 Markeita Cellars
15 Nioka Ridge
21 Ruberto's Winery
5 Sand Hills Vineyard
19 The Silos
25 Tilba Valley Wines
8 Tizzana
20 Trentham Estate
9 Vicary's
13 Woodonga Hill
23 Woodrow Wines

much of it falling in January and February as harvest draws near. Its MJT is 22.5, but like the Hunter the apparent heatload is offset both by high humidity and that heavy rainfall.

Much of the vineyard development, which at mid-1990 stood at 204 hectares, has been financed by Sydney investors anxious to take advantage of a cleverly structured tax scheme with Claude Cassegrain called Clos Farming. The sophistication of the legal and tax framework is matched only by the professionalism of the viticulture, now under the direction of Dr Richard Smart (see page 332). Whether at the end of the day the hot, wet summers will allow wines of high quality to be made remains to be seen. Chardonnay is clearly the best variety (in better vintages), while much faith is being placed on the fungal-resistant properties of a French hybrid called Chambourcin, which produces intensely coloured wines in even the wettest years.

ABOVE: *Chardonnay greets the first light of a new day.*

ADDITIONAL WINERIES OF NEW SOUTH WALES

BARWANG   NR
Barwang Road
Young 2594
Established   1974
Winemaker   Jim Brayne
Production   Not fixed at this stage.
Principal Wines   The initial Barwang releases
under McWilliam's ownership will be a Semillon
and a Shiraz.
Best Vintages   Irrelevant because of change
of ownership and winemaking.
Not long before the 1989 vintage, Barwang was
acquired by McWilliam's. The plans are to
significantly increase plantings, and the wines
will be made as regional wines specifically
attributed to the Barwang vineyard. The first
two wines made, from 1989, are of outstanding
quality, the Semillon deservedly winning gold
medals at national shows within months of its
making, showing remarkable intensity of flavour
and a striking herbaceous cut to the fruit. The
Shiraz is very nearly as good, with strong,
peppery fruit and excellent oak.

CAMDEN ESTATE   B-B
Lot 32, Macarthur Road
Camden 2570   (046) 58 8337
Established   1974
Winemaker   Norman Hanckel
Production   9600 cases
Principal Wines   Chardonnay, Chablis, Classic
White (Traminer blend) and Cabernet
Sauvignon.
Best Vintages   W and R 1988, '89

A long established vineyard which for many
years sold its substantial output (there are 18 ha
of vines) to Hungerford Hill (Lower Hunter
Valley and Coonawaarra, South Australia); a
small quantity of wine was first made in 1980,
but it was not until 1988 that Norman Hanckel
decided to seriously develop the commercial
potential of the vineyard. Its Chardonnay is by
far the best wine, once again demonstrating
what a flexible grape this is.

CASSEGRAIN   CA-B
Hastings Valley Winery
Pacific Highway
Port Macquarie 2444 (065) 83 7777
Established   1980
Winemaker   John Cassegrain
Production   Not for publication.
Principal Wines   The wines are increasingly
made from Hastings Valley grown grapes, the
principal wines being Chardonnay, Pinot Noir,
Chambourcin, Cabernet Merlot and Cabernet
Sauvignon; the other principal wines come from
Hunter Valley grown material.
Best Vintages   W 1986, '88, '89
                      R 1986, '87, '88
John Cassegrain is a very interesting man who
holds strongly to the apparently improbable
theory that the Hastings Valley on the mid-New
South Wales north coast hosts a microclimate
uniquely suited to the Burgundian varieties.
Without wishing to be too cynical, it is possible
to argue that the Hastings Valley proves yet
again how malleable is Chardonnay. Some

excellent wines from this variety (in particular)
have appeared under the Cassegrain label; it
should be noted in passing that some
contaminated new oak caused problems for some
of the 1988 vintage wines — not John
Cassegrain's fault, and a great pity given the
potential quality of the vintage.

CHARLES STURT WINERY   CB-B
Boorooma Street
North Wagga Wagga 2650 (069) 23 2435
Established   1977
Winemaker   Rodney Hooper
Production   5000 cases
Principal Wines   A wide range of varietal
white and red table wines from an equally
diverse number of areas, all of which vary from
year to year. Labels clearly identify both. The
estate-grown wines from the College vineyards
are labelled Booranga.
Best Vintages   Not relevant owing to
                      diverse fruit sources.
The College winery has served a dual function:
as a training laboratory for the viticulture and
oenological students enrolled at the Charles
Sturt University (Western Australia) and as a
commercial winery. The two functions have sat
unhappily with one another, and some very
disappointing — if not downright embarrassing
— wines have resulted. A new administration
under Dr Brian Freeman, and the appointment
of the extremely capable Rodney Hooper, should
see a veritable transformation in quality. A
marketing arrangement with American
Express/Cellarmasters will also help.

THE COWRA ESTATE   CB-B
Boorowa Road
Cowra 2794   (063) 42 3650
Established   1973
Winemaker   Simon Gilbert
Production   6000 cases
Principal Wines   Chardonnay, Sauvignon
Blanc, Pinot Noir and Cabernet Sauvignon.
Best Vintages   W 1986, '88, '89

ABOVE: Dr Norman Hanckel enjoying the fruits of the vine at Camden Estate.

The Cowra Estate is a very substantial operation, with a 40 ha vineyard largely planted to Chardonnay, but without a winery of its own — although there is a sales and tasting area at Cowra for tourists to visit. It has been a major grower in the Cowra region for many years. The wines have been contract-made at various wineries, and as the early Petaluma Chardonnays (made entirely from Cowra fruit) attest, base quality is not in dispute. The flavours are invariably generous, with potent peach/melon fruit, and while exceptional vintages are long-lived, most mature within 2 to 3 years.

NIOKA RIDGE   CB-CB
Barwang Road
Young 2594   (063) 82 2903
Established   1979
Winemaker   Phil Price
Production   1000 cases
Principal Wines   Chardonnay, Rhine Riesling, Late Harvest Rhine Riesling,Cabernet Malbec, Cabernet Sauvignon and Vintage Port.
Best Vintages   W and R 1986, '87, '89
The quantity of wine made each year under the Nioka Ridge label varies according to the percentage of grapes sold to other makers, with significant quantities going to the Canberra District. However, the Cabernet Malbec can be quite impressive, and certainly underlines the potential of the district. In 1987 Phil Price also produced a splendidly flavoured toasty/lime Rhine Riesling — the best white wine to have come from the Hilltops prior to the Mc-William's acquisition.

CHARLES STURT
U N I V E R S I T Y

CHARDONNAY 1989

TRENTHAM ESTATE   CA-B
Sturt Highway
Trentham Cliffs 2738 (050) 24 8747
Established   1985
Winemaker   Tony Murphy
Production   3800 cases
Principal Wines   *Méthode Champenoise* Chardonnay, Chardonnay, Sauvignon Blanc, Colombard Chablis, Traminer Riesling, Late Harvest Taminga, Pinot Nouveau, Merlot, Cabernet Merlot and Tawny Port.
Best Vintages   W 1986, '87, '89
                                   R 1987, '88
The Murphy family have been substantial grape growers in the Mildura district for many years; son Tony Murphy was one of the senior members of the Mildara winemaking team before the family established a new winery and restaurant complex on their property. The wines first appeared in retail outlets in 1989. The quality of all of them is exemplary, given the limitations of Riverland fruit. A 1989 Chardonnay tasted early in its life promised to transcend those limitations and to be quite exceptional; likewise a 1989 Pinot Noir was extraordinarily good.

VICARY'S   B-B
Northern Road
Luddenham 2750   (047) 73 4161
Established   1923
Winemaker   Chris Niccol
Production   Around 4000 cases.
Principal Wines   Semillon, Chablis, Fumé Blanc, Chardonnay, Traminer Riesling, Gewurztraminer, Cabernet Sauvignon, Shiraz and the full array of cellar door styles of the kind found inthe Murrumbidgee Irrigation Area.
Best Vintages   W 1984, '86, '87, '88
                                   R 1985, '86, '87, '89
By far the best wines from this little-known winery are made from Hunter Valley grapes, with a honeyed/buttery Chardonnay occasion-ally excellent, and a generously proportioned sweet chocolate/berry Cabernet Sauvignon very good.

OTHER WINERIES

HILLTOPS REGION

CARTOBE NR
Young Road
Boorowa 2586 (063) 85 3128

HERCYNIA NR
RMB 97, Prunevale Road
Kingsvale 2587 (063) 84 4243

WOODONGA HILL D-D
Cowra Roa
Young 2594 (063) 82 2972

OTHERS

COGNO'S COBBITTY WINES DC-C
Cobbitty Road
Cobbitty 2570 (046) 51 2281

D'AQUINO WINES NR
129–133 Bathurst Road
Orange 2800 (063) 62 7381

ENFINLASS C-B
Elysian Farm, Parkes Road
Wellington 2820 (068) 45 2011

ETTAMOGAH WINERY C-CB
Tabletop Road
Tabletop via Albury 2640 (060) 26 2366

GILGAI NR
Tingha Road
Gilgai 2360 (067) 23 1304

GREVILLEA ESTATE C-CB
Buckajo Road
Bega 2550 (064) 23 006

THE GUM RIDGE VINEYARD NR
4 Griffith Road
Orange 2800 (063) 62 5631

JASPER VALLEY WINES C-CB
RMB 880, Croziers Road
Berry 2535 (044) 64 1596

MARKEITA CELLARS NR
Mitchell Highway
Neurea 2820 (068) 46 7277

RUBERTO'S WINERY NR
Moama Street
South Hay 2711 (069) 93 1480

SANDHILLS VINEYARD NR
Sandhills Road
Forbes 2871 (068) 52 1437

THE SILOS DC-C
180 Princes Highway
Jaspers Brush 2535 (044) 48 6082

TILBA VALLEY DC-C
Glen Eden Vineyard
Corunna Lake via Tilba 2546 (044) 73 7308

TIZZANA DC-DC
Tizzana Road
Ebenezer 2756 (045) 79 1150

WOODROW WINES C-C
'Woodrow' Olympic Way
Junee 2663 (069) 24 1516

VICTORIA

In 1886 Hubert de Castella published a book about Victoria's vineyards, winemakers and wines glorying under the title of *John Bull's Vineyard*. The title reflected not only the fact that the State was then by far the most important wine producer in Australia, but that a substantial part of that production found its way to England.

From a tentative start in the early 1840s, the growth of viticulture quickened: that decade saw the establishment of the Melbourne Metropolitan, Yarra Valley and Geelong districts, areas which were to remain of prime importance for the next 40 years at least. The centre of Victoria followed in the wake of the discovery of gold in 1851, and viticulture soon extended over all of the centre and the north-east.

It was a golden age, in which the stories of those who planted vineyards and established vines were every bit as romantic as the stories of those who feverishly dug for gold. Gold and vines were inextricably linked, the former giving the impetus for the development of the latter. While history proved what was in any event inevitable — that easily won gold would soon be exhausted — the start of the long decline of the wine industry was triggered by an altogether different cause: the discovery of phylloxera at Fyansford, near Geelong, in 1875.

I follow the progress of phylloxera and its past and future implications at pages 108 to 109. Suffice to say that it led to the immediate demise of the Geelong district and cut a swathe through Central Victoria, finally reaching the north-east in 1899. While the vignerons of this district replanted their vineyards on grafted rootstock, many others did not bother.

In 1886 Hubert de Castella railed against the production of 'sweet full bodied red, and sweet full bodied white wines — abomination of desolation' and forecast that within 10 years there would be a swing back to 'clean, dry wines, as light as their climate can produce'. He spoke after visiting the Rutherglen Show, and of course his prophecy was not fulfilled. Heavy, fortified wines, by no means all as good as those produced in the north-east, came to dominate the Australian industry.

However, the central and southern districts of the State were totally unsuited to fortified wines, and as the chart below shows, the decline in production was not reversed until 50 years had passed. Federation, the removal of State duties and tariffs, and the rapid growth in the South Australian industry all combined to decisively end Victoria's dominance. What phylloxera started, fashion finished.

By the early 1960s the only wineries south of Glenrowan were Best's and Seppelt at Great Western, and Chateau Tahbilk and Osicka in the Goulburn Valley. As at the end of 1989, there were 169 licensed wineries spread across the length and breadth of the State, and the rate of growth showed no sign of slackening.

It is exceedingly unlikely that Victoria will ever seriously challenge South Australia for the crown it lost at the end of the 1890s as the major producer in terms of volume. The quirk of history which drew the South Australian and Victorian State boundary just to the east of Coonawarra and Padthaway may also deny — and will at the least delay — a challenge on the grounds of quality, but there is no question that the importance of Victoria in the production of premium wine is growing day by day.

In the north-west it houses Australia's largest (and probably most efficient) winery: Lindemans' Karadoc, which has crushed up to 60,000 tonnes in a single vintage, well over 10 per cent of the Australian crush. It is also the operational headquarters of Lindemans, a role it will presumably retain notwithstanding its acquisition by Penfolds. Mildara likewise has its chief production facilities at nearby Mildura. The Sunraysia and Kerang–Swan Hill irrigation regions, spread along the Murray River, provide 65,000 tonnes of the State total of 78,400 tonnes — keeping it in touch with South Australia, at least.

The quality areas start with the north-east, and fan out southwards, ultimately extending to Drumborg in the far south-west, and Gippsland in the far south-east. An immense diversity of wines and wine styles emerges, ranging from the luscious fortified Tokays and Muscats of the north-east through to the delicate but intense Pinot Noirs and Chardonnays from the Geelong, Mornington Peninsula and Yarra Valley regions around Melbourne.

One is never far from a vineyard in the arc running from Portland in the south-west up through Great Western and Bendigo to Rutherglen, thence south-east to Lakes Entrance, then back through Geelong to Melbourne. A great deal of the countryside is beautiful, some very beautiful — and it is constantly changing. Wine tours using Melbourne as a base can take anything from a day to a week: every winery, every district brings something new, something fresh.

ABOVE: The very attractive winery and residential complex run by the Bazzani family at Warrenmang.

PREVIOUS PAGES: Coldstream Hills with the Yarra Valley beneath.

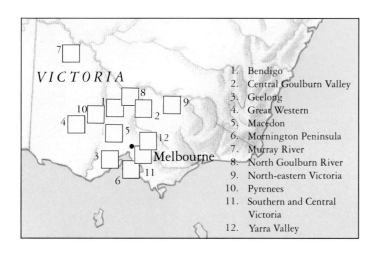

VICTORIA

1. Bendigo
2. Central Goulburn Valley
3. Geelong
4. Great Western
5. Macedon
6. Mornington Peninsula
7. Murray River
8. North Goulburn River
9. North-eastern Victoria
10. Pyrenees
11. Southern and Central Victoria
12. Yarra Valley

Melbourne

VICTORIAN WINE PRODUCTION '000 LITRES

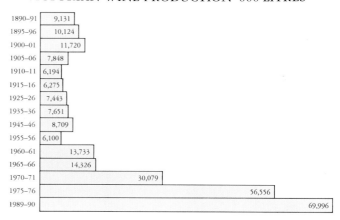

Year	Production
1890–91	9,131
1895–96	10,124
1900–01	11,720
1905–06	7,848
1910–11	6,194
1915–16	6,275
1925–26	7,443
1935–36	7,651
1945–46	8,709
1955–56	6,100
1960–61	13,733
1965–66	14,326
1970–71	30,079
1975–76	56,556
1989–90	69,996

ABOVE: *In winter, the most abundant vineyard can seem austere.*

VICTORIA

BENDIGO

Whether vines preceded or followed the discovery of gold at the end of 1851 is not clear, but in 1864 there were more than 40 vineyards. By 1880, 216 hectares supported over 100 wineries — a term which one must suppose included a lean-to at the back of the house containing a few wine barrels and a motley assortment of Heath Robinson-inspired pieces of winemaking equipment.

Phylloxera heralded a brutal end to winemaking when it arrived in 1893, but no doubt the bank crash of the same year and the move to fortified wines also played their part in the cessation of winemaking in the region.

A gap of over 60 years followed until Bendigo pharmacist Stuart Anderson planted vines at Balgownie in 1969, and within 5 years captured the imagination of wine drinkers from Melbourne to Sydney with his startling red wines — wines with a colour, character and strength which were to set the pace for the many who followed in his path.

And in the sprawling Bendigo district there were indeed many. For a start, it has a number of quite distinct subregions: Bridgewater, Big Hill, Heathcote, Harcourt, Mount Ida, Maiden Gully, Kingower, Baynton and Mandurang. Dense eucalypt forest and undulating hills mean

AUSTRALASIAN WINE REGIONS
1980 – 1990

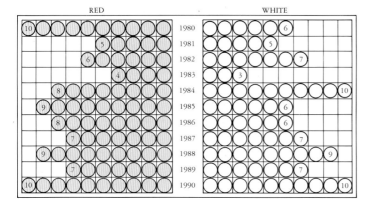

THE REGION IN BRIEF

LOCATION AND ELEVATION
36°45'S 144°17'E
240–390 m

SUBREGIONS
Bridgewater, Kingower, Harcourt, Maiden Gully, Heathcote, Mandurang, Big Hill, Baynton and Mount Ida.

CLIMATE
The climate varies significantly in the various subregions. In the demographic centre (the town of Bendigo) the HDD summation is 1708 (at the top end of the warm-climate group) while at Heathcote the figure is 1593, at the middle of the same group. It is quite possible that individual vineyards could report even greater variations. Rainfall, too, varies, but is a very modest 500 mm at Bendigo rising to 625 mm at Harcourt. The pattern is essentially winter-spring dominant, and irrigation is essential if economically viable crop levels are to be assured.

SOIL
Once again, there is variation, but the majority of the soils fall in the Dr2.22, 2.23 and 2.33 group, with brownish surface loamy sand to clay loam soils over a stony clay base, through to the Dy 3.41 and 3.42 soils which are extremely common in south-eastern Australia. These are yellow-brown in colour, and often quite acidic: generous applications of lime — particularly to the subsoil — are needed if vine vigour is to be promoted.

HARVEST TIME
Vintage commences in early to mid-March, and continues through to the end of April. Cold nights help, and vintage rain is seldom a major problem.

PRINCIPAL GRAPE VARIETIES
Chardonnay,24.66 ha	*Shiraz, 45 ha*
Rhine Riesling, 11.78 ha	*Cabernet Sauvignon, 43 ha*
Semillon, 1.60 ha	*Pinot Noir, 13.38 ha*
TOTAL WHITE *39 ha*	*Cabernet Franc, 6.94 ha*
	Merlot, 2.15 ha
	TOTAL RED *112 ha*

ABOVE: Cabernet Sauvignon, the prince of grapes, naturally produces great wine in Bendigo.

FACING PAGE: Investment in new oak is a heavy cost for the quality-conscious small winery everywhere, and not always understood by outsiders.

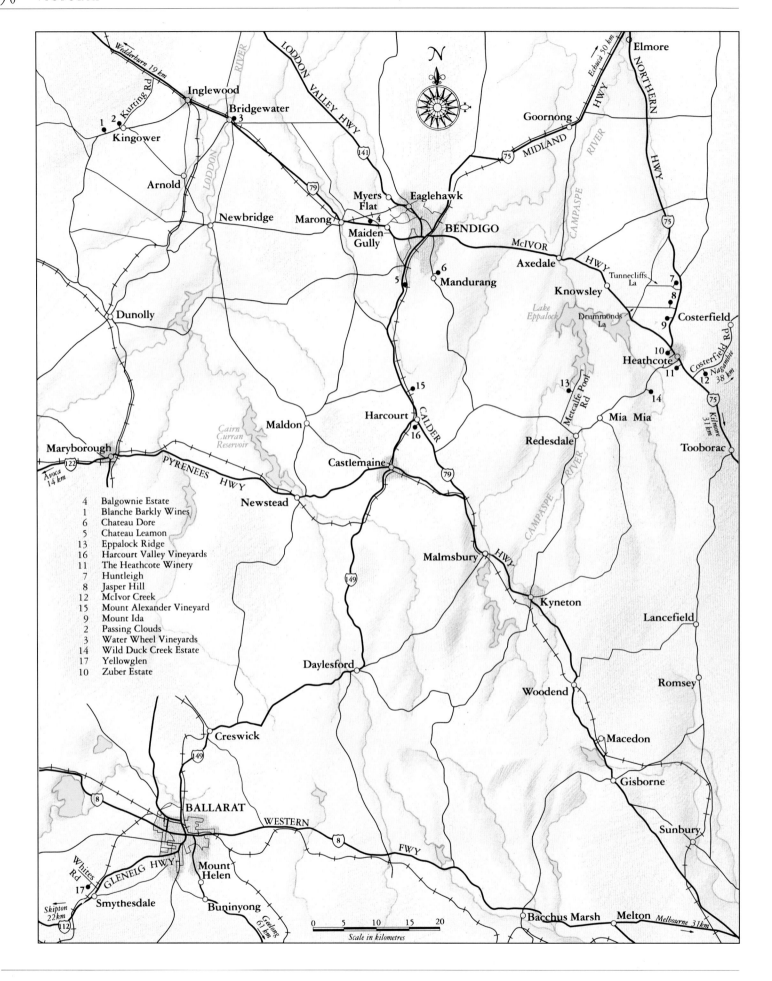

4 Balgownie Estate
1 Blanche Barkly Wines
6 Chateau Dore
5 Chateau Leamon
13 Eppalock Ridge
16 Harcourt Valley Vineyards
11 The Heathcote Winery
7 Huntleigh
8 Jasper Hill
12 McIvor Creek
15 Mount Alexander Vineyard
9 Mount Ida
2 Passing Clouds
3 Water Wheel Vineyards
14 Wild Duck Creek Estate
17 Yellowglen
10 Zuber Estate

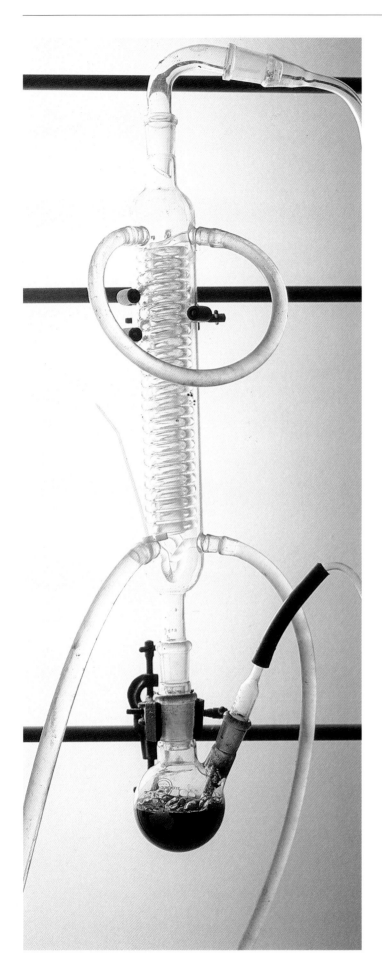

each vineyard hides in its own little enclave: many are humble, none grand, but almost all have a distinctive charm, perhaps from the stone used in their construction, perhaps from the way they look out over their vineyards, perhaps from their Lilliputian scale — or even from the sheer improbability that wine could actually be made there.

PRINCIPAL WINE STYLES

CABERNET SAUVIGNON

This is red wine country first and foremost, and it is inevitable that most attention focuses on Cabernet Sauvignon. There is a character which runs right across Central Victoria (from Great Western to the Pyrenees and onwards, in slightly diminishing strength, to the Goulburn Valley) which was first noted 100 years ago: Francois de Castella recorded that the red wines of the Bendigo region were noted for a 'faint curious character, resembling sandalwood', and that this even persisted in brandy distilled from the wine. In modern winespeak, we use the term mint (meaning mint in the eucalypt-to-peppermint spectrum, as opposed to garden mint) to describe this character. Its intensity varies from vintage to vintage, and from wine to wine, but it is seldom entirely absent. This apart, the wines have great depth of colour, a rich texture with abundant tannins, and fruit flavours ranging from faintly tobacco/herbaceous (in the coolest years), through to the far more common blackberry/blackcurrant flavours. They are long-lived, seldom showing their best inside 7 to 8 years. Many of the wineries produce Cabernet Sauvignon, with Balgownie Estate Chateau Le Amon and Passing Clouds among the most distinguished.

SHIRAZ

This is the other great red wine of the region. Indeed, in the Heathcote subregion and at nearby Great Western, many think it reaches its greatest expression, and for that reason I examine its role in Australia on pages 92 to 93. It follows the style set by Cabernet Sauvignon, and blends particularly well with it here — witness the wines of Mount Ida, Jasper Hill, Passing Clouds and Walkershire Wines (in the central Goulburn Valley) among many. The colour is deep, and the wine almost voluptuous in the way the flavour and texture fill the mouth. Pepper/spice may accompany mint, but frequently replaces it, with red berry and sometimes cherry fruit to support these more exotic flavours. It is every bit as long-lived as Cabernet Sauvignon.

WHITE WINES

White grapes are sparingly grown; only the Heathcote Winery has more than a token quantity. Chardonnay once again demonstrates its flexibility, and the trophies won by Heathcote for this variety should come as no great surprise. That winery's success with Gewurztraminer is altogether surprising: rich, spicy and smooth, without excessive phenolic or oily characters. Balgownie Estate, too, has produced a few first class and very complex Burgundian-style Chardonnays. But, as I say, this is essentially red wine country.

ABOVE: *The laboratory is an essential part of the small winery; this is part of the equipment for measuring sulphur dioxide levels.*

SHIRAZ — A MULTI-FACETED GEM

The origins of Shiraz are as uncertain as those of any other grape variety. In the broadest possible sense, we have some ideas about the places in which vines were first domesticated, and certainly about the places in which wine was first made. But even the immaculately researched and detailed *Story of Wine* by Hugh Johnson (Mitchell Beazley, 1989) cannot provide definitive answers to the origins of the modern day varieties.

Part of the difficulty stems from the fact that while we know a considerable amount about the historical, social and economic importance of wine (and how it was made) we have scant knowledge about how it tasted, and even less about the types of grapes used to make it. This is because grape types mutate — rapidly when propagated from seed, far more slowly when grown from cuttings.

Finally, from prehistory until well into the nineteenth century, there has been absolutely no discipline in the naming of grapes. Phonetic and linguistic corruptions, whimsical local variants or downright inventions, and finally sheer lack of ampelographical skills or knowledge have all contributed to near endless confusion about the true identity of grape varieties.

So it is sufficient to say that Shiraz may have originated in the ancient Persian city of Shiraz, but found its way — probably through the Romans — to the Rhône Valley, France, at the northern end of which it established its European home. In the first half of the nineteenth century the red wines from Tain L'Hermitage and the Côte Rotie were the most famous (and most expensive) in all France, outranking the greatest reds of Burgundy and Bordeaux. It was from this district that James Busby obtained cuttings for the collection he brought back with him in 1832, which were used to form the basis of Australian viticulture. His task had been to obtain the widest possible selection of varieties as he travelled across Europe for 4 months (he brought back 400 different vines), and it is not possible to guess whether he realised that the warm climate of the northern Rhone might be duplicated in many areas of Australia.

The fact is nonetheless that Shiraz has a warm-climate ancestry, and that it quickly consolidated its position as one of the most appropriate quality grapes for Australian conditions. By the end of the nineteenth century it had shrugged off all the other classic varieties (Cabernet Sauvignon, Pinot Noir, Malbec and Petit Verdot) and for the next 60 years was virtually the only red wine grape used in quality wine (the bulk market was supplied by Grenache and Mataro).

Since then Cabernet Sauvignon (aided in recent times by Merlot and Cabernet Franc) has supplanted Shiraz in the eyes of virtually all Australian wine drinkers, and it is left to experts from overseas to remind us that it produces the most distinctively Australian red wine in our repertoire — *and* that its quality can be every bit as high as that of Cabernet Sauvignon.

It is something of a chameleon, particularly when it is young, responding quite dramatically to the influence of climate and *terroir*. It would be difficult not to immediately perceive the difference in a 2 year old Shiraz from each of Bendigo, and the Yarra (Victoria), the Hunter (New South Wales), and Barossa (South Australia) Valleys. Yet with 20 or more years bottle age the wines move close to a common destiny, and even more remarkably, no less close to a common destiny than with an equivalently aged Rhône Shiraz such as Jaboulet's La Chapelle Hermitage.

Whether one prefers the vibrancy (and individuality) of youth or the softer, gentler supple and velvety characters of age is a matter of personal choice. Perhaps the most wise position is to have one's cake and eat it by preferring both, choosing youth on one occasion, age the next.

And so to the styles. There are many good judges who see the Heathcote subregion of Bendigo as Australia's greatest area for Shiraz, notwithstanding the far greater (historic) reputation of the Hunter and Barossa Valleys. In almost all of the Central Victoria regions it produces a wine of almost voluptuous fruit flavour when young, with flavours in the dark berry and dark red fruit spectrum (blood plum, to dark cherry to raspberry), yet happily avoids the stewed fruit character which can intrude in full flavoured Shiraz from some districts.

Depending on the season and the particular vineyard site, overtones of ground pepper and spice can intrude to a greater or lesser degree. As one moves towards Great Western (and in particular to vineyards such as Mount Langi Ghiran) that pepper/spice character is apt to increase; as one goes further south or higher (notably in the Macedon district) the pepper/spice character becomes more frequent and more flamboyant.

In the mid-1980s it became fashionable to regard pepper/spice as a sure indication of great style and quality;

ABOVE: Bud-burst, an annual miracle of rebirth, is a time filled with emotion for grapegrowers.

wiser counsel and the views of such authorities as Gerard Jaboulet (of the Rhône Valley) now put it into a better perspective. It should be part only of a tapestry of flavour and structure, with sufficiently generous berry fruit and tannin to allow the wine to mature, in the process of which much of the spice will fade. Too much pepper/spice is simply the sign of an unripe wine from a poor year, says Jaboulet.

At its greatest, Barossa Valley Shiraz moves into another dimension: Penfolds Grange Hermitage. Here the secret is old, low yielding unirrigated bush vines which hug the soil and seldom yield much more than 3.5 tonnes to the hectare. The thick-skinned but small berries retain surprising acid levels while effortlessly achieving vigneron Max Schubert's specification of 12.5 baume. There have been no serious pretenders to the Shiraz throne occupied by Grange, but many courtiers: traditional Barossa Shiraz makes one of the most immediately recognisable and obviously Australian wines, at its best voluptuously warm and at its worst baked and jammy.

The reputation of Coonawarra in South Australia was forged over a 60 year period in which Shiraz was to all intents and purposes the only grape grown. The fact that the region is now the source of Australia's greatest Cabernet Sauvignon should not obscure the greatness of the wines made by the Redman family between 1930 and 1960 nor the glory of 1955 Wynns Michael Hermitage, indisputably one of the best red wines ever made in Australia.

There are stories aplenty that between 1955 and 1965 (particularly) the distinction between Coonawarra Shiraz (of which there was plenty) and Coonawarra Cabernet Sauvignon (of which there was very little) was what might euphemistically be described as elastic. This came about simply because Coonawarra Shiraz had the cool grown elegance which one associated with Cabernet from places such as Bordeaux.

In its youth, no one can confuse Hunter Valley Shiraz (or Hermitage, as it is still called there) with Coonawarra Shiraz and even less with Bordeaux Cabernet Sauvignon. The most picturesque description of older-generation Hunter Hermitage is 'sweaty saddle after a hard day's riding'. Against all the odds, this is not considered pejorative but purely descriptive. And the sundry smelly, tarry, leathery — even cabbagey — aromas are accompanied by a frequently mouth-ripping level of tannin. Yet these magically soften into a slightly sweet, faintly earthy and gently luminous old wine which in its prime of life (remembering that life begins at 50) merges with Coonawarra, the Rhône Valley and almost anywhere else Shiraz is grown.

ABOVE: *It is on old Shiraz vines such as these that the Barossa Valley's reputation for this wine type is based.*

WINERIES OF THE BENDIGO REGION

BALGOWNIE ESTATE   A-A
Hermitage Road
Maiden Gully 3551 (054) 49 6222
Established   1969
Winemakers   Stuart Anderson, Lindsay Ross
Production   7000 cases
Principal Wines   Chardonnay, Cabernet
Sauvignon, Pinot Noir and Hermitage.
Best Vintages   W 1984, '86, '87, '89
                             R 1973, '75, '76, '80, '85,
                             '87, '88, '90

The senior winery of the numerous Bendigo
district operations, both in terms of the length
of time it has been established and the quality of
its best wines; Stuart Anderson has made a
lasting contribution to the reputation and
development of small wineries in Australia.
Outstanding is its long lived and concentrated
Cabernet Sauvignon, at its best in a classic
Bordeaux mould; some of the Chardonnays and
one or two of the Pinots have also been
exceptionally good.

CHATEAU LE AMON   B-BA
140 km post, Calder Highway
Bendigo 3550   (054) 47 7995
Established   1977
Winemaker   Ian Leamon
Production   2500 cases
Principal Wines   Semillon/Rhine Riesling,
Rhine Riesling, Chardonnay, Shiraz and
Cabernet Sauvignon.
Best Vintages   R 1980, '82, '83, '85, '86,
                             '87, '88, '90
Produces some of the most interesting red wines
to come from the district; while quality is
almost invariably very good, the style differs
markedly from year to year. Sometimes the
Shiraz shows strong pepper/spice characteristics,
and in other vintages none at all; in some years
the Cabernet Sauvignon has strong mint/
eucalypt aroma and flavour (itself a hallmark of
Central Victoria), while in other years there are
much riper red berry flavours and higher tannin
levels.

THE HEATHCOTE WINERY   BA-B
183–185 High Street
Heathcote 3523   (054) 33 2595
Established   1982
Winemaker   Stephen Reed
Production   Usually in the vicinity of
                             5000 cases.

Principal Wines   Chardonnay, Chenin Blanc,
Gewurztraminer, Shiraz, Pinot Noir, Cabernet
Shiraz, Cabernet Sauvignon and Viognier.
Best Vintages   W 1984, '85, '87, '88, '90
                             R 1984, '86, '87, '89
The Heathcote Winery consistently produces
some of the district's finest white wines, an
ironical twist given that its own vineyards are
planted exclusively to red grapes. Chardonnay is
the star performer, complex, rich and tangy,
with Burgundian overtones from barrel
fermentation. It also demonstrates a sure touch
with Gewurztraminer, which typically has
attractive lychee-spice fruit flavours without
unwanted phenolics.

JASPER HILL   A-BA
Drummonds Lane
Heathcote 3523   (054) 33 2528
Established   1976
Winemaker   Ron Laughton
Production   2500 cases
Principal Wines   Georgia's Paddock Riesling,
Georgia's Paddock Shiraz and Emily's Paddock
Shiraz/Cabernet Franc. Beautiful and innovative
packaging a feature of the wines.

Best Vintages   R 1982, '84, '85,' 86, '88, '90
Ron and Elva Laughton's response to the
bushfires which devastated their vineyards early
in 1987, not to mention the help they
subsequently received from vignerons across
Central Victoria, goes to the very heart of
everything that is great about Australians and
Australian mateship. It is fitting that Jasper
Hill's reds should be so strong in aroma, flavour
and body, with a wiry strength to take them
into the next century.

MOUNT IDA   A-A
Northern Highway
Heathcote 3523 (vineyard only)
Established   1976
Winemaker   Jeff Clarke
Production   1000 cases
Principal Wines   Shiraz and Cabernet Shiraz.
Best Vintages   R 1982, '84, '85, '86, '89, '90

Mount Ida suffered the same fate in the 1987
bushfires as did Jasper Hill. Perhaps it was this
which persuaded famous Australian artist
Leonard French (and partner Dr James Munro)

*ABOVE: The vines at Jasper Hill, still undergoing drastic remedial
surgery in the aftermath of the 1987 bushfires.*

to sell the Mount Ida vineyard to Tisdall (North Goulburn River), which had long made the wines under contract. In any event, Tisdall acquired a superb vineyard, which has consistently produced voluptuous, minty red wines with a softness which belies their longevity.

PASSING CLOUDS BA-A
Kurting Road
Kingower 3517   (054) 38 8257
Established   1974
Winemaker   Graeme Leith
Production   2500 cases
Principal Wines   Red table wines only estate-produced; Pinot Noir, Shiraz Cabernet and Cabernet Sauvignon. Some white wines madeunder contract by others.
Best Vintages   R 1982, '84, '85, '86, '88, '90
Graeme Leith is a great character, with a diverse range of interests running from winemaking to fly fishing, and a sense of humour second to none. Why this should equip him to make such wonderful reds I do not know. The flavour varies in much the same way as does that of Chateau Le Amon, but the greatest, such as the '84 wines (or the 1987 Cabernet Sauvignon), transcend all other Bendigo reds.

WATER WHEEL VINEYARDS   B-B
Bridgewater-on-Loddon
Bridgewater 3516   (054) 37 3213
Established   1972
Winemaker   Peter Cumming
Production   5500 cases
Principal Wines   Rhine Riesling, Chardonnay, Chablis, Hermitage, Cabernet Sauvignon, Liqueur Port and Vintage Port.
Best Vintages   R and W 1988, '89
Once notorious for its inconsistency and (in my view, at least) for its recurrent sulphide problems, Water Wheel Vineyards has turned the corner with the arrival of Peter Cumming as winemaker. The rating given is very much a compromise between the past and what I expect the future to be.

YELLOWGLEN   B-B
White's Road
Smythesdale 3551   (054) 42 8617
Established   1975
Winemaker   Jeffrey Wilkinson
Production   Very large, as befits the market leader in its price bracket.
Principal Wines   *Méthode Champenoise* specialist, offering NV Brut, Brut Cremant, Brut Róse and Cuvée Victoria (the last a vintage wine).
Best Vintages   W 1980, '86, '87
I have been quietly critical of the standard Yellowglen releases, but in mid-1990 it seemed that quality might be returning to the wine in the bottle to accompany the superb marketing skills which have propelled the Yellowglen juggernaut. The rating is given in the hope and expectation that this will not be a flash in the pan.

OTHER WINERIES

BLANCHE BARKLY WINES   DC-C
Rheola Road
Kingower 3517 (054) 43 3664

CHATEAU DORE   NR
Mandurang 3551 (054) 39 5278

EPPALOCK RIDGE   CB-B
Metcalfe Pool Road
Redesdale 3444 (054) 25 3135

HARCOURT VALLEY VINEYARDS NR
118 km post, Calder Highway
Harcourt 3453 (054) 74 2223

HUNTLEIGH   C-C
Tunnecliffes Lane
Heathcote 3523 (054) 33 2795

McIVOR CREEK   C-CB
Costerfield Road
Heathcote 3523 (054) 33 2711

MOUNT ALEXANDER VINEYARD DB-C
Calder Highway, North Harcourt
3453 (054) 74 2262

WILD DUCK CREEK ESTATE   NR
Cnr Spring Flat Road and Carboons Lane
Heathcote 3606 (03) 781 2939

ZUBER ESTATE   CB-B
Northern Highway
Heathcote 3523 (054) 33 2142

ABOVE: Morning dew and spider web, a jewelled fantasy known to every vigneron, but one which never palls.

CENTRAL
GOULBURN VALLEY

The story of the establishment of viticulture in the Goulburn Valley has all the ingredients for a television epic: high-stakes gambling, initial failure, gory and premature death quickly followed by overnight success. The success was that of a syndicate headed by R H Horne and John Pinney Bear, which in 1860 raised £25,000 ($50,000) for the 'purpose of forming the company to be entitled the Tahbilk Vineyard Proprietary'.

Within two years 80 hectares had been planted with 700,000 vines, and by the end of the decade 90-metre-long 'old' cellars had been constructed, followed by the 'new' cellars in 1875. By this time Tahbilk was producing the equivalent of 70,000 cases of wine a year, and even though production declined somewhat in the ensuing years to around 35,000 cases, a thriving trade with England was quickly established.

Phylloxera spelt the end for the other smaller vineyards and wineries in the district, and when the Purbrick family purchased Chateau Tahbilk in 1925 it was the only operating

winery, a situation which was to continue until the arrival of the Paul Osicka in 1955. Indeed, to this day the only other significant winery (in commercial terms) to be established has been Mitchelton (in 1969).

These two wineries more than compensate for the lack of numbers: the National Trust-classified Chateau Tahbilk retains more of its nineteenth century atmosphere than any

AUSTRALASIAN WINE REGIONS
1980 – 1990

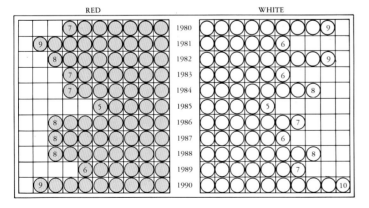

THE REGION IN BRIEF

LOCATION AND ELEVATION
36°47'S 145°10'E
131 m

SUBREGIONS
Tahbilk, Seymour, Graytown, Mitchellstown, Nagambie, Mount Helen, Strathbogie Ranges and Yarck.

CLIMATE
As befits its status as primarily a producer of full bodied red wines, this is a relatively warm region if judged by its centre around the towns of Seymour and Nagambie with an HDD of 1680 (which, for example, compares with 1710 for Nuriootpa in the Barossa Valley). Nor is the rainfall especially generous: at 560 mm (winter-spring dominant), irrigation, or vine access to the underground water table (as in the case of Chateau Tahbilk), is essential. The climate of subregions such as Mount Helen in the Strathbogie Ranges is much cooler, and careful site selection to minimise the danger of frosts is important. The principal risk, however, is heavy vintage rain which causes problems two or three times a decade.

SOIL
There are three principal soil types: red and brown sandy clay loams in the Dr2.22, 2.23 and 2.33 group; similar hard duplex soils, but yellow-brown in colour (Dr2.62); and gritty/gravelly quartzose sands laid down by the prehistoric wanderings of the Goulburn River in the Uc1.22 and 1.23 group. The sandy soils held phylloxera at bay, and it is for this reason that Chateau Tahbilk has Shiraz vines in production which date back to 1864.

HARVEST TIME
Early March — early May. Shiraz ripens late, and for this reason is sometimes troubled by late season rain.

PRINCIPAL GRAPE VARIETIES

Rhine Riesling, 61 ha	*Shiraz, 89 ha*
Chardonnay, 58 ha	*Cabernet Sauvignon, 80 ha*
Sauvignon Blanc, 23 ha	*Pinot Noir, 16 ha*
Marsanne, 20 ha	*Merlot, 15 ha*
Semillon, 18 ha	*TOTAL RED, 285 ha*
TOTAL WHITE, 268 ha	

NOTE: *These figures are for both the Central and Northern Goulburn Valley.*

ABOVE: Stalks and marc ultimately break down to provide useful fertilizer but are usually simply discarded or sent to Tarac Distillery in the Barossa Valley.

FACING PAGE: A fine display of Pinot Noir.

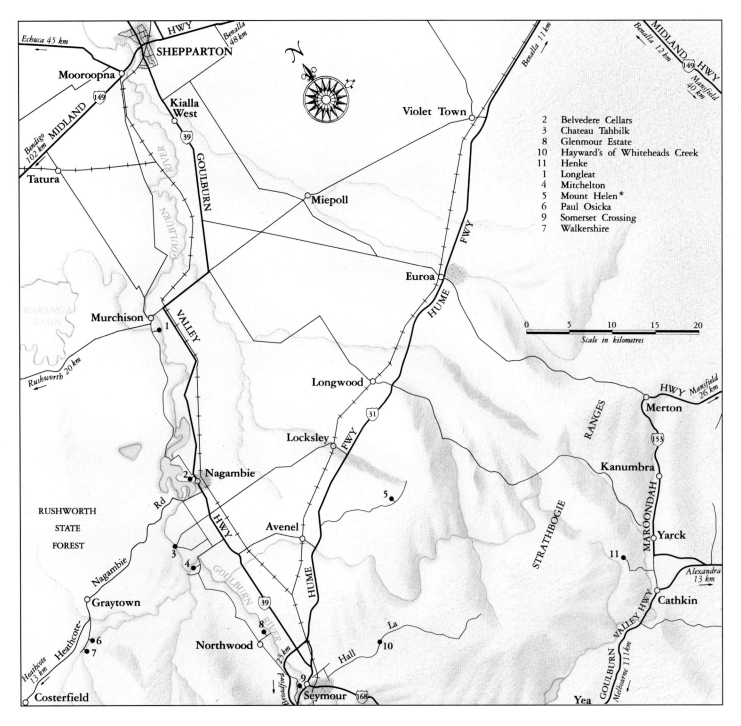

other winery in Australia. New buildings have been added with the utmost care and sensitivity, and are barely noticed.

Chateau Tahbilk is surrounded by the billabongs and backwaters of the Goulburn River (and by the river itself on one side), a setting it shares with Mitchelton. There the similarity ends: the massive red wines of Chateau Tahbilk look backwards to the last century, the futuristic architecture and strongly oak-influenced Marsanne of Mitchelton are the harbingers of the next century.

The essentially flat countryside is never boring: white-trunked eucalypts (frequently massive), a profusion of bird life and the wandering watercourses create a unique atmosphere. In the height of summer, when the temperatures soar and the canopy of the vines starts to wilt under the heat, a cool and shady spot is never far away.

Nor, in some directions, are the hills, and with the hills, a far cooler climate. The mountain ranges on either side of the valley give rise to diverse subregions including Mansfield, Mount Helen and the Strathbogie Ranges, while Graytown and Seymour also have a different atmosphere. Mansfield is white wine country, Mount Helen sits on the fence, but the Central Goulburn region — like so much of Central Victoria — is best suited to the production of full bodied, archetypal Australian dry reds.

PRINCIPAL WINE STYLES

SHIRAZ

The flatlands — or, if you prefer, the central valley floor — is uncompromisingly red wine country, producing red wines of awesome proportions. The old vines of Chateau Tahbilk take Shiraz into another dimension, but even its standard Shiraz is as compelling in its consistency of style as it is in its concentration and tannic strength. Longleat and Walkershire Wines throw their weight in along the same track; the wines unlock their secrets slowly and reluctantly, gradually revealing flavours of dark fruits, a hint of mint, dark chocolate and soft, supple leather. Paul Osicka Shiraz shows that pepper and spice can be part of the matrix, with a slightly softer and more accessible fruit structure.

CABERNET SAUVIGNON

Not surprisingly, there are more Cabernet Sauvignon-based (or Cabernet dominant) wines these days than there are Shiraz, and the style is more diverse. Those of Tahbilk, Longleat and Walkershire Wines are at one extreme, those of Mitchelton at the other: raw power contrasted with sophistication. (In the case of Mitchelton the game is complicated somewhat by diverse fruit sources) Those of Mount Helen (Cabernet Sauvignon, Cabernet Merlot and Merlot) vary according to vintage, but can achieve all the concentration and strength any lover of traditional Australian reds could ever ask for, with an extra dimension of new oak to satisfy the modernists.

MARSANNE

This is the only district in which Marsanne is grown and made in commercial quantities — All Saints Estate (North-east Victoria) and Yeringberg (Yarra Valley) are the other wineries in Australia offering the wine, but they do so in minuscule quantities. For both Mitchelton and Chateau Tahbilk, the variety is very important: in many ways it is the flagbearer for each, even though each makes greater quantities of other wines. Yet the style of the two wines could not be more different: that of Mitchelton is heavily oak influenced, lemon-accented and gains a pungent, almost oily, richness with age. Oak plays no part at all in the Tahbilk wine: it is delicate and faintly chalky in its youth, but in the best years is extremely long-lived, building the honeysuckle bouquet and taste which typifies the variety.

RHINE RIESLING

While showing a degree of variability from one vintage to the next, it is arguable that the Central Goulburn region produces Victoria's best Rhine Riesling. Mitchelton has been particularly successful (and most consistent), but Chateau Tahbilk and Mount Helen have done very well at times. The wines have considerable weight and flavour, with marked lime juice and tropical fruit aromas and flavours intermingling. Despite their early appeal, the wines also have the capacity to age attractively for up to 5 years, holding their peak for some further years thereafter.

ABOVE: *The unmistakeable hedgehog effect of mechanically-pruned vines (at Mitchelton).*

CHATEAU TAHBILK —
A PRICELESS INHERITANCE

There can be no counting the worth of an institution such as Chateau Tahbilk. In a world in which change has become an end in itself, in which wine styles, labels and varieties come and go overnight, and public loyalty is uncertain, Chateau Tahbilk stands firm. Twenty years ago it had an overnight dalliance with a new label, but woke up the following morning thoroughly ashamed of itself, and has shown no sign of such frivolity since. The leaves still blow from the plane trees onto the smooth earth surroundings, catching at the base of the horse-hitching rails and rustling against the fading cream painted walls of the winery buildings as they have done for over a century. The horses are gone from the stables, but the saddlery and the implements they pulled are still there, gradually rusting but quietly awaiting the day when they will provide the nucleus of a priceless museum to show the saucer-eyed children (and even adults) of the twenty-first century how things used to be done.

The octogenarian, Cambridge-educated Eric Purbrick has guided Tahbilk since he arrived as a young man when his family purchased the property in 1925. Unfailingly courteous, his mind and his understated sense of humour remain as razor sharp as they ever were. It is unlikely I shall ever forget the way he and Len Evans set me up the first night I stayed at the Purbricks' house: I alone was unaware it was the custom of the house to 'dress' for dinner. My sportscoat, tie and corduroy trousers were no match for the dinner jackets of the others, and even less for Eric Purbrick's dark red velveteen smoking jacket. The succession is guaranteed: grandson Alister has long since assumed the winemaking role, and while there could never be two Eric Purbricks, Alister's gentle charm and modesty are more than worthy of the dynasty.

Chateau Tahbilk was borne of wild and exciting days: for once the gold rush played no direct role, but that did not dampen the spirits or imagination of those involved. Major Thomas Mitchell was the first white man to cross the Goulburn River — on 9 October 1836 — and his reports of flat, fertile and easily farmed land quickly encouraged settlers. In 1840 the Mantons claimed the Noorilim run; 2 years later the Tahbilk run was excised from it, and some years later Noorilim was purchased by Andrew Sinclair.

In 1860 Sinclair formed a joint venture with R H Horne: the Goulburn Vineyard Proprietary was to raise £30,000 from the public, spending £6000 to acquire Noorilim and the balance in developing the vineyard and winery. The prospectus seeking funds from the public emphasised the centuries-old benefits of wine: 'The means we possess here of making wines of the most delicious quality, and better suited to the inhabitants of these colonies as a healthy beverage than most of the light wines which are imported, has also been equally well known to those who are conversant with the subject. The wines of the Rhine and the Moselle can certainly be equalled, but in some instances will probably be surpassed by vintages of the Goulburn, the Loddon, the Campaspe, and, in fact, of the whole valley of the Murray . . . Besides the commercial benefits, the best sanitary and moral results may be anticipated, because a wine-drinking population is never a drunken population.'

Sinclair should have heeded his own words: a few weeks later, his body 'disfigured by insects, reptiles and the native cat . . . was discovered in the scrub off the seashore near St Kilda, where it appeared he had wandered after having been hocussed by some brandy he had drunk at one of the evil villas of the suburbs.'

That was the end of the first fund-raising effort, but within months Horne had formed the Tahbilk Vineyard Proprietary, and with John Pinney Bear, raised the necessary funds to plant an 80 hectare vineyard and (by the end of the 1860s) to construct the 90-metre-long underground cellars built of stone quarried on the estate. The so-called 'new cellars' were completed at the end of 1875: the vintages of 1874 and 1875 had both produced the equivalent of 70,000 cases of wine, and the old cellars were overflowing.

This in fact represented the high point of Chateau Tahbilk's production: due to phylloxera and declining fertility it did not exceed 35,000 cases in any subsequent

ABOVE: A priceless history and tradition.

year. However, Tahbilk built a thriving export trade with the United Kingdom, which by 1890 reached 50 hogsheads (the equivalent of 1750 cases) a month.

First federation and then the onset of the First World War reduced Tahbilk to a shadow of its former self. When the Conservative MP for Walton, England, Reginald Purbrick, purchased Chateau Tahbilk in 1925 it was in a thoroughly run-down state. One wonders how his Melbourne born and schooled son Eric Purbrick, with a Cambridge degree and a recent admission to the Bar of the Inner Temple, was equipped to take over the management of what was then (and still is) a substantial farming as well as winemaking business. But he did so in 1931, retaining Francois de Castella as consultant and persuading an initially reluctant Tom Seabrook to take on the Melbourne distribution of the wine. Rehabilitation and recognition did not occur overnight, but is now complete.

Tahbilk has fashioned a reputation for its Marsanne, thanks in no small measure to the fact that it was served to a youthful Queen Elizabeth II at the winery in 1953 and subsequently became firmly established on the House of Commons' wine list. It has also produced several outstanding Rhine Rieslings and one or two very good Chardonnays, but its forte is its massively constructed Shiraz and Cabernet Sauvignon.

The factors at play are some extremely old, low yielding vines (one planting of the original 1864 Shiraz remains); a warm climate which in the majority of years produces high sugar and tannin levels; and a very traditional (and unchanging) approach to vinification and maturation of the red wines. Quite deliberately, the red wines are made and handled precisely the same way today as they were 50 years ago.

This involves the unbridled extraction of colour, flavour, alcohol and tannin during fermentation, with reliance on longer than normal maturation, first in large old oak casks and then in bottle to soften the often highly astringent tannins. New oak and newly fashionable varieties such as Merlot play no part. Variation exists from one year to the next, but it is due solely to differing vintage conditions and is, in any event, variation within a theme.

All of these wines are very long-lived, and in their youth positively demand time. The question often is whether the tannins will soften before the fruit starts to fade, a question seldom answered in less than ten years, sometimes twenty. Recent vintages holding every promise of balance are 1980, '83, '85 and '86, while I cannot think the 1984 wines will ever soften sufficiently to give pleasure.

Each year one outstanding cask is selected and given a non-repeating bin number: usually it is a Cabernet Sauvignon, occasionally a Shiraz. Here the flavour (though mercifully not necessarily the tannin) moves into another dimension, and the wine is not released until it is 6 years old. While writing these words I have been savouring the 1968 Cabernet Sauvignon Bin 51: its colour is a brilliantly clear but deep red, the bouquet fresh and strong with eucalypt mint overtones, the palate smooth and fleshy with youthful red berry and mint fruit, and the tannins are perfectly balanced. It is near to its peak, but will easily see in the year 2000, and still give pleasure well into the next century.

ABOVE: *Eric Purbrick above the 'new' cellars (1875) of Chateau Tahbilk; a keen mind still and a wonderful sense of humour, and loved by all who have the privilege to know him.*

WINERIES OF THE CENTRAL GOULBURN VALLEY

CHATEAU TAHBILK   BA-A
Off Goulburn Valley Highway
Tahbilk 3607   (057) 94 2555
Established   1860
Winemaker   Alister Purbrick
Production   58,000 cases
Principal Wines   Rhine Riesling, Semillon,
Chardonnay, Marsanne, Marsanne (blend),
Cabernet Sauvignon and Shiraz, together with a
yearly release of Private Bin red (usually though
not invariably Cabernet Sauvignon and usually 8
years old).
Best Vintages   W 1980, '82, '87, '88, '90
                       R 1968, '71, '76, '79, '81,
                       '86, '88, '90

In the world of changing fashions, Chateau
Tahbilk is a rock of ages. There is a continuity of
style of the kind rarely encountered in Australia.
The red wines invariably show generous, warm-
area berry and chocolate flavours, with enormous
supporting tannin. They need a minimum of 10
years, and they will unhesitantly repay 20 years
in the cellar. They are not for the faint of heart
or the quick business lunch.

LONGLEAT   C-B
Old Weir Road
Murchison 3610   (058) 25 2294
Established   1975
Winemakers   Alister Purbrick,
                       Peter Schulz
Production   3000 cases
Principal Wines   Under the Longleat (estate-

grown) label, wines comprise Shiraz, Cabernet
Sauvignon, Spatlese Rhine Riesling and Rhine
Riesling. Under the Murchison label, wines
made from other regions comprise Champagne,
Muscat and Vintage Port; also King Valley
Chardonnay and Sauvignon Blanc.
Best Vintages   R 1982, '83, '86, '87, '88

Given the Chateau Tahbilk influence, it is not
surprising that the Longleat red wines are so
formidable. Some, indeed, have been even more
than that, and the softening in the style of the
most recent releases is welcome.

MITCHELTON   CA-BA
Mitchellstown via
Nagambie 3608   (057) 94 2710
Established   1974
Winemaker   Don Lewis
Production   1.8 million litres.
Principal Wines   There are three groups. At
the top end, Classic Release wines, being re-
releases of aged Show Reserve stocks. Then come
the Print label and Mitchelton label series while
the Thomas Mitchell range comes at the bottom.
Marsanne is a winery specialty; the other wines
are Rhine Riesling, Semillon, Chardonnay, Shiraz
and Cabernet Sauvignon.
Best Vintages   W 1978, '80, '81, '85, '86,
                       '88, '90
                       R 1980, '82, '85, '86, '88, '90

The wines have an utterly distinctive style: oak
is always pronounced, sometimes a little too
much so, but the fruit simply will not give in,
and all of the wines —white and red — age
gracefully for up to a decade. This also includes
the unwooded Rhine Riesling, which is

ABOVE: Chateau Tahbilk.

Victoria's best example of the variety. The Thomas Mitchell range, incidentally, usually offers exceptional value for money.

MOUNT HELEN BA-BA
Strathbogie Ranges (vineyard only)

Established	1972
Winemaker	Jeff Clarke
Production	Not for publication.

Principal Wines   Rhine Riesling, Chardonnay, Fumé Blanc, Pinot Noir, Cabernet Merlot, Merlot and limited quantities of Chardonnay and Pinot Noir *Méthode Champenoise.*

Best Vintages   **W** and **R** 1980, '81, '82, '84, '86, '88, '90

These are the flagship wines of Tisdall, separately grown and marketed. The low-yielding vineyard provides wines of unusual concentration of flavour and colour; apart from complex, mouthfilling butterscotch Chardonnays, incredibly potent blackcurrant/plum Merlot, and intense, briary Cabernet Sauvignon in the right year can lift the label to rare heights.

PAUL OSICKA BA-B

Graytown 3608	(057) 94 9235
Established	1955
Winemaker	Paul Osicka
Production	Not for publication.

Principal Wines   Chardonnay, Hermitage, Cabernet Sauvignon and Vintage Port.

Best Vintages   **R** 1976, '78, '85, '87, '89, '90

The only winery in Victoria to be established in a 20 year span from the end of the Second World War until the mid-1960s, and one which has never sought publicity. Vibrant and spicy/peppery, Hermitage is, without doubt, its best wine and deserves a far wider audience.

WALKERSHIRE WINES B-B
Rushworth Road

Bailieston 3608	(057) 94 2726
Established	1976
Winemaker	John Walker
Production	1000 cases

Principal Wines   Shiraz, Cabernet Shiraz and Cabernet Sauvignon.

Best Vintages   **R** 1983, '85, '86, '87, '90

Pity the palate that has to arbitrate between the power, tannin and longevity of Chateau Tahbilk on the one hand and Walkershire Wines on the other. These are massive wines, constructed in a deliberately rustic fashion by the imposing figure of Yorkshireman and builder-turned-winemaker, John Walker.

OTHER WINERIES

BELVEDERE CELLARS   CB-C
399 High Street
Nagambie 3608 (057) 94 2514

GLENMOUR ESTATE   CB-C
Johnsons Lane
Northwood 3660 (057) 92 1229

HAYWARD'S OF WHITEHEADS CREEK   DC-C
Lot 18A, Hall Lane
Seymour 3660 (057) 92 3050

HENKE   CB-CB
Lot 30A, Henke Lane
Yarck 3719 (057) 97 6277

SOMERSET CROSSING   NR
Old Hume Highway (1 Emily Street)
Seymour 3660 (057) 92 2445

ABOVE: Mitchelton — from stone-age to space-age.

VICTORIA

GEELONG

It will come as a major surprise to many readers to find that 130 years ago Geelong was the most important wine-making district in Victoria, if not Australia. In 1861 there were 225 hectares under vine, and by the end of the decade 400 hectares. It also shares with the Yarra Valley the unusual distinction of being primarily established by Swiss vignerons, drawn to Australia by the Swiss-born wife of the first governor of Victoria.

By 1875 the vineyards extended along each side of the valleys formed by the Moorabool, Leigh and Barwon Rivers; on the slopes and plains around Ceres and Waurn Ponds, and on to German Town (or Marshall, as it is called today). Either in that year, or a little later, phylloxera was discovered at Fyansford, and neither for the first nor the last time, the politicians became involved and demonstrated that — whatever their understanding of the political process — they knew nothing whatsoever about the wine industry. In a knee-jerk reaction to public pressure (some say fuelled by a jealous Rutherglen industry, then vying for pre-eminence with Geelong) the Government ordered the wholesale eradication of the Geelong vineyards.

It has been generally accepted that this spelt the end of viticulture until Daryl and Nini Sefton planted in 1966, but Francois de Castella speaking in 1942 said Pilloud and Deppler — descendants of some of the original Swiss vignerons — still owned vineyards planted subsequent to the

government-ordered eradication. There is, however, no record of winemaking or surviving wines from the interregnum, so for the time-being the honour for the revival of the district must go to the Seftons, followed almost immediately by Tom Maltby at Mount Anakie (now called Zambelli Estate).

While some outstanding wines have been made in Geelong since its rebirth, and while land values — relatively speaking — remain modest and broad hectare viticulture likewise remains free from urban or alternative land use pressure, the

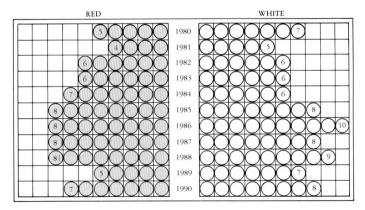

AUSTRALASIAN WINE REGIONS
1980 – 1990

Year	RED	WHITE
1980	5	7
1981	4	5
1982	6	6
1983	6	6
1984	7	6
1985	8	8
1986	8	10
1987	8	8
1988	8	9
1989	5	7
1990	7	8

THE REGION IN BRIEF

LOCATION AND ELEVATION
30°07'S 144°22'E
20 m

SUBREGIONS
Anakie, Bannockburn and Moorabool.

CLIMATE
This strongly maritime-influenced region belies its cool climate with a puzzling HDD summation of 1470. Wind chill — wind is a significant limiting factor on yields — provides part of the explanation, as do lesser diurnal temperature fluctuations. Perhaps, too, the MJT of 19°C is a better indication. Certainly it has handsomely proved its suitability for the temperamental and hard-to-please Pinot Noir, yet has the capacity to fully ripen potent spicy Shiraz and deep-coloured Cabernet Sauvignon. Irrigation has proved quite essential, not the least surprising given the 540 mm rainfall and the absence of useful summer rains to follow on after the wet spring.

SOIL
The principal soil type is one of the commonest to be found in viticultural regions in Australia: red-brown clay loam over a hard clay base, ranging from mildly acidic to mildly alkaline, technically known as hard red duplex soil of the Dr2.23 classification. Somehow or other it seems to take on a tougher face in Geelong: perhaps it is the windswept aspect of many of the vineyards. There are also patches of a not dissimilar-looking group of dark black cracking clays in the Vg5.15 and 5.16 band.

HARVEST TIME
Pinot Noir has been harvested as early as the last week of February, but is normally picked in the first half of March, with Rhine Riesling and Cabernet the last to come in towards the middle to end of April.

PRINCIPAL GRAPE VARIETIES
Chardonnay, 11 ha	*Cabernet Sauvignon, 16 ha*
Rhine Riesling, 8 ha	*Shiraz, 13 ha*
Gewurztraminer, 4 ha	*Pinot Noir, 3 ha*
Sauvignon Blanc, 3 ha	*TOTAL RED, 34 ha*
TOTAL WHITE, 25 ha	

ABOVE: *After a brief winter's rest, the pink-tipped bud-burst signals another growing season.*

FACING PAGE: *The crop harvested, the vines start to take on the hues of cool-climate autumn.*

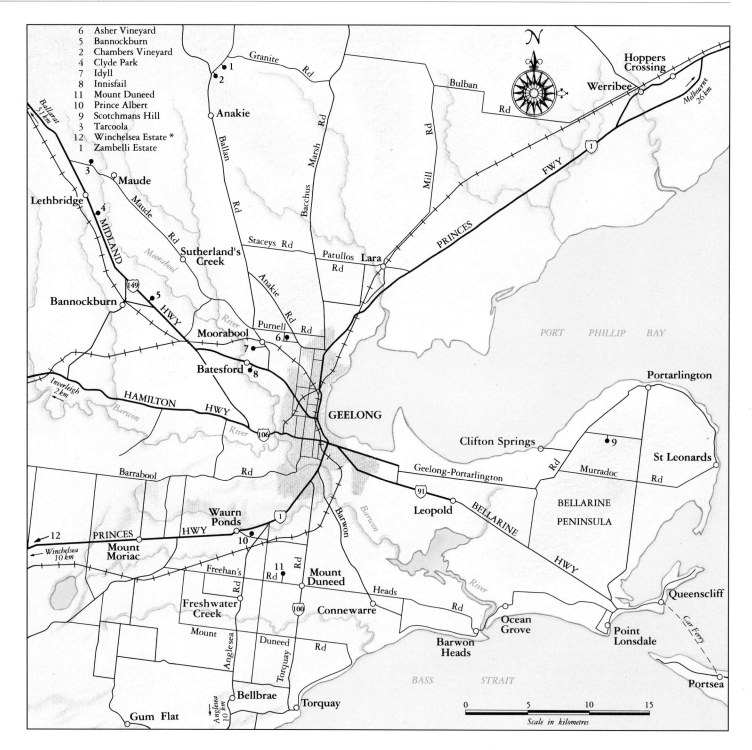

Scale in kilometres

region has shown no sign whatsoever of regaining the glory it once had. Six of the ten existing wineries have been in operation since 1975; since that time there has been phenomenal growth in the other two districts near Melbourne (the Yarra Valley and the Mornington Peninsula).

Quite why this should be so is not easy to say. A facile explanation is that the district has had only two market-oriented operators: the transient Hickinbotham family and the enduring Seftons at Idyll Vineyard. A slightly more convincing thesis is that the nineteenth century was far more accommodating financially to modest yields in good seasons

and to derisory yields in poor ones. For Geelong today is not an easy place to grow grapes. Spring frosts, wind during flowering and fruit set, the mysterious abortion of varieties such as Sauvignon Blanc after fruit set, generally hard soils and a miserable rainfall (making irrigation all but a necessity) all have an impact in one year or another somewhere in the district.

On the other hand, wineries such as Bannockburn have established international reputations for excellence, and Idyll has laboured unremittingly to do likewise. The quality is there, it is just that it is difficult (and expensive) to achieve.

PRINCIPAL WINE STYLES

PINOT NOIR

Given that there are only two wineries making Pinot Noir in the region, and then in extremely limited quantities, it may seem strange that this wine style is given pride of place. But in the early days of cool climate Pinot Noir, Prince Albert was one of the leaders in Australia, and since 1985 Bannockburn has assumed an even more prominent role in the development of this fickle and often misunderstood variety. The capacious hands of Bannockburn's Gary Farr fashion a wine of piercing varietal character — plums, tobacco, violets, strawberries, truffles — which has all the structure, weight and power one could ever ask for. It comprehensively gives the lie to the oft-repeated assertion that all Australian Pinot Noirs are thin and lacking in body. The climatic areas suited to Pinot Noir are few and far between: Geelong is one of them.

SHIRAZ

If there is a unifying feature in all of the Geelong wines it is their strength and depth of colour, bouquet and flavour. Almost all the wineries produce striking Shiraz (at Idyll Vineyard it is blended with Cabernet Sauvignon) which sometimes shows pepper/spice overtones, but more often than not relies on potent dark cherry fruit, with persistent but balanced tannins providing structure and longevity.

CABERNET SAUVIGNON

Zambelli Estate (formerly Mount Anakie) Bannockburn and Clyde Park all produce concentrated, powerful and long-lived Cabernets, with those of Zambelli Estate showing intense blackcurrant/cassis characters at their best. In all sites, limited yields are of prime importance in shaping the style and the intensity of the wine.

CHARDONNAY

Not much Chardonnay is made, but that of Bannockburn is so rich, complex and not infrequently controversial that it must be mentioned. Burgundian winemaking techniques and philosophies are applied to grapes which can happily carry this approach. The result is a wine which always appeals to the heart and sometimes, but not always, to the intellect.

GEWURZTRAMINER

Another winery specialty — this time Idyll Vineyard — and fittingly made in a highly individual style, crammed with lusty spicy flavour and sometimes surprisingly fleshed out further with oak. One might think there was little need to add another dimension to the flavour, but the wine succeeds more often than it fails.

ABOVE: Birds will not enjoy these Pinot Noir grapes.

PHYLLOXERA — STILL NO CURE

*P*hylloxera vastatrix — to give the full name bestowed on it by a French professor of pharmacy, M J E Planchon, in August 1868 — is an American genus of aphid. From the late 1860s it progressively laid waste to the vineyards of Europe, ending what many still consider to be the golden age of French wine and winemaking.

It lost little time in coming to Australia, Geelong enjoying the doubtful claim to fame as the first region in which it appeared — either in 1875 or 1876. By that time French academia was engaged in a furious debate over the most appropriate form of defence, with the chemists opposed to the so-called Americanists. The chemists advocated chemical control (through the highly dangerous and difficult technique of injecting carbon bisulphide into the soil) while the Americanists advocated grafting the European *Vitis vinifera* onto American root stocks (*Vitis rupestris/Vitis riparia*).

The grafting solution had been suggested as early as 1869, but 120 years later it is still possible to find those who claim this will in some way encourage the spread of phylloxera. On the other hand, 120 years later there is still no effective insecticide — the poisonous and potentially explosive carbon bisulphide, with its limited effectiveness, still remains as good as any other form of chemical control.

The reasons for the comparative success/failure ratio of the two approaches are at once simple and exceedingly complicated. The simple (or seemingly simple) answer is that the roots of American vines are resistant to phylloxera (having cohabited with it for countless centuries) whereas those of European vines are not. The unanswered question is precisely how this resistance comes about, but it is of largely academic interest. The complicated answer lies in the extraordinary life cycle of the phylloxera, which may (but does not necessarily) go through 19 distinct phases in a full creative cycle — five underground and 14 above ground.

The reproductive mechanisms (and options) which the phylloxera has at its disposal are as bizarre and as difficult to grasp as Einstein's theory of relativity. Parthenogenesis — reproduction without mating — plays a major role; the life cycle moves in erratic and unpredictable ways; there are multiple egg and adult phases within a full cycle; there is a sexuparous (or hermaphroditic) phase; at one stage a female may lay 500 to 600 eggs, at another (the last in the cycle), only a single egg — the 'winter egg' which is however

potentially the forbear of 4800 million gall-living females by midsummer. If all this were not enough, most of the forms (and the eggs) are too small to be seen by the naked eye.

But it is the ability of the parthenogenetic root-living forms to pass through endless successions of three stages (of the full 19 stage cycle) on the roots of *Vitis vinifera* which makes chemical control all but impossible. The solution im-posed by the Victorian Government in 1881 was different again, but equally ineffective: the compulsory eradication of all infected (and ultimately all) vineyards, first in Geelong and then Bendigo — all in a fruitless endeavour to prevent its spread to North-east Victoria, where it duly arrived around the turn of the century.

A thoroughly alarmed South Australia imposed strict quarantine laws which to this day have prevented the occurrence of phylloxera in that State. But for reasons which no one fully understands phylloxera has never come to the Yarra Valley in Victoria nor the Hunter Valley, Mudgee or the Riverland in New South Wales — though it is present in the Sydney metropolitan area. It has been found in suburban Brisbane, but nowhere else in Queensland, and has not appeared in Western Australia or Tasmania.

Nonetheless, vines grafted onto American rootstock are to be found all over Australia, and are likely to become increasingly common. The most important reason is to combat nematodes, a type of microscopic worm which infests many regions and attacks the roots of the vine with less devastating but still very debilitating effects.

The obvious question in all this is whether — as was strongly believed by legendary writers such as Professor George Saintsbury — wines produced from ungrafted vines are inherently greater than those made from grapes grown on grafted vines. There is evidence to suggest that wines made in the last great prephylloxera vintages (1864, 1865, 1874) will never be equalled for their power and longevity — and I, for one, will add greatness to power and longevity.

But if this be true, the reason probably does not lie in grafting, and certainly not grafting alone. Rather it stems from the greater age of the vines, the far greater density of planting, the previous absence of diseases such as downy and powdery mildew, the strictly controlled use of even the most natural forms of fertiliser and the much, much lower yields per hectare (let alone yield per vine).

ABOVE: *Phylloxera nymphs feeding on vine roots (Department of Agriculture trials).*

In Australia today, we have ample opportunity to compare grapes from grafted and ungrafted vines, and it is barely an issue. What is increasingly interesting viticulturists are the vigour-control possibilities of grafting: almost all the worldwide research has been into vigour-enhancement. But in the more favoured southern wine growing regions of Australia — notably Victoria — reducing yields without the 'bandaid' solutions of chemical control or bunch-thinning (cutting off a percentage of the bunches around the time of veraison, or colour change) is going to be of increasing interest to those for whom quality — rather than quantity — is paramount.

The other, and distinctly more contentious issue, is whether phylloxera will spread to regions (or States) hitherto unaffected, and if it does, whether it will be the unmitigated disaster it might appear at first sight. In the wider perspective there are those who say the rigid quarantine imposed by South Australia has caused far greater damage — in terms both of economics and of wine quality — than phylloxera would have caused.

In the narrower view, vignerons in all parts of the world have had to come to grips with living with phylloxera. For while phylloxera over a period of years will kill the vine, there is ample evidence of its arrival as the growth diminishes and the leaves prematurely turn red and gold towards the end of the growing season. What is more, the rate of spread across a vineyard is slow, particularly if the soil is sandy: the phylloxera likes to travel through the cracks which open up in clay-based soils during dry weather.

So one of the newer techniques is to interplant replacement vines on grafted rootstock, and continue to crop and harvest (albeit at a reduced rate) fruit from the affected vines. After 2 or 3 years the replacement vines are ready to bear a crop, and the infected plants are then removed. This eliminates the 2 to 3 year crop loss which occurs with wholesale removal.

As mechanical harvesters, semitrailers and tankers move with increasing frequency around Australia, it becomes increasingly unlikely that those areas previously free from phylloxera will remain so indefinitely. One only has to look to New Zealand, where it has spread from the North Island to Marlborough in the South Island, and is moving through the vineyards there at an alarming speed. But there are ways to minimise its economic impact, and it may even be that in the long term wine quality will improve.

ABOVE: *The typical spread of phylloxera: soon the healthy vines in the background will come under attack.*

WINERIES OF GEELONG

BANNOCKBURN   A-A
Midland Highway
Bannockburn 3331   (052) 81 1363
Established   1974
Winemaker   Gary Farr
Production   5000 cases
Principal Wines   Chardonnay, Sauvignon Blanc, Pinot Noir, Cabernet Sauvignon and Shiraz.
Best Vintages   W 1980, '85, '87, '88, '90
R 1985, '86, '87, '89, '90

Those who accuse Australian Pinot Noir of being limp-wristed should wrap their tongues around a Bannockburn Pinot Noir. Those who think cool climate, southern Victorian Chardonnay lacks body and opulence should confront a bottle of Bannockburn Chardonnay. These are great wines by any standards; the fact that they may not appeal to all does no more than prove the eternal fascination of wine.

CLYDE PARK B-B
Midland Highway
Bannockburn 3331   (052) 81 7274
Established   1980
Winemaker   Gary Farr
Production   1000 cases
Principal Wines   Chardonnay and Cabernet Sauvignon.
Best Vintages   W 1985, '87, '88, '89, '90
R 1985, '86, '88, '90
The wines are produced from a vineyard owned by Gary Farr, and are made by him at Bannockburn. Perhaps fittingly, they do not challenge the majesty of the Bannockburn wines; I prefer the complex, mouth-filling Chardonnay to the spicy/mulberry flavours of the Cabernet Sauvignon.

IDYLL VINEYARD   B-B
265 Ballan Road
Moorabool 3221   (052) 76 1280
Established   1966
Winemaker   Daryl Sefton

Production   4000 cases
Principal Wines   Classic Dry Gewurztraminer, Gewurztraminer Oak Aged, Chardonnay, Idyll Blush, Idyll Glow, Bone Idyll and Cabernet Sauvignon/Shiraz.
Best Vintages   W 1976, '77, '82, '84, '86, '87
R 1971, '75, '76, '80, '81, '82, '84, '86, '87

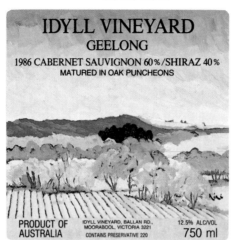

Daryl and Nini Sefton have never bowed to convention (and never will) in making, naming or labelling their wines. Nor do they brook criticism easily; but they are old hands at it now, and over the years both they and their wines have mellowed, without losing their individuality.

MOUNT DUNEED   CB-B
Feehan's Road
Mt Duneed 3216   (052) 64 1281
Established   1972
Winemakers   Ken Campbell, Peter Caldwell
Production   1000 cases
Principal Wines   Dry White (Semillon/Sauvignon blend), Dry Red Blend (Cabernet Sauvignon/Malbec/Merlot/Shiraz), Malbec, Cabernet Sauvignon and Botrytised Blend (Semillon/Muscadelle).
Best Vintages   W 1986, '87, '89
The partially botrytised (semi-sweet) and fully botrytised (sweet) white wines of Mount Duneed are challenging and at times exciting, with all of the multi-faceted flavours (from lime through to apricot) that botrytis can bring. They are often harsh and disjointed when young, but come together remarkably with 4 to 6 years bottle age.

PRINCE ALBERT   B-B
Lemins Road
Waurn Ponds 3221   (052) 43 5091
Established   1975
Winemakers   Bruce Hyett, Neil Everist
Production   800 cases
Principal Wine   Pinot Noir

Best Vintages   1978, '83, '84, '85, '87, '88, '90
Australia's only mono-cru: a 100 per cent estate-grown Pinot Noir, with not another grape (nor wine) in sight. The sad thing is that it was once one of the leaders in the field; others have since caught it up and passed it by. One suspects that problems in the vineyard may be contributing to a lack of power and concentration in the wine, but it still retains varietal authenticity and a rather delicate charm.

ZAMBELLI ESTATE   B-B
Staughton Vale Road
Anakie 3221   (052) 84 1256
Established   1969
Winemaker   Paul Chambers
Production   4000 cases
Principal Wines   Rhine Riesling, Semillon, Chardonnay, Shiraz, Biancone and Cabernet Sauvignon.
Best Vintages   R 1986, '87, '88, '90
Formerly Mount Anakie, established by Tom Maltby, and operated by the Hickinbotham family for many years, but now owned by Igor Zambelli and family. Despite the changes of ownership and winemaking style and direction, quality has not suffered: the vineyard produces grapes with all the flavour one could wish for, resulting in reds with an almost kaleidoscopic array of red berry fruit flavours allied with a tantalising touch of spice.

OTHER WINERIES

ASHER VINEYARD   NR
360 Goldsworthy Road
Lovely Banks RMD
Geelong 3220 (052) 76 1365

CHAMBERS VINEYARD   CB-B
20 Staughton Vale Road
Anakie 3221 (052) 84 1229

INNISFAIL VINEYARD   NR
Ballan Road
Moorabool 3221

SCOTCHMANS HILL   B-B
Scotchman's Road
Drysdale 3222 (052) 51 3176

TARCOOLA   C-C
Maude Road
Lethbridge 3332 (052) 81 9245

WINCHELSEA ESTATE   CB-CB
Lorne-Deans Marsh Road
Winchelsea 3241

ABOVE: *Early growth on spur-pruned Cabernet Sauvignon.*

VICTORIA

GREAT WESTERN

Gold fever reached its peak in Central Victoria: the towns of Ballarat, Beechworth and Bendigo are all testaments to the extraordinary changes it wrought on the fabric, not just of Victorian, but of Australian, society. Nowhere is its legacy for the wine industry more evident than at Great Western, and in particular in the vast underground tunnels (or drives) at what is now Seppelt Great Western.

Great Western is also unique in that it is the only district in Australia to have directly and significantly benefited from French winemaking experience: Trouette, Blampied, Pierlot in the last century, Landragin in this century. Pierlot played a key role in establishing the reputation of the district as a sparkling wine producer, and (after a 70 year hiatus) Dominique Landragin continued that role.

Simply because Great Western is the best-known sparkling wine brand in Australia, and because of the historic Seppelt winery and cellars, the assumption is that it is indeed still a major producer. The reality is that only a tiny percentage of

AUSTRALASIAN WINE REGIONS
1980 – 1990

	RED	WHITE
1980	8	7
1981	7	7
1982	7	7
1983	6	5
1984	9	9
1985	10	7
1986	7	8
1987	8	7
1988	8	9
1989	5	6
1990	8	9

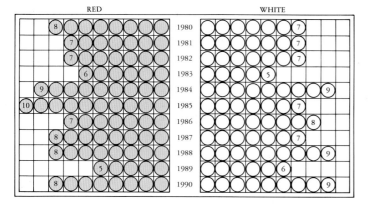

THE REGION IN BRIEF

LOCATION AND ELEVATION
37°09' S 142°50' E
750 m

SUBREGIONS
The region is more correctly (or technically) known as the Grampians; the subregions are Great Western, Halls Gap, Stawell and Ararat.

CLIMATE
The heat summation (HDD) of 1406 (taken at the Stawell Meteorological Station) is significantly lower than that of Bendigo (1708), and is certainly reflected in the wine style. But in both areas varying altitude and site exposure play critical roles in determining microclimatic variation, and in common with all Central Victorian areas, the climate is continental. In short this means the nights, even in the height of summer, are very cool, resulting in better-than-expected acid retention. Annual rainful is 525 mm, with only 207 mm falling between October and March; in the absence of irrigation, yields will not exceed 5 tonnes per hectare, leading to some exceptional flavour concentration but making production economics very difficult indeed. Spring frosts are also a constant threat once one moves off free-draining slopes.

SOIL
There are two principal soil types, both of them common to the grape growing regions of the southern parts of Australia. The first group is Dy3.41 and 3.42, with grey and grey-brown loamy sands and clay loam surface soils which are quite acid and which need lime adjustment; the subsoils are less permeable than the surface soil, and can lead to drainage problems. These soils are known as hard yellow duplex soils, and are closely related to the other group, Dr2.21 and 2.22 — hard red duplex soils. Once again, these are acidic, and once again need lime adjustment. Here the subsoils are of structured clay which is usually reasonably well drained, but can cause temporary water-logging. Neither group is especially fertile, and unless the pH is significantly increased by liming both the surface and the subsoil, it will militate against vine vigour and restrict crop levels.

HARVEST TIME
Mid-March – late May

PRINCIPAL GRAPE VARIETIES

Chardonnay, 71 ha	*Shiraz, 58 ha*
Sauvignon Blanc, 29 ha	*Cabernet Sauvignon, 58 ha*
Trebbiano, 22 ha	*Pinot Noir, 23 ha*
Rhine Riesling, 15 ha	*Merlot, 14 ha*
TOTAL WHITE, *149 ha*	TOTAL RED, *168 ha*

NOTE: These figures are for the Central Highlands, which encompass Bendigo, Great Western and the Pyrenees.

ABOVE: Rosellas cause only minor damage during vintage, and their beauty year round is more than sufficient compensation.

FACING PAGE: 70-year-old Shiraz vines at Seppelt Great Western, recently re-trellised and irrigated.

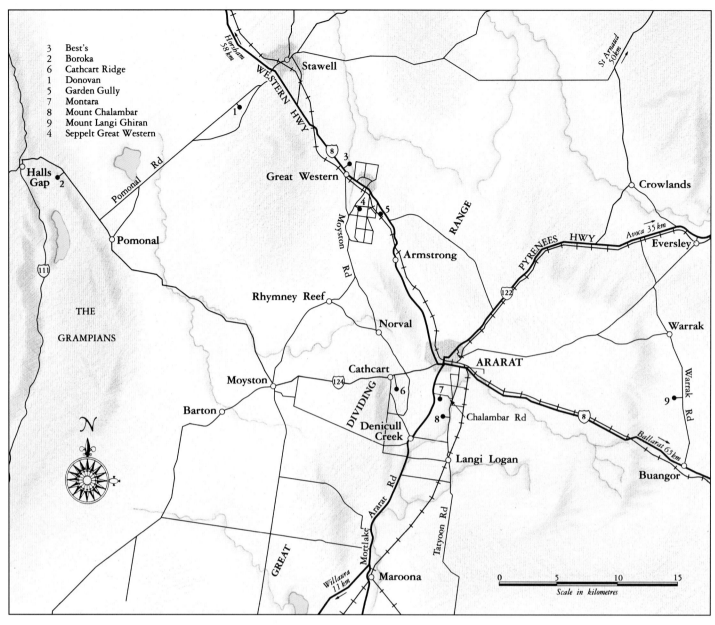

3   Best's
2   Boroka
6   Cathcart Ridge
1   Donovan
5   Garden Gully
7   Montara
8   Mount Chalambar
9   Mount Langi Ghiran
4   Seppelt Great Western

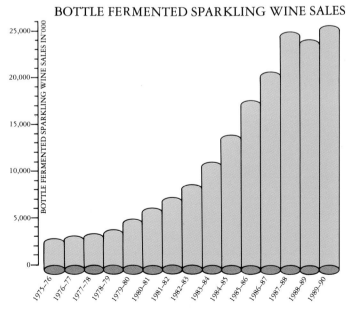

BOTTLE FERMENTED SPARKLING WINE SALES

the grapes used in the Seppelt sparkling wines is grown in the region, even if the vinification, maturation and bottling of all the wines are carried out there.

Great Western is in fact primarily a producer of fine table wine, and is especially suited to Shiraz and to Chardonnay, but is also capable of providing high quality Rhine Riesling, Cabernet Sauvignon and even Pinot Noir — together with its 'district specials', Ondenc and Chasselas. These are produced from a diverse array of vineyards: the scenic hillsides of Montara, the remote plantings of Boroka under the stark outline of the Grampian Mountain range, the historic vines of Best's, and the recent arrivals of Mount Langi Ghiran, Cathcart Ridge and Mount Chalambar.

It is a compact area, with the wineries clearly signposted. A

weekend, with an overnight stay in the historic town of Ballarat, will provide ample opportunity to visit all the wineries and enjoy the quiet beauty — and palpable sense of history — which is the hallmark of the region.

ABOVE: *Winter pruning: slow, wet and cold work.*

PRINCIPAL WINE STYLES

SHIRAZ
Frequently labelled Hermitage, this is the district's finest variety, white or red. It makes wines of diverse but great style, ranging from the silky smooth, almost understated, red cherry/plum wines of Best's to the complex, gamey, chocolate and spice wines of Seppelt Great Western through to the crisp, delicately peppery characters of Cathcart Ridge, then moving up the scale of intensity with Montara and finally arriving at the superbly concentrated, textured dark fruits and potent pepper/spice of Mount Langi Ghiran — the latter at its best one of the great red wines of Australia.

CHARDONNAY
As elsewhere in Australia, a relatively recent arrival, but one which has lost no time in establishing its class and quality. Best's and Seppelt Great Western are consistent producers of wines with tremendous flesh and mouth-feel; opulent citric/buttery fruit is given a complex coating of barrel fermented oak at the hands of Seppelt.

CABERNET SAUVIGNON
Over the years, sparingly grown and often blended with Shiraz (and other varieties), Cabernet Sauvignon performs well in adverse conditions and wonderfully when — as in vintages such as 1988 and 1990 — everything goes right. Then blackcurrant, blackberry and even raspberry flavours run riot without threatening that elegant, almost svelte Great Western style. Best's and Montara have produced some outstanding examples in the latter part of the 1980s.

RHINE RIESLING
Mount Chalambar, Garden Gully, Best's and Seppelt Great Western are among those who exploit the potent and intense tropical/lime juice aroma and flavour of the richer years, the reserved, toasty styles — still with a hint of lime juice — of the lighter vintages. These can be striking wines; once again, the evidence suggests that for Australian Rhine Riesling style, there is much to commend the slightly warmer regions.

PINOT NOIR
A somewhat surprising inclusion perhaps, and prompted by only one maker: Montara. Over the years — most recently in 1987 — it has produced some Pinots of remarkable varietal character and verve. At their best these show sappy/plummy fruit evocative of the top Pinots of Pommard in Burgundy, and no less surprisingly have the capacity to age for up to 5 years.

SPARKLING WINES
A nominal inclusion, they are however closely associated with the district; I explain why at pages 116 and 117.

SEPPELT AND SPARKLING WINE

Seppelt is synonymous with Great Western, and Great Western is synonymous with sparkling wine. Yet the reality is that Seppelt Great Western winery and vineyards are but a part of a far wider empire which is based in South Australia, and that despite a fantastically rich history, next to none of the sparkling wine made at Great Western comes from grapes grown in the region. The answer to this conundrum comes in large part from that history.

Gold and grapes formed the same partnership in Great Western as they forged in Bendigo. One of the early arrivals was Joseph Best, a butcher who invested the profits he earned from the ever-hungry miners in establishing a vineyard and winery. When the gold ran out Joseph Best employed out-of-work goldminers to tunnel through the seams of decomposed granite under the winery to create the underground cellars which are such a feature of Seppelt today.

His first vintage in 1868 produced 175 litres of wine; by the time he died in 1887, unexpectedly and intestate, his wines had won gold and silver medals as far afield as London, Philadelphia, Bordeaux and Amsterdam.

The winery was purchased by a local businessman, Hans Irvine; he rapidly expanded production, buying the grapes from all the independent growers in the Great Western/ Rhymney region. Within a few years he had decided to specialise in sparkling wine, hiring Charles Pierlot, a Frenchman who had worked in Reims, and importing all of the necessary winemaking equipment from France. The relationship between Irvine and Pierlot was a stormy one, but the business prospered even though the attempts to build up significant exports to the United Kingdom failed in the face of what Francois de Castella described as 'unreasonable prejudice'.

Irvine extended both the winery (to a capacity of over 1.3 million litres) and the underground drives, which by 1907 extended for 1.6 kilometres. He also imported what he thought was Chardonnay, but which became known as Irvine's white, as the base for his sparkling wine. In fact it was Ondenc, and we are left to speculate what he might have achieved had the variety really been Chardonnay.

Once again there was no family to carry on the business, and in 1918 (only a few years before his death) Irvine sold out to Seppelt. Expansion continued, with an additional 50 hectares of vineyard being planted by 1923, the year in which a young winemaker called Colin Preece arrived to assist Reginald Mowatt, who was the manager and chief winemaker.

In 1932 Colin Preece succeeded Mowatt and proceeded to establish himself as one of the great winemakers of the twentieth century, in a reign which extended for over 30 years until his retirement in 1963. His talents extended across the full range of sparkling and table wine: sparkling Burgundy, sparkling white wine, dry white, dry red and Sauternes-style wines. I have drunk more than my fair share of Preece's wines, and still have some precious bottles of each style (dating from 1944) in my cellar. Quite simply, they were (and are) some of the greatest Australian wines I have encountered.

Preece's retirement coincided with the start of the table wine boom in Australia, and the quality of the wines slumped alarmingly in the second half of the 1960s, a decline which continued well into the '70s. The tide turned with the coming of age of Seppelt's vineyards at Padthaway (South Australia), Drumborg (Southern and Central Victoria) and Barooga — the last unfashionable but of enormous importance in providing Seppelt's winemakers with large quantities of Chardonnay for both sparkling and table wine. The special importance of Barooga (on the New South Wales side of the Murray River, 67 kilometres west of Corowa/Rutherglen) is its ability to produce grapes of surprisingly yet consistently high quality at the lowest possible cost.

Changes in the winemaking team were also significant. History repeated itself with the appointment of Champagne-born and trained Dominique Landragin in 1979 (and one suspects in the at-times stormy relationship before he departed for Yellowglen (Bendigo) in March 1982), but of more lasting importance was the appointment of Ian McKenzie as chief winemaker in June 1983.

It would be wrong to suggest that the face of Australian sparkling wine changed overnight, or that Seppelt alone has been responsible for the changes. The Wynn/Seaview group has certainly played its part too, and particularly in the all-important move towards the widespread use of Chardonnay and Pinot Noir in the base wines. Equally, Yellowglen partly created and then rode the swelling wave of mid-priced bottle fermented sparkling wine sales (shown in the **chart** on page 114), while Croser at Petaluma (in the Adelaide Hills) and Domaine Chandon (in the Yarra Valley) have added another

ABOVE: *Riddling sparkling wine in Seppelt's Great Western cellars: a dying but not yet dead art.*

dimension to that very significant wave.

But Seppelt has played the single most important role in reshaping the style and quality of *Méthode Champenoise* (which for brevity I will call MC) wines in Australia. In 1970 it broke new ground by producing an experimental quantity from 100 per cent Pinot Noir. The pink-bronze colour was considered entirely unacceptable by the standards of the time, and the amount of Pinot Noir available was in any event very limited, so it caused little excitement and even less favourable comment.

Nonetheless, it was a symbol of things to come. Until that time the premium wines came entirely or predominantly from varieties such as Ondenc and Semillon, and the cheaper versions overwhelmingly from Muscat Gordo Blanco; these latter wines were tempered by more neutral grapes such as Trebbiano. What is more, most of these grapes came from warm-area vineyards, and were necessarily picked while still green.

The importance of the subsequent shift to Chardonnay, Pinot Noir (and a little Pinot Meunier), and to cooler growing regions cannot be over-emphasised. The 1980s witnessed an absolute revolution in the quality of our MC wines, and there are no better commercial examples than the Seppelt Fleur de Lys range or Great Western vintage Brut. There are better MC wines, but none offer better value for money.

The style is distinctively Australian: we instinctively value and protect varietal grape flavour, and instinctively reject off-aromas and flavours, however much they may add to complexity. There is no doubt this style will continue to evolve — after all, its genesis is so recent — and little doubt that there will be a gradual shift to more complexity and away from simple fruit flavour, but the basic pattern has been established.

A substantial proportion of MC production is still based wholly or partly on inferior grape varieties, but it is only a question of time — I suspect a relatively short time frame — before Chardonnay becomes the dominant variety in almost all of our quality sparkling wines. When it does, we can thank Seppelt.

ABOVE: *The underground drives (or cellars) at Seppelt are a priceless inheritance of the nineteenth century.*

WINERIES OF THE GREAT WESTERN REGION

BEST'S   A-A
2 km off Western Highway
Great Western 3377 (053) 56 2250
Established   1866
Winemaker   Viv Thomson,
                     Simon Clayfield
Production   14,000 cases
Principal Wines   Chardonnay, Rhine Riesling,
Gewurztraminer, Pinot Meunier, Hermitage Bin
Number 0, Pinot Noir, Cabernet Sauvignon and
Concongella Brut.
Best Vintages   W 1979, '81, '84, '85, '87,
                       '88, '89, '90
                       R 1964, '67, '70, '76, '80,
                       '84, '87, '88, '90

One of the quiet achievers, with a long and
proud history and some of the oldest and rarest
vines to be found in Australia. It has long made
a silky, cherry/plum flavoured Hermitage which
seduces one into drinking it long before its due
time, but more recently has produced
increasingly impressive citric/grapefruit-toned
Chardonnay, fruit rather than oak driven.

CATHCART RIDGE   B-B
Byron Road
Cathcart via
Ararat 3377   (053) 52 4082
Established   1978
Winemaker   Dr Graeme Bertuch
Production   1600 cases
Principal Wines   Chardonnay, Shiraz and
Cabernet Merlot.
Best Vintages   W 1987, '89, '90
                       R 1986, '88, '89, '90
Local Doctor Graeme Bertuch, with consultancy

advice from Trevor Mast, consistently produces
very fine and elegant red wines; the Shiraz
almost invariably shows fragrant spicy/peppery/
cherry aroma and flavour, while the Cabernet
Merlot moves up a notch in terms of weight and
structure with penetrating, ripe cassis/dark berry
fruits. I am not so enamoured of the Chardonnay.

GARDEN GULLY   B-B
Western Highway
Great Western 3377
Established   1987
Winemaker   Warren Randall
Production   Not for publication.
Principal Wines   A mixture of estate-grown,
Great Western-grown and selected blended
wines covering a range of Rhine Riesling,
Traminer, Chardonnay, Shiraz, Cabernet
Sauvignon and *Méthode Champenoise* releases.
Best Vintages   Not relevant due to varied
grape sources.
A very visible and charming cellar door sales
outlet has been established on the site of the
original Hockheim Winery, which still retains
the original underground wine tanks of
handmade bricks. The wines are in fact contract
made at Seppelt Great Western, where a number
of the syndicate owning Garden Gully presently
or previously worked.

MONTARA   BA-B
Chalambar Road
Ararat 3377   (053) 52 3868
Established   1970
Winemaker   Michael McRae
Production   4000 cases

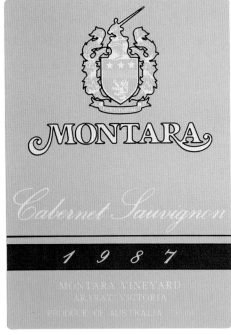

Principal Wines   Chardonnay,   Ondenc,
Chasselas, Rhine Riesling, Pinot Noir, Shiraz,
Cabernet Sauvignon and Vintage Port.
Best Vintages   W 1982, '85, '86, '88, '89, '90
                       R 1980, '82, '84, '86, '88, '89,
                       '90
Without question, the most impressive wine
from Montara is its Pinot Noir, which in
favoured years such as '84, '87 and '89 shows
magnificent plummy/sappy/strawberry varietal
character and challenges all of my neatly
packaged preconceptions about areas and
climates suited to Pinot Noir. An opulently
oaked Ondenc and a tropical/honeysuckle,
slightly sweet Chasselas are also winery
specialties, while the Cabernet Sauvignon can be
as good as any from the district.

MOUNT CHALAMBAR   B-B
Off Tatyoon Road
Ararat 3377   (053) 52 3768
Established   1978
Winemaker   Trevor Mast
Production   1800 cases
Principal Wines   Rhine Riesling, Chardonnay,

ABOVE: *Corrugated iron, the universal Australian building material
when these cellars were constructed.*

Pinot Noir and *Méthode Champenoise* Chardonnay.
Best Vintages W 1985, '88, '89
This is the 'home vineyard' of former Best's winemaker Trevor Mast, who has long-term aspirations to become a sparkling-wine specialist. The Rhine Riesling, in particular, invariably has abundant lime juice aroma and flavour, while the *Méthode Champenoise* is highly regarded, even if the oak-influenced style is somewhat idiosyncratic.

MOUNT LANGI GHIRAN   BA-A

Vine Road

Buangor 3375	(053) 54 3207
Established	1970
Winemaker	Trevor Mast
Production	9800 cases
Principal Wines	Rhine Riesling, Chardonnay,

Shiraz, Pinot Noir and Cabernet Sauvignon.

Best Vintages   W 1986, '87, '88, '90
    R 1983, '84, '85, '87, '88, '90
At its best, exemplified by years such as '83, '84, '85 and '88, the Shiraz is magnificent, showing abundant pepper/spice yet at the same time having tremendously rich fruit and finely balanced tannins to give warmth and fullness in the mouth. The Cabernet Sauvignon, too, often shows a background touch of spice which adds to its attraction. The other wines under the label are good, but not in the same class.

SEPPELT GREAT WESTERN   A-A

Moyston Road

Great Western 3377	(053) 56 2202
Established	1866
Winemakers	Ian McKenzie,
	Michel Kluczko, Tony Royal
Production	Not for publication.

Principal Wines   The most important wines from Seppelt's viewpoint are the *Méthode Champenoise* wines. Though the majority of these come from a variety of fruit sources, all are fermented, tiraged and matured at Great Western. The most important quality labels are Salinger, Great Western Vintage Brut and Fleur de Lys, with occasional releases of single area varietal wines such as Great Western Chardonnay Brut and Drumborg Chardonnay Brut. The Great Western table wines comprise Rhine Riesling, Chardonnay, Hermitage and Cabernet Sauvignon, which are produced in strictly limited quantities.

Best Vintages   Largely irrelevant to the making of sparkling wine; for table wines

    W and R 1971, '80, '84, '86, '88.
Seppelt deservedly dominates the quality end of the sparkling wine market, even though the competition grows day by day. Overall, the style of the sparkling wines is generous and soft, aided by the inclusion of a percentage of Pinot Meunier. The occasional district releases of table wines are invariably of very high quality.

OTHER WINERIES

BEN NEVIS ESTATE   NR
Brewster Road
Ararat 3377 (053) 52 1620

BOROKA D-C
Pomonal Road
Halls Gap 3381 (053) 56 4252

DONOVAN   CB-B
Pomonal Road
Stawell 3380 (053) 58 2727

ABOVE: Montara Vineyards, Great Western: as ever, room to move.

MACEDON

To suggest to a Frenchman that the Macedon region should be treated as a single viticultural area for the purposes of appellation control would bring a stare of total disbelief. For it encompasses three principal subregions which, topographically, geologically and climatically, bear little or no resemblance to each other.

The three districts in question are Sunbury, on the flat, windswept plains just to the north-east of Melbourne's Tullamarine Airport; the Macedon Ranges, due north of Sunbury, sharing Sunbury's ferocious winds but at a much higher altitude and in more hilly country; and further north again, the band of high country vineyards running east and west of Kyneton (which is technically a separate region of its own). The union of the districts is purely a marriage of convenience: while there is a rich history of winemaking at Sunbury, viticulture in the other districts is very much the product of the 1970's move to expand the frontiers of cool-climate viticulture.

That rich history centred on the wineries of Craiglee Vineyard and Goonawarra, both now producing wine again, even if bureaucracy has prevented Pat Carmody of Craiglee from using the beautiful bluestone winery of his nineteenth century predecessor James S Johnston.

THE REGION IN BRIEF

LOCATION AND ELEVATION
37°30's 144°33'E Gisborne
50–510 m

SUBREGIONS
The subregions of Macedon are Sunbury, Mount Macedon, Newham, Lancefield and Romsey. Kyneton is a single district without subregions.

CLIMATE
Not surprisingly, the climate varies significantly from south to north, in large part responding to altitude. The Mount Macedon Ranges subregion is the coolest, and Kyneton has the lowest temperature summation (1030 (HDD of any recognised Australian mainland district, and yet surprisingly few vignerons have had problems with spring frosts — autumn frosts in April and May have posed a greater threat. The winter dominant rainfall (necessitating summer irrigation) varies between 750 and 880 mm; the principal climatic problem is wind, which causes problems ranging from moderate to severe, and has led to extensive planting of windbreaks in most vineyards.

SOIL
Once again, these are extremely varied, ranging from sandy grey loam over gritty yellow clay (in the hard yellow and red duplex family Dr2.21 and 2.22) to black basalt clay, often weathered and poor, but offering good drainage. The soils all allow adequate yields if wind and the summer rainfall deficit are overcome.

HARVEST TIME
Varies from late March to mid-May, according to variety and subregion. The normal mid-May finish for non-botrytised wines is the latest on the Australian mainland.

PRINCIPAL GRAPE VARIETIES

Chardonnay	*Cabernet Sauvignon*
Rhine Riesling	*Shiraz*
Semillon	*Pinot Noir*
Traminer	

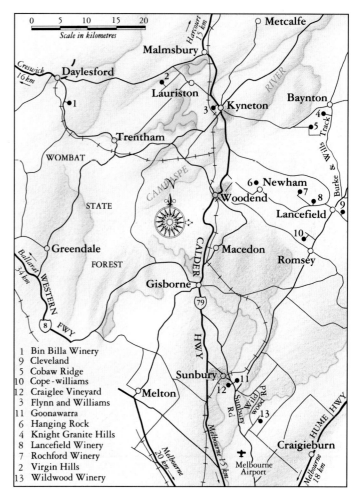

1 Bin Billa Winery
9 Cleveland
5 Cobaw Ridge
10 Cope-williams
12 Craiglee Vineyard
3 Flynn and Williams
11 Goonawarra
6 Hanging Rock
4 Knight Granite Hills
8 Lancefield Winery
7 Rochford Winery
2 Virgin Hills
13 Wildwood Winery

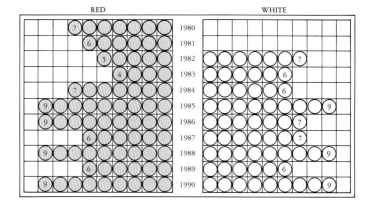

AUSTRALASIAN WINE REGIONS
1980 – 1990

FACING PAGE: Hanging Rock vineyard.

ABOVE: *Cool climate viticulture: tiny vines grown close together
(Hanging Rock).*

PRINCIPAL WINE STYLES

SHIRAZ

Shiraz vies with Cabernet Sauvignon as the most successful variety, making striking wine both in the Sunbury subdistrict (notably Craiglee Vineyard) and at Kyneton (Knight Granite Hills). In the hands of both these makers the wine has an almost overwhelming aroma and taste of black pepper and sundry spices, supported by red cherry fruit. In the best vintages that fruit has sufficient weight and texture to balance the pepper/spice, but not all wine lovers enjoy this cool-climate style. For those who do, these are the best wines of the region.

CABERNET SAUVIGNON

The most widely propagated variety, assuming pride of place at Virgin Hills and Flynn and Williams, and grown at Knight Granite Hills, Rochford, Goonawarra, Craiglee, Wildwood and Romsey Vineyards. It does best in the north around Kyneton and at the southern end of Sunbury: in the centre it seldom ripens sufficiently, and many vignerons who planted it have since grafted it or removed it altogether. Both Virgin Hills and Flynn and Williams make a deep-coloured, richly-textured and intensely-flavoured wine in the best vintages, Knight Granite Hills and Craiglee a more elegant but still excellent wine with strong blackcurrant fruit edged with a touch of herbaceousness. Those green, leafy characters become dominant in less favoured years. If you like the red wines of Chinon (in the Loire Valley of France) you may find the wines appealing, but they are certainly not typically Australian.

CHARDONNAY

Chardonnay is grown over most of the region, in the warmer parts for table wine, in the cooler sites for sparkling wine — the latter notably at Hanging Rock and Romsey Vineyards. Craiglee and Goonawarra Vineyards have produced the best table wines, those of Knight Granite Hills and Wildwood Winery being less convincing.

PINOT NOIR

Like Chardonnay, much of the Pinot Noir grown in the region is used in sparkling wine production. Only Romsey Vineyards has produced table wine from it, with delicate but clear varietal flavour in a slightly — but not unpleasantly — sappy/vegetative style.

Overall there are 30 vineyards servicing 10 small wineries, Hanging Rock being the largest, Virgin Hills being the oldest. Each vigneron has found it is a long and slow process to determine which grape varieties are best suited to their particular site, and no less difficult to establish which pruning, trellising and canopy management techniques give the best results. It is quite certain that a high degree of skill is required, and that even where all the correct decisions are taken, in some years satisfactory colour, flavour and sugar levels may be impossible to achieve. Given the marginal economic viability of a small vineyard and winery under even the most favourable circumstances, it seems unlikely that the Macedon region as a whole will ever become a significant commercial region.

Equally, some outstanding wines have been made in the past and will be made in the future.

ABOVE: *Some of the last Cabernet Sauvignon to be picked in Australia each year (typically early May) at Knight Granite Hills.*

WINERIES OF THE MACEDON REGION

CRAIGLEE VINEYARD   A-A
Sunbury Road
Sunbury 3429   (03) 744 1160
Established   1976
Winemaker   Pat Carmody
Production   Under 2000 cases.
Principal Wines Chardonnay, Shiraz, Pinot
Noir and Cabernet Sauvignon.
Best Vintages   W 1985, '86, '87, '90
                    R 1979, '80, '84, '85, '86,
                    '87, '88, '90

Craiglee is the reincarnation of a famous
nineteenth century vineyard established by
James S Johnston, the label of today being a
slightly modernised version of that of 100 years
ago. Then and now Shiraz is the outstanding
wine: low in tannin but intense in flavour, with
spicy fruit which sparkles when young, but has
the ability to age with grace — as those who
have been lucky enough to taste the 1872
Hermitage will attest.

GOONAWARRA VINEYARD   NR
Sunbury Road
Sunbury 3429   (03) 744 7211
Established   1863
Winemaker   John Barnier, John Ellis
Production   700 cases
Principal Wines Cabernet Franc, Chardonnay
and Semillon.
Best Vintages   Too recent for proper
evaluation.

Like Craiglee Vineyard, Goonawarra is the
reincarnation of a famous nineteenth century
vineyard established by a former Victorian
Premier. Unlike Craiglee the winery is situated
in the historic bluestone building in which the
wine was made last century; it also boasts a
splendid restaurant. It is early days yet to finally
assess wine quality, but the '88 and '89 vintages
hold out much promise.

HANGING ROCK   CA-B
The Jim Jim, Jim Road
Newham 3442   (054) 27 0542
Established   1982
Winemakers   John Ellis, Gary Duke
Production   10,000 cases
Principal Wines   The winemaking follows a
philosophy of producing, where possible,
individual vineyard wines, marketed with a
regional identification, eg Faraday Chardonnay
and Heathcote Shiraz. Others have a more
general Victorian origin, including the Cabernet
Sauvignon and Merlot blend and Wood Matured
Semillon. A range of 'Reserve' wines is made
from small parcels of outstanding grapes from
individual vineyards. Quantities may be as low
as 20 dozen for each label, and they are available
only from cellar door. The estate vineyard at
'The Jim Jim' near Hanging Rock is principally
planted for sparkling wine production, with the
first release in late 1990. Small quantities of
estate-grown Semillon and Sauvignon Blanc are
also produced and available now.
Best Vintages   W and R 1988, '90
An immense range of wines of at times varying
quality and of varying style. The best to date have
been exceptionally strong, concentrated Shiraz
releases from various parts of Central Victoria.

ABOVE: The 120-year-old bluestone winery of Craiglee.

KNIGHT, GRANITE HILLS   CA-B
Lancefield–Mia Mia Road
25 km east of Kyneton (054) 23 7264
Established   1979
Winemaker   Lew Knight
Production   5000 cases
Principal Wines   Estate-grown wines comprise
Rhine Riesling, Chardonnay,Shiraz and
Cabernet Sauvignon; small parcels of Shiraz are
also being processed from Heathcote.
Best Vintages   W 1981, '82, '84, '85, '86,
                    '88, '90
                    R 1976, '80, '81, '85, '86,
                    '88, '90
Knight Granite Hills was the first of the cool
region Victorian wineries to introduce the
public to peppery/spicy Shiraz, and it is for this
wine that Knight is best remembered by many.
However, its intensely flavoured and structured
lime/passionfruit Rhine Riesling can be
outstanding (in years such as 1988), while over
the years there have been some no less fine
Cabernets.

ROMSEY VINEYARDS   B-B
Glenfern Road
Romsey 3434   (054) 29 5428
Established   1977
Winemakers   Gordon and Michael Cope-
                    Williams
Production   3000 cases
Principal Wines   Chardonnay, Pinot Noir
and *Méthode Champenoise* backed by red and white
blends of estate-grown and contract-grown fruit.
Best Vintages   W 1986, '87, '88
                    R 1985, '86, '87, '88, '90
Romsey Vineyards vies with Virgin Hills in
taking the cool climate syndrome to its extreme.
There is no problem with that part of the
Romsey Vineyards' production given over to
sparkling wine (even though it is often harvested

in April) but the mid-May picking for Pinot
Noir and Chardonnay destined for table wine
poses a real challenge. All of the viticultural
problems are yet to be surmounted, but there
have been some exciting Chardonnay and Pinot
Noir table wines from this winery.

VIRGIN HILLS   A-A
Salisbury Road
Lauriston West via
Kyneton 3444   (054) 23 9169
Established   1968
Winemaker   Mark Sheppard
Production   1500 cases
Principal Wines   One wine so far commercially
released, simply called Virgin Hills. No other
description, varietal or generic, is provided on
the label. It is in fact a Cabernet-dominated
blend, with the Cabernet content increasing
substantially from 1982 and now accounting for
approximately 75 per cent of the blend, with
the remainder made up by Shiraz and a little
Malbec and Merlot.
Best Vintages   R 1974, '75, '76, '82, '85,
                    '86, '88, '90

VIRGIN HILLS

1988

GROWN, VINTAGED AND BOTTLED AT
DOMAIN GILBERT VIRGIN HILLS VINEYARD, KYNETON, VICTORIA.
12.0% ALC/VOL.   375 ml.
PRODUCT OF AUSTRALIA

They always said — and Tom Lazar readily
agreed — that he (Tom Lazar) was a little mad.
Who else would have picked this ultra cool,
high altitude spot with no viticultural history.
The choice proved to be not only sane but
brilliant, with a magnificent line of concentrated, deep-flavoured briary/berry wines with
an almost indefinite cellaring capacity. The new
owners, the Gilbert family, have protected their
inheritance without compromise.

OTHER WINERIES

BIN BILLA WINERY   C-C
Hogan's Road
Daylesford (053) 48 6539

CLEVELAND   NR
Shannon's Road
Lancefield 3435 (054) 29 1449

COBAW RIDGE   NR
Perc Boyer's Lane
Pastoria East via Kyneton 3444
(054) 23 5227

FLYNN AND WILLIAMS   B-B
Flynns Lane
Kyneton (054) 22 2427

LANCEFIELD WINERY   NR
Woodend Road
Lancefield 3435 (054) 29 1217

ROCHFORD WINERY   C-CB
Woodend Road
Romsey Park,
Rochford 3422 (054) 29 1428

WILDWOOD WINERY   CB-CB
St John's Lane
Wildwood, Bulla, 3428 (03) 307 1118

*ABOVE: Knight Granite Hills: wild, windswept and cold, but capable of
producing great wine.*

MORNINGTON PENINSULA

Contrary to most accounts, vineyards did exist on the Mornington Peninsula (chiefly in the Hastings area) in the nineteenth century, albeit on a small scale. They disappeared without trace, and the next attempt to establish a vineyard — by the Seabrook family at Arthurs Seat at the end of the 1940s — likewise faded away after several trial vintages. A chance lunchtime conversation between David Wynn and Baillieu Myer at Elgee Park in 1971 ignited the flame once more, this time to burn brightly. Wynn told Myer of the Seabrook experiment, and expressed regret that it had lapsed. Baillieu Myer resolved to establish a vineyard, which he did the following year.

There are now 80 vineyards and 26 producers, a number sharing wineries or winemakers with a further three planning to come on stream by the time this book is published. Yet the pace of development after 1972 was initially slow, accelerating progressively through to the end of the 1980s. When one then takes into account the undoubted quality of the wines of the region, and the quite remarkable consistency of that quality, it might seem inevitable that the Mornington Peninsula will become a nationally important wine producing region.

However, many of its strengths are also limitations. The Peninsula has long been Melbourne's chief weekend playground, the physical beauty of its softly rolling pastured hills and the proximity of its beaches acting as a powerful magnet. Land values are high, and are bound to go higher as demand inexorably grows for what is a finite resource. Substantial agricultural holdings are already extremely rare, and are dwindling rapidly. The prospect of a major Australian wine company seeking to buy 100 hectares — the minimum holding such a company would even contemplate — is remote.

What we in fact have is a patchwork quilt of tiny vineyards (by Australian standards), only four of which are larger than 3 hectares and most of which can never be economic units to run on conventional financial yardsticks. This is of little if any concern to those who own them, for a great number of the wineries are the weekend lifestyle occupations of wealthy

professional or businessmen, with economic return of secondary importance.

But it is also true that this has meant the owners have had both the financial ability and the intelligence to do things correctly, and not to baulk at spending the money to obtain

THE REGION IN BRIEF

LOCATION AND ELEVATION
38°20'S 144°58'E Dromana
25–250 m

SUBREGIONS
Nil, although there is a surprising climatic variation between sites, with the Red Hill/Main Ridge region far colder than the central coastal vineyards around Dromana, while Rye is colder still.

CLIMATE
Once again, there is both variation and mystery in the HDD figures, with 1570 attributed to Mornington, which appears at odds with the wine style. The figure for Dromana Post Office is 1240, while the total drops to around 1080 in locations near Main Ridge, and lower still at Rye. Yet the Mornington figure is not much greater than that of Healesville, and both regions (Mornington and Yarra Valley) have similar ripening patterns and wine styles. In lay terms, though not technical terms, this is a cool climate, with wind chill adding an edge which is not easy to measure in statistical terms but which undoubtedly delays (and ultimately inhibits) ripening in some vineyard sites, compounded further by the heavier red soils of some of the Red Hill/Main Ridge vineyards. The rainfall grades from 875 mm on the coast to 950 mm on the highest sites, once again tending to inhibit ripening.

SOIL
There are four principal soil types. The hard mottled yellow duplex soils (Dy3.21 and 3.22) with a very distinct break (marked by a thin, acid cement/sand pan) between the surface soil and the underlying friable well drained clay are to be found in the Dromana area. Around Red Hill and Main Ridge, red soils of volcanic origin predominate; these are very deep and fertile. At Stoniers Merricks there are brown duplex soils (in the Db group), while much sandier soils are in evidence at Moorooduc.

HARVEST TIME
Vintage usually commences later and finishes later than the Yarra Valley — end March for Pinot Noir, mid-May for Shiraz and Rhine Riesling. In 1990 some Shiraz was picked on 2 June.

PRINCIPAL GRAPE VARIETIES

Chardonnay	*Cabernet Sauvignon*
Rhine Riesling	*Merlot*
Sauvignon Blanc	*Pinot Noir*
Gewurztraminer	*Shiraz*

AUSTRALASIAN WINE REGIONS
1980 – 1990

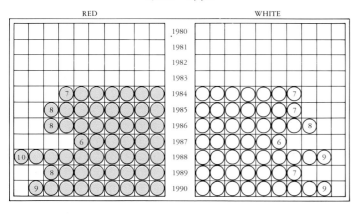

FACING PAGE: The Chardonnay of Mornington Peninsula offers the promise of greatness.

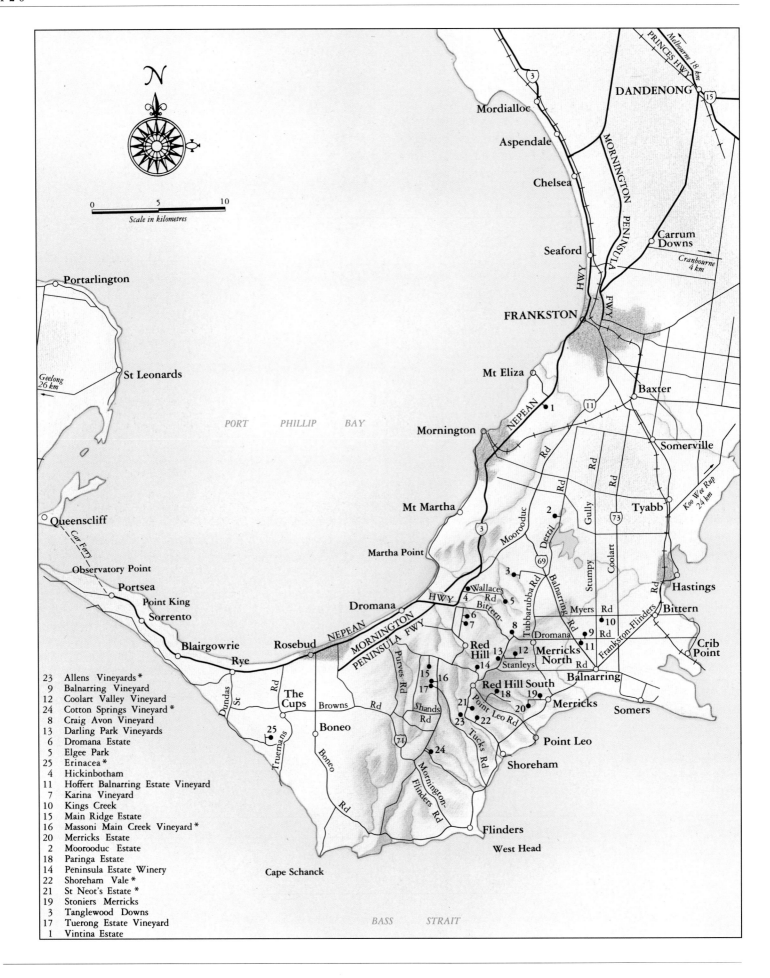

skilled viticultural and oenological consultancy advice. This has paid immediate dividends in terms of wine quality — which is uncharacteristically consistent — and may well pay modest financial dividends in the long run.

This professionalism comes through in the packaging of the wines, and in their marketing through mailing list and (increasingly) cellar door. On the other hand, only Dromana Estate enjoys national retail distribution on any consistent basis, and only it, Hickinbotham winemakers and Main Ridge Estate are full time occupations for their owners. So Mornington Peninsula is living proof of the old adage that small is beautiful, and will remain so.

PRINCIPAL WINE STYLES

CHARDONNAY
By and large the wines are of light to medium body, with quite delicate melon/citric/fig fruit flavours and well balanced acidity. This delicacy of flavour demands sensitive oak handling, and this too is a pleasing feature of the region's Chardonnays. One or two wines, however, have shown startling richness and concentration: as the vineyards mature, we may well see more of these. Dromana Estate and Stoniers Merricks are usually excellent; Massoni Main Creek Vineyard (made in tiny quantities) is an example of the soft and richer style.

CABERNET SAUVIGNON
Something of a misnomer, for almost all the Cabernets are in fact blended with up to 20 per cent Merlot and Cabernet Franc, a practice which accentuates the natural tendency to suppleness and elegance: these are the equivalent of the right bank of the Gironde in Bordeaux (St Emilion and Pomerol) compared to the left bank (Haut Médoc and Graves) of — say — Coonawarra (South Australia). The flavours can be intense if not downright piercing, running the full gamut of red into black berries, but the wines are never heavy and certainly not tannic. Karina Vineyard, Dromana Estate and Moorooduc Estate are among the best, with a sparkling multi-flavoured core of fruit.

PINOT NOIR
Once again, the characteristic delicacy of the region's wines manifests itself, raising the question whether greater depth and strength will materialise as the average age of the vines increases (and possibly as high yields are brought under control). The wines are typically bright but light in colour, extremely fragrant and with the aroma and flavour of red cherries. Main Ridge Estate, Kings Creek and Dromana Estate are the leading producers.

RHINE RIESLING AND GEWURZTRAMINER
Like the wines of the Yarra Valley from these varieties, they are uncompromisingly European, with a faintly chalky overlay and almost none of the rich lime/tropical characters of South Australian examples.

TOP: *Bird netting at Dromana estate: starlings and Indian Mynas are a major problem in parts of southern Victoria.*

ABOVE: *Netting in place, the only sure way of preventing the birds picking the crop first.*

COOL-CLIMATE VITICULTURE

The major development in the premium sector of the wine industry over the past 30 years has been the establishment — or in many instances re-establishment — of viticulture in the cooler parts of Australia.

If one accepts that Coonawarra in South Australia was teetering on the brink of extinction when David Wynn made his far-sighted decision to buy Chateau Comaum (now known as Wynns Coonawarra Estate) in 1951, the cool climate resurgence covers the entire south-western corner of Western Australia; the Adelaide Hills, Coonawarra and Padthaway (South Australia); the whole of Tasmania; most of Central Victoria and all Southern Victoria.

The Barossa Valley in South Australia remains the focal point of wine production, but its relative importance as a grape growing region has been steadily declining for decades. In New South Wales the Hunter Valley is in a not dissimilar position: its hectares under vine are half what they were 20 years ago, and the major producers increasingly rely on grapes grown outside its borders. The Swan Valley (Western Australia), too, is shrinking, sustained almost entirely by one company — Houghton.

If one looks at a mid-50s map, that leaves Mudgee (New South Wales), the Clare Valley and Southern Vales – Langhorne Creek (South Australia) as the only other significant producers of premium wine. The engine room of the Australian industry — the riverland regions spread along the Murray River and around Griffith on the Murrumbidgee River — continues to produce over 60 per cent of Australian wine, but only a minuscule proportion of that aspires to the premium tag: De Bortoli Semillon Sauternes(Murrumbidgee Irrigation Area, New South Wales) and Renmano Chairman's Selection Chardonnay (the Riverland, South Australia) are two of the exceptions proving the rule.

It is not surprising that this shift has caused considerable anxiety to the vested interests in the traditional warmer regions, or that it has led to a great deal of hype about the perceived merits of cool-climate viticulture. The truth is that many of Australia's greatest Chardonnays and almost all its great Semillon are made in the Upper or Lower Hunter Valley; that Clare Valley Rhine Riesling is challenged only by that of the Eden Valley; while our greatest red wine — Penfolds Grange Hermitage — is based on Barossa Valley Shiraz.

Even more is it true that growing grapes in cool climates is neither a licence to print money nor a passport to the automatic production of premium wine. As quickly as new regions have come into production so have viticultural problems emerged. The past decade has witnessed a veritable revolution in both theory and practice, with consultants such as Dr Richard Smart (see page 332) suddenly becoming

household — well, wine-household — names and ultimately leaving academia to become professional consultants.

Nor does the revolution show any signs of finishing. Today's truth will become tomorrow's fallacy as the bewildered vigneron is caught in the cross currents, with economics pulling him in one direction, the desire for quality in another, the ebb and flow of theoretical opinion all the while creating a vicious and often unseen undertow.

To take one practical example, compare the minimal pruning regime with the Swiss-inspired Tasmanian experiments conducted over 1989 and 1990. The former, widespread in Coonawarra, largely leaves the vine to its own devices. Conventional pruning ceases altogether, the only manipulation of the vine coming in late spring when the bottom of the canopy is skirted (or trimmed) by machine to facilitate airflow under the vines.

Tasmania took the thin vertical canopy to its logical extreme. Not only were the vines meticulously hand-pruned in winter, all of the growing shoots precisely positioned by hand and the foliage wires moved progressively upwards, but all of the 'laterals', the second shoot which forms at the base of each leaf on a new cane, were removed by hand.

The cost of the minimal pruning regime is under $200 per hectare, that of the Swiss-Tasmanian over $10,000 per hectare — probably much over. Yet curiously both have the same aim: to gain maximum exposure of the grape bunches and next year's fruiting buds to the sunlight.

For what we have learnt about cool-climate viticulture is that it is easy to grow big vines with large leaf canopies, and much less easy to grow a vine which is in balance — in which there is the correct ratio between wood, leaf and grapes, and in which there is proper light penetration. If that balance is lost, grapes deficient in colour and tannin, with excessively high pH and producing a soapy/squashy taste, will be the result.

On a next-worse scenario, cool-grown grapes produce pretty wines, wines with pure but delicate varietal flavour which bloom as briefly as the most overworked hot area Chardonnay. The latter quickly turns to unattractive fat, the former simply wilts and fades away into skeletal thinness.

The challenge of any wine region, cool climate included, is to produce wines with texture, structure, vinosity and the requisite concentration and balance to ensure they will age with grace. To this end we have seen the emergence of the Lyre Trellis, the Te Kauwhata 2 Tier, the Scott-Henry and a host of other trellises, all expensive and elaborate. 'Leaf plucking' has become the buzz word of the end of the '80s, Pellenc 'knitting machines' (a tractor-driven machine which knits the vine into a thin vertical plane) and leaf trimmers the latest (and most expensive) vineyard toy.

We have also witnessed the return of the winemaker to the vineyard, a tacit recognition of the fact that 9 times out of 10 it is in the vineyard, not in the winery, that great wines are made. The winemaker will tell his or her viticulturist what yields are required, what sugar and acid levels, how much tannin and so on: if the team works well enough, the winemaker's job is largely complete by the time the grapes come in the winery door, for from that point on the principal task is simply to protect what the vineyard has given.

The Mornington Peninsula is no different to any other new (or not so new) cool-climate region. If an appropriate viticultural regime is used, wines of the highest quality can be made, wines with intensity of flavour which simultaneously achieve a 'European' elegance and finesse.

ABOVE: Cool-climate viticulture can yield good results.

WINERIES OF THE MORNINGTON PENINSULA

BALNARRING VINEYARD   CB-B
Bittern-Dromana Road
Balnarring 3926   (059) 89 5258
Established   1982
Winemaker   David Wollan (contract)
Production   Not stated.
Principal Wines   Chardonnay, Rhine Riesling, Traminer, Pinot Noir and Cabernet Merlot.
Best Vintages   **W** and **R** 1987, '88
This vineyard demonstrates that all things are feasible on the Mornington Peninsula, and in particular that it is possible to produce extremely strong, full bodied red wines. Some, indeed, have gone over the edge, almost denying their varietal base — Pinot Noir included. However, too much flavour is better than too little, and while the wines of Balnarring Vineyard have been erratic in the past, the more recent releases show real promise.

DROMANA ESTATE   A-A
Cnr Harrison's and
Bittern-Dromana Roads
Dromana 3936   (059) 87 3275
Established   1982
Winemaker   Garry Crittenden
Production   2000 cases Dromana Estate; 3000 cases Schinus Molle.
Principal Wines   The principal label is Dromana Estate, which is exclusively reserved for estate-grown and made Chardonnay, Pinot Noir and Cabernet Merlot. Winemaker/proprietor Garry Crittenden has also developed a second label, Schinus Molle, the wines of which are not necessarily Mornington Peninsula-sourced. These comprise Sauvignon Blanc, Chardonnay and Cabernet.
Best Vintages   **W** 1988, '89, '90
                     R 1987, '88, '89, '90

In an area producing an impressively high percentage of excellent wines, Dromana Estate nonetheless stands apart as the most consistent of all. Its light but intensely-flavoured dark cherry Pinot Noir with a backdrop of spicy oak, its beautifully modulated melon and grapefruit-flavoured Chardonnay with strong barrel ferment influence, and its almost dazzlingly fruity Cabernet Merlot win only the highest praise from those who understand what cool climate wines are all about. From vineyard to bottle, Garry Crittenden is a perfectionist. The Schinus Molle wines, incidentally, are very nearly as good, with a striking Sauvignon Blanc making its debut in 1989.

ELGEE PARK   B-B
Wallaces Road
Merricks North 3926 (059) 89 7338
Established   1972
Winemakers   Daniel Green with Gary Baldwin
Production   2000 cases
Principal Wines   Rhine Riesling, Chardonnay and Cabernet Merlot (the latter with Cabernet Franc in the blend). Experimental quantities of Viognier.
Best Vintages: **W** 1986, '88, '89
                      R 1980, '85, '87, '88, '90
Elgee Park boasts by far the oldest vineyards in the Mornington Peninsula, and has played a focal role in the development of viticulture and winemaking in the region. Very elegant wines are produced, the best being the Rhine Riesling and Chardonnay, both of which take a surprising time to develop in bottle. The Cabernet Merlot needs more richness and structure to lift it into the top category.

HICKINBOTHAM   B-B
Cnr Wallaces Road and
Nepean Highway
Dromana 3936   (059) 81 0355
Established   1981
Winemakers   The Hickinbotham family and Peter Cummings.
Production   An absolutely astonishing number of different parcels of wine, all made in small quantities, but adding up to a very substantial amount in total.
Principal Wines   Hickinbotham winemakers' specialty is taking small parcels of grapes (perhaps as little as one tonne at a time) and turning these into distinct lots of wine (in quantities as small as 50 dozen) identified by variety and by the vineyard name. These are then made available either by mailing list or, if through a retailer or restaurant, often on a single outlet exclusive basis. A number of the individual wines come from the Mornington

Peninsula but others do not: the Hickinbotham net extends to the Bellarine Peninsula, Geelong, Gippsland and the Yarra Valley to name a few districts.
Best Vintages   Not relevant owing to varied fruit sources.
Many superb wines of all styles have appeared under the Hickinbotham label in the past few years, none better than its voluptuous, plummy 1988 Geelong Pinot Noir. The 1989 Chardonnays were less convincing, however, and winemaking operations were suspended in 1990.

KARINA VINEYARD   B-B
Harrisons Road
Dromana 3936   (059) 81 0137
Established   1984
Winemaker   Graeme Pinney
Production   700 cases
Principal Wines   Rhine Riesling, Sauvignon Blanc and Cabernet Merlot.
Best Vintages   **W** 1988, '89
                     R 1988, '90

To this point, Karina has only proved itself as a white wine vineyard, but a very good one at that, with extremely potent gooseberry Sauvignon Blanc and a passionfruit-accented Rhine Riesling in 1988.

KINGS CREEK   BA-B
237 Myers Road
Bittern 3918   (059) 83 2102
Established   1981
Winemakers   Kathleen Quealy, Brian Fletcher
Production   660 cases
Principal Wines   Chardonnay, Pinot Noir and Cabernet Sauvignon.
Best Vintages   **W** 1986, '88, '89, '90
                     R 1987, '88, '90
Kings Creek is unusual amongst Peninsula producers in offering wines with 2 or 3 years bottle age. Quality and style are still to gain consistency, but it has done best with full flavoured Chardonnay, particularly 1989, and brought to the Peninsula the first gold medal won at a capital city show with its 1990 Pinot Noir.

ABOVE: *Garry Crittenden of Dromana Estate: skilled viticulturist and fine wine producer.*

MAIN RIDGE ESTATE   A-BA
Lot 48, William Road
Red Hill 3937   (059) 89 2686
Established   1975
Winemaker   Nat White
Production   1000 cases
Principal Wines   Chardonnay, Pinot Noir,
Cabernet Sauvignon and Cabernet Franc, and
Pinot Meunier in tiny quantities.
Best Vintages   W 1985, '86, '88, '89, '90
                     R 1980, '85, '86, '88, '90
Nat White's attention to detail is legendary;
there is no question he knows the shape of every
vine on the vineyard, and he takes endless care in
making the wines of Main Ridge Estate. Some
quite beautiful wines have appeared over the
years: a fragrant spicy Pinot Noir, a Chardonnay
with the aroma and taste of white peaches, and a
surprisingly assertive Cabernet Sauvignon have
all delighted. It seems likely that the wines will
always have a particular vineyard style, one
which is bound to appeal to many. Changes in
viticulture have resulted in increased colour and
flavour in the more recent vintages and the
already high reputation of Main Ridge can only
increase.

12.0% Alc. Vol. Produce of Australia 750ml.
PRESERVATIVE (220) ADDED

MERRICKS ESTATE   BA-BA
Thompsons Lane
Merricks 3916   (059) 89 8352
Established   1984
Winemakers   George Kefford and family
and Selma Lowther. Chardonnay made by Alex
White.
Production   1200 cases
Principal Wines   Chardonnay, Pinot Noir,
Shiraz and Cabernet Sauvignon.
Best Vintages   W 1986, '87, '88, '90
                     R 1984, '86, '88, '90
The 1984 Merricks Estate Shiraz set a standard
(and a style) for this variety in the areas around
Melbourne. Few vineyards have bettered it since,
and in 1989 Merricks Estate Shiraz swept all
before it in the local shows. If pepper/spice is
your bag, Merricks Estate Shiraz is your wine.

MOOROODUC ESTATE BA-BA
Derril Road
Mooroduc 3936   (059) 78 8585
Established   1984
Winemaker   Dr Richard McIntyre
                     (consultant Nat White)
Production   1000 cases
Principal Wines   Chardonnay, Pinot Noir
and Cabernet Sauvignon.
Best Vintages   W 1988, '89, '90
                     R 1988, '89, '90
As each vintage passes, the wines of Mooroduc
Estate grow in stature. Opulent Chardonnay,
running the flavours between peach and
grapefruit, and an extremely finely crafted,
Bordeaux-like Cabernet (a prolific gold medal
winner) are the best wines so far. A winery —
and yet another medical winemaker — to watch.

PARINGA ESTATE   NR
44 Paringa Road
Red Hill South 3937 (059) 89 2669
Established   1985
Winemaker   Lindsay McCall
                     (consultant Tod Dexter)
Production   550 cases
Principal Wines   Chardonnay, Shiraz and
Cabernet Sauvignon are the only wines presently
made; however, subsequent plantings of Merlot,
Cabernet Franc and Pinot Noir will extend the
range.
Best Vintages   R 1988, '90
School teacher Lindsay McCall had a dream
debut with his 1988 reds, the Shiraz showing
clean red berry fruit with marked spice/pepper,
the Cabernet Sauvignon strong cassis/dark berry
flavours. The oak handling was excellent, and
the overall depth of flavour for young vines
particularly impressive. It will be interesting to
watch the estate as the vines mature.

STONIERS MERRICKS   A-A
62 Thompsons Lane
Merricks 3916   (059) 89 8352
Established   1978
Winemaker   1982–1986 vintages: the
late Stephen Hickinbotham. From 1987 Tod
Dexter at Elgee Park Winery with private
consultancy.
Production   850 cases
Principal Wines   Chardonnay,   Cabernet
Sauvignon and Pinot Noir.
Best Vintages   W 1985, '87, '88, '90
                     R 1984, '86, '87, '88, '90
Brian Stonier, perhaps best known in book
publishing circles, enlivens the Mornington
Peninsula with his sardonic wit and his at times
magnificent wines. The '84 and '88 Cabernet
Sauvignons are the best of this variety to come
from the Peninsula to date, while both the
Chardonnay and the Pinot Noir show exemplary
varietal character and good depth of flavour. At
their best, the Cabernets have beautifully

modulated flavour with perfectly ripened
varietal fruit showing all of its many flavours
and aroma nuances.

OTHER WINERIES

ALLENS VINEYARDS   NR
Red Hill-Shoreham Road
Red Hill 3937 (059) 89 2044

**COOLART VALLEY VINEYARD
CB-CB**
Thomas Hill Road
Red Hill South 3937 (059) 89 2087

COTTON SPRINGS VINEYARD NR
9B Musk Creek Road
Flinders 3929 (059) 89 6193

CRAIG AVON VINEYARD   NR
Craig Avon Lane
Merricks North 3926 (059) 89 7465

DARLING PARK VINEYARDS NR
Browne Lane and Red Hill Road
Red Hill 3937 (059) 892732

ERINACEA   NR
Devonport Drive
Rye 3941 (059) 88 6336

**HOFFERT BALNARRING ESTATE
VINEYARD   NR**
87 Bittern-Dromana Road
Balnarring 3926 (059) 89 5330

**MASSONI MAIN CREEK VINEYARD
BA-B**
Mornington-Flinders Road
Red Hill 3937 (059) 89 2060

PENINSULA ESTATE WINERY NR
Red Hill Road
Red Hill 3937 (059) 89 2866

SHOREHAM VALE   NR
Red Hill-Shoreham Road
Red Hill South 3937

ST NEOT'S ESTATE   NR
63 Red Hill-Shoreham Road
Red Hill South 3937 (059) 89 2023

TANGLEWOOD DOWNS   NR
Bulldog Creek Road
Mornington Rural (059) 74 3325

TUERONG ESTATE VINEYARD B-B
Mornington-Flinders Road
Red Hill 3937 (059) 89 2129

VINTINA ESTATE   D-C
1282 Nepean Highway
Mount Eliza 3930 (03) 787 8166

THE MURRAY AND
NORTH GOULBURN RIVERS

The riverlands of Australia are a remarkable achievement in a continent which has only grudgingly provided a habitat for its European invaders around its eastern and south-western coastline and in its south-eastern corner. Attempts to impose order and infrastructure on the dry centre have been few and far between: the Ord River scheme was a failure, while plans to turn the east-flowing river system of New South Wales and Queensland inland remain the dream of a few visionaries.

Only along the giant Murray River (and on a lesser scale, the Murrumbidgee) has the parched red sand and stunted growth of saltbush and spinifex grass been transformed into a giant orchard, and a vegetable and rice garden. Because the country is so monotonously flat, and the distances so vast, only by flying along the Murray can one gain any real perspective of the extent of the achievement.

In the relentless dry heat of summer the road stretching in front of the intrepid driver shimmers, wobbles and suddenly disappears into a wonderful mirage, the classic oasis of water and trees. As you sweep past barren earth into another area under irrigation, the lush green of the vines and orange trees momentarily seems to be yet another mirage, but it is not. With the magic elixir of water, plants grow with an almost savage fury, bearing crops which are if anything altogether too bountiful, too perfect to be true. In the dry air, diseases

AUSTRALASIAN WINE REGIONS
1980 – 1990

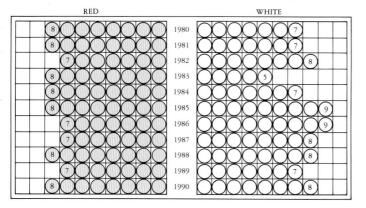

THE REGION IN BRIEF

LOCATION AND ELEVATION
*36°13'S 144°46'E Echuca to 34°10'S 142°10'E Mildura
50–60 m*

SUBREGIONS
There are four distinct subregions: Mildura, Robinvale, Swan Hill and Echuca, although the federal and Victorian authorities differ on how they should be described (and grouped).

CLIMATE
As one moves west from Echuca to Mildura, the climate becomes progressively hotter, rising from a heat summation (HDD) of 2017 at Echuca to 2240 at Mildura. The rainfall varies from 347 mm in the east to 275 mm at Mildura, less than half of which falls in the 6 months growing season — it hardly need be said that irrigation is absolutely essential. The absence of rain and the relatively low humidity sharply reduces both the incidence of fungal disease and vintage variation.

SOIL
The soils are remarkably uniform along the length of the Murray, almost all being calcareous earths (Gc1.22). The surface soil is red-brown sandy loam which ranges from neutral to alkaline; the subsoil becomes progressively more alkaline with depth, thanks to the increasing accumulation of carbonates. While the surface soil is permeable, the subsoil is less so, necessitating elaborate drainage works to alleviate the salinity build up which would otherwise occur.

HARVEST TIME
White varieties picked for sparkling wine usage start proceedings in late January to early February; the principal activity takes place in a frenetic burst between mid-February and mid-March, tailing off rapidly thereafter.

PRINCIPAL GRAPE VARIETIES
The figures are for Mildura, Robinvale and Swan Hill; note also that only 20 per cent of the sultana production is used in winemaking, the rest is used in the dried fruits industry

*Sultana (Thompsons Seedless), 7922 ha   Cabernet Sauvignon, 113 ha
Muscat Gordo Blanco, 1090 ha   Shiraz, 110 ha
Chardonnay, 342 ha   Grenache, 77 ha
Colombard, 181 ha
Rhine Riesling, 141 ha
Crouchen, 101 ha*

ABOVE: Chardonnay glows translucent in the early morning sun.　　*FACING PAGE: Growing tips at sunset.*

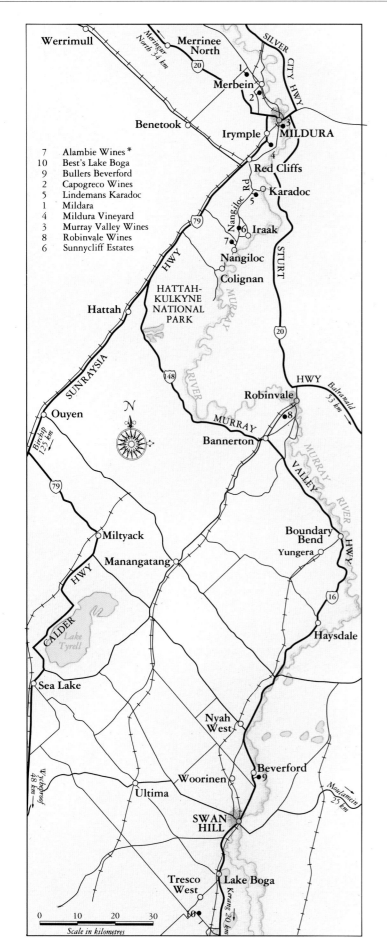

7   Alambie Wines *
10 Best's Lake Boga
9   Bullers Beverford
2   Capogreco Wines
5   Lindemans Karadoc
1   Mildara
4   Mildura Vineyard
3   Murray Valley Wines
8   Robinvale Wines
6   Sunnycliff Estates

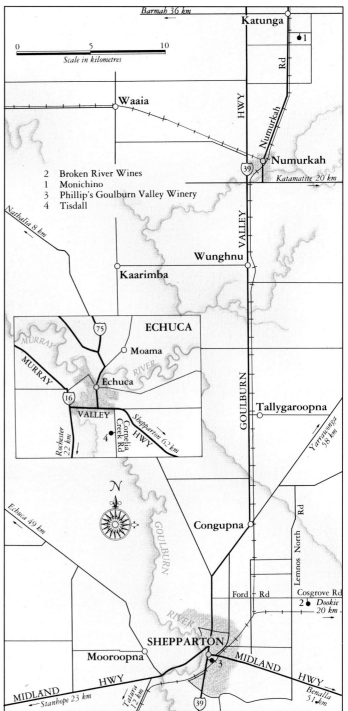

2   Broken River Wines
1   Monichino
3   Phillip's Goulburn Valley Winery
4   Tisdall

seldom take hold, and the maintenance of a healthy vineyard is (relatively speaking) an easy matter. It is also relatively inexpensive; the large size of the average holding, the degree of mechanisation, the reliability of the weather and the abundant yields all reduce the cost of producing each tonne of grapes to an absolute minimum. Most of the grapes are produced by growers who sell to a few very large wineries — some situated in the Riverland, others far away. The wineries have all of the atmosphere of a petrol refinery, and the landscape is monotonously flat. This is not the glamorous face of winemaking, it is simply the most efficient.

PRINCIPAL WINE STYLES

Australian wine is distinguished from that of almost all other nations by its softness and its fruitiness. In the Riverland the softness moves to another dimension, sometimes to the point of blandness, producing wines which give everything to and demand nothing from the consumer. These are not wines to be analysed, and in a sense not even criticised: they serve a functional purpose, and it is idle to impose the judgmental yardstick of fine or premium wine. Yet for all that some varieties do fare better than others, and some worse, with an overwhelming bias in favour of white varieties.

CHARDONNAY
Almost inevitably, Chardonnay seems to rise above its constraints, producing wine which has that distinctive soft peachy fruit which is its birthright — and birthmark. In one or two locations — notably Seppelt's Barooga vineyard at the extreme eastern end on the New South Wales side — it rises higher still, producing wine of real substance, flavour and style.

RHINE RIESLING
This is one of the relative failures: it is a variety which must retain its crispness to achieve any quality, and here it tends to be soft and excessively bland.

COLOMBARD
A variety which has never become fashionable, partly because of its own inherent limitations and partly because it has been skilfully used in blends to produce generic wines labelled Chablis, White Burgundy and so on. Its great virtue is its ability to retain high natural acidity, a virtue all the more valuable in the hot Riverland climate, and which has contributed to the steady increase in its plantings.

CHENIN BLANC
This is a somewhat vapid variety at the best of times, with its blurred fruit salad flavour seldom giving a wine of distinction. These characteristics are no handicap in this region, however, and the variety is a useful 'filler' with others.

MUSCAT GORDO BLANCO
Still the workhorse of the bulk end of the market, its spicy/grapey taste providing flavour to otherwise neutral and washy blends. Even if the purist says the character so given is rather common, it is flavour nonetheless.

SULTANA (THOMPSONS SEEDLESS)
The unspecified and totally undistinguished base of bulk white wine destined for casks of lesser quality.

CABERNET SAUVIGNON
This is a chameleon: a few producers — notably Tisdall, Lindemans' Karadoc (via its Matthew Lang label) and Mildara (via its Church Hill Flower label) produce wines of at times surprising quality. None are better than Tisdall, which blends the variety with Merlot to produce a wine which, for over a decade, has consistently shown that in Australia nothing is impossible. It has strong colour, a crystal clear taste of red berries and blackcurrant, and even has some real structure and length to the palate.

SHIRAZ
By and large, a failure: ordinary wines which tire quickly are the rule, and simply emphasise that with the exception of Cabernet Sauvignon (and Merlot) this is white wine country.

ABOVE: *The Goulburn River, ever beautiful.*

THE RIVERLAND AND AUSTRALIAN WINE
1900 TO 1950

The story of the development of the irrigation areas along the Murray River has all the ingredients for an epic television series. Starting in California where the protagonists, brothers George and William Chaffey, learnt how to make large scale irrigation work (and made a small fortune in so doing), switching to Victoria where Government perfidy destroyed all of their plans, moving to South Australia and their successful establishment of Renmark, and then coming back to a chastened Victoria where they oversaw the development of Mildura between 1887 and 1890.

The saga continued: on 28 January 1893 the great bank crash commenced, ultimately forcing the biggest bank of all — the Commercial Banking Company of Sydney — to temporarily close its doors. If this were not enough, the Murray River dried up unusually early, largely cutting off the all-important Melbourne market. Then it was discovered that yabbies were undermining the main irrigation channels, while salt seepage was killing young vines and fruit trees in some locations.

In 1895 a Royal Commission found the brothers guilty of mismanagement (a debatable finding at best) and a broken and bankrupt George Chaffey returned to America. William Chaffey persevered, however. A believer in temperance, he had founded Chateau Mildura in 1891 to make table wine, but was opposed to spirits or fortified wine. It soon became clear the population had other ideas, and Chaffey was forced to allow the distillation of part of the unsold 1892 and 1893 vintages, and ultimately — in 1897 — to install a still himself. But it was to no avail; by 1908 the winery had closed, and the vineyards grafted to table grapes.

The pendulum swung again, and almost overnight things turned for the better. A market for fortifying spirit developed in North-east Victoria, and the indomitable William Chaffey formed Mildura Winery Proprietary Limited, reopening the winery in time for the 1914 vintage, and soon establishing a second operation at Merbein.

Prosperity was all too brief: Returned Soldier Settlement Schemes sponsored by the New South Wales, Victorian and South Australian governments produced a sudden grape surplus. The business went into liquidation, but a new company (with some different shareholders but having the same name and retaining William Chaffey as its chairman) was formed in 1920 to acquire the assets of the old company.

The next 4 years were a struggle, but in 1925 the federal Government passed the Wine Export Bounty Act, which was followed in 1926 by the introduction of preferential tariffs in the United Kingdom for wines produced by British Empire countries. Another violent swing of the pendulum led to a time of unprecedented activity and prosperity for the vignerons of the Riverland, and for Australia as a whole.

The extent of the impact on the Australian wine industry of those initiatives is best appreciated through some raw statistics. In 1921 England had imported 21,044,000 litres of wine from France and 2,439,000 litres from Australia. In 1927 it imported 19,010,000 litres from Australia, and 15,935,000 litres from France. From this point on, French imports declined sharply, while those from Australia held their ground. Between then and 1940 the cumulative value of Australian wine exports to England dwarfed those of France — 164,153,000 litres to 92,657,000 litres.

Almost all of this wine was fortified: sweet sherry and tawny port (very young tawny port) were the staple items, and it was the ultimate conclusion of a steady shift away from the table wine exports of the nineteenth century. It also mirrored domestic consumption, the wine bars which existed everywhere dealt exclusively in fortified wine, their clientele coming entirely from the working classes — a far cry from the chic London or Sydney wine bar of today.

However, even in the height of the frenzied prosperity and gaiety of the jitterbug 1920s, problems were mounting up in the bond warehouses of the London docks where much of the Australian wine (exported almost entirely in cask) was accumulating. The fault lay partly in Australia, partly in London. Due to a lack of understanding of the biochemistry of fortified wine, wines which were inherently susceptible to bacterial spoilage were exported, but the problem was made infinitely worse by the storage conditions (and the complete lack of skilled winemaking care) in the London warehouses. The wines needed topping up, racking and sulphur dioxide corrections, but received none of these things. In the outcome, much was ruined by bacterial spoilage, and Australia's reputation suffered greatly in consequence.

The onset of the Depression was no less sudden and no less severe for the wine industry than it was for the rest of Australian business. Production, which had peaked at 93,000,000 litres in 1927, fell to 59,500,000 litres in 1931. Grape surpluses accumulated across Australia, and led to the creation of some of the largest cooperatives, including Kaiser Stuhl in the Barossa Valley.

It enforced the trend towards fortified wine production, and to production of the cheapest possible wine. Plantings of premium varieties decreased to the point where quality table wine ceased to play any meaningful role in the industry. Only three varieties — Shiraz, Rhine Riesling and (on a much

smaller scale) Semillon — kept a toehold. Palomino, Muscat Gordo Blanco, Sultana (a multi-purpose grape also extensively grown for drying), Grenache and Mataro ruled the roost.

But the industry survived, thanks to two factors. First and foremost, the extraordinary level of exports, and thereafter (from 1940 to 1950) the effects of beer rationing and the unavailability of imported spirits. As the chart on the right shows, between 1926-27 and 1939-40 exports reached levels which in terms of simple litres were not exceeded until 1986-87, and which in percentage terms will never be equalled. It took Australian wine a long time to throw off the unfortunate reputation it gained — as a producer of indifferent quality port and sherry — but the economic benefits at the time were of crucial importance.

And so, too, was the wartime shortage of alcohol, a drought which continued until the early 1950s. The one readily available form was fortified wine, dispensed by every hotel across Australia (and from its myriad of seedy wine salons). The end of beer rationing saw a 10 year period of economic stagnation until the table wine boom of the 1960s started and the industry we know today began to take shape.

AUSTRALIAN WINE EXPORTS

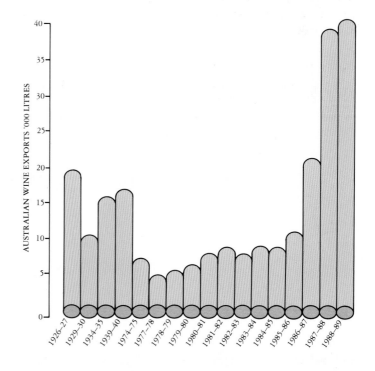

ABOVE: *Much of the vast Murray River production ends up in tanks like these.*

WINERIES OF THE MURRAY AND NORTH GOULBURN RIVERS

MURRAY RIVER

BEST'S LAKE BOGA   CB-BA
St Andrew's Vineyard
Lake Boga 3584   (050) 37 2154
Established   1929
Winemakers   Viv Thomson, Simon Clayfield
Production   25,000 cases
Principal Wines   A number of table wines, both white and red, are produced; not all are released under the Bests label. By far the most important estate release is Bests Victorian Cabernet Sauvignon. Other regular releases are Victorian Shiraz, Victorian Rhine Riesling, and Victorian Chenin Blanc.
Best Vintages   W and R 1983, '85, '87, '89, '90

Supremely honest wines which at times have quite remarkable flavour and style, and which more often than not represent outstanding value for money. The winery, of course, is an offshoot of Best's Great Western.

BULLERS BEVERFORD   CB-B
Murray Valley Highway
Beverford 3590   (050) 37 6305
Established   1952
Winemaker   Richard Buller Junior
Production   About 1300 tonnes of grapes crushed; a little over 50 per cent is for distillation to make fortifying spirit.
Principal Wines   A full range of generic and varietal table wines, principally white but also red, offered in bottle and in 10 litre and 20 litre soft-pack cases. Likewise, a range of fortified wines including sherries of all styles. Most of the tawny and vintage ports are made at Rutherglen. Table wines include Rhine Riesling, Colombard, Chenin Blanc, Chablis, White Burgundy, Riesling, Cabernet Merlot, and Cabernet Sauvignon.
Best Vintages   Largely irrelevant.

Like Best's Lake Boga to Best's Great Western, Bullers Beverford is an offshoot of Buller's principal operations in North-east Victoria, and it provides much of the table wine to be released under the Buller label. The accent is on reliability and value.

LINDEMANS' KARADOC   B-BA
Nangiloc Road
Karadoc on Calder Highway,
27 km east of Mildura 3500   (050) 24 0303
Established   1963
Winemakers   A team directed by company oenologist, Phillip John.
Production   Estimated around 3.5 million cases.
Principal Wines   Lindemans Premier Selection Chardonnay, Bin 65 Export Chardonnay, Bin 95 Export Sauvignon Blanc and Bin 45 Export Cabernet Sauvignon all basically made from locally grown fruit. Matthew Lang range is also nominally housed here, although the base material comes both from the Murray River and from elsewhere.
Best Vintages   Completely irrelevant.
Karadoc is now the operational base for the Lindemans' group, and presumably will remain so notwithstanding its acquisition by Penfolds. Its chief oenologist Phillip John is stationed there, and all of the key decisions, and many of the wines, are made there. Lindemans does, however, operate substantial wineries in the Hunter Valley, Coonawarra and the Barossa Valley. The wines of those regions are separately discussed and rated at pages 51, 221 and 199.

MILDARA   CB-BA
Wentworth Road
Merbein 3505   (050) 25 2303
Established   1888
Winemakers   Alan Harris (senior winemaker), Andrew Fleming, Andrew Peace and David Tierney.
Production   In excess of one million cases.
Principal Wines   Church Hill Range comprises Chardonnay, Fumé Blanc, Chablis, Cabernet Merlot, Rhine Riesling. Fortifieds comprise Cavendish Port, Benjamin Port, George Fino Sherry, Chestnut Teal, Supreme Dry, Stratford Port and the Rio Vista range. Brandy includes Morgon Brown Pot Still, Supreme and Special.
Best Vintages   Largely irrelevant.
The Merbein winery of Mildara fulfills much of the same function as Lindemans' Karadoc: nerve centre of the empire, and principal operational base. The cheaper Riverland-sourced wines are adequate for the task, with the Cabernet Merlot occasionally reaching surprising heights. The great wines under the Mildara label come from Coonawarra, and are separately discussed at page 221.

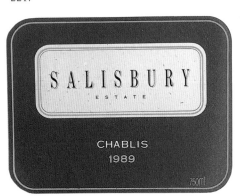

OTHER WINERIES

CAPOGRECO WINES   DC-C
Riverside Avenue
Mildura 3500   (050) 23 3060

MILDURA VINEYARD   NR
Campbell Avenue
Irymple 3498   (050) 24 5843

MURRAY VALLEY WINES   DC-C
15th Street
Mildura 3500   (050) 23 1500

ROBINVALE WINES   DC-C
Sea Lake Road
Robinvale 3549   (050) 26 3955

SALISBURY ESTATE   B-A
Nangiloc Road
Nangiloc 3494   (050) 29 1546

SUNNYCLIFF ESTATES   CB-BA
Nangiloc Road
Iraak 3496   (050) 291426

NORTH GOULBURN RIVER

MONICHINO   CB-BA
Berrys Road
Katunga 3640   (058) 64 6452
Established   1968
Winemaker   Carlo Monichino
Production   9000 cases
Principal Wines   Premium varietal releases comprise Rhine Riesling, Sauvignon Blanc, Semillon, Chardonnay, Spatlese Frontignac, Orange Muscat, Malbec, Cabernet Sauvignon, Vintage Muscat and Liqueur Raisin. Also a limited range of generic fortified wines sold in bottle, flagon and bulk containers.
Best Vintages   W and R 1980, '82, '84, '85, '86, '87, '88

A little known winery, which for many years has been a favourite of mine, partly because Carlo Monichino is one of the most pleasantly modest winemakers one is ever likely to meet, and partly because of the quite surprising quality of many of his wines. Quality comes from innovations such as a stainless steel field crushing unit which places the grapes under an immediate carbon dioxide blanket, with a further precaution that picking only takes place in the cool of the morning. The same care is then taken in the winery, and very fragrant, fruity wines are the result.

TISDALL   CB-BA
Cornelia Creek Road
Echuca 3564   (054) 82 1911
Established   1979
Winemaker   Jeff Clarke
Production   Around 50,000 cases of bottled wine; substantial bulk sales to other wineries.
Principal Wines   Chardonnay, Rhine Riesling, Chablis, Chenin Blanc, Fumé Blanc, Sauvignon Blanc, Semillon, Shiraz Cabernet, Cabernet Merlot and Cabernet Sauvignon under the standard Tisdall label. Selection Series and Hopwood Estate wines available at cellar door only. Premium label is Mount Helen, for which see separate entry in Central Goulburn section, page 103.

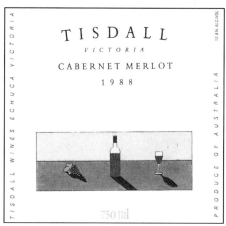

Best Vintages   W 1982, '84, '86, '89, '90
                     R 1980, '82, '84, '86, '88, '90.
Tisdall proves once again what many grape growers know: grapes grown under conditions of total irrigation can produce wines of good — at times very good — quality. There is probably an increasing awareness that this is so in relation to Chardonnay, but Tisdall Cabernet Merlot, year in and year out, shows what can be achieved with red wines. It has clean and fresh red berry/cherry fruit, often with quite surprising tannins, and can happily live for at least 5 years.

OTHER WINERIES

BROKEN RIVER WINES   NR
RMB 4881
Shepparton 3630 (058) 29 9293

HERITAGE FARM WINES   NR
RMB 1005, Murray Valley Highway
Cobram 3655 (058) 72 2376

PHILLIPS' GOULBURN VALLEY WINERY   C-C
52 Vaughan Street
Shepparton 3630 (058) 21 2051

ABOVE: Cabernet Sauvignon just completing veraison.

VICTORIA

NORTH-EASTERN VICTORIA

One of the first vignerons in the north-east was Lindsay Brown, who took up the Gooramadda run in 1839. Gold came later, but Brown was convinced there was greater (and surer) wealth in viticulture. Victoria's great wine historian and chronicler Hubert de Castella records that Brown 'was in the habit of settling miners' discussions as to the depth to which sinking of shafts should be carried. "To get gold", he would say, "you need sink only about 18 inches and plant vines".'

As in so much of Victoria, gold and vines remained intertwined during the extraordinary boom days of 1860 to 1893 — with Ned Kelly and the River Murray providing local colour — each in a different way facilitating the flow of wealth. The bank crash of 1893 and the onset of phylloxera then struck hard at what had become Victoria's most important wine producing region, but it had the resilience to survive.

Right from the outset it was obvious the shimmering heat of the summer days, not to mention the acid-retention counterbalance of the cold nights, were ideally suited to the production of full bodied red wines and even more to fortified wines. For reasons which are lost in the mists of time the emphasis fell on Muscat and Tokay, but the significance of the heavy red table-wine market which the region developed in the United Kingdom cannot be overemphasised.

It was this market which led to the establishment of the three great vineyards and wineries of the region: Mount Ophir (280 hectares), Fairfield (250 hectares) and Graham's (also 250 hectares). These produced massive quantities of both heavy table and fortified wine, most of which was exported in barrel to the United Kingdom. They survived the Second World War, sustained by the local market, and re-established their export franchise at its conclusion, but the shift away from fortified wine (and heavy table wine) led to their demise in the second half of the 1950s.

Almost all the smaller wineries and vineyards which replanted after the onslaught of phylloxera survived, even if some changed names and/or owners. Largely for this reason

AUSTRALASIAN WINE REGIONS
1980 – 1990

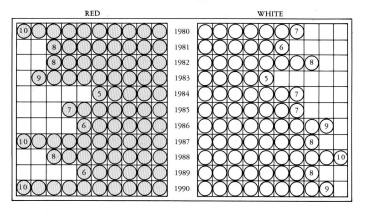

THE REGION IN BRIEF

LOCATION AND ELEVATION
36°01'S 140°19'E
160–770 m

SUBREGIONS
King Valley, Ovens Valley, Rutherglen, Wahgunyah, Milawa, Barnawatha, Glenrowan, Buckland River Valley and King Valley.

CLIMATE
It hardly needs saying that the climate varies dramatically across the region. Even the plains have a significant altitude, with the nights made colder still by the air draining off the nearby mountains. Small wonder that spring frosts are a continuing hazard, or that they can destroy an entire vintage (witness 1968). It is no doubt also the reason why Rutherglen has a heat summation (HDD) of 1770, and although this is not far removed from Bendigo (1708) and the Clare Valley (1773), in reality the climates are simply not comparable. The rainfall at Rutherglen is 585 mm, with a bias towards winter and spring. As one goes up the King Valley towards Whitlands, the temperature summation drops and the rainfall increases, finally reaching 1250 mm.

SOIL
The soils are remarkably diverse, falling into three main groups in the traditional (lowland) areas. First are the hard red duplex soils (Dr2.22, 2.23 and 2.33). Next are the gritty, gravelly quartzose sands, grey-brown in colour, which are extremely free draining (Vc1.21 and 1.22). The third group are the sandy, mottled yellow duplex soils (Dy5.41 and 5.42) which have clay subsoils. The soils at Whitlands form yet another group, deep red well-drained clay of volcanic origin, which is extremely fertile, over a basalt base.

HARVEST TIME
Vintage is an unusually prolonged affair, one which makes vintage charts more than ordinarily useless: for the table wine vintage is one thing, the fortified wine vintage another. Thanks to the cold nights, vintage starts far later than the heat summation might suggest, with the early ripening varieties picked at the end of February or early March. When the last of the Muscadelle and Tokay will be picked depends upon the state of the vines and the prospects for sugar accumulation, with late season rain a major factor. Usually, however, this will be between 21 April and 10 May.

PRINCIPAL GRAPE VARIETIES
Chardonnay, 83 ha	*Shiraz, 128 ha*
Rhine Riesling, 77 ha	*Cabernet Sauvignon, 104 ha*
Muscadelle, 39 ha	*Pinot Noir, 41 ha*
Muscat à Petits Grains, 31 ha	*TOTAL RED, 434 ha*
Gewürztraminer, 24 ha	
Sauvignon Blanc, 23 ha	
Chenin Blanc, 21 ha	
Semillon, 20 ha	
TOTAL WHITE, 369 ha	

FACING PAGE: All Saints Vineyard: the Murray River provides essential water for irrigation, occasionally to excess.

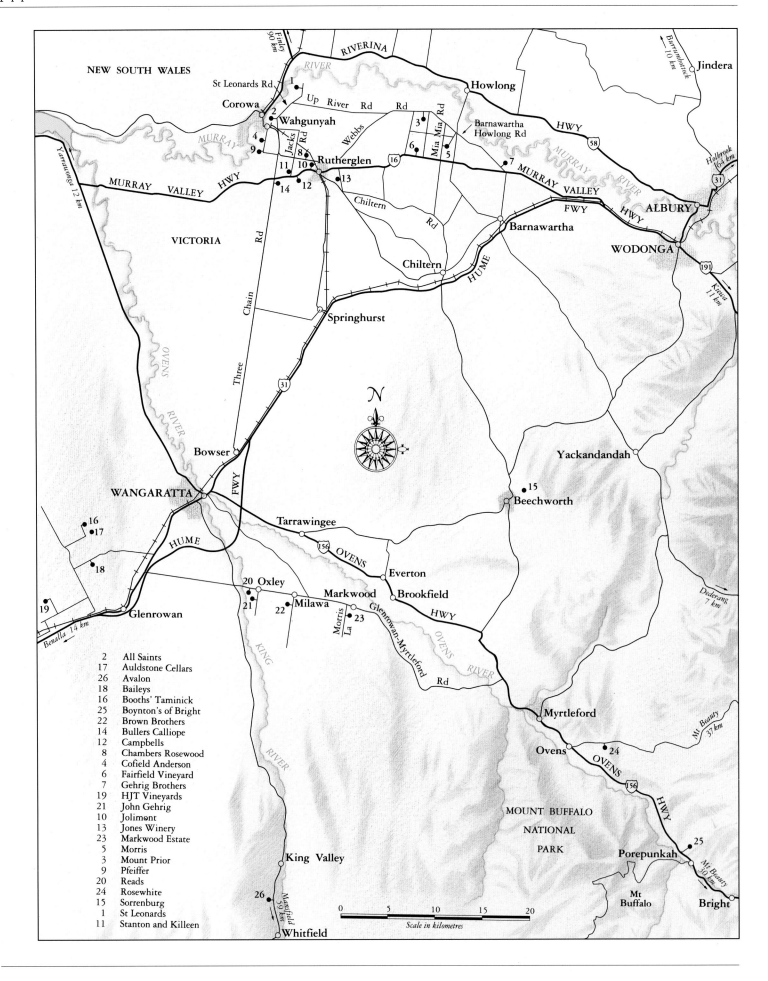

NEW SOUTH WALES

Jindera

RIVERINA

RIVER

Finley 90 km

Barrumbidgee 10 km

St Leonards Rd

Corowa

Howlong

HWY

58

Holbrook 64 km

Up River Rd Rd

Webbs Rd

Wahgunyah

Mia Mia Rd

Barnawartha Howlong Rd

MURRAY

31

Jacks Rd

Rutherglen

16

MURRAY RIVER

ALBURY

MURRAY VALLEY HWY

Yarrawonga 12 km

Chiltern Rd

VICTORIA

Rd

MURRAY VALLEY FWY

Barnawartha

WODONGA

191

HUME

Chiltern

Kiewa 11 km

OVENS RIVER

Springhurst

Chain Rd

Three Rd

N

31

Yackandandah

Bowser

Beechworth

Dederang 7 km

FWY

WANGARATTA

Tarrawingee

HUME

OVENS

156

Everton

Ovens River Rd

Glenrowan

Benalla 14 km

Oxley

Markwood

Brookfield

Mt Beauty 37 km

Milawa

Morris La

Glenrowan-Myrtleford Rd

HWY

KING RIVER

OVENS RIVER

Myrtleford

Ovens

OVENS HWY

156

MOUNT BUFFALO

NATIONAL

Porepunkah

Mt Beauty 30 km

King Valley

PARK

Mt Buffalo

Bright

Mansfield 59 km

Whitfield

2	All Saints
17	Auldstone Cellars
26	Avalon
18	Baileys
16	Booths' Taminick
25	Boynton's of Bright
22	Brown Brothers
14	Bullers Calliope
12	Campbells
8	Chambers Rosewood
4	Cofield Anderson
6	Fairfield Vineyard
7	Gehrig Brothers
19	HJT Vineyards
21	John Gehrig
10	Jolimont
13	Jones Winery
23	Markwood Estate
5	Morris
3	Mount Prior
9	Pfeiffer
20	Reads
24	Rosewhite
15	Sorrenburg
1	St Leonards
11	Stanton and Killeen

0 5 10 15 20

Scale in kilometres

the north-east is richly endowed with wineries and buildings which are as full of character (and history) as the people who inhabit them. Mercifully, the twentieth century has done little to destroy the inheritance of the nineteenth century, and the North-east stands proud among Australia's most interesting wine regions.

The character of the wineries comes both from the richness of the architecture, whether it be the main street of Rutherglen or the magnificence of the Victorian mansions of Fairfield and Mount Ophir, the humble galvanised iron of the working areas of wineries such as Chambers Rosewood and Morris, or the striking (and bizarre) castellated red brick walls of the pseudo Scottish castle of All Saints Estate.

It also comes through the equally startling diversity of wine styles: as a purist I look uneasily at the production of dry white table wine in an area such as this (notwithstanding the undoubted skills of St Leonards and others, and even acknowledging the supreme cleverness of Brown Brothers in moving to the foothills of the Alps) but wearing my other

hat of a vigneron trying to make a modest living from making and selling wine I have every sympathy.

My eulogy for the great Muscats and Tokays of the region follows, so I need say no more here. But if you have a choice of visiting only two of the regions covered in this book, North-east Victoria should surely be one of them.

PER CAPITA CONSUMPTION (LITRES) AND MARKET SHARE OF TABLE WINE BY CONTAINER TYPE

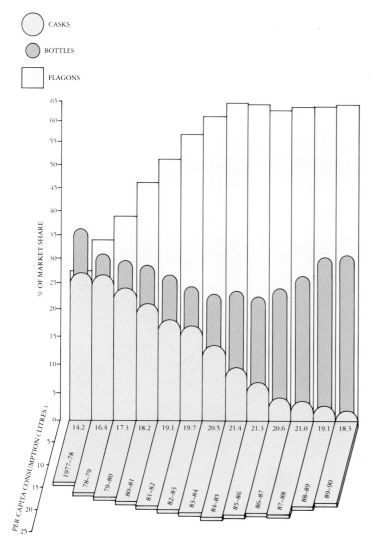

CASKS

BOTTLES

FLAGONS

PRINCIPAL WINE STYLES

MUSCAT AND TOKAY
These two sublime (and unique) wines are discussed at length in a moment, so I will say no more now — except for one thing: if you have anything more than a passing interest in wine, and you have never tasted either, please buy a bottle of each today. Remember that the wine will live for many weeks (months, even) after you have opened it: each glass, each night, will bring a new perspective, and at the smallest imaginable cost given the extraordinary quality of the wines.

WHITE TABLE WINES
In no small measure due to the influence of Brown Brothers (supported by Jolimont, St Leonards, Baileys and Campbells to name but a few) there is a kaleidoscopic range to choose from. Brown Brothers in particular has dramatically extended the canvas by converting the Italian-extraction tobacco growers of the King Valley (along with several distinguished Anglo-Saxon pastoralists) to grape growing. It is Brown Brothers, too, which has taken this move to its ultimate logical conclusion with its pioneering development of its Whitlands vineyard. At an altitude of 770 m, it has a climate as cool as any in Victoria, even if (as in this case) the altitude does produce a different type of cool climate to more maritime (and southerly) regions. So one has a matrix of great complexity: on the one hand vineyards with climates ranging from hot to cool, and on the other hand a Noah's Ark of white grape varieties ranging from the common to such exotics as Orange Muscat, Flora, Sylvaner, Emerald Riesling and Fetayaska. Suffice it to say that quality (and style) is principally dependent on the maker, and to a lesser degree on (or in) the eye of the beholder.

RED TABLE WINE
Brown Brothers' experiments with high altitude Pinot Noir may yet bear fruit, but for the time being it is Shiraz, Cabernet Sauvignon and a little Merlot which have provided the principal wines of note. One honourable exception is Morris' Durif (a monumental if not lethal wine based on a Rhône Valley hybrid bred by Dr Durif in the 1880s) and another is Mondeuse, used by Brown Brothers and Bullers Calliope in intriguing blends of Shiraz and Cabernet Shiraz. But whatever the variety, the climate of the lowlands (inhabited by all except Brown Brothers) demands that the winemaker does not attempt to scale down the wines to accord with effete contemporary tastes, but lets them run riot. The red wines of Baileys or Campbells Shiraz are prime examples — wines to be matched with the thickest, rarest charcoal-grilled rump steak on the coldest winter night.

MUSCAT AND TOKAY —
UNIQUELY AUSTRALIAN: UNIQUELY GREAT

Part of the magic of wine stems from the intensely personal — or subjective — response it elicits from all those who drink it. Whether raw novice or expert, each person will have his or her own likes or dislikes, and experts are just as likely to differ from their peers as are novices. For liking (or disliking) a wine by no means necessarily involves a quality judgment. We can quite cheerfully admit we like a particular wine while recognising a technical flaw or fault in its makeup. Conversely, we can recognise a high quality wine for what it is without particularly liking it, or ever being tempted to buy it.

What is true of dry table wines is even more true of less widely known styles — notably sweet table wines and, above all else, fortified wines. So it is truly remarkable that virtually every observer I have ever spoken to or read pays unstinting homage to the Muscats and Tokays of North-east Victoria.

What is more, the recognition proceeds along three fronts. These are wines of superb quality; they are of a unique style among the great fortified wines of the world; and they are enormously — indeed dangerously — enjoyable. (As to the last character-istic, they are often unfairly blamed for the hangover following a first class dinner party, simply because they are the last wines to be consumed, and the first bottles which greet your eyes as you stagger in to survey the wreckage the following morning. It makes just as much sense to blame the champagne with which you started proceedings, or any of the intervening wines.)

The two wines are made in identical fashion: the difference between them derives from the different grapes. Muscat is made from the brown clone (or type) of Muscat à Petits Grains, more commonly known as Brown Muscat or Brown Frontignac. Tokay is made from Muscadelle, and for this reason has an even greater claim to being unique than has Muscat, for nowhere else in the world is Muscadelle put to this use. (Its best known role is as a minor component in French Sauternes.)

The grapes are allowed to hang on the vine long after normal maturity, gradually concentrating their sugar (and acid) as they commence to shrivel and raisin. Although

botrytis plays no role (or at least should play no role), the process is no less finely balanced and no less unpredictable than that of botrytised dessert wines.

If all goes well, the baume levels will increase to 16 or 17 degrees in good years, 20 degrees or above in great vintages. In the lesser years, the grapes start to collapse and become mushy, quickly turning rotten with grey or black mould if they are not picked. In these circumstances the baume will not have risen much above 14 degrees.

The grapes are crushed (an extreme-ly difficult process when the baume is above 17 degrees), and then some makers allow fermentation to start, but stop it very quickly by the addition of fortifying spirit, giving a typical final analysis of 17 to 18 degrees alcohol and residual (or unfermented) grape sugar of 9 to 14 degrees baume. Other makers simply fortify the unfermented grape juice with spirit before fermentation com-mences, with a similar analysis.

The wine is then placed in small oak barrels (old oak is preferred; the flavour of new oak is entirely inappro-priate in such wines) to begin what is a gradual but quite miraculous transformation. Young Tokay is a pale gold colour; young Muscat light reddish brown, with an almost pink tinge. The aroma of both is intensely grapey, with the spirit providing a distinct cut to that grapiness. The Tokay will already have its distinct varietal aroma, variously described as like cold tea, malt extract or fish oil — I must confess to understanding the first two descriptions much better than the latter.

Over the next 10 to 20 years the colour turns dark brown, with a tell-tale olive green rim. The Muscat retains some of the red embers of its youth; the Tokay (often but not always a little lighter in depth) tends more to burnt sienna. The transformation in the bouquet and palate is no less dramatic. The bouquet acquires complexities which have no parallel in table wines: if ever it is possible to sense texture without touching it, it is with these wines. There is an almost indescribable complexity in the combination of fruit, alcohol, the gentle oxidation caused by the prolonged storage in barrels and (very importantly) the concentration caused by

ABOVE: *One-hundred-year-old Muscat essence: as thick as treacle.*

evaporation through the oak — the so-called 'angel's share'.

The concentration becomes steadily more apparent with age: when very young the consistency of the wine is only a little thicker than that of table wine. A great old Muscat or Tokay pours in an oily stream, in which the viscosity is readily apparent, and which coats the side of the glass as you swirl it. Chambers and Morris both have tiny quantities of wine from the last century which is — literally — the consistency of treacle.

This effect is not, however, to be confused with the all-important development of rancio, a Spanish term used to describe the cumulative effect of prolonged barrel aging on all the constituents of the wine. Rancio is a character which is exceedingly difficult to describe, but once recognised, never forgotten. It derives partly from aldehydes and partly from volatile acidity, and gives the fortified wine the cleansing cut which prevents it from cloying. It develops only in cask: once a Muscat or Tokay has been bottled it ceases to develop — nor, interestingly, will that development recommence once the bottle has been opened. Neither will the wine deteriorate when opened, although leaving quarter-full bottles around for 6 months is not recommended.

In my *Australian Wine Compendium* (Angus & Robertson, 1985) I wrote 'Like Narcissus drowning in his reflection, one can lose oneself in the aroma of a great old Muscat. All this, and one has not yet felt the necessity of actually tasting the wine. That moment destroys the calm which preceded it: an old muscat has an explosive intensity of luscious flavour, combined with high acid and a twist of wood-derived volatility, which strips the saliva from the sides of the taster's mouth, leaving the flavour in undiminished magnificence for minutes after the last millilitre has been swallowed.' I do not think I can improve on that.

There should be no question of preferring Muscat to Tokay or vice versa. The choice should come down to a question of mood, one night favouring one, the next night the other. Muscat tends to be richer and sweeter (in fruit, rather than unfermented sugar), Tokay more elegant and less fleshy. You can taste the raisined grapes in even the oldest Muscat; Tokay seems more remote.

In much the same way, the choice between makers is a question of style more than quality. Baileys' are the richest and most voluptuous; Morris' the most complex and classic; Chambers' the most elegant, intense and perfectly balanced; while the All Saints Lyrebird range can claim affinities with all three styles. Campbells and Stanton and Killeen make younger, fresher, more grapey styles which are a great alternative if you are looking for something lighter.

While these wines are seen as after-dinner drinks, I personally drink much of my Muscat and Tokay as an aperitif, particularly during winter. A small glass goes a very long way, warming the mind as well as the stomach.

ABOVE: Muscat skins left after fermentation.

WINERIES OF NORTH-EAST VICTORIA

ALL SAINTS ESTATE   CA-CA
All Saints Road
Wahgunyah 3687   (060) 33 1922
Established   1864
Winemakers   Andrew Sutherland Smith,
Max Cofield
Production   50,000 cases
Principal Wines   The wines of All Saints

Estate have recently received a major facelift and new labels, starting at the bottom with the Elm Tree Drive range followed by Swan Crest, and finally the Premium Lyrebird range. Table wines include Marsanne, Chardonnay Semillon, Chardonnay, Rhine Riesling, Chenin Blanc, Shiraz, Cabernet Shiraz, Cabernet Merlot and Hermitage. Fortified wines include Tawny Port, Liqueur Muscat and Liquer Tokay.
Best Vintages   **W** and **R** 1988, '89 (truncated owing to recent change of ownership) Ex-marketing director of Wolf Blass wines, Mike Fallon, headed a syndicate which acquired control of All Saints in 1988 and is proceeding to restore the battered reputation of this historic and imposing castellated hundred-year-old red brick winery. The Lyrebird Muscat and Tokay are superb, arguably representing the best value for money in this style at the present time. Mike Fallons untimely death in mid-1990 may well precipitate another change in ownership.

BAILEYS   A-A
Cnr Taminick Gap Road
and Upper Taminick Road
Glenrowan 3675   (057) 66 2392
Established   1870
Winemaker   Steve Goodwin
Production   30,000 cases

Principal Wines   One of the greatest fortified wine producers in North-east Victoria, also producing a range of table wines including Chablis, Chardonnay, Colombard, Rhine Riesling, Auslese Aucerot, Auslese Rhine Riesling, Classic Hermitage, Winemakers Selection Hermitage, Cabernet Sauvignon and Cabernet Sauvignon Hermitage. Great fortified Muscat and Tokay released under three labels: Warby Range, Founder and Winemakers Selection (the last formerly HJT).
Best Vintages   **R** 1983, '85, '88, '89
Producer of the richest and most treacly of all of the North-east Victorian fortified wines; whether one prefers the more complex wines of Morris or the more elegant wines of Chambers Rosewood is purely a matter of style preference. These are the three great names, which is not to denigrate the others in the district. The table wines are more than adequate; best are the Shiraz-based reds which have undergone a number of style changes over the past 20 years, but which are never less than monumental in weight. As with Morris and Chambers, the rating is given for the fortified wines.

BROWN BROTHERS   B-BA
Off main Glenrowan-
Myrtleford Road,
Milawa 3678   (057) 27 3400
Established   1889
Winemaker   John G Brown
Production   Over 200,000 cases of premium bottled wine, plus substantial bulk wine for sale to others.
Principal Wines   An extremely wide range of varietal table wines, released in several series. First, there is the traditional Milawa range (comprising 6 different white and red varietals and 2 red blends); then follows the Limited Production series (13 or 14 different varietals);

then come the King Valley wines including Koombahla, Meadow Creek and Whitlands; the Family Reserve wines, being the best Riesling, Chardonnay and Cabernet or Cabernet blend of each vintage; and finally the Classic Vintage releases, principally of red wines, but also including Noble Riesling, released after 5 years or more, and the red wines often after 10 or more years.
Best Vintages   **W** 1970, 72, '76, '78, '80, '82, '86, '87, '90
R 1966, '70, '78, '79, '82, '84, '85, '86, '88, '90
Every member of the prolific Brown family is a thorough gentleman or gentlewoman. With their gentle, easy smiles and soft, slow voices, they run a winery in outback Australia in much the same way they have for the past 100 years. Where illusion stops and reality starts is hard to pinpoint, but the financial and marketing brilliance of the family is truly breathtaking. From a tiny operation in the early 1960s, Brown Brother's products not only span Australia, but the world.

BULLERS CALLIOPE   CB-BA
Three Chain Road
Rutherglen 3685   (060) 32 9660
Established   1921
Winemakers   The Buller Family;
Richard senior and Andrew.
Production   2000 cases
Principal Wines   Principally red table and fortified wines from the Calliope vineyard at Rutherglen (cheaper generic table wines, white varietal table wines and Cabernet Sauvignon come from Beverford Vineyard on the Murray River). Vineyard specialty is Calliope Vintage Port; also very good Liqueur Muscat and Liqueur Frontignac in a somewhat lighter style than those of Bailey and Morris.
Best Vintages   Not relevant.
This is a low-key, no-frills operation which has always specialised in fortified wines, and which markets these at yesterday's prices.

CAMPBELLS   B-B
Murray Valley Highway
Rutherglen 3685   (060) 32 9458
Established   1870
Winemaker   Colin Campbell
Production   35,000 cases
Principal Wines   Table wines comprise Rhine Riesling, Chardonnay, Bobbie Burns Shiraz, Rutherglen Shiraz, Malbec and Durif; fortified wines comprise Vintage Port, Old Rutherglen Port, Old Rutherglen Tokay, Old Rutherglen Muscat and Merchant Prince Muscat.
Best Vintages   **W** and **R** 1980, '86, '88, '89

One of the more progressive wineries of the region, apt to produce surprisingly good Rhine Riesling and Chablis, a marvellously rich and imposing Shiraz, and fortified wines which deliberately offer an alternative to the rich style exemplified by Baileys. The fortified wines of Cambells are fresher, more lively and grapey, and made to be drunk by the mouthful rather than sipped.

CHAMBERS ROSEWOOD A-A

Off Corowa-Rutherglen Road
Rutherglen 3685 (060) 32 9641
Established 1864
Winemaker Bill Chambers
Production 10,000 cases plus bulk wine.
Principal Wines An unusual array of table wines and some great fortified wines. Table wines include Rhine Riesling, Moselle-style Trebbiano, Riesling Gouais, Spatlese Rhine Riesling, Cabernet Shiraz, Cabernet/Blue Imperial/Alicante Bouchet and Lakeside Cabernet Sauvignon. Fortified wines include a range of old sherries including ports, and excellent Flor Fino and an even better Amontillado; Liqueur Muscat and Liqueur Tokay, Special Liqueur Muscat; and intermittent releases of very old Tokay and Muscat of the highest possible quality.
Best Vintages Not relevant.
The table wines of Chambers Rosewood are very cheap, but not terribly good. The fortified wines (at the top end) are expensive, but worth every cent. They are, in a word, quite magnificent, and if I had to choose between the big three fortified winemakers (Baileys and Morris being the other two), my choice would always be on Chambers' top Tokay and Muscat.

GEHRIG BROTHERS C-CB

Cnr Murray Valley Highway and
Howllong Road
Barnawartha 3688 (060) 26 7296
Established 1858
Winemaker Brian Gehrig
Production 5000 cases
Principal Wines Chenin Blanc, Rhine Riesling, Sauternes, Pinot Noir, Shiraz, Cabernet Sauvignon; also a range of 7 different ports, 5 sherries and Brown Muscat.
Best Vintages W 1983, '86, '88, '89
R 1986, '88
A winery which remained firmly locked in the nineteenth century until a few years ago, but which is slowly being modernised and producing better wines as each year passes. The Tawny and Vintage Ports are the pick.

HJT VINEYARDS BA-BA

Keenan Road
Glenrowan 3675 (057) 66 2252
Established 1979
Winemakers Harry and Catherine Tinson.

Production 1000 cases
Principal Wines Rhine Riesling, Chardonnay, Pinot Noir and Cabernet Sauvignon.
Best Vintages W 1984, '86, '87, '90
R 1985, '86, '87, '90.

Harry Tinson ensured a lifetime reputation when in 1972 he, quite accidentally, became winemaker at Baileys. After many happy years he and winemaker wife Cath retired to do their own thing and startled the Australian wine world by producing a 1984 Chardonnay which still ranks as one of the greatest made in Australia, a wine of exceptional complexity and uncannily Burgundian style.

JOHN GEHRIG C-B

On Oxley to Milawa Road
Oxley 3678 (057) 27 3395
Established 1976
Winemaker John Gehrig
Production 10,000 cases
Principal Wines Rhine Riesling, Rhine Riesling-Kabinett, Chenin Blanc, Chardonnay, *Méthode Champenoise*, Brut Reserve Blanc de Noir, Pinot Noir, Merlot, Cabernet-Merlot, Vintage Port and Tawny Port.

Best Vintages W 1982, '84, '87, '88
R 1982, '84, '85, '87, '88
John Gehrig for many years sold grapes to Brown Brothers and learnt his winemaking as a cellar hand there. His wines often display unexpected elegance; even Pinot Noir succeeds in a warm-climate fashion, but the Cabernet-Merlot and Merlot releases are the most reliable, with the odd surprising Chardonnay.

JOLIMONT B-B

Cnr Murray Valley Highway
and Corowa Road
Rutherglen 3685 (060) 32 9922
Established 1986
Winemaker Steven Warne
Production 9000 cases
Principal Wines Wines produced principally from Rutherglen grown fruit, comprising table wines, *Méthode Champenoise* and traditional Rutherglen fortified styles. Rougenfant, a soft,

early drinking, dry red style is produced from Cabernet Sauvignon grown at Cowl Cowl Station on the Lachlan River near Hillston in Central New South Wales.

Best Vintages   W 1986, '89, '90
                R 1987, '88, '89, '90

Jolimont has had a peripatetic life, with its base moving around but finally establishing itself in the historic former Seppelt winery at Rutherglen in 1986 (which is treated as its year of establishment). Former Great Western winemaker Howard Anderson made an innovative and challenging array of wines which I invariably enjoyed. His departure and the closure of the superb restaurant in 1990, came as a blow to regular visitors to the region.

MORRIS   A-A
Mia Mia Vineyard
Rutherglen 3685   (060) 26 7303
Established   1859
Winemaker   Mick Morris
Production   55,000 cases
Principal Wines   In addition to producing some of North-east Victoria's greatest fortified wines (principally Muscat and Tokay), Morris also offers a full range of cask wines and premium varietal table wines including Rhine Riesling, Sauvignon Blanc, Chardonnay, Durif, Cabernet Sauvignon, Pinot Noir, Shiraz and Blue Imperial. The full range of fortified wines is headed by Liqueur Muscat and Liqueur Tokay, and at the top of the range are Old Premium Liqueur Muscat and Old Premium Liqueur Tokay. The rating is given for Baileys' fortified wines.
Best Vintages   Irrelevant
The Orlando ownership manifests itself in the table wines, which are invariably well made and generously flavoured, the massive Durif almost overwhelmingly so. But the great wines are the Tokay and Muscat; many devotees of this style would place Morris first.

PFEIFFER   CB-B
Distillery Road
Wahgunyah 3687   (060) 33 2805)
Established   1980
Winemaker   Chris Pfeiffer
Production   6000 cases

Principal Wines   Rhine Riesling, Chardonnay, Spatlese Frontignac, Auslese Tokay, Shiraz Cabernet, Pinot Noir, Gamay and Cabernet Sauvignon; Liqueur Muscat and Liqueur Tokay, Tawny Port, Vintage Port.
Best Vintages   W and R 1987, '88
Chris Pfeiffer was for many years fortified winemaker at Lindemans' Corowa winery before its closure. He now makes wine in the historic Seppelt Masterton winery, which is suited to fortified winemaking but not altogether to table wine, and this has obviously posed difficulties in the establishment period. Recent vintages have seen a sharp improvement in table wine quality, while the fortified wines are, as one would expect, reliably good.

ST LEONARDS   BA-BA
Wahgunyah 3687   (060) 33 1004
Established   1975
Winemakers   Roland Kaval, Eddie Price
Production   12,000 cases
Principal Wines   Chardonnay, Semillon, Gewurztraminer, Orange Muscat, Chenin Blanc, Sauvignon Blanc, Shiraz, Cabernet Sauvignon, Cabernet Franc/Merlot and Malbec.
Best Vintages   W 1980, '82, '84, '87, '88, '90
                R 1982, '83, '86, '87, '88, '90

A winery which has always challenged preconceptions and generalisations; it produces a few unremarkable fortified wines, and a great number of very good table wines, with the white varieties (headed by Chardonnay) performing even better than the reds. Flavours are full, mouth-filling and precise to the variety of the grape, and the wines all seem to blossom with 3 to 5 years bottle age. A beautifully situated winery and excellent tasting facilities make it one of the compulsory stops on the north-east tourist trail.

STANTON AND KILLEEN   B-B
Murray Valley Highway
Rutherglen 3685   (060) 32 9457
Established   1925
Winemaker   Chris Killeen

Production   10,000 cases
Principal Wines   Red table and fortified wine specialist; top-quality table wines released under the Moodemere label, including Cabernet Shiraz and Durif; fortified wines include Special Old Liqueur Muscat, Liqueur Muscat, Liqueur Tokay, Vintage Port, Liqueur Port and Old Tawny Port. A range of cheaper sherries is also produced.
Best Vintages   R 1972, '75, '76, '80, '83, '86, '87, '90
Probably one of the most predictable of the wineries of the north-east, producing appropriately full bodied and robust red wines, vintage ports which can be quite delicious at 10 to 15 years of age, and a (relatively) light bodied and fresh Muscat which does nothing to harm the reputation of the district.

OTHER WINERIES

AVALON   CB-CB
RMB 9556
Whitfield Road
Wangaratta 3678 (057) 29 3629

BOOTHS' TAMINICK   C-B
Taminick via Glenrowan 3675 (057) 66 2282

BOYNTON'S OF BRIGHT   NR
Ovens Valley Highway
Bright 3747

COFIELD ANDERSON   CB-B
Distillery Road
Wahgunyah 3687 (060) 333798

FAIRFIELD VINEYARD   NR
Murray Valley Highway
Browns Plains via Rutherglen 3685
(060) 32 9381

JONES WINERY   C-C
Chiltern Road
Rutherglen 3685 (060) 32 9496

MARKWOOD ESTATE   NR
Morris Lane
Markwood via Milawa 3678
(057) 27 0361

MOUNT PRIOR   NR
Cnr River Road and Popes Lane
Rutherglen 3685 (060) 26 5591

READS   C-CB
Pound Road
Oxley 3678 (057) 27 3386

ROSEWHITE   CB-B
Happy Valley Road
Happy Valley (057) 52 1077

FACING PAGE: Muscat and Morris: a marriage made in heaven.

PYRENEES

If ever a region belied its name, it is the Pyrenees: anyone who has driven up and down the twisting mountain roads of that wonderfully scenic area which runs along the boundary between Spain and France, and who has then traversed the gentle rolling hills around the towns of Redbank, Moonambel and Avoca, will know what I mean.

It is a quiet region, off the main highways and — like Coonawarra in South Australia — on the way to nowhere. Both its prior and present winemaking history has been similarly undramatic, even if the slings and arrows of outrageous fortune have hit their mark here as elsewhere.

The first vines were planted by the Mackereth family in 1848; the winery came to be quite substantial, ultimately passing into the control of two brothers, one a bank manager by training, the other an art and music teacher. Towards the end of the First World War negotiations began for the sale of the winery to Seppelt, but fell through apparently because Seppelt felt one of the brothers intended to continue winemaking in opposition to it. The winery was ultimately sold to a Methodist Minister in 1929, who promptly closed the winery, destroyed the cellars and pulled out the last 20 hectares of vines.

Winemaking continued at Moonambel until 1945 through Kofoed's Mountain Creek winery, but a hiatus followed until the establishment in 1963 of the Chateau Remy vineyards. Then began a decidedly curious phase in the history of the

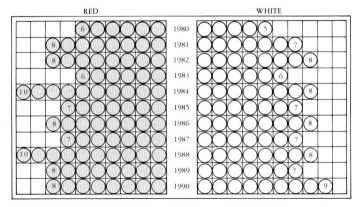

AUSTRALASIAN WINE REGIONS
1980 – 1990

	RED								WHITE						
			6				1980					5			
	8						1981						7		
	8						1982							8	
			6				1983					6			
10							1984							8	
	7						1985						7		
	8						1986							8	
	7						1987						7		
10							1988							8	
	8						1989						7		
	8						1990								9

THE REGION IN BRIEF

LOCATION AND ELEVATION
37°05'S 143°29'E
220–375 m

SUBREGIONS
Redbank and Moonambel.

CLIMATE
Due principally to the inland location of the Pyrenees (and to a lesser degree, to its elevation) the temperature range from day to night is substantial. One instinctively distrusts its lower heat degree summation (1530 HDD) when compared to, for example , Barker (1620 HDD): the Pyrenees is inherently warmer than Mount Barker despite the figures. Higher midday peaks (with lower early morning and late afternoon temperatures) must be part of the reason, and the MJT of 20.9°C may be a better indication. The rainfall of 544 mm is strongly winter-spring dominant, and yields in vineyards without irrigation are low.

SOIL
The grey-brown sandy loam soils which predominate fall into the hard mottled yellow duplex groups (Dy3.41 and 3.42), although the brown loamy sand soils in the hard red duplex category (Dr2.21 and 2.22) are also quite common. Both soil groups are improved by the addition of gypsum, and tend to be acidic, needing amelioration by lime.

HARVEST TIME
Grapes destined for sparkling wine production are picked from late February onwards, with the table wine season commencing early March and concluding 5 to 6 weeks thereafter.

PRINCIPAL GRAPE VARIETIES
Sauvignon Blanc   *Cabernet Sauvignon*
Semillon   *Shiraz*
Rhine Riesling   *Merlot*
Chardonnay
Trebbiano

ABOVE: Underground cellars at Taltarni.

FACING PAGE: Warrenmang: remote, unspoilt beauty.

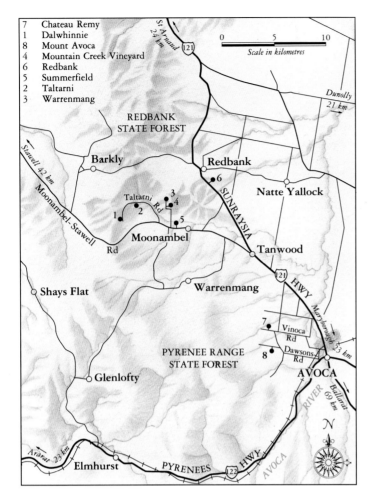

7	Chateau Remy
1	Dalwhinnie
8	Mount Avoca
4	Mountain Creek Vineyard
6	Redbank
5	Summerfield
2	Taltarni
3	Warrenmang

region. The area was selected by Remy as suitable for the production of quality brandy, and the vineyard was planted accordingly, with Trebbiano the principal variety. The best laid plans notwithstanding, the brandy market collapsed, so production switched to another type of wine the Remy Martin group knew about — sparkling wine.

It is hardly surprising that even Remy Martin's expertise (it controls Krug) was unable to make a silk purse out of a sow's ear — unable to produce high quality sparkling wine from brandy grapes grown in what is first and foremost a red wine area. Reworking of the vineyard, grafting and replanting with Chardonnay and Pinot Noir has helped, but I still find the wines rather heavy and clumsy, no doubt partially reflecting the unsuitable climate.

It was not until 1970 that the other wineries arrived: there was a frantic burst of activity as first Mount Avoca and Summerfield, then Taltarni, Redbank, Warrenmang and finally Dalwhinnie were established over the ensuing 6 years. Since that time there has not been a single arrival, a pattern unique to this area.

As with the other Central Victoria regions, it is first and foremost a red wine district, producing full blooded and richly textured styles. Only Mount Avoca and Taltarni have produced white wines of any consequence, and these have been largely limited to Sauvignon Blanc.

PRINCIPAL WINE STYLES

CABERNET SAUVIGNON
The most widely propagated variety, which produces a wine which is never less than substantial and is at times of awesome proportions, notably when made by Dominique Portet at Taltarni. Here the most striking feature is often the massive tannins evident in the young wines, which are quite clearly made with the future — indeed the long term future — in mind. At Redbank Neil Robb crafts an entirely different style — far softer and fleshier — with the recurrent aroma and flavour of eucalypt mint which is so much the hallmark of Central Victoria. Somewhere in between fall the Cabernets of the other producers, with a dash of blackcurrant the unifying feature.

SHIRAZ
Once again Shiraz demonstrates just how suited it is to the climate and terroir of Central Victoria. From the at times exuberant pepper and spice of the best Summerfield vintages, the flavour (and texture) progressively moves to the more urbane rounded flavours of Mount Avoca and Dalwhinnie, and at the far edge to the Taltarni-like power of Warrenmang.

MERLOT
This is not a major variety in terms of total plantings, but it does play a vital role in shaping (and slightly softening) Taltarni's Cabernet Sauvignon, which (both in terms of volume and prestige) is the most important wine made in the district.

SAUVIGNON BLANC
For reasons which I do not profess to understand, and which simply serve to underline the glorious unpredictability of wine, this variety usually does well, sometimes brilliantly so, in the Pyrenees. Wines such as the 1987 and 1989 Mount Avoca and the '84 '86 '87 and '89 vintages of Taltarni (with the '87 Mount Avoca quite outstanding) show exhilarating gooseberry/passionfruit flavours and a crisp, lingering finish.

SPARKLING WINES
Chateau Remy is, of course, the leader, but Summerfield and Taltarni both throw in their hand. I simply wish I could be more enthusiastic about any of these wines, but all I can say is that there are better examples made elsewhere in Victoria (and in other States too).

ABOVE: Winter pruning at Taltarni: a trellis system built to last.

WINERIES OF THE PYRENEES

CHATEAU REMY   CB-CB

Vinoca Road
Avoca 3467   (054) 65 3202
Established   1963
Winemaker   Vincent Gere
Production   Sparkling wine 30,000 cases; table wines 10,000 cases.
Principal Wines *Méthode Champenoise* under Chateau Remy labels, Cuvée Speciale, Royal Vintage and Rosé Premier; red wine under Blue Pyrenees Estate label; white wines Clos St Charles and 'S' Semillon.
Best Vintages   Basically irrelevant.

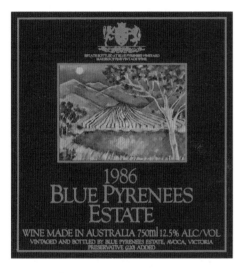

Owned by the Remy Martin group, Chateau Remy was originally established for the specific purpose of making Australian Brandy, but it has now converted to a table and sparkling wine operation. Expert packaging and marketing does not cover up the deficiencies in the wines themselves, although there is no question the sparkling wines are improving as the base changes from Trebbiano to Chardonnay and Pinot Noir.

DALWHINNIE   B-B

Taltarni Road
Moonambel 3478   (054) 67 2388
Established   1976
Winemaker   Rodney Morrish (contract)
Production   3000 cases
Principal Wines Chardonnay, Shiraz and Cabernet Merlot.
Best Vintages   W and R 1980, '82, '84, '86, '88, '90

Initially only a producer of strongly-flavoured and structured red wines, but now with a melon/peach barrel fermented Chardonnay, expertly made by Rodney Morrish, to fill out the range. It has a loyal clientele in Victoria, but deserves a wider audience.

MOUNT AVOCA   BA-BA

Moates Lane
Avoca 3467   (054) 65 3282
Established   1978
Winemakers   John Barry, Rodney Morrish
Production   10,000 cases
Principal Wines Cabernet Sauvignon, Shiraz, Trebbiano, Chardonnay, Semillon and Sauvignon Blanc.
Best Vintages   W 1987, '88, '89, '90
                    R 1980, '84, '85, '86, '89, '90
Smooth, gently minty, red berry flavoured Shiraz and Cabernet were the wines which founded the reputation of Mount Avoca, but in recent years the white wines have gained much attention, with a startlingly good Sauvignon Blanc, full of grassy/gooseberry tang, making its appearance in 1987.

REDBANK   BA-B

Sunraysia Highway
Redbank 3467   (054) 67 7255
Established   1973
Winemaker   Neill Robb
Production   4000 cases
Principal Wines Sally's Paddock is the principal estate-grown red wine followed by Redbank Cabernet. A number of other red wines are also made each year from grapes purchased in and around the Pyrenees region. A few years ago the first white wine (Alexandra Kingsley Chardonnay) made its appearance under the Redbank label.
Best Vintages   1981, '82, '83, '86, '88, '90
A very highly respected red wine producer, with Redbank Cabernet Sauvignon enjoying the distinction of being the highest priced red wine sold on mailing list allocation in Australia, but being eagerly snapped up for all that. Sally's Paddock is a red wine of rare balance and complexity with minty, dark berry flavours and finely judged oak. I do not like the Chardonnay.

SUMMERFIELD   BA-A

Moonambel-Stawell Road
Moonambel 3478   (054) 67 2264
Established   1980
Winemaker   Ian L Summerfield
Production   2400 cases
Principal Wines Champagne *Méthode Champenoise* (made from Trebbiano), Hermitage and Cabernet Sauvignon.
Best Vintages   R 1979, '80, '83, '84, '87, '88, '90
A small and relatively unknown producer which gained attention with two spectacularly-flavoured 1988 reds, both showing abundant American oak, but also more than sufficient fruit to carry that oak. Magnificent in cask, they suffered a little going to bottle.

TALTARNI   A-A

Taltarni Road
Moonambel 3478   (054) 67 2218
Established   1972
Winemakers   Dominique Portet, Greg Gallagher
Production   60,000 cases
Principal Wines Taltarni Cuvée Brut, Brut Tache and Royal and Blanc de Blanc (Chardonnay) (three *Méthode Champenoise* sparkling wines), Blanc Des Pyrenees (Chablis style), Fumé Blanc, Rhine Riesling, Rosé des Pyrenees, French Syrah (the Taltarni adopted name for Shiraz), Cabernet Sauvignon, Reserve Des Pyrenees (Cabernet Malbec blend), and Merlot (100 per cent).
Best Vintages   R 1979, '82, '84, '86, '88, '90

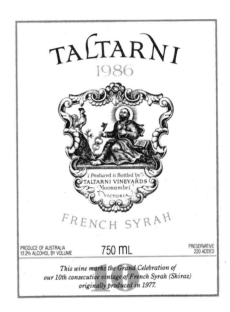

Dominique Portet is part of a distinguished international winemaking family: Chateau Lafite in Bordeaux, Clos du Val in California and Taltarni in Australia are or were in the care of various members of the family. The Bordeaux influence is strong, as are the red wines — at times mouth-rippingly so. In more recent years they have softened somewhat.

OTHER WINERIES

MOUNTAIN CREEK VINEYARD NR
Mountain Creek Road
Moonambel 3478 (054) 67 2230

WARRENMANG   C-C
Mountain Creek Road
Moonambel 3478 (054) 67 2233

SOUTHERN AND CENTRAL VICTORIA

It is pragmatism rather than logic which brings these districts (and their wineries) together. If there be a common bond it is their isolation — isolation both from large urban markets and from fellow producers. Perhaps, too, they serve to demonstrate that almost anywhere you look in Southern and Central Victoria, it is possible to grow high quality grapes.

The westernmost region is Drumborg, pioneered by Seppelt in 1964 as part of the company's drive to gain access to early-ripening premium grape varieties: in 1963 it had led the move into Padthaway (South Australia). Padthaway performed rather differently to initial expectations, but nowhere to the extent of Drumborg. The latter has a heat summation (HDD) of 1207, but a combination of wind, spring rain, summer drought, soil, grape varieties and inappropriate viticultural practices meant that for almost 20 years Seppelt failed to achieve adequate ripeness in most vintages.

Drumborg was literally under sentence of death, and was saved only by the exceptional quality of the few vintages which did succeed and by the stubbornness of the viticulturists who argued that it had to be possible to unlock the key. The second half of the 1980s has seen the tide turn, and barring a succession of disasters, Drumborg has been reprieved. It is producing some excellent base material for Seppelt's top sparkling wines (and the occasional vineyard release) and an outstanding Cabernet Sauvignon (not every year, but often enough to make it worthwhile).

Crawford River is the most successful of the handful of small wineries in the district, winemaker John Thomson having had remarkable success with three styles: dry white, dry red and — most surprisingly — botrytised Riesling.

Central Victoria is represented by Giaconda, Delatite, Flowerdale and Murrindindi. Once again, it is a strange grouping: technically, one can say that Giaconda, at Beechworth, is part of North-east Victoria, and that Delatite, at Mansfield, is part of the Goulburn Valley. The difficulty is that in terms of their respective physical locations and their wine styles they do not happily fit those classifications.

AUSTRALASIAN WINE REGIONS
1980 – 1990

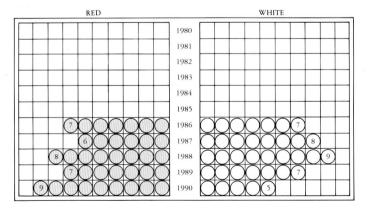

Delatite, spectacularly situated with snow clad alps rising high behind it, has a very cool climate which imposes its stamp on all of its wines: the white aromatic wines are very delicate, fragrant and crisp in a true European style, while the red wines rarely escape a vineyard stamp of eucalypt-mint, which transcends the variety and which I take to be associated with difficulties in achieving full ripeness. Exceptions such as the wonderful 1987 Delatite Devils River (a Cabernet family blend) tend to prove the rule.

Giaconda specialises in Pinot Noir and Chardonnay in a climate which is technically too warm for Pinot Noir, but Rick Kinzbrunner has never bowed — and never will bow — to conventional wisdom, having learnt much at the feet of Warren Winiarski of Stags Leap (in the Napa Valley). Giaconda is one of the trendiest small wineries in Australia,

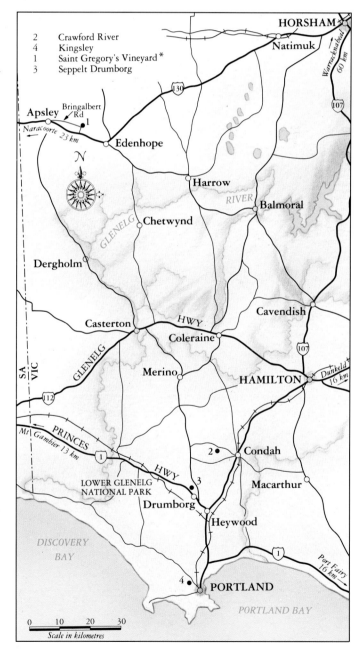

FACING PAGE: *Alpine light is an ever-changing joy at Delatite.*

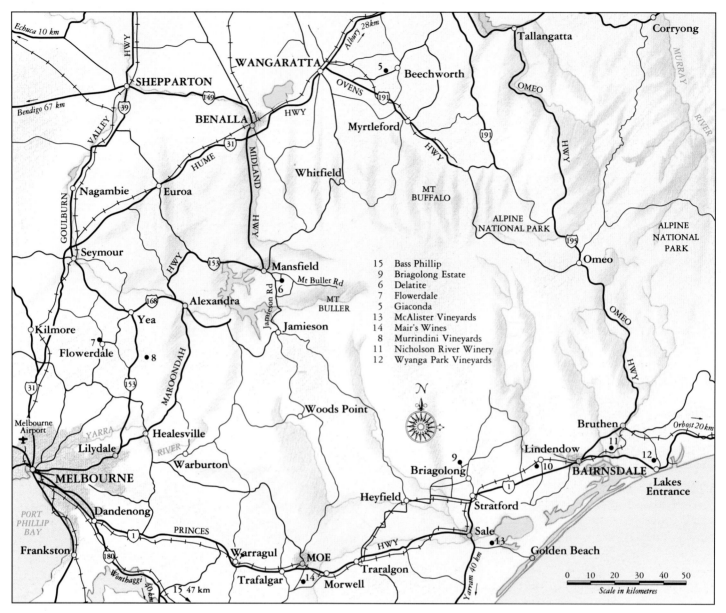

15 Bass Phillip
9   Briagolong Estate
6   Delatite
7   Flowerdale
5   Giaconda
13 McAlister Vineyards
14 Mair's Wines
8   Murrindini Vineyards
11 Nicholson River Winery
12 Wyanga Park Vineyards

and its tiny production will almost certainly guarantee a continuation of that position.

Murrindindi Vineyards and Flowerdale fall just outside the northernmost extremity of the Yarra Valley, however much they might wish to fall within it. There seems no reason why — with careful site selection — they should not be joined by other vineyards in the future and form the nucleus of a new region in the Dandenong Valley.

Gippsland is the final district: according to the classification suggested by the Victorian Wine Industry Association it is two distinct regions, each with subregions. They are West and South Gippsland, with Leongatha, Moe and Traralgon as its subregions; and East Gippsland, with Maffra, Bairnsdale, Dargo, Lakes Entrance and Orbost.

It was a not unimportant wine producing region in the nineteenth century, and with the renaissance in cool climate viticulture in the 1970s at least one major wine company gave it more than a passing glance. The temperature summations (1414 HDD at Lakes Entrance, 1457 HDD at Bairnsdale) put it firmly into the cool climate basket; once again, however, these figures tell only part of the tale. The most difficult feature of the climate is the lack of reliable winter-spring rain. Throughout almost all of the 1980s East Gippsland, in particular, suffered from a winter drought. This, in conjunction with soils of low to moderate fertility, has tended to reduce crop yields to subeconomic levels and to add to the economic difficulties confronting any small winemaker.

Wine quality has also suffered: contrary to public opinion, excessive stress on a grapevine does not produce high quality grapes. To add insult to injury, in several years much of the annual rainfall has fallen shortly before or during vintage, rather as it is wont to do in New South Wales' Hunter Valley. Yet despite this, the Gippsland region can and does produce some excellent wine, with Nicholson River Chardonnay quite magnificent in 1987 and 1988.

THE SMALL WINERY AND ITS MARKETS

Once upon a time it was possible to start a small winery and know that the moment you offered your wine for sale it would all be purchased by eager buyers within a matter of weeks. Up would go the 'sold out' sign, and 11 months later it would briefly come down.

To the new entrant into the hyper-competitive market of the late 1980s and early 1990s that may seem like a fairytale to exceed anything invented by Hans Christian Andersen, and indeed there may be a measure of exaggeration — but not much, particularly for the early birds of the late 1960s.

There are now almost 600 wineries fighting for a share of the market, more than double the number of 20 years ago. Indeed, if you take Victoria as an example, in 1960 the only licensed vignerons outside North-east Victoria were Mildara, Darvensia, Chateau Tahbilk, Osicka, Seppelt and Best's (and perhaps one or two other obscure growers on the Murray River). Now there are over 170.

What is more, over 90 per cent of all Australian wine is now made by the 20 or 30 largest wineries, leaving 550 competing for the last 10 per cent. Yet statistics are, as always, damned lies, because the small winery does not compete in the cask and flagon market, which still accounts for 65 per cent of overall sales.

But that crumb of good news is all the hopeful new entrant can expect. For unless the new winery is backed by a virtually limitless promotional budget and produces gold medal winning wines into the bargain, it will find it impossible to attract a financially secure and reasonably competent distributor. Undaunted, our vigneron may reason that he or she will be able to supply retailers and restaurants direct. Well, our vigneron will not even make it past the front door of the top retailers and the best restaurants.

Oh well, there is always the mailing list and the cellar door. All sorts of stories are told about mailing lists: just look how much the Westpac Wine Club and Cellarmasters sell. Yes, in their case they do sell a great deal. If you have 5 or 10 years, a handsome budget, and you are the creative director of a major advertising agency when you are not pottering around making wine, you may end up selling several thousand cases of wine a year this way. If not, count on several hundred cases, and if you achieve that, know you have done better than some of your competitors.

This leaves the cellar door. Immediately our ever-vigilant health inspectors start rubbing their evidently grubby little hands. While no one who I know of has male and female toilets in their house (and cellar door may be house door) you can be perfectly certain they will be required by our health guardians. As one vigneron acquaintance of mine plaintively asked 'What the hell do they think my customers come here to do? Sit on the loo all day?'

You can also be sure that a glass-washing facility worthy of a surgical operating theatre will have to be installed. And if the list of expensive health-related demands stops there, think yourself lucky.

Having spent $80,000 or so on this marvellous facility, you then have to staff it. Family labour costs nothing, but if you are sitting in the cellar door you are not in the vineyard pruning nor in the winery topping up the barrels, racking them, gassing tanks or whatever. Somewhere there will be a substantial labour bill, and the truth is that in real terms family labour does have a cost.

All will be well, you nonetheless think. After all, there is the 2.4 times multiplier working in your favour. (This multiplier is the rule of thumb used to convert the ex-cellar price to a distributor to a standard retail price: in other words, if you sell to your distributor for $10 a bottle, it will retail for $24 a bottle.) If you get only half that back after expenses and taxes, you will be happy. Unhappily, it is highly probable you won't get anywhere near 50 per cent.

First, there are the insatiable demands of the Sales Tax Commissioner, who over the life of your winery ownership is quite certain to make more money from your investment and your unremitting labour than you. For a start, his base 20 per cent margin will be greater than you will ever achieve. You carry the cost of collection, of filling out the forms, and sending off the money. All he has to do is bank it.

You might think the commissioner would be satisfied with that. Of course he is not: he also taxes at 20 per cent the wine you do *not* sell — the wine you are expected to so happily give to your customers as free tastings. No matter that you often writhe as it turns into a free drinking session, with the so-called customer havingf no intention at all of buying anything. Your misfortune is compounded by the thought of the commissioner profiting from your loss.

However, all this is predicated on the assumption that you actually have customers to serve. Wherever you may hang up your shingle, weekdays are usually a disaster. You stay open partly because you are haunted by the prospect of missing out on the occasional thousand dollar sale, partly because you know people remember if your brochure or sign says 'open 7 days', but cannot (or will not) remember more restricted opening hours — and are then apt to miss you out.

If you think this is all something of a beat-up, just talk to a vigneron in Coonawarra (South Australia) or the Margaret River (Western Australia), and ask them how much they sell cellar door. If the answer is heaps, count their sales over any 2 hour period on a peak weekend and you will come up with a different answer. And just remember when you console yourself by drinking a glass of your own wine, that the commissioner wants his 20 per cent.

WINERIES OF SOUTHERN AND CENTRAL VICTORIA

CENTRAL VICTORIA

DELATITE   BA-BA
Stoney's Road
Mansfield 3722   (057) 75 2922
Established   1982
Winemaker   Rosalind Ritchie
Production   11,500 cases
Principal Wines   Riesling, Dead Man's Hill
Gewurztraminer, Chardonnay, Late-picked
Riesling, New Shiraz, Pinot Noir, Cabernet
Sauvignon Merlot, Malbec, Shiraz and a
Cabernet blend Devil's River.
Best Vintages   W 1982, '83, '86, '87, '88, '90
                R 1984, '86, '87, '88, '90
Delatite produces wines of immediately
recognisable style: crisp, delicate and elegant
white wines which slowly fill out and evolve in
bottle, and equally meticulously crafted red
wines which have a similar delicacy, but also
have a trade mark stamp of eucalypt mint
character in their bouquet and palate. Winemaker Rosalind Ritchie is both skilled and
dedicated, and Delatite has won a loyal band of
followers within Australia and the United
Kingdom.

GIACONDA   BA-B
McClay Road
Beechworth 3747   (057) 27 0246
Established   1985
Winemaker   Rick Kinzbrunner
Production   700 cases
Principal Wines   Chardonnay, Pinot Noir
and a Cabernet Sauvignon Cabernet Franc
Merlot blend.
Best Vintages   W 1986, '88, '89
                R 1986, '88, '90
The tiny output at Giaconda is instantaneously
purchased by a fanatical band of supporters.
Rick Kinzbrunner is a creative winemaker who
relies heavily on intuition and on a strongly
developed perspective of style. His wines may
not always please the purist, but Kinzbrunner
would be the first to say they are not intended to
do so.

OTHER WINERIES

FLOWERDALE C-C
Yea Road, Flowerdale
3717 (057) 80 1432

MURRINDINDI VINEYARDS CB-B
RMB 6070, Cummins Lane
Murrindindi 3717

GIPPSLAND

NICHOLSON RIVER WINERY   A-BA
Liddells Road
Nicholson 3882 (051) 56 8241
Established   1978
Winemaker   Ken Eckersley
Production   700 cases
Principal Wines   Chardonnay, Semillon,
Cabernets, Rhine Riesling, Pinot Noir and
Shiraz; second label is 'Mountview'.
Best Vintages   W and R 1987, '88

After years of single-minded dedication, former
school teacher Ken Eckersley made a glorious
Chardonnay in 1987, and an even greater one in
1988. The latter has the weight and
concentration of a Corton Charlemagne or
Batard Montrachet from a top producer in a
good year, and has almost no parallel in

Australia. The Gippsland climate remains
unpredictable, but given half a chance, Ken
Eckersley is liable to produce something quite
out of the ordinary.

BASS PHILLIP   A-A
Tosch's Road
Leongatha South 3953 (03) 818 3358
Established   1979
Winemaker   Phillip Jones
Production   1000 cases
Principal Wines   Pinot Noir (90 per cent
plus) and Chardonnay.

Best Vintages   1984, '86, '88, '89
Tiny quantities of some of the most exciting
Pinot Noir to be made in Australia came onto
the market in late 1990. The wines have
tremendous concentration of flavour, power and
length, yet retain the essence of Pinot Noir's
varietal character. In style they are akin to the
best wines of Vosne-Romanée, Burgundy, and
will be very long-lived.

OTHER WINERIES

BRIAGOLONG ESTATE   C-C
Valencia-Briagolong Road
Briagolong 3860 (051) 47 2322

GOLVINDA   C-C
RMB 4635, Lindenow Road
Lindenow South via
Bairnsdale 3865 (051) 57 1480

McALISTER VINEYARDS   CA-B
Golden Beach Road, Longford
3851 (051) 49 7229

MAIR'S WINES   CB-CB
Coalville Vineyard, Moe South Road
Moe South 3825 (051)27 4229

WYANGA PARK VINEYARDS   C-C
Baades Road, Lakes Entrance
3909 (051) 55 1508

ABOVE: Ros Ritchie, young, talented – and happy.   *TOP: Rick Kinzbrunner, disciple of the international wine god.*

SOUTH-WESTERN VICTORIA

CRAWFORD RIVER   B-B
Crawford via Condah
3303 (055) 78 2267
Established   1982
Winemaker   John Thomson
Production   2200 cases
Principal Wines   Rhine Riesling, Beeren-
auslese Rhine Riesling, Semillon/Sauvignon
Blanc and Cabernet Sauvignon.
Best Vintages   **W** and **R** 1986, '88, '90

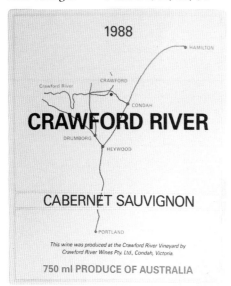

Crawford River has repeatedly risen above the
limitations imposed by its isolation, its relatively small size, and the essentially part time nature
of the winemaking of its grazier-owner John
Thomson. Some truly excellent wines have
appeared under the Crawford River label, the
best seemingly throwing down the gauntlet to
Seppelt Drumborg. Its wines have ranged in style
from botrytised Riesling through to Cabernet
Sauvignon, the latter outstanding in 1988.

SEPPELT DRUMBORG   A-A
Drumborg 3304   (055) 27 9257
Established   1964
Winemaker   Ian McKenzie
Production   Not stated
Principal Wines   Rhine Riesling, Cabernet
Sauvignon and *Méthode Champenoise*.
Best Vintages   **W** and **R** 1978, '80, '82,
                       '86, '88, '89
It was doubly ironical that in a generally
difficult vintage such as 1989 Seppelt
Drumborg should have produced such
outstanding wines. Seppelt winemakers and
viticulturists have long struggled with the
temperamental climate, and with grapes which
refused to ripen sufficiently in 2 years out of 3.
By late 1988 it duly produced the expected fine
wines; 1989 came as a gift from the Gods. At
their best, the steely, lime juice Rhine Rieslings
and intense, blackcurrant flavoured Cabernet
Sauvignons (the latter with surprising depth and
generosity to the structure) can only be
described as outstanding.

OTHER WINERIES

KINGSLEY   CB-CB
50 Bancroft Street
Portland3305 (055) 23 1864

ST GREGORY'S VINEYARD NR
Bringalbert South Road
Bringalbert South via Apsley
3319 (055) 86 5225

ABOVE: The snow is never far away from Delatite.

YARRA VALLEY

Let there be no doubt about it: I am hopelessly biased when it comes to the Yarra Valley, for it is where I live, where I work making and writing about wine, and it is where I hope I will die when my time comes. It is a place of extreme beauty, of constantly changing light, of colour and of mood. It offers landscapes on an heroic scale with the same profligacy as it offers intimate vistas. Once you have seen it, you cannot help but love it.

Yet my love affair started before I set foot in it, when I tasted the first vintages of Seville Estate, Yeringberg and Mount Mary, followed soon thereafter by Yarra Yering. In the second half of the 1970s these wines opened up a new horizon; the Pinot Noirs, a new world.

Within a year I had traversed its length, and although I did not know it then, my fate was sealed, my life to change direction from that of a senior partner in a major law firm specialising in corporate law to that of full time winewriter and winemaker without (as I am fond of saying) visible means of support.

The antecedents of the Yarra Valley were (and are) impeccable, with a proud and rich history of grape growing and winemaking stretching back to the first settlers (in 1838) and reaching the height of its fame in 1881. I trace the rise and fall of the Yarra Valley's first incarnation at pages 166 to 167; here I shall follow the course of its renaissance which burst like a spring flower between 1968 and 1971, inexplicably all but stopped growing throughout the rest of the 1970s and flourished in an extraordinary fashion in the 1980s.

The **figures** below give a raw statistical picture of that growth, which in terms of percentage increase outstrips that of all other Australian regions over the same period. Yet they raise an obvious question: for how long, and at what rate, will the growth continue? And is it possible the Yarra Valley will suffer the same fate as the Hunter Valley, and sharply contract as the Hunter has done since its flood-tide of 1968?

RATE OF GROWTH IN THE YARRA VALLEY

1964 2 ha   1978 61 ha   1986 209 ha   1990 513 ha

AUSTRALASIAN WINE REGIONS
1980 – 1990

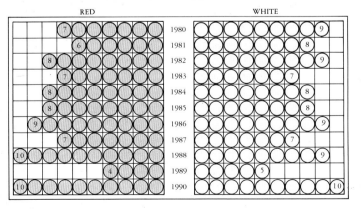

THE REGION IN BRIEF

LOCATION AND ELEVATION
37°45'S 145°22'E Lilydale
50–400 m

SUBREGIONS
Coldstream, Dixons Creek, Steels Creek, Yarra Glen, St Andrews, Seville and Lilydale.

CLIMATE
Given the considerable variation in altitude, and the significance of aspect (ie north or south) on the many hillside vineyards, it is not surprising that there is substantial variation in climate. However, even the warmest sites are, comparatively speaking, cool: the MJT at Healesville is 19.4°C, which is lower than at Bordeaux or Burgundy, but it has an aberrationally high heat summation (HDD) of 1490; that of the highest vineyards is not much over 1100. The greatest problem is wind, which principally affects the traditionally-preferred north-facing slopes. This, in conjunction with rain, can be particularly damaging during flowering and fruit set, but it also acts to inhibit ripening in what can be a marginal climate in windy years. The other viticultural hazard is birds, which cause substantial crop losses in some years. Spring frosts are not at all common, but the rainfall of between 750 mm and 950 mm does make drip irrigation from January to March highly desirable.

SOIL
There are two basic soil types: the 'traditional' areas between Lilydale, Yarra Glen, Dixons Creek and Healesville are almost all in the Dr2.21 and 2.22 group — hard red duplex soils. Despite the technical name, these are grey to grey-brown to brown in colour on the surface and range from loamy sand to clay loam in consistency. They have red-brown clay subsoils, frequently impregnated with rock. Most are relatively acidic and low in fertility, but are well drained. The other major soil type is the immensely deep and fertile vivid red volcanic soil to be found at Seville, Hoddles Creek and elsewhere on the Warburton side of the Yarra Valley.

HARVEST TIME
Pinot Noir and Chardonnay destined for sparkling wine are picked in early March; the table wine season usually starts mid-March with Pinot Noir, and runs through to late April/early May for Cabernet Sauvignon.

PRINCIPAL GRAPE VARIETIES
Chardonnay, 163 ha
Sauvignon Blanc, 27 ha
Rhine Riesling, 16 ha
Semillon, 11 ha
Cabernet Franc, 14 ha

Pinot Noir, 127 ha
Cabernet Sauvignon, 93 ha
Shiraz, 27 ha
Merlot, 22 ha

FACING PAGE: *Seville Estate, looking towards the Dandenongs.*

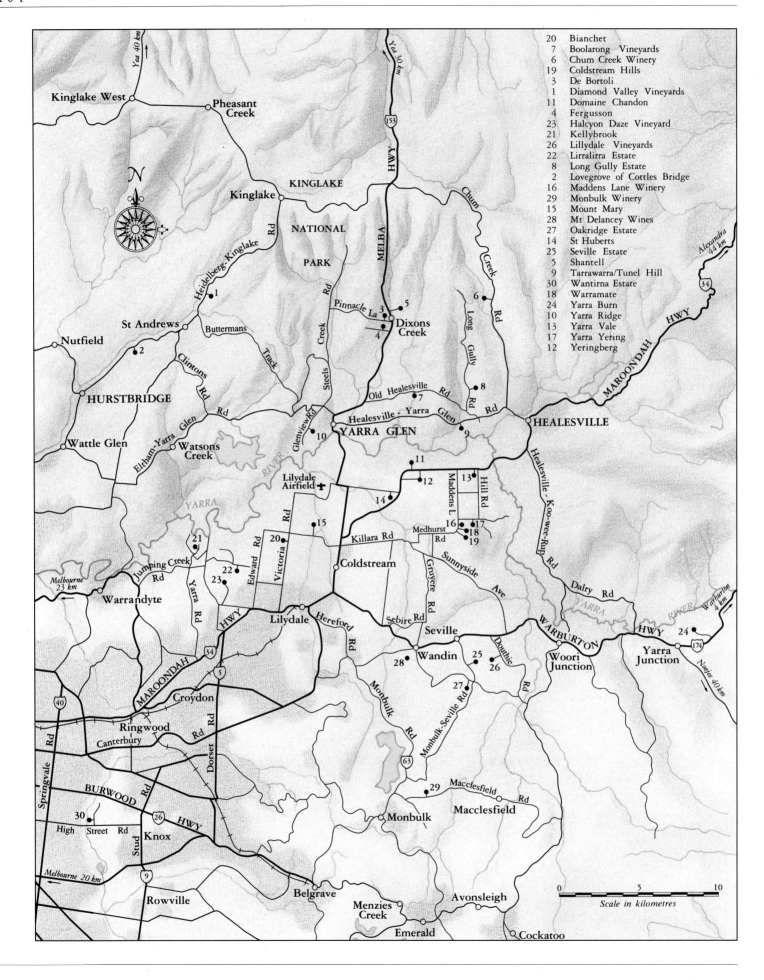

20 Bianchet
7 Boolarong Vineyards
6 Chum Creek Winery
19 Coldstream Hills
3 De Bortoli
1 Diamond Valley Vineyards
11 Domaine Chandon
4 Fergusson
23 Halcyon Daze Vineyard
21 Kellybrook
26 Lillydale Vineyards
22 Lirralirra Estate
8 Long Gully Estate
2 Lovegrove of Cottles Bridge
16 Maddens Lane Winery
29 Monbulk Winery
15 Mount Mary
28 Mt Delancey Wines
27 Oakridge Estate
14 St Huberts
25 Seville Estate
5 Shantell
9 Tarrawarra/Tunel Hill
30 Wantirna Estate
18 Warramate
24 Yarra Burn
10 Yarra Ridge
13 Yarra Vale
17 Yarra Yering
12 Yeringberg

The answer is that the Yarra Valley will continue to grow at an exceptional rate, overtaking the Hunter Valley (New South Wales) in terms of plantings and winery numbers (though not total production) by the turn of the century — if the Victorian State Government does not prevent it. For the real danger confronting the Yarra Valley is urban pressure, and the temptation to open the floodgates to suburban housing development is great.

As it is, continuous housing and full services and infrastructure have spread to Lilydale, 10 minutes drive or a few kilometres from the heart of the vineyards. The Yarra Valley has received a major imprimatur from Moët et Chandon with the establishment of the $8 million headquarters of Domaine Chandon Australia, while the giant Goodman Fielder Wattie (through its subsidiary Baileys) has purchased St Huberts. De Bortoli has invested several million dollars in Yarrinya Estate, while Coldstream Winemakers Limited (which trades as Coldstream Hills) at the time of writing was capitalised at $3 million on the Stock Exchange. Finally, the $2 million Hoddles Creek vineyard development will be supplying more than 1000 tonnes of grapes a year to winemakers all over Australia by 1992.

All this is but the tip of the iceberg, however. One study suggests that within 20 years the Yarra Valley could have 5000 hectares of vineyards and 100 wineries producing 3,000,000 cases of wine worth over $200,000,000 (in today's dollars) in annual sales. But this will only happen if the present zoning is retained, keeping land prices within reason, and allowing major wine companies to purchase large holdings (which still exist) for development.

PRINCIPAL WINE STYLES

PINOT NOIR
Pinot Noir takes pride of place simply because the Yarra Valley has achieved more with this difficult variety than any other Australian wine region. For all that, it still causes great dissension, simply because it is the least widely understood of all wine varieties and — in Australia as elsewhere — some wine lovers expect it to look and taste like any other red wine. For those who understand true Burgundy (typically Domaine-bottled) the sappy/strawberry/plum spectrum of fruit flavours to be found in the Yarra is very exciting. The leading producers (alphabetically) are Coldstream Hills, Diamond Valley, Mount Mary, St Huberts, Seville Estate, Yarra Burn, Yarra Ridge, Yarra Yering, Yarrinya Estate and Yeringberg.

CABERNET SAUVIGNON
As in the Mornington Peninsula, Cabernet Sauvignon is usually blended with up to 20 per cent (sometimes more) of Cabernet Franc and Merlot. The wines are invariably elegant, but can vary from light bodied (such as Lillydale Vineyards and Diamond Valley) through to full bodied (Yeringberg and Yarra Yering). The one common feature is the softness of the tannins — they are almost silky. This can trap the unwary into assuming the wines will not cellar well, but they do. It is hard to single out other producers as almost every winery in the Yarra Valley makes a Cabernet, but Oakridge, Mount Mary and Seville Estate have produced some great wines.

CHARDONNAY
The style of Yarra Valley Chardonnay tends to be delicate and restrained. For Australian palates used to the luscious wines of the Hunter Valley or McLaren Vale the taste (and texture) may seem pale and insipid. These delicate wines can mature wonderfully well in bottle, but for those with less patience St Huberts, Yarrinya Estate and Yarra Ridge have produced some more precocious (and luscious) wines recently, while Tarrawarra makes a masculine wine of enormous complexity which demands time in bottle.

RHINE RIESLING
Rhine Riesling produces two styles: a faintly spicy, dry, crisp wine with pronounced European overtones (exemplified by Lillydale Vineyards) but which seems to lack the heart which most Australians expect, or an intensely rich, searingly luscious botrytised style (Seville Estate and, occasionally, St Huberts).

SHIRAZ
Sparingly produced, with Yarra Yering Dry Red No 2, Seville Estate and Warramate frequently outstanding — redolent with pepper/spice some years, velvety red berry fruit in the others.

SAUVIGNON BLANC
A relative newcomer. So far Yarra Burn and Yarra Ridge have done best, but others are trying.

ABOVE: Roses and the young vines of Domaine Chandon: as beautiful in the Yarra Valley as anywhere.

YARRA VALLEY — A SOUTHERN BELLE

The history of grape growing and winemaking in the Yarra Valley in the period from 1837 to 1921 is a microcosm of nineteenth century Australia. It was a country populated by men and women of amazing ingenuity and courage, who accepted wild swings of fortune as an inevitable adjunct of a turbulent society in which the risks of failure were high, the rewards of success no less so. Shortly put, it was a land — and a time — in which nothing was impossible.

It was in a sense inevitable that the Ryrie brothers carried vines with them when in 1837, only 2 years after John Batman had founded Melbourne, they set out from their cattle station Arnprior in the Monaro, the high plains surrounding what is now Cooma in New South Wales, to traverse the Snowy Mountains and find a way to the country around Melbourne. Donald Ryrie subsequently wrote his recollections of the planting of those vines in August 1838, 'They were taken from Arnprior and were the Black Cluster or Hamburg and a white grape, the Sweet Water. We afterwards had sent from Sydney other vines taken from MacArthur's vineyard at Camden. The first wine was made in March, 1845; a red wine resembling Burgundy and a white wine resembling Sauterne and both very good. Dardel, a Swiss (afterwards at Geelong) used to come to prune the vines. He also put us in the way of making the wine.'

Just as Germans dominated the development of viticulture in the Barossa Valley (South Australia), Yugoslavs in the Swan Valley (Western Australia), and Italians (excepting the McWilliam clan) in the Murrumbidgee Irrigation Area (New South Wales), so the Swiss were the leading figures in the development of the Yarra Valley and Geelong. Persecution or poverty led to the emigration of all but the Swiss: they came from an altogether different socio-economic strata. Charles la Trobe, who arrived as Administrator in 1839 and who became the State's first governor when it separated from New South Wales in 1851, had married the Neuchatel-born daughter of the Swiss Counsellor of State.

Her impeccable connections led to the establishment of vineyards in Geelong in 1842 by Swiss — Pettavel, Belperroud and Brequet — and to the arrival of Paul de Castella in the Yarra Valley in 1849. He purchased Yering

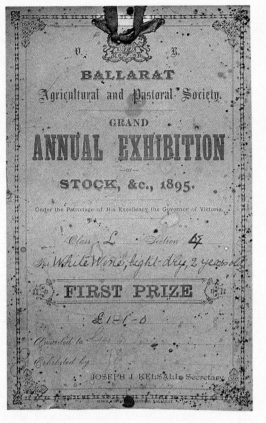

Station from Ryrie, and with it the 0.4 hectare vineyard. One hundred years later Francois de Castella, Hubert de Castella's son and Paul's nephew, recounted how Paul de Castella had brought with him a quantity of Pommard from Burgundy. One fateful night the Pommard ran out, and a Yering wine from the one acre vineyard had to be substituted — to be acclaimed by the guests as 'better than the Pommard'.

Through family connections in Europe, Paul de Castella obtained 20,000 vine cuttings, mainly from Chateau Lafite, and between 1855 and 1857 the vineyard was extended to 40 hectares, supplemented by vines obtained in Sydney and Geelong. By 1861 it was able to win the 100 guinea gold cup offered by *The Argus* for the best vineyard in Victoria, famous for its 'Sauvignon', which was in fact Cabernet Sauvignon.

Baron Guillaume de Pury was the nephew of Mrs La Trobe, and followed her to Victoria in 1852. In 1854 he formed a partnership with the newly-arrived Hubert de Castella and purchased Dalry Station (near Healesville) from the Ryrie brothers. Within a few years Hubert de Castella returned to Switzerland, leaving de Pury in charge. The property was soon sold, and de Pury followed de Castella back to Switzerland in 1861.

Both men returned to Victoria in late 1862, this time to stay and soon to establish the other two great nineteenth century vineyards of St Huberts and Yeringberg. By 1875 St Huberts had 80 hectares under vine; by 1890 this had increased to 100 hectares, and the property supported 40 permanent and 87 part time workers — it also carried 800 dairy cattle and 3400 turkeys.

Yeringberg, like St Huberts and Yering, ran a mixed grazing and winemaking business, with vineyards occupying only a small part of the total property. However, de Pury soon had 28 hectares under vine, and in 1885 built the magnificent three-storey wooden winery which is still in exceptional condition and in which the Yeringberg wines of today are made by de Pury's grandson (Baron Guillaume de Pury — known to all as Guill de Pury).

By the end of the century there were 45 separate vineyards and 1080 acres (440 hectares) under vine in the Yarra Valley. Well known vineyards of the time included Auguste

---

ABOVE: Yeringberg: first prizes were par for the course in the nineteenth century.

Deschamps' Lillydale Vineyards (planted on land which is now in the heart of the town); Yeringa, established by two sons of Auguste Deschamps near Yeringberg; the Huttons' Cooring; and David Mitchell's Coldstream (on the slopes above what is now Coldstream Airport). David Mitchell is perhaps best known as Dame Nellie Melba's father. Mitchell also purchased the financially troubled St Huberts from Andrew Rowan, and it was Mitchell's decision to cease wine production there.

The end came with devastating suddenness. It was not, as commonly supposed, due to phylloxera. Rather it was a combination of declining soil fertility, a cycle of frosty springs, and — most importantly of all — the shift away from table to fortified wine consumption. The closure of St Huberts was also a grave psychological blow; Cooring lingered on until 1920, and Yeringberg made its last vintage in 1921 — with the wine made in its previous three vintages lying unsold in its cellars.

Yet the three major vineyards had achieved extraordinary success and fame in their brief hours of glory. In 1881 the Melbourne International Exhibition was staged in the building specially constructed for the event (and which still stands today). In the manner of the times, this was a grand event, comparatively more so than Brisbane's Expo in Queensland, and attracted worldwide interest and participation. The Emperor of Germany's contribution was a Grand Prize to be awarded to 'the Australian exhibitor whose artistic and industrial progress is best displayed by the outstanding qualities of his product.' Eighteen sections contested the prize: wool, fabrics, agricultural machinery, steam engines, tobacco, printing, various manufactured goods and wine (and in the wine section alone there were 711 entries). Thus it was that by beating (inter alia) a felt hat and a steam engine, St Huberts won the Emperor's prize.

The purists might argue that Yering's award of a Grand Prix at the Paris Exhibition of 1889 was even more significant. Only 14 Grand Prixs were awarded to the thousands of entries, and only one to a southern hemisphere winery. But Francois de Castella, speaking to the Victorian Historical Society on 5 September 1942, puts it into the best perspective: 'The three vineyards were prized for their wines, which had the unmistakable imprint of quality — of breeding — that makes the disappearance of all the vineyards from the Yarra Valley the more regrettable, and scarcely comprehensible. Of the three, the palm sometimes was awarded to Yering for its reds; sometimes to Yeringberg for its whites, while St Huberts consistently held its own in both categories.'

ABOVE: Sunset from Yeringberg.

WINERIES OF THE YARRA VALLEY

BIANCHET   CB-B
Lot 3, Victoria Road
Lilydale 3140   (03) 739 1779
Established   1976
Winemaker   Lou Bianchet
Production   2000 cases
Principal Wines   Chardonnay, Gewurztraminer,
Verduzzo, Semillon, Pinot Noir, Shiraz,
Cabernet Sauvignon and Merlot.
Best Vintages   **W** and **R** 1982, '85, '86,
                       '88, '90
Lou Bianchet makes generous full flavoured
white and red wines from now largely mature
vines. A little more expenditure on new oak
could lift the quality into a higher category, but
would no doubt also increase the presently fairly
modest prices charged. Verduzzo, an Italian
white variety, is a winery speciality.

COLDSTREAM HILLS   NR
Lot 6, Maddens Lane
Coldstream 3770   (059) 64 9388
Established   1985
Winemaker   James Halliday
Production   16,000 cases
Principal Wines   Chardonnay, Fumé Blanc,
Pinot Noir, Merlot, Cabernet Merlot and
Cabernet Sauvignon (the latter a Bordeaux blend
of approximately 80 per cent Cabernet
Sauvignon and equal quantities of Merlot and
Cabernet Franc). There are often two releases
each year, particularly with Pinot Noir and
Chardonnay. Coldstream Hills now has 15 ha of
its own vineyards but also has long term
contract purchase arrangements with other Yarra
Valley growers.
Best Vintages   **W** 1986, '88, '90
                       R 1985, '86, '88, '90
The author's own winery, and accordingly no
subjective assessment is given. However, in
1988 and 1989 Coldstream Hills received more
trophies and gold medals for its Pinot Noir than
any other Australian exhibitor, and also enjoyed
significant international success in Paris and
California. Its Chardonnays and Cabernet
Sauvignon-based wines have fared very nearly as
well.

DE BORTOLI   BA-B
Pinnacle Lane
Dixons Creek 3775 (059) 65 2271
Established   1971
Winemakers   Stephen Webber,
                      David Ellis
Production   20,000 cases
Principal Wines   Riesling, Gewurztraminer,
Chardonnay, Pinot Noir, Shiraz and Cabernet
Sauvignon.
Best Vintages   **W** 1987, '88, '89
                       R 1977, '82, '88, '89, '90

Since its acquisition by De Bortoli, the former
Yarrinya Estate has gone from strength to
strength. Unusually rich and full flavoured
Chardonnay has been the flag bearer, closely
followed by a complex and well structured
Cabernet Sauvignon. The Pinot Noir has faired
well in the show ring, but I have found it less
impressive than the other two wines.

DIAMOND VALLEY VINEYARDS   BA-A
Kinglake Road
St Andrews 3761   (03) 710 1484
Established   1976
Winemaker   Dr David Lance
Production   4500 cases
Principal Wines   Estate-grown Rhine Riesling,
Pinot Noir and Cabernets (a blend Cabernet

Sauvignon, Merlot, Cabernet Franc and Malbec).
A range of Blue label wines (including
Chardonnay) produced from fruit grown in
neighbouring vineyards has also been developed.
Best Vintages   **W** 1983, '84, '86, '87, '88
                       R 1982, '85, '86, '87, '88
If the Yarra Valley finally establishes its
reputation as Australia's finest Pinot Noir
region, Diamond Valley will have played the
major role in creating that reputation. All of its
red wines are light and elegant, and Pinot Noir
(in its true manifestation) is of this description
in any event. Those who enjoy traditional
Barossa or Hunter Valley reds are unlikely to
ever either understand or enjoy such wines, but
then that is no more than part of the endless
fascination of wine.

ABOVE: *The one-in-four slopes of the Coldstream Hills vineyards.*

DOMAINE CHANDON   A-A
'Green Point'
Maroondah Highway
Coldstream 3770   (03) 739 1110
Established   1988
Winemaker   Dr Tony Jordan with Wayne Donaldson (with input from Moët et Chandon through Edmond Maudiere and Richard Geoffroy).
Production   15,000 cases

Principal Wines   *Méthode Champenoise* wines only are produced; the first release in May 1989 (cuvée 86.1) was a Blanc de Blanc (100 per cent Chardonnay). The second release (cuvée 87.1) late in 1989 was a blend of Chardonnay and Pinot Noir. The principal release each year is a blend of Pinot Noir, Chardonnay and Pinot Meunier. A significant part of the cuvée comes from Yarra Valley grapes, particularly from Domaine Chandon's own extensive vineyards. Each cuvée also incorporates contract grown fruit from many parts of South-eastern Australia and Tasmania.
Best Vintages   Irrelevant.
In every conceivable way, Domaine Chandon will be an enduring landmark in the Yarra Valley. Tens of thousands of people will visit it every year, and if its early releases are anything to go by, it will certainly be accepted as one of Australia's top three sparkling winemakers.

FERGUSSON'S   CB-CB
Wills Road
Yarra Glen 3775   (059) 65 2237
Established   1968
Winemaker   Chris Kies
Production   5000 cases
Principal Wines   Chenin Blanc, Rhine Riesling, Chardonnay, Shiraz, Cabernet Sauvignon and Cabernet Franc Merlot.
Best Vintages   W 1984, '86, '87, '88, '90
    R 1979, '80, '84, '86, '88, '90
Fergusson's is one of the show pieces of the Yarra Valley, and has been fully rebuilt after being almost totally destroyed by fire shortly after the 1989 vintage. It sells wines from the Yarra Valley and from other districts. Those from the Yarra Valley are good; those from other districts are adequate for the purpose. Its receivership in late 1989 cast a shadow of uncertainty over its future.

KELLYBROOK   CA-CB
Fulford Road
Wonga Park 3115   (03) 722 1304
Established   1960
Winemaker   Darren Kelly
Production   1200 cases
Principal Wines   Kellybrook produces table wines and various forms of cider, the latter produced using classic fermentation and maturation techniques and employing specially grown cider apples. Table wines include Chardonnay, Traminer, Rhine Riesling, Pinot Noir, Brut *Méthode Champenoise*, late picked Rhine Riesling, Shiraz, Cabernet Sauvignon and Vintage Port. Ciders include Vintage Champagne Cider Brut, Farmhouse Cider, Old Gold (Vintage), Liqueur Cider and Yarra Valley Apple Brandy (Calvados-style).
Best Vintages   W 1982, '84, '87, '90
    R 1982, '84, '86, '88, '90
Kellybrook produces some quite wonderful ciders in various forms (sparkling, still and Calvados-style) and, in vintages such as 1988, produces very good Cabernet Sauvignon. It also offers a weekend restaurant in pleasant surroundings.

LILLYDALE VINEYARDS   BA-B
Davross Court
Seville 3139   (03) 642 016
Established   1976
Winemakers   Alex White,
    Martin Grinbergs
Production   8500 cases
Principal Wines   Rhine Riesling, Gewurztraminer, Chardonnay, Yarra Dry White, Sauvignon Blanc, Pinot Noir and Cabernet Sauvignon.
Best Vintages   W 1984, '86, '88, '90
    R 1983, '86, '88, '90
One of the leading wineries in the Yarra Valley, it now has its own home base (formerly the wines were made at St Huberts), and makes elegant wines all with a distinct Lillydale stamp. Alex White does not believe in the excessive use of new oak, and aims to present wines which are fully drinkable at the time of their release. The high reputation of the vineyard bears witness to the success of this philosophy.

LONG GULLY   B-B
Long Gully Road
Healesville 3777   (03) 807 4246
Established   1982
Winemaker   Peter Florence
Production   4800 cases
Principal Wines   Sauvignon Blanc, Rhine Riesling, Chardonnay, Semillon, Pinot Noir, Cabernet Sauvignon, Merlot, Malbec and Cabernet Franc.
Best Vintages   W 1986, '87, '89, '90
    R 1986, '87, '88, '90
A new but rapidly growing winery with a

substantial vineyard providing 100 per cent estate-grown wines. The best so far has been its Cabernet Sauvignon, with great flavour and concentration, but an excellent 1989 Chardonnay also showed much promise.

LOVEGROVE OF COTTLES BRIDGE   B-B
Lot 21, Kinglake Road
Cottles Bridge 2099   (03) 718 1569
Established   1988
Winemaker   Malcolm Lovegrove (and consultants).
Production   1100 cases
Principal Wines   Chardonnay, Cabernets and Pinot Noir.
Best Vintages   W and R 1987, '88, '90

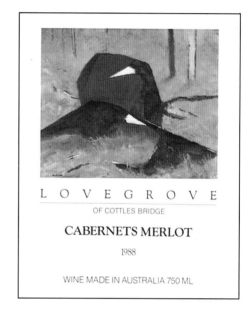

Situated in the hills of the Diamond Valley region, and aided by skilled consultancy advice, Lovegrove's initial releases show considerable promise. The Chardonnay, in particular, is rich and peachy; the Cabernet Merlot is in the lighter style which the Diamond Valley region seems to produce.

MOUNT MARY   CA-CA
Coldstream West Road
Lilydale 3140   (03) 739 1761
Established   1971
Winemaker   Dr John Middleton
Production   2500 cases but increasing.
Principal Wines   Two dry whites and two dry reds, with a blended wine and a varietal wine in each group. The white wines are Chardonnay, and Sauvignon Blanc, Semillon, Muscadelle blend; red wines are Pinot Noir, and Cabernets, a Cabernet Sauvignon (50 per cent), Cabernet Franc (20 per cent), Merlot (25 per cent), Malbec (3 per cent) and Petit Verdot (2 per cent) blend. These percentages are for vines in the vineyard and not necessarily for the wine in the bottle.

Best Vintages R 1977, '79, '80, '82, '84, '85, '86, '88

A reputation as exalted as that of Mount Mary carries its penalties: if any of the wines are less than perfect, it is apt to create tremendous anxiety for all concerned. Fortunately, Mount Mary's red wines are usually above criticism, the impossibly Bordeaux-like Cabernets consistently proving itself one of the finest reds made in Australia each year, and the plummy Burgundian Pinot Noir is only a whisker behind. For many good judges, myself included, the whites are decidedly less satisfactory.

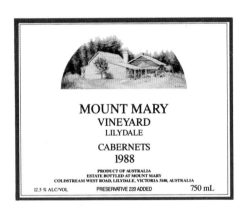

**MOUNT MARY
VINEYARD
LILYDALE
CABERNETS
1988**

PRODUCT OF AUSTRALIA
ESTATE BOTTLED AT MOUNT MARY
COLDSTREAM WEST ROAD, LILYDALE, VICTORIA 3140, AUSTRALIA

12.5 % ALC/VOL   PRESERVATIVE 220 ADDED   750 mL

OAKRIDGE ESTATE   BA-B
Aitken Road
Seville 3139   (059) 64 3379
Established   1982
Winemaker   Michael Zitzlaff
Production   2000 cases
Principal Wines   Cabernet Sauvignon and Cabernet Shiraz Merlot.
Best Vintages   R 1984, '85, '86, '90
With its vineyard situated on the rich, red volcanic soils shared by Seville Estate, Oakridge has produced one of the Yarra Valley's best Cabernets, with tremendous depth of flavour to its cassis/red berry/mint fruit, and enough tannin to allow it to reach its full potential in 10 to15 years. The '87 and '88 vintages are very much lighter (and I must say less attractive) in style; hopefully they are aberrations.

ST HUBERTS   BA-B
Cnr St Huberts Road
and Maroondah Highway
Coldstream 3770   (03) 739 1421
Established   1966
Winemaker   Brian Fletcher
Production   20,000 cases
Principal Wines   Rhine Riesling, Chardonnay, Shiraz, Pinot Noir and Cabernet Sauvignon. Second label is Andrew Rowan.
Best Vintages   W 1984, '86, '87, '88, '90
                      R 1977, '80, '81, '84, '86, '88, '90
The future control, and indeed destiny, of St Huberts was exceedingly uncertain at the time of writing, but there is no question that the arrival of Brian Fletcher as winemaker has seen St Huberts fulfil the potential which it only intermittently realised prior to 1988. In that year a brilliant grapefruit/melon/fig Chardonnay, with superb supporting oak, and a Cabernet Sauvignon which was, if anything, even better, were made. The Cabernet Sauvignon is powerful, with dark fruits and finely balanced sweet oak.

SEVILLE ESTATE   A-A
Linwood Road
Seville 3139   (059) 64 4556
Established   1972
Winemaker   Dr Peter McMahon
Production   1700 cases
Principal Wines   Chardonnay, Riesling, Beerenauslese, Shiraz, Pinot Noir and Cabernet Sauvignon. Occasionally Rhine Riesling Trocken-beerenauslese is also made when vintage conditions permit.
Best Vintages   W 1980, '81, '82, '85, '86, '88, '90
                      R 1977, '79, '80, '81, '84, '85, '86, '88, '90
The quietly but eternally humorous Dr Peter McMahon occasionally makes a less than perfect wine, but does not let it concern him unduly — rightly so, because the majority are superb, spanning the range from beautifully balanced peach/melon Chardonnay through herbaceous/passionfruit Rhine Riesling to spicy/pepper Shiraz to berry flavoured Cabernet Sauvignon with just the right amount of green capsicum tartness to a searingly luscious botrytised Rhine Riesling, the last of which has no parallel elsewhere in Australia.

SHANTELL   B-B
Off Melba Highway
Dixons Creek 3775   (059) 65 2264
Established   1981
Winemakers   Shan and Turid Shanmugam, Kathleen Quealy (consultant)
Production   1400 cases
Principal Wines   Chardonnay, Semillon, Pinot Noir and Cabernet Sauvignon.
Best Vintages   W and R 1988, '90
The Shanmugams have been grape growers for a number of years. Prior to the 1988 vintage they erected a substantial winery in which their first, and remarkably good, vintage was made. With mature vines and competent consulting winemaking, the future looks good, even if the winery (and the cellar door sales area) is a little off the beaten track. It is worth the effort.

TARRAWARRA   BA-B
Healesville Road
Yarra Glen 3775 (059) 62 3311
Established   1983
Winemaker   David Wollan
Production   Not stated as a matter of policy, but estimated at around 3000 cases.
Principal Wines   Chardonnay specialist, with small quantities of Pinot Noir. Second label is Tunnel Hill.
Best Vintages   W 1987, '88, '90
Until Domaine Chandon came along to spoil the game, TarraWarra was the Yarra Valley's answer to the wonder-wineries of the Napa Valley. Built without regard to cost, and absolutely dedicated to making the best possible Chardonnay, TarraWarra has stirred all sorts of emotions. The wine style, too, is controversial: exceedingly complex, with fruit subservient to style, it is a love it or leave it wine.

WANTIRNA ESTATE   B-B
Bushy Park Lane
Wantirna South 3152 (03) 801 2367
Established   1963

ABOVE: The onset of autumn at Seville Estate.

Winemaker	Reg Egan,
	assistant Maryann Egan.
Production	1000 cases
Principal Wines	Chardonnay, Pinot Noir

and Cabernet Merlot.

| Best Vintages | R 1969, '70, '74, '77, '78, |
| | '81, '82, '84, '87, '88, '90 |

I have long held the supremely elegant red wines of Wantirna Estate in very high regard; these days the sparkle seems to be a little dimmer, and as I doubt very much whether the wines are in fact regressing, it seems it simply must be that the world is getting more competitive day by day. A little more new oak might help arrest the tide.

WARRAMATE   BA-B

4 Maddens Lane

Gruyere 3770	(059) 64 9219
Established	1970
Winemaker	Jack Church
Production	1500 cases
Principal Wines	Rhine Riesling, Shiraz and

Cabernet Sauvignon.

| Best Vintages | 1977, '79, '82, '86, '88, '89, '90 |

The tiny but beautifully situated Warramate, with Yarra Yering on its northern boundary and Coldstream Hills on its southern, can produce wines of very high quality. Retention of consultant winemaking assistance in 1988 (and again in 1989 and 1990) has paid handsome dividends, with the best wines for over 5 years being produced.

YARRA BURN   CB-B

Settlement Road

Yarra Junction 3797	(059) 67 1428
Established	1976
Winemaker	David Fyffe
Production	7000 cases
Principal Wines	Pinot Noir, Chardonnay,

Sauvignon Blanc/Semillon, Cabernet Sauvignon, Pinot Noir *Méthode Champenoise* and Light Shiraz.

| Best Vintages | R 1982, '84, '85, '86, '90 |

Yarra Burn has made great wines in the past, and will make great wines in the future. Its rating does not do the winery justice, but then neither do the majority of the releases of the past couple of years. No one in the entire valley works harder than do David and Christine Fyffe, and they will surely come out on top. I have no reservations about their first class restaurant nor the extremely beautiful surrounds of the vineyard and winery.

YARRA RIDGE   BA-A

Glenview Road

Yarra Glen 3755	(03) 73 01613
Established	1983
Winemakers	Louis Bialkower, Peter Steer
Production	10,000 cases
Principal Wines	Chardonnay, Sauvignon

Blanc, Pinot Noir and Cabernet Sauvignon.

| Best Vintages | W and R 1989, '90. |

Yarra Ridge is a fast rising star in the Yarra Valley. After a slightly uncertain start, the wine quality has been exemplary, and its aggressive approach to pricing has won it a substantial market share in a short period of time. Sweet, peachy Chardonnay (with a background hint of American oak), an excellent '89 Sauvignon Blanc, and rich, plummy Pinot Noirs have been its best wines.

YARRA YERING   A-A

Briarty Road

Coldstream 3770	(059) 649267
Established	1969
Winemaker	Dr Bailey Carrodus
Production	3000 cases
Principal Wines	Dry White No 1 (Semillon

and Sauvignon Blanc), Chardonnay, Pinot Noir, Dry Red No 1 (a blend of Cabernet Sauvignon, Malbec and Merlot) and Dry Red No 2 (85 per cent Shiraz plus various other Rhône varieties).

| Best Vintages | R 1978, '80, '82, '83, '84, |
| | '87, '88 |

I have long been a staunch and vocal supporter of Yarra Yering's dry reds. These are wines with a quite extraordinary depth and concentration of flavour; just when you think you have found everything the wine has to offer, yet another aspect of its character appears. They are wines which appeal to the heart rather than the mind, and those with a cerebral or over-technical approach may find fault — which is just as well, because there is not enough Yarra Yering to go round.

YERINGBERG   A-A

Maroondah Highway

Coldstream 3770	(03) 739 1453
Established	1862
Winemaker	Guill de Pury
Production	1000 cases
Principal Wines	Marsanne, Chardonnay,

Pinot Noir and 'Yeringberg' (the last a blend of Cabernet Sauvignon, Merlot and Malbec).

| Best Vintages | W and R 1977, '79, '80, |
| | '81, '85, '86, '87, '88, '90 |

As its establishment date suggests, Yeringberg has history on its side. It also has quite superb

wines, with a concentration of flavour and with layers of complexity rivalled only by Yarra Yering. If I had to lay a case of wine down to be drunk in the year 2090, it would be of Yeringberg.

YARRA RIDGE

1 9 8 9

PINOT NOIR

PRODUCE OF AUSTRALIA   750 ml

OTHER WINERIES

BOOLARONG VINEYARD   NR
Old Healesville Road
Yarra Glen 3775 (03) 439 7425

HALCYON DAZE VINEYARD   CB-CB
Uplands Road
Chirnside Park 3116 (03) 726 7111

LIRRALIRRA ESTATE   C-CB
Paynes Road
Lilydale 3140 (03) 735 0224

MADDENS LANE WINERY   NR
Maddens Lane
Gruyere 3770 (059) 64 9279

MONBULK WINERY   C-CB
Macclesfield Road
Monbulk 3793 (03) 756 6965

TUNNEL HILL   B-B
Tarrawarra Winery
Healesville Road
Yarra Glen 3775 (059) 62 3311

YARRA VALE   C-CB
Lot 7, Maroondah Highway
Coldstream 3770 (059) 62 5266

ABOVE: A 90-year-old bottle of 'Sauvignon' (Cabernet Sauvignon)
perfectly preserved in its original straw wrapping.

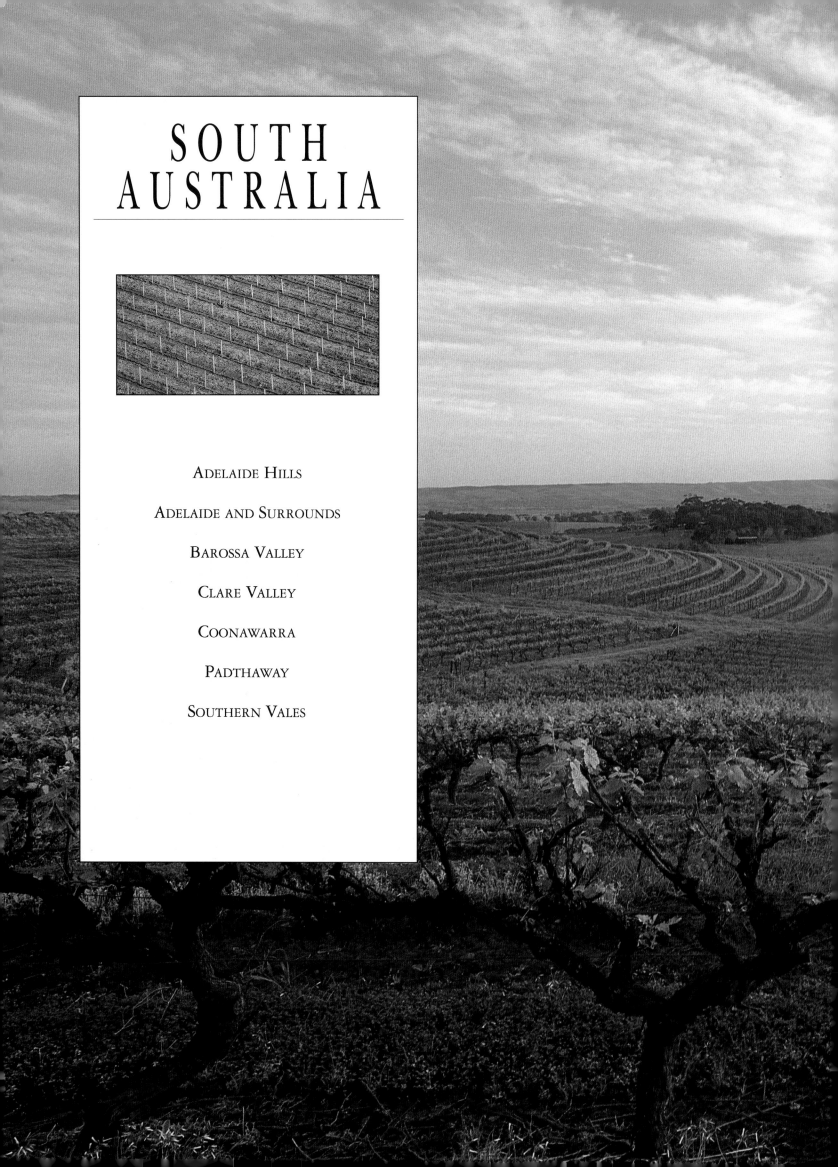

SOUTH
AUSTRALIA

ADELAIDE HILLS

ADELAIDE AND SURROUNDS

BAROSSA VALLEY

CLARE VALLEY

COONAWARRA

PADTHAWAY

SOUTHERN VALES

South Australia has been the centre of wine production in Australia for so long that it is difficult to comprehend that it was ever otherwise. But as the Australian wine production chart opposite shows, it was not until this century that it achieved the dominance it now enjoys.

Victoria's early prosperity was paid for by gold, and in no small measure it was ended by the twin impact of phylloxera and federation. It is an interesting academic question to consider what would have eventuated if phylloxera had not intervened.

The answer is almost certainly that South Australia would still be the major producer, albeit with a distinctly smaller share. For its climate and soils are (and were) ideally suited to the production of full bodied table wine and, with increasing importance after 1900, of sherry and tawny port. Here the Riverland region of South Australia was the key in the heady years following the First World War, and they have remained equally important in the subsequent shift of the production base from fortified to table wine.

But of course the engineroom of the ship is a lot less obvious, and less glamorous, than the bridge, and traditionally South Australian winemaking was equated with that of the Barossa Valley. Needless to say, not only is there the engine room of the Riverland, but the State has substantially more premium areas than just the Barossa: as the wine regions chart on the facing page shows, Coonawarra, Southern Vales and Clare Valley all make major contributions, while that of the Adelaide Hills (for which separate figures are not available) grows day by day.

In the fashion of New South Wales, the first vines were planted in what is now metropolitan Adelaide. John Reynell, Richard Hamilton, Walter Duffield and John White have all laid claim to making the first wine, Duffield receiving particular support from *The South Australian Register* of 25 June 1845. The newspaper reported that he had made six hogsheads of wine (210 dozen bottles) and congratulated him on being the first to produce wine on a commercial scale. Duffield capitalised (so he thought) on the publicity by sending Queen Victoria a case of 1844 white wine made from grapes grown in the Adelaide Hills, and was promptly prosecuted for making wine without the requisite licence.

The first vineyards were established in the Southern Vales by John Reynell and Dr A C Kelly between 1838 and 1840; the Clare Valley by John Horrocks in 1842; at Magill by Dr Christopher Rawson Penfold in 1844; at Langhorne Creek by Frank Potts in the early 1840s; at Pewsey Vale by Joseph Gilbert in 1847 and at Rowland Flat in the Barossa Valley by Johann Gramp in the same year; followed by Samuel Smith at Angaston in 1851, and J E Seppelt and William Jacob in 1854.

Until the 1890s the Barossa Valley provided most of South Australia's wine; the major expansion of the Clare Valley, the Southern Vales and the establishment of the Riverland then followed and ultimately resulted in the production mix we know today. Where any future expansion will take place is

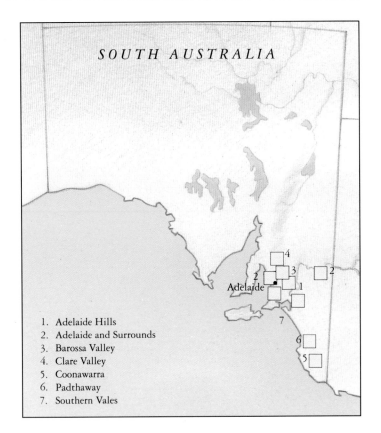

SOUTH AUSTRALIA

1. Adelaide Hills
2. Adelaide and Surrounds
3. Barossa Valley
4. Clare Valley
5. Coonawarra
6. Padthaway
7. Southern Vales

not clear. Coonawarra is fully developed, some would say over-developed. Growth at Padthaway is restricted by the water-sharing agreement between Victoria and South Australia which means no new irrigation rights will be granted. The Barossa Valley has contracted sharply, while the Southern Vales faces relentless urban pressure. The Clare Valley, too, has contracted, and lack of suitable ground water is a continuing fetter on new plantings.

The Adelaide Hills is an area of tremendous potential: that of the northern end has been known (and indeed utilised) for many years, but that of the southern end – from Lenswood through to the Piccadilly Valley – has only started to manifest itself in the second half of the 1980s. Quality is not in dispute: land availability, restrictions imposed by the water catchment authorities, and alternative land-use pressures may nonetheless limit the growth of this exciting cool-climate region.

Perhaps the vineyard established by former Wine and Brandy Corporation chief executive Robert Hesketh near Keith (near the Victorian/South Australian border) points to another new direction. Continued growth along the Riverland is also possible if salinity problems can be controlled — and if there is increased demand for cask rather than premium quality wine. Given the continuing resurgence in the Victorian wine industry, growth needs to come from one source or another for the chart of Australian wine production on the facing page shows just how far South Australia's share of production has fallen since the start of the table wine boom in the early '60s.

PREVIOUS PAGES: *The sweeping expanse of the Southern Vales, looking over Seaview and Coriole Vineyards.*

AUSTRALIAN WINE PRODUCTION IN '000 LITRES
(also given as percentage of the annual total)

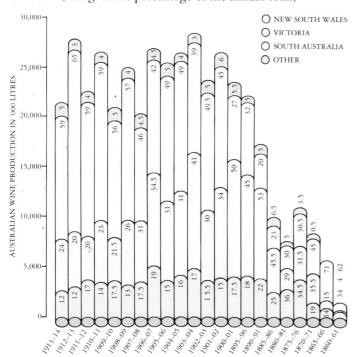

○ NEW SOUTH WALES
○ VICTORIA
○ SOUTH AUSTRALIA
○ OTHER

SOUTH AUSTRALIA WINE REGIONS
HECTAREAGE & PRODUCTION

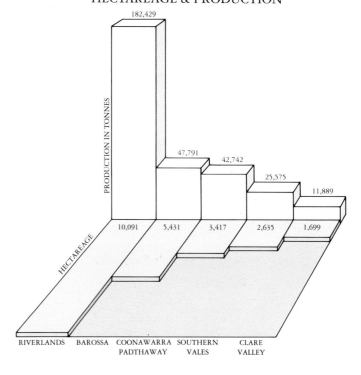

ABOVE: *The windswept slopes of Moutadam.*

SOUTH AUSTRALIA

ADELAIDE HILLS

The northern part of the Adelaide Hills has been home to viticulture for well over a hundred years, and until recently the East Barossa Ranges and the Eden Valley have been regarded as part of the Barossa Valley. Even now the region of origin scheme proposed by the Australian Wine and Brandy Corporation recognises only the Piccadilly subregion (in the south) as falling within the Adelaide Hills, ascribing the numerous subregions in the centre and north to the Barossa Valley.

Yet the winemakers of the Adelaide Hills have themselves defined their area as that part of the Mount Lofty Range which has an altitude of at least 400 metres and an annual rainfall of at least 625 millimetres, incorporating a north-east slanting oblong region extending from the southern edge of Adelaide to 70 kilometres north of Adelaide and which includes the East Barossa Ranges and Eden Valley. The answer to the apparent contradiction is that most of the large Barossa Valley floor wineries buy grapes from or own vineyards in the northern sector, and from a marketing and prestige viewpoint would prefer that the historical annexation continue.

But the reality is that the climate is radically different to that of the Barossa Valley proper, and the style of the wines is only slightly less so. It was for this very reason, for example, that Yalumba progressively developed its Pewsey Vale, Heggies Vineyard and Hill-Smith Estate vineyards in the East Barossa Ranges between 1961 and the end of the 1970s.

This northern end, running from Keyneton south through High Eden, Eden Valley, Flaxmans Valley and Springton, is open, windswept country, with Orlando Steingarten its most famous and extreme manifestation. It is in turn the home of Australia's finest Rhine Riesling: if I had to choose between the Eden Valley and the Clare Valley, that choice — however reluctantly — would fall on the Eden Valley. It, or rather the adjacent Flaxmans Valley, is also the producer of Australia's finest Gewurztraminer: the only difference here is that there is no challenger.

But wineries such as Henschke (in particular) and Mountadam show that this northern end can produce quite

THE REGION IN BRIEF

LOCATION AND ELEVATION
34°34'S 139°8'E Keyneton 35°7'S 138°36'E Clarendon 400—500 m

SUBREGIONS
Keyneton, Eden Valley, Flaxmans Valley, High Eden, Pewsey Vale, Springton, Mount Pleasant, Partalunga, Piccadilly, and Clarendon.

CLIMATE
Notwithstanding the unifying influence of the 400 m altitude base for the district, the diverse topography ensures substantial variation in climate (and microclimate). The only question is whether (in the general Australian usage of these terms) the climate is cool or very cool. One yardstick is the fact that even in the slightly warmer northern parts, vintage starts later than it does in Coonawarra, consistent with the heat degree (HDD) summation for Lenswood of 1392 (compared with 1414 for Coonawarra). At Stirling the summation is significantly less again, falling to less than 1300. The rainfall, as one would expect, is strongly winter/spring dominant, with around 38 per cent of the 750 mm falling between October and April — once again, supplementary irrigation is just as essential in cool climate areas as it is in hot ones. With appropriate site selection, frosts should not be a problem. The real disabilities of the area lie in the wind which is present throughout the growing season (in the north) and in the misty, wet weather which prevails during flowering and fruit set (in the south). These influences operate to sharply reduce potential yields, a reduction which may be partially offset again in quality, but which can nonetheless make the economics of grape production very difficult.

SOIL
The East Barossa Ranges have predominantly grey, grey-brown or brown loamy sands and clay loams falling in the Dy3.22 and 3.61 groups (hard mottled yellow duplex soils). There are also patches of much sandier and more weakly structured soil which run into the duplex soils, but are of lesser quality. Fertility varies, tending to be higher in the southern and central areas.

HARVEST TIME
This basically spans the months of March and April, with Pinot Noir and Chardonnay destined for sparkling wine being picked in the first 2 weeks of March, and the table wine season commencing thereafter (again with those two varieties), finishing sometimes into May with botrytised Rhine Riesling.

PRINCIPAL GRAPE VARIETIES
Rhine Riesling	*Cabernet Sauvignon*
Chardonnay	*Shiraz*
Sauvignon Blanc	*Pinot Noir*
Gewurztraminer	*Merlot*
	Cabernet Franc

AUSTRALASIAN WINE REGIONS
1980 – 1990

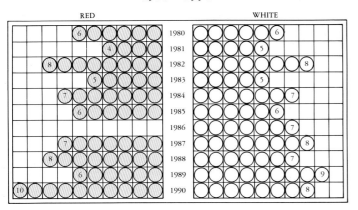

FACING PAGE: *The blue sky above Petaluma will soon give way to wintery grey.*

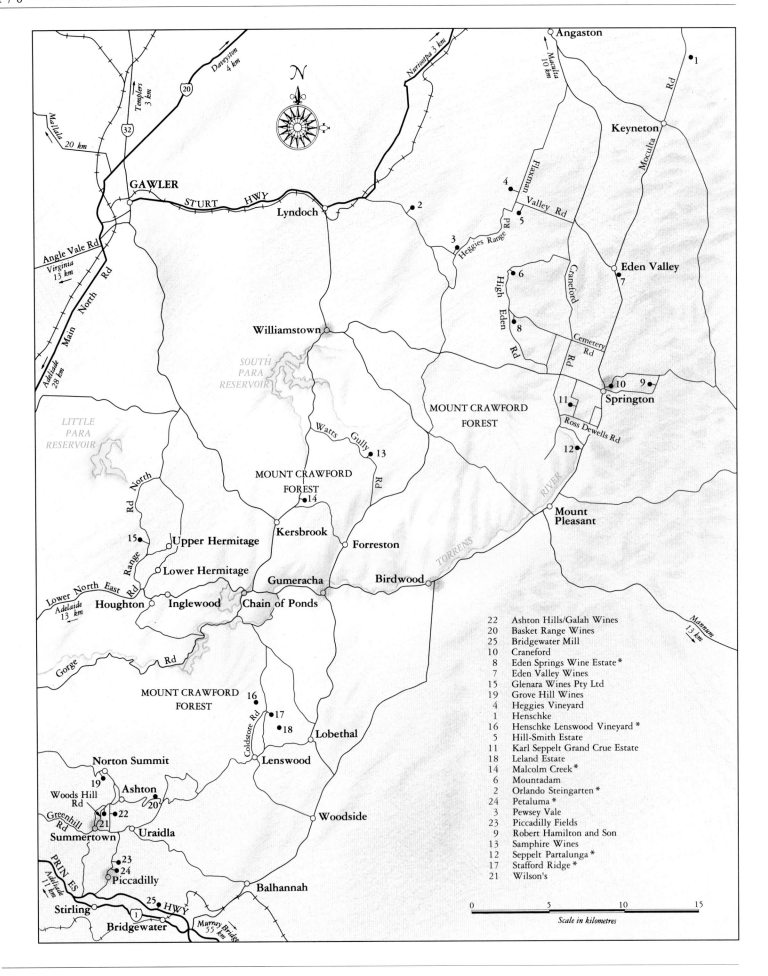

Angaston

1

Keyneton

Moculta
10 km

4

Flaxman

Valley Rd

5

3

Heggies Range Rd

Eden Valley

7

High

6

Craneford

Rd

Eden

Rd

8

Cemetery Rd

Springton

10   9

11

MOUNT CRAWFORD
FOREST

Ross Dewells Rd

12

RIVER

Mount
Pleasant

Mannum
13 km

TORRENS

GAWLER

STURT   HWY

Lyndoch

2

20

32

Templers
3 km

Daveyston
4 km

N

Mallala
20 km

Angle Vale Rd

Virginia
13 km

Main North Rd

Adelaide
28 km

Williamstown

SOUTH
PARA
RESERVOIR

LITTLE
PARA
RESERVOIR

Watts   Gully

13

MOUNT CRAWFORD
FOREST

14

Rd

North   Rd   Range

15   Upper Hermitage

Kersbrook

Forreston

Lower Hermitage

Gumeracha

Birdwood

Lower North East Rd

Adelaide
13 km

Houghton   Inglewood   Chain of Ponds

Gorge   Rd

MOUNT CRAWFORD
FOREST

16

Coldstore Rd

17

18

Lobethal

Norton Summit

19

Ashton

Woods Hill
Rd

20

22

Greenhill
Rd

21

Summertown

Uraidla

23

24

Piccadilly

PRINCES

Adelaide
11 km

Balhannah

25   HWY

Stirling

1

Bridgewater

Murray Bridge
55 km

Lenswood

Woodside

22	Ashton Hills/Galah Wines
20	Basket Range Wines
25	Bridgewater Mill
10	Craneford
8	Eden Springs Wine Estate*
7	Eden Valley Wines
15	Glenara Wines Pty Ltd
19	Grove Hill Wines
4	Heggies Vineyard
1	Henschke
16	Henschke Lenswood Vineyard*
5	Hill-Smith Estate
11	Karl Seppelt Grand Crue Estate
18	Leland Estate
14	Malcolm Creek*
6	Mountadam
2	Orlando Steingarten*
24	Petaluma*
3	Pewsey Vale
23	Piccadilly Fields
9	Robert Hamilton and Son
13	Samphire Wines
12	Seppelt Partalunga*
17	Stafford Ridge*
21	Wilson's

0   5   10   15

Scale in kilometres

bears Croser's name. But right from the first vintage in 1985, Bollinger made two things clear: it did not intend that its name be used in any way in marketing the product, and it had no intention of telling Croser how to make sparkling wine in the Adelaide Hills.

Petaluma now produces five different wine styles: Croser (100 per cent Adelaide Hills) Rhine Riesling (100 per cent Clare Valley), Chardonnay (100 per cent Adelaide Hills, though not originally Adelaide Hills, having moved from Cowra to Coonawarra and thence to the Hills), botrytis Rhine Riesling (100 per cent Coonawarra, but produced only when vintage conditions permit, so far being 1982, '84, '85 and '88) and a single red wine, simply named Coonawarra (first made in 1979, always containing more than 80 per cent Coonawarra Cabernet Sauvignon with a passing parade for the remaining percentage, but now fixed on Merlot, also from Coonawarra).

Despite their radically differing styles, all the wines have a number of things in common. They are elegant and understated in their youth, and all age gracefully and relatively slowly. Each reflects the gradual evolution in Croser's perception of style, particularly in the wake of the Petaluma vineyards in Coonawarra, the Clare Valley and the Adelaide Hills all reaching maturity.

So if one looks at the evolution of the Coonawarra red over the 1985, 1986, 1987 and 1988 vintages, one can immediately see a pay-back for the discipline with which Croser rated his efforts between 1979 and 1984 (where would he be had he rated those wines at 6 and 7?), but more importantly, a marvellous build-up in the strength, structure and complexity of the style, without sacrificing the hallmarks of elegant, crystal clear varietal fruit flavour.

The Rhine Riesling has always been out of the ordinary: the 1980 has now reached the peak of its power, although the leisurely pace it has followed to date suggests it will plateau and hold its form for another 5 years at least. Given that these vineyards were already fully mature when purchased by Petaluma, and that the making of Rhine Riesling is essentially simple (deceptively simple perhaps, and requiring care and discipline), it is hard to see much scope for improvement. In a different way, the same comment applies to the intermittent releases of botrytis Riesling, so much depends on the vineyard.

It is with the Chardonnay that the greatest scope lies. The early vintages were absolutely outstanding by the measure of their times, but in the mid-1980s the gap between Petaluma and its competition (the other 400 or so wineries making one or more Chardonnays each year) narrowed to an uncomfortable degree. In part that reflects Croser's refusal to indulge in the 'fly now, pay later' approach to Chardonnay, which results in precocious peaches and cream styles which bloom all too briefly. The problem is, of course, that most comparisons are made at the time the wines are first released, rather than three, five or seven years down the track when the Petaluma Chardonnay reaches the peak of its development.

If I know Croser as well as I think I do, that rationalisation is not enough. So watch this space, it is quite certain something will fill it.

ABOVE: *The brightly coloured end to another vintage.*

WINERIES OF THE ADELAIDE HILLS

ASHTON HILLS   B-B
Tregarthen Road
Ashton 5137   (08) 390 1243
Established   1982
Winemaker   Stephen George
Production   1280 cases
Principal Wines   Rhine Riesling, Chardonnay,
Pinot Noir and Cabernet.

Best Vintages   Too early to assess.
Ashton Hills is the fulfilment of a long-held
dream for Stephen George, who also releases
wine under his brand Galah Wine, and who has
assisted Tony Brady in the making of
Wendouree wines for over 5 years. Early
indications are that the Ashton Hills vineyard
will give of its best reluctantly, but when it does
give its best the wines will be superb.

BRIDGEWATER MILL   A-A
Mount Barker Road
Bridgewater 5155   (08) 339 3422
Established   1985
Winemaker   Brian Croser
Production   Not for publication.
Principal Wines   Chardonnay, Sauvignon
Blanc, (from the Clare Valley and Coonawarra),
Cabernet Malbec, Rhine Riesling (from the
Clare Valley) Bridgewater Brut, McLaren Vale
Pinot Noir and Chardonnay (from the Clare
Valley).
Best Vintages   W and R 1987, '88, '89, '90

Bridgewater Mill houses the sparkling winemaking facilities of Petaluma, producing the wine
simply known as Croser. It also gives its name to
a second range of wines produced by Petaluma,
and made to similarly high standards. The
building itself is one of the most beautiful and

historic in a State abundantly blessed with old
buildings, and the restaurant (in two parts) is
second to none. Less than half an hour's drive
from Adelaide, a visit cannot be too highly
recommended.

CRANEFORD   C-B
Main Street
Springton 5235   (085) 68 2220
Established   1978
Winemaker   Colin Forbes
Production   2200 cases
Principal Wines   Rhine Riesling, Chardonnay,
Cabernet Sauvignon, Shiraz and Sparkling
Burgundy.
Best Vintages   W 1988, '89, '90
                        R 1987, '88, '90
Craneford was for many years a label without a
winery; Colin Forbes has now purchased the
Holmes Estate winery and cellar door sales
facility, and that label (Holmes Estate) will be
seen no more. Forbes is a very experienced
winemaker, but it has to be said that quality has
been disappointing.

HEGGIES VINEYARD   BA-BA
Cnr Heggies Range and
Tanunda Creek Roads
Adelaide Hills   (085) 64 2423
Established   1971
Winemaker   Alan Hoey, Simon Adams
Production   14,000 cases
Principal Wines   Chardonnay, Rhine Riesling,
Botrytis Affected Late Harvest Rhine Riesling
and Cabernet/Merlot.
Best Vintages   W 1979, '82, '84, '86, '88, '90
Heggies Vineyards was the second of the
Yalumba high country vineyards to be establish-
ed, and a part of the very carefully thought out
strategy of the Yalumba group for sourcing the
highest quality grapes for table wines. Rhine
Riesling, both dry and botrytised, has been the
vineyard's strength, with strong lime juice
aroma and flavour. The range has expanded now,

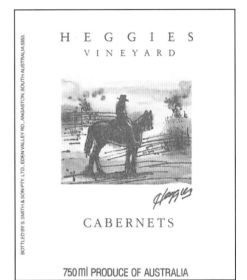

and the best of the new wines is a peachy/buttery
Chardonnay with pronounced oak.

HENSCHKE   A-A
Moculta Road
Keyneton 5353   (085) 64 8223
Established   1868
Winemaker   Stephen Henschke
Production   40,000 cases
Principal Wines   Hill of Grace, Cyril Henschke
Cabernet Sauvignon, Mount Edelstone, Keyneton
Estate, Malbec, White Burgundy, Semillon,
Chardonnay, Sauvignon Blanc, Rhine Riesling,
Dry White Frontignac, Rhine Riesling Spatlese
and Rhine Riesling Auslese.Tilley's Vineyard
White Burgundy is a new addition to the range.
Best Vintages   W 1972, '73, '78, '79, '82,
                        '84, '87, '88, '90
                        R 1972, '73, '77, '78, '82,
                        '84, '85, '86, '90
On any view of the matter, one of the top half
dozen small wineries of Australia, consistently
producing a superb range of both white and red
wines. Exceptional oak handling is a feature of

the whites, while the reds all have quite exceptional colour, flavour and depth — directly deriving from the very old but outstanding vineyards.

HILL-SMITH ESTATE   B-B
Flaxman Valley Road
Adelaide Hills   (085) 64 2423
Established   1980
Winemakers   Robert Hill-Smith,
                       Alan Hoey (consultant)
Production   7500 cases
Principal Wines   Fumé Blanc, Semillon, Chardonnay, Shiraz and Late Harvest Semillon.
Best Vintages   W 1984, '87, '88, '89, '90
                       R 1988, '90
A competitively priced range of wines, once overly dependent on oak but no longer so, which, I suspect, was primarily developed for the export market. Late Harvest Semillon is often very good; the Shiraz may also yet prove to be a winner.

KARL SEPPELT GRAND CRU ESTATE   B-A
Ross Dewell's Road
Springton 5235   (085) 68 2378
Established   1981
Winemaker   Presently made by contract at various wineries, including Petaluma, Yalumba.
Production   2800 cases
Principal Wines   Rhine Riesling, Chardonnay, Shiraz and Cabernet Sauvignon.
Best Vintages   W and R 1986, '87, '88
In the wake of SA Brewing's takeover of Seppelt, Karl Seppelt relinquished his position as marketing director and turned his attention to the family estate. Curiously, the winemaking side has more than competently looked after itself; it is the marketing which is still to take shape and direction. In consequence, the wines are underappreciated and underpriced.

MALCOLM CREEK   BA-B
Bonython Road
Kersbrook 5231 (vineyard only)
Established   1982
Winemaker   Reg Tolley
Production   500 cases

Principal Wines   Chardonnay and Cabernet Sauvignon.
Best Vintages   W 1986, '88, '90
                       R 1986, '89, '90
The first commercial vintage from the family vineyard of Reg Tolley of Tolley Pedare (Adelaide Metropolitan Region) fame was in 1986. With the dual advantages of the Adelaide Hills climate and the totally professional winemaking at Tolley, Malcolm Creek is a label worth watching.

MOUNTADAM   BA-B
High Eden Road
High Eden Ridge
5235   (085) 64 1101
Established   1970
Winemaker   Adam Wynn
Production   7000 cases
Principal Wines   Riesling, Chardonnay, Pinot Noir, Cabernet Sauvignon and Chardonnay Pinot Noir Sparkling.
Best Vintages   W 1981, '84, '85, '86, '87, '89, '90
                       R 1979, '84, '85, '86, '87, '88, '90
It is hard to imagine greater dedication to quality; Mountadam represents the culmination of the unmatched wine industry career of David Wynn, and the start of that of son Adam. Robert Parker is amongst the most prominent of those who revere the Mountadam Chardonnay, but I had real difficulties with the style up until the 1989 vintage, which I greatly like. I have no such reservations about the Pinot Noir or about most of the Cabernets. It should be noted that most writers would accord Mountadam an A-A rating.

ORLANDO STEINGARTEN   BA-B
Eastern Barossa Ranges
due east of Rowland Flat,
north of Trial Hills Road
off Sturt Highway 5350 (085) 21 3111
Established   1962
Winemaker   Robin Day
Production   Limited quantity made.
Principal Wines   Only Orlando Steingarten Riesling, normally as a dry white wine but a Spatlese was made in 1976 and 1979.

ABOVE: The vines are made to struggle at Mount Adam, but grape quality is not in doubt.

ABOVE: *Petaluma and the Piccadilly Valley: a distinctly European feel
prevails through most of the year.*

Best Vintages 1976, '79, '80, '82, '84, '86, '87, '88, '90

Impossible dream, romantic folly, call it what you will, but even the large companies occasionally fall prey to sentiment. Colin Gramp was the instigator, but happily Orlando has kept this windswept hill of rock in production, and are indeed taking steps to increase it through the establishment of much needed windbreaks. Quality is often a just reward, but not always.

PETALUMA   A-A
Spring Gully Road
Piccadilly 5151   (08) 339 4011
Established   1976
Winemaker   Brian Croser
Production   50,000 cases (of both Petaluma labels and of Croser).
Principal Wines   The principal Adelaide Hills release is the *Méthode Champenoise* simply named Croser. Adelaide Hills Chardonnay has been a component of Petaluma Chardonnay from 1985 in increasing proportion. The first Pinot Noir table wine was made in 1989. For other Petaluma entries see the Clare Valley and Coonawarra sections on pages ***.
Best Vintages   W 1978, '80, '82, '86, '87, '88, '90
          Sparkling 1987, '88, '89, '90

Croser (the sparkling wine) follows a unique style path, diametrically opposed to that of, say, Seppelt Salinger, and demonstrating that extreme finesse and elegance does not mean lack of flavour intensity. Much the same comment applies to the very long-lived Chardonnay, understated in its youth but growing slowly and surely in bottle.

PEWSEY VALE   BA-BA
Browne's Road
Adelaide Hills Pewsey Vale (085) 64 2423
Established   1961
Winemaker   Alan Hoey

Production   22,000 cases
Principal Wines   Rhine Riesling, Botrytis Rhine Riesling and Cabernet Sauvignon.
Best Vintages   W 1970, '71, '73, '78, '79, '80, '82, '84, '86, '88, '90
          R 1975, '76, '81, '82, '84, '86, '87, '88, '90

Yalumba showed extraordinary foresight in re-establishing viticulture in the Adelaide Hills after a gap of over 60 years. Pewsey Vale has both symbolic and practical importance. Its Rhine Riesling has long been at the forefront of the style, remarkable for its longevity and for the largely unseen steely strength of its structure. The Cabernet Sauvignon is not in the same class, tending to lightness and leafiness.

ROBERT HAMILTON & SON   CB-B
Hamilton's Road
Springton 5235   (085) 68 2264
Established   1981
Winemaker   Robert Hamilton (and consultants).
Production   4000 cases
Principal Wines   Rhine Riesling, Semillon, Chardonnay, Shiraz, Cabernet Sauvignon and Cabernet Shiraz.
Best Vintages   W and R 1982, '85, '86, '87
The label marks the re-entry of the Hamilton family into winemaking on its own account; the family purchased the historic winery back from Mildara wines in 1981, continuing a family tradition which commenced in 1837.

STAFFORD RIDGE   BA-BA
Stafford Ridge (vineyard only)
Lenswood 5240   (08) 272 2105
Established   1980
Winemaker   Geoffrey Weaver
Production   3500 cases
Principal Wines   Rhine Riesling, Chardonnay and Cabernet Merlot.
Best Vintages   W 1986, '88
          R 1988, '89
Geoff Weaver, chief winemaker at Thomas Hardy, has his employer's permission (which he does not abuse) to produce small quantities of wine from his own vineyard. Stafford Ridge (formerly Ashbourne) is the result, with a passionfruit flavoured Rhine Riesling invariably excellent.

WILSON'S   B-B
No winery established or planned at present; wines made by contract at Petaluma under Ian Wilson's direction.
(08) 231 9555
Established   1987
Winemaker   Ian Wilson
Production   12,000 cases
Principal Wines   One wine: Wilson's, a premium non-vintage sparkling wine presently utilising McLaren Vale Chardonnay and Pinot Noir, but in the near future moving to pre-

dominantly Adelaide Hills grown material.
Best Vintages   Not relevant.
Ian Wilson is genuinely committed to producing the best possible sparkling wine from grapes largely sourced in the Adelaide Hills. For the time being, he has to be content with McLaren Vale fruit, but not for too long.

OTHER WINERIES

BASKET RANGE WINES   NR
Blockers Road
Basket Range 5138   (08) 390 1515

EDEN SPRINGS WINES ESTATE   NR
Boehm Springs Road
Springton 5253   (085) 64 1056

EDEN VALLEY WINES   NR
Main Street
Eden Valley 5235   (085) 64 1111

GALAH WINES   CB-BA
Box 231
Ashton 5137   (08) 390 1243
(mail order only)

GLENARA WINES PTY LTD   CB-BA
126 Range Road
North Upper Hermitage 5131 (08) 380 5056

GROVE HILL WINES   NR
120 Old Norton Summit Road
Norton Summit 5136   (08)390 1437

PICCADILLY FIELDS   NR
Udy's Road,
Piccadilly 5151

SAMPHIRE WINES   NR
Watts Gully Road
Kersbrook 5231   (08) 389 3183

SEPPELT PARTALUNGA   BA-B
Adelaide Hills (vineyard only)
(085) 68 2470

ADELAIDE AND SURROUNDS

The South Australian Riverland constitutes the engine room which drives the Australian wine industry. Typically it produces almost 60 per cent of all South Australia's grapes and around 30 per cent of the national crush, although the precise contribution will vary from year to year according to vintage.

That variation does not come about, as one might expect, solely because of climatic conditions. These play a part in expanding and shrinking production, but the essence of the Riverland is its reliable climate and dependable production yield. The wild cards are sultana, a white variety known as a multi-purpose grape, and to a lesser degree Muscat Gordo Blanco. These grapes may be used either for winemaking or for drying (or as fresh grapes for the table) and act as a safety valve for fluctuating supply and demand in the various sectors. It is here more than anywhere else that one comes

AUSTRALASIAN WINE REGIONS
1980 – 1990

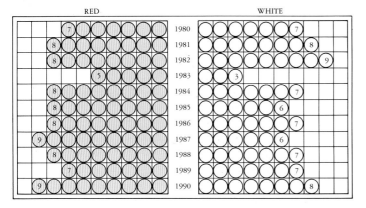

THE REGIONS IN BRIEF

LOCATION AND ELEVATION
RIVERLAND
34°02'S 139°40'E Morgan 34°10'S 140°45'E Renmark
20 — 65 m

ADELAIDE PLAINS
34°41'S 138°34'E
20 m

SUBREGIONS
RIVERLAND
Ramco, Barmera, Morgan, Kingston, Qualco, Renmark, Loxton, Lyrup, Murtho, Berri, Waikerie, Moorook and Monash.

ADELAIDE PLAINS
Gawler River and Evanston.

CLIMATE
Both regions are uncompromisingly hot. Waikerie has a heat summation (HDD) of 2245, Berri 2330, Renmark 2384; each has an MJT in excess of 23°C. These figures are higher than that of the Adelaide Plains, but not so as to materially change the nature of the climate or the style of the wines. The total rainfall is around 275 mm, of which only 130 mm falls between October and March.

SOIL
The soils along the vast length of the Murray River are remarkably uniform, dominated by red-brown sandy loams known as calcareous earths, falling principally into the Gc1.22 classification. The subsoils gradually become more clayey and calcareous (and hence more alkaline), but there is no sharp dividing line as there is with the duplex soils. Fertility is moderate, and both surface and subsoils are permeable. However, the flat countryside and the build-up of salinity with continuous irrigation has made drainage essential.

HARVEST TIME
Mid-February to late March, sometimes extending into early April.

PRINCIPAL GRAPE VARIETIES
The figures given are for the Riverland; those for the Adelaide Plains/Adelaide metropolitan region are not separately recorded and are, in any event, very small by comparison. Usually 50 per cent or more of the Sultana plantings are used for drying.

Sultana, 1866 ha	*Grenache, 778 ha*
Muscat Gordo Blanco, 1771 ha	*Shiraz, 667 ha*
Boradillo, 677 ha	*Mataro, 396 ha*
Palomino, 481 ha	*Cabernet Sauvignon, 392 ha*
Trebbiano, 331 ha	TOTAL GRAPES, 3038 ha
Rhine Riesling, 329 ha	
Chardonnay, 315 ha	
Colombard, 216 ha	
TOTAL GRAPES, 7052 ha	

ABOVE: Newly formed leaves glow with the iridescence of a butterfly emerging from its cocoon.

FACING PAGE: Afternoon shade brings relief from the heat of the Adelaide Plains.

ABOVE: *The flat terrain makes good drainage essential.*

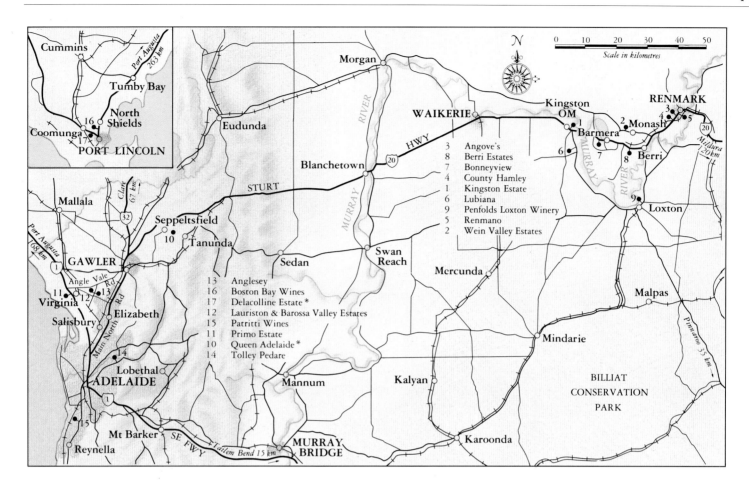

face to face with the reality that fundamentally grapes are no different to any other agricultural commodity, their price determined not by their cost of production but by the laws of supply and demand.

Neither the countryside, the vineyards, the wineries (few in number and all more like petrol refineries than traditional wineries) nor the wines produced will have any particular appeal to those who are sufficiently interested in wine to have taken the trouble to purchase or read this book in the first place. But cast your mind back to the first glass of wine you purchased: you will very probably have forgotten it, but there is a very good chance it came from a wine cask, and — although you did not know it then — that it was made from grapes grown somewhere along the Murray or Murrum-bidgee Rivers.

Also included in this chapter are the Adelaide metropolitan region and the Adelaide Plains (once known as Angle Vale). While the Adelaide Plains is geographically discontinous, it has many features in common: a hot, dry climate (reducing fungal diseases), coupled with near-total reliance on irrigation, makes the economics of grape growing both predictable and (in normal market conditions) favourable.

The peculiar thing about winemakers is that no matter where they may be and no matter what their theoretical station in life, they are forever driven by the belief that next vintage they can produce a greater wine than they have ever done hitherto, and that in doing so they can rise above the theoretical limitations of their region. And technically Australian winemakers (and wineries) are second to none. The result is that companies such as Angove's, Barossa Valley Estates, Primo Estate, Woodley Queen Adelaide, Renmano and Tolley Pedare can all produce wines (principally white) which rise far above the ordinary — and which help give the industry the formidable reputation it enjoys in so many of the markets of the world.

ABOVE: *The region is a highly efficient producer of medium quality table wines destined for use in casks.*

WINERIES OF ADELAIDE AND SURROUNDS

ADELAIDE PLAINS

ANGLESEY   CB-B
Heaslip Road
Angle Vale 5117   (085) 24 3157
Established   1969
Winemaker   Lindsay Stanley
Production   10,000 cases
Principal Wines Semillon, Chardonnay, Sauvignon Blanc Chenin Blanc, Chablis, Cabernet/Malbec, Shiraz/Cabernet, Cabernet/Merlot, and QVS Red (Cabernet/Shiraz/Malbec).
Best Vintages   W and R 1984, '86, '88, '90

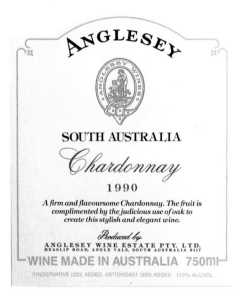

Anglesey has struggled bravely and tenaciously to establish a satisfactory position in the market place, but has not succeeded. A change of ownership seems likely; where the brand is headed is not certain.

LAURISTON AND BAROSSA VALLEY ESTATES   BA-A
Heaslop Road
Angle Vale 5117   (085) 24 3100
Established   1984
Winemaker   Colin Glaetzer
Production   110,000 cases
Principal Wines   There are now two principal releases from Lauriston: the Barossa Valley Estates range comprising Sauvignon Blanc, Rhine Riesling, Semillon, Chardonnay, Late-picked Frontignac, Hermitage and Cabernet Sauvignon; and the Lauriston range comprising Chardonnay, Sauvignon Blanc, Cabernet Shiraz and *Méthode Champenoise* Vintage Brut, which may be made at Lauriston or alternatively purchased from other makers either within the Berri Renmano group or outside it.
Best Vintages   Irrelevant.
The quality of the wines coming out under these labels — and particularly Barossa Valley Estates — never ceases to amaze me. The feature of both the white and red wines is the depth and richness of the flavour; one can only assume there are some traditional, dry-land Barossa farmers still supplying high quality grapes grown from low-yielding vineyards to the group.

PRIMO ESTATE   A-A
Old Port Wakefield Road
Virginia 5120   (08) 380 9442
Established   1979
Winemaker   Joe Grilli
Production   9000 cases
Principal Wines   Riesling, Sauvignon Blanc, Colombard, Chardonnay, Auslese Riesling, Beerenauslese Riesling, Shiraz, Cabernet Sauvignon, 'Joseph' Double Pruned Cabernet Sauvignon and 'Joseph' Cabernet Merlot Moda Amarone.
Best Vintages   W 1982, '85, '87, '88, '90
   R 1984, '85, '87, '88, '90

Those who top their graduation year from university (or other tertiary institutions) not infrequently disappear back into the academic world, or sink from sight in the commercial world. Joe Grilli took away the gold medal as dux of Roseworthy Agricultural College, and has put it to brilliant use at Primo Estate, producing a fascinating array of wines using a galaxy of innovative winemaking techniques.

OTHER WINERIES

BOSTON BAY WINES   CB-CB
Lincoln Highway
Port Lincoln 5606   (086) 84 3600

DELACOLLINE ESTATE   CB-CB
Whillas Road
Port Lincoln 5606   (086) 82 5277

PATRITTI WINES   DC-C
13-23 Clacton Road
Dover Gardens 5048   (08) 296 8261

ADELAIDE METROPOLITAN REGION

QUEEN ADELAIDE   CB-A
Seppeltsfield
via Tanunda 5352   (085) 62 8028
Established   1858
Winemaker   Ian McKenzie
Production   Very substantial, but not for publication.

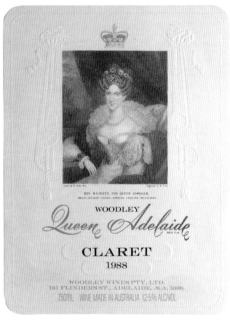

Principal Wines   Queen Adelaide Riesling, Queen Adelaide Chardonnay, Queen Adelaide Spatlese Lexia, Queen Adelaide White Burgundy, Queen Adelaide Chablis, Queen Adelaide Claret, Queen Adelaide Vintage Brut Champagne, Three Roses Sherry, Lord Melbourne Port are the principal brands, with Queen Adelaide Riesling one of the largest brand sellers in Australia. Also very limited occasional releases of high-quality Cabernet Sauvignon from Coonawarra such as the Queen Adelaide Classic Hermitage 1985.
Best Vintages   To all intents and purposes irrelevant.
The establishment date is a somewhat notional one, going back to the forerunner of Woodley wines, which was the company to first develop the Queen Adelaide label as part of a historic series of labels from the early 1950s. Queen Adelaide is now Seppelt's answer to Boadicea, or, if you prefer, Queen of the fighting varietals. Unwooded Chardonnay is the spearhead. (Cellar door sales at Seppelts Barossa Valley.)

TOLLEY PEDARE   B-B
30 Barracks Road
Hope Valley 5090   (08) 264 2255
Established   1892
Winemakers   Chris Tolley, Robert Scapin

Production 250,000 cases
Principal Wines Rhine Riesling, Gewurztraminer, Chardonnay, Chablis, Colombard/Semillon, Sauvignon Blanc, Spatlese Frontignac, Pinot Noir, Shiraz Cabernet and Cabernet Sauvignon. Also a limited range of fortified wines and a Chardonnay/Pinot Noir bottle fermented Vintage Brut.
Best Vintages W 1982, '86, '87, '88, '90
R 1981, '82, '86, '87, '90
Listed in the Adelaide metropolitan area, simply because that is where the winery happens to be; most of the grapes are grown in the company's large vineyards in the Barossa Valley, some are grown in the Riverland. Gewurztraminer has long been an unlikely specialty of the winery, with the Cabernet Sauvignon consistently justifying the high rating for value.

THE RIVERLAND

ANGOVE'S CB-BA
Bookmark Avenue
Renmark 5341 (085) 85 1311
Established 1886
Winemaker Frank Newman
Production Not for publication but substantial.
Principal Wines A complete range of table and fortified wines is made. The table wines are Angove's Varietal releases (8 white wines and a red wine); Bin Reference Claret Sauvignon/Shiraz and Shiraz/Malbec; The Reserve Series Tregrahan Claret, Brightlands Burgundy,

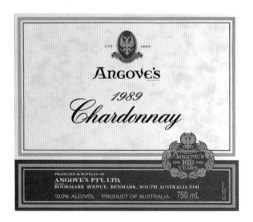

Bookmark Riesling, Nanya Moselle and Golden Murray Sauterne, Special Riesling, Moselle and Claret; and the 2 litre flagon and 5 litre flagon and 5 litre cask range. The range of brandies includes St Agnes Old Brandy, Old Liqueur Brandy and Three Star Brandy.
Best Vintages Theoretically irrelevant, but I have the sneaking suspicion more attention should be paid to it.
Angove's never produces bad wines, but every second or third vintage it comes up with a range of varietals (either white or red) which shows why Riverland winemakers become irritable when their wines are assumed to be of cask quality and no more. It is in years such as these that the A portion of the value rating applies with full force.

BERRI ESTATES C-B
Sturt Highway
Glossop 5344 (085) 83 2303
Established 1922
Winemaker Reg Wilkinson
Production The equivalent of 3 million cases.
Principal Wines Specialists in 5 litre wine casks, fine old fortifieds and bulk sales to other wineries. A range of 750 ml bottles in low to medium price bracket called Brentwood.
Best Vintages Irrelevant.
Almost exclusively a bulk and cask wine producer, with a small amount released under the Brentwood label at prices reminiscent of the 1970s; these are honest but unambitious wines.

RENMANO BA-A
Sturt Highway
Renmark 5341 (085)86 6771
Established 1914
Winemaker Paul Kassebaum
Production The equivalent of 1.4 million cases.
Principal Wines Renmano 2 litre wine casks and 750 ml table wines released under Chairman's Selection range comprising Chardonnay Bin 104, Traminer Riesling Bin 204, Sauvignon

Blanc, Rhine Riesling Bin 604, Cabernet Sauvignon Bin 460 and Merlot Bin 540; Rumpole Tawny Port, Cromwell Tawny Port; Paringa Hill Hermitage, Lockley Ridge Colombard Chardonnay, and Chabrel VSOP Brandy. Very large sales in bulk also made.
Best Vintages Conventionally treated as irrelevant, but in fact the quality and style of each particular wine varies markedly.
The Renmano Chairman's Selection range has really made people sit up and pay attention to what goes on in the Riverland. The 1988 Chairman's Selection Chardonnay was the most decorated show wine of the 1988 show year, winning the Tucker Seabrook Caon Trophy for the Champion Wine (white or red) to appear in that show year. The Dolly Parton description was invented for bosomy, peaches and cream, full bodied Chardonnays long before that particular wine appeared, but if ever this was an apt description it is for this wine.

OTHER WINERIES

BONNEYVIEW DC-C
Sturt Highway
Barmera 5345 (085) 88 2279

COUNTY HAMLEY NR
Cnr Bookmark Avenue and
Twenty-Eighth Street, Renmark 5341
(085) 85 1411

KINGSTON ESTATE
Kingston-on-Murray 5331 (085) 83 0244

LUBIANA DC-C
School Road
Moorook 5332 (085) 83 9320

WEIN VALLEY ESTATES NR
Nixon Road,
Monash 5342 (085) 83 5225

ABOVE: The stainless steel screw in the receival bin takes the grapes into the crusher.

SOUTH AUSTRALIA

BAROSSA VALLEY

The Barossa Valley is a paradox. It is the most important wine producing region in Australia, and will always remain so. Penfolds, Orlando, Seppelt, Wolf Blass, Yalumba, Saltram, Krondorf and Peter Lehmann produce considerably more than 50 per cent of Australian wine, and are all headquartered in the Barossa Valley.

But as a wine growing region it is of much lesser importance. The Commonwealth statistics include the Adelaide Hills plantings, and even with these taken into account, in the record vintage of 1989 the Barossa Valley provided only 8.5 per cent of the national crush. Viticulturally, it has been (and is being) restructured at a faster rate than any area other than the Hunter Valley. As the chart below implies, between 1979 and 1989 there was a decline of 35 per cent in overall plantings, which is almost twice the national average of 18.4 per cent over the same period. Yet tonnage has remained more or less constant (this time tracking the national average) edging up from 45,956 tonnes in 1979, to 47,791 tonnes in 1989.

Two things have happened: the varietal mix has changed radically, and the majority of the old, unirrigated, bush-pruned low yielding vineyards have gone out of production

BAROSSA VALLEY HECTAREAGE / GRAPE VARIETIES

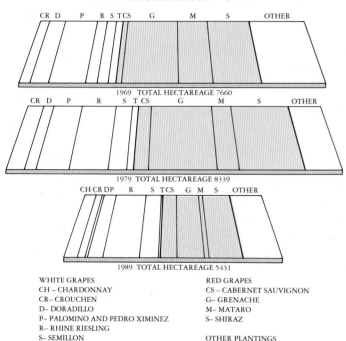

1969 TOTAL HECTAREAGE 7660

1979 TOTAL HECTAREAGE 8339

1989 TOTAL HECTAREAGE 5431

WHITE GRAPES
CH – CHARDONNAY
CR– CROUCHEN
D– DORADILLO
P– PALOMINO AND PEDRO XIMINEZ
R– RHINE RIESLING
S– SEMILLON
T– TREBBIANO

RED GRAPES
CS – CABERNET SAUVIGNON
G– GRENACHE
M– MATARO
S– SHIRAZ

OTHER PLANTINGS

AUSTRALASIAN WINE REGIONS
1980 – 1990

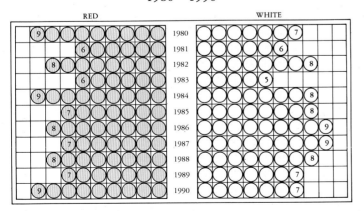

THE REGION IN BRIEF

LOCATION AND ELEVATION
34°29'S 139°00'E Nuriootpa
274 m

SUBREGIONS
Rowland Flat, Nuriootpa, Dorrien, Barossa Valley, Gomersal, Seppeltsfield, Lyndoch, Greenock, Tanunda and Angaston.

CLIMATE
In an era in which cool climate viticulture has become so fashionable, the Barossa Valley and its climate are often treated as passé (or unfashionably warm). The HDD summation of 1710 and the MJT of 21.4°C seem to support that view, but there are off-setting factors. The fact is that the winters are cold, spring is usually mild and relatively wet, while temperatures start to fall significantly by the start of April. The problem — if it be a problem — lies with the very hot weather which can come from Central Australia in February and March, placing extreme stress on the vines (and on the wineries) at the end of the ripening cycle. Adding to the stress is the winter/spring oriented rainfall, with only 210 mm of the annual (and itself sparse) rainfall of 520 mm falling from October to April. The traditional viticultural answer was to prune the vines very hard, resulting in low yields which the vines could handle even in these adverse circumstances. The modern solution has been to install drip irrigation and to thereby substantially increase yield.

SOIL
The soil types fall into two groups: brown, loamy sand to clay loam surface soils falling in the hard red duplex groups of Dr2.23 and 3.23; and the light brownish grey to dark grey-brown sandy soils falling in the Dy5.43, 5.82 and 5.83 group (sandy, mottled grey duplex soils). As with most soils suited to viticulture, fertility is moderately low (and distinctly low in the case of the sandy yellow duplex soils), and overall there is a tendency to acidity which increases with depth and which will restrict vigour unless altered by the application of lime and gypsum.

HARVEST TIME
Varieties destined for sparkling wine are harvested at the end of February; early ripening table wine varieties usually commence in the first week of March, and picking continues steadily through to mid to late April before tapering off to a few specially selected sites or varieties.

PRINCIPAL GRAPE VARIETIES
See chart at left

FACING PAGE: *The 'Old Block' of St Hallett: Shiraz planted 100 years ago, and still going strong.*

So if you turn the coin over, it is possible to argue that the Barossa Valley's efficiency as a grape producer has increased by a far greater degree than the national average.

What it unquestionably means is that the viticultural face of the Barossa Valley and the style of the wines it produces have changed forever. In terms of production economics — particularly of those of the big companies — it is simply reality born of necessity. But it led to an alarming erosion of the spirit and pride of the Barossa Valley throughout the 1970s and much of the 1980s — an erosion which has since been halted by a curious (and at times uneasy) mixture of conservationists and developers.

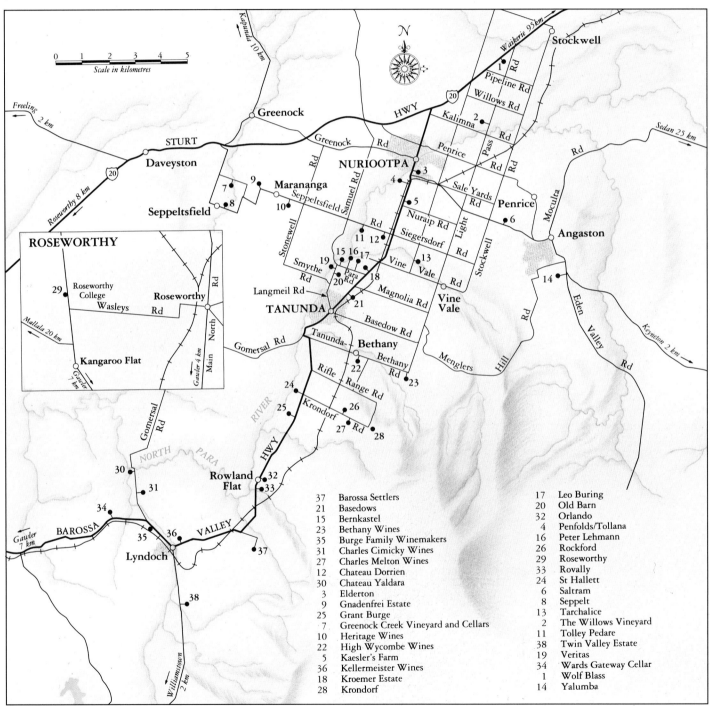

No.	Winery	No.	Winery
37	Barossa Settlers	17	Leo Buring
21	Basedows	20	Old Barn
15	Bernkastel	32	Orlando
23	Bethany Wines	4	Penfolds/Tollana
35	Burge Family Winemakers	16	Peter Lehmann
31	Charles Cimicky Wines	26	Rockford
27	Charles Melton Wines	29	Roseworthy
12	Chateau Dorrien	33	Rovally
30	Chateau Yaldara	24	St Hallett
3	Elderton	6	Saltram
9	Gnadenfrei Estate	8	Seppelt
25	Grant Burge	13	Tarchalice
7	Greenock Creek Vineyard and Cellars	2	The Willows Vineyard
10	Heritage Wines	11	Tolley Pedare
22	High Wycombe Wines	38	Twin Valley Estate
5	Kaesler's Farm	19	Veritas
36	Kellermeister Wines	34	Wards Gateway Cellar
18	Kroemer Estate	1	Wolf Blass
28	Krondorf	14	Yalumba

ABOVE: *Seppelt has almost certainly forgotten it won these first prizes.*

Their common bond is the fabulously rich heritage of the Barossa Valley, which is visibly and permanently reflected in the wonderful stone buildings of the towns, the farms and the vineyards. A quick look at the town of Tanunda, or at the Seppelt, Yalumba, Saltram, Grant Burge and Rockford wineries will say it all. Stucco, plate glass and 'progress' in all its ugly manifestations has wrought some damage, but the essential physical fabric is still there.

And the metaphysical is now also receiving succour from a group whose most active members include Peter Lehmann, Robert O'Callaghan (of Rockford), Bob Maclean (of St Hallett), Grant Burge, Graeme Melton (of Charles Melton Wines), Maggie Beer (of the Pheasant Farm restaurant) and artist Rod Schubert. The role of the various planning authorities can best be described as ambiguous, but the momentum for sensible preservation and conservation of the Barossa Valley as a viticultural region seems secure.

There will be hiccups along the way, and the sheer size of the Barossa Valley, its beauty, its history, and its Germanic culture will always generate a certain degree of tourist-driven veneer. But the links with Johann Gramp (who planted his first vines at Rowland Flat in 1847), Samuel Hoffman (who followed suit in the same year), J E Seppelt (shortly after), and William Jacob (at Jacobs Creek in 1854) grow stronger rather than weaker.

ABOVE: *A patchwork quilt of 100-year-old German improvisation at Rockford stands defiantly against the elements.*

PRINCIPAL WINE STYLES

SHIRAZ
Shiraz is given pride of place because the Barossa Valley is the birthplace of Penfolds Grange Hermitage, the greatest red wine made from this variety outside of the confines of the northern Rhône Valley. Penfolds Bin 28 Shiraz is another famous marque; almost every Barossa Valley winery has a Shiraz or Shiraz blend somewhere on the books, but in recent years Elderton, Kaiser Stuhl Red Ribbon and Peter Lehmann have been among the most consistent and best contributors. The style is full blooded — dark in colour, rich in dark red fruits with a touch of chocolate, a hint of roasted character, and sometimes eucalypt/mint. The structure is round and velvety, and the wines are almost invariably extremely long lived.

CABERNET SAUVIGNON
Cabernet Sauvignon follows a similar track to Shiraz. Wonderfully strong and rich in flavour and colour, it does manage to cling to its varietal character, but it is often best blended with grapes from other regions such as the Eden Valley, McLaren Vale or Coonawarra. That, certainly, was the view of Max Schubert, and the illustrious Penfolds Bin 707 Cabernet Sauvignon is now a wholehearted marriage between the Barossa Valley and Coonawarra.

RHINE RIESLING
Just as almost every Barossa Valley winery has a Shiraz, so does it have a Rhine Riesling. Increasingly these are sourced wholly or partially outside the valley (usually from the adjacent East Barossa Ranges), although that is not always apparent from the labels. The style is quintessentially Australian: strong, passionfruit/tropical fruits/lime flavours which can build magnificently with prolonged bottle age, although only a tiny percentage are given the opportunity. If you wish to see for yourself the effect of age, Leo Buring and Orlando both regularly release old wines from their museum stocks.

CHARDONNAY
Chardonnay is still something of an orphan in the Barossa Valley; even more than in the case of Rhine Riesling, it tends to be blended with grapes from other regions, in this case principally McLaren Vale. Saltram with its Mamre Brook and Pinnacle Selection series has been conspicuously successful, as has Krondorf with its Show Reserve wines. Both develop quickly into super-luscious styles, that of Krondorf even more quickly than that of Saltram — and for this reason my choice falls on the latter.

SEMILLON
Semillon has had a distinct renaissance, notably at the hands of Basedows where it is given a seductive coating of American oak and labelled White Burgundy, and proceeds to win multiple gold medals and trophies (and to invariably receive top points whenever I am called upon to judge it in blind tastings). Peter Lehmann also does better than most with the variety, finding a second use for it with his outstanding Semillon Sauternes style.

MAX SCHUBERT AND GRANGE HERMITAGE

Honour has come to the prophet in his own lifetime. Max Schubert, OA, has received the national and international recognition which he so richly deserves, but which he never actively sought or expected. For he is not only the most gifted winemaker of his time — arguably of all time — but one of the most humble and gentle of men.

By chance, the night before I wrote these words, on 22 June 1990, the most prestigious gathering of wine industry leaders I have ever seen in one place met in Sydney to witness the presentation of the inaugural Mount Pleasant Maurice O'Shea Award. This will be awarded each year to someone who has made an outstanding contribution to the industry. In 1990 it went to Max Schubert, adding to his Order of Australia, his 1988 award as Decanter Magazine Man of the Year and numerous other accolades. Yet his emotion and his humility as he received the award caused tears to come to the eyes of more than a few in the audience, and led to a prolonged standing ovation.

How unlikely all this would have seemed to Max Schubert when Grange Hermitage was first unveiled to the Sydney trade in 1956 (there were no winewriters then, or not as we understand that term today). The experimental '51 and '52 vintages, along with the semi-commercial '53, were shown. Schubert recalls the reaction in words which show how deeply he was hurt, 'The result was absolutely disastrous. Simply, no one liked Grange Hermitage'. Further tastings were hurriedly arranged in Adelaide; the results were, if possible, even worse. 'Schubert, I congratulate you. A very good dry port — which no one in their right mind will buy — let alone drink,' said one prominent wine man. Another caustically observed, 'A concoction of wild fruits and sundry berries, with crushed ants predominating'. Yet another, recalls Schubert, 'wanted to buy it and use it as an aphrodisiac. His theory was that the wine was like bull's blood in all respects and would raise his blood count to twice the norm when the occasion demanded'.

Yet in a sense the greatest improbability of all was that Schubert should be there in the first place having judgment of any description passed on him. One of six children of a Barossa Valley blacksmith, he left school at the age of 16 to join Penfolds as a messenger boy. The year was 1931, and he must have counted himself lucky to get a job of any description. Within a year, he was seconded to help the newly-appointed wine chemist, Penfolds first chemist, and soon enrolled in night school to learn more about chemistry. He was befriended by Leslie Penfold Hyland, and rose first to the position of cellar hand and then, in 1940, to assistant winemaker.

In 1949 an undreamt of opportunity came his way: he was sent to Jerez for a month to learn more about the making of sherry, thereafter spending a fortnight in the Douro during the port vintage. Almost as an afterthought, he returned via Bordeaux, where his host was Christian Cruse. It was the turning point in Schubert's life: 'Mr Cruse showed me magnificent old French wines, some 60 to 70 years old but which still had so much life in them. I have never forgotten those wines, and I don't think I have ever tasted wines like them since.'

It is somehow appropriate that in his retirement Schubert has gone back to making small quantities of sherry, his first and, until 1950, only love. For between 1930 and 1950 the Australian wine industry was concerned almost exclusively with making fortified wine (it accounted for 90 per cent of all sales), and in turn most of this was sweet sherry. Dry red and dry white table wine sales were negligible and largely anonymous — much was sold as non-vintage wine under generic labels such as hock, chablis, claret and burgundy.

It would be hard to imagine a less hospitable environment for the creation of an entirely new style of premium quality red wine. Why Schubert even entertained the idea is hard to comprehend, and that is with the wisdom of hindsight. But, shortly put, he decided to endeavour to make a wine which had as much as possible of the character and the longevity of the wines which Christian Cruse had served him. This in turn meant a total revolution in the fermentation and maturation of wine in Australia, requiring the use of (with liberal adaptations) the fermentation techniques he had observed in Bordeaux and perhaps even more importantly the new small oak barrels he had seen there.

Simply because neither Cabernet Sauvignon nor French oak were readily available, Schubert elected to use Shiraz and American oak, 'knowing full well that if I was careful enough in the choice of area and vineyard, coupled with the correct production procedure, I would be able to make the type and style of wine I wanted'.

ABOVE: *Max Schubert OA, loved and respected by all who know him.*

Ever the professional, Schubert made a 'control' wine as well, using the same grapes but utilising conventional large fermentation vessels and conventional fermentation techniques. Almost immediately the fermentation had finished, Schubert was sure he had succeeded. 'After 12 months, both wines were crystal clear with superb dark, full rich colour and body — but there the similarity ended. The experimental wine was bigger in all respects. It was a big wine in bouquet, flavour and balance. The raw wood was not so apparent [as it had been earlier] but the fruit characteristics had become more pronounced and defined, with more than a faint suggestion of cranberry. It was almost as if the new wood had acted as a catalyst to release previously unsuspected flavours and aromas from the Hermitage grape.'

Grange Hermitage was born. After the debacle of 1956 Schubert was formally instructed to discontinue its production, but he quietly ignored the instruction — even though he was denied the all important new oak, with inevitable consequences for the '56, '57 and '58 vintages. But by 1960 the mood had changed, enough wise men recognised the quality of the wine to persuade the Penfolds' board to relent, and production 'officially' recommenced. In 1962 Penfolds re-entered the show circuit, and the 1955 Grange swept all before it. The rest as they say, is history. Schubert had not only created Australia's greatest red wine, but laid the ground for the revolution in Australian red winemaking which has led to the high reputation that it now enjoys in the major wine markets of the world.

ABOVE: *Ancient Shiraz at bud-burst.*

WINERIES OF THE BAROSSA VALLEY

BAROSSA SETTLERS   CA-BA
Trial Hill Road
Lyndoch 5351   (085) 24 4017
Established   1983
Winemakers   Howard Haese, Douglas Lehmann (contract)
Production   2100 cases
Principal Wines   Rhine Riesling, Late Harvest Rhine Riesling, Auslese RhineRiesling, Shiraz Claret, Cabernet Sauvignon, Sweet Sherry and Vintage Port.
Best Vintages   Not considered relevant, because not all wines are made each year.

The Haese family have been grape growers for over 100 years, and the picturesque cellar door sales area is now in a converted horse stable built in 1860. With a contract winemaker of the skill of Douglas Lehmann, it is not surprising that the best wines are quite outstanding.

BASEDOWS   BA-A
161-165 Murray Street
Tanunda 5352   (085) 63 2060
Established   1896
Winemaker   Douglas Lehmann
Production   Over 30,000 cases.

Principal Wines   White Burgundy, Chardonnay, Rhine Riesling, Spatlese White Frontignac, Hermitage, Cabernet Sauvignon, Special Release reds and Old Tawny Port.
Best Vintages   W 1983, '84, '86, '88, '89, '90
R 1980, '82, '84, '86, '88, '90
All of Basedows' white wines deserve an A-A rating; the B is reserved strictly for the reds. The cunningly oaked and voluptuous White Burgundy, indeed, deserves an A-A rating for value (and consistency), but the Rhine Riesling and Chardonnay are also both extraordinary wines at their price.

BETHANY WINES   B-B
Bethany Road, Bethany via
Tanunda 5352   (085) 63 2086
Established   1977
Winemakers   Robert Schrapel, Geoff Schrapel
Production   5000 cases
Principal Wines   Chardonnay, Fumé Blanc, Bethany Reserve Rhine Riesling, Steinbruch Spatlese Rhine Riesling, Auslese Rhine Riesling, Schlenke's Gully Shiraz, Cabernet Sauvignon, Cabernet Merlot, 'Old Quarry' Vintage Port and Frontignac White Port.
Best Vintages   W 1986, '87, '88, '90
R 1987, '88, '90
Rhine Riesling, both dry and sweet, has always been Bethany's strength, but recently it has commenced producing excellent Chardonnay, followed by a modern-style Cabernet Merlot, with crisp fresh berry fruit and low tannin.

BURGE FAMILY WINEMAKERS   CB-B
Gomersal Road
Lyndoch 5351   (085) 244 644
Established   1928
Winemakers   Noel and Rick Burge
Production   3000 cases
Principal Wines   Chardonnay, Rhine Riesling, White Frontignac, Trinity and Clochemerle (a Cabernet/Merlot/Malbec blend). Fortified wines have for long been the strength of the winery, and continue to be so.
Best Vintages   Not relevant owing to radical changes in winemaking.
A winery with ambition and (in the form of Rick Burge) considerable marketing expertise. The move into premium table wines has met with a few teething problems, but presumably will succeed.

CHARLES CIMICKY WINES   BA-BA
Gomersal Road
Lyndoch 5351   (085) 24 4025
Established   1972
Winemaker   Charles Cimicky
Production   2000 cases

Principal Wines   Sauvignon Blanc, Rhine Riesling, Shiraz and Cabernet Merlot.
Best Vintages   W 1986, '87, '88, '90
R 1987, '88, '89, '90
Charles Cimicky is the super deluxe label of Karlsburg, the latter name being largely phased out. The wines released under the Cimicky label represent the best of a far larger crush, and are very impressive, with a beautifully balanced and structured Cabernet Merlot leading the way, and one of the few good Barossa Sauvignon Blancs I have so far encountered.

CHARLES MELTON WINES   B-BA
Krondorf Road
Tanunda 5352   (085) 63 3606
Established   1986
Winemaker   Graeme Melton
Production   1000 cases
Principal Wines   An esoteric, small range of red wines including Rosé, Hermitage Pinot Noir, Nine Popes (a Grenache Shiraz blend) and Sparkling Burgundy.
Best Vintages   Not relevant due to recent establishment.
Wines full of flavour and individuality are made by Graeme (Charlie) Melton, himself strictly one of a kind. If you visit the little timber winery, you are sure to leave feeling happier than when you arrived. The voluptuously soft and velvety Nine Popes is especially good.

CHATEAU YALDARA   CB-B
Gomersal Road
Lyndoch 5351   (085) 24 4200
Established   1965
Winemakers   Hermann Thumm (Chateau Yaldara), Jim Irvine (Lakewood)
Production   40,000 cases
Principal Wines   Wines released under three labels: Acacia Hill, Lakewood and Yaldara. Between them they cover Semillon Sauvignon Blanc, Chardonnay Chenin Blanc, Rhine Riesling, Chablis, Riesling, Moselle, Cabernet Merlot, Hermitage, Cabernet Shiraz, Cabernet Sauvignon and anything else you care to name.
Best Vintages   Not relevant with such a large range.
Striking packaging and low prices are the most attractive features of the wines made at Chateau Yaldara; wine quality is, however, steadily improving.

ELDERTON   B-B
3 Tanunda Road
Nuriootpa 5355   (085) 62 1058
Established   1982
Winemakers   Neil Ashmead, James Irvine (contract)
Production   20,000 cases

ABOVE: *Roger Harbord, assistant winemaker to Doug Lehmann at Basedows.*

Principal Wines Rhine Riesling, Chablis style, Hermitage, Domain Nouveau (light red), Pinot Noir, Cabernet Merlot and *Méthode Champenoise.*
Best Vintages W 1984, '85, '87, '88, '90
R 1982, '84, '86, '90
Neil Ashmead has made a more than successful transition from grape grower to winemaker, by putting in a great deal of hard work in marketing and promotion. All of the wines are reliable, the Hermitage on occasion rising above itself.

GRANT BURGE B-BA
Sturt Highway
Jacobs Creek via Tanunda 5352 (085) 63 3700
Established 1988
Winemaker Grant Burge
Production 20,000 cases
Principal Wines Eden Valley Rhine Riesling, Semillon, Chardonnay, Sauvignon Blanc, Barossa Frontignac, Non Vintage Sparkling Wine, Merlot, Very Old Liqueur Frontignac and Very Old Tawny Port.

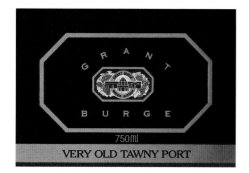

Best Vintages Too recent to assess.
Grant Burge, like former partner Ian Wilson, is building another wine empire. It is based on the vast vineyard holdings which Grant Burge has in the Barossa Valley, and it seems quite certain that the Grant Burge label will come to be a dominant force in the middle-upper sector of the wine market.

HERITAGE WINES CA-CA
Seppeltsfield Road
Marananga via Tanunda 5352 (085) 62 2880
Established 1984
Winemaker Stephen Hoff
Production 3200 cases
Principal Wines Semillon, Chardonnay, Rhine Riesling, Shiraz, Cabernet Sauvignon and Cabernet Franc.
Best Vintages W and R 1986, '87, '88, '90
Stephen Hoff has the happy knack of coming up with an outstanding wine every now and then. Sometimes it is a Chardonnay, sometimes a Rhine Riesling. Other wines produced by Heritage are distinctly less memorable, but it is a winery always worth trying on your way through the Barossa Valley.

KAISER STUHL CA-B
Tanunda Road
Nuriootpa 5355 (085) 62 0389
Established 1931
Winemakers John Duval (chief winemaker), Rod Chapman (production manager)
Production Not for publication but around 1.8 million cases equivalent (ie including casks).
Principal Wines Table wines centre on the Ribbon range, comprising Green Ribbon Rhine Riesling and Red Ribbon Shiraz. Brands also include a Black Forest range in three styles: Soft Light Red, Crisp Dry White and Moselle style. The Kaiser Stuhl Rosé also fits into this group. Next come Bin 22 Beaujolais, Bin 33 Claret, Bin 44 Riesling, Bin 55 Moselle, Bin 66 White Burgundy and Bin 77 Chablis. Summer Wine is one of the largest selling sparkling wines (non-bottle fermented) in Australia.
Best Vintages W 1978, '79, '82, '84, '86, '88, '90
R 1980, '82, '85, '86, '87, '88, '90
The Green Ribbon Rhine Riesling and Red Ribbon Shiraz are exemplary examples of mid-range commercial wines; both are capable of winning (and occasionally do win) major show trophies competing against the best wines in the country. The Riesling shows strong lime/toast aroma and fruit; the Shiraz, soft velvety fruit with seductive vanillin oak.

KRONDORF B-BA
Krondorf Road
Tanunda 5352 (085) 63 1245
Established 1978
Winemaker Nicholas Walker
Production 200,000 cases
Principal Wines Top of the range releases are the Show Reserve Burge and Wilson Chardonnay and Burge and Wilson Cabernet Sauvignon. Next follow limited edition Chardonnay, Sauvignon Blanc, Cabernet Sauvignon and Cabernet Franc Cabernet Sauvignon. At the bottomend come the standard releases of Chablis, Shiraz Cabernet, Barossa Valley Rhine Riesling and Coonawarra Hermitage.
Best Vintages W 1985, '87, '88, '90
R 1979, '80, '86, '87, '88, '90

An ultra-consistent producer of wines in three quality grades, which equally consistently represent exceptionally good value for money. Occasional releases are of the highest quality, notably the toasty/lime Eden Valley Rhine Riesling, and some voluptuous, peachy Show Reserve Chardonnay.

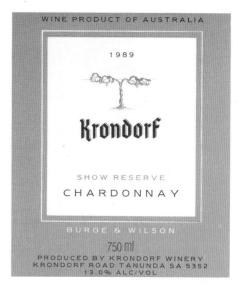

LEO BURING A-A
Sturt Highway
Tanunda 5352 (085) 63 2184
Established 1931
Winemaker John Vickery
Production Not for publication.
Principal Wines The highest quality wines, both white and red, are released under the Reserve Bin labels incorporating a system of bin numbers that change each year. Releases of Show Reserves include some of the greatest Rhine Rieslings in the country. These are followed by the Leo Buring Varietal Collection of white and

ABOVE: A symbol of the Leo Buring heritage.

red table wines: Chardonnay, Fumé Blanc, Rhine Riesling, Shiraz, Cabernet and Pinot Noir. Next come such popular wines as Leibrauwine.

Best Vintages   W 1972, '73, '75, '79, '84, '86, '87, '90

The greatest maker of Rhine Riesling in Australia, with the best absolutely majestic when 10 to 15 years old. The commercial releases, even from the humble Shiraz, seem to get better as each year passes.

ORLANDO   A-A

Sturt Highway
Rowland Flat 5350   (085) 24 4500
Established   1847
Winemakers   Robin Day, Ivan Limb, Leon Deans, Bernie Hickin, Tom Van der Hoek, David Morris, Stephen Obst
Production   Around 3 million cases equivalent (including casks).
Principal Wines   Orlando takes grapes from all over South Australia, the principal regions being Barossa, Eden and Clare Valleys, Coonawarra, Padthaway, McLaren Vale and the Riverland. The Eden Valley is the most important source of high quality Rhine Rieslings and Traminer; Coonawarra, Padthaway, McLaren Vale and the Riverland for Chardonnay; and Coonawarra and Padthaway for Cabernet Sauvignon. The wines, in descending order of quality are released under the following labels; Jacaranda Ridge, Steingarten, Flaxmans, St Helga, St Hilary, St Hugo, Gramps, RF, Jacobs Creek and finally Coolabah casks and flagons. Carrington is a major sparkling wine brand.
Best Vintages   To all intents and purposes irrelevant given the enormous range of wine, but basically conforming to the South Australian pattern.

A brand-builder extraordinaire, Orlando is one of the three giants of the Australian industry, producing wines of the utmost reliability and consistency. Its majority ownership by Pernod-Ricard of France will no doubt assist its international marketing efforts.

PENFOLDS   A-A

Tanunda Road
Nuriootpa 5355   (085) 62 0389

Established   1844
Winemakers   The Penfolds' winemaking team headed by John Duval.
Production   1.8 million cases equivalent (including casks).
Principal Wines   Specialist red winemakers of the highest reputation and quality; in descending order of price, Australia's greatest red wine, Grange Hermitage, Bin 707 Cabernet Sauvignon, Magill Estate, St Henri Claret, Bin 389 Cabernet Shiraz, Bin 28 Kalimna Shiraz and Bin 128 Coonawarra Shiraz. Koonunga Hill Claret has, since 1976, established itself as one of the best value-for-money red wines in the lower half of the market. Over the years some quite magnificent Show Release wines have appeared under non-repeating bin numbers. For many, 1962 Bin 60A is the greatest red produced in Australia in the last 30 years; others of note are Bin 58 of 1961, Bins 61, '62, '63 and '64 of 1963 and Bin 7 of 1967. In more recent times the Show Bins have made a more than welcome reappearance with a magnificent 1980 Bin 80A and the equally great 1982 Bin 820. The limited range of white wines comprise Chardonnay, Chardonnay Semillon, Fumé Blanc and Bin 202 Traminer Riesling.

Best Vintages   W 1978, '80, '82, '88, '90
                     R 1955, '62, '66, '71, '76, '80, '82, '83, '86, '88, '90

'1844 to Evermore', ran the old sales slogan of Penfolds, and it is indeed hard to see the day when this long-standing institution will no longer be Australia's greatest red wine producer. Grange Hermitage, the unique creation of Max Schubert, which remains in good hands now that Schubert has retired, is known to wine-lovers across the world. In the last few years there have been increasing signs that Penfolds may yet become a white wine producer of note, with Chardonnay leading the way.

PETER LEHMANN   B-BA

Samuel Road off Para Road
Tanunda 5352   (085) 63 2500
Established   1979
Winemakers   Peter Lehmann, Andrew Wigan, Peter Scholz, Leonie Bain
Production   65,000 cases.
Principal Wines   Specialist winemakers of quality Barossa Valley table wines and Vintage Ports under the Peter Lehmann and Masterson labels. Wines under the Peter Lehmann label include Rhine Riesling, Dry Semillon, Chenin Blanc, Fumé Blanc, Semillon Chardonnay, Chardonnay, Botrytis Semillon Sauternes, Brut Absolu, Cabernet Sauvignon, Pinot Noir, Shiraz Dry Red, Shiraz/Tokay, Shiraz Cabernet, Beaujolais and Vintage Port. The Masterson label is represented by Rhine Riesling, Dry Chablis and Dry Red.

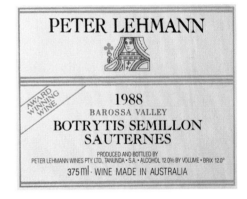

Best Vintages   W 1979, '82, '87, '88, '90
                     R 1980, '82, '83, '84, '87, '88, '90

The grape growers of the Barossa Valley owe an everlasting debt to Peter Lehmann; he risked all and has worked ferociously hard in their cause. Consistently smooth, generously flavoured and supremely honest wines are some compensation for his dedication.

ROCKFORD   B-B

Krondorf Road
Tanunda 5352   (085) 63 2720
Established   1984
Winemaker   Robert O'Callaghan
Production   3500 cases
Principal Wines   Rhine Riesling, Sauvignon Blanc, White Frontignac, Rhine Riesling Botrytis Cinerea, Alicante Bouchet, Shiraz Cabernet, and Cabernet Sauvignon, increasingly sourced from the Barossa Valley and Eden Valley.
Best Vintages   W and R 1984, '86, '87, '88, '90

Rocky O'Callaghan, Charlie Melton, Bob McLean (of St Hallett) and Peter Lehmann are all formidable characters, and are all motivated by an intense pride in and loyalty to the Barossa

Valley. O'Callaghan, no less than the others, produces wines which show why that loyalty exists. The Rhine Rieslings and the Basket Press Shiraz are, like their creator, frequently larger than life.

ROSEWORTHY   B-B
Roseworthy Agricultural College
Roseworthy 5371 (085) 24 8057
Established   1883
Winemakers   Andrew Markides,
                  Clive Hartnell
Production   6000 cases
Principal Wines   Chardonnay, Rhine Riesling, *Méthode Champenoise*, Spatlese, Cabernet Sauvignon/Merlot, Angaston Shiraz, Amontillado Sherry, Old Liqueur Tawny Port, Vintage Port and Old Liqueur Brandy.
Best Vintages   W 1983, '87, '88, '90
                     R 1984, '86, '87, '88, '90

Roseworthy has had much greater success with its commercial winemaking than its counterpart, the College (ie Charles Sturt University). Given its function as a teaching facility, the consistency is quite surprising — if one ignores one or two poor wooded whites.

ST HALLETT   BA-A
St Hallett's Road
Tanunda 5352   (085) 63 2319
Established   1967
Winemaker   Stuart Blackwell
Production   20,000 cases
Principal Wines   A revamped range of white and red table wines and fortified wines, including Colombard Rhine Riesling, Semillon Sauvignon Blanc, Chardonnay, Cabernet Merlot and Old Block Shiraz (the grapes for which come from a 100 year old vineyard).
Best Vintages   W 1986, '88, '90
                     R 1976, '80, '82, '86, '87, '88, '90

Each of the three partners contributes to the success of St Hallett: the Lindner family vineyards, the winemaking skills of Stuart Blackwell (and a very well equipped winery), and the marketing skills of Bob McLean. The style of each wine has been carefully thought

out, and no less successfully realised. In the result, you get rather more than you pay for, more particularly with the dark berry, dark chocolate Old Block Shiraz and the restaurant-aimed Cabernet Merlot.

OLD BLOCK SHIRAZ
1986

LINDNER McLEAN
HALLETT VALLEY BAROSSA

750ml

SALTRAM   CA-BA
Angaston Road
Angaston 5353   (085) 64 2200
Established   1859
Winemakers   Mark Turnbull,
                  David Norman
Production   500,000 cases
Principal Wines   At the top of the quality and price tree come the Pinnacle range and the Mamre Brook range; there is then a considerable gap to the varietal wines of Chardonnay, Rhine Riesling, Sauvignon Blanc, Cabernet Sauvignon, Shiraz, and the generics: Chablis, White Burgundy and Claret. The best fortified wine is Mr Pickwick's Particular Port.

Best Vintages   W 1982, '83, '87, '88, '89, '90
                     R 1967, '71, '76, '80, '82, '85, '86, '87, '90

Since 1982 the Pinnacle and Mamre Brook Chardonnays have been leading examples of the full blown, peaches and cream style — deep yellow in colour and flooding the mouth with flavour. Across the board the white wines at the top end have been far better than the reds. In the commercial range of varietals and generics, quality is more uniform and value likewise. Saltram excelled itself in the difficult 1989 vintage, pointing to the continuing upsurge in overall quality.

RHINE RIESLING
1989
A classic example of Rhine Riesling, selected from the best Riesling areas in South Australia

750ML

SEPPELT   A-A
Seppeltsfield via
Tanunda 5352   (085) 63 2626
Established   1850
Winemakers   James Godfrey,
                  Nigel Dolan

ABOVE: Dust storms in the Barossa Valley, a reminder that the red centre of Australia is little more than a two hour drive to the north.

Production 2.5 million cases
Principal Wines Seppeltsfield Winery produces Seppelt's famed Para Liqueur Port, Seppeltsfield Tawny, Seppeltsfield Tawny-21, Old Trafford and Mount Rufus. Each year a 100 year old vintage Para Liqueur Port is released in tiny quantities, selling for over $2000 per bottle. DP90 Tawny Port is legendary for its quality and scarcity, while Seppelt's equally distinguished range of sherries (Flor Fino DP117, Amontillado DP116 and Oloroso DP38) are also matured at Seppeltsfield. Most the company's red wines are made in the Barossa Valley; the white wines (including the outstanding value Gold Label Chardonnay) are made at Great Western.
Best Vintages R 1978, '81, '84, '86, '89, '90

Seppelt remains the country's leading maker of fortified wine, even though that role is of sharply declining commercial significance. It is also the largest grower of Chardonnay, and it produces the best value Chardonnays on the Australian market —Seppelt Gold Label and Queen Adelaide. In between the extremes of chardonnay and fortified wines come many finely-crafted wines of every conceivable shape, colour and hue, released under a bewildering range of labels.

TOLLANA   BA-BA
Tanunda Road off Sturt
Highway Nuriootpa 5355   (085) 62 0389
Established   1888
Winemakers   John Duval, Rod Chapman
Production   750,000 cases equivalent (not all released under Tollana labels).
Principal Wines   A recent reappraisal of wines led to Tollana diversifying its grape sources and no longer relying solely on its excellent Woodbury vineyard in the High Eden Hills. Woodbury continues to supply Eden Valley Rhine Riesling and the great Cabernet Sauvignon Bin TR 222. The range has been rationalised since Penfolds' takeover of Tollana and will now comprise mainly premium 750 ml Cabernet Sauvignon, Shiraz, Chardonnay, Sauvignon Blanc, Riesling and Botrytis Rhine Riesling.
Best Vintages   W 1978, '82, '87, '88, '90
R 1976, '80, '82, '86, '88, '90
Tollana was a spinsterish, undiscovered treasure when acquired by Penfolds. It had great vine-

yards, a fine winemaker and superb wines, all of which were largely ignored by the public, although they were well known to other winemakers more than happy to buy bulk wine from Tollana. Sooner or later the winery had to be purchased and the buyer happened to be Penfolds. Penfolds must be more than happy with its acquisition. Superb, concentrated lime juice/pineapple Rhine Riesling, bursting with flavour at 5 years of age, has been consistently the greatest, but several glorious botrytised Rhine Rieslings have also starred in national wine shows.

TWIN VALLEY ESTATE   NR
Hoffnungsthal Road
Lyndoch 5351   (085) 24 4511
Established   1969
Winemaker   Fernando Martin
Production   Not stated.
Principal Wines   Chardonnay, Semillon Blanc, Cabernet Sauvignon, Cabernet Franc, Shiraz, Rhine Riesling, Traminer and Muscat of Alexandria.
Best Vintages   W and R 1976, '80, '84, '86, '87, '88, '90
After four name changes (Karrawirra to the Redgum Estate to Kies Estate to Twin Valley Estate) and three ownership changes in a little over 5 years, a certain sense of schizophrenia might seem inevitable. However, the new owners Fernando and Jeanette Martin are undaunted, and plan to restore the winery 'to its former glory'.

VERITAS WINERY   CA-B
94 Langmeil Road
Tanunda 5352   (085) 63 2330
Established   1951
Winemaker   Rolf Binder
Production   6500 cases
Principal Wines   Semillon, Sauvignon Blanc,

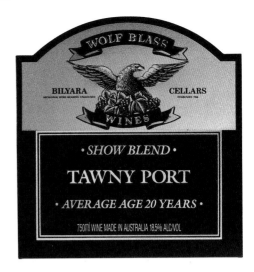

Rhine Riesling, Tramino, Rhine Riesling White Frontignac, Spatlese, Leanyka, Cabernet Franc Merlot, Cabernet Sauvignon, Shiraz Cabernet Sauvignon Malbec, Bikaver Bull's Blood and a range of ports, sherries, vermouths and even an Oom Pah Pah Port.
Best Vintages   W 1984, '86, '88, '90
R 1980, '82, '84, '87, '89, '90.
A producer little known outside of South Australia, but deserving a better fate, particularly for its red wines, which can be of exceptional quality, ranging according to vintage from light and elegant to rich, juicy and full blooded. The white wines are less appealing.

WOLF BLASS   BA-A
Bilyara Vineyards
Sturt Highway
Nuriootpa 5355   (085) 62 1955
Established   1973
Winemakers   John Glaetzer, Stephen John, Chris Hatcher, Christa Binder
Production   400,000 cases

ABOVE LEFT: A proud history and tradition.   *ABOVE RIGHT: The Orlando production line.*

Principal Wines The range comprises Classic Dry White, Yellow Label Rhine Riesling, Traminer Riesling, Spatlese Rhine Riesling, Green Label Frontignac Traminer, White Label (Chablis style), South Australian Chardonnay, Yellow Label Cabernet Shiraz, Grey Label Cabernet Sauvignon, Black Label Cabernet Sauvignon Shiraz, Brown Label Hermitage, Red Label Shiraz Cabernet, Presidents Selection Cabernet Sauvignon, Chardonnay Cuvée Champagne and 15 year old Tawny Port.

Best Vintages   W 1982, '84, '86, '87, '88, '90
R 1972, '75, '78, '80, '82, '84, '85, '86, '88, '90

Wolf Blass is the most accomplished marketer the Australian industry has seen, something which tends to obscure the fact that he has also made consistently outstanding wines across the spectrum from commercial to deluxe. Sophisticated oak treatment is the most obvious feature of the winemaking, but skilful blending of varieties and regional components has been no less important, particularly with the red wines. If only there were a little less oak, or a little more fruit.

YALUMBA   B-BA

Eden Valley Road
Angaston 5353   (085) 64 2423

Established   1863

Winemakers   Described by Yalumba as the 'Yalumba Team' headed by Brian Walsh and Geoff Linton.

Production   700,000 cases
(group production).

Principal Wines   The wines of S Smith & Son Pty Ltd are marketed under four distinct labels. The first is the traditional Yalumba label, covering a range of wines and styles made from grapes not necessarily estate grown. Premium wines include Signature Collection Varietals, 'D'*Méthode Champenoise*, Brut de Brut Vintage Champagne and Galway Pipe Tawny Port. Two new series of budget-priced wines under the Country Wines and Gourmet series have further expanded the range (see separate entries for Hill-Smith Estate, Heggies Vineyard and Pewsey Vale at pages 182 to 185).

Best Vintages   W 1982, '87, '88, '90
R 1976, '77, '84, '86, '88, '90

A great family institution, which has nonetheless often found itself at the cutting edge of vineyard, winery and market developments. Wine quality surged in the '60s and '70s, faltered in the late '70s and early '80s, but has since made a strong recovery, even if one would like to see a little less oak and a little more fruit in some of the wines.

ABOVE: Firing barrels at Yalumba.

OTHER WINERIES

BERNKASTEL   C-CB
Cnr Para and Langmeil Roads
Tanunda 5352   (085) 63 2597

CHATEAU DORRIEN   DC-C
Cnr Sturt Highway and
Seppeltsfield Road
Dorrien 5352   (085) 62 2850

GNADENFREI ESTATE   NR
Seppeltsville Road
Marananga 5353, 6 km north-east
of Tanunda   (085) 62 2522

GREENOCK CREEK VINEYARD NR
Seppeltsfield Road
Manunga 5353

HIGH WYCOMBE WINES NR
Bethany 5353
3 km east of Tanunda (085) 63 2776

HOFFMANS   CB-B
Para Road, North Para via
Tanunda 5352 (085) 63 2983

KAESLER'S FARM   C-CB
26 Washington Street
Angaston 5353 (085) 64 2607

KELLERMEISTER WINES C-B
Barossa Valley Highway
Lyndoch 5351 (085) 24 4304

KROEMER ESTATE   NR
Tanunda 5352 (085) 63 3375

OLD BARN   NR
Langmeil Road
Tanunda 5352

ROVALLEY   D-D
Sturt Highway
Rowland Flat 5352 (085) 24 4537

TARCHALICE   DC-C
Research Road
Vine Vale via Tanunda 5352 (085) 63 3005

TOLLEY PEDARE   NR
Seppeltsfield Road
Nuriootpa 5355 (085) 62 1366

WARD'S GATEWAY CELLARS   C-CB
Lyndoch 5351, between Sandy Creek and
Lyndoch (085) 24 4138

THE WILLOWS VINEYARD   NR
Light Pass Road, Light Pass
Nuriootpa 5355 (085) 62 1080

SOUTH AUSTRALIA

CLARE VALLEY

The Clare Valley occupies the same special place in my heart as does Tuscany: if I were to live elsewhere in Australia, I would wish it to be in Clare; elsewhere in the world, Tuscany. They share the same softness, the same intimacy, the same palpable sense of history, the same lack of twentieth century pressure. Tuscany has these characteristics in greater abundance, no doubt, but that in no way diminishes the particular appeal of the Clare Valley. Tim Knappstein, doyen of the Clare Valley winemakers, puts it beautifully: 'There are only two kinds of people: those who were born in Clare, and those who wish they were born in Clare.' He, of course, is in the former category; I am in the latter.

The feeling stems in part from its abundant stone buildings (banks, halls, houses, wineries, farm houses and sheds); in part from its convoluted geography, ever promising a little creek or a spring, though not always providing it; in part from the interplay between eucalypts and vines; in part from its people; and in part from its surrounding districts, notably Mintaro (with such wonderful places as the Magpie and Stump Hotel and Martindale Hall) and Burra (the old copper mining town with its unique terraces of miners' cottages, now converted to bed and breakfast accommodation).

Clare was founded by an extraordinary Englishman, John Horrocks, when he established Hope Farm in 1840 and planted the first vines. Minerals provided the first surge in population: copper was discovered at Burra in 1845 and at Wallaroo and Moonta between 1859 and 1861. When the first flush of minerals was depleted, the wheat boom started, creating great wealth in a short time. High quality slate was discovered at Mintaro, and in 1885 the Broken Hill Proprietary Company Limited was formed to mine silver at Broken Hill. Clare was the town through which much of the trade (and the people) generated by these developments passed: it became known as the 'Hub of the North'.

Vineyards (and wineries) grew steadily. Sevenhill planted its first vines in 1852, those of Spring Vale (later to become Quelltaler Vineyards and now — lamentably — Eaglehawk

Estate) in 1853. By 1890 there were 100 hectares of vineyards, but expansion (at a rate reminiscent of the late 1960s in the Hunter Valley) lifted hectareage by almost 500

THE REGION IN BRIEF

LOCATION AND ELEVATION
33°50'S 138°38'E
400 m

SUBREGIONS
Clare, Sevenhill, Watervale, Leasingham, Auburn, and Polish Hill River.

CLIMATE
More than any other district, the Clare Valley throws into question the accuracy of the heat summation index as a measure of climate, yet as I explain at pages 28 to 31, it still remains the best shorthand method we have. The HDD summation is 1770, which compares with 1770 for Rutherglen and 1710 for Nuriootpa. Nor does the MJT of 21.9°C help much. All one can say is that the style of the wines is entirely inconsistent with a climate seemingly so warm, and many of the factors discussed in those pages no doubt come into play here. Over 60 per cent of the annual rainfall is between May and September; the growing season rainfall of a mere 200 mm makes irrigation highly desirable, although the absence of ground water makes this difficult to supply in many parts of the Clare Valley, and the vines have traditionally been grown using dry land farming techniques. The low humidity means fungal diseases are seldom a threat but water stress late in the growing season often leads to partial or total defoliation of the vines, contributing to occasional ripening problems with Rhine Riesling.

SOIL
While there is considerable variation in slope and aspect, by far the most common soil is the hard red duplex soil (Dr2.23), and brown to brown-grey loamy sand, which overlies a calcareous subsoil. In the southern part of the Clare Valley, and in particularly at Eaglehawk Estate, the lime content increases significantly. These are excellent vineyard soils, and no doubt make some contribution to the quality and style of the Clare Valley wines.

HARVEST TIME
From early March until mid to late April, with Rhine Riesling frequently coming in last of all.

PRINCIPAL GRAPE VARIETIES
Rhine Riesling, 465 ha   *Cabernet Sauvignon, 277 ha*
Chardonnay, 184 ha   *Shiraz, 222 ha*
Palamino and Pedro Ximinez, 123 ha   *Grenache, 78 ha*
Sauvignon Blanc, 59 ha   *TOTAL RED, 684 ha*
Crouchen, 49 ha
Semillon, 44 ha
TOTAL WHITE, 1015 ha

AUSTRALASIAN WINE REGIONS
1980 – 1990

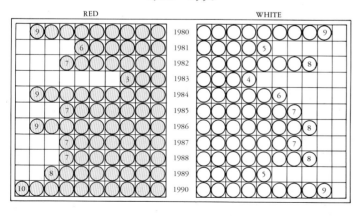

FACING PAGE: *Sun sets over Clare Valley.*

per cent in the next 7 years. By 1897 there were 580 hectares under vine, and in 1903 the Stanley Wine Company produced 450,000 litres of wine (mostly exported to London), the same quantity as produced by Penfolds. The twentieth century slowed the rate of growth, and a number of the nineteenth century wineries disappeared. The Stanley Wine Company and Quelltaler Vineyards dominated production, but Sevenhill and Wendouree both continued to make and market wines to a small but appreciative market.

Thomas Hardy now owns Stanley Leasingham, Wolf Blass owns Eaglehawk Estate and majority control of Tim Knappstein Wines, and Penfolds has established its major vineyard on the Polish Hill River side of the Clare Valley known as the Clare Estate. But the atmosphere has not

ABOVE: *The Clare Valley – always a palpable sense of history.*

changed, and the Clare Valley vignerons remain one of the most dedicated and harmonious of groups. One of many achievements has been the annual wine and food weekend held in May, at which the public is given the rare opportunity of tasting the weeks-old wines from the current vintage (on the Saturday) and touring the wineries on the Sunday (when each winery teams up with a prominent local or Adelaide restaurant to provide a matched glass of wine and small plate of food).

But whenever you visit the Clare Valley, you will be assured of a specially warm welcome and seduced by its gentle beauty.

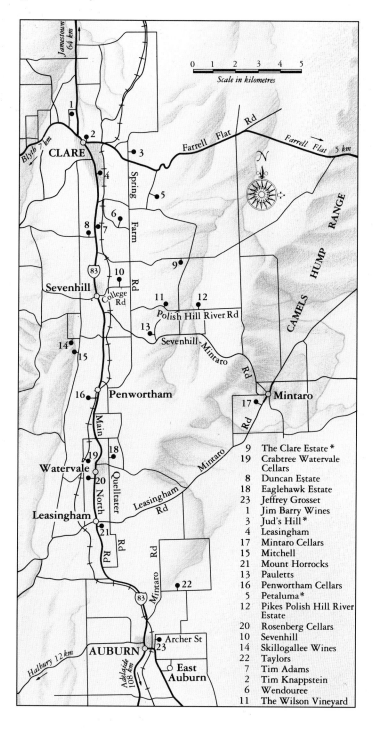

9 The Clare Estate *
19 Crabtree Watervale Cellars
8 Duncan Estate
18 Eaglehawk Estate
23 Jeffrey Grosset
1 Jim Barry Wines
3 Jud's Hill *
4 Leasingham
17 Mintaro Cellars
15 Mitchell
21 Mount Horrocks
13 Pauletts
16 Penwortham Cellars
5 Petaluma *
12 Pikes Polish Hill River Estate
20 Rosenberg Cellars
10 Sevenhill
14 Skillogalee Wines
22 Taylors
7 Tim Adams
2 Tim Knappstein
6 Wendouree
11 The Wilson Vineyard

PRINCIPAL WINE STYLES

RHINE RIESLING

Much of Australia's finest Rhine Riesling is grown in the Clare Valley, and it is the most important wine for the region. Typically it starts life in a fairly austere mode, with faint aromas of passionfruit, a touch of lime, and a steely strength. Almost immediately a telltale touch of lightly browned toast starts to emerge, and as the wine ages and becomes more complex, the intensity of that toasty character grows. These are long lived wines: only in the weakest years will they not benefit from 5 years in bottle, many of the better wines improving for up to 10 years. Among many fine producers Jeffrey Grosset, Mitchell, Petaluma, Stanley Leasingham and Tim Knappstein Wines stand out. Tim Knappstein Wines has produced some superlative Beerenauslese styles, none better than in 1989.

CABERNET SAUVIGNON

This is the other great wine of the region. Here the character and the style is less homogeneous, in part reflecting the philosophy of the winemaker and in part the imperatives of the vineyard terroir. Mitchell makes a very elegant style which grows gracefully in bottle for a decade or more; Wendouree's Cabernet Sauvignon (often blended with a touch of Malbec) is a wine which will seemingly last a century, so concentrated and layered is its flavour and structure.

SHIRAZ

There are those who think that Clare Shiraz is every bit as good as Cabernet Sauvignon, and over the years the two have frequently been blended, sometimes with the addition of a little Malbec. The wines are deep in colour and flavour, rounder and softer than the Cabernet Sauvignon, but with similar strength and depth. Mitchell sometimes produces a wine with pronounced pepper/spice character, however, normally the wines have a silky, red berry fruit, and are best exemplified by the superb but very expensive offering from Jim Barry Wines, the Armagh.

CHARDONNAY

Until Thomas Hardy showed the way with its excellent, softly peachy Domaine series from Stanley Leasingham, Chardonnay was a shadowy and elusive variety in the Clare Valley. It seemed to swing violently between pale anaemia in its youth, missing normal maturity altogether, and several years later presenting itself as overblown and over the hill. Given the climate and soil, others should achieve more consistent results with it, and may well do so in the future.

SEMILLON

Eaglehawk Estate (in the days when it was known as Quelltaler Vineyards), Stanley Leasingham Domaine and Tim Adams have all produced some wonderful oaked examples of Semillon; Mount Horrocks produces both a dry and late harvest (Cordon-cut) style, the latter in company with Eaglehawk Estate; and Mitchell has recently joined the band. The wines age and grow in bottle in a fashion reminiscent of the richer Hunter Valley (New South Wales) styles, albeit a little more quickly.

EAGLEHAWK ESTATE —
A MODERN-DAY PHOENIX

The first vineyard owned by Wolf Blass was its Clare Valley venture in the Polish Hill River region, which it established in 1979. The first crusher, the first press, the first fully operational winery owned by Wolf Blass was Quelltaler Vineyards, which it acquired in 1987. In other words, Wolf Blass had managed to create a major Australian wine company with none of the things which less lateral thinkers would regard as essential prerequisites.

Yet no one would accuse Blass of producing anonymous blends. Every Blass wine ever made shows the full impact of Wolf Blass' winemaking philosophy: every tiny facet of the character and style of each wine has been deliberately and precisely calculated and built in. Wolf Blass has had a unique ability to read the mind and the palate of the public, and to anticipate changing trends in style long before his competitors. Blass has never tried to dictate to the public what kind of wine it should like: he has simply responded to its needs. His skill in doing this has been so great that many think he creates the style first, and the demand follows, but it is not so.

Why Wolf Blass was prepared to outlay millions of dollars to acquire Quelltaler Vineyards, and millions more to upgrade the winery and resuscitate the vineyards is not immediately obvious, and it may even be that by 1990 he was regretting his impetuosity. In the longer term the acquisition will surely make sense: a priceless piece of Australian history in one of our premium grape growing regions, blessed with some of the best (or potentially best) vineyards in that region.

And it is quite certain that it was this quality potential which led to the establishment of the Polish Hill River vineyard, and that it had much to do with the acquisition of Quelltaler Vineyards and Tim Knappstein Wines. These acquisitions were also intimately bound up in the transformation of Wolf Blass from a specialist red wine producer to one of the leaders in the production of premium Rhine Riesling, if not the leader — a transformation which occurred overnight, so it seemed, and without initially at least, the fanfare of trumpets which usually accompanies every achievement of this remarkable man and his no less remarkable company.

It is no doubt sheer coincidence that the flamboyant careers of a number of Quelltaler Vineyards' owners parallel that of Wolf Blass, but the coincidence remains nonetheless. In 1842 Francis Treloar left his native Cornwall, and after 10 years in the Cape of Good Hope, the Victorian goldfields and the copper mines of South Australia, he purchased a 47 hectare property near Watervale which he named Spring Vale, and the following year planted vines obtained from his neighbour.

In 1860 he sold Spring Vale to Walter Hughes, who had captained a whaling ship and a trading ship to the Orient before discovering what became the Wallaroo and Moonta copper mines on one of his pastoral properties, and rapidly acquiring great wealth. In 1869 Hughes began the construction of the first part of the cellars which stand proud today, and progressively extended them as the vineyards grew to 30 hectares and annual production to 45,000 litres by 1880.

Hughes' winemaker since 1868 was German immigrant, Carl Sobels. Following Hughes' death in 1887, his nephew J M Richman inherited the property and in 1890 sold it to a partnership formed between Carl Sobels and Adelaide wine merchant Herman Buring. The two rapidly and aggressively expanded the business in a manner reminiscent of Wolf Blass 80 years later. By 1896 Spring Vale had 2.25 million litres of oak storage, and 2 years later a youthful Leo Buring (Herman's son) joined elder brother Rudi Buring at Spring Vale. It was at this time that the Quelle Tal brand name made its appearance (soon changing to Quelltaler). Its genesis was simple enough: it was German for Spring Vale.

Quelltaler Hock, Quelltaler Sauternes, San Carlo Claret and Granfiesta Sherry quickly became nationally prominent brands, and underpinned the continued growth of the company between 1900 and 1950. Once again, Wolf Blass would have been in his element. But with the family involvement waning, and the generous cheque books of the 1960s table wine boom opened at a moment's notice, ownership of Quelltaler passed first to Nathan and Wyeth, and then to Remy Martin.

Ten years of relative calm followed, but in 1980 Francois Henry arrived in Australia as managing director of Remy

Martin, installed Alsace born and trained Michel Dietrich as winemaker from 1981, and embarked on a costly public relations exercise designed to put Quelltaler Vineyards into the super prestige bracket of wineries along with labels such as Leeuwin Estate and Petaluma. Despite some very good, slow developing wines and continuing heavy promotional expenditure, Quelltaler Vineyards absolutely failed to achieve the goals set for it.

In the meantime, Wolf Blass and Remy Martin had merged their wine distribution businesses, and so knew each other well. It was also wholly appropriate that Blass, a German-born adventurer–winemaker, who had arrived in

Australia in 1961 as a young man without financial resources (albeit with the job of helping Kaiser Stuhl get on the Barossa Pearl sparkling wine bandwagon), should be the purchaser — via the company he controlled — of Quelltaler Vineyards.

Just where Eaglehawk Estate is headed in the long term is not clear. The adoption of the new name, the seemingly mandatory design of new labels, and the launch of the new product range were accompanied by the usual Blass fanfare. Since that time the Eaglehawk has seldom ventured to the skies, but that is not a state of affairs the perpetual motion man, Wolf Blass, will suffer to continue indefinitely.

ABOVE: *Well-used oak barrels in the even older stone cellars at Eaglehawk; some traditions, at least, are maintained.*

WINERIES OF THE CLARE VALLEY

THE CLARE ESTATE   B-B
Polish Hill River
Sevenhill 5453
Established   1980
Winemakers   The Penfolds' winemaking team headed by John Duval.
Production   Not stated.
Principal Wines   Two wines only released: Chardonnay and the Clare Estate (a Merlot/Malbec/Cabernet Sauvignon/Cabernet Franc Blend).
Best Vintages   **W** 1987, '88, '90
                     R 1986, '87, '90
Most of the production from the 100 hectare vineyard is used for blending in Penfolds' other premium wines and the Clare Estate label is reserved for the pick of the crop. In these circumstances one expects great wines; in reality they are good, not great — they seem too smooth, too polished.

EAGLEHAWK ESTATE   B-BA
Main North Road
Watervale 5452   (088) 43 0003
Established   1865
Winemaker   Stephen John
Production   90,000 cases
Principal Wines   Fumé Blanc, Rhine Riesling, Shiraz Merlot Cabernet, Quelltaler Hock, Granfiesta Flor Sherry, Treloars Tawny Port. Also Premium Wood Aged Semillon and Noble Gold Semillon under the Quelltaler brand name.
Best Vintages   **W** and **R** 1987, '89, '90
The adoption of the name Eaglehawk Estate in

place of Quelltaler Estate severely ruffled local feathers, but this Wolf Blass-owned operation has once again been accepted into the local fold as one of the most important Clare Valley wineries. Its wines have been placed firmly in the mid-market range, but I wonder whether that will do full justice to its potential, for there are certainly some great vineyards.

JEFFREY GROSSET   BA-BA
King Street
Auburn 5451   (088) 49 2175
Established   1981
Winemakers   Cate and Jeffrey Grosset.
Production   4500 cases
Principal Wines   White and red table wines including Polish Hill Rhine Riesling, Chardonnay and Cabernet Sauvignon.
Best Vintages   **W** 1982, '86, '87, '89, '90
                     R 1984, '86, '87, '90
If there is a more fastidious winemaker in Australia than Jeffrey Grosset, I am yet to meet him or her. Classic toasty/lime Rhine Rieslings, and spotlessly clean, medium bodied but intensely flavoured Cabernet Sauvignon are by far the two best wines, as noteworthy for their consistency as for their style.

JIM BARRY WINES   CA-B
Main North Road
Clare 5453   (088) 42 2261
Established   1974
Winemaker   Mark Barry
Production   25,000 cases

Principal Wines   Watervale Rhine Riesling, Chardonnay, Sauvignon Blanc, Lavender Hill Moselle, Armagh Shiraz, Cabernet Sauvignon, Cabernet Merlot, Sentimental Bloke Port and Old Walnut Tawny Port.
Best Vintages   **W** 1983, '84, '86, '87, '90
                     R 1971, '78, '79, '80, '86, '87, '88, '90
A once relatively unfashionable and correspondingly unexciting family-owned and run (there are many Barrys) winery which has suddenly produced a series of marvellous oaked reds (from the 1987 and '88 vintages) conspicuously headed by the expensive, imaginatively labelled Grange-pretender, the Armagh.

JUD'S HILL   B-B
Farrell Flat Road
2 km east of Clare 5343
Established   1977
Winemaker   Brian Barry
Production   12,000 cases
Principal Wines   Chablis, Rhine Riesling, Cabernet Sauvignon and CabernetSauvignon Merlot
Best Vintages   **W** 1984, '86, '87, '90
                     R 1984, '86, '87, '90
Brian Barry, a winemaker of enormous experience, has curiously been content to let others make the wine from his Clare Valley vineyard. It is perhaps for this reason that the wine has never really developed a personality or secure place in the market; these elegant wines deserve better.

LEASINGHAM   B-A
7 Dominic Street
Clare 5453   (088) 42 2555
Established   1893
Winemakers   Chris Proud, Neil Paulett
Production   The equivalent of 2 million cases, much of it in cask.
Principal Wines   The Domaine range of Chardonnay, Semillon, Rhine Riesling, Shiraz and Cabernet Malbec was introduced in 1990 with outstanding success. One of the leaders in the cask market, challenging Orlando Coolabah.
Best Vintages   **W** 1969, '71, '73, '77, '78, '80, '82, '84, '86, '87, '89, '90
                     R 1966, '71, '75, '78, '84, '86, '88, '90
By far the largest of the Clare Valley wineries, acquired by H J Heinze from the Knappstein family in 1971 and by Thomas Hardy from H J Heinze in 1987. Over the years, some of the Clare Valley's greatest Rhine Rieslings, Cabernet Sauvignon and Cabernet Malbec have been made here; after years of uncertainty under Heinze ownership Thomas Hardy promises to turn the tide with the new Stanley Leasingham Domaine range.

ABOVE: Mintaro in the style of Gainsborough.

MINTARO CELLARS   B-B
Leasingham Road
Mintaro 5415   (088) 43 9046
Established   1984
Winemaker   James Pearson
Production   2000 cases
Principal Wines   Rhine Riesling and Cabernet
                        Sauvignon.
Best Vintages   W 1985, '87, '89, '90
                        R 1986, '87, '88, '90
A tiny winery which had its moment of glory at the 1989 Small Makers Wine competition with its winning 1985 Rhine Riesling. The wine was in fact no flash in the pan; the Rhine Rieslings are consistently good to very good, the red wines less attractive.

MITCHELL   A-A
Hughes Park Road
(known locally as Skillogalee or Skilly Road)
Skillogalee Valley
Sevenhill via Clare 5453 (088) 43 4258
Established   1975
Winemaker   Neil Pike
Production   12,000 cases
Principal Wines   Watervale Rhine Riesling,
Wood Aged Semillon, Chardonnay, Peppertree Vineyard Shiraz and Cabernet Sauvignon.
Best Vintages   W 1977, '80, '82, '84, '87, '90
                        R 1977, '80, '82, '84, '86, '87,
                        '90
One of Australia's finest small wineries, making a long-lived steely/toasty Rhine Riesling and

intensely flavoured but finely balanced red berry/cassis Cabernet Sauvignon; the more recent arrivals (Semillon, Chardonnay and Shiraz) have not harmed the reputation of the winery, but do not yet challenge its best two wines.

MOUNT HORROCKS   CB-CB
Mintaro Road
Leasingham 5452   (088) 43 0005
Established   1981
Winemaker   Jeffrey Grosset
Production   4000 cases
Principal Wines   Watervale Rhine Riesling,
Watervale Semillon, Chardonnay, Cordon-cut Rhine Riesling and Cabernet Merlot.
Best Vintages   W 1985, '86, '87, '90
                        R 1984, '85, '86, '87, '90
The Ackland brothers have been major grape growers in the Clare Valley for many years, and decided to establish their own label when they saw their best grapes disappearing into the anonymity of large company blends. Some excellent wines have appeared under the label, others seem to me to be affected by volatility (although I am forever worried that this technical fault may be completely irrelevant to the wine-buying public). Certainly, the wines are full of flavour.

PAULETTS   BA-BA
Polish Hill Road
Polish Hill River   (088) 43 4328
Established   1983
Winemaker   Neil Paulett
Production   3000 cases
Principal Wines   Rhine Riesling, Sauvignon
Blanc, Shiraz and Cabernet Merlot.
Best Vintages   W and R 1987, '88
Neil Paulett was winemaker at Penfolds Wybong Estate when Rosemount acquired it so many years ago, and stayed on in the Hunter Valley for some time thereafter; his Australia-wide search for his own vineyard and winery ended in the Polish Hill River area of the Clare Valley where he has made some lovely wines, with minty Shiraz and fine Cabernet Merlot the best. Just to keep his hand in, Paulett is also assistant winemaker at Stanley Leasingham.

PETALUMA   A-A
Off Farrell Flat Road
Clare 5453   (08) 42 2858
Established   1977
Winemaker   Brian Croser
Production   10,000 cases
Principal Wines   Rhine Riesling, wholly from
Petaluma's own vineyard at 500 m above sea level. Chardonnay used for Petaluma Chardonnay between 1984 and 1988.
Best Vintages   W 1980, '84, '85, '86, '87, '90
Apart from the aged Rhine Rieslings of Leo Buring, that of Petaluma stands tall in the Australian Riesling wine scene. Like the wines

of Leo Buring, however, it needs far more bottle age than it usually gets: extremely discreet and reserved when young, it ever so slowly matures into magnificence, as the 1980 vintage clearly shows, and as the '90 will show.

PIKES POLISH HILL
RIVER ESTATE   BA-BA
Polish Hill River Road
Sevenhill 5453   (088) 43 4249
Established   1985
Winemaker   Neil Pike
Production   6000 cases
Principal Wines   Rhine Riesling, Chardonnay,
Sauvignon Blanc, Cabernet Sauvignon, Cabernet Franc Merlot Blend and Shiraz.
Best Vintages   W 1985, '86, '87, '90
                        R 1984, '86, '87, '88, '90

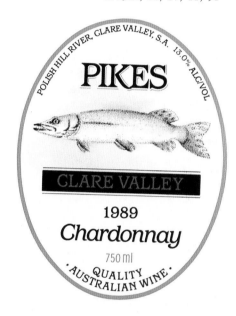

The Pike brothers, Neil and Andrew, have full time occupations elsewhere: Andrew in charge of Penfolds' nearby vineyards, Neil as wine-maker at Mitchell. Both bring their professional skills to bear with their own vineyard, producing sparkling gooseberry flavoured Sauvignon Blanc (always one of my favourites), relatively slow maturing Chardonnay, and striking, full flavoured minty/berry/leafy red wines.

SEVENHILL   BA-A
College Road
Sevenhill via Clare 5453 (088) 43 4222
Established   1851
Winemakers   Brother John May,
                        John Monten
Production   14,500 cases
Principal Wines   White Burgundy, Rhine
Riesling, Traminer Frontignac, Dry Tokay, Clare Riesling, Shiraz, Cabernet Sauvignon, Merlot Cabernet Franc and Cabernet Sauvignon Malbec, together with a limited range of fortified wines, including Liqueur Tokay,

Verdelho, Touriga Portand Vintage Port, and a substantial output of sacramental wines.

Best Vintages   W 1975, '76, '77, '80, '86, '87, '88, '90
R 1975, '76, '77, '82, '86, '88, '90

As Brother John May once said to me, 'There have only been seven winemakers here since 1851. We've all been happy with our job and the pay is just right.' In this Jesuit-run winery, there is of course no pay, but there is a divine touch to the wines. For long famous in wine circles for its reds, Sevenhill has over the past decade steadily built the quality of its white wines, with its humble White Burgundy outstanding at its price.

TAYLORS   B-BA

Mintaro Road
Auburn 5451   (088) 49 2008
Established   1972
Winemaker   Andrew Tolley
Production   170,000 cases
Principal Wines   Chardonnay, Rhine Riesling, White Burgundy, Chablis, Hermitage, Pinot Noir and Cabernet Sauvignon.
Best Vintages   W 1979, '82, '87, '89, '90
R 1976, '78, '79, '87, '88, '90

The once lofty ambitions of Taylors have long since been subjugated to the dreary reality of marketing table wine in substantial quantities, so much so, indeed, that Taylors is often not accorded the respect it deserves. Ironically, its Cabernet Sauvignon is now achieving much of that quality originally sought, with complex cigar box/leafy/tobacco/spicy characters intermingling in a wine of balance and substance.

TIM ADAMS   BA-A

Warenda Road
Clare 5453   (088) 42 2429
Established   1986
Winemaker   Tim Adams
Production   3000 cases
Principal Wines   Semillon, Rhine Riesling, Tim Adams Shiraz and Tim Adams Aberfeldy Vineyard Shiraz.
Best Vintages   W 1988, '89, '90
R 1986, '87, '88, '90

Tim Adams was winemaker at Stanley Leasingham for many years, and elected to leave the largest winery in the district for one of the smallest. Initial releases were good, but in 1988 and 1989 he produced wonderful wines, with a classic toasty/lime Rhine Riesling and a concentrated, firm, textured Shiraz the best.

TIM KNAPPSTEIN WINES   A-A

2 Pioneer Avenue
Clare 5453   (088) 42 2600
Established   1976
Winemaker   Tim Knappstein
Production   38,000 cases

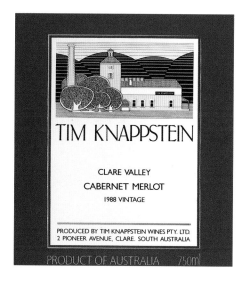

Principal Wines   Rhine Riesling, Fumé Blanc, Chardonnay, Gewurztraminer, Cabernet Sauvignon Cabernet Merlot and Beerenauslese Rhine Riesling.
Best Vintages   W 1977, '80, '82, '85, '87, '89, '90
R 1975, '80, '84, '86, '87, '90

Tim Knappstein is the Peter Pan of the Australian wine industry: looking at him one can hardly credit that he has 23 vintages under his belt. He has been instrumental during that period in establishing the Clare Valley as one of the premium wine regions of Australia, making immaculate Rhine Riesling, Cabernet Sauvignon and Cabernet Merlot.

WENDOUREE   A-A

Wendouree Road
Clare 5453   (088) 42 2896
Established   1895
Winemaker   Tony Brady
Production   3000 cases
Principal Wines   Cabernet Sauvignon, Caber-

net Malbec, Shiraz, Shiraz Mataro and Muscat of Alexandria.

Best Vintages   R 1975, '78, '80, '83, '86, '87

The most heroic reds made in Australia by Tony and Lita Brady. Yet the power and longevity of these wines does not hit you like a sledgehammer when they are young; like the Bradys, they do not offer up their secrets easily.

THE WILSON VINEYARD   BA-A

Polish Hill River
Sevenhill via Clare 5453 (088) 43 4310
Established   1974
Winemaker   John Wilson
Production   3200 cases
Principal Wines   Rhine Riesling, Chardonnay, Cabernet Shiraz/Malbec, Cabernet Sauvignon, Pinot Noir and Zinfandel.
Best Vintages   W 1986, '88, '89, '90
R 1981, '84, '85, '86, '87, '88, '90

Almost every year, John Wilson manages to produce at least one outstanding red, typically showing ripe, red berry fruit with a haunting touch of cigar box.

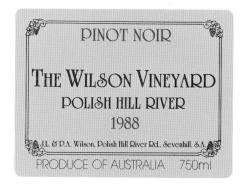

OTHER WINERIES

CRABTREE WATERVALE CELLARS CB-B
North Terrace
Watervale 5452 (088) 43 0069

DUNCAN ESTATE   DC-C
Spring Gully Road
Clare 5453 (088) 43 4335

PENWORTHAM CELLARS   NR
Main North Road
Penwortham

ROSENBERG CELLARS   D-C
Main North Road
Watervale 5452 (088) 43 0131

SKILLOGALLEE WINES   NR
Off Hughes Park Road, Skillogallee Valley
Sevenhill via Clare 5453
3 km south-west of Sevenhill

FACING PAGE: The Polish Hill River subregion has an atmosphere and a beauty all of its own.

ABOVE: An improvised fire beater made from old leather gloves at Wendouree.

SOUTH AUSTRALIA

COONAWARRA

Coonawarra's pre-eminent position as Australia's greatest red wine region today stands in stark contrast to Bill Redman's famous dictum: 'From 1890 to 1945 you can write failure across the face of Coonawarra.' For much of that time most of the wine produced was distilled into brandy, while in the 1930s the South Australian Government implemented a mini vine-pull scheme, offering all ex-servicemen in the area a bounty of £4.10.0 an acre (.4 hectare) for removing their vines and converting the land to dairying.

Indeed, there is every reason to argue that 1951 should be substituted for 1945, for in the intervening period what is now Wynns Coonawarra Estate was nearly sold to the Department of Lands and Forests. Had that occurred, the only working winery would have been the then tiny Rouge Homme of the Redman family. It was in 1951 that David Wynn made his fateful decision to buy the now famous stone winery and cellars which had been built with such hope and enterprise by John Riddoch exactly 60 years earlier.

Until this time the only table wine made in Coonawarra was Redman's Shiraz, which had been sold in bulk to Woodley since 1920. Woodley bottled some of the wine, and sold the rest in bulk to other South Australian wineries. From 1952 Redman started selling to those companies direct, while continuing to supply Woodley with its requirements for bottling (and enabling it to produce the famous Treasure Chest series, the labels of which are reproduced on page 217).

Thomas Hardy (Pathaway, Southern Vales), Chateau Reynella (Southern Vales) and Leo Buring and Yalumba (both of the Barossa Valley) were among the first purchasers of Redman's wine; in 1953 Ronald Haselgrove of Mildara joined the queue, and — unable to purchase as much as he needed — commissioned Bill Redman to find a suitable vineyard block and develop a vineyard. This was done in 1955, and Penfolds followed suit in 1957. The quest for land was on in earnest, and has still not run its course.

More than that, the unrelenting pressure is now causing problems which even Ronald Haselgrove did not foresee when in 1955 he observed that 'within 15 years every major

THE REGION IN BRIEF

LOCATION AND ELEVATION
37°18'S 140°49'E
59 m

CLIMATE
With a heat summation (HDD) of 1430, Coonawarra was the first cool climate viticultural region to gain national prominence. With no maritime influence whatsoever, the winters are cold, wet and windy, and throughout much of the growing season, the night time temperatures are likewise low. Frost used to be a major problem, but viticultural adaptation has significantly reduced the danger. The annual rainfall is 647 mm, 282 mm of it falling between October and April — continuing the winter-spring pattern across south-east Australia and necessitating the use of supplementary water from December onwards. In almost all vintages Coonawarra receives intermittent bursts of very hot weather in February/March. The other climatic problems in a basically favourable climate are wind and rain during flowering (frequently upsetting Merlot and sometimes Cabernet Sauvignon) and mid to late vintage rains, impacting particularly on Rhine Riesling and Shiraz.

SOIL
Coonawarra boasts the most celebrated vineyard soil in Australia, commonly known as terra rosa, a distinctive, albeit thin, band of at times vivid red soil 100 cm to 500 cm deep overlying a bed of soft limestone. In truth there are two technically different soils which are treated as one and the same: a subplastic medium clay classified as Uf5.31, which is in fact very friable and well drained, whatever its name may suggest to the contrary, and shallow friable loams falling in the Um6.41, 6.42 and 6.43 groups. On the western side of the terra rossa strip are black cracking clays falling in the Ug group which overlay limestone, but which are fertile and prone to waterlogging. Experience has shown it is extemely difficult to obtain full ripeness on these soils, and many of the plantings are now devoted to sparkling wine production. On the eastern side of the strip are duplex sandy soils over a clay base (Dr2.23).

HARVEST TIME
Vintage extends from early March (sparkling wine base) through to the end of April; if the grapes are not ripe by this time, climatic conditions seldom allow or justify May picking.

PRINCIPAL GRAPE VARIETIES
The hectares quoted include Padthaway plantings; the districts are not separately recorded in the Australian Bureau of Statistics figures, but the relative importance does not vary significantly.

Rhine Riesling, 839 ha	*Cabernet Sauvignon, 859 ha*
Chardonnay, 420 ha	*Shiraz, 617 ha*
Traminer, 112 ha	*Pinot Noir, 167 ha*
Sauvignon Blanc, 63 ha	*Merlot, 65 ha*
TOTAL WHITE, *1595 ha*	*Cabernet Franc, 33 ha*
	TOTAL RED, *1822 ha*

AUSTRALASIAN WINE REGIONS
1980 – 1990

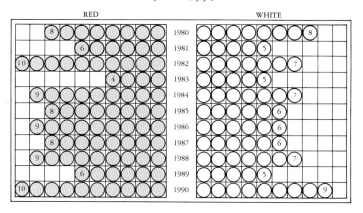

FACING PAGE: *Machine pruned Cabernet Sauvignon with winter growth of capeweed, the latter tolerated but certainly not encouraged in Coonawarra.*

PRINCIPAL WINE STYLES

CABERNET SAUVIGNON

Whatever yardstick one adopts, Coonawarra produces most of Australia's great Cabernet Sauvignon. The best grapes and the best oak are used in making prestige labels such as Wynns John Riddoch, Lindemans St George, Mildara Alexanders and Katnook Estate. In these wines the fruit flavours are very concentrated (particularly in the John Riddoch) and luscious, covering a broad spectrum of individual fruit flavours ranging from blackcurrant to plum to red cherry to prunes. Notwithstanding the impact of oak tannins, the wines are seldom astringent or tannic, and indeed Coonawarra winemakers invest much effort in extracting every last grain of available tannin.

SHIRAZ

To all intents and purposes, Shiraz was the only wine grape grown in Coonawarra between 1900 and 1950; there were a few vines of Cabernet Sauvignon and a little Grenache. The grape that in effect created Coonawarra's reputation seemed to be taking a slow ride to obscurity in the face of the success of Cabernet Sauvignon until Wynns Coonawarra Estate (with its Hermitage) and Mildara (with Jamieson's Run) turned the tide. A straw poll of wine writers in 1990 would almost certainly put those two wines first and second (the order being debatable) as Australia's greatest red wine bargains. The flavour varies significantly according to vintage.

RHINE RIESLING

Rhine Riesling is seemingly a fickle variety in Coonawarra: Lindemans has given up the struggle altogether, consigning its Coonawarra Rhine Riesling to blended anonymity; Mildara makes a token effort; only Wynns (in a very large way and very successfully), Katnook Estate and Hollick (in a small but also successful way) carry the banner. Once again the crisp and aromatic Wynns Coonawarra Estate Rhine Riesling represents extraordinary value for money, and while most of the wine is consumed within hours of purchase, it also demonstrates an utterly unexpected capacity to mature superbly well in bottle.

CHARDONNAY

A variety which has taken time to find its feet, initially being diverted in large part to sparkling wine usage, but now establishing a strong reputation through the efforts of Katnook Estate, Rouge Homme and Wynns Coonawarra Estate. These three producers typically produce rich, peachy wines with surprising weight and mouthfeel, and of reasonable (3 to 4 years) longevity.

OTHER VARIETIES

Lindemans is starting to do some interesting things with Pinot Noir, and Wynns Coonawarra Estate succeeded admirably with its 1986 vintage. While the limestone soil is clearly suited to the variety, the climate may be a little too warm. Katnook Estate has caused the most excitement with Sauvignon Blanc, occasionally producing wines of marvellously concentrated gooseberry flavour, and tremendous length to the palate.

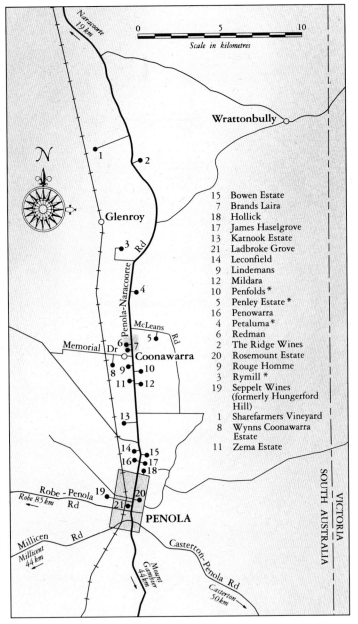

15	Bowen Estate
7	Brands Laira
18	Hollick
17	James Haselgrove
13	Katnook Estate
21	Ladbroke Grove
14	Leconfield
9	Lindemans
12	Mildara
10	Penfolds *
5	Penley Estate *
16	Penowarra
4	Petaluma *
6	Redman
2	The Ridge Wines
20	Rosemount Estate
9	Rouge Homme
3	Rymill *
19	Seppelt Wines (formerly Hungerford Hill)
1	Sharefarmers Vineyard
8	Wynns Coonawarra Estate
11	Zema Estate

wine company will be clamouring for Coonawarra vineyard land'. For the whole thrust of viticulture in Australia serves to deny the French view of *terroir* and of the importance of soil. Yet in Coonawarra there exists a classic example to support the French view. The exception may do no more than prove the rule elsewhere in Australia (it is an issue I deal with at greater length in pages 26 to 27) but it is causing real anxiety in Coonawarra in the 1990s. There are three soil types in Coonawarra: the famous red soils; the grey sandy soils which abut on the east; and the heavy black soils on the west. Experience shows that the last soil simply will not allow grapes to ripen properly for table wines, as it is too fertile and not sufficiently well drained. It can, however, produce satisfactory grapes for sparkling wine. The sandy soils to the east are entirely unsuited to viticulture.

It is this dichotomy, not readily apparent from the dead flat perspective of ground level, which has given rise to the

anxiety. There are those who would like to retrospectively define and delimit Coonawarra by reference to the red soils (possibly incorporating some of the black soils), but it may well be they have waited too long. The concern is, of course, that inferior wines from inferior soils will tarnish Coonawarra's reputation.

The difficulty is compounded by the isolation and extremely compact size of Coonawarra. As Dr Sam Benwell said, 'It lies between Melbourne and Adelaide, but never quite on the way between the two cities, no matter which way one goes.' It is completely flat, and one can drive through its 15 kilometre length without seeing anything much other than some vines. It is bitingly cold in winter, and can be fiercely hot in summer. The township of Coonawarra is a motley general store, a phone box, and one or two insignificant buildings (all on a side street). The wineries are functional but little more; only Wynns Coonawarra Estate vies — albeit handsomely — with what is commonplace in, for example, the Barossa Valley. But it is the Mecca to which all true wine pilgrims must travel.

ABOVE: *The famous Woodley Treasure Chest labels; it is amazing that they are printed on a single sheet then cut.*

MODERN AUSTRALIAN VITICULTURE

For better or worse, Coonawarra has been the crucible in which much of modern viticultural practice has been forged over the past 20 years. This has come about because of the dominance of major companies, each with large holdings; the ease of mechanisation on absolutely flat land with easy year-round access; the economic value of the crops, which has justified the research and development component of the expenditure; and the lack of an available labour-pool for hand-pruning and hand-picking.

The original plantings in Coonawarra were laid out in rows 2.1 metres apart, with a diminutive single wire trellis 60 centimetres above the ground. (Brands Laira and Redman each have a precious small block of these plantings.) The first change, introduced from the 1950s, was to widen the row spacing to 3 metres or more to accommodate tractors in place of horses, and to lift the trellis to 1.2 metres to reduce frost damage, and to install a second fruiting wire to allow more canes and so compensate for the reduced yield from the wider spacings.

The next change came at the end of the 1960s with the introduction of a T trellis — in other words, a 0.3 metre cross-piece was placed on top of the trellis, with wires running along the length of the trellis attached to the ends of the cross-pieces. This allowed up to eight canes to be laid down each year, and permitted far greater yields than the 5 tonnes per hectare which had hitherto been accepted as normal.

Frost control (through overhead irrigation sprays) also gradually became standard procedure, but surprisingly enough, it is now increasingly recognised that insufficient use has been made of this capacity to alleviate water stress during the growing season — in other words, to irrigate.

The transformation in viticulture started a few years later in the early 1970s: the architects were Colin Kidd of Lindemans, Bob Hollick of Mildara and Vic Patrick of Wynns Coonawarra Estate (now of Mildara). First was the introduction of mechanical harvesting, which occurred at much the same time as in the rest of Australia. At the time it was seen as somewhat controversial and as inimical to wine quality, but no more. Although precise figures are not available, it is probable that over 90 per cent of all grapes in Australia are now mechanically harvested, and speed, flexibility and the ability to harvest at night are accepted as at least compensating for the downsides (maceration and

MOG, or material other than grapes, eg leaves, canes, snails, etc) in large vineyards.

There were a number of consequences. Vic Patrick had already demonstrated that, contrary to long-held local opinon, the cheaper and quicker spur pruning was as successful (in terms of yield) as was cane pruning. So immediately following the introduction of mechanical harvesting, the first trials in mechanical pruning began, using a circular saw (sometimes a reciprocating bar cutter) attachment on either a mechanical harvester or tractor. (Mechanical pruning results in an inelegant but highly effective form of spur pruning.)

The wide T trellis quickly proved unsuited to both mechanical harvesting and mechanical pruning, and was abandoned in favour of a vertical spreading system. The vines looked dreadful in winter: like rows of ruffled hedgehogs, with a tangled, crowded mess of viable and dead shoots. Traditional opinion was outraged, confidently forecasting the speedy death of the vines. Clearly only the big companies, with a mixture of hard-nosed economic pragmatism and strong scientific back-up from Peter Clingeleffer at the CSIRO (Commonwealth Scientific and Industrial Research Organisation), who was and is the inspiration for so much of this work, had the will and ability to persevere.

The next development was even more radical, and remains controversial to this day. In 1979 Bob Hollick, in conjunction with Clingeleffer, took the logic one step further. The mechanically-pruned vines had indeed survived (and flourished) because of a hitherto unsuspected capacity to self-regulate their own growth. So why prune at all? Following earlier trials at the CSIRO near Merbein, minimal pruning was introduced. Minimal pruning means no winter pruning at all, and a light mechanical trimming (or skirting) of the vines in late spring to open up the area underneath the vines (where the foliage hangs down) to encourage air circulation.

The consequence of this treatment is that all of the grapes form on the outside of the canopy, and the interior is barren of grapes (and leaves). Contrary to what one would expect, the size of the canopy does not increase significantly each year, attesting to the ability of the vine to self-regulate, and to the effect of competition between the vines seeking to support such a large canopy.

These changes were accompanied by equally radical moves in soil management. The old vineyards were regularly

ABOVE: *Vic Patrick, formerly Wynns and now Mildara chief viticulturist, knows every square centimetre of soil in Coonawarra.*

ploughed to control weeds and grasses, and to help (so it was thought) water penetration. Now in most vineyards there is total herbicide control, and the soil is no longer ploughed or disced. Instead there is a hard, completely smooth and bald earth surface, which (coupled with the lift in the trellis height and the use of overhead sprays) has reduced the incidence of frost damage. The smooth surface of the soil means the cold air is not trapped by weeds, grasses or the ploughed surface, and instead 'slips' down infinitesimal slopes off the slightly raised 'red bank' or terra rosa soil.

The impact on annual costs has been dramatic. Even with the economics of the large scale holdings which are common in Coonawarra, the cost of maintaining a hectare of vineyard using traditional methods is around $4520, while the fully mechanised/minimal pruning approach is $1550. At a typical yield of 12 tonnes per hectare, the production cost per tonne of grapes comes down from $380 per tonne to $130 per tonne.

The implications for wine quality and wine style are less clear-cut. It is common that in the immediate aftermath of the introduction of either machine or minimal pruning yields increase dramatically and quality suffers somewhat. The vine then catches up with itself, yields come back to 9 to 10 tonnes per hectare, but with a much larger number of smaller bunches with small individual berries giving a better skin to juice ratio (and hence better colour and flavour), or so the

supporters argue. The critics say that strange flavours emerge. I have described these as 'Coonawarra pie and peas', a curious melange of very ripe/gamey/meaty flavours on the one hand and a grassy/leafy herbaceousness on the other. Colin Kidd rejects outright the notion that this is due to uneven ripening on minimally pruned vines, but the fact remains that the flavour is there. Furthermore, some viticulturists admit there can be ripening problems in cool or wet years.

In apparent recognition of these problems, Katnook Estate and Wynns Coonawarra Estate are both looking at reverting to high density plantings with machine pruned and machine-trained vertical canopies, which will cost more per hectare to manage but which will provide similar yields of higher quality grapes. Likewise, there are experimental trellis designs which will almost certainly lead to an improvement in grape quality.

The story is far from finished. Many of the developments have taken place with a background of unsatisfied demand for grapes (pushing yields higher) and downwards pressure on production costs (supporting higher yields but also supporting other practices which on some views do not enhance quality). Coonawarra's reputation has positively flowered during this period, so it is simply not possible to say quality has been degraded. But the question for the future remains: can Coonawarra do better still?

ABOVE: *Minimally pruned (left hand side) and machine pruned (right hand side) Chardonnay vines at Old Penola Estate Vineyard.*

WINERIES OF COONAWARRA

BOWEN ESTATE   A-A
Main Penola-Naracoorte Road
Penola 5277   (087) 37 2229
Established   1972
Winemaker   Doug Bowen
Production   7000 cases
Principal Wines Rhine Riesling, Chardonnay,
Shiraz and Cabernet Sauvignon Merlot.
Best Vintages   W 1981, '82, '84, '87, '89, '90
                     R 1979, '80, '82, '84, '87, '89,
                     '90

Since its foundation, Bowen Estate has been the dominant force among the small Coonawarra wineries. It is still generally regarded as the foremost red wine maker among the small producers, notable for their spicy/peppery Shiraz and for exceptionally fine, textured Cabernet Sauvignon with fruit lusciousness varying according to vintage from dark berry/cassis through to a more herbaceous, Bordeaux-style.

BRANDS LAIRA   BA-B
Penola-Naracoorte Highway
Coonawarra 5263   (087) 36 3260
Established   1965
Winemakers   Bill and Jim Brand.
Production   18,000 cases
Principal Wines Chardonnay, Shiraz, Cabernet Sauvignon, Cabernet Merlot, Cabernet Sauvignon Sparkling Burgundy. Limited special releases of Original Vineyard Shiraz and of Family Reserve Wines. Individual varietal wines Merlot, Pinot Noir, Malbec and Rhine Riesling available at cellar door only.
Best Vintages   R 1966, '68, '76, '77, '84, '86,
                     '87, '88, '90

The Brand family has had a leading role in winemaking in Coonawarra for a quarter of a century, and have been grape growers there since 1950. The red wines are consistently very good, with full, soft and ripe fruit flavours and minimal oak influence shaping wines with a 10 to 15 year maturity optimum.

HOLLICK   BA-B
Racecourse Road
Coonawarra 5263   (087) 37 2318
Established   1983
Winemakers   Ian Hollick, Pat Tocaciu
Production   15,000 cases
Principal Wines Rhine Riesling, Chardonnay,
Cabernet Merlot, Pinot Noir and Shiraz.
Best Vintages   W 1984, '86, '88, '89, '90
                     R 1984, '85, '87, '88, '90

The partnership of Pat Tocaciu and Ian Hollick should be a tremendously potent one; Tocaciu put his skill as a white wine maker beyond any doubt during his time at Tollana (Barossa Valley), and he no doubt knows more than most people have forgotten about red wine making. Ian Hollick has already shown a masterly touch with Cabernet and Cabernet Merlot, reflected to the fullest in the most recent red releases from Hollick. With the expectation of Rhine Riesling and Chardonnay of equal quality, Hollick must be headed to an A-A rating.

JAMES HASELGROVE   CB-B
Main Penola-Naracoorte Road
Coonawarra 5263   (087) 37 2734
Established   1980
Winemaker   James Haselgrove
Production   10,000 cases
Principal Wines Rhine Riesling, Gewurztraminer, Late Harvest Riesling, Auslese Riesling, Nouveau, Shiraz, Cabernet Sauvignon and Cabernet Shiraz.
Best Vintages   W 1982, '85, '86, '87, '89, '90
                     R 1982, '83, '85, '86, '87, '88,
                     '90

An unusually large number of wines are typically on offer at any one time from James Haselgrove, most from his extensive Coonawarra vineyards, but one or two from McLaren Vale. Quality and style varies substantially, however, the best are good —particularly the lime-juice flavoured botrytised Rieslings.

KATNOOK ESTATE   A-AB
Off main Penola-Naracoorte Road
Coonawarra 5263   (087) 37 2394
Established   1980
Winemaker   Wayne Stehbens
Production   5000 cases (estimated)
Principal Wines Rhine Riesling, Sauvignon Blanc, Chardonnay and Cabernet Sauvignon.
Best Vintages   W 1980, '82, '83, '85, '87, '90
                     R 1980, '83, '84, '86, '87, '88,
                     '90

Katnook Estate is the super-premium label of the vast Coonawarra Machinery Company plantings owned by the Yunghanns family, and is able to pick the very best grapes out of each vintage. This luxury results in fleshy, gooseberry flavoured Sauvignon Blanc, highly aromatic Rhine Riesling with strong Germanic overtones, and startlingly intense and deeply coloured Cabernet Sauvignon.

LECONFIELD   B-B
Main Penola-Naracoorte Road
Coonawarra 5263   (087) 37 2326
Established   1974
Winemaker   Dr Richard Hamilton
Production   11,000 cases
Principal Wines Rhine Riesling, Chardonnay, Cabernet Sauvignon, Cabernet Shiraz and Cabernet Merlot.
Best Vintages   W 1986, '88, '89, '90
                     R 1978, '80, '82, '84, '86, '88,
                     '90

A winery founded by the legendary Syd Hamilton when he was 77 years young, and reluctantly sold by him to his nephew when he was 84. Syd Hamilton leaves behind the achievement of his great '78 and '80 Leconfield Cabernets. Recent vintages have seen some of the best reds since Syd Hamilton's days and a sharp improvement in the white wines. Definitely a winery on the way back and headed to a higher rating.

LINDEMANS   A-A
Main Penola-Naracoorte Road
Coonawarra 5263   (087) 36 3205

ABOVE: The transition from terra rosa to limestone: a large part of the Coonawarra magic.

Established 1908
Winemakers Greg Clayfield with Phillip John.
Production Not for publication.
Principal Wines Limestone Ridge Shiraz Cabernet, St George Vineyard Cabernet Sauvignon and, in the wake of its 1986 Jimmy Watson Trophy, Pyrus, a blend of Cabernet Sauvignon, Cabernet Franc Merlot and Malbec.
Best Vintages W and R 1976, '78, '80, '82, '86, '88, '90

The red wines released under the Lindemans label (as opposed to the separate Rouge Homme, see below) are generally regarded as the finest to come from the major companies in Coonawarra. The style is quite different to that of Wynns Coonawarra Estate (which I personally rate on a par with Lindemans), with less concentrated fruit, but more elegance, and quite distinctive oak handling. The subtlety of the oak is growing better day by day, and Lindemans may yet show a clean pair of heels to the entire field.

MILDARA   BA-BA

Main Penola-Naracoorte Road
Coonawarra 5263   (087) 36 3380
Established 1955
Winemaker Gavin Hogg
Production Not for publication; estimated 90,000 cases.
Principal Wines A tightly controlled and selected range of brands falling in distinct price categories. At the bottom end is Coonawarra Rhine Riesling and Coonawarra Hermitage; then comes Jamieson's Run (predominantly Shiraz); next is Coonawarra Cabernet Sauvignon and finally Alexanders (a Bordeaux blend).
Best Vintages W 1979, '85, '86, '88, '90

R 1963, '64, '69, '79, '82, '85, '86, '88, '90
Mildara seems to be marginally missing the boat with its white wines from Coonawarra, but it is certainly challenging the best with its red wines. The first two vintages of Jamieson's Run ('85 and '86) offered unprecedented value for money, and after a slightly weak '87, it seems it has returned to top form with a Jimmy Watson Trophy to its credit. The humble Hermitage, although light in body, offers fresh, fruity drinking at a no less remarkable low price.

PENFOLDS   B-B

Main Penola-Naracoorte Road
Coonawarra 5263 (vineyard only)
Established 1960
Winemakers John Duval and assistants.
Production Not for publication.
Principal Wines Bin 128 Coonawarra Claret only.
Best Vintages Bin 128 1963, '66, '68, '80, '82, '85, '86, '87, '90

Penfolds has been content to take a very low-key approach with Bin 128, its only 100 per cent Coonawarra-sourced red wine on regular release. If it allocated more new oak to the wine, and lifted the price correspondingly, I think the interests of consumers would be better served.

PETALUMA   A-A

Evans Vineyard
Main Penola-Naracoorte Road
Coonawarra 5263 (vineyard only)
Established 1979
Winemaker Brian Croser
Production Estimated 12,000 cases.
Principal Wines A Cabernet Merlot blend simply entitled Coonawarra and sometimes a Botrytis Affected Rhine Riesling. Some Chardonnay used between 1980 and 1985 for Petaluma Chardonnay.
Best Vintages R 1979, '86, '87, '88, '89, '90

In according Bowen first rank among the small producers in Coonawarra, I was including only winemakers in the district. Petaluma would vigorously contest the overall number one position, of course, and in my opinion, would win. For all that, after a brilliant debut in 1979, the wines seemed to lack something until 1986. Since that year, however, each succeeding vintage (including the yet to be released vintages up to

and including 1988, all of which I have tasted) have gone from one level of excellence to the next. They have the flavour and structure which some of the excessively elegant wines from the early 1980s lacked. The occasional searingly luscious botrytised Riesling adds further lustre to the label.

REDMAN   C-B

Main Penola-Naracoorte Road
Coonawarra 5253   (087) 36 3331
Established 1966
Winemaker Bruce Redman
Production 20,000 cases
Principal Wines Only two wines are made: Claret and Cabernet Sauvignon (the latter in bottles, magnums and imperials).
Best Vintages 1966, '68, '69, '70, '76

Redman is, quite simply, a fallen idol, which seems to survive partly on its past glories, and partly on a modest retail price (the wines are often savagely discounted). One tangible reason is the lack of new oak but the wines also lack body and flavour, quite apart from an array of minor winemaking faults.

ROSEMOUNT ESTATE   BA-B

Main Penola-Naracoorte Road
Penola 5270 (vineyard only)
Established 1981
Winemaker Philip Shaw
Production Not for publication.
Principal Wines The Kirri Billi vineyard

ABOVE LEFT: Gavin Hogg with offspring.

ABOVE RIGHT: The gnarled and tortured limbs of Shiraz planted a century ago under the gaze of John Riddoch, and owned by the Redmans.

ABOVE: *Wynns Coonawarra Estate, with some of the original vines.*

range, with Cabernet Sauvignon and Merlot the first releases.

Best Vintages   1986, '88, '89, '90
Rosemount has bided its time, but the 1990 release of its 1986 vintage reds under the Kirri Billi range confirm that it is very serious about its Coonawarra operation. It will be interesting to see what future releases will bring.

ROUGE HOMME   BA-A

c/o Lindemans
Main Penola-Naracoorte Road
Coonawarra 5263
Established   1963
Winemakers   Greg Clayfield with Phillip John.
Production   Not for publication.
Principal Wines   Chardonnay, Export Estate Dry White, Pinot Noir, Claret and Cabernet Sauvignon. Old vintages of Cabernet Sauvignon and Claret from time to time.
Best Vintages   W 1986, '88, '90
R 1963, '70, '78, '80, '84, '86, '88, '90

Once a Cabernet Sauvignon and Claret (the latter indicating a predominantly Shiraz-based wine) specialist, the Rouge Homme label now extends to distinguished Chardonnay and (as from 1988) a Pinot Noir which has some real style. The best wine remains the Cabernet Sauvignon, with perfectly ripened Cabernet flavour, good structure and prominent but not overweening oak.

SEPPELT   CB-CB

Main Penola-Naracoorte Road
Penola   (087) 37 2613
Established   1971
Winemaker   Gerry Sissingh
Production   Not known.
Principal Wines   Rhine Riesling, Chardonnay, Shiraz, Cabernet Merlot and Cabernet Sauvignon.
Best Vintages   W 1986, '87, '88, '90
R 1978, '80, '82, '84, '86, '88, '90
Hungerford Hill has produced superb Coonawarra Cabernet Sauvignon over the years, and some very good Shiraz. The acquisition of Hungerford Hill by Seppelt should herald a sharp lift in both quality and consistency.

WYNNS COONAWARRA ESTATE   A-A

Memorial Drive
Coonawarra 5263   (087) 36 3266
Established   1891
Winemaker   Peter Douglas
Production   450,000 cases
Principal Wines   Rhine Riesling, Chardonnay, Pinot Noir, Hermitage, Cabernet Hermitage, Cabernet Sauvignon and John Riddoch Cabernet Sauvignon.
Best Vintages   R 1955, '62, '66, '75, '76, '80, '82, '84, '86, '88, '90
Having regard to the fact that Wynns Coonawarra Estate produces a Rhine Riesling and a Hermitage which in early 1990 had a real retail price of $6 a bottle or less, the A-A rating may seem, at the very least, inconsistent. However, the quality of those wines deserves honorary A status. The opulently oaked and increasingly complex Chardonnay, the rich cassis/berry Black Label Cabernet Sauvignon and the amazingly concentrated, super-rich John Riddoch Cabernet Sauvignon need no honorary elevation. As always, style preferences matter: I enjoy the style more than others, but I have to admit that I would not wish to drink the wines every day of the week — the flavour does tend to build up in the bigger red wines such as the John Riddoch Cabernet Sauvignon.

ZEMA ESTATE   B-B

Main Penola-Naracoorte Road
Coonawarra 5263   (087) 36 3219
Established   1982
Winemaker   Ken Ward
Production   3000 cases

Principal Wines   Rhine Riesling, Late Harvest Rhine Riesling, Shiraz and Cabernet.
Best Vintages   R 1982, '84, '86, '88, '90
In an area in which mechanisation is ubiquitous, hand-pruned, hand-picked vines are a rarity. Zema Estate has these, and the traditionalists would no doubt like to put that as one of the reasons for the outstanding wines produced by Zema — deep in colour, rich in flavour and without any of the errant characters one sometimes finds in the Coonawarra flavour jungle.

OTHER WINERIES

LADBROKE GROVE   D-C
Millicent Road
Penola 5277 (087) 37 2997

PENLEY ESTATE   NR
McLeans Road
Coonawarra 5263 (08) 366 4106
(vineyard only)

PENOWARRA   NR
Main Penola-Naracoorte Road
Penola 5277 (087) 37 2458

RYMILL WINES   A-B
Old Penola Estate
Penola 5277 (087) 37 2317
(vineyard only)

THE RIDGE WINES   DC-C
Naracoorte Road
Coonawarra 5263 (087) 36 5071

ABOVE LEFT: Greg Clayfield and a young Rouge Homme Cabernet Sauvignon.   *ABOVE RIGHT: Peter Douglas, Wynns winemaker.*

SOUTH AUSTRALIA

PADTHAWAY

If Coonawarra is not quite on the way to anywhere, Padthaway is on the way to nowhere. If you can pass through Coonawarra without noticing very much, you can pass through Padthaway without noticing anything at all. Its birth was both recent and humble, and initially the major wine companies (which have a near monopoly on its plantings) entirely misread its potential. Although it is only 25 years since the first vines were planted there, it is, notwithstanding the degree of trial and error, now clearly one of Australia's premium white wine producers.

The region's potential was pinpointed by a Seppelt committee appointed in the early 1960s to select suitable vineyard sites for large scale planting of early ripening grape varieties. The requirements were ready availability of land (at a modest price), a cool climate, and plentiful water for irrigation. The committee's research turned up a 1944 CSIRO (Commonwealth Scientific and Industrial Research Organisation) report which focused on a 3200 hectare block of country north of Naracoorte, and which concluded, 'The soil type is variable in depth and there are usually some stony portions on each of the small patches in which it occurs. It is a terra rosa soil . . . the deeper sites of the terra rosa soils should make first class garden soils'.

Only then did the Seppelt viticulturists visit the region, and duly identify a strip running for 16 kilometres along the Naracoorte to Padthaway road, which fell within the narrow 550 millimetre rainfall belt — but with unlimited underground water. One of the nearby principal farming and grazing properties was Keppoch Park, and Seppelt gave the name Keppoch to the region, a choice initially adopted by Thomas Hardy when it purchased its first land in 1968. Lindemans arrived the same year, but selected land further north at Padthaway, and used that name. Wynns, the other big company holder, has never made a regional wine (all of its production is blended, much of it into sparkling wine), and so did not enter the tug-of-war over the name.

After a decade or more of confusion, all have agreed on Padthaway, which has gone some way to giving the region a sense of identity. However, the absence of any winery (Thomas Hardy and Seppelt have field crushing stations, but no more) and the presence of only one cellar door sales outlet (that of the one small player, Padthaway Estate) means the district is little known and seldom visited.

To add historical insult to injury, Seppelt initially decided to concentrate on red wines, relying on Drumborg to produce the white wines, while Lindemans envisaged the region as a producer of medium quality wine to go into its lower to mid-priced bottle range (casks were then but a bright idea

THE REGION IN BRIEF

LOCATION AND ELEVATION
36°36'S 140°30'E
60 – 80 m

SUBREGIONS
Padthaway and Keppoch (in some schemes the two subregions are treated as separate wine producing regions which seems an entirely unnecessary and confusing division).

CLIMATE
Not surprisingly, the climate is very similar to that of Coonawarra, albeit with a higher heat summation (HDD) of 1610. Rainfall is around 550 mm, and strongly winter-spring dominant, and irrigation has always been regarded as essential. The principal climatic hazard is spring frosts, which devastated Padthaway in 1988, and which overall occur more frequently than in Coonawarra.

SOIL
The landscape avoids the dead flat monotony of Coonawarra, but the slopes are very gentle. The principal 'garden soil' identified by the CSIRO in 1944 is in fact the same soil which dominates the Barossa Valley, Clare Valley, Watervale and the Southern Vales: red-brown loamy sand soils in the hard red duplex group Dr2.23. The subsoils are strongly alkaline, and on some of the ridges sandy soils in the Uc2.21 group overlie a limestone base similar to that found in Coonawarra. There are also patches of surface soil identical to the bright red soil of Coonawarra falling into the shallow friable loam group of Um6.41, 6.42 and 6.43.

HARVEST TIME
Again, similar to Coonawarra, commencing early March for sparkling wine purposes and concluding mid to late April for dry table wines, with botrytised Riesling harvested in May.

PRINCIPAL GRAPE VARIETIES

Rhine Riesling	*Cabernet Sauvignon*
Chardonnay	*Shiraz*
Sauvignon Blanc	*Pinot Noir*
	Merlot

(The hectareage is combined with that for Coonawarra, see page 215.)

AUSTRALASIAN WINE REGIONS
1980 – 1990

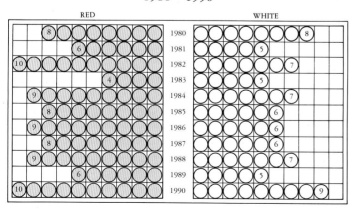

FACING PAGE: *Wynns' and Seppelt's vineyards make a brilliant Padthaway mosaic.*

for the future, with numerous technical problems unsolved). That Padthaway is now to white wine what Coonawarra is to red is due simply to the quality of the wine it has produced, quality which has overridden prejudice, isolation and lack of glamour (for want of a better word).

Padthaway falls within a buffer zone between Victoria and South Australia which imposes strict controls on water usage. No further irrigation rights are being granted, and this has restricted (and will in the future restrict) the spread of viticulture. The one major independent grower supplies Orlando, which has however recently acquired 165 hectares of land and already planted 40 hectares. The only other acquisitions (in 1989) have been by Andrew Garrett (Southern Vales) and by Tolley Pedare (Adelaide Metropolitan Region).

To this day the one great drawcard is Padthaway Estate, a magnificent two-storey Victorian homestead now offering luxurious Relais et Chateaux type accommodation to a handful of lucky guests. Padthaway Estate is also in the course of establishing its own sparkling wine and table wine winery on the property in a superb stone shearing shed; by the time of publication this should be fully functional, and Padthaway itself that little bit better known.

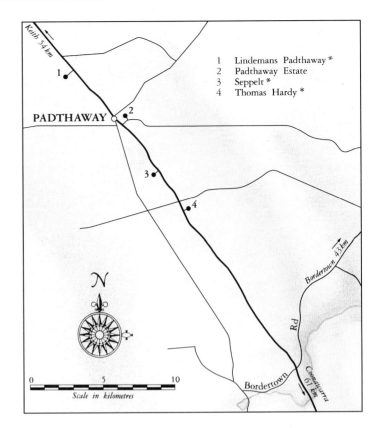

1 Lindemans Padthaway *
2 Padthaway Estate
3 Seppelt *
4 Thomas Hardy *

ABOVE: *Buds burst at the most unexpected spots on old vines.*

PADTHAWAY—PREMIUM WHITE WINE PRODUCER

There is no question that the quality of the white wine produced in Padthaway has come as a great surprise to the companies which have invested so heavily in it. Part of the reason is historical: all of the major players had taken up their positions 3 years before the first Chardonnay (Tyrrell's — of the Lower Hunter Valley — 1971 Vat 47) was made, and long before Chardonnay became readily available for planting in South Australia. It may seem incredible, but in 1981 only 323 tonnes of Chardonnay were crushed in the whole of South Australia, 118 tonnes of which came from the south-east — in other words, Padthaway and Coonawarra.

Inevitably, too, there was a lack of accumulated knowledge about the suitability of the district to the various grape varieties. As recently as 1982 the Lindemans plantings were a veritable oriental fruit salad, with some decidedly strange components. It is a fair bet many of those varieties have been grafted over or pulled out and replanted, but the list remains a fascinating one:

Rhine Riesling, 216 ha	*Chardonnay, 61 ha*
Traminer, 51 ha	*Shiraz, 49 ha*
Grenache, 42 ha	*Crouchen, 29 ha*
Tokay, 21 ha	*Tokay, 21 ha*
Sauvignon Blanc, 19 ha	*Verdelho, 19 ha*
Sylvaner, 15 ha	*Frontignac, 12 ha*
Semillon, 12 ha	*Pinot Noir, 10 ha*
Chenin Blanc, 10 ha	*Cabernet Sauvignon, 8 ha*
Oeilliade, 6 ha	*Müller-Thurgau, 1 ha*
Experimental varieties, 5 ha	

Towards the end of 1982 I obtained samples from Seppelt, Lindemans and Thomas Hardy of almost all the wines they had made and bottled from Padthaway grapes. They comprised 17 Rhine Rieslings from 1975 to 1981, mainly dry but including a handful of Spatlese and Auslese styles; three Frontignacs; four Traminers; two Sylvaners; two Fumé Blancs; a Verdelho; three Pinot Noirs; three Shiraz; nine Cabernet Sauvignons; and a single Chardonnay.

Significantly, the Chardonnay came from Thomas Hardy which, together with Lindemans, has done so much since to establish Padthaway as one of Australia's great Chardonnay districts. The style of the wine is very distinctive, and the flavour very consistent. Time and again I find myself recognising Padthaway Chardonnay in large blind tastings, and the characteristic I immediately identify is the strong aroma and taste of grapefruit. Obviously, there are other flavours — after all, the wine is made from grapes, not grapefruit — and there is the inevitable influence of oak, sometimes spicy, sometimes vanillan, sometimes lemony. But grapefruit is my taste mnemonic. The structure, too, is distinctive: the grapefruit character can occur in Chardonnay grown in a remarkably diverse range of climates, but a second identifier is the overall elegance and length to the flavour.

Those voluptuous Chardonnays from the Hunter Valley (New South Wales), McLaren Vale and the Riverland tend to cloy after the second glass, and to tire after 2 or 3 years in the bottle. The typical Padthaway Chardonnay, with its crisp acidity and elegance, provides as much pleasure from the last glass as the first; what is more, with a limited track record, they are showing remarkable longevity. The Lindemans Padthaway Chardonnays from 1984 and 1985 were both superb (and remarkably similar) at 5 years of age, yet Lindemans believe (and I agree) that the more recent vintages have even greater potential.

Thomas Hardy, having won many gold medals with its Collection Series Chardonnays from Padthaway, has gone one better with its Eileen Hardy Chardonnays, also from Padthaway. The Collection wines have been made using the most basic techniques, and with little or no new oak. They are fruit-driven wines, lasting testimonials to the quality of Padthaway fruit; those under the Eileen Hardy label employ the full range of techniques and are much more complex.

These two companies have also made some outstanding Sauvignon Blancs (labelled Fumé Blanc). Here Lindemans is the leader, making a miraculous wine from the frost-ravaged 1988 vintage. These wines have clear-cut gooseberry varietal flavour, but also have richness and weight in the mouth, an uncommon combination in Australia.

Seppelt has elected, by and large, to use most of its Padthaway wine in multi-region blends, but it and Thomas Hardy have produced some of Australia's greatest botrytised Rhine Rieslings in the 1984, '85 and '87 vintages. The purity, intensity and length of flavour of these wines elevates them into world class. Dry Rhine Riesling is more workmanlike than brilliant; lower cropping levels might work wonders, but the price-position of Rhine Riesling and big-maker wine economics make such restraint highly unlikely. For all that, Hardys Siegersdorf Rhine Riesling is now (according to the year) wholly or largely sourced from Padthaway.

ABOVE: *Chardonnay a few weeks from harvest.*

WINERIES OF PADTHAWAY

LINDEMANS PADTHAWAY   A-A
Padthaway via Naracoorte 5271
(vineyard only)

Established	1968
Winemakers	Greg Clayfield assisted by Phillip John
Production	Not for publication.

Principal Wines   Chardonnay, Sauvignon Blanc (Fumé Blanc), Verdelho, Rhine Riesling, Pinot Noir and Cabernet Sauvignon.

Best Vintages   W 1983, '85, '86, '87, '88, '90
R 1980, '83, '87, '88, '90

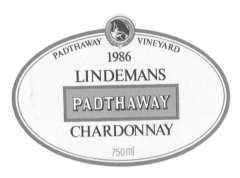

Lindemans Padthaway Estate is the white wine jewel in the Penfolds-Lindemans crown. The best wine is the long-lived grapefruit/melon Chardonnay, the vast proportion of which is sold and consumed within 2 years of vintage, but which is quite superb at 4 or 5 years of age. The Fumé Blanc is also outstanding, with wonderfully rich tropical/gooseberry fruit; it reaches its best a year or two earlier.

PADTHAWAY ESTATE   BA-BA
Padthaway township, adjacent
to highway   (087) 65 5039

Established	1986
Winemaker	Leigh Clarnette
Production	5500 cases

Principal Wines   Pinot Chardonnay Brut, Pinot Noir Brut Rosé and two table wines, Chardonnay and Pinot Noir.

Best Vintages   W 1986, '88, '90
R 1986, '89, '90

Padthaway Estate is three things: a major grape grower (selling much of its output to Thomas Hardy), a winemaker (with its wines formerly made by Thomas Hardy but now being made on-site) and a sumptuous mini-hotel in the manner of the Relais and Chateaux chain in Europe (it is not in fact a member). It is not the only place to stay in Padthaway, but it is *the* place to stay.

SEPPELT   BA-A
Adjacent to Padthaway township
(087) 65 5047

Established	1963
Winemakers	Ian McKenzie plus others.

Production	Not for publication.

Principal Wines   Only occasional individual vineyard releases (such as Padthaway Cabernet-Merlot 1987 and the superlative 1984 Rhine Riesling Auslese), but Rhine Riesling, Chardonnay, Shiraz and Cabernet Sauvignon play a major role in many of the more important Seppelt wines, such as the Seppelt Black label and Gold label ranges and Chardonnay and Pinot Noir in premium sparkling wines.

Best Vintages   W 1984, '86, '87, '90
R 1978, '81, '84, '86, '88, '90

Apart from confusing the situation for many years by doggedly referring to Padthaway as Keppoch (it has now recanted), Seppelt has seemingly preferred to use its Padthaway material as a blend component in wine such as its large volume Black label series, rather than producing single area wines which have a specific identity.

THOMAS HARDY   A-A
Padthaway, adjacent to highway
(087) 65 6060

Established	1968
Winemakers	Tom Newton (white); David O'Leary (red).
Production	Not for publication.

Principal Wines   A wide range of varietal table wines is produced, with the Padthaway vineyard providing by far the greatest part of Thomas Hardy wines. Siegersdorf Rhine Riesling now contains Padthaway material; various varietals under various labels have been released over the years, with the Hardy Collection range introduced mid-1985 and including Chardonnay, Sauvignon Blanc, Fumé Blanc, Chardonnay, Beerenauslese Rhine Riesling, Pinot Noir and Rhine Riesling. Classic Cuvée *Méthode Champenoise* first released in 1987.

Best Vintages   W 1980, '82, '85, '86, '90
R 1978, '79, '82, '87, '90

As with Lindemans, the Chardonnay and Fumé Blanc produced from Padthaway grapes are outstanding; the occasional Eileen Hardy Chardonnay is absolutely magnificent, in a textured grapefruit/melon style. Thomas Hardy has also produced two glorious Beerenauslese Rhine Rieslings of world class, but its recent efforts with Pinot Noir have been unconvincing.

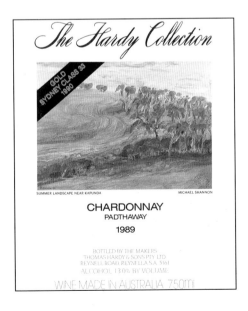

ABOVE: *Padthaway Estate, jewel of the district.*

ABOVE: *The military precision of large-scale planting.*

SOUTH AUSTRALIA

SOUTHERN VALES

The development of viticulture in the Barossa Valley (and to a lesser degree the Clare Valley) was fostered almost entirely by Germans from Silesia. That of the Southern Vales — from Reynella to McLaren Vale to Langhorne Creek — was almost exclusively due to the efforts of Englishmen. More precisely, to the efforts of three men: John Reynell, Thomas Hardy and Dr A C Kelly, with a lesser contribution from George Manning at Hope Farm.

Despite the early start — John Reynell laid the foundations for Chateau Reynella in 1838 — viticulture initially played second fiddle to wheat, which enjoyed a brief boom during the 1850s and 1860s. As in the Clare Valley, the fertility of the soil was soon exhausted; the wheatfields disappeared as quickly as they had arrived, and by the mid-1870s the once thriving township of McLaren Vale was all but deserted.

In large part due to the success of Thomas Hardy, who acquired Tintara from Dr A C Kelly in 1876, the pace of viticultural development steadily picked up through the 1880s and 1890s. In 1903 over 3 million litres of wine (almost

AUSTRALASIAN WINE REGIONS
1980 – 1990

	RED	WHITE
1980	9	10
1981	6	7
1982	10	8
1983	7	7
1984	9	9
1985	7	8
1986	9	8
1987	8	9
1988	9	8
1989	8	7
1990	9	10

THE REGION IN BRIEF

LOCATION AND ELEVATION
35°14'S 138°33'E   McLaren Vale
50–100 m

35°15'S 138°53'E   Langhorne Creek
30 m

SUBREGIONS
Cormandel Valley, Morphett Vale, Currency Creek, McLaren Flat, Seaview, Happy Valley, Reynella, Willunga and Clarendon.

CLIMATE
There is substantial meso-climatic variation in the Southern Vales region with varying exposure to the cooling influence of the nearby ocean. As one moves to Currency Creek and Langhorne Creek, the influence becomes very marked, with a heat summation (HDD) of 1520, which is cooler than that of Padthaway. The summations are greater as one moves north-east across Hill Range, with a different maritime influence coming to bear, and different wind patterns; McLaren Vale has an HDD reading of 1913. The annual rainfall here is 656 mm, of which only 182 mm falls between October and April. It is even lower at Langhorne Creek, the figures being 410 mm and 135 mm respectively. Overall, the climate is very much suited to full bodied white wines and to dry reds, as well as to producing Australia's finest vintage ports.

SOIL
There is a wide variety of soil types, even though the red-brown loamy sands of the hard red duplex group Dr2.23 dominate. The structurally similar grey-brown loamy sand in the Dy3.43 classification (hard mottled yellow duplex soils) with yellow clay subsoils interspersed with limey deposits, and a slightly more sandy version of the same (Dy5.42), are common. This tendency to a more sandy character reaches a peak around the Blewitt Springs region. Finally, there are patches of black or red friable loams falling in the Um6.2 and 6.4 groups — the Coonawarra type, called terra rosa. At Langhorne Creek dominant soils are sandy loams varying in colour from red-brown to dark grey; they are in the Uc1.43 and 1.44 firm siliceous groups. There are also isolated patches of heavy black self-mulching cracking clays in the Ug5.15 classification.

HARVEST TIME
In February/early March for sparkling wine varieties, running through to mid to late April for table wines.

PRINCIPAL GRAPE VARIETIES

Chardonnay, 331 ha	*Cabernet Sauvignon, 495 ha*
Rhine Riesling, 249 ha	*Shiraz, 491 ha*
Palomino and Pedro Ximinez, 136 ha	*Grenache, 350 ha*
Sauvignon Blanc, 108 ha	*Pinot Noir, 106 ha*
Semillon, 68 ha	*Merlot, 60 ha*
TOTAL WHITE, *1051 ha*	TOTAL RED, *1584 ha*

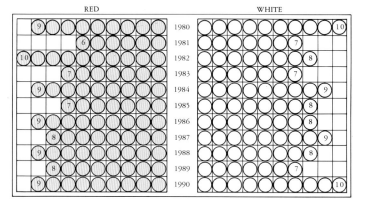

ABOVE: *The old underground cellars at Chateau Reynella are lovingly guarded both by Thomas Hardy & Sons Pty Ltd and the National Trust.*

FACING PAGE: *Contour planting is no longer fashionable, but creates tapestry patterns, particularly when cover crops are planted between the rows.*

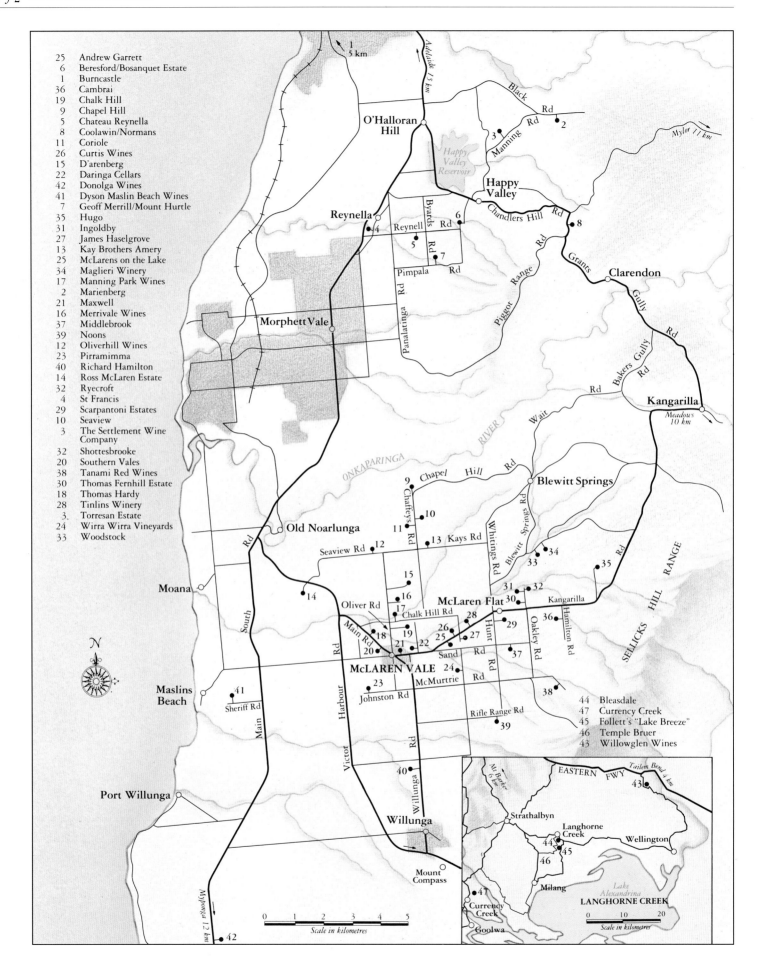

25 Andrew Garrett
6 Beresford/Bosanquet Estate
1 Burncastle
36 Cambrai
19 Chalk Hill
9 Chapel Hill
5 Chateau Reynella
8 Coolawin/Normans
11 Coriole
26 Curtis Wines
15 D'arenberg
22 Daringa Cellars
42 Donolga Wines
41 Dyson Maslin Beach Wines
7 Geoff Merrill/Mount Hurtle
35 Hugo
31 Ingoldby
27 James Haselgrove
13 Kay Brothers Amery
25 McLarens on the Lake
34 Maglieri Winery
17 Manning Park Wines
2 Marienberg
21 Maxwell
16 Merrivale Wines
37 Middlebrook
39 Noons
12 Oliverhill Wines
23 Pirramimma
40 Richard Hamilton
14 Ross McLaren Estate
32 Ryecroft
4 St Francis
29 Scarpantoni Estates
10 Seaview
3 The Settlement Wine Company
32 Shottesbrooke
20 Southern Vales
38 Tanami Red Wines
30 Thomas Fernhill Estate
18 Thomas Hardy
28 Tinlins Winery
3. Torresan Estate
24 Wirra Wirra Vineyards
33 Woodstock

44 Bleasdale
47 Currency Creek
45 Follett's "Lake Breeze"
46 Temple Bruer
43 Willowglen Wines

entirely red table and fortified) was made by the 19 wineries in the district. Thomas Hardy was the largest, followed (in order) by Reynella, Horndale, Vale Royal, Tatachilla, the Wattles, Kay Brothers Amery, Clarendon Vineyard, Pirramimma, Wirra Wirra Vineyards, Mount Hurtle, Potts Bleasdale, Hope Vineyard, Mrs Douglas, Ryecroft, Katunga, Formby and E Potts.

The prosperity was in large part founded on the English trade, with the staple export dark coloured, high-alcohol, tannic dry red wine of legendary medicinal value. This trade continued (with a brief hiatus between 1940 and 1945) until well into the 1950s, largely through the agency of the Emu Wine Company, which was ultimately acquired by Thomas Hardy from its English owners.

The Southern Vales shared in the prosperity of the 1960s and 1970s, and quickly became the spiritual home of the small winery in Australia, boasting more small wineries than any other region by the early 1970s. The one threat was urban sprawl, which progressively swallowed up the large vineyards which once existed between Reynella and Adelaide, and reduced the vineyards around Reynella to token levels.

Hopefully, there will be no more major inroads. Because Adelaide's population base is small, it exerts less pressure on the Southern Vales than, for example, Melbourne does on the Yarra Valley, and winemaking plays a much greater role in the economy and hence the political consciousness of South Australia than it does elsewhere.

What is more, grape growing and winemaking have changed dynamically since 1975. McLaren Vale has proved to be an exceptionally fine producer of rich Chardonnay and intense Sauvignon Blanc: these two varieties, together with some help from Rhine Riesling and Semillon, have radically changed the perception (and reputation) of the region. Indeed, in the grape price boom years of 1988 and 1989, McLaren Vale became the pace setter (and the record setter) for premium varieties such as Chardonnay, Sauvignon Blanc and Cabernet Sauvignon. In other words, the winemakers of the major companies voted with their money in placing the Southern Vales at the top end of the quality market.

ABOVE: 100-year-old Shiraz.

PRINCIPAL WINE STYLES

CABERNET SAUVIGNON

The wines are full bodied, rich, and warm, often with a touch of dark chocolate intermixed with blackcurrant, but they avoid overripe, jammy characteristics. Perhaps the capacity of the district to produce excellent wine in large volume is best demonstrated by Seaview Cabernet Sauvignon. Other good producers include Coriole, Marienberg, Norman's and Pirramimma.

CABERNET MERLOT

Clearly, the softening influence of Merlot has been seen by many producers as synergistic, and many such blends are produced. Those of Andrew Garrett, Chateau Reynella, Maxwell, St Francis, Shottesbrook and Wirra Wirra Vineyards are good examples.

CHARDONNAY

With 225 ha in bearing and 106 ha still coming into production, Chardonnay is the boom grape in the region. This reflects the huge demand for McLaren Vale Chardonnay generated as much by wineries outside the district as those inside. It produces a particularly rich, peachy and buttery wine, yet producers such as Wirra Wirra Vineyards show it is possible to have richness and flavour without sacrificing elegance and longevity. Hugo and Blewitt Springs let the style have full rein and develop maximum lusciousness relatively quickly, proving once again the flexibility of Chardonnay.

SHIRAZ

As in so many of the premium wine growing districts of Australia, Shiraz was the backbone of the industry for much of this century. It produces a densely coloured, richly flavoured wine which quickly develops a velvety texture. This is not the region for the peppery/spicy type of Shiraz, but the style of Australian wine which, in bygone years, was always labelled Burgundy. Producers such as Coriole, Thomas Hardy and Woodstock all demonstrate why the region depended on the variety for so long.

RHINE RIESLING

Although substantial quantities of Rhine Riesling are grown and made, the wine seldom scales great heights. The flavours are full and rich, living up to the reputation of the district overall, but the wines often tend to be rather broad and blowzy: the finish coats the tongue somewhat. There are exceptions, and one suspects that these come through the varying micro-climates. Wirra Wirra Vineyards has consistently produced one of the best Rhine Rieslings.

SAUVIGNON BLANC

Although the plantings are not particularly large, there is a strong case to be made that McLaren Vale is the premier region for Sauvignon Blanc in Australia. As with Chardonnay, substantial quantities go outside the region but Currency Creek, Ingoldby, Norman's, Scarpantoni Estates, Wirra Wirra Vineyards and Woodstock have all produced outstanding wines from time to time, none more frequently than Wirra Wirra.

THOMAS HARDY AND
THE HARDY WINE COMPANY

When 20-year-old Devonshire farmer Thomas Hardy stepped ashore from the sailing ship *British Empire* on 15 August 1850 he had £30 in cash and a single wooden box of personal possessions. Today the company he founded, which bears his name and which is still owned by his descendants, is the third largest winemaker in Australia, and in many ways the most dynamic.

The story of the Hardy Wine Company is rich in coincidence. Thomas Hardy's first job as a labourer for John Reynell at Reynella farm came 8 days after he arrived. Hardy wrote in his diary, 'Although it was low wages, I thought I had better embrace the opportunity as I have no doubt I shall soon be able to better myself'.

A year in the Victorian goldfields did just that. In 1853 he purchased Bankside on the Torrens River. By 1857 he had made his first wine (no doubt drawing on his experience with John Reynell), and by 1859 he had commenced to export to England as well as establishing markets throughout South Australia.

A mini-recession in the 1860s gave Hardy the opportunity of buying wine in bulk from small producers at low prices. His superior marketing skills found profitable outlets, and when in 1876 Dr A C Kelly's 283 hectare property Tintara went into receivership, Thomas Hardy purchased it and recouped the price out of the first year's sales of Tintara's accumulated wine stocks.

One hundred years later Thomas Hardy and Sons Pty Limited made its next major acquisition. In the meantime it had grown steadily if unspectacularly until eventually it was ranked as one of South Australia's larger wine companies. It resisted the overtures of numerous foreign multinationals during the heady days of the late 1960s and early 1970s when so many old, family-owned companies were sold. But it gave little sign of what was to come.

In 1976 Hardy purchased the English-owned Emu Australian Wine Company, beating (so it is said) a mumps-suffering Robert Holmes à Court. The chief asset of Emu was Houghton wines of the Swan Valley in Western Australia, and Houghton's chief asset (spectacularly undervalued, one suspects) was Houghton White Burgundy, now Australia's largest selling dry white wine and a major contributor to group profits and cash flow. Another intangible and undervalued asset was Emu's large share of the then Australian wine export market. There were other choice tangible assets,

including the historic cellars and homestead at Houghton and one which has been talked about many times: an English bank account with a very large sum of money in it. Old Tom must have smiled and approved: while this sort of thing tends to remain closely guarded, it is quite certain the company recovered its purchase price almost as quickly as had Thomas Hardy 100 years before, and the present value of Houghton dwarfs its acquisition cost.

In 1982 the Hardy Wine Company moved again. Having unsuccessfully bid for Kaiser Stuhl (Penfolds was the purchaser), it purchased Chateau Reynella from Rothmans of Pall Mall. This time old Tom could barely have contained himself with delight: his descendants had purchased the company which his first employer had founded. More than that, they had acquired one of the grandest and most beautiful winery complexes in Australia, which has since been lavishly refurbished and upgraded, and now serves as corporate headquarters as well as providing the chief white wine making base for the company. But that was not all: right at that time urban rezoning of much of the land at Reynella was taking effect. It was not so much the case of the jam tin in the garden as the garden itself. Again, the company does not talk of such matters, but local observers are adamant that Thomas Hardy's surplus land sales through the 1980s substantially reduced the effective cost of the purchase.

In early 1988 the company made its third major Australian acquisition, buying Stanley Leasingham (Clare Valley) from H J Heinz of the United States for more than $20 million. It was the third time Hardy had bought back a major piece of the farm from foreign ownership, and would have again brought a smile to old Tom's face. For in May 1892 he had visited Clare Valley and addressed a large public meeting at the Mechanics Institute; in his speech (reported at length in *The Chronicle* on 7 May 1892) he urged the planting of more vineyards and the making of more wine. (Later in the same month Benno Seppelt said more of the same.) Two years later the Stanley Wine Company was formed; it made its first wine in 1895, but by 1903 was producing 450,000 litres a year, placing it among the top six wineries in South Australia.

Having secured its Australian base the Hardy Wine Company turned its attention overseas, where it had long enjoyed a disproportionately large share of export markets. If

ABOVE: The Tintara brand goes back to the mid-nineteenth century and the founding of Thomas Hardy.

the giant Penfolds-Lindeman group has perceived the importance of the European Economic Community after 1992 (and surely it must have), it has given scant indication of having done so. Hardy, on the other hand, has moved with elan. In late 1989 it bought and merged two significant English wine distributors, now known as Whiclar and Gordon Wines Limited, investing $4 million in so doing. Then in early 1990 it purchased Ricasoli, one of the major Tuscan producers of Chianti. Ricasoli is the oldest wine company in Italy (founded in 1141) and at one time formed part of the Seagram group. It currently produces 850,000 cases a year, and

has the capacity to lift that to 2 million cases. In February 1990 Hardy purchased La Baume winery and vineyards in the Midi, in the south of France; the refurbished winery made its first vintage in 1990 with Peter Dawson, senior winemaker at Houghton (Swan Valley, Western Australia), in charge.

It seems highly likely that before 1990 the Hardy Wine Company will have placed the final piece of the jigsaw puzzle by securing ownership of its own distribution company in the United States, making it Australia's foremost multinational wine company with 500 employees world wide. Old Tom's £30 was indeed invested wisely.

ABOVE: *Old bottles in Thomas Hardy's famous 'black hole' museum.*

WINERIES OF THE SOUTHERN VALES

ANDREW GARRETT   B-BA
Kangarilla Road
McLaren Vale 5171   (08) 323 8853
Established   1983
Winemakers   Andrew Garrett,
   Warren Randall
Production   Not stated.
Principal Wines   Limited range of premium-quality table wines including Chardonnay, Fumé Blanc, Rhine Riesling, Pinot Noir, Shiraz, Cabernet Merlot and NV Pinot Noir *(Méthode Champenoise)*. McLarens On The Lake has limited retail distribution but frequently offers outstanding value.
Best Vintages   W 1986, '88, '90
   R 1985, '86, '87, '88, '90
Once the fastest moving of the stars in the vinous firmament, now owned by Japanese wine and spirit giant, Suntory. Notwithstanding the rapidity of the growth of the business, and the flamboyance of Andrew Garrett, it has managed to produce some serious wines, particularly Chardonnay and Cabernet Merlot.

BERESFORD   B-B
Old Heritage Horndale Winery
Fraser Avenue
Happy Valley 5067   (08) 322 2344
Established   1985
Winemaker   Robert Dundon
Production   13,000 cases
Principal Wines   Sauvignon Blanc, Chardonnay, Pinot Noir and a blend of Cabernet Sauvignon/ Cabernet Franc.
Best Vintages   W 1987, '89, '90
   R 1986, '87, '88, '90
Robert Dundon elects to make full bodied whites and light bodied reds, arguing that this creates the best food styles. He has also established a considerable reputation for a carbonic maceration-style Pinot Noir, in which the making technique positively transcends the variety.

BOSANQUET ESTATE   CB-B
Old Heritage Horndale Winery
Fraser Avenue
Happy Valley 5067   (08) 322 2344
Established   1989
Winemaker   Robert Dundon
Production   40,000 cases
Principal Wines   Fumé Blanc, Riesling, Semillon Chardonnay, St Helene Cabernet/Shiraz and sparkling wine.
Best Vintages   Too recent to assess.
A new entrant into the toughest sector of the market: the lower-middle price bracket of under $7 as at early 1990. Quality is certainly adequate, but it is impossible to see how an operation such as this can match the economies of scale achieved by the largest companies and groups.

CHATEAU REYNELLA   BA-A
Reynella Road
Reynella 5161   (08) 381 2266
Established   1838
Winemakers   Bill Hardy (fortified);
   David O'Leary (red);
   Tom Newton (white); and
   Tom Newton (sparkling).
Production   Not stated, but large.
Principal Wines   Vintage Reserve Chablis, Chardonnay, Rosé, Vintage Reserve Claret, Cabernet Sauvignon, Cabernet Malbec Merlot, Vintage Port (one of Australia's two greatest) and an Old Cave Tawny Port (10 years).
Best Vintages   W 1980, '81, '85, '86, '88, '90
   R 1978, '80, '82, '86, '87, '90

This is the beautifully restored and refurbished headquarters of the Thomas Hardy group, still producing fine wines under its own label. At the bottom end there is great value for money; at the top end there is the superlative Vintage Port, with its almost lantana-like spicy flavour and strong brandy spirit influence; a perfumed, spicy Chardonnay, and small volumes of a Cabernet Malbec Merlot which is usually fine and elegant, but occasionally shows great richness and flavour.

COOLAWIN   B-A
Chandlers Hill Road
Clarendon 5157   (08) 383 6138
Established   1969
Winemakers   Brian Light,
   Gregory O'Keefe
Production   50,000 cases
Principal Wines   Rhine Riesling, Frontignac Spatlese, White Burgundy, Chablis and Shiraz made from selected grapes grown in the Southern Vales region.
Best Vintages   W and R 1984, '86, '87, '88, '90

Since its acquisition by the Norman's group, Coolawin has become the second label for Norman's, but it is of sufficient importance to justify a separate entry. The winemaking team at Norman's does not know how to make bad wines, and those under the Coolawin label can be extraordinarily attractive at the price.

CORIOLE   B-A
Chaffeys Road
McLaren Vale 5171   (08) 323 8305
Established   1969
Winemakers   Mark Lloyd, Stephen Hall
Production   12,000 cases
Principal Wines   The principal wines are Shiraz, Cabernet Sauvignon and Chenin Blanc. Also small quantities of Chardonnay and Sangiovese.
Best Vintages   W 1984, '87, '88, '90
   R 1974, '76, '80, '84, '86, '88, '90
The Lloyd family were grape growers for generations before establishing the Coriole brand, and accordingly have some of the finest vineyards in McLaren Vale under their control. The winemaking team has also shown a sure touch in handling oak, resulting in consistently complex, full flavoured and stylish reds.

D'ARENBERG   B-B
Osborn Road
McLaren Vale 5171   (08) 323 8206
Established   1928
Production   60,000 cases
Principal Wines   Rhine Riesling, White Burgundy, Noble Riesling, Chardonnay, Gloucester Blanc, Burgundy, Shiraz, Cabernet Sauvignon, Claret, Tawny Port, Vintage Port and White Muscat.
Best Vintages   W 1985, '87, '88, '90
   R 1967, '73, '76, '82, '86, '88, '90
One of the landmarks of McLaren Vale, but it is still easy to forget the contribution d'Arry Osborn made in lifting the reputation of the district as a premium wine region with his red wines of the second half of the 1960s. The style has not changed much since, but the wines are all the better for that; soft, velvety, gently earthy but never tannic or astringent. The white wines have changed quite radically, and are now thoroughly modern in style.

GEOFF MERRILL   A-A
Mount Hurtle Winery
Cnr Pimpala and Byards Roads
Reynella 5161   (08) 381 6877
Established   1980
Winemaker   Geoff Merrill
Production   12,000 cases

ABOVE: The homestead at Chateau Reynella now serves as the most beautiful corporate headquarters in Australia.

FACING PAGE: Coriole's vineyards produce some of the finest grapes in the Southern Vales region.

Principal Wines Only two wines are made each year, one white, one red: a Semillon/ Chardonnay blend and a Cabernet/Cabernet Franc blend (labelled Cabernet Sauvignon).
Best Vintages W 1981, '84, '86, '87, '88, '90
R 1980, '83, '84, '86, '87, '90
Geoff Merrill is a larger-than-life figure who makes surprisingly elegant, crisp and fruity reds from grapes picked a little earlier than most, and long-lived lemony/oaky white wines which are seldom released at less than 2 years of age. Merrill may always be ready for a laugh or a beer, but his commitment to quality is absolute.

HUGO   BA-B
Elliott Road
McLaren Flat 5171 (08) 383 0098
Established   1982
Winemaker   John Hugo
Production   8000 cases
Principal Wines Six wines made: Rhine Riesling, Late-picked Rhine Riesling, Chardonnay, Shiraz, Muscat of Alexandria and Tawny Port.
Best Vintages W 1984, '86, '87, '88, '90
R 1986, '87, '89, '90
Both the quality and quantity of the Hugo wines has increased sharply over the past few years, with an eye catching peachy Chardonnay showing sophisticated use of oak, and some rich spicy/berry Shiraz with strong American oak, the pick of the releases.

INGOLDBY   BA-B
Ingoldby Road
McLaren Flat 5171 (08) 383 0005
Established   1973
Winemaker   Walter Clappis
Production   6000 cases released
Principal Wines Rhine Riesling, Sauvignon Blanc, Cabernet Shiraz, Hermitage, Cabernet Sauvignon and also a Late-picked Frontignac.
Best Vintage W 1984, '86, '88, '89, '90
R 1985, '86, '87, '88, '90
Walter William Wilfred Clappis is yet another of the many and varied characters — eccentrics

if you will — who so richly endow the wine industry. There seems to be some magic alchemy which means that eccentrics make very good wine; the Ingoldby tour de force is its Cabernet Sauvignon, which was quite superb in 1985 and 1987, with consistent cherry/red berry fruit and spicy charred oak.

KAY BROTHERS AMERY   DB-CB
Kays Road
McLaren Vale 5171 (08) 323 8211
Established   1890
Winemaker   Colin Kay
Production   3500 cases
Principal Wines A full range of table and fortified wines comprising Rhine Riesling, Late Harvest Frontignac, Late Harvest Rhine Riesling, Cabernet Shiraz, Pinot Noir, Blackwood EstateShiraz, Block 6 Shiraz, Cabernet Sauvignon, Vintage Port,Ruby Port, Tawny Port and Liqueur Muscat. Shiraz and Ruby Port also offered in 10 litre casks and 200 litre drums.
Best Vintages W 1973, '75, '80, '87, '88, '90
R 1971, '75, '78, '82, '86, '87
'88, '90
An historic family-owned winery with some marvellous vineyards; Block 6 Shiraz was planted in 1892. The red wines — and in particular Block 6 Shiraz — fulfil the promise of the history, but the white wines are really not good enough in this day and age.

MARIENBERG   CB-B
Black Road
Coromandel Valley 5051
Established   1968
Winemaker   Ursula Pridham
Production   15,000 cases
Principal Wines White Burgundy, Chablis, Rhine Riesling, Sauvignon Blanc Rosengarten, Beerenauslese, Pinot Noir, Shiraz, Cabernet Shiraz and Cabernet Sauvignon.
Best Vintages W 1984, '86, '87, '88
R 1977, '81, '82, '83, '85, '86
Marienberg has established a reputation with a

consistently good and stylish Cabernet Sauvignon which, remarkably, is not released until it is 5 years old, by which time its minty, red berry fruit has developed attractive, secondary cigar box aroma and flavour. The other wines in the stable are not in the same class.

MAXWELL   B-B
24 Kangarilla Road
McLaren Vale 5171 (08) 323 8200
Established   1979
Winemaker   Mark Maxwell;
meadmaker Ken Maxwell.
Production   5000 cases, although some
is sold in bulk.
Principal Wines Chardonnay, Rhine Riesling, Frontignac, Adelaide Nouveau, Cabernet Merlot, Old Tawny Port and Maxwell Meads (various).
Best Vintages W 1982, '86, '88, '90
R 1980, '82, '86, '87, '89, '90
The winemaking equipment at Maxwell is interesting: the inventor Heath Robinson would feel very much at home here. The wines, too, are invariably full of interest, while those expert in mead agree that the meads are outstanding.

MOUNT HURTLE   BA-A
Mount Hurtle Winery
Cnr Pimpala and Byards Roads
Reynella 5161   (08) 271 2267
Established   1897
Winemakers   Joe Di Fabio, Geoff Merrill
Production   8000 cases
Principal Wines Sauvignon Blanc/Semillon, Grenache (Rosé style) and Cabernet Sauvignon.
Best Vintages W 1986, '87, '90
R 1987, '88, '89, '90

Mount Hurtle is the beautifully restored stone winery in which both the Geoff Merrill and Mount Hurtle wines are now made. As the suburban sprawl continues, it will become a veritable oasis, with its tangy Sauvignon Blanc Semillon and sparkling strawberry Grenache particularly irresistible on a warm summer's day.

ABOVE: Geoff Merrill had his moustache before Merv Hughes grew his.

NOON'S   C-B

Rifle Range Road
McLaren Vale 5171 (08) 323 8290
Established   1976
Winemaker   David Noon
Production   2850 cases
Principal Wines   Burgundy, Cabernet Sauvignon, Dry Red, Grenache Shiraz, Hill-side Red, Maceration Carbonique, Mulled Red, Rosé, Shiraz Cabernet, Traditional Red, Vintage Port, Chablis and Semillon. Most reds sold with 2 or 3 years bottle age.
Best Vintages   R 1976, '80, '84, '85
These are totally individual hand-crafted wines which bowled me over with their quality and style when I first encountered them. It has to be said, however, that vintages since 1985 have been very disappointing.

NORMAN'S   B-A

Grants Gully Road
Clarendon 5157   (08) 383 6138
Established   1851
Winemakers   Brian Light with Gregory O'Keefe.
Production   120,000 cases
Principal Wines   Chardonnay, Sauvignon Blanc, Rhine Riesling, Chenin Blanc, Shiraz, Pinot Noir, Cabernet Sauvignon, Conquest Brut, Pinot and Chardonnay Brut Premier, 1066 Tawny, 12 year old King William Tawny and XO 30 year old Tawny Port. The grapes are sourced from the company's vineyards at Evanston Estate, Adelaide Plains and Clarendon in the Adelaide Hills. Additionally, grapes are purchased from selected growers at McLaren Vale and Coonawarra. Norman's also produces a top quality range of limited-release table wines under the Norman's Chais Clarendon label.
Best Vintages   W 1982, '85, '87, '89, '90
                                    R 1980, '82, '86, '87, '90
The consistency of the quality of the Norman's wines is wholly admirable; within their price bracket, they are indeed outstanding. Those with the greatest appeal are the Cabernet Sauvignons (concentrated cassis fruit with a nice varietal cut to the edge) and honeyed, relatively oaky Chardonnay; the Sauvignon Blanc (wooded and unwooded) follows close behind.

PIRRAMIMMA   CB-B

Johnston Road
McLaren Vale 5171 (08) 323 8205
Established   1892
Winemaker   Geoff Johnston
Production   50,000 cases
Principal Wines   Chardonnay, Rhine Riesling, Rhine Riesling Spatlese, Cabernet Sauvignon, Shiraz, Special Selection Shiraz, Vintage Port, Tawny Port and Liqueur Port. Shiraz and Shiraz Grenache sold in 20 litre packs and 205 litre drums; 5 year Old Tawny Port also sold in 205 litre drums.

Best Vintages   W 1979, '80, '83, '85, '87, '88, '90
                                    R 1966, '70, '72, '80, '84, '86, '88, '90
Pirramimma built on the early success of D'Arenberg in lifting the reputation of the McLaren Vale district, first with its red wines and then, in the late '70s with its whites. A little of the sparkle seems to have gone off the edge in recent years, but the wines remain honest and workmanlike.

RICHARD HAMILTON   CB-B

Willunga Vineyards
Main South Road
Willunga 5172   (085) 56 2288
Established   1972
Winemaker   John Innes
Production   10,000 cases
Principal Wines   Chardonnay, Rhine Riesling, Chenin Blanc, Semillon, Sauvignon Blanc, Cabernet Sauvignon and *Méthode Champenoise* sparkling wine.
Best Vintages   W 1972, '73, '75, '76, '84, '86, '87, '90
Both the quality and style of the Richard Hamilton white wines have varied significantly over the past decade; very often the wines come within a whisker of excellence, but fall away with some minor fault. To be so near and yet so far must be very frustrating.

RYECROFT   B-B

Ingoldby Road
McLaren Flat 5171 (08) 383 0001
Established   1888
Winemaker   Nick Holmes
Production   30,000 cases
Principal Wines   A full range of varietal table wines including Wood Matured Semillon, Chardonnay, Sauvignon Blanc, Cabernet Sauvignon and Shiraz; wine of special quality and greater bottle age released under the Reserve label.
Best Vintages   W and R 1987, '88, '90
Ryecroft is a phoenix risen again from the ashes; the new generation wines are smooth and uncontroversial, consciously aimed at the mid-market and designed to stir neither the mind nor the wallet unduly.

ST FRANCIS   B-A

Bridge Street
Old Reynella 5161 (08) 381 1925
Established   1852
Winemakers   Rob Dundon, James Irvine
Production   25,000 cases
Principal Wines   Rhine Riesling, Fumé Blanc, Chardonnay, Late Harvest Frontignac, Chablis, Pinot Noir, Hermitage, Shiraz Cabernet and Cabernet Sauvignon. A second label, Governor Phillip, is also used.
Best Vintages   Not relevant owing to varied fruit sources.

St Francis runs a highly successful *négociant* business; it is not itself a winemaker, but buys wine in bulk (often already in bottle) from other producers over the length and breadth of South Australia. The St Francis consultants have done a superb job, with some absolutely remarkable wines (particularly Rhine Riesling with 4 to 6 years bottle age) appearing under the label.

SCARPANTONI ESTATES   B-BA

Scarpantoni Drive
McLaren Flat 5171
Established   1979
Winemakers   Domenico Scarpantoni, Michael Filippo
Production   5000 cases
Principal Wines   Block 1 Rhine Riesling, Sauvignon Blanc, Late Harvest Rhine Riesling, Botrytis Rhine Riesling, Chardonnay, Shiraz, Cabernet Merlot, Gamay (a red maceration style), Cabernet Sauvignon, Liqueur Riesling (fortified) and Vintage Port.
Best Vintages   W 1980, '82, '84, '85, '88, '90
                                    R 1980, '82, '84, '85, '86, '88, '90

The winery name may suggest rocket fuel wines made for an ethnic community and to be drunk within months of vintage; however, the reality could not be more different: right across the board, from crisp, herbaceous/lime Sauvignon Blanc to spicy, dark chocolate, chewy Vintage Port, Scarpantoni Estates is capable of producing wines of excellent quality.

SEAVIEW   B-BA

Chaffeys Road
McLaren Vale 5171 (08) 323 8250

Established	1850
Winemakers	Robin Moody, Mike Farmilo
Production	Not for publication.

Principal Wines Rhine Riesling, Traminer Riesling, Chardonnay, White Burgundy, Cabernet Sauvignon (one of the bottled-wine brand leaders in Australia), Cabernet Shiraz and Tawny Port.

Best Vintages W 1985, '87, '89, '90
R 1972, '76, '82, '84, '86, '88, '90

Seaview is largely a brand, with the grape sources spread across South Australia, and many of the wines multi-region blend. The Cabernet Sauvignon, however, is almost entirely sourced from McLaren Vale, with a little Coonawarra and Padthaway material incorporated in varying percentages. It is invariably good, while every now and then Seaview comes up with a gold medal standard Rhine Riesling or Chardonnay. The Penfolds' influence, particularly so far as oak is concerned, grows stronger day by day in the shaping of the Cabernet Sauvignon.

SHOTTESBROOKE   B-B

Ryecroft Vineyard
Ingoldby Road
McLaren Flat 5171

Established	1984
Winemaker	Nick Holmes
Production	4000 cases

Principal Wines Sauvignon Blanc and a Cabernet Sauvignon Merlot Cabernet Franc (or Malbec) blend simply labelled Shottesbrooke.

Best Vintages R 1984, '86, '88, '90

Much of Shottesbrooke's wine is sold without fuss to a loyal South Australian clientele, and it is not as well known in the eastern states as it deserves to be. The reds are usually very elegant, with spotlessly clean fruit flavours.

VALES WINE COMPANY   NR

151 Main Road
McLaren Vale 5171 (08) 323 8656

Established	1901

Winemakers	Roland Wahlquist, Jane Paull
Production	Not for publication.

Principal Wines The wines are sold under the Tatachilla name. Wines under the newly released The Wattles range include Semillon, Rhine Riesling, Chenin Blanc, Frontignac and Dry Red.

Best Vintages R 1972, '76, '77, '80, '88, '89, '90

Given the complete change at Southern Vales, both in ownership and winemaking, quality rating becomes impossible. For the last 10 years Southern Vales has been in a quality recess, but the 1989 wines, tasted early in their life, gave promise of much better things.

THOMAS FERNHILL ESTATE   CB-B

Ingoldby Road
McLaren Flat 5171 (08) 383 0167

Established	1975
Winemaker	Wayne Thomas
Production	4000 cases

Principal Wines Chardonnay, Sauvignon Blanc, Rhine Riesling, Shiraz, Cabernet Sauvignon, Old Tawny Port and Fernhill Brut.

Best Vintages W 1985, '86, '89, '90
R 1979, '82, '86, '88, '90

Wayne Thomas is an immensely experienced winemaker, and over the years he has produced some outstanding wines. The quality in recent years has been surprisingly variable.

THOMAS HARDY   A-A

Reynella Road
Reynella 5161 (08) 381 2266

Established	1853
Winemakers	Bill Hardy (fortified); David O'Leary (red); Tom Newton (white); and Tom Newton (sparkling).
Production	2 million cases

Principal Wines Thomas Hardy produces a full range of wines including Australia's greatest Vintage and Tawny Ports, the principal source being McLaren Vale Shiraz. The majority of the premium table wine produced comes from Padthaway, with Chardonnay, Rhine Riesling and Semillon being the backbone of the whites, and Pinot Noir and Cabernet Sauvignon leading the resurgence in quality of the dry reds. Hardy's leading brand-seller, Siegersdorf, is basically made from Padthaway and Clare Valley material. The two principal lines are the Collection Series (premium quality) and the Bird Series (mid-range commercial).

Best Vintages W 1976, '78, '80, '86, '88, '90
R 1979, '80, '82, '86, '87, '89, '90

White wines still remain Thomas Hardy's greatest strength if one ignores its small volume but superlative quality Vintage Port; however, with winemaking changes, there are strong signs

of a continuing resurgence in red wine quality, with flavour, fruit and depth returning to formerly vapid wines.

WIRRA WIRRA VINEYARDS   A-A

McMurtrie Road
McLaren Vale 5171 (08) 323 8414

Established	1968
Winemaker	Ben Riggs
Production	25,000 cases

Principal Wines Hand-picked Rhine Riesling, Late-picked Rhine Riesling, Chardonnay, Sauvignon Blanc, Semillon-Sauvignon Blanc, Cabernet Sauvignon, Church Block (Cabernet-Shiraz-Merlot) and the Cousins (Pinot Noir-Chardonnay) *Méthode Champenoise*.

Best Vintages W 1979, '82, '84, '86, '88, '90
R 1980, '82, '84, '86, '87, '90

The white wines of Wirra Wirra Vineyards, headed by the Sauvignon Blanc and Sauvignon Blanc Semillon blend, with Chardonnay in close attendance, are of a consistently high quality; the fruit flavours show precise varietal definition, and the oak handling is sensitive and skilled. The red wines always seem pale and uninteresting in comparison.

WOODSTOCK   A-A

Douglas Gully Road
McLaren Flat 5171 (08) 383 0156

Established	1973
Winemaker	Scott Collett
Production	25,000 cases

Principal Wines Rhine Riesling, Sauvignon Blanc, Semillon, Chardonnay, Botrytis Sweet White, Cabernet Sauvignon, Shiraz, Tawny Port and Vintage Port. Tawny Port also sold in 25 litre containers.

Best Vintages W 1983, '85, '87, '88, '90
R 1982, '84, '85, '87, '89, '90

Scott Collett plays harder than almost anyone I have ever met, and works very nearly as hard, producing very substantial quantities of consistently very good dry white, botrytised white and red wines. It is hard to single out any one style as being better than the other, particularly given the full bodied, fruity Cabernet Sauvignons which show all of the best characters in McLaren Vale, the at times impossibly complex and luscious botrytised sweet whites, and the smooth, honeyed flavours of the wooded whites.

ABOVE: Greg Trott, the wonderfully eccentric and much loved owner of Wirra Wirra.

OTHER WINERIES

BURNCASTLE   NR
Bowker Street
Somerton Park 5044 (08) 296 9178

CAMBRAI   CB-B
Hamiltons Road
McLaren Flat 5171 (08) 323 0251

CHALK HILL WINES   NR
Brewery Hill Road
McLaren Vale 5171 (08) 323 8815

CHAPEL HILL   CB-B
Chapel Hill Road
McLaren Vale 5171 (08) 323 8429

CURTIS WINES   NR
Kangarilla Road
McLaren Vale 5171

DARINGA CELLARS   CB-CB
Kangarilla Road
McLaren Vale 5171 (08) 323 8665

DONOLGA WINERY   NR
Main South Road
Aldinga 5173 (085) 56 3179

JAMES HASELGROVE   C-C
Foggo Road
McLaren Vale 5171 (08) 323 8706

McLARENS ON THE LAKE   B-B
Kangarilla Road
McLaren Vale 5171 (08) 323 8853

MAGLIERI WINERY   C-CB
Douglas Gully Road
McLaren Flat 5171 (08) 383 0177

MANNING PARK WINES   NR
Chalk Hill Road
McLaren Vale 5171 (08) 323 8209

MASLIN BEACH   C-CB
Sherriff Road
Maslin Beach 5171 (08) 386 1092

MERRIVALE   NR
Olivers Road
McLaren Vale 5171 (08) 323 9196

MIDDLEBROOK   C-B
Sand Road
McLaren Vale 5171 (08) 383 0004

ROSS McLAREN ESTATE   NR
Cnr Main South Road and Budgen Roads
McLaren Vale 5171 (08) 323 8614

THE SETTLEMENT WINE COMPANY C-CB
Temporary premises at Torresan Estates
Martins Road, McLaren Vale (08) 323 8808

TANAMI RED WINES   NR
McMurtrie Road
McLaren Vale 5171 (08) 383 0351

TINLINS WINERY   D-C
Kangarilla Road
McLaren Flat 5171 (08) 323 8649

TORRESAN ESTATE   DC-C
Manning Road,
Flagstaff Hill 5159 (08) 270 2500

LANGHORNE CREEK

BLEASDALE   CB-B
Wellington Road
Langhorne Creek 5255 (085) 37 3001
Established   1850
Winemaker   Michael Potts
Production   45,000 cases
Principal Wines   Rhine Riesling, Verdelho, Colombard, Cabernet Sauvignon, Shiraz Cabernet, Malbec, Special Vintage Shiraz and Private Bin Hermitage. Tiny quantities of very old, high-quality Heysen Madeira also available at the winery (one bottle per customer limit).
Best Vintages   W and R 1978, '80, '82, '84, '86, '88, '90

The red wines of Bleasdale are always sold with considerable bottle age, showing the soft, fruity characteristics which make Langhorne Creek such an important region for the major wine companies, who buy its wines in bulk and use them to blend with harder wines of other regions. The style of Bleasdale's wines is very traditional but honest.

CURRENCY CREEK   B-B
Winery Road
Currency Creek 5214 (085) 55 4069
Established   1968
Winemakers   Brian Croser/Petaluma (white, under contract); Phillip Tonkin/Brian Barry, consultant (red); Phillip Tonkin (cellar door).
Production   Not stated.
Principal Wines   Semillon, Rhine Riesling, Late Harvest Rhine Riesling, Chardonnay, Sauvignon Blanc, Shiraz, Cabernet Sauvignon, Pinot Noir and *Méthode Champenoise*.
Best Vintages   W 1984, '86, '87, '89, '90
R 1982, '83, '86, '87, '90

Currency Creek has not helped the establishment of its identity by successive name changes from Tonkins to Santa Rosa to Currency Creek — all under the continuing ownership of Wally Tonkin, I might add. Its identity crisis is further strengthened by the fact that I, at least, have always treated it as part of the Southern Vales, when in truth it really is situated in the Langhorne Creek area. Throughout all of this confusion, consistently excellent white wines have been made, attesting both to the quality of the fruit from the vineyard and the skills of contract winemaker Petaluma. It has also defied convention with several respectable Pinot Noirs.

OTHER WINERY

WILLOWGLEN WINES   NR
Jervois Road
Murray Bridge 5253 (085) 32 2632

ABOVE: *Scott Collett of Woodstock, renowned for his Cabernet Sauvignon.*

WESTERN
AUSTRALIA

LOWER GREAT SOUTHERN REGION

MARGARET RIVER

PERTH HILLS AND SURROUNDING DISTRICTS

SOUTH-WEST COASTAL PLAIN

SWAN VALLEY

Western Australia was founded in 1829, 5 years before Victoria and 7 years before South Australia. The botanist Thomas Waters planted vines at his 20 hectare Guildford property (called Olive Farm) that year, commencing the excavation of cellars the following year. By 1842 he was in commercial production and sales, antedating both Victoria and South Australia. Two years earlier John Septimus Roe planted vines at Sandalford, and by 1843 a contemporary observer was able to write 'the colony is possessed with a vine mania'.

Although there were sporadic attempts to establish vineyards and wineries throughout a number of towns in the southern part of the State, until the late 1960s the industry was focused almost entirely on the Swan Valley. In 1920, 730,000 litres of wine were made in the Swan Valley; in 1930, 1.4 million litres; in 1950, 3.6 million litres (sourced from 3690 hectares of table and wine grapes). Production elsewhere was virtually non-existent.

The change in emphasis between 1980 and 1989 has been quite dramatic, as the chart below shows. In looking at the chart you should also realise that around half of the Swan Valley plantings are of table grapes, whereas less than 3 per cent of the 'rest of State' plantings are used for this purpose.

For a while (between 1984 and 1989) it seemed the shift in emphasis might be halted. Houghton Wines was underpinning the Swan Valley, purchasing just about every tonne of quality grapes it could lay its hands on, while the Margaret River and Lower Great Southern region seemed to have stalled after 20 years of strong growth. Now the massive developments for Goundrey Wines Limited north of

Denmark, Houghton Wines at Pemberton (80 hectares by 1991) and the Omrah Vineyard at Mount Barker (88 hectares), together with several smaller developments at Manjimup and Pemberton, will add more than 4000 tonnes to the 'rest of State' production, taking it to four times the size of the present-day Swan Valley wine output (and with little indication of any renaissance there).

This phenomenal growth has been market-driven. The great problem for the numerous small wineries of the State was the limited size and capacity of the Perth market, and the cost and expense of successfully attacking the lucrative markets of the eastern states. I touch on the troubles of the Margaret River wineries at page 255, and the same difficulties applied here. Houghton, of course, was one obvious exception, dominating Australian sales of dry white wine in bottles with its brand leader, Houghton White Burgundy. Now Goundrey has broken free, too, although its feat is not something which one can necessarily easily duplicate.

Overall, Western Australia provides a mini-version of the Australian industry as a whole. The Swan Valley is Western Australia's answer to South Australia's Barossa Valley: a

WESTERN AUSTRALIAN WINE REGIONS PRODUCTION & HECTAREAGE

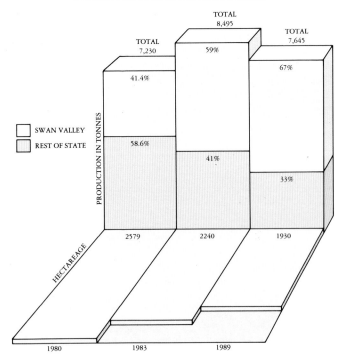

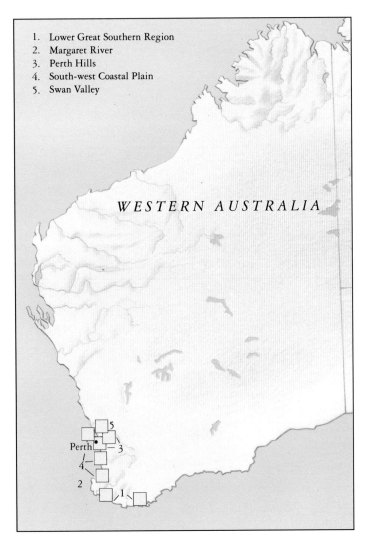

1. Lower Great Southern Region
2. Margaret River
3. Perth Hills
4. South-west Coastal Plain
5. Swan Valley

WESTERN AUSTRALIA

PREVIOUS PAGES: Oats and rye interplanted between the vines at Leeuwin Estate: windbreaks, mulch and an alternative food source for the birds.

traditional, warm area region of declining viticultural importance but continuing to play a pivotal role in production and in tourism (with Houghton and Sandalford to the fore). As one moves south, the emphasis switches to a multiplicity of cooler regions with the accent on premium, hand-made wine production, but with Houghton (in the manner of the big eastern companies) sourcing increasing quantities of its grapes from there. The degree to which Western Australia succeeds or fails will mirror the success or failure of Australia as a whole.

ABOVE: *Prickly pears and grapevines: strange bedfellows.*

LOWER GREAT
SOUTHERN REGION

markets and technical expertise). Only one large vineyard was established, Frankland River Wines with 100 hectares of vines. This was leased by Houghton in 1981. Plantagenet however dominated proceedings, making wine not only for itself but for a number of other well known labels, and only Goundrey ran an operation of any real size in competition with Plantagenet.

In 1987 that all changed, and changed quite dramatically. Michael and Alison Goundrey formed an unlisted public company, and with the aid of substantial capital, built a large new winery and acquired several new vineyards. In May 1990 a major public issue of units and shares raised $3.7 million to develop 90 hectares of vineyards (including the then existing plantings) which will provide Goundrey Wines Limited with 1200 tonnes of grapes a year by 1996. At the same time Goundrey Wines Limited announced a major distribution agreement with Hokuriku Coca-Cola Limited of Japan which will result in 35 to 40 per cent of Goundrey's wines being exported to that country.

No other boutique Australian winery has ever grown so fast, and the impact on this far flung and still remote region will inevitably be considerable. However, the nearby development of the Omrah Vineyard, and the opening up of what is really a whole new district within the Lower Great Southern Region, between Manjimup and Pemberton, means that Goundrey is in good company.

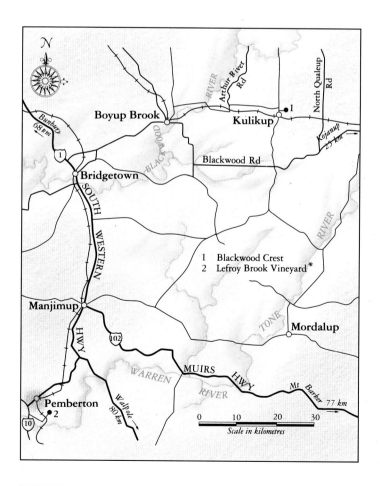

PRINCIPAL WINE STYLES

CABERNET SAUVIGNON

Cabernet Sauvignon thrives across the length and breadth of the region, producing long-lived wines of deep colour, intense flavour and powerful structure. They are in every sense classic Cabernets, with little of the errant (if attractive) characteristics of other noted Australian districts, such as the complex 'pie and peas' lifted fruit of Coonawarra in South Australia or the eucalypt mint of Central Victoria. There is instead an austerity to the flavour, and a briary toughness to the young wines which demands patience but which richly rewards it. The outstanding producers are Goundrey, Alkoomi, Plantagenet, Howard Park, Castle Rock Estate and Karrelea Estate.

RHINE RIESLING

The style of the Rhine Rieslings is the white wine correlative of that of the Cabernet Sauvignon: crisp, lean and elegant, but often reclusive in its youth, slowly developing and unfolding with age. Once again, the term classic has to be used, as all of the aromas and flavours are precisely correct. Everyone — myself included — accepts the common wisdom that Australia's greatest Rieslings come from the Eden and Clare Valleys of South Australia, but I wonder what would have happened had Australia's wine industry been centred around Perth rather than Adelaide. The top producers are too numerous to list, but Castle Rock Estate, Forest Hill, Goundrey, Karrelea, Plantagenet and Tinglewood are usually among the best.

SHIRAZ

Not surprisingly, another variety which does very well, even if — like Rhine Riesling — its relative unfashionability denies it the full recognition it deserves. Plantagenet has had the greatest success, producing supple wines of warmth and complexity, and often with a rich tapestry of fruit and spice.

CHARDONNAY

A relative latecomer and still sparingly produced, although one imagines that Goundrey will change all that. Once again, Plantagenet has done best, making intense grapefruit-tinged wines with power and elegance, and achieving much the same for Forest Hill when it made Forest Hills' wines under contract. Wignalls and Goundrey have also provided wines of distinction.

SAUVIGNON BLANC

Even rarer than Chardonnay, with Alkoomi, Forest Hill, Wignalls and Goundrey the principal contributors of a delicate, fresh and relatively understated style.

PINOT NOIR

Only one winery has succeeded, but it has done so spectacularly: Wignalls, with its unique strongly maritime influenced microclimate. The plummy varietal character is excellent, and the wine develops a very good soft, slightly smoky complexity with several years bottle age.

SIZE AND OPPORTUNITY —
THE NEEDLE IN THE HAYSTACK

The vignerons of the south-western corner of Western Australia have found themselves in a classic Catch 22 situation: because their customers would never come to their wineries in sufficient numbers to provide a sufficient business base to grow their markets, they needed to reach out to those markets and service them direct. But the cost of effectively doing that — repeatedly visiting the eastern states to drum up media, retail and restaurant support — was way in excess of their cash flow or profit capacity.

A number did not even make the effort. I will never forget visiting a producer in the south in 1980. To reach the property we drove along a series of unmade and unmarked roads in the middle of a major sheep grazing region, and finally arrived at the kitchen door of a farm house. The very friendly owners were delighted to see us, and took us down to the cellar to fetch two bottles for sampling. This we reached by climbing over several fences en route to the farm dam, into one wall of which had been excavated the 'cellar'. (Quite what the dam builder thought of this cunning means of having an underground cellar in dead flat sheep country I did not learn.)

Triumphantly returning to the house with our bottles (made under contract at a proper winery over 100 kilometres away), several duralex glasses were retrieved from the breakfast table, the milk rinsed out, and the wine poured for our consideration. Although it was a little difficult to be precise, the wines, a dry and semi-dry Rhine Riesling, seemed quite acceptable, and anyone calling at the cellar door would have been pleased with the price. Needless to say, few made the trip, and the farmer — who was simply trying to find ways to diversify — now limits his efforts to grape growing, his label having disappeared as quietly as it arrived.

David Hohnen of Cape Mentelle in the Margaret River region seemingly broke free of the Catch 22 situation when he elected to take on Veuve Clicquot as a major (or majority, no one is saying) partner. It gave him access to world markets on a scale even Cloudy Bay, his New Zealand venture, has been unable to achieve, not to mention an inexhaustible supply of capital to satisfy the inexhaustible appetite of the small to medium sized winery.

In the Lower Great Southern region, the biggest break-through has been made by Goundrey Wines Limited. With a combination of highly sophisticated corporate and taxation planning and a no less impressive marketing agreement with a Japanese company, it has embarked on an expansion programme which will lift its production from 19,000 cases in 1989 to almost 100,000 cases by 1996.

The first move was to convert Goundrey to an unlisted public company in 1987, with an expanded shareholding to finance the early phases of the group's expansion, which included the erection of a large, modern winery at Langton. Then in June 1990 a prospectus was issued to the public offering units in the Agrilink Equitus Limited Partnerships and shares in Blue Wren Estates Limited which raised $3.7 million. These funds will be used to develop the vineyards which will be supplying 1200 tonnes of grapes to Goundrey by 1996.

Of equal importance was the signing of a distribution agreement with Hokuriku Coca-Cola Limited, a Japanese sake brewer and Coca-Cola bottler which also owns 58 per cent of Mountarrow Wines Limited (ie Arrowfield), of the Upper Hunter Valley. It is anticipated that between 35 per cent and 45 per cent of each year's production will be marketed in Japan.

When it started its aggressive expansion programme, Goundrey was known to only the most dedicated wine lovers in Australia. Its wines were distributed in the eastern states, but in small volume. If its business plan succeeds, it will become one of the best known medium sized wineries in Australia — if not *the* best known winery.

It will require an exceptional public relations promotion and marketing programme. The pressures on the winemaking team will be immense: it will have to deal with grapes coming predominantly from young vines for the first 5 years, which are the 5 years of massive volume growth. Also, to successfully build a major export business, it is all but essential to have a strong domestic base. In the ultra-critical Australian market, this means the wines must be of a consistently high quality — for by the very nature of the region, Goundrey must be in the premium sector of the market in terms of both price and quality.

In many ways, Goundrey Wines Limited will be a bell-weather for the prospects of success or failure for all recent premium winemaking ventures in Australia. If it succeeds, there is absolutely no reason why others should not do likewise. Let us hope that it does.

ABOVE: Michael Goundrey, mover and shaker.

WINERIES OF THE LOWER GREAT SOUTHERN

ALKOOMI   A-A
Wingeballup Road
Frankland 6396   (098) 55 2229
Established   1971
Winemakers   Kim Hart and Merv Lange
Production   8000 cases.
Principal Wines   Rhine Riesling, Semillon,
Sauvignon Blanc, Chardonnay, Shiraz Malbec and
Cabernet Sauvignon.
Best Vintages   **W** and **R** 1977, '80, '82,
'83, '84, '86, '89

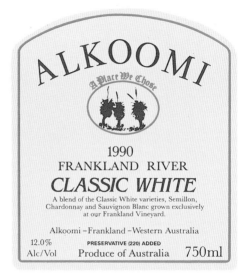

Alkoomi is one of the more remote wineries in
this remote region, but is more than worth the
effort of a visit. It produces crisp, pungent and
varietally precise white wines, and immensely
long-lived, concentrated and deep flavoured
reds. One of the more unusual winery specialties
is its malbec, giving a glimpse of why this
variety was so important in Bordeaux before the
advent of phylloxera.

CASTLE ROCK ESTATE   A-A
Porongurup Road
Porongurup 6324   (098) 41 1037
Established   1983
Winemaker   Angelo Diletti.
Production   1000 cases.
Principal Wines   Rhine Riesling, Late Harvest
Riesling and Cabernet Sauvignon.
Best Vintages   **W** and **R** 1986, '87, '88, '90
A spectacularly-situated winery with sweeping
vistas of the hillsides under the lee of the
Porongurups, the massive, rounded boulders of
which often seem like an Antipodean answer to
Stonehenge. Castle Rock is a relatively recent
arrival on the scene, but has produced some
finely-chiselled, steely/toasty Rhine Riesling
providing further evidence (if such is needed) of
the suitability of the area for this variety. Its
initial release of Cabernet Sauvignon from 1988

was outstanding, with piercing red berry fruit
and a lingering finish.

CHATSFIELD   CA-B
34 Albany Highway
Mount Barker 6324 (098) 51 1266
Established   1976
Winemaker   Goundrey Wines (contract).
Production   1500 cases.
Principal Wines   Rhine Riesling, Traminer,
Chardonnay and Shiraz.
Best Vintages   **W** 1987, '88
                       R 1986, '88.
Originally called Watermans, Chatsfield is a
somewhat shadowy and elusive operation so far
as eastern states wine lovers are concerned

because of its very limited distribution. No
doubt much of its excellent wine is consumed in
Western Australia, but it does deserve a wider
audience. The outstanding wines to date have
been the fragrant and aromatic varieties such as
gewurztraminer and rhine riesling, the best of
which had had an almost piercing delicacy. It
must be said, however, that quality has been a
little variable.

FOREST HILL   BA-BA
142 km peg, Muir Highway
Forest Hill via Mount Barker 6324
(098) 51 1724
Established   1966
Winemaker   Bernard Abbott.

ABOVE: *Immaculately tended vines at Castle Rock in the aftermath of
the rainstorm.*

Production 4000 cases.
Principal Wines Rhine Riesling, Traminer and Chardonnay
Best Vintages **W** and **R** 1975, '85, '86, '88

By far the longest established vineyard in the Lower Great Southern area, and now part of (the late) Australian millionaire businessman Robert Holmes a Court's personal empire. Forest Hill (which has never had its own winery) is now integrated with the Margaret River winery Vasse Felix, which Mr Holmes a Court purchased first. The Forest Hill label will continue, albeit limited to its white wines, which is good news for all concerned. Its Rhine Riesling and Chardonnay can be sublime; the former intense and toasty, the latter with no less intense grape-fruit/melon.

GALAFREY   CB-B

145 Lower Sterling Terrace
Albany 6330   (098) 41 6533
Established   1975
Winemaker   Ian Tyrer
Production   3000 cases.
Principal Wines   Rhine Riesling, Chardonnay, Muller Thurgau, Shiraz, Pinot Noir and Cabernet Sauvignon.
Best Vintages   **W** and **R** 1986, '88

Galafrey's winery and cellar door tasting facilities fit comfortably inside a large wooden woolstore built around the turn of the century, and situated well within the town limits of Albany. Owners Ian and Linda Tyrer are determined to build the business, and to reach eastern states markets. A number of interesting wine styles are produced, even if quality is somewhat inconsistent; there can, however, be no quarrel with wines such as the 1988 Rhine Riesling.

GOUNDREY   A-BA

Muir Highway
Mount Barker 6324 (098) 511 777
Established   1971
Winemaker   Michael Goundrey

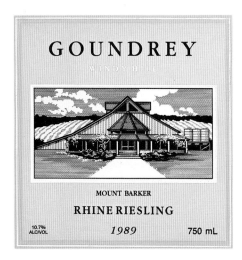

Production 18,000 cases.
Principal Wines Rhine Riesling, Chardonnay, Sauvignon Blanc, Pinot Noir, Cabernet Shiraz and Cabernet Sauvignon.Mailing list and cellar door sales; extensive retail distribution through I.H.Baker Wines & Spirits (eastern states) and own sales represenrive (Perth); WA country through H.M. Beigew & Co. Cellar door sales 10 am to 4 pm Monday to Saturday, 12 to 4 pm Sunday.
Best Vintages **W** 1982, '85, '88, '89, '90
                           R 1981, '85, '87, '88

A substantial injection of capital through the introduction of shareholder partners has allowed founders Michael and Alison Goundrey to establish a spendid new winery and to acquire and/or establish substantial additional vineyards. Wine quality has never been in doubt, but has gone from strength to strength over the past few years. It is difficult to choose between the striking lime/passionfruit Rhine Riesling, the tangy, charred-oak grapefruit flavoured Chardonnay, and the herbaceous/gooseberry Sauvignon Blanc, but overall the honours must go to the Cabernet Sauvignon, hotly pursued by the Shiraz and Cabernet Shiraz.

HOWARD PARK   A-BA

Lot 11, Little River Road
Denmark 6333   (098) 48 1261
Established   1986
Winemaker   John Wade.
Production   850 cases.
Principal Wines   Riesling and Cabernet Sauvignon.
Best Vintages   **W** 1986, '87, '89, '90
                           R 1987, '88, '89

Owner winemaker John Wade is best known for his time as chief winemaker at Wynns Coonawarra, followed by a stint with Goundrey and now as chief winemaker at Plantagenet. The tiny production under his own Howard Park label is eagerly sought by winelovers; the blackcurrant/red berry flavoured Cabernet Sauvignon is of exceptional quality and style.

KARRELEA ESTATE   B-B

Duck Road
Mount Barker 6324 (098) 511 838
Established   1986
Winemaker   Plantagenet Wines
                           (contract).
Production   500 cases.
Principal Wines   Rhine Riesling, Sauvignon Blanc, Pinot Noir and Cabernet Sauvignon Cabernet Franc Merlot.
Best Vintages   **W** and **R** 1986, '87, '88

An as yet small and relatively new winery which had a dream debut with its 1987 Rhine Riesling, winning a gold medal in open class company at the 1987 Perth show of that year. The wines are all in mainstream Lower Great

Southern style, with finely structured, toasty Riesling and intense although not heavy, leafy/berry Cabernet Sauvignon.

KARRIVALE   B-B

(formerly Narang)
Woodlands
Porongurup 6324   (098) 53 1009
Established   1979
Winemaker   John Wade (contract)
Production   550 cases.
Principal Wines   Rhine Riesling.
Best Vintages   **W** 1988, '89, '90

Formerly known as Narang, Karrivale nestles at the foot of one of the most striking of the rounded granite hills of the Porongurups. Rhine Riesling is the only wine so far produced, but recent plantings of Chardonnay and Shiraz will broaden the range. Thanks to highly competent contract winemaking, the quality of the wines so far released has been of exemplary consistency, even if supply is extremely restricted.

PLANTAGENET   BA-A
Albany Highway
Mount Barker 6324   (098) 51 1150
Established   1968.
Winemaker   John Wade.
Production   11,200 cases.
Principal Wines   Rhine Riesling, Chenin
Blanc, Chardonnay, Frontignac, Fleur, Pinot
Noir, Shiraz, Cabernet Sauvignon and Cabernet
Shiraz.
Best Vintages   **W** 1977, '83, '85, '87, '89, '90.
                    R 1977, '83, '85, '86, '89
For over a decade Plantagenet stood un-
challenged as the leading winery in the Lower
Great Southern Area. Goundrey has now thrown
down the gauntlet, and it is quite certain
Plantagenet will respond. It produces the most

comprehensive range of wines in the region,
most extremely good and the remainder simply
outstanding. In some years the Rhine Riesling
and the Chardonnay scale the heights, in other
years it is the Shiraz and the Cabernet
Sauvignon. The red wines particularly can show
unusual complexity and balance.

WIGNALLS   A-A
Chester Pass Road (Highway 1)
Albany 6330 (098) 41 2848
Established   1982
Winemaker   John Wade (contract)
Production   2000 cases.
Principal Wines   Chardonnay, Sauvignon
Blanc and Pinot Noir.
Best Vintages   **W** and **R** 1986, '87, '88, '89, '90
The strong maritime influence of the nearby
ocean gives Wignalls an entirely different
climate to the majority of the regions in the
Lower Great Southern Area. The days are cooler,
the nights warmer, and the result is an
exceptionally long growing season. It was an
inspired decision by owners Bill and Pat
Wignall to plant the three varieties they had
chosen, for they do exceptionally well with all,
and are indeed making one of the top half dozen
pinot noirs in Australia.

OTHER WINERIES

BLACKWOOD CREST   CB-C
RMB 404A Boyup Brook 6244

DALYUP RIVER ESTATE   NR
Murray's Road
Esperance 6450 (090)76 5027

HAY RIVER   B-B
Denmark Road
Mount Barker 6324

JINGALLA   CA-CB
RMB 114 Bolganup Dam Road
Porongurup 6324 (098) 53 1023

KARRI VIEW   NR
Scotsdale Road
Denmark 6333 (098) 40 9381

LEFROY BROOK VINEYARD   NR
Cascades Road,
Pemberton, near Manjimup, 6258

SHEMARIN   B-B
19 Third Avenue
Mount Lawley 6050 (098) 51 1682

TINGLE-WOOD WINES   CB-BA
Glenrowan Road
Denmark 6333 (098) 40 9218

ABOVE: *Resident snail-catchers at Wignalls: no strikes or work bans here.*   TOP: *John Wade, winemaker at Plantagenet, the twinkle ever in his eyes.*

WESTERN AUSTRALIA

MARGARET RIVER

Whether it is in part due to the subliminal suggestion of the name I do not know, but I have always felt there is a feminine quality to the soft beauty of the Margaret River region. Yet at one and the same time it is uncompromisingly Australian: Western Australia is home to many of our most striking native plants, and they grow in profusion in the Margaret River. Stately eucalypts, gnarled banksias and ancient blackboys, their trunks blackened by centuries of bushfires, stand above carpets of flowering kangaroo paws, desert peas and countless other flowers.

The doctors-cum-winemakers who, for some strange reason dominated the early development of viticulture and who still have a strong presence, were unusually sensitive to the environment, and the wineries tend to merge into the countryside rather than stand superimposed on it. Stone or rammed earth walls, and skilful use of local timber are commonplace, with subtle bush landscaping adding to the overall effect.

When the first Margaret River reds came onto the market in the eastern states in the mid-1970s they made a huge impression. There was a clarity and a delicacy to their red fruit flavours and an elegance in their structure which immediately set them apart. In retrospect it seems likely that part of this 'difference' was due to the absence of naturally-occurring malolactic fermentation in the bacterially sterile confines typical of new wineries in a new wine region.

Almost overnight Margaret River became the most fashionable address in Australia, and — for many good

reasons — it still retains much of its allure. But its isolation from Perth and, even more obviously, the markets of the eastern states seems to have slowed its subsequent growth, notwithstanding the unique public relations extravaganzas of Leeuwin Estate.

That isolation also contributed to its relatively recent arrival on the scene. Its potential had been recognised by Californian viticulturist Professor Harold Olmo in his pioneering viticultural study of 1955, but the critical spark came from research carried out by Dr John Gladstones and published in December 1965. Dr Gladstones concluded that the Margaret River had distinct advantages over Manjimup

AUSTRALASIAN WINE REGIONS
1980 – 1990

	RED	WHITE
1980	6	4
1981	7	5
1982	9	8
1983	6	6
1984	7	6
1985	6	8
1986	8	9
1987	9	8
1988	7	8
1989	9	8
1990	8	9

THE REGION IN BRIEF

LOCATION AND ELEVATION
33°57'S 15°03'E
40 m

CLIMATE
Perhaps because of the reputation which the Margaret River gained for itself in the early to mid-'70s, it has always been regarded as having a particularly cool climate. The reality is a little different, as the HDD summation of 1690 and the MJT of 20.4°C attest. To use singularly loose language, the climate might be described as soft; certainly, this is reflected in the largely languorous wine styles. It is also reflected in the fact that true winter dormancy is seldom achieved: the Margaret River has the lowest Mean Annual Range of any Australian wine region of only 7.6 degrees. It also has the most exaggerated Mediterranean climate in terms of rainfall: annual rainfall is a towering 1160 mm, but only 200 mm of that falls between October and April.

SOIL
The vast majority of the Margaret River soils are sandy: grey-brown loamy sand topsoil gradually passes into sandy to sandy clay loam subsoils, which are yellow or brown (Uc4.21 and 4.22). The soils are highly permeable when moist, but when dry, can shed moisture from sloping sites. Overall, water capacities are low, and the nature of the soil exacerbates the extreme break in the rainfall pattern, placing enormous importance on irrigation — an importance which has not always been fully recognised in the region. There are also patches of brownish grey quartzsose sands (Uc1.22) and smaller areas of sandy mottled yellow duplex soils (Dy5.81).

HARVEST TIME
End February — mid-April

PRINCIPAL GRAPE VARIETIES

Chardonnay	*Cabernet Sauvignon*
Semillon	*Shiraz*
Sauvignon Blanc	*Merlot*
Chenin Blanc	*Pinot Noir*
Rhine Riesling	

ABOVE: Margaret River wild flowers.

FACING PAGE: The soft beauty of Margaret River.

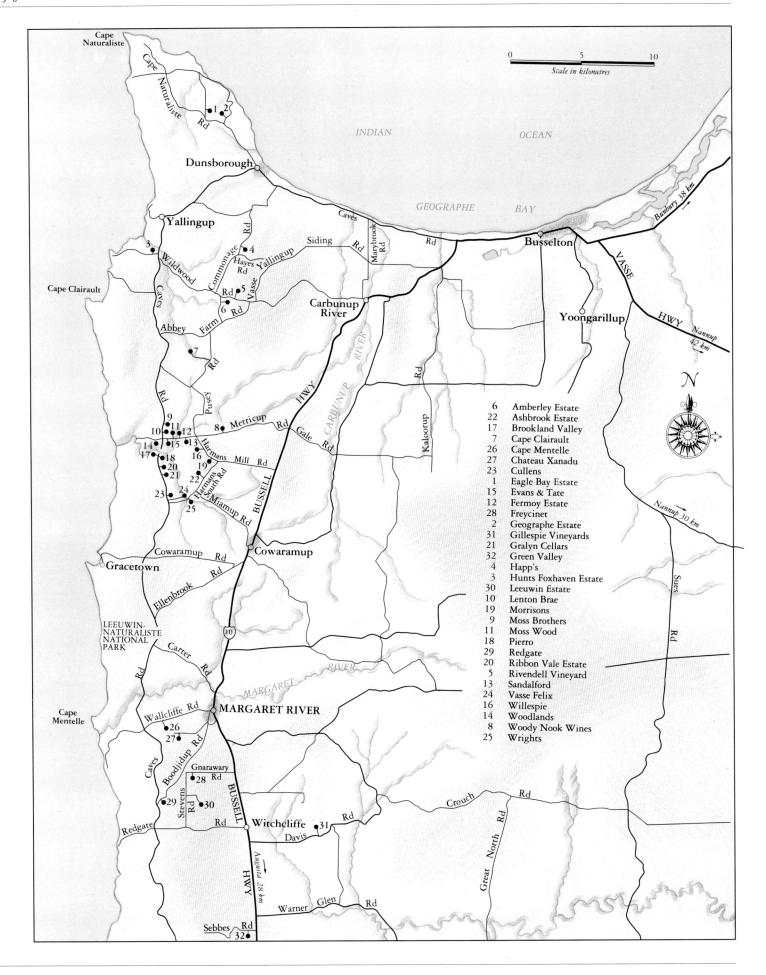

(the boom district of the 1990s) and Mount Barker, and that 'it should be ideal for table wines generally'.

One and a half years later Perth cardiologist Dr Tom Cullity planted the first vines at Vasse Felix and the curtain went up on the 'greatest show in the West'. Dr Bill Pannell followed suit in 1969 with Moss Wood, and Dr Kevin and Diana Cullen in 1971 with Cullens.

Growth may have slowed, but it certainly has not stopped. Veuve Clicquot now controls a sizeable chunk of Cape Mentelle; the Robert Holmes à Court family bought Vasse Felix (and Forest Hill, in the Mount Barker area); and a substantial number of new wineries have opened their doors over the past few years.

PRINCIPAL WINE STYLES

CABERNET SAUVIGNON

Margaret River Cabernet Sauvignon was the first wine style to catch the imagination and respect of the markets of the eastern states in the mid-1970s. By the standards of the day, the wines had a striking clarity of flavour, with beautifully modulated cherry and dark currant fruit flavours. The weight varied from the light and elegant Vasse Felix and Moss Wood wines through to the much stronger structure of Cullens and Cape Mentelle. Then in the early 1980s Cape Mentelle had its double Jimmy Watson success, putting the final seal of approval on the style. As the vines have matured, and as malolactic fermentations have become widespread (in the early years they were often absent), the style seems to have changed somewhat. That core of fruit is still there, but there is a particular, regional 'gravelly' overlay which is quite distinctive and which requires an element of understanding. In addition to the 'big four', Cape Clairault (regularly) Happ's, Leeuwin Estate (sometimes spectacularly) and Ribbon Vale Estate (less regularly), produce classic Cabernet Sauvignon and Cabernet Merlot (Merlot is in fact frequently blended with Cabernet Sauvignon).

CHARDONNAY

Chardonnay has taken a long time to establish itself as a major variety for the district, notwithstanding the outstanding early success of Leeuwin Estate. Those with early Leeuwin wines (notably the 1982) in their cellars are indeed privileged. But it has been a difficult variety from a viticultural viewpoint, and many of the vignerons have been content with other white varieties. In more recent years, Moss Wood, Cape Mentelle, and Pierro in particular, have shown what can be achieved. In the hands of these makers the wines show wonderfully rich and supple texture, with peachy fruit and tremendous length and concentration of flavour.

SEMILLON

Arguably the most important, and certainly the most striking, white wine variety. For some obscure reason, Semillon performs quite differently here to the way it performs in any other Australian wine region, producing wines with a marked herbaceous cut in three vintages out of four, leaving the unwary to believe the wine is in fact Sauvignon Blanc. One finds the same pattern in New Zealand, but in much cooler

climates. Moss Wood is the foremost producer of Semillon, releasing wooded and non-wooded versions each year which are almost invariably outstanding. Evans and Tate, too, has done exceptionally well with this variety, although Ashbrook Estate and Willespie also succeed handsomely.

SHIRAZ

Usually labelled Hermitage, it is a variety which does well in the Margaret River region, even though the marketing Ides of March tell against it. Taking all of the wines of the 1980s into account, I would place the Cape Mentelle Hermitage in front of its Cabernet Sauvignon (and probably put the Cape Mentelle Zinfandel in front of the Hermitage). Vasse Felix, too, has done very well with this variety, even if it does not attain the same depth of zesty spicy/cherry fruit of Cape Mentelle.

SAUVIGNON BLANC

Truly, it is often difficult to establish Margaret River Sauvignon Blanc from Semillon, and for this reason the two are not infrequently blended (with Chenin Blanc added to fashion the so-called Classic or Margaret River Classic style). The most distinguished varietal Sauvignon Blancs have come from Leeuwin Estate (consistently), Chateau Xanadu, Ashbrook Estate and Willespie.

CHENIN BLANC

An important variety, but usually found in a two or three grape blend. Occasional varietal releases tend to show the same herbaceous character as does Semillon and Sauvignon Blanc, which is extremely confusing. A few makers have attempted to differentiate it by leaving a certain amount of residual sugar in the wine, a solution which I wholeheartedly condemn.

PINOT NOIR

The special preserve of Moss Wood and Leeuwin Estate: both producers are extremely proud of their efforts, which can be easily understood if you have access to the 1981 Moss Wood or the best of the Leeuwin Estate wines. However, at the end of the day, I think that Albany and other subregions of the Lower Great Southern area may emerge triumphant.

ABOVE: Erl Happ's bird netting: the only recipe for a good night's sleep.

LEEUWIN ESTATE

Icarus flew too close to the sun, and paid the price accordingly. In mid-1990 it seemed very likely that Denis Horgan had done likewise, and it was far from clear whether he would retain ownership of Leeuwin Estate — and if he did, whether he would be able to keep it in the fashion to which it was accustomed.

But nothing can take away from the achievements of Leeuwin Estate and of Denis Horgan in their unrelenting pursuit of excellence since 1974, when a vine nursery was established on site and the clearing of timber commenced. Most of the 90 hectare vineyard was planted in 1975 and 1976; an additional 9 hectares of Chardonnay were planted in 1978; and the 1982 grafting of 3 hectares of Shiraz to Sauvignon Blanc has been the only subsequent change.

That Leeuwin Estate got it right so early on (remembering that the mid-70s were a time of rapid and largely unforseen change in the industry) was no doubt partially due to the involvement of Robert Mondavi, the Napa Valley's most famous vigneron. (Mondavi was acting as consultant to a group of American investors who initially had a share in Leeuwin Estate; they forfeited that share in bizarre circumstances which had nothing to do with any personal disagreement between Mondavi and Horgan, who remained good friends.)

In typical fashion, the decision was taken to establish the vineyard without recourse to the use of irrigation. Yields have accordingly remained exceedingly low by contemporary commercial standards: in full maturity the vines are yielding only 4.5 tonnes per hectare on average, with Chardonnay a miserable 3.5 tonnes per hectare. These yields are less than half those which are regarded as normal for premium wine in Australia (and a fraction of those for cask wine), and are less than those of the top French appellations.

LEEUWIN ESTATE PLANTINGS

Rhine Riesling,	30 ha	Cabernet Sauvignon,	28 ha
Chardonnay,	17 ha	Pinot Noir,	5 ha
Sauvignon Blanc,	4 ha	Gewurztraminer,	3.5 ha
Malbec,	1.5 ha		

If this were not enough, Leeuwin Estate has never hesitated to downgrade or 'declassify' wine which it does not consider is of sufficiently high standard for its label. This is quietly disposed of in bulk, and instead of a theoretical production of around 26,000 cases from its 400 tonne crush, the most recent figure available was of 18,000 cases.

The winery has likewise been built and equipped without regard to cost. One oft-repeated detail is of the acquisition not of one but of two new Willmes tank presses, each big enough to handle the crush on its own. Another is of 'insurance' against breakdown, a risk which less fortunate

wineries have no option but to accept. The building itself is on a massive scale for the size of the crush, and extensive use of off-form concrete adds to the feeling that Leeuwin Estate will be here for centuries to come.

It hardly needs be said that the hospitality, restaurant and tasting facilities are second to none, and it is in the area of promotion and marketing that Leeuwin Estate has so unashamedly and successfully engaged in the 'pursuit of excellence'. If that phrase is now a cliché, Horgan must take part of the credit, for he was one of the initiators of the game.

He started by taking a leaf out of Baron Philippe de Rothschild's book, and commissioning leading artists to produce paintings which were then reproduced on each year's label. In 1985 this not-altogether-altruistic patronage of the arts was extended in spectacular fashion to music. Denis Horgan was asked by the Festival of Perth to underwrite the London Philharmonic Orchestra's Australian tour. He agreed on one condition: that it stage an open-air concert in the grounds of Leeuwin Estate.

The sheer improbability of the idea, and its audacity, guaranteed not only Australian, but world-wide publicity. To say it was a success is a masterpiece of understatement, and an ordinary mortal would have taken the conventional course and said, 'Well, it is impossible to top such an event, and exceedingly difficult — and expensive — to even seek to repeat it.' Not Horgan: over the ensuing year Leeuwin Estate hosted such diverse attractions as the Berlin State Orchestra, Ray Charles, Dionne Warwick, and the handicapped pianist David Helfgott. In what may conceivably be Leeuwin Estate's swansong, its 1990 concert featured Kiri Te Kanawa and James Galway, with the backing of the Western Australian Symphony. If there has to be a finale, that concert was as close to perfect as even Horgan could have wished.

But what of Leeuwin Estate's wines? For some the most noteworthy feature has been the price, around $35 a bottle for the Chardonnay, $30 for the Pinot Noir, and $27 for the Cabernet Sauvignon. Next to Penfolds Grange Hermitage, these are Australia's highest-priced wines at the time of their release. Yet even at these levels it seems inconceivable Leeuwin Estate could be making a profit if any part of the cost of its promotion and marketing were borne by it. The probability is the cost is (or was) effectively borne by the other much larger companies in the Barrack House group, which has interests concentrated in mining and real estate. (However, the group appears to have fallen prey to the 1990 recession.)

Indeed, even excluding these costs, it is unlikely Leeuwin Estate could operate at a profit given the size of its vineyard and winery relative to production, unless of course one ignored the capital cost involved and if the whole project was

financed without recourse to debt. Only then would one be likely to arrive at a profit.

The effective cost of production has been exacerbated by Leeuwin Estate's quality-driven decision to hold the Cabernet Sauvignon for 6 years before release, and the Chardonnay and Pinot Noir for 5 years. This alone makes the Chardonnay unique in Australia, but I also happen to believe it is a great wine, and by far the most distinctive and convincing wine to bear the Leeuwin Estate label. It is by no stretch of imagination in the mainstream of the Australian Chardonnay style: the structure is much tighter and more concentrated, the aromas and flavours often tending to those of Burgundy, and the finish is longer and finer. In comparative tastings against younger Australian Chardonnays which are more direct in the lush, simple fruit of their appeal, the Leeuwin Chardonnays do not always fare well. I think that this is as much a reflection on the judge as on the wine: or, put another way,

that blind tastings do not always produce the right result, regardless of the experience and skill of the judges.

The Leeuwin Cabernet Sauvignons can be very nearly as good. The 1985 vintage released in late 1990 is a classic wine in every sense, inviting comparisons with Bordeaux. The last reserve stocks of Leeuwin's 1979 Cabernet Sauvignon, a wine in a similar mould, were also offered in late 1990. These wines show the same intensity as the Chardonnay, yet are fine, supple and elegant — rare commodities in Australia.

I am not so sure the same policy pays dividends with the Pinot Noir. While it sometimes shows remnants of excellent varietal character, I think it should be released young, as are the Rhine Riesling and the exemplary Sauvignon Blanc.

So much passion, so much time and so much money have been invested in Leeuwin Estate that it has become a hallmark for the Australia wine industry. It deserves to stay that way.

ABOVE: *Contour planting and oats and rye grass catch the eye of man and bird alike (Leeuwin Estate).*

WINERIES OF MARGARET RIVER

ASHBROOK ESTATE   BA-A
Harman's South Road
Willyabrup 6284 (097) 55 6262
Established   1976
Winemakers   The Devitt family.
Production   4000 cases.
Principal Wines   Semillon, Chardonnay, Verdelho, Rhine Riesling, Sauvignon Blanc and Cabernet Sauvignon.
Best Vintages   1986, '87, '90
Ashbrook is one of the most elusive of all wineries, notwithstanding its substantial production and notwithstanding the considerable expertise and industry experience of Tony Devitt. It does not participate in the show judging system, and Devitt chooses not to submit any wines for tasting by journalists. He says "We prefer to let the client make up his or her mind; the business is very small and we deal with our clients on a very personal basis." However, a recent tasting of the full range of wines, with the 1990's to the fore, left me in no doubt that this is a first class winery.

CAPE CLAIRAULT   B-B
Henry Road
Willyabrup 6284   (097) 55 5229
Established   1976
Winemaker   Ian Lewis.
Production   2500 cases.
Principal Wines   Semillon Sauvignon Blanc, Sauvignon Blanc, Rhine Riesling, Cabernet Sauvignon and Vintage Port.
Best Vintages   W 1987, '88, '89, '90.
               R 1982, '83, '85, '86, '87
Geologist Ian Lewis and school teacher-wife Arni Lewis have never let success go to their heads. As long ago as 1984 their 1982 Cabernet Sauvignon won the *Canberra Times* Trophy for the best dry red table wine (firm finish) in the premium classes of the Canberra National Show. More recently, their '83 Cabernet was judged Best Red of Show at the 1987 Lord Forrest competition (the local show), while their Sauvignon Blanc won the gold medal in its class at the 1988 Sheraton Wine Awards. Despite all this, they have continued to seek to improve the

quality and consistency of their wines with the retention of qualified consultancy advice, which has paid particular dividends with the white wines centred around Sauvignon Blanc and Semillon Sauvignon Blanc; both of these show the pungent gooseberry/grassy characters for which Margaret River is becoming increasingly well known.

CAPE MENTELLE   A-A
Off Wallcliffe Road
Margaret River 6285   (097) 57 2070
Established   1969
Winemakers   David Hohnen and John Durham.
Production   13,000 cases.

Principal Wines   Now famous as a Cabernet Sauvignon specialist, but offers an eclectic choice of Semillon (which includes a touch of sauvignon blanc and chenin blanc), Chardonnay, Rhine Riesling, Zinfandel, Hermitage and Cabernet Sauvignon.
Best Vintages   W 1985, '88, '89, '90.
               R 1978, '82, '83, '85, '86, '87, '88, '90
Winning the Jimmy Watson Trophy once is a dream come true for a small winery; winning it twice in a row is so improbable that one does not even dream of it, but David Hohnen achieved that double with his 1982 and 1983 Cabernet Sauvignon. Not content with that, Hohnen then established the spectacularly successful Cloudy Bay winery in New Zealand and topped off his achievements by acquiring Veuve Cliquot as a substantial shareholder in 1990. The red wine quality of Cape Mentelle is really unquestioned, but my personal choice falls unashamedly on the wonderfully textured, spicy, Zinfandel. Veuve Clicquot has given its imprimatur by taking a majority shareholding in the venture (including Cloudy Bay).

CHATEAU XANADU   CA-B
Railway Terrace, off Wallcliffe Road
Margaret River 6285 (097) 57 2581
Established   1979
Winemaker   Conor Lagan.

Production   5000 cases.
Principal Wines   Chardonnay, Semillon, Semillon II, Sauvignon Blanc, Cabernet Sauvignon and Cabernet Franc.
Best Vintages   W 1986, '87, 89, '90
               R 1985, '87, '89
Chateau Xanadu has established a particular reputation for its pungently herbaceous Semillon which in years such as 1987 reaches the apogee of this somewhat idiosyncratic style. The version with a touch of residual sugar (Semillon II) is far less convincing, if not downright illogical, but evidently pleases those calling at the cellar door. The Chardonnay and Sauvignon Blanc are reliable, the Cabernet Sauvignon unreliable.

CULLENS   A-A
Caves Road, Willyabrup
via Cowaramup 6284 (097) 55 5277
Established   1971
Winemaker   Vanya Cullen.
Production   8000 cases.
Principal Wines   Chardonnay, Semillon, Sauvignon Blanc, Rhine Riesling, Sauvignon Blanc Sauternes style, Pinot Noir and Cabernet Merlot.
Best Vintages   W 1977, '82, '86, '88, '89, '90.
               R 1975, '76, '84, '86, '89

Father Dr. Kevin Cullen, mother Diana and daughter Vanya are both part of a family of quite wonderful individuals, individuals who have made Cullens what it is: one of the most highly rated yet intensely individualistic of the better known Margaret River wineries. Barrel fermentation looms large in the fashioning of the white wines, and not all of these will please the purists. However, they have tremendous strength, flavour and character, while the Cabernet Merlot is a model of consistency with its concentrated, classic dark berry Cabernet varietal character and its long, pleasantly tannic finish.

ABOVE LEFT: Blackboys, so much part of an ancient landscape, point the way to Ashbrook Winery.
CENTRE: David Hohnen of Cape Mentelle: nothing succeeds like success.

ABOVE RIGHT: Mother Diana and daughter Vanya Cullen: first ladies of the Margaret River.

EVANS AND TATE   BA-A
Metricup Road
Willyabrup 6284 (097) 55 6244
Established   1974
Winemaker   Krister Jonsson.
Production   11,000 cases.
Principal Wines Semillon, Sauvignon Blanc, Chardonnay, Hermitage, Merlot and Cabernet Sauvignon.
Best Vintages   **W** and **R**, 1981, '82, '84, '87, '89, '90

Evans and Tate has played a large role in reshaping perceptions of Western Australian wine. If there is to be the barest hint of criticism, it is that at times the wines have become almost too elegant. In more recent years there has been a move back to fruit richness and greater complexity, with some particularly striking Semillon and Sauvignon Blanc in both 1989 and 1990.

FERMOY ESTATE   NR
Metricup Road, Willyabrup
via Cowaramup 6284 (097) 55 6285
Established   1985
Winemaker   Michael Kelly.
Production   1000 cases.
Principal Wines Semillon/Sauvignon Blanc and Cabernet Sauvignon.
Best Vintages   **W** and **R** 1988, '89.
One of the most recent arrivals on the scene in Margaret River, which announced its arrival in a blaze of glory at the 1989 Sheraton Wine Awards winning the gold medal (there being only one gold medal ever awarded in each class) in the light bodied red class. The wine in question was spotlessly clean, with fragrant spicy/berry fruit and oak, and just an appropriate hint of leafy astringency. If subsequent vintages are of the same quality, Fermoy Estate will be headed to an A-A rating, and its owner (Western Mining Corporation Director John Anderson) will no doubt be persuaded there is gold above the ground as well as underground.

FREYCINET   CB-B
Lot 1, Gnarawary Road
Margaret River 6285 (097) 57 6358
Established   1978
Winemaker   Peter Gherardi.
Production   3500 cases.
Principal Wines Sauvignon Blanc, Semillon, Chenin Blanc, Chardonnay and Cabernet Sauvignon/Merlot/Cabernet Franc blend.
Best Vintages   **W** 1986, '88, '89.
                     R 1986, '87, '88
Winemaker/owner Peter Gherardi is a highly experienced viticulturist with the Western Australian Department of Agriculture. Over the years a number of stylish Semillons and Chenin Blancs have appeared under the Freycinet label, but more recently the fairly austere and long-lived Cabernet Sauvignon, with that particular gravelly edge which seems so much part of Margaret River style, has been more impressive.

HAPP'S   B-B
Commonage Road
Dunsborough 6281 (097) 55 3300
Established   1978
Winemaker   Erland Happ.
Production   5000 cases.
Principal Wines Chardonnay, Cabernet Merlot, Merlot, Shiraz, Verdelho Muscat and Port.
Best Vintages   **R** 1986, '87, '88, '90
Erl Happ, economics teacher turned potter turned winemaker, sets high standards for himself, and sees no reason why others should not live up to the same high standards. All in all, a complex man who makes complex wines, wines which sometimes mirror the ascerbic edge to Erl Happ's character.

LEEUWIN ESTATE   A-B
Gnarawary Road
Margaret River 6285 (097) 57 6253
Established   1974
Winemaker   Bob Cartwright
Production   18,000 cases.
Principal Wines Chardonnay, Rhine Riesling, Sauvignon Blanc, Pinot Noir and Cabernet Sauvignon.
Best Vintages   **W** 1982, '85, '86, '87, '90.
                     R 1980, '82, '85, '87, '90
Owner Dennis Horgan was in pursuit of excellence long before it became a cliche. A wealthy and very successful businessman, he has been in the fortunate position of not having to count the cost of owning and promoting Leeuwin Estate in a fashion not approached by any other Australian winery. But it is not a mere facade: the best Chardonnays are amongst the best made to date in Australia, there have been some outstanding Cabernet Sauvignons and one or two somewhat delicate Pinot Noirs which nonetheless have shown excellent varietal character and style.

MOSS WOOD   A-A
Metricup Road
Willyabrup via
Cowaramup 6284   (097) 55 6266
Established   1969
Winemaker   Keith Mugford
Production   4000 cases.
Principal Wines Chardonnay, Semillon, Pinot Noir and Cabernet Sauvignon.
Best Vintages   **W** and **R** 1977, '81, '83, '85, '87, '89, '90

If I had to nominate the Margaret River winery I hold in the highest regard, I would hedge the answer with all sorts of qualifications, but in the end the choice would have to fall on Moss Wood. In turn, it would rest upon the quality of the Semillons (both in the wood matured and unoaked versions) and upon the perfectly constructed Cabernet Sauvignon, with its near perfect amalgum of berry and leafy aromas, and its classically modulated balance and weight. What Dr. Bill Pannell started so long ago has been more than ably continued by owner/ winemaker Keith Mugford.

PIERRO   BA-B
Caves Road
Willyabrup via
Cowaramup 6284   (097) 55 6220
Established   1980
Winemaker   Michael Peterkin.
Production   2500 cases.
Principal Wines Les Trois Cuvees (a blend of Sauvignon Blanc, semillon and Chardonnay), Chardonnay and Pinot Noir.
Best Vintages   **W** and **R** 1980, '82, '87, '88, '89, '90

Michael Peterkin is yet another of the extraordinary band of Margaret River medical practitioners who have combined vine and scalpel. Unlike most doctors, who have been content to rely on their scientific training and their palate, Peterkin added a Roseworthy degree in Oenology to his medical degree, and adds consulting to his twin lives of winemaker and doctor. Rather like Erl Happ, his wines reflect a strong personality: by far the most successful are the Chardonnays made in varying styles, at their best potent and complex.

ABOVE: Keith Mugford of Moss Wood with his vintage Massey Ferguson.

REDGATE CB-B

Boodjidup Road
Margaret River 6285 (097) 57 6208

Established 1977
Winemakers Bill and Paul Ullinger.
Production 5000 cases.
Principal Wines Semillon, Chenin Blanc, Sauvignon Blanc, Spatlese Riesling, Pinot Noir, Cabernet Shiraz and Cabernet Sauvignon.
Best Vintages **W** and **R** 1985, '86, '88, '89.
The Redgate wines fall fairly and squarely in the mainstream of Margaret River style: almost all of the white varietals show some of the grassy characteristics one expects from the region, while the red wines have that taught astringency underlying blackcurrant and capsicum fruit. Overall, the reds have been more successful, with the Cabernet Sauvignons leading the way in 1985 and 1987.

RIBBON VALE ESTATE CB-B

Lot 5 Caves Road
Willyabrup via
Cowaramup 6284 (097) 55 6272
Established 1977
Winemaker John James
Production 1500 cases.
Principal Wines Semillon, Sauvignon Blanc, Semillon Sauvignon Blanc, Cabernet Sauvignon and Merlot.
Best Vintages **W** and **R** 1986, '87, '88, '90
Ribbon Vale takes its name from its quite extraordinary shape: the vineyard block is 150 metres wide and 1.5 kilometres long, a kindly neighbour having acceded to John James' pleas and subdivided the unused edge of his property. It has been developed slowly, with a winery built on site well after the first vintages were contract made. Some attractively herbaceous Semillon and Sauvignon Blanc (and a blend of the two) has emerged, followed more recently by typical Margaret River Cabernet Sauvignon.

SANDALFORD CB-CB

Metricup Road
Willyabrup via
Cowaramup 6284 (097) 55 6213
Established 1972
Winemakers Christian Morlaes, Tony Rowe and Candy Jonsson.
Production 25,000 cases.
Principal Wines Semillon, Rhine Riesling, Verdelho, Late Harvest Rhine Riesling, Auslese Rhine Riesling, Cabernet Sauvignon, Shiraz and Vintage Port.
Best Vintages **W** and **R** 1988, '89.
The Sandalford vineyard is the largest in the Margaret River region, and provides at least three quarters of Sandalford's total output. Changes in management and winemaking have resulted in sharply increased quality (commencing with the 1988 vintage) and — although there is still some distance to go —

Sandalford may yet realise the potential of its excellent vineyard resources. The Verdelho, in particular, is worth watching for.

VASSE FELIX A-A

Cnr Caves Road and Harmans
South Road, Cowaramup 6284 (097) 55 5242
Established 1976
Winemaker Bernard Abbott
Production 10,000 cases.
Principal Wines Rhine Riesling, Verdelho, Classic Dry White, Hermitage, Cabernet Sauvignon and Classic Dry Red.
Best Vintages **W** and **R** 1976, '78, '79, '84, '85, '86, '87, '89
The acquisition of Vasse Felix by the Holmes a Court family might have been expected to generate a flurry of publicity and promotional activity. Apart from the initial announcements, there has been none: Vasse Felix seemingly goes on as much as ever producing the most elegant of all of the Margaret River Cabernet Sauvignons, as finely strung as any of the late Mr Holmes a Court's racehorses. The red wines of Vasse Felix are a natural complement to the white wines of Forest Hill, also owned by the Holmes a Court interests.

WILLESPIE BA-BA

Harmans Mill Road
Willyabrup via
Cowaramup 6284 (097) 55 6248
Established 1976
Winemakers Kevin Squance; J. and M. Davies (consultants).
Production 3000 cases.
Principal Wines Rhine Riesling, Semillon, Verdelho, Cabernet Sauvignon and Vintage Port.
Best Vintages **W** and **R** 1986, '87, '89, '90

Since 1987, Willespie seems to have made better wines year by year. Again and again one returns to the underlying fruit structure of Margaret River: grassy whites and intense, concentrated and textured Cabernet Sauvignon with a cut as authoritative as any ever delivered by school headmaster and owner Kevin Squance.

OTHER WINERIES

AMBERLEY ESTATE NR
Wildwood and Thornton Road
Yallingup 6282

BROOKELANDS VALLEY NR
Caves Road
Willyabrup 6280 (097)55 6250

EAGLE BAY ESTATE C-C
Eagle Bay Road
Eagle Bay 6281 (09) 325 7488

GILLESPIE VINEYARDS C-C
Davis Road
Witchcliffe 6286 (097) 57 6281

GRALYN CELLARS C-C
Caves Road
Willyabrup via Cowaramup 6284

GREEN VALLEY NR
2 Cornwall Street
Swanbourne 6016 (09) 384 3131

HUNTS FOXHAVEN ESTATE NR
Canal Rocks Road
Yallingup 6282 (097) 55 2232

LENTON BRAE C-C
Caves Road
Willyabrup 6280
(097) 55 6255

MORRISONS DC-DC
Harmans Mill Road
Willyabrup via Cowaramup 6284
(097) 55 6234

MOSS BROTHERS NR
Caves Road
Willyabrup 6280 (097) 55 6290

WOODLANDS CB-C
Cnr Caves Road and Metricup Road
Willyabrup via Cowaramup 6284
(09) 294 1869 (home)
(097) 55 6226 (vineyard).

WOODY NOOK WINES B-B
Metricup Road
Metricup 6280

WRIGHTS C-C
Harmans South Road
Cowaramup 6284 (097) 55 5314

FACING PAGE: The all pervasive beauty of Margaret River; Leeuwin Estate Cabernet Sauvignon.   *ABOVE: The geometric patterns of a tapestry (Willespie).*

WESTERN AUSTRALIA

PERTH HILLS
AND SURROUNDS

The Perth Hills is not only Australia's newest wine region, but its smallest: it boasts a mere 25 hectares of vines and eight wineries, most of which produce less than 1000 cases of wine a year. It is situated in the Darling Ranges, 30 kilometres east of Perth, and although the vignerons have now decided otherwise, the region is still officially called the Darling Ranges.

The vineyards are established at an altitude of between 150 and 410 metres; this elevation means that the climate, while still warm, is markedly cooler than that of the Swan Valley. Because of its complex, tightly-folded, hilly topography there is substantial mesoclimatic variation, and the HDD figures vary from 1550 to 1800 across a relatively small distance. The rainfall (which is winter dominant) is much higher than that of the Swan Valley at around 1200 millimetres.

It is a very pretty region, with constantly changing vistas. The exotic native plant vegetation grows in rich profusion: Western Australia was given far more than its fair share by nature, and this is shown to full advantage in the Perth Hills, with patches of introduced exotics from Europe and elsewhere adding an unexpected contrast near streams and in home gardens.

The soils are principally red and brown duplex, with some more gravelly patches. They are not ideal soils for the summer drought and heat which occurs in some (though not all) years, and drip irrigation is needed to guard against defoliation and stress. Birds — silvereyes — can cause substantial crop losses in years when alternative food sources, notably from the flowering gums, are not available.

Cabernet Sauvignon and Chardonnay are the two dominant varieties, and both do well. Darlington Vineyard showed just what could be achieved with Chardonnay in its 1989 wine, and with Cabernet Sauvignon in its 1988 vintage. Piesse Brook produced a lovely Cabernet Shiraz in the same year, while Scarp Valley makes pleasant Hermitage. I have no reservations about the suitability of these varieties, nor for that matter about the suitability of Semillon or Sauvignon Blanc (particularly when the two are blended). I am less

convinced that Gewurztraminer or Pinot Noir should be grown. This is a pity, because Peter Fimmel of Hainault — a tireless ambassador for the region, proprietor of its largest winery, and with a deep knowledge of and interest in all aspects of wine — has directed much of his energy towards these two varieties.

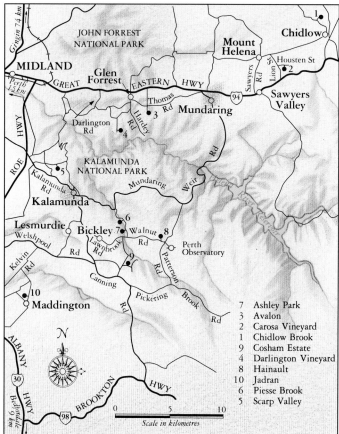

AUSTRALASIAN WINE REGIONS
1980 – 1990

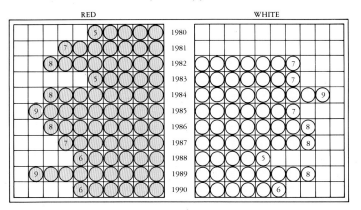

Map legend:

7 Ashley Park
3 Avalon
2 Carosa Vineyard
1 Chidlow Brook
9 Cosham Estate
4 Darlington Vineyard
8 Hainault
10 Jadran
6 Piesse Brook
5 Scarp Valley

PRINCIPAL GRAPE VARIETIES

Cabernet Sauvignon, 9.5 ha	*Gewurztraminer, 1.0 ha*
Chardonnay, 6.0 ha	*Shiraz, 1.0 ha*
Semillon, 3.2 ha	*Verdelho, 0.4 ha*
Merlot, 2.1 ha	*Cabernet Franc, 0.3 ha*
Pinot Noir, 1.6 ha	*Rhine Riesling, 0.2 ha*

FACING PAGE: Darlington Estate Chardonnay vines produce one of the best wines of the region.

ABOVE: Traminer budburst.

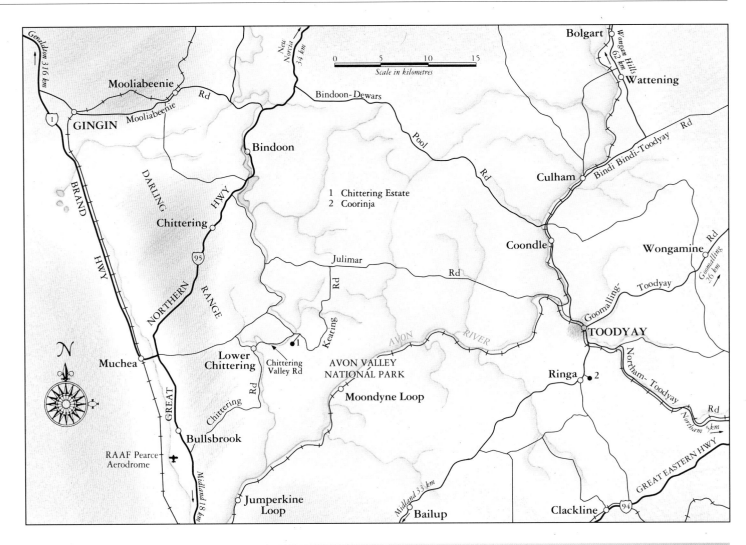

1 Chittering Estate
2 Coorinja

ABOVE: *The upper vineyard at Chittering Estate enjoys the highest altitude of any West Australian vineyard.*

WINERIES OF PERTH HILLS AND SURROUNDS

CHITTERING ESTATE   B-B
Chittering Valley Road
Lower Chittering 6084 (09) 571 8144
Established   1982
Winemaker   Steven Schapera
Production   2000 cases
Principal Wines   Semillon/Sauvignon Blanc,
Chardonnay and Cabernet Sauvignon/Merlot.
Best Vintages   Too recent to assess. If
ambition and dedication can create great wine,
then Chittering Estate will produce it. With the
financial backing of Perth seafood entrepreneur
George Kailis, viticultural advice from leading
eastern states consultant Di Davidson, and the
quiet — even shy — determination of Steven
Schapera, this most beautifully situated and
handsomely equipped winery has everything
going for it. It seems that wine style is yet to
achieve coherence, with the concentrated and
tannic Cabernet Sauvignon Merlot superior to
the somewhat chalky/hessiany white wines.

DARLINGTON VINEYARD   BA-BA
Lot 39, Nelson Road
Glen Forrest 6071   (09) 299 6268
Established   1983
Winemakers   Balt Van der Meer
Production   15,000 cases
Principal Wines   Chardonnay, Semillon,
Sauvignon Blanc, Gamay Beaujolais, Shiraz,
Cabernet Sauvignon, Merlot and Port.

Best Vintages   Too recent to assess.
Owner Balt Van der Meer made some superb
wines in 1989 with consultancy advice from Rob
Bowen (who has since departed to New
Zealand). The high quality rating is something
of an article of faith, and what is more, assumes
that those wines made it safely to bottle. I shall
watch the future of Darlington with more than a
little interest.

HAINAULT   CB-CB
Walnut Road
Bickley 6076   (09) 293 8339
Established   1980
Winemaker   Peter Fimmel

Production   1500 cases
Principal Wines   Chardonnay, Gewurztraminer, Semillon, Pinot Noir and Cabernet Merlot.
Best Vintages   W 1984, '86, '87, '89
                       R 1984, '87, '88, '89
Peter Fimmel is a tireless ambassador for the
Perth Hills in particular and for wine in general.
His background as a biochemist gives him a
basic grounding in both viticulture and
winemaking, and he applies himself to both
with great zeal. Wine quality is variable, and I
remain to be convinced that he has chosen the
best varieties for the district.

B I C K L E Y
PERTH HILLS • WESTERN AUSTRALIA
ESTATE BOTTLED • 75 CL • PRESERVATIVE (220) ADDED • 12.2% ALC/VOL
HAINAULT VINEYARD WALNUT RD BICKLEY 6076 W.A.

OTHER WINERIES

ASHLEY PARK   NR
284 Aldersyde Road
Bickley 6076 (09) 293 1451

AVALON   NR
Lot 156 Bailey Road
Glen Forrest 6071 (09) 298 8049

CAROSA VINEYARD   NR
Lot 3, Houston Street,
Mount Helena 6555 (09) 572 1603

CHIDLOW BROOK   NR
Lot 318, Lakeview Road
Chidlo 6556 (09) 572 4021

COSHAM ESTATE   NR
4 Giles Road
Lesmurdie 6076 (09) 291 6514

PIESSE BROOK   B-A
Lot 731, Aldersyde Road
Bickley 6076 (09) 386 7872

SCARP VALLEY   C-B
6 Robertson Road
Gooseberry Hill 6076 (09) 454 5748

ABOVE: Chittering Estate Winery and cellar door sales: a unique ambience.

TOP: Francesca Van der Meer among the Cabernet vines at Darlington Estate.

WESTERN AUSTRALIA

SOUTH-WEST
COASTAL PLAIN

The South-west Coastal Plain is surely the largest (perhaps longest is the better term) wine region in the world. It stretches 150 kilometres from the western outskirts of Perth down to the south-west coastal town of Bunbury. The softening influence of the always-nearby Indian Ocean notwithstanding, the climate varies significantly, being much warmer at the northern end than at the southern end. There the heat summation is around 1740 and slightly warmer than that of the nearby Margaret River; Bunbury has an MJT of 22°C.

The unifying influence is the unique soil, the fine grey tuart sands which all the vineyards share. These have the remarkable characteristic of being impassable to conventional cars when dry, but driveable after rain. They take their name from the massive tuart gum trees which they (sometimes insecurely) support: the extremely free-draining nature of the soils means that the roots of the gums tend to spread out saucer-like near the surface, and windstorms can wreak a heavy toll. This free-draining character also means that drip irrigation is essential to counterbalance the very dry summer months: the winter bias of the Swan Valley, Margaret River and South-west Coastal Plain is the most extreme in Australia.

So far the most impressive wines have come from the southern end, with Capel Vale very much in the ascendancy. It, however, has steadily increased its spread of vineyard sources, just for good measure extending into the Lower Great Southern region more than the somewhat closer Margaret River district. The move has been very successful: Capel Vale regularly produces Rhine Riesling and

PRINCIPAL WINE STYLES

CHARDONNAY
Produced by Capel Vale, Leschenault, Baldivis Estate and Paul Conti, Chardonnay comes in a Joseph's coat of many colours, attesting once again to the versatility and flexibility of the variety. That of Capel Vale can be almost searing in its pungency and intensity, with strong grapefruit flavours; that of Leschenault much finer and more restrained, although some of the same characters are present. That of Paul Conti is rich and buttery, that of Baldivis Estate is at the opposite end of the spectrum, almost to the point of attenuation — although their young vines may be partly responsible.

CABERNET SAUVIGNON
With the exception of the robust wines of Capel Vale, the Cabernets tend to be rather fine and delicate, with soft tannins and cherry/red fruit flavours. Peel Estate, Paul Conti and Thomas Wines have produced some attractive wines over the years, but not of the same style or intensity as those of the Margaret River or Lower Great Southern area.

SHIRAZ
This follows the pattern set by Cabernet Sauvignon, tending to the soft, elegant style exemplified by the best wines of Peel Estate. Paul Conti Mariginiup Hermitage, too, is a softly seductive wine with its core of cherry and mint fruit.

RHINE RIESLING
Rhine Riesling is the virtual sole preserve of Capel Vale, which does quite magical things with the wine, matching the intensity of its Chardonnay, and at times exceeding it. It has more affinity with the Rieslings of Mount Barker in the Lower Great Southern region than with those of the Margaret River, and at its best is among the top half dozen Rhine Rieslings in Australia.

AUSTRALASIAN WINE REGIONS
1980 – 1990

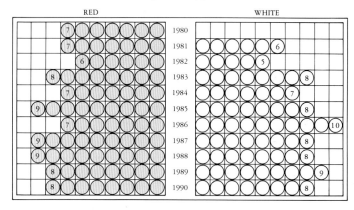

Year	RED	WHITE
1980	7	
1981	7	6
1982	6	5
1983	8	8
1984	7	7
1985	9	8
1986	7	10
1987	9	8
1988	9	8
1989	8	9
1990	8	8

*FACING PAGE: **Minimally pruned vines***

ABOVE: Life and death in the tuart forest between Capel and Busselton.

Chardonnay of the highest quality, and the recent appointment of the very experienced Rob Bowen as winemaker can only assist the ambitious expansion plans of Capel Vale owner Dr Peter Pratten.

Leschenault also backs up the potential of the south for high quality wine production, even if on a smaller scale. In its case, all the grapes are estate grown, helping cement district identity. It is likely this will focus primarily on white wines, with Capel Vale drawing a substantial part of its red wine requirements from the Lower Great Southern region.

In the north, Baldivis Estate is the newcomer concentrating on white wines, while Paul Conti is the general all-rounder and rock of ages. Here more than anywhere the sandy soil provides cohesion: the wineries are geographically spread far and wide, and the varying styles reflect differing making philosophies.

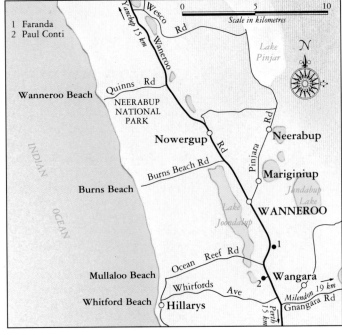

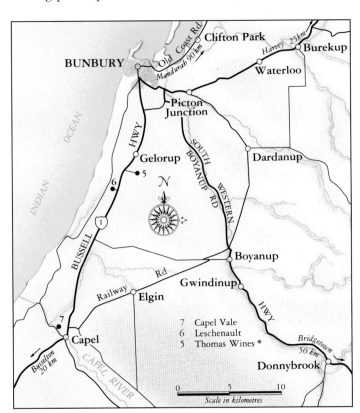

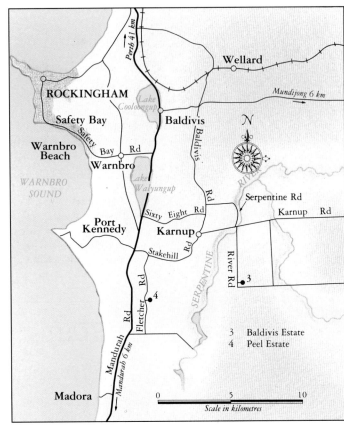

ABOVE: *Jackson, an Australian champion British Bulldog reputed to enjoy a glass of port, on guard at Leschenault.*

Two waves of immigration by Yugoslavs, the first at the turn of the century (principally from Dalmatia) and the second after the Second World War gave the Swan Valley two claims to fame. The first is that, most surprisingly, for a time it had more wineries in operation than either New South Wales or Victoria; the second is that, more obviously, it joined the Barossa Valley (German) and the Riverlands (Italian) as a significant ethnically-driven wine producing region.

It was not always so. Viticulture was started by English settlers, most notably Thomas Waters who dug the cellar at Olive Farm in 1830, thus giving this winery the distinction of being the oldest winemaking establishment in Australia to be in use today. Perhaps fittingly, it passed into the ownership of a Yugoslavian family in 1933, with present-day winemaker Ian Yurisich making some of the best Swan Valley wines of the present time.

The main link with the past comes through the colonial surgeon Dr John Ferguson who purchased part of a substantial land grant owned by three Indian Army Officers, the most senior of whom was Colonel Houghton. Even though Houghton never came to Australia, the property was named after him — likewise the Houghton wines of today (Western Australia's largest wine company).

The Swan Valley has always been a friendly place in which to grow vines and make wine. The completely flat alluvial river plain provides soils which are immensely deep and well drained (or are so in the prime vineyard locations) and the hot, dry summer means that grapes ripen easily and quickly. This was and is an ideal climate for table grapes (huge quantities were produced for export markets in bygone years) and for fortified wines. It was likewise suited to the production of bulk table wine which was sold to a large but uncritical local clientele, many of this clientele were of Yugoslavian origin, and they brought their own flagons, drums and sundry other containers to be filled up at their chosen winery.

The export market for table grapes has shrunk, the fortified wine market likewise, and third generation Yugoslavs have

entirely forgotten their cultural heritage and abandoned their parents' ways. Also the big wine companies of the eastern states have put cask wine on supermarket shelves for less than it costs local wineries to produce, let alone sell. And it must

THE REGION IN BRIEF

LOCATION AND ELEVATION
31°50'S 116°E
45 m

SUBREGIONS
Upper Swan, Herne Hill, Middle Swan, West Swan and Guildford.

CLIMATE
Whichever yardstick you take, the Swan Valley has an unequivocally hot climate. It has the highest mean January temperature (24.3°C) of any significant district. It has the lowest summer rainfall of any Australian region (107 mm), the lowest relative humidity (47 per cent) and the most sunshine hours per day (9.7 hours). Its heat summation (HDD) almost comes as an anticlimax at 2340. Its one risk is torrential rain which can come in February (before the vintage is finished) dumping all of the nominal 107 mm for the 6 months in a matter of days. It therefore follows that irrigation on all except the most favoured sites is essential.

SOIL
The best soils fall in the Gn2.15 and 2.25 subgroups of the red massive earths. These have brown or yellow-brown loamy sand surface soils passing gradually through lighter coloured (and slightly more clayey) subsurface soils, thence into porous sandy clay loam subsoils. This structure allows deep penetration by the vine roots to tap the reserves of the heavy winter rainfall, allowing low-yielding vines to survive without irrigation and produce high quality fruit. The other principal soil group is Dy5.81 (sandy mottled yellow duplex) which suffers from waterlogging at relatively shallow depths after the heavy winter rains, but then dries out rapidly, making irrigation absolutely essential.

HARVEST TIME
From the end of January for the sparkling wine base through to the end of February — a very early and usually very compressed vintage occasionally prolonged by rain.

PRINCIPAL GRAPE VARIETIES

Chenin Blanc, 58 ha	*Grenache, 75 ha*
Muscat Gordo Blanco, 36 ha	*Shiraz, 43 ha*
Verdelho, 15 ha	*Cabernet Sauvignon, 15 ha*
Muscadelle, 14 ha	TOTAL RED
Semillon, 13 ha	*(for winemaking), 140 ha*
TOTAL WHITE	
(for winemaking), 173 ha	

AUSTRALASIAN WINE REGIONS
1980 – 1990

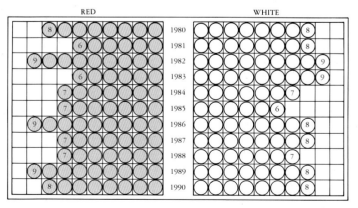

FACING PAGE: *Houghton's Swan Valley vineyard: the vine is as old as the post.*

12	Adriatic Wines
18	Banara Wines
20	Bassendean
9	Cobanov
1	Ellendale Estate Wines
3	Evans & Tate
2	Henley Park Wines
13	Highway Wines
14	Houghton Wines
15	Jane Brook Estate
6	Lamont Wines
8	Little River Wines
19	Olive Farm
17	Pinelli Wines
10	Revelry
16	Sandalford
7	Talijancich Wines
5	Twin Hills
11	Vindara
4	Westfield

be said that the big company cask wine is far easier to live with the morning after.

Inevitably, the ethnic base of the Swan Valley winemaking has declined steadily through the years, while the dominance of Houghton Wines has grown in leaps and bounds since Thomas Hardy acquired its parent (the English-based Emu Wine Company) in 1976. Sandalford continues on in a somewhat fitful fashion in terms of quality, and Evans and Tate, Westfield, Lamont and Talijancich Wines join Olive Farm in providing credible alternatives to the main contender, but Houghton (riding on the back of its charger, Houghton White Burgundy, Australia's largest selling white wine) is these days to all intents and purposes synonymous with the Swan Valley industry in most people's minds.

PRINCIPAL WINE STYLES

WHITE BURGUNDY

That Houghton White Burgundy, a generically named blend of three varieties – Chenin Blanc, Muscadelle (or Tokay) and Chardonnay – should be the principal wine style of a region as old, established and important as the Swan Valley might seem surprising until one finds that it is Australia's largest-selling white wine. Its style, its past, its present and its future are discussed at length at page 276, so I will pass on from here.

CHENIN BLANC

This variety dominates plantings in the Swan Valley, contributing roughly 25 per cent of the annual crush. Arguably, the Swan Valley is the one region in Australia in which this grape (and the wine it makes) rises above mediocrity. In the hot climate it produces a wine with a certain luscious richness, which responds well to bottle age, producing (as Jack Mann realised) an almost voluptuous White Burgundy style. Houghton has also shown what can be achieved with a 100 per cent varietal with the use of new oak, particularly if enhanced by bottle age. Olive Farm, Westfield, Jane Brook, Lamonts, and Moondah Brook Estate (a Houghton brand) have also produced some lovely honeyed wines from the variety.

CHARDONNAY

The plantings are still surprisingly small, but Westfield has produced some very good, buttery/peachy wines from it, sometimes with an almost Burgundian tang which comes from a measure of barrel ferment. For the time being, Houghton seems content to divert most of its Chardonnay into its White Burgundy.

VERDELHO

A traditional variety which was appreciated well before the eastern states vogue of the 1980s. Almost all of the best wineries produce a varietal wine from this grape, and are usually content to allow the honeyed/honeysuckle flavour free reign without introducing new oak.

SHIRAZ

Although it comes a distant second to Grenache in terms of hectares, this is the most important red wine grape in what is essentially white wine country. It produces a warm, fleshy wine in the hands of most makers: Evans and Tate (under its Gnangara brand name) has managed to invest it with a degree of elegance and style which other makers do not seem able to emulate.

CABERNET SAUVIGNON

Westfield, Olive Farm, Lamonts and Moondah Brook (to a lesser degree) produce respectable Cabernet Sauvignon, usually in a soft, dark chocolate-tinged mould, although Lamont sometimes contributes a note of astringency, particularly in its version which does not see oak. But without question the best manifestation and variety is in the form of Houghton's vivid (in colour, aroma and flavour) Cabernet Rosé. Year in, year out this is Australia's finest example of this wine style. Why we do not drink tens of thousands of cases of it every summer I will never know.

FACING PAGE: Ivan Gugic washing barrels at Houghton: after 35 years on the job, he doesn't need to be told how.

JACK MANN AND HOUGHTON

To the end of his long and happy life, Jack Mann extolled the virtues of the three Cs: cricket, Christianity and Chablis. Poor eyesight and frozen hips did not diminish his razor-sharp wit nor his essentially good humoured rapier tongue. In the 10 years before his death I met and talked with him at length on a number of occasions and count myself richer for having done so.

Jack Mann was of the old school, and unashamedly proud of it. His touchstones were many and colourful, but he believed in them absolutely: grapes should never be picked until the vine could support them no longer, and no wine was worthy of the name unless it could be diluted by an equal quantity of water without adversely affecting its flavour. 'Wine', he said, 'should be resplendent with generosity', and he made it in his own image.

Jack's father George was appointed winemaker at Houghton in 1920. Jack came west from the Barossa Valley 2 years later. In 1930 he succeeded his father as chief winemaker, and presided over the next 52 vintages, retiring in 1972.

In the years immediately prior to the Second World War he delighted in doing battle with Bill Chambers senior in the sherry classes at Royal Melbourne Show, although he was denied the pleasure of ever travelling to Melbourne to collect the Trophy in the years he came out on top.

It was in this time of fortified and heavy red table wine that he devised Houghton White Burgundy, a white table wine with the weight to do battle with those red and fortified wines. In the mid-1970s I shared in a bottle of 1944 Houghton White Burgundy (at least I think it was a 1944 wine) with an old yellow heart or grape-leaf shaped label, and which still had sweet fruit at its core. I can clearly remember drinking it in the late 1950s, and up until the mid-1960s it was the only Western Australian wine to be readily found on eastern states shelves. By that time it had adopted its distinctive blue striped label.

The wine that Jack built was made from more or less equal quantities of Tokay (as he called Muscadelle) and Chenin Blanc. The grapes were crushed by being passed through a butcher's meat mincer: every grape Jack Mann picked was treated that way. Given the very high sugar levels, a conventional crusher might have had problems in any event, but the maceration effect of the mincer also promoted the type of phenolic extraction which is these days achieved by skin contact (for Chardonnay and other White Burgundy types) before fermentation.

Mann's wine would then be heavily sulphured, and the cloudy juice fermented at ambient temperatures. It was an approach which worked very well. The opulence, weight and richness of the juice begged for a degree of harsh handling to pull it back into balance and give it shape.

Nor, on the other hand, did it need propping up with oak, and in that respect it conformed very much to the standards of its day. The changes came in the second half of the 1970s, sparked partly by Thomas Hardy's acquisition of Houghton (in 1976), partly by the white wine boom of the 1970s and partly by changes in the style and taste of Australian white wine generally.

I believe the changes to Houghton White Burgundy have been entirely beneficial. It may seem an extraordinary statement to make about Australia's largest selling table wine (with sales of around 150,000 cases a year in 1990), but it is quite certain the real quality of the wine is not understood or noticed by most of those who would consider themselves 'wine buffs'. For it is difficult to have one's cake and eat it (or one's wine and drink it). National best sellers are marketed to consumers on price, on store position and on the likes and dislikes of the mass wine market. Few such consumers want to read about wine or talk about wine: as a wise observer once said, 'The wine industry constantly overemphasises the consumer's desire to know and constantly underemphasises his/her palate'.

It is no doubt the consumer's ability to instinctively tell a good wine which has helped Houghton White Burgundy break another icon: to sell in volume, a white wine must have some residual sugar (or sweetness). Houghton White Burgundy has none, what it does have is smoothness, balance and just the right amount of fruit aroma and flavour.

That aroma and flavour is provided by a blend of Chenin Blanc (predominant), Chardonnay (increasing year by year), and Muscadelle. The introduction of Chardonnay in 1987 was done carefully, due to limitations on supply, but also common sense, meant that only a small percentage was included in the first year. Winemaker Peter Dawson was, and is, sensitive of the need to carefully monitor any change in style. The 1989 vintage had 15 per cent Chardonnay, and in Dawson's view (with which I agree) is the best wine yet.

It is not so many years since Lindemans Ben Ean Moselle was not only the number one seller, but dominated the Australian bottled wine market like no wine before or since. It is now out of the top ten, and seemingly dying a slow death. Will the same thing happen to Houghton White Burgundy?

The answer to that question is no, notwithstanding my personal belief (hotly disputed by marketing experts) that almost all mass-market wine brands have a limited life expectancy. The reasons for my faith in Houghton White Burgundy are first that it is a dry white wine (and not a sweet one); secondly, its perfect style positioning between the aromatic non-oaked wines such as Rhine Riesling on the one side and the opulent, oaked Chardonnays on the other; and thirdly its extraordinary ability to age in the bottle.

ABOVE: *The late Jack Mann, much loved and respected, was Houghton winemaker from 1930 to 1972.*

WINERIES OF THE SWAN VALLEY

EVANS AND TATE   B-B
Swan Street
Henley Brook 6055 (09) 296 4666
Established   1972
Winemakers   Bill Crappsley (chief wine-
maker) and Krister Jonsson (winemaker).
Production   5000 cases.
Principal Wines   High quality table wines
made from two vineyards: Redbrook inthe
Margaret River (see separate entry) and
Gnangara Estate in the Swan Valley. The latter
produces Gnangara Shiraz (a blend of 80%
Shiraz and 20% Cabernet Sauvignon); a wider
range of wines comes from Redbrook.
Best Vintages   R 1977, '82, '84, '87, '88
In 1975 an unknown and small winery in the
unfashionable and remote Swan Valley entered
its 1974 Gnangara Shiraz in the national show
ring. It won medals in the open classes at
Sydney, Canberra and Melbourne. The 1977
vintage of the same wine was the most successful
dry red table wine in the history of Australian
winemaking, winning 14 medals and two
trophies in capital city wine shows. But not only
were the wines excellent, so was the publicity
and marketing, and it not only brought Evans
and Tate to the forefront, but lifted the entire
image of the Swan Valley. Houghton has since
taken over much of the running, and the focus of
Evans and Tate's attention these days is on the
Margaret River, but its Gnangara Shiraz is a
lovely wine in good years.

HOUGHTON   A-A
Dale Road, Middle Swan 6055 (09) 274 5100
Established   1836
Winemaker   Peter Dawson.
Production   300,000 cases.
Principal Wines   A substantial range of
wines from a wide diversity of vineyard sources
ranging from the Swan Valley and nearby
Gingin, and from the Margaret River,
Manjimup and Mt Barker regions. At the top
come the show reserve releases, followed by the
gold reserve range, then the largest selling white

wine in Australia, Houghton White Burgundy,
and Australia's best Cabernet Rose. At the
bottom end price-wise come the Wildflower
Ridge range.
Best Vintages   W and R 1982, '83, '86,
                     '88, '89
The A-A rating may appear controversial, but
really it is hard to know how one could expect
more from a company of the size of Houghton,
and with a product range spanning the price
categories in the fashion it does. More
importantly still, Australia is indeed a lucky
country when its largest volume selling white
wine is of such quality, excellent in the year of
its release but repaying five to seven years
cellaring in the manner of a thoroughbred.

JANE BROOK ESTATE   CB-B
Toodyay Road
Middle Swan 6056 (09) 274 143
Established   1972
Winemaker   David Atkinson.
Production   10,000 cases.
Principal Wines   Wood Aged Chenin Blanc,
Chardonnay, Sauvignon Blanc, Late Harvest
Frontignac, Cabernet Merlot, Tawny Port,
Vintage Port, Liqueur Tokay, Liqueur Muscat
and Liqueur Verdelho.
Best Vintages   W and R 1983, '88, '89,
                     '90

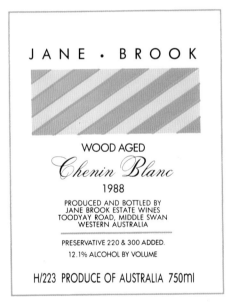

David and Beverley Atkinson have worked
tirelessly to promote Jane Brook Estate, and also
to improve the quality of its wines. In the past
few years that quality (and consistency) has
improved, thanks to some skilled consultancy
advice and to a move away from the all-pervasive
German oak which was the hallmark of earlier
vintages.

LAMONT WINES   B-B
Bisdee Road
Millendon 6056 (09) 296 4485
Established   1978
Winemaker   Corin Lamont.
Production   3300 cases.
Principal Wines   White Burgundy, Chard-
onnay, Cabernet Rose, Cabernet Sauvignon,
Vintage Port and a marvellous and exclusive
fortified wine called Navera, the latter made in
minuscule quantities.
Best Vintages   W and R 1986,'88,'90

The legacy left by the late Jack Mann of
Houghton White Burgundy was not his only
gift: his daughter Corin Lamont founded Lamont
Wines in 1978 to continue the winemaking
tradition and methods of her father. These are
wines made in Jack's image, resplendent in their
generosity (as he would say).

MOONDAH BROOK ESTATE   B-B
Mooliabeenie Road
Gingin 6503 (09) 279 4944
Established   1968
Winemaker   Paul Lapsley.
Production   30,000 cases.
Principal Wines   Verdelho, Chenin Blanc,
Chardonnay and Cabernet Sauvignon.
Best Vintages   W 1980, '83, '87, '88, '89
                     R 1981, '83, '86, '88, '89
The Moondah Brook wines are models of
consistency; every now and then a superb aged
version bobs up in the show ring (such as the
1983 Wood Matured Chenin Blanc) which
shows what a little patience can do. The
Verdelho, the Chenin Blanc and more recently
the Chardonnay are all wines to be approached
with confidence.

OLIVE FARM   B-B
77 Great Eastern Highway
South Guildford 6055 (09) 277 2989
Established   1829
Winemaker   Ian Yurisich.
Production   5000 cases.
Principal Wines   Verdelho, Chenin Blanc,
Semillon, Late Harvest Semillon, Chardonnay,

ABOVE: The old C.W. Fergusson homestead at Houghton.   *ABOVE RIGHT: Lamont Winery, where the spirit of Jack Mann lives on.*

Cabernet Shiraz, Cabernet Sauvignon, Oloroso Sherry, Old Madeira, Vintage Port and Tawny Port.
Best Vintages No information available.
Olive Farm is the oldest winery in Australia to have remained in continuous use since its establishment in 1829 (or 1830 — this was the year in which Thomas Waters dug his wine cellar, the remains of which can be still seen today). Under the skilled hand of Ian Yurisich, wine quality is very good indeed, even if he is singularly uninclined to in any way promote Olive Farm wines or answer correspondence from pestilential wine journalists.

SANDALFORD   C-CB
West Swan Road
Caversham 6055 (09) 274 5922
Established 1840
Winemakers Christian Morlaes (Managing Director),Tony Roe and Candy Jonsson.
Production 5000 cases.
Principal Wines Chenin/Verdelho,Semillon/Chardonnay, Matilda Rose, Caversham Estate Cabernet Sauvignon and Zinfandel, Liqueur Port, Liqueur ƒSandalera and St.Nicolas Tawny Port.
Best Vintages W and R 1987, '88, '89.
The date of establishment of Sandalford really depends on which view one takes of history. While grapes have been grown on the property since it was granted to John Septimus Roe in 1840, winemaking only became a commercial venture after the second World War, and the corporate structure presently existing came into being in 1970. So you pay your money and you take your choice. More relevant is the recent revitalisation of winemaking, which has seen quality improve significantly, even if a few ghosts (of sulphide) of the past still bob up from time to time.

TALIJANCICH WINES   B-B
121 Hyem Road
Herne Hill 6056 (09) 296 4289
Established 1932
Winemakers Peter and James Talijancich.
Production Not for publication.
Principal Wines Wooded Verdelho, Wooden Semillon, Grenache Rose, Late Picked Verdelho, Shiraz, Vintage Port, Liqueur Tokay, Liqueur Muscat, Vintage Port and Tawny Port.

Best Vintages W and R 1987, '88, '89.
Formerly called Peter's Wines and best known for some outstanding reserves of old fortified wines (muscat, tokay and tawny port), Talijancich has now made a concerted move into table wine production. With consultancy advice, a range of truly excellent wines were made in 1989; I hope the momentum continues.

WESTFIELD   B-BA
Cnr Memorial Avenue and Great Northern Highway, Baskerville 6056 (09) 296 4356
Established 1922
Winemaker John Kosovich
Production 3500 cases.
Principal Wines Chardonnay, Verdelho, Chenin Blanc, Semillon, Cabernet Blanc, Riesling, Shiraz, Merlot and Cabernet Sauvignon.
Best Vintages W 1984, '86, '87, '89.
R 1985, '86, '87, '89.
John Kosovich is one of the quiet achievers of the Swan Valley, a region in which his family's roots go as deep as those of the vines. He would never contemplate leaving it, but I have often speculated how good his wines might be if he moved to an area such as Coonawarra. The quality extends across the range of both white and red wines, with the Chardonnay frequently exceptional, the Verdelho in close pursuit.

OTHER WINERIES

ADRIATIC WINES   NR
Great Northern Highway
Herne Hill 6056 (09) 296 4518

BANARA WINES   NR
Banara Road
Caversham 6055 (09) 279 6823

BASSENDEAN   NR
147 West Road
Bassendean 6054 (09) 276 1734

BONANNELLA & SONS   NR
3 Pinjar Road
Wanneroo 6065 (09) 405 1084

COBANOV   NR
Lot 1, Stock Road
Herne Hill 6056 (09) 296 4210

COORINJA   NR
Box 99, Toodyay Road
Toodyay 6566 (096) 26 2280

ELLENDALE ESTATE WINES   C-CB
18 Ivanhoe Street
Bassendean 6054 (09) 279 1007

GLENORA WINES   NR
Lot 38, Nelson Road
Glen Forrest WA 6071 (09) 378 2000

HENLEY PARK WINES   C-C
Swan Street
West Swan 6055 (09) 296 4328

HIGHWAY WINES   NR
Great Northern Highway
Herne Hill 6056 (09) 296 4353

JADRAN WINES   NR
445 Reservoir Road
Orange Grove 6109 (09) 459 1110

LAKEVILLE VINEYARDS   NR
1921 Albany Highway
Maddington 6109 (09) 459 1637

LITTLE RIVER WINES   C-CB
Cnr West Swan and Forrest Roads
West Swan 6055 (09) 296 4462

PINELLI WINES   NR
8 Bennett Street
Caversham, 6055 (09) 279 3805

REVELRY   NR
200 Argyle Street
Herne Hill 6056 (09) 296 4271

TWIN HILLS   NR
Great Northern Highway
Baskerville 6056 (09) 296 4272

VINDARA   NR
Great Northern Highway
Herne Hill 6065 (09) 296 4556

ABOVE LEFT: Olive Farm, established in 1830.

ABOVE RIGHT: John Kosovich of Westfield talking to a young Chardonnay vine; viticulture is in his blood.

CANBERRA DISTRICT

CANBERRA

It has always struck me as a wry commentary on the unreality of the political hothouse of Canberra that none of the Canberra district vignerons should actually have a vineyard in Canberra, and even more appropriate that none is a politician. The reason for the territorial exclusion is essentially a pragmatic one, however much the concept might have pleased Lewis Carroll: freehold does not exist within the Australian Capital Territory, and land used for anything other than housing, commerce or industry is liable to be rezoned (and the lease terminated) at short notice.

So the vignerons cluster just outside the Territory's borders in two groups: in the Yass Valley around Murrumbateman, and along the shores of Lake George. It was indeed within a few hundred metres of the edge of Lake George that Dr Edgar Rick planted the first vines in 1971, and others — mainly from the scientific community, most with Doctorates

of Philosophy to their credit — quickly followed in his wake. By 1974 the Canberra District Vignerons Association had been founded, and it now has over 15 members.

Overall, growth has been steady rather than spectacular, and the general quality of the wines has been equally modest. This has been due to three main reasons: first, the virtual absence of qualified winemakers; secondly, the initial lack of understanding of the particular problems posed by the Canberra climate and *terroir*; and thirdly, the inherent difficulty of small scale winemaking of white wines.

The lack of technical expertise has been partially overcome by the use of consultants (notably at Doonkuna Estate), partially by skills learnt on the winery floor (chiefly at Lark

12	Affleck Vineyard *
1	Benfield Estate
11	Brindabella Hills
13	Brook Creek Winery *
6	Clonakilla
5	Doonkuna Estate
2	Helm's Wines
8	Jeir Creek Wines
4	Kyeema *
10	Lake George *
14	Lark Hill
16	Madew Wines
3	The Murrumbateman Winery
17	Simons Wines
15	Warralonga
9	Westering Vineyard *
7	Yass Valley Wines

THE REGION IN BRIEF

LOCATION AND ELEVATION
35°0'S 149°20'E
500 m

SUBREGIONS
Lake George, Murrumbateman, Yass and Bungendore.

CLIMATE
With its extremely continental climate, the Canberra District shows just how inadequate a single index of climate can be. If one looks purely at the heat summation (HDD) of 1410 it would lead one to believe that this is a genuinely cool region, but it is not — or at least, its wine styles do not suggest it is. A hot dry summer (but with cool nights) gives way to a cool autumn, with harvest not infrequently interrupted by significant rain. The major viticultural limitation lies in the very dry spring and summer months. Spring frost has been a problem too, but can be largely avoided with appropriate site selection.

SOIL
The soils are principally in the hard red duplex group, with brownish clay loam surface soils which are usually shallow. The subsoils are not particularly water-retentive, adding to the need for irrigation.

HARVEST TIME
From mid-March for the earliest ripening varieties through to the end of April for dry wines and early May for late-harvested Rhine Riesling.

PRINCIPAL VARIETIES

Chardonnay, 16.28 ha	*Cabernet Sauvignon, 14.93 ha*
Rhine Riesling, 14.34 ha	*Merlot/Cabernet Franc, 7.45 ha*
Traminer, 5.07 ha	*Pinot Noir, 7.34 ha*
Sauvignon Blanc, 4.05 ha	*Shiraz, 4.45 ha*
Semillon, 3.4 ha	TOTAL REDS, 36.38 ha
TOTAL WHITES, 43.59 ha	

PREVIOUS PAGES: *Brindabella Hills Pinot Noir.*

Hill), although this has been supplemented by the undertaking of external studies at the oenological course at Charles Sturt University, and partially by the acute intelligence and high scientific qualifications of many of the winemakers who — strictly speaking — are unqualified in the making of wine. But it has to be said that there is still a long way to go for many of the wineries.

The climatic question has been better addressed: it took a long time for the vignerons to realise to what extent the summer drought made irrigation essential, and — having recognised the problem — to do something about it. The other learning curve was in respect to the danger of spring frost in sites with poor or non-existent air drainage. Taken together, these problems reduced yields to subeconomic levels without providing increased quality.

The third problem is in some ways an extension of the first, but is by no means unique to Canberra. It is a simple fact of life that white wine is much harder to make in small quantities than is red wine: it requires much greater discipline and attention to detail, and requires much more sophisticated plant and equipment.

For all that, the overall quality and range of the Canberra District wines has improved greatly in the last decade, and the best wines — though few in number — can acquit themselves with honour in open competition with those of the rest of Australia's small wineries.

PRINCIPAL WINE STYLES

CABERNET SAUVIGNON
Overall, this appears to be the variety most suited to the idiosyncratic Canberra climate, although the best example (that of Lark Hill) is usually blended with Merlot, and others are blended with Shiraz. Helm's, Jeir Creek Wines and Affleck Vineyard also contribute wines of merit, if of varying style, ranging from austere and leafy to rich, dark and chocolatey. As with all varieties, the varied climatic conditions which prevail from one vintage to the next (and a certain element of unpredictability in the wineries) make generalisations unusually hazardous.

RHINE RIESLING
Once again, Lark Hill demonstrates just what can be achieved with this variety, particularly when it is made in a traditional Australian spatlese style, ie non-botrytised. The lime juice characters of both bouquet and palate are intensified, and that extra bit of sweetness fleshes out the palate. All of which is not intended to denigrate the crisp gently toasty, dry Rieslings made by Doonkuna Estate, and Lark Hill.

CHARDONNAY
As I say in the introduction to this chapter, it is not easy for small wineries to make high quality white table wines. But once the basic technique is mastered, a variety such as Chardonnay seldom fails to do well. Doonkuna Estate provides vivid evidence of this, with Lark Hill and Westering Vineyard in solid support.

SAUVIGNON BLANC
Sauvignon Blanc is the virtual monopoly of Doonkuna Estate, which consistently makes a fresh, lively wine, with attractive lemony/spice oak lending well-judged support to the fruit.

PINOT NOIR
Statistically an important grape, but the vast majority of the wines made to date have shown little or no varietal character. One must conclude the climate is too hot or, if not too hot, simply unsuited to the variety.

AUSTRALASIAN WINE REGIONS
1980 – 1990

Year	RED	WHITE
1980	7	7
1981	8	8
1982	7	7
1983	7	7
1984	5	5
1985	7	7
1986	8	8
1987	7	7
1988	9	10
1989	5	6
1990	8	8

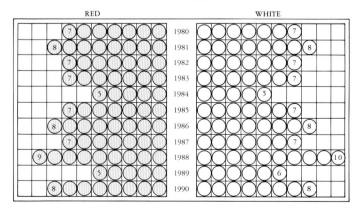

ABOVE: Not a Mexican, but Dr David Carpenter of Lark Hill.

WINE AND THE WEEKEND VIGNERON

It is an insidious thing, wine. It creeps up on you, casting its spell like a drug — but not the sort of drug the neoprohibitionists would have us believe it is. It all starts so innocently: the first glass of wine one drinks may well have been diluted with 50 per cent of water by a solicitous parent, and the taste — even so diluted — will have been strange and sour. Some take to the taste more quickly than others; until they reached the age of 18 or so, my children treated the whole subject with bored indifference, having the occasional sip or two to please me, and plainly not particularly enjoying it. (I hasten to add that this is no longer the case.)

Some will go through life drinking wine when it is offered, even conforming to the expectations of society by purchasing bottles for special events or dinner parties, but otherwise ignoring it. Others will regularly drink wine with meals but never wander beyond the confines of Chateau Cardboard. Some will suddenly realise there is something quite special — magical even — in the taste of each wine they drink, and find themselves fascinated by its infinite variation. The latter group will then split into two: those who are happy to enjoy wine for its own sake, and those who want to learn more about it.

A few will become so engrossed that they will conceive the idea of establishing their own vineyard. I was one such: along with two close friends (lawyers like myself), I bought a 4 hectare block at the end of 1970, and in the winter of 1971 we planted our first hectare of grapes at Brokenwood. The idea was simple enough, we all led busy professional lives in Sydney, and the vineyard was intended as therapy, a release from workday pressures. Everyone, we said, should have an interest outside his or her professional career to provide a balanced lifestyle.

It is hard to remember just how idyllic we thought vineyard ownership would be, but any illusions were quickly dispelled with the physical agony involved in planting that first hectare. But we were young (well, 30 or so) and that memory quickly faded as the first tiny green shoots appeared, and as each weekend passed the vineyard started to miraculously take shape. The first phase of addiction was complete.

Then, only 12 months later in the spring of 1983 came the next miracle: as the leaves on our 15 month old vines unfolded, tiny flowers appeared, and, within a few weeks, the first grapes were formed. We witnessed their growth, their change of colour; we worried about hail, lack of rain, too much rain, caterpillars and fungal diseases. But by the end of January it became clear we were going to harvest one tonne of Shiraz, and — a few weeks later — half a tonne of Cabernet Sauvignon.

We had always intended to make the wine, but this is the witching point for many vignerons who start off thinking they will be content simply to grow grapes, realising the time, the capital cost and the expertise required to make wine will be beyond them. The heartbreak involved in selling the grapes and seeing them taken away to the anonymity of someone else's winery however, is often all too much. Somehow, some way, you realise, you must make the wine, or — at the very least — have it made for you. The second and terminal phase of addiction for us was now well under way, with death, bankruptcy or divorce the only probable cures.

For it is one thing to grow grapes, yet another thing to make wine, and yet another thing to successfully market it. The first few vintages seldom present much of a problem as, unless you are very lucky (we were), the first year or two are likely to be what is sometimes euphemistically described as experimental: the bottles, replete with handwritten labels, are given away to friends, relatives (even enemies) with humorous instructions for use as weed killers.

Then come the first few commercial releases, and for a variety of motives (and quite possibly with a range of emotions), your friends, workmates and relatives will dutifully buy a case or two. But the novelty soon wears off, and your still unbounded enthusiasm for the vineyard (as yet untempered by the cynicism of your bank manager) has no doubt seen production go up each year as more and more vines are planted and come into production.

It is here that the divorce cure may come into play. More and more time has to be spent in the vineyard; vintage ceases to be a bit of fun and instead becomes a month of fierce and unremitting labour, with sleep a forgotten luxury. You have to find new and better ways of selling the wine, which likewise involves much more time. The purchase of a new car has to be postponed because the winery absolutely has to have a new press. The bank manager ceases to be your best friend and is quite unmoved by the cases of wine delivered (free of course) to his doorstep. Your children refuse point blank to come to the vineyard, and friends suddenly have social calendars brimful of engagements which stretch long into the future. The marital ultimatum is delivered, and the choice must be made.

Obviously, it does not always go this way. For the Canberra district vignerons it has not (or at least so far as I know it has not), and the original plan — a second interest outside their respective chosen professions — remains largely intact. A few have sold out, but most have happily persevered, bolstered by three advantages. First, their vineyards and wineries are but a short drive from Canberra, bringing that captive market of potential buyers to their cellar door sales doorstep. Secondly, although none of the proprietors were qualified winemakers when they started their operations, almost all had impressive scientific backgrounds which enabled them to avoid major winemaking disasters. Thirdly, most have been content to limit the scale of their operations and accept the fact that profits would be both distant in time and modest in scope.

For at the end of the day, the weekend vigneron has to decide whether he or she has a hobby or a business. If it is a hobby, it is likely to cost money (a fact increasingly known to the Commissioner of Taxation) but it will not unduly disrupt one's lifestyle. If it is a business, it may end up consuming all involved — sometimes happily (and eventually profitably), sometimes not so happily. But in the best Australian tradition, you can at least console yourself with the knowledge that you had a go.

ABOVE: *The sight of a flourishing vineyard has enticed many a wine-lover to turn vigneron.*

WINERIES OF THE CANBERRA DISTRICT

BRINDABELLA HILLS WINERY   NR
Woodgrove Close via Hall
2618   (062) 302 583
Established   1989
Winemaker   Roger Harris
Production   800 cases
Principal Wines   Rhine Riesling, Chardonnay, Sauvignon Blanc, Pinot Noir, Cabernet (Bordeaux blend), most produced from grapes grown on the Hercynia and Nioka Ridge vineyards in the Hilltops region of New South Wales.
Best Vintages   Too recent to assess.
The first wines made by distinguished wine research scientist Roger Harris were magnificent in cask, but some failed to make the transition to bottle, showing strong aldehyde, presumably from inadequate sulphur dioxide. Hopefully, these were sheer aberrations; certainly there is enormous potential for quality.

DOONKUNA ESTATE   BA-A
Barton Highway
Murrumbateman 2582 (06) 227 5885
Established   1973
Winemaker   Sir Brian Murray

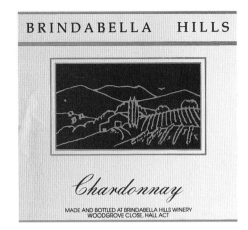

Production   1200 cases
Principal Wines   Rhine Riesling, Chardonnay, Sauvignon Blanc, Pinot Noir, Shiraz and Cabernet Sauvignon.
Best Vintages   W and R 1987, '88
With the aid of skilled consultancy advice, Doonkuna Estate (under the ownership and direction of retired Victorian Governor, Sir Brian Murray) has produced some outstanding wines, with a classically restrained, almost Chablis-like Chardonnay and an immaculately oaked Fumé Blanc; Rhine Riesling, in a full blown style, has also appealed. The red wines have been more variable, particularly the Pinot Noir, but wines such as the 1988 Cabernet Sauvignon are beyond reproach.

HELM'S   DB-C
Butt's Road
Murrumbateman 2582 (06) 227 5536
Established   1974
Winemaker   Ken Helm
Production   1400 cases
Principal Wines   Rhine Riesling, Traminer, Chardonnay, Müller-Thurgau, Cabernet Sauvignon and Hermitage.
Best Vintages   W 1988
                       R 1983, '84, '86, '88
Retired CSIRO (Commonwealth Scientific and Industrial Research Organisation) scientist Ken Helm is a tireless worker, and promoter, of his wines and of those of the Canberra district. He is also one of the few to regard winemaking as a commercial venture, and to expect a financial return from it. Wines such as his 1986 Cabernet Sauvignon can only help his efforts, but white wine quality in particular seems to me to fall behind current commercial standards.

LAKE GEORGE   CB-B
Federal Highway
Collector 2581 (048) 48 0039 or (062) 48 6302
Established   1971
Winemaker   Dr Edgar Riek
Production   550 cases
Principal Wines   Chardonnay, Pinot Noir, Semillon, Cabernet Sauvignon and Merlot.
Best Vintages   W and R 1986, '87, '88

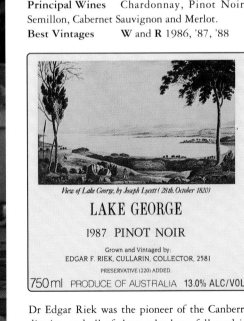

Dr Edgar Riek was the pioneer of the Canberra district, and all of those who have followed in his footsteps owe much to his ever-inquiring mind. His Lake George winery continues to be a

ABOVE: *Jean-Michel Garcian of the Loire Valley, France, gaining vintage experience (the hard way) at Doonkuna.*

somewhat off-beat wine research facility, with Dr Riek constantly trying new ideas, and equally persisting in eschewing safe, commercial approaches to winemaking and style.

LARK HILL   A-A
RMB 281, Gundaroo Road
Bungendore 2621 (062) 38 1393
Established   1978
Winemakers   Dr Dave Carpenter,
                      Sue Carpenter
Production   1200 cases
Principal Wines   Chardonnay, Rhine Riesling,
Semillon, Cabernet Sauvignon/Merlot blends,

Pinot Noir. All wines made from estate-grown or Canberra district grapes. Botrytis styles in some years.
Best Vintages   W 1988, '89
                         R 1987, '88
Lark Hill is clearly the leading winery in the Canberra district, consistently producing wines of quality on a par with the best of the small wineries of better-known regions. Particularly outstanding are the late harvest Rhine Rieslings, with pungent lime aroma and flavour; some excellent Chardonnay, with a beguiling touch of spicy oak, and minty/leafy Cabernet Merlot are also strongly recommended.

OTHER WINERIES

AFFLECK VINEYARD   C-CB
RMB 244, Gundaroo Road
Bungendore 2621 (062) 36 9276

BENFIELD ESTATE   DC-C
Fairy Hole Road
Yass 2582 (062) 26 2427

BROOK CREEK WINERY   NR
RMB 209, Brooks Road
Bungendore 2621 (062) 36 9221

CLONAKILLA   C-CB
Crisps Lane off Gundaroo Road
Murrumbateman 2582
(062) 51 1938 (after hours)

JEIR CREEK WINES   CA-CA
Gooda Creek Road
Murrumbateman 2582
062) 58 8292 (after hours)
or (06) 227 5999 (winery)

KYEEMA   C-C
PO Box 282
Belconnen 2616 (062) 54 7557
or (062) 49 9392(business hours)

MADEW WINES   C-C
Furlong Road
Queanbeyan 2620 (062) 97 2742

THE MURRUMBATEMAN WINERY NR
Barton Highway
Murrumbateman 2582 (062) 27 5584

SIMONS WINE   D-DC
RMB 274, Badgery Road
Burra Creek 2620 (062) 36 3216

WARRALONGA   NR
Sutton Road
Queanbeyan 2620 (062) 97 8898

WESTERING VINEYARD   B-B
Federal Highway
Collector 2581 (062) 95 8075

YASS VALLEY WINES   NR
Crisps Lane
Murrumbateman 2582 (062) 27 1592

ABOVE: Chardonnay in the Australian bush.

ABOVE RIGHT: Dr Dave Carpenter of Lark Hill tests the fruits of his labour.

QUEENSLAND

GRANITE BELT

Queensland is the forgotten State. According to the Australian Bureau of Statistics, it had 83 hectares of vineyard in bearing in 1989, compared with Tasmania's 62 hectares: both of these figures are understatements (because the Bureau does not collate figures for establishments with an estimated value of agricultural operations (EVAO) of less than $25,000) but the comparison remains valid. It is true Tasmania had 42 hectares coming into bearing compared with Queensland's 4 hectares, but on the other hand Queensland has a very substantial table grape production, with 925 hectares of vineyard providing 3600 tonnes in 1989.

What is more, it was a significant producer in the latter part of the nineteenth century: in 1890 it made 750,000 litres of wine, more than twice that of Western Australia, and more than a quarter of that of South Australia. A great deal of this wine came from Bassett's Winery at Roma, which was established in 1863 by Samuel Bassett, a 23 year old Cornishman who had worked for his uncle at Maitland in the Hunter Valley for the previous 7 years and had learnt the rudiments of viticulture and winemaking there.

By the 1890s Bassett's had 180 hectares of vineyard, and profited greatly from the disruption which phylloxera caused in Victoria. In 1901 Bassett's won 10 of the 11 medals awarded at the Royal Brisbane Show, and the winery produced every conceivable wine style — even so-called champagne. But the fiercely hot climate (it has an HDD summation of 3140 and an MJT of 27.3°C) has always meant that Bassett's best wines have been its fortifieds: to this day it makes Australia's best Madeira (or at least the best fortified wine bearing that name), even though the scale of operations is but a fraction of what it was in its heyday.

An equally outlandish and unexpected winery is situated at Herberton on the Atherton Tablelands south-west of Cairns. Here Fosters produce rustic table and fortified wine much appreciated by the Italian community. But the real centre of activity these days is the Granite Belt in the Southern Queensland highlands around Stanthorpe, only a few kilometres north of the New South Wales border. The first vines were planted here in 1878 by Father David, an Italian-born Roman Catholic priest who was sufficiently enlightened to urge his parishioners to follow suit. The remains of Father David's winery and cellars can still be seen, but while vineyards multiplied, no other winemaking enterprises were established until 1928, when Musumeci and Constanza commenced to make wine from table grapes. For the next 40 years all of the wine was made from this source: a lethal brew which was sold in bulk and (necessarily) consumed with rapidity. I take up the subsequent events in the Granite Belt in the next chapter.

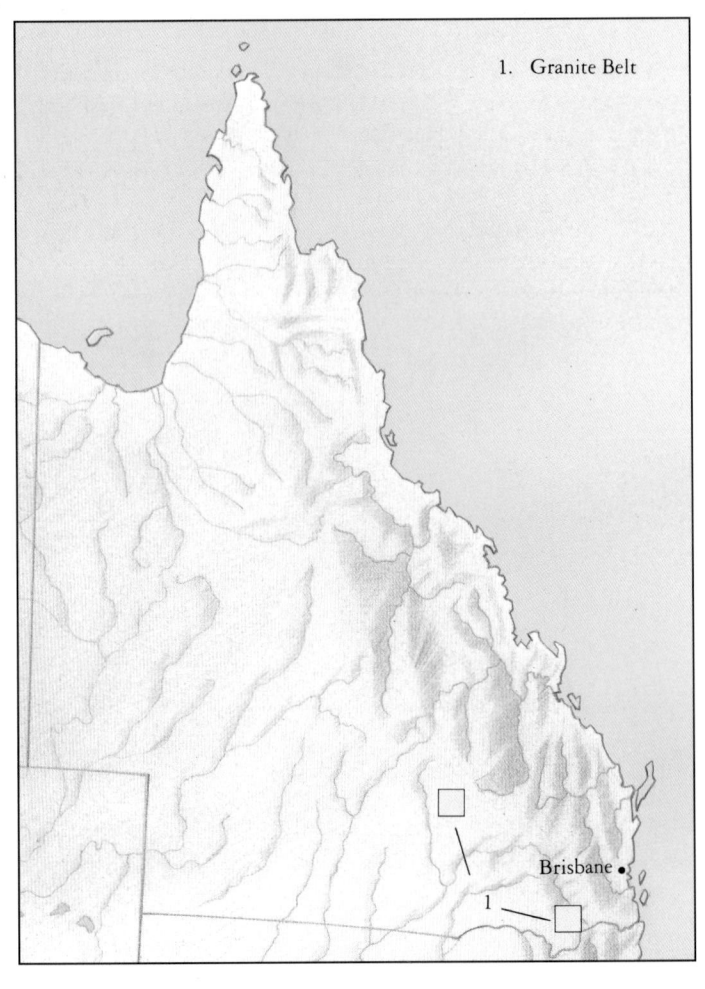

1. Granite Belt

PREVIOUS PAGES: *The tones of autumn in a young vineyard.*

ABOVE: *Graftlings in the nursery waiting to be planted out.*

THE GRANITE BELT

In 1965 the first wine grapes were planted in the Granite Belt: 1 hectare of Shiraz. It was an appropriate choice because this variety outshone all others (with the possible exception of Semillon) over the next 25 years. The Ricca Family were the pioneers, but have since faded from the scene.

However, it was not long before others followed suit. Toowoomba solicitor John Robinson and wife Heather established Robinsons Family vineyard in 1969, while the following year third-generation farmer Angelo Puglisi commenced what was initially called Sundown Valley Vineyards but is now called Ballandean Estate. These two wineries remain the largest in the district, and both enjoy the distinction of having their products marketed nationally (if on a restricted scale).

The Granite Belt is an interesting region. It owes much to Sydney-based wine consultant John Stanford, who became involved in the early '70s, and was something of a Messiah for its potential. Angelo Puglisi, too, gained recognition for the district when he was awarded a Churchill Fellowship in 1977 to study European winemaking techniques (an honour also accorded to his then winemaker Rodney Hooper a decade later).

But its present and future prosperity hinge to a large degree on the parochial Queensland market and on the steady flow of tourists passing up and down the New England Highway. For although many of the local vignerons would have it otherwise, the Granite Belt is no more a 'natural' grape growing region than is the Hunter Valley.

The principal drawbacks are spring frosts and vintage time rainfall. True, these do not occur every year, and appropriate site selection can significantly reduce the risk of frost. But then there is the vexed question of the climate, and how one really

AUSTRALASIAN WINE REGIONS
1980 – 1990

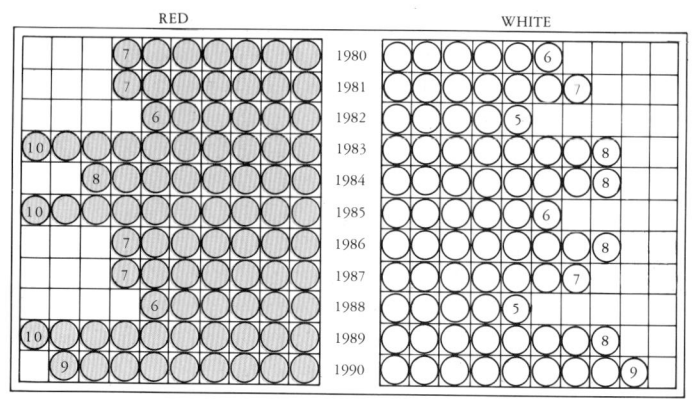

ABOVE: Bud-grafting onto American rootstock is a job for the expert.

THE REGION IN BRIEF

LOCATION AND ELEVATION
28°40'S151°56'E Stanthorpe
790 m

SUBREGIONS
Stanthorpe and Ballandean.

CLIMATE
As I say in the introduction, the climate of a region such as the Granite Belt is not easy to pigeonhole. Because vintage is relatively late, and because it is fashionable to say so (one producer even announces the fact in large letters on his wine label), there are those who categorise this as a cool climate region. The hard facts are an HDD summation of 1703 (others report it as 1814 and 1868!) and a MJT of 20.5°C. This is warmer than Rutherglen. The rainfall is strongly summer dominant: 550 mm, or 70 per cent of the annual total, falls between October and April.

SOIL
There are two principal soil types: highly permeable speckled, sandy grey-black soils in the Uc2.21 group, and light brownish-grey sandy mottled yellow duplex soils in the Dy5.41 and 5.81 groups. Each type has a white, bleached sandy subsurface soil, the latter two then passing into clays at depth.

HARVEST TIME
Mid-March– mid-April.

PRINCIPAL GRAPE VARIETIES

Chardonnay, 6 ha	*Shiraz, 21 ha*
Rhine Riesling, 41 ha	*Cabernet Sauvignon, 9 ha*
Semillon, 3 ha	*Pinot Noir, 3 ha*
Muscat Gordo Blanco, 3 ha	TOTAL RED, 42 ha
Chenin Blanc, 2 ha	
TOTAL WHITE, 41 ha	

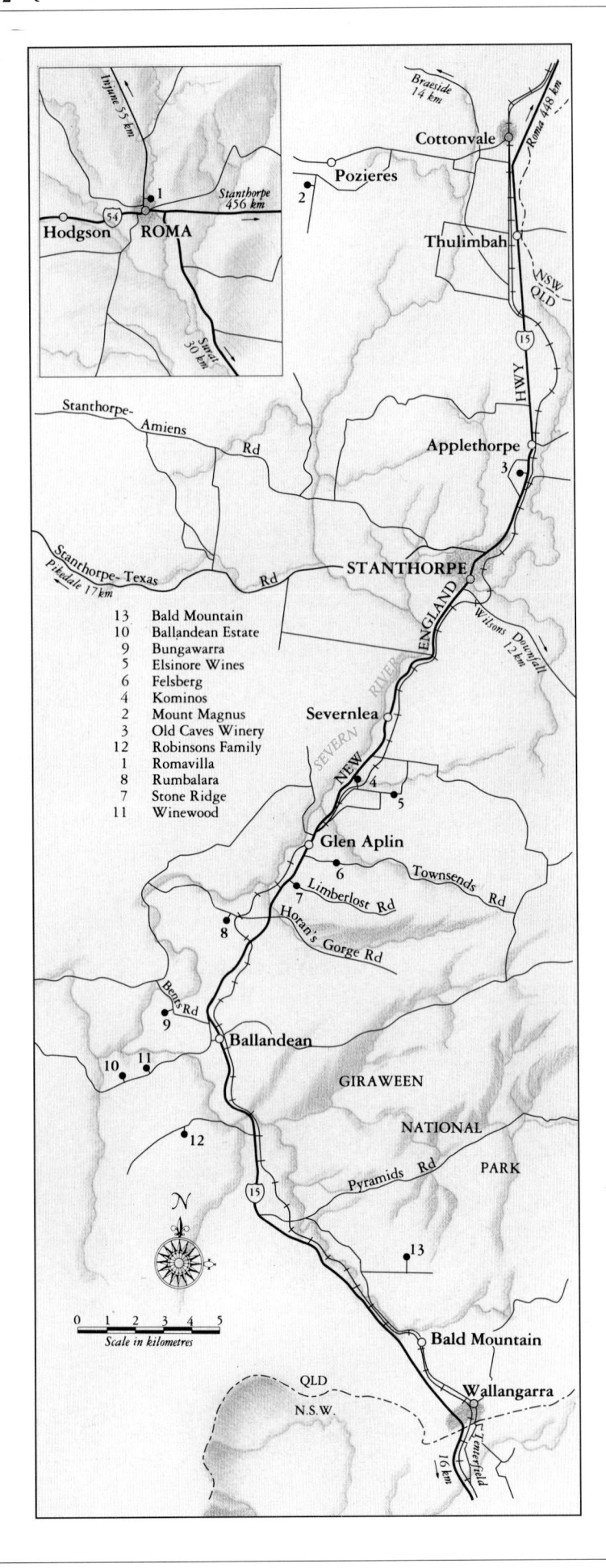

13 Bald Mountain
10 Ballandean Estate
9 Bungawarra
5 Elsinore Wines
6 Felsberg
4 Kominos
2 Mount Magnus
3 Old Caves Winery
12 Robinsons Family
1 Romavilla
8 Rumbalara
7 Stone Ridge
11 Winewood

assesses a high altitude region with a continental climate. Finally, there are the variable soils, some far too sandy and granitic, others much better suited to viticulture — a distinction ignored by some of the plantings made in the 1970s.

All of these factors make viticulture and winemaking that little bit more difficult. While I have tasted many enjoyable and a few outstanding wines over the years, a proverbial bucket of cold water was thrown over the region during the 1989 Royal Brisbane Wine Show. Prior to that year, there were special classes for Queensland wines, but in 1989 they were simply entered in the general classes (albeit with specially reduced volume requirements for entry) to compete against wines from the rest of Australia. Not one wine from the Granite Belt (or anywhere else in Queensland) won so much as a bronze medal.

So clearly the region has the task in front of it. It has some talented and enthusiastic viticulturists and winemakers, and its physical beauty is a major asset in marketing terms. It can succeed, but it must recognise and respond to the formidable challenge of other comparable Australian wine regions.

PRINCIPAL WINE STYLES

SHIRAZ
This is the one consistently distinctive wine style of the region: dark in colour; strong in body, flavour and tannin; and above all else, redolent with spice when young, but developing soft, sweet velvety fruit with time in bottle, reminiscent of Shiraz of the Hunter Valley (New South Wales). It is also used extensively in the making of Ballandean Nouveau, an early-picked, early-bottled and early-released carbonic maceration style which has been effectively used as a regional promotion. Bald Mountain, Ballandean Estate, Kominos Wines and Stone Ridge Vineyards are among the best producers of Shiraz made in the normal fashion, and Robinsons Family has produced wines of at times fearsome intensity.

SEMILLON
Echoes of the Hunter Valley also appear in the Semillons of the region, wines which grow gracefully in bottle for 5 years or more. Early in its life, Semillon can exhibit striking tropical fruit characters (possibly botrytis influenced) but with age, classic honeyed/toasty characters emerge. The foremost examples over the years have come from Rumbalara and Ballandean Estate; Kominos Wines is a promising newcomer.

CABERNET SAUVIGNON
Like Shiraz, the wine is full, dark and rich in flavour — at times perhaps rather too much so, but arguably too much is better than too little. Cassis/red berry/sweet fruit flavours predominate, attesting to the warm climate, and the often warm vanillan oak. Ballandean Estate, Kominos Wines, Robinsons Family and Rumbalara (the last superb in 1986 and 1987) are fine examples.

WINERIES OF THE GRANITE BELT

BALD MOUNTAIN   NR
Old Wallangarra Road
Wallangarra 4383   (076) 84 3186
Established   1987
Winemakers   Denis Parsons,
     John Cassegrain (contract)
Production   1000 cases
Principal Wines   Sauvignon Blanc, Chardonnay, Shiraz and Cabernet Sauvignon.
Best Vintages   Too recent to assess.
Denis Parsons brings the skills learnt as a General Manager of Exxon (with a background in chemical engineering) to his early-retirement venture with wife Jackie at Bald Mountain. He has applied discipline and energy in more or less equal parts in rejuvenating the vineyard he purchased, which is acknowledged to be on some of the most suitable soils and in one of the best positions in the entire Granite Belt. He is determined to produce top quality fruit, and I have every confidence he will do so. Some of the early wines (made under contract) have been exciting, but one or two problems (mouldy oak, for example) have partially obscured the underlying quality.

BALLANDEAN ESTATE   B-BA
Sundown Road
Ballandean 4382   (076) 84 1226
Established   1970
Winemaker   Peter Scudamore-Smith
     (consultant)
Production   5000 cases
Principal Wines   There are two distinct ranges: Ballandean Estate and Sundown Valley Vineyards, the former including Sauvignon Blanc, Semillon, Chardonnay, Shiraz, Cabernet Sauvignon and light red Shiraz, the latter devoted to generic (and cheaper) styles. Fortified wines are also made.
Best Vintages   W 1979, '81, '83, '87, '89
     R 1974, '80, '83, '87, '89
Ballandean Estate (formerly Sundown Valley Vineyards, and before that Angelo's Winery) is the largest and arguably the most important winery in the Granite Belt. Owner Angelo Puglisi was one of the first to break free of the shackles of traditional Italian winemaking (basically from table grapes) and deservedly received a Churchill Fellowship in 1977 to study winemaking overseas. A little more than a decade later, his then winemaker Rodney Hooper followed in his footsteps, and the benefits show in the wide range of wines and styles, both white and red, coming from the winery.

KOMINOS WINES   B-B
New England Highway
Severnlea 4352   (076) 83 4311

Established   1976
Winemaker   Tony Comino
Production   2,500 cases
Best Vintages   W and R 1986, '89
Tony Comino is one of the bright young lights of the Granite Belt, and has the enthusiastic backing and commitment of his solicitor-father and family. The new winery is one of the focal points of the district; spicy/peppery Shiraz and herbaceous Semillon show once again how suited these varieties are to the district.

ROBINSONS FAMILY   CB-CB
New England Highway
Lyra 4352   (076) 32 8615
Established   1969
Winemakers   Rod McPherson, Philippa
     Hambleton
Production   3000 cases
Principal Wines   Chardonnay, Cabernet Sauvignon, Shiraz, Pinot Noir, *Méthode Champenoise* — Chardonnay, Pinot Noir blend. Ballandean Nouveau Light Red (maceration carbonique).
Best Vintages   W 1976, '82, '88, '89
     R 1981, '82, '83, '86, '87
Toowoomba-based solicitor John Robinson has given his heart and soul to his vineyard and winery for more than a decade. Some incredibly concentrated, deeply coloured and tannic reds have resulted, while Chardonnay has gyrated from one extreme of style and quality to the other. There is some great potential here, but overall the wines suffer from lack of attention to detail and from over-enthusiasm in the quest for flavour and structure.

RUMBALARA   CA-BA
Fletcher Road
Fletcher 4381   (076) 84 1206
Established   1974
Winemaker   Bob Gray
Production   4000 cases
Principal Wines   Rhine Riesling, Semillon, Rosé, Cabernet Sauvignon, Pinot Noir, Shiraz, Vintage Port and Muscat.
Best Vintages   W 1979, '83, '84, '86, '87
     R 1984, '85, '86, '87
Some glorious wines have appeared under the Rumbalara label over the years, arguably the best to so far appear from the Granite Belt. Particularly outstanding were the 1984 Semillon, with its riotous tropical fruit flavours, and the complex, weighty and fruit-sweet berry/cassis/plum Cabernet Sauvignons from 1986 and 1987.

STONE RIDGE   B-B
Limberlost Road
Glen Aplin 4381   (076) 83 4211

Established   1981
Winemaker   Jim Lawrie
Production   500 cases
Principal Wine   Shiraz
Best Vintages   R 1987, '88, '89
Stone Ridge has built a disproportionate reputation for itself with its vibrant, peppery/berry Shiraz, a wine which reaffirms the synergy between the Granite Belt and this variety. Production is tiny but well worth seeking out.

PRODUCE OF AUSTRALIA

STONE RIDGE VINEYARDS
1988
SHIRAZ
100% GRANITE BELT GROWN GRAPES

Produced and bottled at
STONE RIDGE VINEYARDS,
LIMBERLOST ROAD, GLEN APLIN. QLD.
750mL   PRESERVATIVE 223 ADDED

WINEMAKERS:
JIM LAWRIE
ANNE KENNEDY
Alc/VOL 12.5%

OTHER WINERIES

BUNGAWARRA   NR
Bents Road (formerly Marshalls
Crossing Road)
Ballandean 4382   (076) 84 1128

ELSINORE WINES   NR
Kerridges Road
Glen Aplin 4381
(076) 83 4234 (winery)
(07) 848 6733 (Brisbane office)

FELSBERG   NR
Newman Road
Glen Aplin 4381   (076) 300 1946

MOUNT MAGNUS   NR
Donnelly's Castle Road off New
England Highway, Severnlea 4352
(076) 85 3213

OLD CAVES WINERY   C-B
New England Highway
Stanthorpe 4380   (076) 81 1494

ROMAVILLA   DB-CB
Northern Road
Roma 4455   (076) 22 1822

WINEWOOD   C-CB
Sundown Road
Ballandean 4382   (076) 84 1187

TASMANIA

NORTHERN TASMANIA

SOUTHERN TASMANIA

Tasmania burst out of the blocks: its first commercial wine was advertised for sale by Bartholemew Broughton in 1827, and it supplied the vine roots (from commercial nurseries established in the same year) which started the Victorian and South Australian industries a decade later.

A mere 20 years later the industry was all but dead, thanks to labour shortages stemming from the Victorian gold rush; a temperance movement induced but government decreed ban on distillation (even for use in fortified wine); lack of suitable sprays to prevent fungal diseases; and simple lack of knowledge of proper viticultural and oenological practices.

The rebirth came in the late 1950s: first a French engineer named Jean Miguet planted a one hectare vineyard near the Tamar River in 1956, followed by Italian textile maker Claudio Alcorso who planted a vineyard on the banks of the Derwent River just north of Hobart in 1958. Alcorso's Moorilla Estate is now one of the three leading Tasmanian wineries, with son Julian Alcorso at the helm, while Miguet's vineyard La Provence has passed into the ownership of Stuart Bryce, but remains tiny.

Given the interest in Tasmanian wine, the supportive attitude of successive Tasmanian Governments, and the high level of skills available at both the viticultural and winemaking level, it is altogether surprising the industry has grown so slowly.

THE REGION IN BRIEF

NORTHERN TASMANIA

LOCATION AND ELEVATION
41°07'S147°05'E
190–210 m Pipers River

SUBREGIONS
Pipers River and Tamar Valley.

CLIMATE
It does not matter which system or terminology one adopts: the climate is uncompromisingly cool. Bridport — just to the north of Pipers River — has an HDD of 1146, Launceston 1020, but nearby Scottsdale is said by one authority to have an HDD of only 868. The MJT is around 17.2°C (compared to 18.3°C for Reims and 19.5°C for Dijon). The annual rainfall is around 750 mm, with 40 per cent (or 300 mm) falling between October and March. Moisture-retaining soils reduce the need for irrigation, but it is used in some vineyards. Onshore wind has proved a major drawback, and windbreaks of various kinds (artificial fabric and trees) have been placed on most less well protected sites. The Tamar Valley subregion is better protected from wind, with a slightly warmer MJT of 18°C, an HDD summation of 1155, and a slightly lower rainfall (680 to 720 mm). In purely pragmatic terms, the differential seems greater still, with the Tamar Valley far better suited to the production of Cabernet Sauvignon than Pipers River.

SOIL
The soils are deep and friable, red to reddish brown in colour, and fall in the Gn group. Many are basalt-derived, with a high ferruginous content and certainly promote vine vigour.

HARVEST TIME
From early April for Pinot Noir in the Tamar Valley through to mid to late May for Cabernet Sauvignon and Rhine Riesling in the Pipers River region.

PRINCIPAL GRAPE VARIETIES
Chardonnay, 19.9 ha
Rhine Riesling, 7.6 ha
Cabernet Sauvignon, 20.4 ha
Pinot Noir, 19.7 ha
Merlot, 4 ha

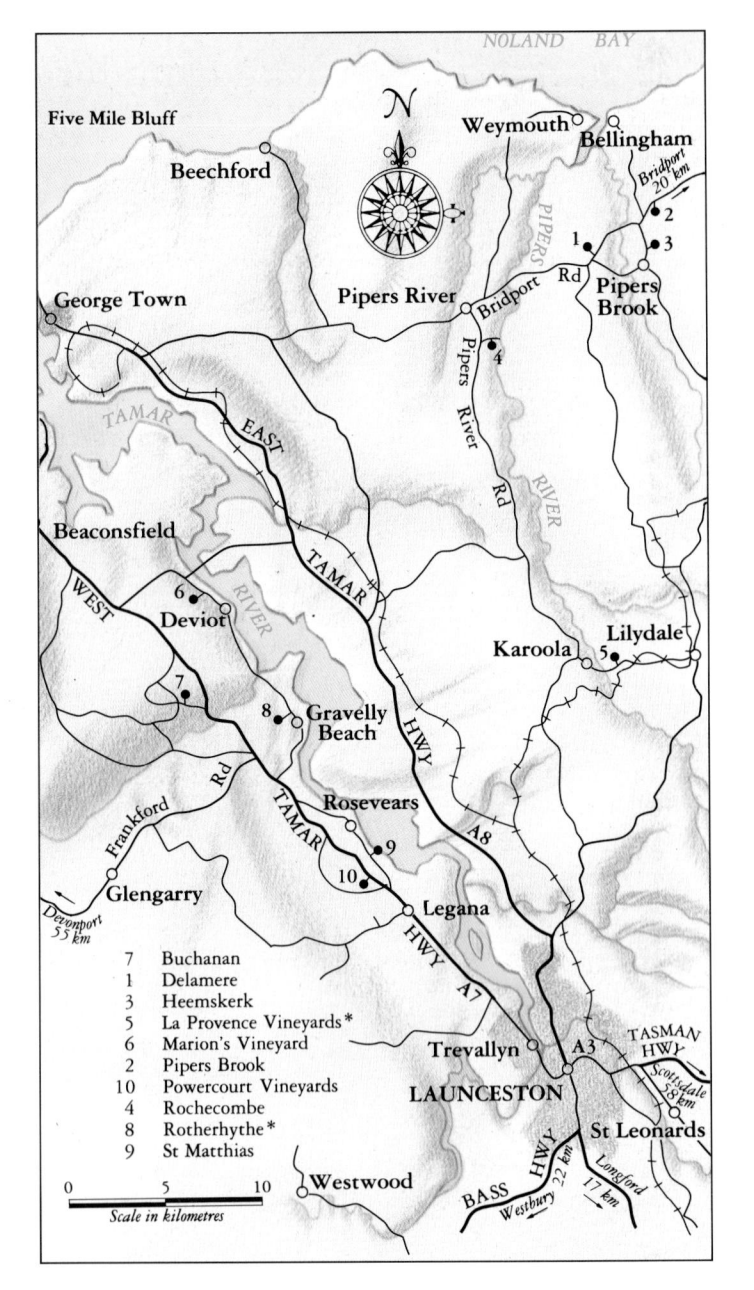

7	Buchanan
1	Delamere
3	Heemskerk
5	La Provence Vineyards*
6	Marion's Vineyard
2	Pipers Brook
10	Powercourt Vineyards
4	Rochecombe
8	Rotherhythe*
9	St Matthias

PREVIOUS PAGES: *French designed and built tractors and harvesters are used in the narrow vine rows at Pipers Brook.*

The chart on page 298 gives the 1989 production by variety and by each of the three major districts in Tasmania: Pipers River, the South (including the Derwent River, the Coal River and the East Coast) and the Tamar Valley. The total crush of 500 tonnes is roughly equivalent to that of one of the Yarra Valley's (Victoria) 31 wineries — St Huberts. However, Department of Primary Industry forecasts suggest that production will rise to 1370 tonnes by 1994 (a prediction that is supported by the 1990 crush of 937 tonnes). Certainly, Pipers Brook Vineyard and Moorilla Estate are both poised on the edge of major expansion, while there are several large vineyard developments under way dedicated for use by sparkling wine makers on the mainland (notably Tolpuddle Vineyards to produce grapes for Domaine Chandon and Clover Hill Vineyard, which will operate for Taltarni).

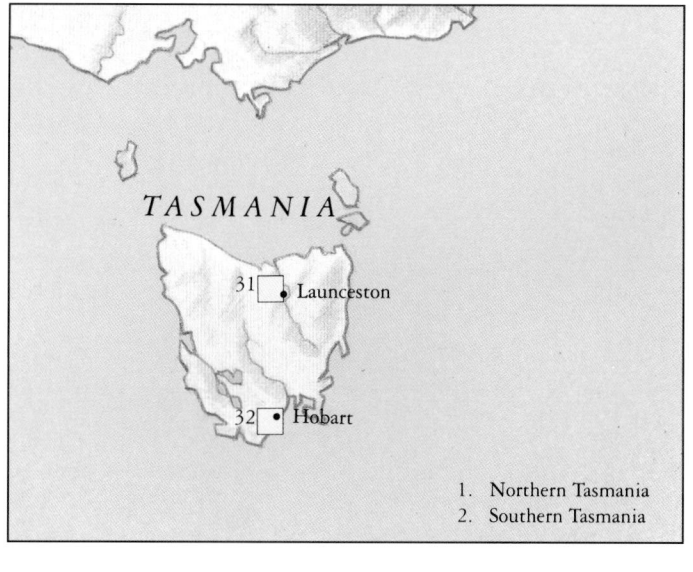

TASMANIA

31 Launceston

32 Hobart

1. Northern Tasmania
2. Southern Tasmania

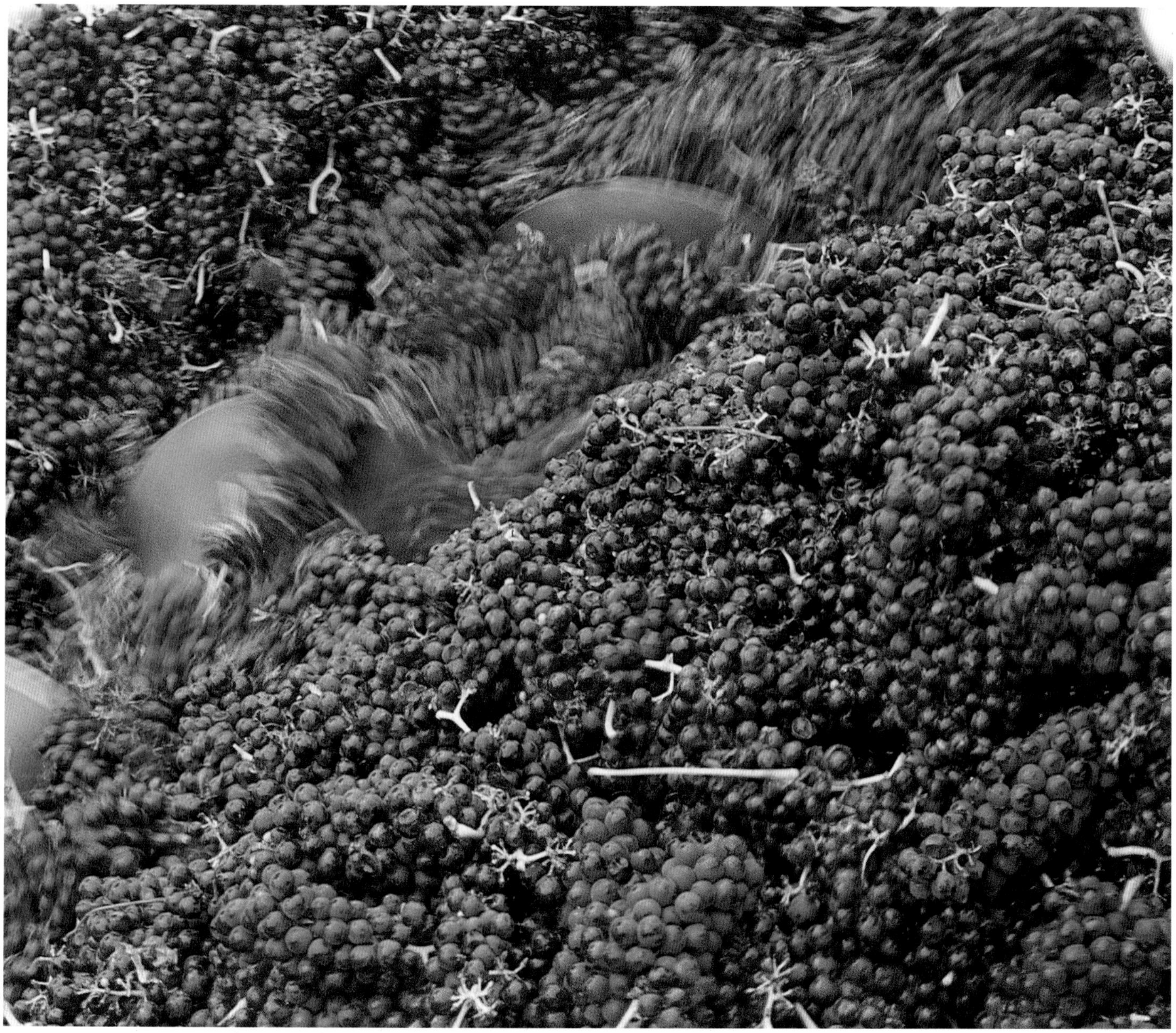

ABOVE: *Pinot Noir headed for the crusher and the birth of a new wine.*

Overall, it is hard to avoid the conclusion that Tasmania has promised far more than it has delivered, particularly given the expertise and intelligence of its major players (and in some instances, their consultants). Excuses have been made for poor vintages, but 1988 provided no such excuse yet it failed to deliver the great wines observers confidently predicted. The reasons hopefully are that it has taken longer than anyone originally anticipated for the viticulturists to fully understand the particular requirements of *terroir* and climate. There has been a massive investment in learning about optimum vine spacing, soil amelioration, windbreak development, and — particularly as the vines mature — that investment can be expected to pay dividends.

One thing is certain: while the correct matching of vineyard site and grape variety is essential, there are few grape varieties that cannot be grown somewhere or other in Tasmania. That truth was brought home to me almost 10 years ago when I tasted a bottle of Zinfandel made by George Park at Stoney Vineyard (in the Coal River area) which forcibly reminded me of a marvellous Californian Zinfandel (from Storybook Mountain) I had encountered only a few months previously. On the other side of the ledger, the disastrous Bream Creek vineyard shows just how unforgiving the wrong match can be.

THE REGION IN BRIEF

SOUTHERN TASMANIA

LOCATION AND ELEVATION
42°45'S 147°00'E Derwent Valley
43°02'S 147°02'E Huon Valley
42°44'S 147°25'E Coal River
41°53'S 148°18'E East Coast, Bicheno
50 – 175 m

SUBREGIONS
Derwent Valley, Huon Valley, Coal River and the East Coast.

CLIMATE
Given the diversity of the sites — some totally maritime influenced, others less so — it is not surprising that there is significant variation. However, Hobart (on the Derwent River) sets the scene with an HDD summation of 918. But as in Northern Tasmania, this figure seems misleading: Dr Andrew Pirie has suggested that sunshine, which is stronger in Southern Tasmania than that encountered in benchmark European regions, explains why (with appropriate protection from wind) in particular sites a surprising range of varieties can be ripened in a majority of years, particularly in the Coal River region. Surprisingly, low and irregular rainfall in all subregions other than the Huon Valley (ranging between 500 mm to something over 650 mm at Bicheno on the East Coast) makes irrigation essential, and wind (particularly from the sea) is a major problem for some vineyard sites.

SOIL
These vary substantially, those on the Lower and Upper Derwent being shallow sandstone-based soils with some schist, which reinforces the necessity for irrigation. The soils at Coal River vary: most are similar to those of the Derwent, being weakly structured, sandy, and low in humus (though with less schist), but there are patches of dark black peaty alluvial soils on which vines are being established.

HARVEST TIME
From early April for Pinot Noir through to early May for Rhine Riesling and for the few sites which endeavour to grow Cabernet Sauvignon.

PRINCIPAL GRAPE VARIETIES
Rhine Riesling, 3.7 ha   *Pinot Noir, 7.9 ha*
Chardonnay, 1.2 ha   *Cabernet Sauvignon, 5.5 ha*

TASMANIA GRAPE VARIETIES / REGION PRODUCTION AND HECTAREAGE

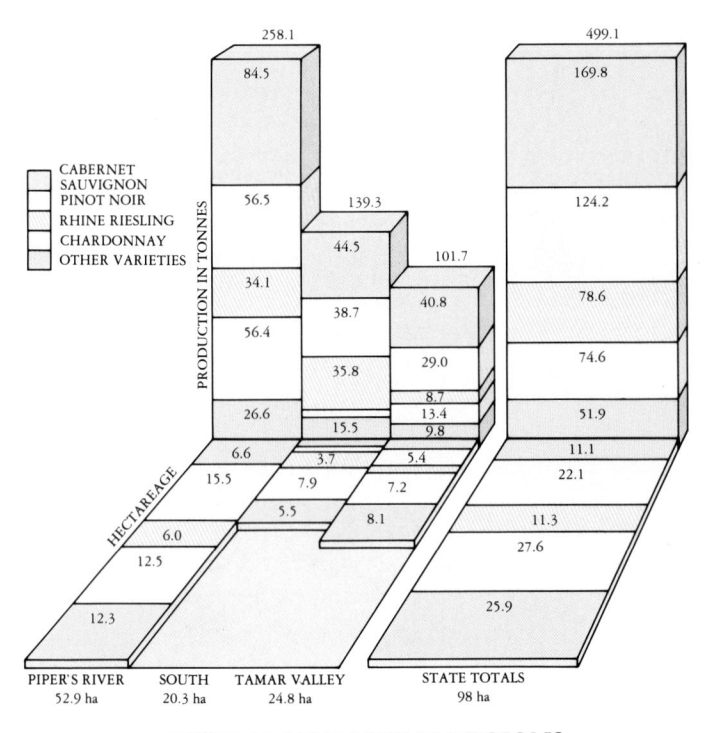

AUSTRALASIAN WINE REGIONS
1980 – 1990

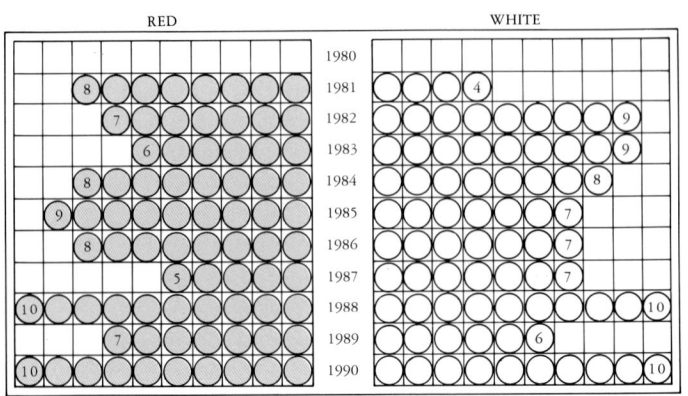

AUSTRALASIAN WINE REGIONS
1980 – 1990

RED		WHITE
7	1980	6
7	1981	6
8	1982	8
5	1983	7
8	1984	8
4	1985	5
4	1986	5
6	1987	7
8	1988	9
8	1989	9
10	1990	9

Map legend:

6 Elsewhere Vineyard
1 Freycinet Vineyard
2 Meadowbank
4 Moorilla Estate
5 Panorama Vineyard
3 Stoney Vineyard

Scale in kilometres 0 10 20

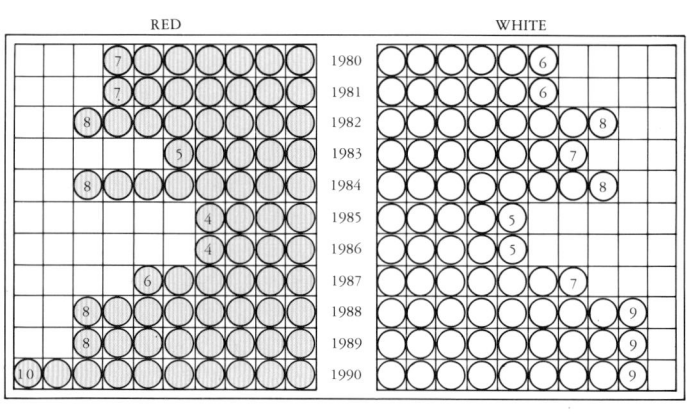

PRINCIPAL WINE STYLES

CHARDONNAY

It is on this variety (and on Pinot Noir) that the ultimate success of Tasmania as a significant wine region will depend. It is grown successfully in all subregions, producing wines of varying style — the style being influenced partly by microclimate, partly by seasonal conditions and partly by winemaking philosophy. They range from rich flavoured, almost viscous wines (sometimes with overtones of botrytis-induced apricot and peach) through to austere, delicate examples fully reflecting the very cool growing conditions commonly encountered. Overall, makers are striving for complexity rather than simple fruit flavours, with Pipers Brook Vineyard in the vanguard, but Heemskerk, St Matthias, Moorilla Estate and Freycinet Vineyard all doing well.

PINOT NOIR

As with Chardonnay, increasing amounts are being devoted to sparkling wine as hectareage increases, but for Moorilla Estate and Pipers Brook Vineyard in particular most of the interest lies in table wine. As long ago as 1981 Pipers Brook Vineyard showed just what could be achieved in the north, while Moorilla Estate has charted its future around Pinot Noir. The best wines (typically from Moorilla Estate and Pipers Brook Vineyard) show good intensity of colour and flavour, and quite good varietal character. Others are startlingly variable, with flavours ranging from eucalypt-mint through to a somewhat flat cherry and on to

dense but over-extracted dark fruits. That the variety will succeed in the long term is beyond doubt, and La Provence, Stoney Vineyard, St Matthias and Rotherhythe will be among the successes.

CABERNET SAUVIGNON

This was the first variety planted in any quantity in Tasmania, but it has become very clear it is not suited to all districts. At Pipers River it tends to produce excessively vegetal and thin wines unless the growing season has been ideal, and it does not normally flourish on the Derwent. The Tamar and Coal River regions can, however, reliably produce wines with good colour and body, distinct fruit (in the red and blackcurrant spectrum) and adequate tannins, and other regions (or sites) may well emerge in the future. For the time being the flag is carried by Meadowbank, St Matthias, Rotherhythe and Stoney Vineyard, with Pipers Brook Vineyard succeeding as much through winemaking wizardry as anything else.

RHINE RIESLING

Some of Tasmania's most lovely wines are Rhine Rieslings, ranging from the classic, long-lived dry styles of Pipers Brook Vineyard and Meadowbank through to the startlingly intense, yet fine and almost steely botrytised style of Moorilla Estate, which emulate the greatest spatleses of the Mosel.

ABOVE: *Chardonnay waiting to be picked; the birds have approved.*

DR ANDREW PIRIE AND PIPERS BROOK VINEYARD

If ever anyone has put his money where his mouth is, it is Andrew Pirie. Having graduated with a Master of Science (Agriculture) from Sydney University in early 1971 (aged 24) he spent that year working in the wine industry across Europe, looking at everything from grape growing to marketing, and spending time in England, Alsace, Burgundy, Bordeaux, Provence, Spain and Italy.

He returned to Australia determined to find a vineyard site comparable to one of the great regions of France, such as Bordeaux or Burgundy. First, of course, he had to devise a valid means of comparing southern hemisphere sites with those of the northern hemisphere, and it was his research on this and on the physiology of the grapevine which led in 1977 to his receiving the first Doctorate of Philosophy from the University of Sydney for viticultural research.

In the meantime he had put his research on homoclimes to practical use. After an exhaustive evaluation of all the possibilities on the south-eastern mainland of Australia, he pinpointed the Pipers River region of North-eastern Tasmania. The only vineyards then in existence in the northern half of Tasmania were two tiny plantings in the Tamar Valley, neither of which were producing wine on a commercial basis: indeed the only winery to be doing so was Moorilla Estate, and then on a very small and somewhat erratic scale.

In 1973 he established Pipers Brook Vineyard, planting the first close-spaced vineyards of the modern era and choosing the then avant-garde varieties Chardonnay and Pinot Noir to accompany the (slightly) more conventional Gewurztraminer and Cabernet Sauvignon. With the wisdom of hindsight it is easy to take the three core decisions (site, planting density and varietal selection) for granted, but all were exceptionally far-sighted.

As with any trail-blazing course, the ensuing years were not without their problems. While the basic viticultural approach has not changed greatly, there has been considerable fine tuning. Pipers Brook Vineyard was the first Australian vineyard to import and use a French over-the-vine tractor, which looks like some strange insect as the driver sits aloft the vinerow, with the tractor's spidery legs coming down to the wheels which run along adjacent rows. It is difficult enough owning and operating a unique piece of equipment close to

Sydney or Melbourne, it is another thing again in a remote part of Tasmania.

Wind has proved a continuing problem, effectively diminishing growing season warmth, and leading to ongoing work in evaluating row orientation, trellis design and canopy management. Andrew Pirie has continued his research efforts, largely at a practical level in his own vineyards, but also at one time on a 12 month Reserve Bank of Australia Agricultural Research Fellowship through the CSIRO (Commonwealth Scientific and Industrial Research Organisation) Division of Food Research. His work was on the potassium content of grapes, a very important issue in Australia given the trendency for pH levels to rise to unacceptably high levels in both cool and warm climates once the vines are placed under any degree of stress.

More recently he worked closely with Dr Walter Eggenberger, a distinguished Swiss viticulturist, seconded to the Tasmanian industry in 1989-90, and who brought a wealth of experience in growing vines in a range of microclimates similar to those of Tasmania.

Research is one thing, commercial success another thing again, but Dr Pirie has been as adept at the latter as the former. He was quickly followed (in 1975) by Heemskerk, which moved from its initial base at Legana in the Tamar Valley to Pipers River, and now has the region's largest plantings (30 ha) under vine. In 1985 the Champagne house Roederer acquired a substantial interest in Heemskerk, and roughly half the production is now used for sparkling wine. Other vineyards have since joined the Pipers' band.

However, few would dispute Pipers Brook Vineyard's claim to first place among all Tasmanian table wine producers. That reputation has been forged on the five wines made since the first vintage in 1981, a bird's-eye view of which comes in the cellar guide prepared by Pipers Brook in 1990.

In the long term, Chardonnay and Pinot Noir will become the most important wines. Riesling and Traminer are suitable varieties, and the quality is impressive, but they lack the market cachet of the other varieties. The Cabernet Sauvignon (which for some years has incorporated around 15 per cent Merlot and Cabernet Franc) is certainly accepted in the market place, and — as the cellar guide attests — can be exceedingly

ABOVE: Dr Andrew Pirie has successfully focussed the attention of the world on Pipers Brook.

long-lived, but in many years its leafy herbaceous style (reminiscent more of Cabernet Franc from Chinon in the Loire Valley) will not appeal to all consumers.

But there are other wines in the wings arising out of a major expansion in Pipers Brook Vineyard's ownership and capital base which took place in 1989. It is now a public company (unlisted), and a substantial share issue led to the expenditure of $2 million dollars in a vineyard and winery expansion.

If acquired the 12.7 hectare Pellion Vineyard (which was previously a joint venture managed by Pipers Brook) and St Patricks (from Leigh and Janet Gawith) a 7 hectare vineyard now called Ninth Island Vineyard. Together with the existing 15.5 hectares of Pipers Brook Vineyard, there are 34.2 hectares of vines, with a planting programme through to the winter of 1993 due to increase the area to 46.2 hectares.

These new vineyard sources provided a Pinot Gris, a Sauvignon Blanc and a botrytis Semillon/Sauvignon Blanc (in small quantities) in 1990. They have also provided Pipers Brook Vineyard with the opportunity of reintroducing its second label (Tasmanian Wine Company) for wines which for one reason or another are not considered appropriate for the Pipers Brook Vineyard label. First crop wines are one example, another is the 1989 Pinot Noir, which simply didn't have the desired intensity or flavour.

The most significant aspect of the expansion is that Pipers Brook Vineyard will become the first Tasmanian producer to market wine nationally and internationally on a fully commercial scale. It will take Tasmania out of the unreality of the Dolls House into the real world, and allow curious consumers everywhere their first real opportunity to see for themselves just what Tasmanian wine is all about.

CELLAR GUIDE

		VINTAGE	OPTIMUM YEARS FOR DRINKING
RIESLING	passed	1981	—
	drinkable now	1983	1990–1992
		1979	1990–1991
		1980	1990–1992
		1984	1990–1992
		1985	1990–1992
		1982	1990–1996
		1988	1990–1998
		1987	1990–1994
		1989	1990–1994
		1986	1990–1994
TRAMINER	drinkable now	1983	1990+
		1984	1990+
		1982	1990+
		1985	1990+
		1988	1990–1993
	cellaring desirable	1989	1990–1993
		1986	1990–1992
		1987	1991–1993
CHARDONNAY	drinkable now	1981	1990–1991
		1983	at peak
		1985	1990
		1984	1990
		1982	1990–1992
		1988	1990–2000
		1986	1990–2000
	cellaring desirable	1987	1990–2000+
		1989	1992–2000
CABERNET SAUVIGNON	drinkable now	1980	Tas Wine Co
		1981	1990
		1983	1990–1992
		1984	1990–1996
		1985	1990–1998
		1986	1992–1998
		1982	1990–2000+
	cellaring desirable	1989	1991–1996
		1987	1993–2000
		1988	1999–2000
PINOT NOIR	drinkable now	1982	at peak
		1981	at peak
		1987	1990–1991
		1983	1990–1992
		1984	1990–1994
	cellaring desirable	1988	1990–1995
		1985	1990–1995
		1986	1994–1996+

This guide is based on wines cellared at less than 20°–21° C year round. The border line between drinking and cellaring should be pushed down by as much as 2 wines for warmer cellars. + May last and improve much longer.

Reproduced with permission of Pipers Brook.

ABOVE: The French-built Howard mechanical harvester is on a Lilliputian scale compared to all others in use in Australia but does the job on the Chardonnay.

WINERIES OF TASMANIA

NORTHERN TASMANIA

BUCHANAN   NR

Glendale Road, Loira
West Tamar 7275   (003) 94 7488
Established   1985
Winemaker   Don Buchanan
Production   4000 cases
Principal Wines   Chardonnay, Sauvignon
Blanc, Pinot and Cabernet Blend.
Best Vintages   W and R 1986, '88, '89

Don Buchanan brought a wealth of practical experience with him when he established his winery in 1985, and was clearly determined to establish Buchanan as one of the leaders in Tasmania. The immaculately tended and beautifully sited vineyards seemed to provide the appropriate base material; the only problem with the initial releases was a decidedly heavy hand with new oak flavours, which made quality assessment difficult.

DELAMERE   B-B

Bridport Road
Pipers Brook 7254   (003) 82 7190
Established   1983
Winemaker   Richard Richardson
Production   500 cases
Principal Wines   Pinot Noir and Chardonnay.
Best Vintages   W 1988, '89, '90
                            R 1987, '88, '90

Richard Richardson's Pinot Noir has excited considerable attention and favourable comment since its first vintage in 1986, which produced a princely 350 bottles. Skilled winemaking (partly throught the agency of Dr Andrew Pirie at Pipers Brook Vineyard where the wines are in fact made) has been a significant factor. Some of the flavours in the Pinot Noir seem to reflect the cool climate more than the variety, and it will be interesting to see how the style develops as the vines mature.

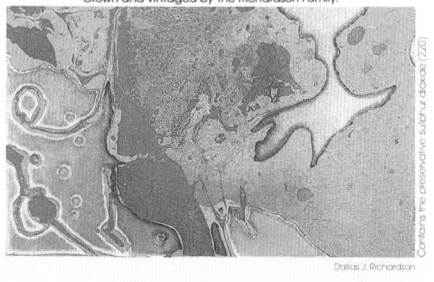

Grown and vintaged by the Richardson Family.

DELAMERE
Pipers Brook

Chardonnay 1989

Alc/Vol 11.0%   Available direct from DELAMERE,
Pipers Brook, Tasmania, 7254 Australia.   750 ml

HEEMSKERK   B-B

Pipers Brook 7254   (003) 31 6795
Established   1975
Winemaker   Graham Wiltshire
Production   The equivalent of 15,000
                            cases.
Principal Wines   Chardonay, Pinot Noir,
Cabernet Sauvignon and sparkling wines.
Best Vintages   W 1982, '85, '86, '88, '90
                            R 1982, '86, '88, '89

One of the 'big 3' Tasmanian wineries (the others being Pipers Brook Vineyard and Moorilla Estate), with its reputation further enhanced by the sparkling wine joint venture with Champagne House Louis Roederer. Some of its early wines were benchmarks in the development of Tasmanian winemaking, but in recent years I must confess to a vague feeling of disappointment. The wines have been good, but never exhilarating, while the production of sparkling wine has been frustratingly slow.

PIPERS BROOK VINEYARD   A-A

Bridport Road
Piper's Brook 7254   (003) 82 7197
Established   1974
Winemaker   Andrew Pirie
Production   7000 cases (but increasing).
Principal Wines   Riesling, Traminer, Chardonnay, Pinot Noir and Cabernet Sauvignon.
Best Vintages   W 1982, '85, '86, '88, '90
                            R 1981, '82, '84, '87, '88, '90

ESTABLISHED BY THE PIRIE FAMILY IN 1974

PIPERS BROOK VINEYARD

1988 PINOT NOIR

Tasmania

Beautifully crafted wines are the norm reflecting the fastidious touch of Andrew Pirie in both the vineyard and the winery. In some years the cherry/plum Pinot Noir (with touches of mint) comes to the fore, in some the complex melon/grapefruit flavoured Chardonnay occasionally showing some tropical botrytis effects is the most successful wine, and in other years it is the turn of the austere and beautifully balanced Rhine Riesling.

ST MATTHIAS   BA-BA

Rosevears Drive
Rosevears 7251   (003) 30 1700
Established   1982
Winemaker   Graham Wiltshire (contract)
Production   2000 cases
Principal Wines   Pinot Noir, Rhine Riesling,
Chardonnay and Cabernet Merlot Blend.
Best Vintages   W 1986, '88, '89, '90
                            R 1987, '88, '89, '90

St Matthias is one of the most superbly situated vineyards and wineries in Australia. The cellar door sales area, with its church-like overtones, is also most attractive. St Matthias was one of disappoint-ingly few vineyards to produce wines living up to the very high expectations held of the 1988 vintage, with its Pinot Noir and Kinburn Cabernet Merlot leading the way.

OTHER WINERIES

HOLM OAK   CB-CB
RSD Rowella 7270 (003) 94 7577

LA PROVENCE VINEYARDS   B-C
Lalla 7267 (003) 95 1290

MARIONS VINEYARD   CB-CB
Foreshore Road
Deviot 7251

NOTLEY GORGE   NR
Loop Road
Glengarry 7275 (003) 96 1166

POWERCOURT VINEYARDS   C-C
McEwans Road
Legana 7251 (003) 30 1700

ROCHECOMBE   NR
Baxters Road
Parker River 7252 (003) 82 7122

ROTHERHYTHE   BA-B
Hendersons Lane
Gravelly Beach
Exeter 7251 (003) 34 0188

ABOVE RIGHT: St Matthias, on the banks of the Tamar River.

SOUTHERN TASMANIA

FREYCINET VINEYARD   B-B
Tasman Highway via
Bicheno 7215   (002) 57 8384
Established   1980
Winemaker   Geoffrey Bull
Production   1000 cases
Principal Wines   Riesling Müller-Thurgau, Chardonnay, Sauvignon Blanc, Pinot Noir and Cabernet Sauvignon.
Best Vintages   W and R 1987, '89, '90
Freycinet Vineyard has produced some exhilarating wines over the years, and some decidedly less satisfactory. The 1988 wines suffered from a variety of problems, including volatility and over-extraction, disappointing given the reputation of the vintage. The rating is something of a soft compromise, simply because I have not had enough opportunity to carefully assess the wines. The whites seem to have been the most successful, hitting a high point in 1987, but doing well in 1989 and better still in 1990.

MEADOWBANK   B-B
Glenora, Derwent Valley
7410
Established   1974
Winemaker   Andrew Pirie (contract)
Production   800 cases
Principal Wines   Rhine Riesling and Cabernet Sauvignon.
Best Vintages   W 1983, '86, '88, '90
    R 1983, '84, '86, '88, '90
Meadowbank is a winery only, its winemaking wandering like a hermit crab from shell to shell, at one stage journeying all the way to Hickinbotham winemakers in Southern Victoria. It came into its own with the 1988 vintage, producing a lime/passionfruit flavoured Rhine Riesling (fulfilling the promise of preceding years), and a Cabernet Sauvignon which showed all of the depth and flavour one would hope for in a perfect vintage, allied with berry/plum/spice fruit.

MOORILLA ESTATE   BA-BA
655 Main Road
Berriedale 7011   (002) 49 2949
Established   1958
Winemaker   Julian Alcorso
Production   8000 cases
Principal Wines   Pinot Noir, Rhine Riesling, Gewurztraminer, Chardonnay and Cabernet Sauvignon.
Best Vintages   W 1982, '83, '84, '87, '88, '90
    R 1981, '84, '87, '88, '90
Julian Alcorso is increasingly turning to Pinot Noir, and overall produces Tasmania's best examples of this variety. Notwithstanding the very high rating given to Moorilla Estate, I have the feeling the best is yet to come: there is a never ending quest for quality both in the vineyard and in the winery, and the secrets of the temperamental and exceedingly demanding Tasmanian climate are still being unlocked.

OTHER WINERIES

ELSEWHERE VINEYARD   NR
Glaziers Bay 7112 (002) 95 1509

GLEN AYR   NR
Back Tea Tree Road
Richmond 7025 (002) 62 2388

SPRINGVALE   NR
Springvale
Swansea 7190 (002) 57 8208

STONEY VINEYARD   BA-BA
Campania 7202 (002) 62 4174

PANORAMA VINEYARD   NR
193 Waterworks Road
Dynnyrne 7005

TASMANIAN VINEYARDS NOT IN COMMERCIAL PRODUCTION IN 1989

PIPERS RIVER DISTRICT

BELLINGHAM VINEYARD
Established 1984. 12 ha. Owners: Dallas Targett and Julie Margaret Targett. Varietal table wines under estate label expected 1991-92.

CLOVER HILL VINEYARD
Established 1987 by Taltarni, Victoria. 11 ha, expanding. Manager: Chris Smith. Longer term plans for an on-site winery.

ROCHECOMBE VINEYARD
Established 1984. 8.4 ha, expanding to 31 ha by 1996. Joint venture involving Bernard Rochaix and manager Alfred Edgecombe. First wine 1990. Future plantings to be Pinot Noir and Chardonnay. Baxter's Road, Parker River 7252. (003) 82 7122.

TAMAR VALLEY

CLIFFHOUSE VINEYARD
Established 1983. 5 ha, expanding. Owner: Cliff House Vineyard (in the Tamar Valley), H S G and C M Hewitt. Winemaker: Julian Alcorso (initially). Camms Road, Kayena 7251. (003) 94 9454.

REBECCA VINEYARDS
Established 1988. 19 ha, expanding to 49 ha. Manager: Heemskerk vineyard. All enquiries to their Launceston office, 85 Elizabeth Street, Launceston 7250. (003) 31 6795.

EAST COAST

BREAM CREEK VINEYARD
Established 1974, 6 ha. Partly owned by Moorilla Estate. Winemaker: Julian Alcorso.

CRAIGIE KNOWE VINEYARD
Established 1979. 4 ha. Owner and winemaker: John Austwick. Small batches of wine have been made at the Swansea vineyard since 1983 and sold commercially since 1984. (002) 23 5620 .

COAL RIVER VALLEY

TOLPUDDLE VINEYARDS
Established 1987. 6.4 ha, expanding to 15.5 ha by 1991. Joint venture involving landowner Bill Caismaty, Domaine Chandon and Dromana Estate. Manager: Chris Harrington. The vineyards will supply Domaine Chandon and Heemskerk (in a joint venture with Roederer) with Pinot Noir and Chardonnay grapes. Back Tea Tree Road, Richmond 7025. (002) 62 2388.

UPLANDS ESTATE
Established 1980, 2 ha. Supplies planting material to the industry. For details write to Viticulture Tasmania, 14 Augusta Road, New Town 7008. (002) 28 5446.

NEW ZEALAND

NORTH ISLAND

AUCKLAND AREA

HAWKE'S BAY

GISBORNE/POVERTY BAY

WAIRARAPA/MARTINBOROUGH

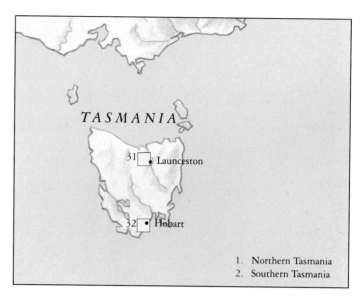

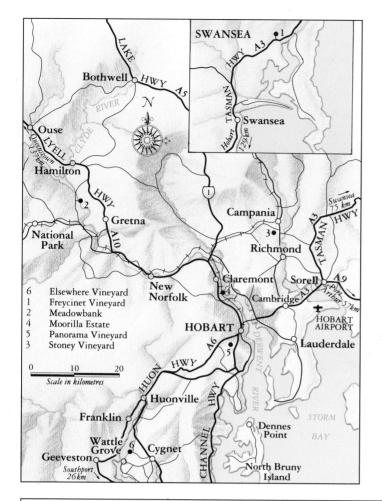

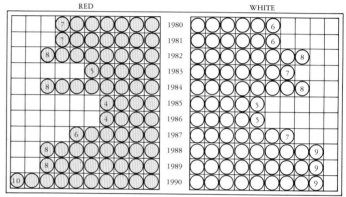

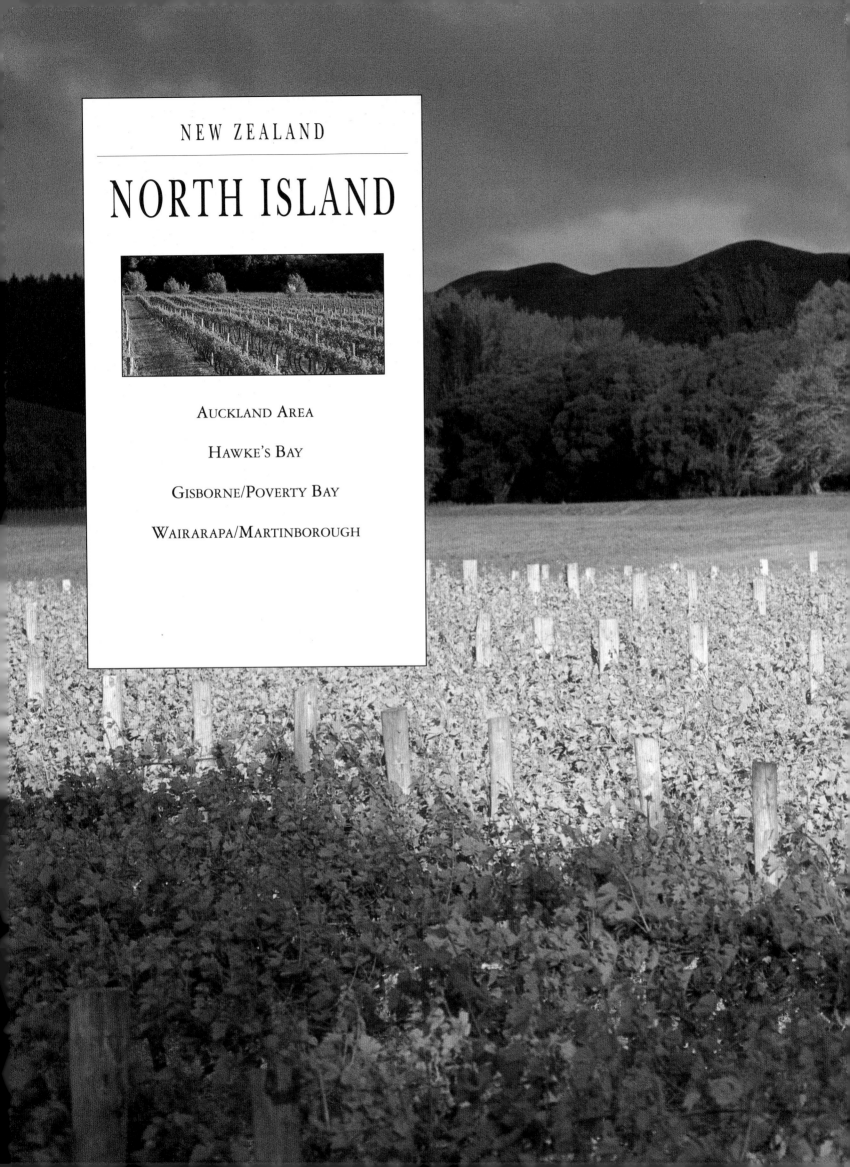

Samuel Marsden, who is perhaps better known in Australia than New Zealand, visited the latter country on several occasions in the role of Anglican Missionary. On 25 September 1819 he wrote in his diary, 'We had a small spot of land cleared and broken up in which I planted about a hundred grape vines of different kinds brought from Port Jackson. New Zealand promises to be very favourable to the vine as far as I can judge at present of the nature of the soil and climate.'

Marsden's vines were planted at Kerikeri, near the Bay of Islands. It was at nearby Waitangi that an even more famous figure in Australian viticulture — James Busby — planted his vineyard in 1836, and subsequently made the first New Zealand wine which French explorer Captain Dumont d'Urville described in 1840 as 'a light white wine, very sparkling, and delicious to taste'.

The first fully commercial winemaking enterprise was owned and run by Charles Levet and Son on an arm of Waipara Harbour (on the Northland west coast) between 1863 and 1907, and W Heathcote Jackman had a celebrated vineyard and winery at Whakapirau at the turn of the century planted to classic varieties. On the east coast near Whangarei, Wendolin Alberts was making 4500 litres of well regarded wine a year, while a year later New Zealand Prime Minister Sir George Grey endeavoured to promote a major (10,500 hectare) vineyard development scheme at Hokianga Harbour on the Northland west coast. Not surprisingly, nothing came of his proposal to bring vignerons from the south of France to develop this huge area.

So it was that Northland was the birthplace of the New Zealand wine industry, but in the manner of Camden, Rooty Hill and the other early vineyards established to the east of Sydney, it is no longer an important viticultural region. With the exception of the brief flare of publicity given to the equally short-lived winery the Antipodean (in my view totally unjustified by the very indifferent quality of at least two of its vintages), Northland and its principal ongoing winery — Continental Wines — are seldom heard of these days. Refer to pages 340 and 341 for maps and wineries of the Northlands regions.

In his excellent book *The Wines and Vineyards of New Zealand* (Hodder & Stoughton, 1988), Michael Cooper observes, 'The history of wine in New Zealand can be portrayed as an industry embarked on a century old rollercoaster ride, soaring and plunging through successive periods of growth and optimism, decline and disillusionment.'

Until 1973 the vast majority of the activity took place on the North Island, although the activity was not, as one might suppose, concentrated solely around Auckland. Joseph Soler ran a highly successful winery at Wanganui (on the south-west coast) between 1869 and 1906, selling wine all over New Zealand. In 1913 Bernard Chambers' vineyard and

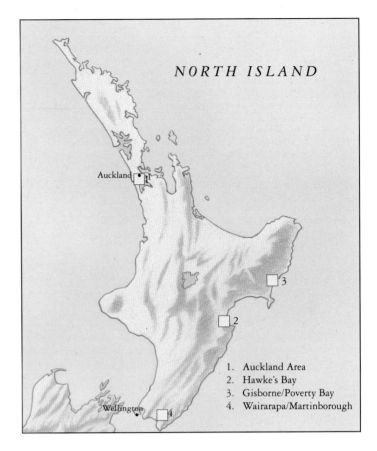

1. Auckland Area
2. Hawke's Bay
3. Gisborne/Poverty Bay
4. Wairarapa/Martinborough

winery Te Mata at Hawke's Bay was the largest in New Zealand, with 14 hectares of vines producing 5000 cases.

The only other operation of comparable size was the government-owned research station at Te Kauwhata which, despite restrictions stemming from a then-flourishing temperance movement, produced the equivalent of 4750 cases from 8 hectares. Te Kauwhata remains the centre of viticultural research in New Zealand, and the Waikato region is home to Cooks, De Redcliffe, Rongopai, Aspen Ridge and (just, as it is in the mouth of the Waihou River at Thames) Totara. Morton Estate, in splendid isolation near the Bay of Plenty (not far north of Tauranga) is usually treated as being in the same group, and I have followed convention. With only 115 hectares, or 2.6 per cent of the New Zealand 1989 total, Waikato is an area of minor importance viticulturally, although it is significant in research and in terms of production (thanks to Cooks and Morton Estate).

In truth, until 1890, wine production however widespread, was on a tiny scale. The temperance movement ebbed and surged between 1860 and 1919, when only the votes of returned servicemen saved the industry from nationwide prohibition. (Various districts, including Henderson, did impose it, and some continue it to this day.) Even short of prohibition, the restrictions imposed on selling wine were stultifying, and lack of winemaking skills and equipment (due in no small measure to the small scale of most winemaking enterprises) meant that the quality of the wine was very poor.

PREVIOUS PAGES: Hawke's Bay lit by a random solar searchlight.

ABOVE: *Ihaumatao Peninsula has its own special climate and grows grapes under contract to Villa Maria.*

Yet further problems came with the arrival of oidium (powdery mildew) in 1876, which was particularly devastating in the humid, high rainfall regions of Northland, Waikato and Auckland (the last region gradually becoming the centre of wine production). The arrival of the first government viticulturist, Romeo Bragato, seconded from Victoria in 1895, coincided with an all too brief period of prosperity for the industry — centred in large part around classic grape varieties in Hawke's Bay.

That brief surge also coincided with the arrival of phylloxera, to which Bragato very properly responded by recommending the importation of American vines for grafting. Initially his advice was not heeded at all, but when it was, growers planted the vines with gusto and did not bother about grafting on *Vitis vinifera* tops. The American vines produced exactly the same sickly, sweet, 'foxy' character for which they are despised the world over, but they had three huge advantages: they resisted the fungal diseases which were such a problem for growers around Auckland, they yielded large crops, and the produce could be sold as table grapes if demand for wine diminished or disappeared altogether in the wake of prohibition. The direct result was Albany Surprise, a clone of the Isabella variety, which produced very inferior wine but which in 1960 was still the most widely grown grape variety in New Zealand.

This tendency was reinforced in 1928 when the first French-American hybrids were imported and distributed from Te Kauwhata. Varieties such as Baco and Seibel cast their baleful influence over the industry for the next 40 years, contributing to the poor reputation it gained. In the early decades of this century, adulteration and concoction of wine was endemic, producing 'wine' which was potentially lethal and which would have been pronounced unfit for consumption in any other country. It also has to be said that the widespread use of sugar to increase alcohol levels followed by dilution with up to 25 per cent water to 'stretch' the quantity of wine, was distressingly common up to the end of the 1960s and continued on a lesser scale for a while thereafter.

The wine industry of today is effectively less than 20 years old. In 1962 only 12 per cent of all wine sold was table wine — just as in Australia — and the rest was fortified (and of truly appalling quality). The burgeoning interest in table wine did not initially produce any improvement in quality (Michael Cooper quotes New Zealand winemaker George Mazuran as saying at the time 'some growers have been getting away with blue murder') but by 1970 the winds of change commenced to blow, and soon became a gale. Between 1960 and 1983 wine production rose from 4.1 million litres to 57.7 million litres, a rate of growth which inevitably produced its own problems in the wake of static sales between 1980 and 1983. Rationalisation, takeovers and a ferocious price war in 1985-86 led to government intervention: in 1985 the industry had crushed 78,000 tonnes of grapes when it needed only 55,000 tonnes, and something had to be done. That 'something' was a vine-pull scheme designed to remove up to 25 per cent of the country's vineyards. In the end 1517 hectares of vines were removed by growers who received NZ$6175 per hectare for doing so.

The impact on production is shown in the chart at the bottom of this page, and more indirectly in the chart below, which shows the present distribution of vineyards across New Zealand, and in the chart at right which shows the varietal mix (and the changes between 1983 and 1989).

Overall, wine quality has improved out of all recognition in the last 10 years. In one style (Sauvignon Blanc) New Zealand leads the New World challenge. In all other styles it produces individual wines of equal stature, which at once demonstrate its potential but also underline the fact that there is still room for improvement. When that occurs the impact New Zealand will make on the world wine markets will utterly belie what will still be a tiny industry.

NEW ZEALAND GRAPE VARIETIES — HECTAREAGE NATIONAL TOTAL AREA OF PLANTED VINES

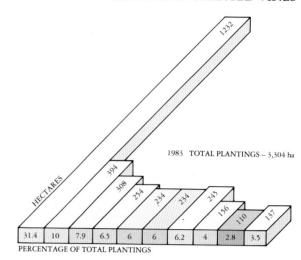

NEW ZEALAND VINEYARD AREAS HECTAREAGE (AND % NZ TOTAL)

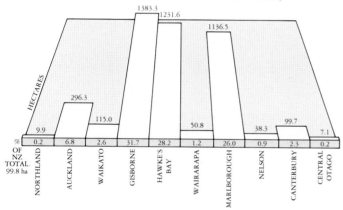

NEW ZEALAND WINE PRODUCTION AND SALES –'000 LITRES

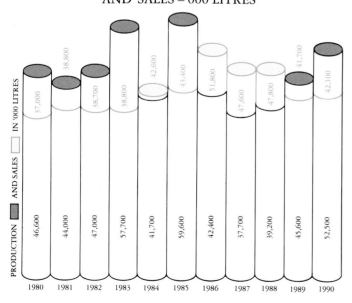

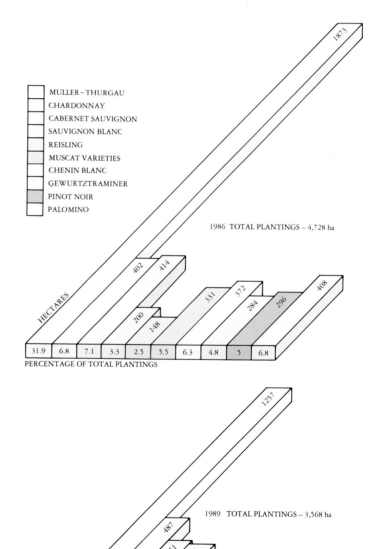

AUCKLAND AREA

From a negligible base at the turn of the century, Auckland steadily grew over the next 65 years to the point where 50 per cent of the country's vines were situated within its confines. Over the next 20 years the apparent decline was spectacular, dipping to 5.6 per cent in 1986 before recovering slightly to 6.8 per cent in 1989. In fact these figures need interpretation: in 1965 the Gisborne/ Poverty Bay plantings began in earnest, in 1973 those at Marlborough began. In other words, it was the explosion in plantings in other regions that caused the change in the figures rather than any particular decrease in Auckland's vineyards. (It is true that 161 hectares were removed during the vine pull, but Hawke's Bay lost 534 hectares.)

Much of the growth was prompted by the Dalmatians (or Yugoslavs) who had migrated to New Zealand in the early 1890s to work in the Kauri gum fields at Henderson. Another wave arrived after the First World War, not to work in the gumfields, but to grow whatever crops were needed.

Sztipan Jelich (in 1902) was the first to turn to viticulture, founding Pleasant Valley, a winery which remains in the family to this day (and is presently undergoing a renaissance). The other pioneer was not a Yugoslav, but a Lebanese: A A Corban, who planted 1.6 hectares at Henderson in 1902 and started a famous family dynasty.

Between 1925 and 1932 there was substantial growth in the New Zealand industry, most of it in the Auckland

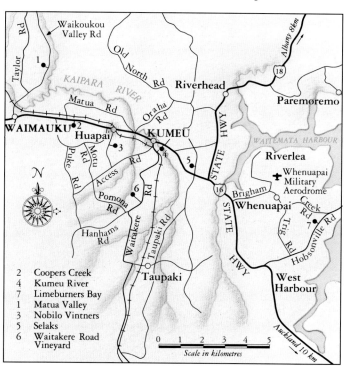

2 Coopers Creek
4 Kumeu River
7 Limeburners Bay
1 Matua Valley
3 Nobilo Vintners
5 Selaks
6 Waitakere Road
Vineyard

AUSTRALASIAN WINE REGIONS
1980 – 1990

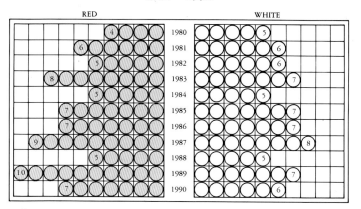

THE REGION IN BRIEF

LOCATION AND ELEVATION

36°47'S 174°34'E	*Kumeu*
36°51'S 174°40'E	*Henderson*
36°49'S 175°08'E	*Waiheke Island*
37°04'S 174°57'E	*Papakura*
50 m – 75 m	

SUBREGIONS
Waimauku/Kumeu, Henderson, Auckland, Waiheke Island and South Auckland.

CLIMATE
The wettest climate in New Zealand places special demands on viticulturists. The HDD summation of 1350 is, somewhat surprisingly, less than that of Hawke's Bay or Gisborne. The annual rainfall is a massive 1370 mm, of which 360 mm falls within the normal vintage span of February to April, and 560 mm falls over the growing season. (It is here that Waiheke Island stands out with its much lower summer rainfall.) However, averages do not tell the tale of vintages disrupted by cyclonic rainfall in the same fashion as the Hunter Valley — and which mean that a tough skinned grape variety such as Cabernet Sauvignon has special value.

SOIL
The shallow clay soils which overlie hard silty-clay subsoils exacerbate the problems associated with the high rainfall; there are some better patches with sandy loam subsoils which offer better drainage, but the vigour and vegetative growth problems have led to the development of the sophisticated U-shaped trellises inspired by Dr Richard Smart (see page 332).

HARVEST TIME
Mid-February — late March

PRINCIPAL GRAPE VARIETIES

Palomino, 55.5 ha	*Cabernet Sauvignon, 58.9 ha*
Chardonnay, 28.7 ha	*Merlot, 18.9 ha*
Semillon, 12.3 ha	*Pinot Noir, 17.6 ha*
Sauvignon Blanc, 11.7 ha	

SHARE OF NEW ZEALAND PLANTINGS
6.8 per cent

FACING PAGE: Peninsula Estate, a new face on Waiheke Island.

region. The number of licensed vignerons increased from 40 to 100, even if the quality of the wine was not particularly distinguished. This growth also laid the basis for the continuing importance of Auckland as a major production region, paralleling the role of the Barossa Valley in Australia: 90 per cent of the most important New Zealand wineries are there, even if they draw their grapes from elsewhere.

The reasons for Auckland's failure to match the viticultural growth of other districts are partly climatic and partly economic. Urban pressure has pushed almost all the vineyards (though not the wineries) out of Henderson to Kumeu/Huapai, but one wonders how long it will be before the same pressures manifest themselves there.

The great success of Matua Valley, Kumeu River, Collards and (to a lesser degree) Nobilo Vintners with locally-grown grapes (chiefly at Huapai and in the Waikoukou Valley) show

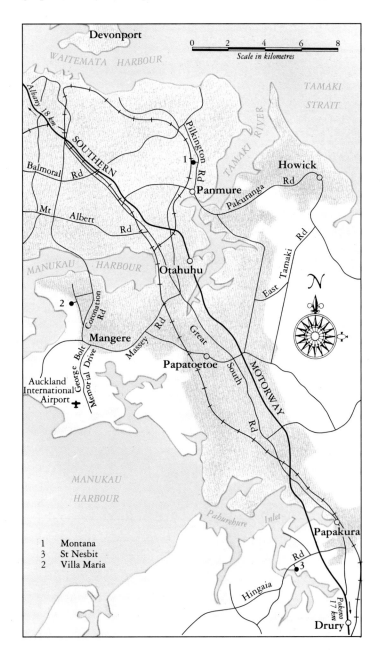

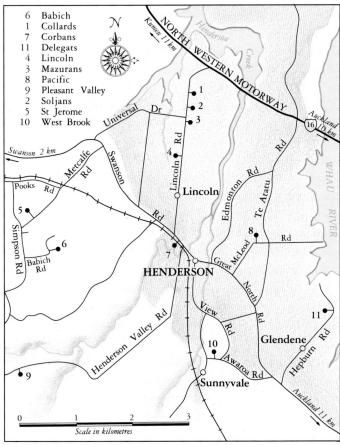

6 Babich
1 Collards
7 Corbans
11 Delegats
4 Lincoln
3 Mazurans
8 Pacific
9 Pleasant Valley
2 Soljans
5 St Jerome
10 West Brook

1 Montana
3 St Nesbit
2 Villa Maria

ABOVE: *Villa Maria contracted vineyards on the Ihaumatao peninsula: cold nights, hot days and a lesser rain fall contribute to quality.*

what can be achieved with appropriate viticulture and canopy management. The logic of growing Cabernet Sauvignon is obvious enough: it is a variety which stands up stoically to excessive rainfall and humidity (the chief problems of the area), and the adequate heat summation means that wines with better structure and fruit flavour are possible.

Then there is the special microclimate of Waiheke Island which has produced the outstanding Cabernets of Stonyridge,

while Auckland Queen's Counsel Dr Tony Molloy seems determined to prove he can do just as well at Papakura, to the south of Auckland. As one would expect of a Queen's Counsel, he makes a most compelling case.

One is simply left to wonder whether the same efforts and precocious skills applied in climates such as those enjoyed in Hawke's Bay or Martinborough might produce even greater wines. Perhaps they would, perhaps they would not.

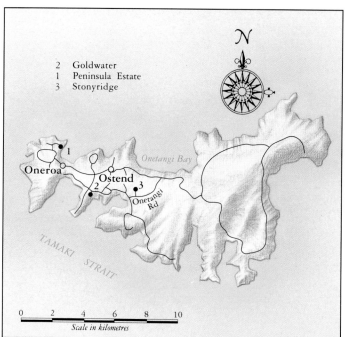

2 Goldwater
1 Peninsula Estate
3 Stonyridge

Scale in kilometres

PRINCIPAL WINE STYLES

CABERNET SAUVIGNON

There is no question: next to Hawke's Bay, Auckland produces New Zealand's best Cabernet Sauvignon, with Waiheke Island looking a strong bet to repulse the future challenge of the Awatere Valley (in Marlborough). Matua Valley produces Cabernet Sauvignon of wholly convincing weight, structure and abundant cherry fruit, while the Stonyridge Larose (80 per cent Cabernet Sauvignon 20 per cent Merlot) customarily does battle with Te Mata and Villa Maria for top place in blind tastings of New Zealand's best Cabernets.

CABERNET MERLOT

The blend of these two varieties is as synergistic here as it is in most other parts of the world, even if the Cabernet component is not as tough as it can be elsewhere. Kumeu River, indeed, makes a Merlot-dominant blend of great elegance and individual style, while in the south St Nesbit consistently produces a superb Bordeaux blend of Cabernet Sauvignon, Merlot and Cabernet Franc. Throughout one finds finely balanced blackcurrant and redcurrant fruit set against a touch of the herbaceous/capsicum flavour which is to be found in all great examples of the style.

CHARDONNAY

As Australia has so handsomely proved, Chardonnay thrives in almost every conceivable combination of climate and terroir. It simply provides wines of differing texture and flavour, but all are immediately recognisable as Chardonnay. Thus it should come as no surprise that Collard Bros should produce a complex, soft, honeyed/buttery wine of great quality even in an extraordinarily difficult vintage such as 1988. Kumeu River takes an entirely different style-path, seeking complexity and longevity, relying on bottle-development rather than simple fruit or on new oak to build flavour and aroma.

SAUVIGNON BLANC

It has to be remembered that most of the Chardonnay and Sauvignon Blanc made by the Auckland wineries is grown elsewhere, and the style of those wines is discussed in the context of the region concerned. The principal local wines are the very idiosyncratic, complex Kumeu River Sauvignon Fumé, with its strong malolactic influence, and the rather more straightforward (but reliable) wines from Collard Bros and Matua Valley. None have the tingling sparkle and zip of Marlborough or even of Hawke's Bay wines, but for some that is a good thing.

ABOVE: *Vine nursery, Stoneyridge Vineyard, Waiheke Island; to be grafted to Cabernet Sauvignon and Petit Verdot.*

MONTANA — INDUSTRY LEVIATHAN

Montana dominates the New Zealand wine industry to an even greater degree than the Penfolds-Lindemans group in Australia. Its annual crush of 30,000 tonnes is approximately half that of the entire country, and it markets all the wine it makes (it is a buyer rather than a seller of bulk wine) under its plethora of brands. Not surprisingly, it controls the retail market like no other because of its all-encompassing distribution, a degree of control strengthened in 1990 when it was appointed distributor of Penfolds' Australian wines in New Zealand. (For outsiders, the move intensified the already-existing confusion caused by Montana's acquisition of Penfolds New Zealand in late 1986: that company had passed out of Penfolds Australia's ownership many years previously, and was in fact sold to Montana by Lion Corporation Limited.)

The Montana brand was established in 1944 by Ivan Yukich from a .2 of a hectare vineyard in the Waitakere Ranges west of Auckland, part of a modest market garden enterprise. By the end of the 1950s his sons Mate and Frank Yukich had increased the vineyard to a modest 10 hectares, which was hardly indicative of the growth which was to follow.

The initial impetus came from Frank Yukich's prescience in foreseeing the move away from fortified to table wines, and his pioneering of aggressive mass-marketing strategies. Some powerful financial backing, which led to the development of a 120 hectare vineyard in the Waikato Valley and a move into Gisborne in 1960, marked the first phase of the expansion.

In 1973 Seagrams acquired a 40 per cent shareholding, and in the same year the company went public, issuing 2.4 million shares. The $8 million raised led to the crucial decision to pioneer vineyards in Marlborough, a move which was ultimately to signal Montana's transformation from a company which relied almost exclusively on marketing skills to one which relies on producing a wide range of wines and on marketing those wines with ruthless discipline. Each wine is of exemplary quality given the price and style parameters within which it is positioned.

All of this was not achieved without a degree of pain along the way: first there were loss years while Marlborough's teething problems were sorted out (it was 4 years before a maiden dividend was paid), and Montana like all others suffered in the price wars of 1985-86. This led to the exit of Seagrams in late 1985, and to Montana becoming a wholly owned subsidiary of Corporate Investments, itself a public company controlled by Montana Chairman Peter Masfen.

Since that time Montana has comprehensively returned to profitability under the direction of Masfen, Managing Director Bryan Mogridge and Production Manager Peter Hubscher, who make a triumvirate of formidable competence. Hubscher, in particular, is a no-frills, no-nonsense executive who joined the company in its troubled years (particularly 1973) and who in the wake of Frank Yukich's departure in 1974, master-minded the company's move to the production of quality wine precisely geared to the needs of the market place.

There is nothing glamorous in the making of wines such as Chardon, Blenheimer, Wohnsiedler Müller-Thurgau, Gisborne Chardonnay, Lindauer (like Chardon, a sparkling wine, though of superior quality), Marlborough Rhine Riesling nor even Marlborough Sauvignon Blanc. Even the most cursory visit to Montana's massive winery in Marlborough tells you this is first and last a production facility based purely on efficiency — a refinery rather than a winery (to reverse the old advertising slogan of Tyrrell's in New South Wales' Lower Hunter Valley).

Those observing Montana from outside New Zealand have to realise that even now 30 per cent of all wine made in New Zealand is Müller-Thurgau, and almost all of that is presented with appreciable residual sugar. So the near-reverence which outsiders accord Montana's Marlborough Sauvignon Blanc is in one sense at odds with the modest contribution which that particular wine makes to Montana's profits.

But what the wine has done is focus world attention on Montana, on Marlborough and indeed on New Zealand. Robert Joseph (the noted English wine writer) made the 1986 vintage his 'Wine of the Year'; in 1990 the 1989 vintage was awarded the Marquis de Goulaine Trophy for the best Sauvignon Blanc at the 21st International Wine and Spirit Competition in London. Indeed, since the initial and still glorious 1980 vintage, every conceivable award and

ABOVE: *Brancott Estate, part of the Montana empire.*

every conceivable word of praise has been lavished on each succeeding vintage of the wine. So it is not unduly fanciful to describe Montana's Sauvignon Blanc as its belated flirtation with glamour.

In 1988 Montana formed a joint venture with Champagne Deutz for the production of a super-premium sparkling wine at Marlborough, the first release taking place in September 1990. The visible focus of the venture (other than the wine itself) is the 18 tonne Cocquard Champagne press, which sits in splendour in its own purpose-built press house — the type of expenditure Montana would never have contemplated in days gone by. A less visible aspect is the degree of control which Montana exercises over the whole venture, which is in truth closer to a franchise/consultancy arrangement.

The other — and economically more important — move to premium quality (and all the trappings which accompany it) came with the 1989 purchase of the historic McDonald Winery at Hawke's Bay. With a quite legitimate sleight-of-hand Montana managed to acquire it for a very modest sum from arch-rival Corbans (the second largest wine group in New Zealand). The purchase cost may have been insignificant, but the subsequent expenditure on refurbishing the winery and acquiring 240 hectares of prime vineyards has been comparable to that spent in establishing Marlborough.

The aim is for the McDonald Winery to produce the highest possible quality Chardonnay, Pinot Noir and Cabernet Sauvignon, starting with the 1990 vintage. The new oak barrels so conspicuous by their absence (relative to its size) at Marlborough are present at the McDonald Winery in their hundreds. Winemaker Tony Pritchard has also been given the small-batch handling equipment, a quality press and a massive cool store — once again not to be found at Marlborough.

Behind the scenes he will be given support not only by the entire winemaking team (headed by John Simes) but through the technical interchange agreements Montana has with Penfolds Australia and, so it is rumoured, a significant consultancy arrangement within New Zealand.

Added to Marlborough Rhine Riesling (itself an excellent wine by any standards), Marlborough Sauvignon Blanc and Deutz Cuvée Marlborough, the McDonald Winery will complete an impressive array of premium wines and bury the no-frills, no-glamour image of Montana once and for all.

ABOVE: *Montana tank farm: like such installations anywhere in the world, more like a refinery than a winery, but very efficient.*

WINERIES OF THE AUCKLAND AREA

WAIMAUKU/KUMEU

COOPER'S CREEK   BA-A
State Highway 16
Huapai (09) 412 8560
Established   1982
Winemaker   Kim Crawford
Production   17,000 cases
Principal Wines   Chardonnay (Swamp Road),
Chardonnay (Hawke's Bay), Fumé Blanc,
Sauvignon Blanc (Marlborough) Riesling,
Gewurztraminer, Cooper's Dry, Cabernet
Merlot, and Cooper's Red.
Best Vintages   W 1984, '86, '89
                     R 1983, '86, '87, '89
Cooper's Creek grows 4 ha of Cabernet
Sauvignon and Merlot at Huapai, but most of its
grapes are sourced in Hawke's Bay where it owns
a 7 ha vineyard and buys grapes under contract.
I have yet to see a bad wine under the Cooper's
Creek label. At the top end, its voluptuous,
barrel fermented Swamp Road Chardonnay has
tremendous depth of peachy flavour, while at the
bottom end its Cooper's Dry (a blend of Chenin
Blanc, Semillon and Chardonnay) offers
wonderfully crisp, lemony/herbaceous flavours
which are a more than adequate New World
substitute for Chablis.

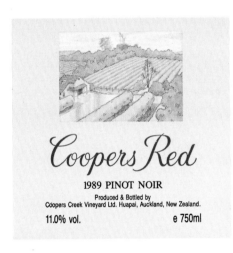

KUMEU RIVER   BA-BA
2 Highway 16
Kumeu (09) 412 8415
Established   1944
Winemaker   Michael Brajkovich
Production   17,000 cases
Principal Wines   Chardonnay, Sauvignon,
and Merlot Cabernet under the Kumeu River
label; Chardonnay, Sauvignon, Merlot and
Cabernet Franc under the Brajkovich label.
Best Vintages   W and R 1986, '87, '89
The youthful Michael Brajkovich graduated dux
of his year at Roseworthy Agricultural College
in South Australia, has made wine for Christian

Moueix in Pomerol, France, and he is New
Zealand's first Master of Wine. He is also a
highly skilled viticulturist and has made it his
mission to show that, with appropriate trellis
and canopy management techniques, Auckland
can produce high quality white and red table
wine. He fearlessly applies his technical and
practical knowledge in the winery, using a
strongly French-influenced non-interventionist
approach which nonetheless has a precisely
defined wine style as its aim. Wine such as the
Botrytised Sauvignon, and the strongly
malolactic-influenced barrel fermented
Chardonnay tend to sharply divide opinons, but
most approve. Overall Brajkovich has
unhesitatingly opted for complexity rather than
pure, simple fruit flavours, and may well prove
to be a prophet before his time.

MATUA VALLEY   BA-A
Waikoukou Road
Waimauku (09) 411 8301
Established   1974
Winemaker   Mark Robertson
Production   67,000 cases
Principal Wines   Sauvignon Blanc, Fumé
Blanc, Chardonnay, Rhine Riesling,Müller-
Thurgau, Chablis, Chenin Blanc, Chardonnay,
LateHarvest Muscat, Gewurztraminer, Semillon,
Pinot Noir, Cabernet Sauvignon, Merlot and
Claret.
Best Vintages   W and R 1977, '83, '85,
                     '86, '87, '89
Owners Bill and Ross Spence are two of the most
well liked and highly respected vignerons in
New Zealand. With intelligent viticulture (with
a heavy emphasis on Auckland-grown fruit but
with substantial purchases from Gisborne and
Hawke's Bay), astute marketing and meticulous
winemaking, Matua Valley has been built in a

relatively short space of time into one of New
Zealand's most successful operations. The
strongly flavoured Cabernet Sauvignon is almost
invariably outstanding, and was the best red
wine I encountered while judging at the 1990
Auckland Wine Show: complex, rich and stylish,
it had weight and abundant ripe fruit, with
lovely overtones of red cherry.

NOBILO VINTNERS   CB-CB
Station Road, Huapai (09) 412 9148
Established   1943
Winemaker   Nick Nobilo
Production   125,000 cases
Principal Wines   Müller-Thurgau, Gewurz-
traminer, Semillon, Sauvignon Blanc,Sauvignon
Fumé, Rosé, Cabernet Sauvignon, Pinotage and
Pinot Noir.
Best Vintages   W 1976, '85, '86, '89
                     R 1970, '76, '78, '83

Nick Nobilo is one of the most flamboyant
members of the flamboyant Dalmatian band of
New Zealand winemakers, and is most certainly
the best-dressed winemaker in Australasia
(particularly if you admire white silk suits). In
the 1970s Nobilo made some of the finest New

ABOVE: *Michael Brajkovich of Kumeu River: early growth of*
Cabernet Franc.

Zealand red wines. The current vintages are but a shadow of their former self, and the emphasis has switched to Chardonnay and Sauvignon Blanc, with varying degrees of success. Rather indifferent, oily oak seems to me to have held back the fruit potential of a number of the wines I have tasted from 1988 and 1989

SELAKS BA-A
Cnr Highway 16 and Old North Road
Kumeu (09) 412 8609

Established 1934
Winemaker Daryl Woolley
Production 29,000 cases
Principal Wines Sauvignon Blanc, Sauvignon Blanc Semillon, Semillon, Chardonnay, Rhine Riesling, Müller-Thurgau, Cabernet Sauvignon, Private Bin Claret, *Méthode Champenoise* and Rose *Méthode Champenoise.*

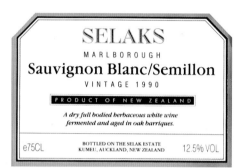

Best Vintages W and R 1983, '85, '86, '89
Australian born and trained Kevin Judd lifted Selaks to Australasian prominence when he joined as winemaker in 1983, producing the 1984 and 1985 vintages; he then departed for Cloudy Bay (in the Marlborough region), but another Australian, Daryl Woolley, has proved a more than able replacement. Despite a great deal of effort being directed to patriarch Mate Selaks' passion, *Méthode Champenoise,* the outstanding (and very consistent) wines are the Sauvignon Blanc and Sauvignon Blanc Semillon. In the same fashion as the early Cloudy Bay wines, the Sauvignon Blanc and Sauvignon Blanc Semillon cunningly counterpoise a touch of residual sugar against the pungent herbal/grassy gooseberry fruit flavours. The red wines of Selaks are, it seems, adequate for the local market, but little more than that.

OTHER WINERIES

LIMEBURNERS BAY CB-CB
112 Hobsonville Road
Hobsonville (09) 416 8844

WAITAKERE ROAD VINEYARD
Waitakere Road
RD1 Kumeu

HENDERSON

BABICH B-BA
Babich Road
Henderson (09) 833 7859
Established
Winemaker Joe F Babich
Production 67,000 cases
Principal Wines Chardonnay (in descending order of price, Irongate, Stopbank and East Coast), Sauvignon Blanc, Fumé Vert (a blend of Semillon, Sauvignon Blanc and Chardonnay), Rhine Riesling, Gewurztraminer, Müller-Thurgau, Riesling Sylvaner, Classic Dry, Chablis, Cabernet Sauvignon, Irongate Cabernet Merlot, Pinot Noir, Dry Red and various fortified wines.
Best Vintages W and R 1985, '86, '89
The Babich family has just under 30 ha of grapes planted at Henderson, but a large part of the crush comes from Hawke's Bay (from their part-owned vineyard there and from contract grape growers), Gisborne, Marlborough and elsewhere in Auckland. The winery is a model of consistency, the wines invariably representing outstanding value for money. The quality leader is, without doubt, Irongate Chardonnay, opulently oaked and very complex, but I find the Sauvignon Blanc and the Fumé Vert even more attractive. They exemplify the crisp, clean, lively New Zealand style. One or two of the Irongate Cabernet Merlots have also impressed, particularly the 1987.

COLLARDS A-A
303 Lincoln Road
Henderson
Auckland 8 (09) 838 8341
Established 1910
Winemakers Bruce and Geoffrey Collard
Production 13,000 cases
Principal Wines Chardonnay (Rothesay), Hawke's Bay, Gisborne and Marlborough), Sauvignon Blanc, Chenin Blanc, Rhine Riesling,

Gewurztraminer, Cabernet Merlot, Private Bin White Burgundy and Private Bin Claret, together with a small range of fortified wines.
Best Vintages W and R 1974, '76, '78, '83, '85, '86, '89
Father Lionel Collard, together with sons Bruce and Geoffrey, are meticulous viticulturists and equally meticulous winemakers. This care has paid handsome dividends with their 16 ha vineyard at Rothesay in the Waikoukou Valley (close to the Matua Valley). In recent years this has produced quite superb Chardonnay, and excellent Sauvignon Blanc. Apart from a small 4 ha planting around the winery, the remainder (roughly 50 per cent) comes from grapes purchased from Marlborough, Hawke's Bay and Te Kauwhata. Hawke's Bay provided a wonderful '89 Chardonnay, equal to anything Australia can produce, while Rothesay triumphed over the adversity of the 1988 vintage. The winery is also recognised as the foremost producer of Chenin Blanc in New Zealand, while the same care (and winemaking skills) shine through in their low priced Private Bin White Burgundy and Private Bin Claret.

CORBANS BA-BA
Great North Road
Hendersen (09) 837 3390
Established 1902
Winemaker Kerry Hitchcock
Production 750,000 cases plus 3 million casks.
Principal Wines Chardonnay, Rhine Riesling, Sauvignon Blanc and Cabernet Sauvignon under the Premium Stoneleigh Vineyard label (Marlborough region); Gewurztraminer, Chardonnay, Fumé Blanc and Cabernet Merlot under the Private Bin label. The full range of other bottled and casked wines come next, often under generic or brand names; there are also fortified wines.
Best Vintages W and R 1983, '85, '86, '87, '89

ABOVE: Collard's Rothesay Vineyard: windbreaks are a common sight in New Zealand vineyards.

The second largest wine group in New Zealand (although dwarfed by Montana), Corbans either owns vineyards or has contract grape growers in most of New Zealand's major grape growing areas, and wineries in Gisborne and Marlborough, the latter the site of a recent joint venture with Wolf Blass wines. In the manner of all of the major companies in Australasia, wine quality is exemplary; you basically get what you pay for with a wide range of product price-positioning.

For Australian palates, the Sauvignon Blancs are outstanding (both under the Stoneleigh and Private Bin label) with those unmistakable pristine gooseberry/herbal fruit flavours of New Zealand. Stoneleigh Chardonnay is one of the better Marlborough wines with smooth, buttery/peachy fruit, but relatively speaking, it is the Cabernet Merlots which, after the Sauvignon Blancs, impress most.

DELEGAT'S   B-B
Hepburn Road
Henderson   (09) 836 0129
Established   1947
Winemaker   Brent Marris
Production   100,000 cases (only a small percentage of which is releasedas premium varietal wine).
Principal Wines   Top of the range are Proprietor's Reserve Chardonnay, Fumé Blanc and Cabernet Sauvignon. Premium varietal wines include Chardonnay, Sauvignon Blanc, Gewurztraminer, Cabernet Sauvignon, Müller-Thurgau and Rhine Riesling.
Best Vintages   W and R 1982, '86, '87, '89
Delegat's does not own any vineyards, relying instead on long term purchase contracts from grape growers in Hawke's Bay, Gisborne and Marlborough. Its early-maturing Chardonnay now has less oak than hitherto, which is all to the good, but still tends to be overblown. On the other hand, its Proprietor's Reserve Sauvignon Blanc can be absolutely outstanding, as witness the quite lovely 1988 wine. It also produces keenly priced and well made Rhine Riesling, Gewurztraminer and Cabernet Sauvignon.

LINCOLN   C-CB
130 Lincoln Road
Henderson   (09) 836 6944
Established   1937
Winemaker   Nick Chan
Production   Not for publication.
Principal Wines   Chardonnay, Sauvignon Blanc, Chenin Blanc, Rhine Riesling, Müller-Thurgau, Brighams Creek White, Gewurztraminer, Cabernet Sauvignon, Brighams Creek Red, Sherry, Tawny and Vintage Port.
Best Vintages   W and R 1986, '88, '89
Lincoln is a former fortified wine specialist which, since 1985, has made a determined effort to lift the quality (and presentation) of its table wines. It has some distance still to go, but conforms to the pattern by producing good Sauvignon Blanc (including an interesting Auckland grown wine in 1989) and full flavoured, soft Chardonnay.

PLEASANT VALLEY   C-B
322 Henderson Valley Road
Henderson   (09) 836 8857
Established   1902
Winemaker   Peter Evans
Production   7000 cases
Principal Wines   Müller-Thurgau, Rhine Riesling, Gewurztraminer, Semillon, Sauvignon Blanc, Fumé Blanc, Chardonnay, White Burgundy, Pinot Noir, Pinotage and Cabernet Sauvignon plus a wide range of sherries and ports.
Best Vintages   W and R 1986, '87, '89
Another former fortified wine specialist which is increasingly turning its attention to varietal table wines, albeit at the bottom end of the market in terms of price. Its white wines in particular are clean and well made, and the range of sherries also offers consistently good value within the New Zealand context.

OTHER WINERIES

MAZURAN'S   NR
255 Lincoln Road
Henderson (09) 836 6945

PACIFIC   C-CB
90 McLeod Road
Henderson (09) 836 9578

ST JEROME   NR
219 Metcalf Road
Henderson (09) 833 6205

SOLJANS   C-B
263 Lincoln Road
Henderson (09) 836 8365

WEST BROOK   B-BA
34 Awaroa Road
Henderson (09) 836 8746

AUCKLAND

MONTANA   BA-A
171 Pilkington Road
Glen Innes   (09) 570 5549
Established   1944
Winemaker   John Symes (senior winemaker)
Production   The equivalent of over 1.8 million cases, though a substantial portion of this is sold in cask form.
Principal Wines   A very large range of brands and varietals; top of the range are Marlborough varietals, Sauvignon Blanc, Chardonnay, Rhine Riesling and Cabernet Sauvignon. Blenheimer and Wohnsiedler are the most important volume selling brands. Other premium wines include Private Bin and Brancott Estate, a wide range of wines under Penfolds labels. Its *Méthode Champenoise* is also a market leader along with Lindauer and the recent Deutz joint venture wine.
Best Vintages   W and R 1980, '82, '83, '86, '87, '88, '89

Controlling almost 50 per cent of the New Zealand market, Montana (with some assistance from Penfolds) sets the pace for the rest of New Zealand to follow. Both in terms of the quantity of its production and of its quality, it is a winemaker of world standing, with its Marlborough Sauvignon Blanc a worthy standard bearer. All of its white wines are of very good quality at their price, and the red wines are pleasant but by and large unremarkable.

WAIHEKE ISLAND

GOLDWATER   B-B
Causeway Road
Putiki Bay   (09) 727 493
Established   1978
Winemaker   Kim Goldwater
Production   1500 cases
Principal Wines   Cabernet Merlot Franc and Sauvignon Blanc Fumé.
Best Vintages   R 1985, '87 '89
At its best, Goldwater Cabernet Merlot Franc vies with the top New Zealand red wines, even if the oak is a fraction assertive for some tastes. The credit goes partly to the climate of Waiheke

Island, partly to the innovative trellising devised by Dr Richard Smart, and partly to the determination of Kim Goldwater to make one of the world's great wines. The Sauvignon Blanc Fumé is much less satisfactory, seldom showing the vibrant fruit which one expects from this variety.

STONYRIDGE   **A-A**
Onetangi Road
Waiheke Island   (09) 72 8822
Established   1982
Winemaker   Stephen White
Production   1000 cases

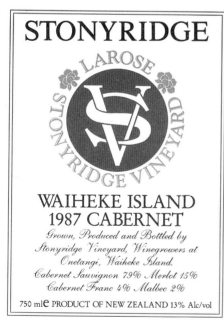

Principal Wines   Stonyridge Cabernet (typically 80 per cent Cabernet, 15 per cent Merlot) and 5 per cent Cabernet Franc and Malbec) and a second label, Airport Cabernet.

Best Vintages   **R** 1985, '87, '89
Stephen White, who graduated in horticulture from Lincoln College (New Zealand) and thereafter worked in Tuscany, California and Bordeaux, has gone further than his neighbour Kim Goldwater in achieving his ambition to make 'one of the best Medoc-style reds in the world'. The 1987 Stonyridge Larose Cabernet Sauvignon is an outstanding wine by any standards, with none of the green grassy characters which seem part and parcel of New Zealand Cabernet style. The oak is strong, but there is the fruit there to balance it. Earlier vintages (particularly the '85) have been no less impressive.

SOUTH AUCKLAND

ST NESBIT   **B-B**
Hingaia Road
R D 1 Papaqu   (09) 790808
Established   1980
Winemaker   Dr Tony Molloy QC
Production   2000 cases (increasing).
Principal Wines   A blend of Cabernet Sauvignon, Cabernet Franc and Merlot.
Best Vintages   **R** 1984, '85, '87, '89

Auckland Queen's Counsel and tax specialist Dr Tony Molloy does not seek publicity; he did not enter his 1987 vintage wine in the 1990 Auckland Wine Show, but it nonetheless walked off with the top gold medal among the dry reds (it was entered by the organisers who purchased it off the retail shelf, an enterprising move on their part). It followed on the outstanding success of the 1984 and 1985 vintages, and consolidated the reputation of St Nesbit.

VILLA MARIA   **BA-A**
5 Kirkbridge Road
Mangere   09) 275 6119
Established   1961
Winemaker   Kim Milne
Production   225,000 cases
Principal Wines   At the top of the range come intermittent Reserve Bin Black label releases of Chardonnay, Gewurztraminer, Sauvignon Blanc, Cabernet Sauvignon and Cabernet Merlot; then follow the Private Bin range of similar wines but also including a Müller-Thurgau.
Best Vintages   **W** and **R** 1985, '86 , '87, '89

Villa Maria's premium wines are made from grapes purchased in the Gisborne, Hawke's Bay, Wairarapa, Te Kauwhata and Kumeu regions. Winemaker Kim Milne (who trained at Roseworthy Agricultural College in South Australia) has consistently produced some of New Zealand's most luscious and highly rated white and red table wines since 1985. Villa Maria was edged out of absolute top position by stablemate Vidal at the 1990 International Small Makers Wine Competition held in Sydney, but the professional panel of Australian judges gave consistently high points to both the Cabernets and Cabernet Merlots of each company. Whether Chardonnay, Sauvignon Blanc, Gewurztraminer or Cabernet Sauvignon or Cabernet Merlot, the hallmark of these wines is the richness and generosity of the flavour. Sometimes this can be a little overwhelming, and it is for this reason that I (somewhat churlishly) pulled Villa Maria out of the absolute top rating which it probably deserves.

TOP: *The Goldwater residence on Waiheke Island.*
CENTRE: *From legal chambers to vineyard is all in a days work for Dr Tony Molloy of St Nesbit.*

ABOVE RIGHT: *Kim Milne, winemaker and rising star of Villa Maria (together with a bit of Ellwood the dog).*

HAWKE'S BAY

The first vines were planted in Hawke's Bay in 1851 by missionaries of the Society of Mary, making Mission Vineyards (still run by the Society of Mary) the only nineteenth century winemaking business to continue in the same ownership. But commercial viticulture and wine-making did not commence until the wine boom of the 1890s, and even then Mission Vineyards made only a modest contribution by commencing to sell a little wine 'of a stomachic and tonic nature' in 1895.

The boom started in 1890, when Henry Stokes Tiffen, a wealthy 71 year old landowner (who had lived in Hawke's Bay since 1857 and who had sporadically endeavoured to support viticulture in the region) plunged into grape growing and winemaking. By 1896 his Greenmeadows Vineyard — planted to varieties such as Chardonnay, Pinot Noir, Pinot Blanc, and Pinot Meunier — was described as 'the premier vineyard in New Zealand'. Romeo Bragato visited the area in 1895, and apart from urging Tiffen to plant Cabernet Sauvignon (advice which Tiffen followed), described Hawke's Bay and Wairarapa Martinborough as two districts 'pre-eminently suited' to viticulture.

In the meantime Bernard Chambers had started planting vines at his Te Mata station in 1892, followed by J N Williams at Frimley Orchards at Hastings in 1893. While these plantings (and the attendant winemaking) were but part of more broadly based pastoral activities of wealthy men who were in no sense dependent on wine for a living, Hawke's Bay was of great importance. By 1913 Chambers not only had the longest vineyard in New Zealand, but Hawke's Bay was producing 30 per cent of the country's wine — and what is more, producing it from the classic grape varieties.

From this point on, those varieties were eclipsed by hybrids and lesser quality high yielding varieties such as Palomino. At the same time the vineyards were removed from the hillsides and re-established on the alluvial river plains. Quantity rather than quality became the aim, and the emphasis switched entirely from table to fortified wine. It was to produce such wine that Jim McLeod at Taradale, Dick

Ellis at Brookfields and Robert Bird at Glenvale (now called Esk Valley) established wineries in the 1930s.

But much, indeed most, of Hawke's Bay's history up to 1980 was dominated by Tom McDonald and McWilliam's Wines. McDonald had acquired a small vineyard and winery from Bartholemew Steinmetz in 1926; in 1944 he sold out to Ballins, a Christchurch-based brewer, but stayed on as manager to achieve the expansion he desired and which was possible with Ballins' financial strength. In 1961

THE REGION IN BRIEF

LOCATION AND ELEVATION
39°31'S 176°50'E
25 – 90 m

SUBREGIONS
Bay View/Eskdale, Taradale, Meanee, Hastings, Havelock North and Ngatarawa.

CLIMATE
The Hawke's Bay climate is self-evidently suited to the production of high quality Chardonnay, Sauvignon Blanc, Cabernet Sauvignon and Merlot. The HDD summation is 1460 (at Napier), and the MJT is 18.8°C. The 7.4 sunshine hours per day in the growing season guarantee full ripening of the grapes, and the only significant hazard is the risk of cyclonic rainfall in March and April (such as happened in 1979 and 1988). The average October to March rainfall of 340 mm is optimal, with the balance of 440 mm falling in the winter and spring months.

SOIL
The soil types vary substantially, notwithstanding that almost all the vineyards are established on old alluvial plains. On one side are the very well drained, infertile Ngatarawa sandy loams which (while ideally suited to premium grapes) need drip irrigation because of their low water holding capacity, on the other there are the heavier silt loams with greater fertility, greater water holding capacity and moderate drainage, which lead to very vigorous growth. At Havelock North sandy loams overlie a clay pan in parts which impedes drainage and may likewise lead to vigour problems.

HARVEST TIME
Mid-March – late April

PRINCIPAL GRAPE VARIETIES
Müller-Thurgau, 394.5 ha   Cabernet Sauvignon, 123 ha
Chardonnay, 114.1 ha   Pinot Noir, 35.6 ha
Chenin Blanc, 104 ha
Sauvignon Blanc, 88 ha
Muscat Dr Hogg, 78.7 ha

SHARE OF NEW ZEALAND PLANTINGS
28.2 per cent

AUSTRALASIAN WINE REGIONS
1980 – 1990

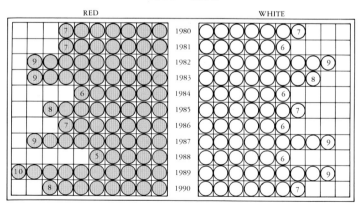

FACING PAGE: *Homestead above the BDM Syndicate vineyard which grows grapes for Te Mata.*

GISBORNE/POVERTY BAY

New Zealand is a country blessed with an abundance of rainfall, well drained moderately fertile soils, and perfect growing season temperatures, and grape vines therefore grow at a prodigious rate and produce no less prodigious crops. But one area nonetheless is superabundant, and performs much the same role for New Zealand as the Riverland does for Australia, providing the fuel for the millions of litres of white cask and cheap beverage wine consumed every year. The area is, of course, Gisborne, which now has 31.7 per cent of the country's vineyards, but has only a handful of wineries.

Between 1921 and 1956 it had only one vigneron, Friedrick Wohnsiedler, and his Waihirere Vineyard was only 4 hectares in size when he died in 1956. Nonetheless it was to be the springboard for massive expansion starting in 1961 and gathering pace from 1965. Montana acquired Waihirere, and has perpetuated Wohnsiedler's name on its premium Müller-Thurgau based wine. Montana now has two large if strictly utilitarian wineries in the region, and Corbans has

one. Neither of these wineries bottle or package wine here, and Montana's Gisborne brand keeps a modest station in life.

It has been left to Matawhero and Millton Vineyard (with Venture Vineyards and Revington Vineyards new and promising players) to show that the region is capable of greater things. Millton Vineyard, despite handicapping itself with organic viticulture in a region which (through humidity and rainfall) is theoretically heavily dependent on fungicide sprays, has done very well indeed with its white wines — albeit acknowledging that this is white wine, not red wine, country. Revington produced a glorious Chardonnay in 1989. It won a richly deserved gold medal at the 1990 Air New Zealand Wine Show, which shows why Gisborne has often provided top quality (if unacknowledged) Chardonnay to the major wine companies.

These small wineries have done much to counter-balance

AUSTRALASIAN WINE REGIONS
1980 – 1990

	RED		WHITE	
1980	6		6	
1981	6			7
1982	7		6	
1983	9			9
1984	6		6	
1985	6			7
1986	8			7
1987	6			7
1988	3		5	
1989	10			9
1990	6		6	

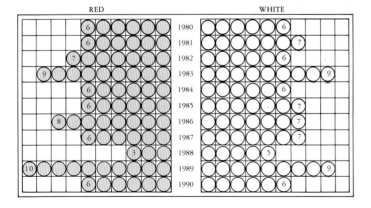

THE REGION IN BRIEF

LOCATION AND ELEVATION
38°40'S 178°01'E
40 m

CLIMATE
The climate is as conducive to growth as are the soils. It is slightly less sunny and hence slightly cooler than the climate of Hawke's Bay, with an HDD of 1380 and an MJT of 18.6°C. The real difference lies in the higher rainfall: 1030 mm annual rainfall, 420 mm between October and March, and 152 mm during February and March. These figures are high, but not distressingly so. The real problems come in years such as 1988 when Cyclone Bola submerged Gisborne, cutting it off entirely from the outside world. (By the time Cyclone Bola reached Hawke's Bay, its intensity had greatly diminished.)

SOIL
The vineyards are grown exclusively on old river flats, with fertile alluvial loams overlying sandy or volcanic subsoils.

HARVEST TIME
Mid-March to mid to late April, and sometimes into May for botrytis styles.

PRINCIPAL GRAPE VARIETIES
Müller-Thurgau, 441 ha
Chardonnay, 151.9 ha
Muscat Dr Hogg, 141.3 ha
Reichensteiner, 86.2 ha
Gewurztraminer, 76.1 ha
Semillon, 75.2 ha
Sauvignon Blanc, 61.3 ha

SHARE OF NEW ZEALAND PLANTINGS, 28.2 per cent

FACING PAGE: *Chardonnay vines and cabbage trees, the latter New Zealand's answer to Western Australia's blackboys; a contracted vineyard for Corbans.*

ABOVE: *A typically verdant and lush Chardonnay planting, the grapes destined for Corbans.*

not only the region's reputation for mediocrity but also the dual blows struck to the region by phylloxera and the vine-pull scheme: between 1983 and 1989 the area under vine fell from 2081 hectares to 1383 hectares, although it has now stabilised, and it is likely that in future we shall see more wines proudly labelled Gisborne.

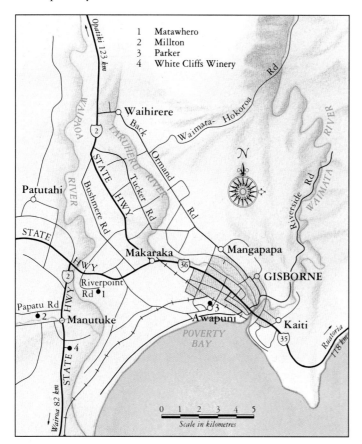

PRINCIPAL WINE STYLES

MÜLLER-THURGAU
Yields from this variety are always high, but here they are gargantuan — 30 tonnes per hectare is common. The resultant wine is bland, and its residual sugar provides it with such flavour as it has.

CHARDONNAY
In a self-perpetuation of what may be an unfair myth, and in a fashion eerily reminiscent of the Australian Riverland, some top quality Chardonnays have been made from Gisborne grapes by major companies, but the source of the grapes has been deliberately suppressed. This is in truth more a tribute to the flexibility of Chardonnay and to winery skills than any indication of unsuspected regional greatness.

GEWURZTRAMINER
It is Gisborne's misfortune that the worldwide view of Gewurztraminer is so jaundiced. New Zealand produces some wonderful wines from this variety, few if any are better than those from Gisborne. At their best, the wines of Matawhero stand supreme — opulently spicy, concentrated and complex yet neither heavy, oily or excessively tannic. When botrytis intervenes, the result is less convincing.

RHINE RIESLING
Millton produces good dry Rhine Rieslings and quite outstanding botrytised versions — the latter presumably occur regularly in the vineyard thanks to the combined effect of viticultural practice (which includes tight netting against birds) and climate.

ABOVE: *Organic growing at Millton Vineyard: wormwood repels insects and helps restrict excess vine vigour.*

DR RICHARD SMART — SOCRATES DISSATISFIED

Dr Richard Smart is, and always has been, a stormy petrel. His ascerbic tongue and pen are driven by a passion for viticulture and an acute intelligence: suffering fools is not one of Dick Smart's strong points. His restless drive has brought him respect — indeed fame — not only in Australasia but right across the New and Old viticultural worlds. He has done more to bring viticulture (and viticulturists) out of the closet than any other person in Australasia, and has immeasurably helped the cause of wine quality in so doing.

In this respect it is true he is simply part of a worldwide trend towards recognition that one grows wine (not grapes) in the vineyard, or — if you prefer — that great wine is made in the vineyard. His particular contribution has been to focus attention on the ways this can be achieved, and to constantly challenge comfortable, conventionally-held views.

Richard Smart began to gain attention shortly after he became a lecturer in viticulture at Roseworthy Agricultural College in South Australia in 1975 (ultimately becoming Dean of the Faculty of Oenology). At that time viticulture was a despised subject on the curriculum — despised by the students, that is — and the same attitudes prevailed in most Australian wineries: the winemaker saw the grapes for the first time when they arrived at the winery door, and picking and winemaking decisions were determined on the laboratory bench. Indeed, the same attitude extended all the way up the corporate management chain — the great game of the period from 1975 to 1987 was to buy wineries and sell off vineyards.

Richard Smart faced entrenched and exceedingly conservative views. Traditional Barossa Valley and Hunter Valley viticulture assumed there would be a drought every year, denied the possibility of irrigation, and pruned accordingly. Typical yields were 2 to 2.5 tonnes per hectare, reducing the grower to financial penury. Smart challenged these views (and others) head-on, and in consequence has always been tagged particularly by his critics as a 'big-vine' proponent.

Inevitably, his views are very much more complex than that tag would suggest. Right from the start his interest has been in efficient utilisation of land to produce maximum yields of premium quality grapes, an aim no one would quarrel with. Nor would anyone deny his central tenet for achieving that aim: a vine in balance, which has an appropriately managed canopy.

It is now generally recognised that the chief problem confronting any grape grower is to train the vine to produce the right amount of vegetative growth to support the desired crop level. The tendency of the vine is to produce excessive vegetation (even in a high-crop situation) and control of vine vigour is of paramount importance.

It is here that the central argument occurs between Richard Smart and others. All sides agree that so far as possible self-regulation of vigour is the desired objective: manual intervention after the growth has occurred is both costly and in certain circumstances partly ineffective. The move to close spacing of vineyards in the New World (emulating as far as terrain and viticultural machinery will permit the vineyards of the Old World) has been prompted by the belief that inter-vine competition will reduce vigour. This in turn means smaller bunches and less bunches per vine, but also a better balance between vegetation and crop.

Richard Smart disagrees. He says first that in most Australian vineyard conditions inter-vine competition is simply not sufficient unless one gets to unrealistically close planting. Secondly, the cost per hectare is needlessly high owing to the far greater number of vines and to significantly increased irrigation and (to a lesser degree) trellis costs. His solution is to space the vine even more widely, but to train it to produce a very large canopy on an elaborate trellis.

Just when the views of the two camps seem irreconcilable, points of agreement start to appear again. For a major part of Richard Smart's research has been directed to measuring the amount of light (or, if you prefer, the degree of shading) on the grape bunches and evaluating the chemical and flavour consequences of increased (or diminished) light. He has made winemakers acutely aware of the importance of adequate sunlight falling on the grapes, and the dire consequences of excessive shading.

The result, a canopy management has become the focus of viticultural attention as the 1990s start. 'Leaf plucking', 'Scott Henry', 'RT2T', 'Lyre', 'canopy surface area' and 'shoot positioning' are among the viticultural buzz words.

After 7 years at Roseworthy Agricultural College, and 8 years with the New Zealand Ministry of Agriculture and Fisheries, Dr Smart has finally left the world of pure academic research and returned to Australia to join a joint venture between Cassegrain vineyards (of New South Wales) and the Commonwealth Scientific and Industrial Research Organisation (CSIRO). The venture's initial project has been the development of a 'slotting' machine to introduce lime into acidic subsoils, lifting pH and thereby enhancing root development and vine growth. We shall hear more, rather than less, from Richard Smart in the future.

ABOVE: *Dr Richard Smart, Australasian guru now returned to Australia's vineyards from those of New Zealand.*

WINERIES OF THE GISBORNE/POVERTY BAY REGION

MATAWHERO   CA-CA
Riverpoint Road
Matawhero   (06) 868 8366
Established   1975
Winemaker   Hatsch Kalberer
Production   8000 cases
Principal Wines   Chardonnay, Gewurztraminer, Sauvignon Blanc, Chenin Blanc, Pinot Noir and Cabernet Merlot.
Best Vintages   **W** and **R** 1978, '82, '83, '87, '89

Both owner Denis Irwin and Matawhero have a formidable reputation as being erratic and unpredictable. I have always had great difficulty with the wines with the honourable exception of the Gewurztraminer, which can be as opulently spicy and flavoursome as the best of Alsace, France. The other wines seem to suffer from excessively idiosyncratic winemaking techniques and philosophies.

MILLTON VINEYARD   BA-B
Papatu Road
Manutuke
Gisborne   (06) 862 8680
Established   1984
Winemaker   James Millton
Production   6000 cases

Principal Wines   Chardonnay, Chenin Blanc, Te Arai River Sauvignon Blanc Semillon, Opou Vineyard Rhine Riesling, Steinberg Müller-Thurgau, Cabernet Rosé and Cabernet Sauvignon.
Best Vintages   **W** and **R** 1985, '87, '89
With remarkable courage James Millton has chosen the difficult Gisborne climate in which to practise organic viticulture, eschewing all chemically-based sprays. The Millton Vineyard is known primarily for its white wines, in particular for its Opou Vineyard Riesling and its late harvest Botrytised Riesling — the '87 and '89 vintages of both styles having won scarce gold medals in New Zealand's show competitions.

OTHER WINERIES

PARKER   NR
91 Banks Street
Gisborne (06) 867 6967

WHITE CLIFFS WINERY   NR
(formerly Revington Vineyards)
PO Box 162
Manutuke (06) 862 8577

ABOVE: Another organic farming method: straw mulch is placed under the vines to retard weed growth (Millton Vineyard).

WAIRARAPA/ MARTINBOROUGH

It is unlikely that Wairarapa will ever challenge Hawke's Bay in terms of production (it presently boasts only 1.1 per cent of the nation's vineyards) but Hawke's Bay owes much to it. In 1890 Henry Stokes Tiffen visited William Beetham's Wairarapa vineyard planted to Shiraz and Pinot Noir, and tasted the wines. Michael Cooper records that Beetham subsequently wrote, 'He [Tiffen] paid us a visit and saw my vineyard; he lunched with us and tasted our wine. He said, "This is enough for me", went back to Napier and planted a vineyard.'

Notwithstanding Romeo Bragato's unqualified endorsement of the suitability of Wairarapa for premium grape growing, Beetham's vineyard (which had been planted in 1883) was removed in 1905 after prohibitionists were victorious in Masterton. The first sign of a renaissance came

in 1978 when Alister Taylor planted a small vineyard, but the real impetus came when leading Department of Scientific and Industrial Research (DSIR) soil scientist Dr Derek Milne became a founding partner in Martinborough vineyards, following up a 1979 report in which he had identified climatic and soil similarities between Wairarapa and Burgundy.

It is an interesting area: one ascends over the imposing Tararua Range to reach it from Wellington, but it in fact sits in a valley which opens directly onto the Cook Strait. It is much cooler and drier than any other North Island region, and shares a climate similar to that of Marlborough.

Notwithstanding that it is surrounded by high mountains, the vineyards are all established on old alluvial gravelly river flats, albeit in carefully delineated patches — carefully

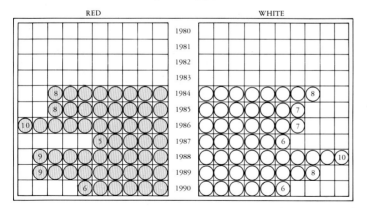

AUSTRALASIAN WINE REGIONS
1980 – 1990

RED				WHITE		
			1980			
			1981			
			1982			
			1983			
8			1984			8
8			1985			7
10			1986			7
	5		1987			6
9			1988			10
9			1989			8
	6		1990			6

THE REGION IN BRIEF

LOCATION AND ELEVATION
41°13'S 175°28'E
50 m

CLIMATE
With an HDD summation of around 1100, the climate is distinctly Burgundian, and it is not hard to see why most of the vignerons have elected to concentrate on early ripening varieties. By March and April, the average daily temperature has fallen to 14.7°C, and there is a long, slow finish to the season, which is intermittently affected by late season rainfall. However, with a winter-spring dominant rainfall of under 700 mm, it is not surprising that drip irrigation is widely used to counteract summer drought. Overall, the principal climatic problem is wind: southerlies blast up from the Cook Strait, while northwesterly gales are also common. Tall windbreaks are to be found in and around almost all vineyards.

SOIL
Centuries ago the Huangarua River laid down strips of gravelly silt loams (similar to those found in parts of Hawke's Bay) over the deep, free draining gravels. These are ideal for premium grapes, but they do exacerbate the effect of summer drought, and make drip irrigation essential.

HARVEST TIME
From late March to early April for Pinot Noir into May for botrytised Riesling and Cabernet Sauvignon.

PRINCIPAL GRAPE VARIETIES
Chardonnay, 13.6 ha   *Pinot Noir, 13.1 ha*
Sauvignon Blanc, 5.6 ha   *Cabernet Sauvignon, 9.6 ha*
Gewurztraminer, 5.6 ha

SHARE OF NEW ZEALAND PLANTINGS, 1.1 per cent

ABOVE: *Te Kairanga boasts a strange assembly of buildings, some converted from quite different duties.*

FACING PAGE: *The Wairarapa Plain, incandescent under the bulwark of the Tararua Range.*

delineated, that is, by the local vignerons who have moved swiftly to set up their own mini appellation control system, and who have differentiated these soils from the heavier clays which are also found in the valley.

Virtually every winery in the district has helped contribute to its ever-growing reputation, a reputation which took a major leap forward at the 1990 Air New Zealand Wine Show.

The star was Ata Rangi, which won the top gold medal in the 1989 Pinot Noir class (a class dominated by Martinborough wineries), a gold medal for its 1989 Celebre (a Cabernet Sauvignon/Shiraz/Merlot blend) and an unpublished but similarly high rating for its 1990 Chardonnay (an 'evaluation' wine submitted under a particular rule of the Show which encourages winemakers to enter wines they are not certain about and which are not officially given points or medals).

Dry River, produced a superlative 1990 Botrytis Riesling of world quality (and which I gave 19.5 points out of 20) and a 1989 Pinot Noir which won a silver medal, adding to its formidable reputation for luscious, mouthfilling Pinot Gris. Palliser Estate received the second gold medal in the Pinot Noir Class for its 1989 Pinot Noir, and a silver medal for its tangy 1990 Sauvignon Blanc. Martinborough Vineyards was (not surprisingly) the third gold-medallist in the 1989 Pinot Noir class and also received a silver medal for a perfectly made 1990 Rhine Riesling.

Finally, there is Chifney Winery which had its moment of glory at the 1988 Auckland Easter Wine Show where its 1986 Cabernet Sauvignon (a wine with long, lingering sweet fruit and just a touch of leafiness) won a gold medal. This did no more than confirm owner/winemaker Stan Chifney's already high reputation as a red wine maker.

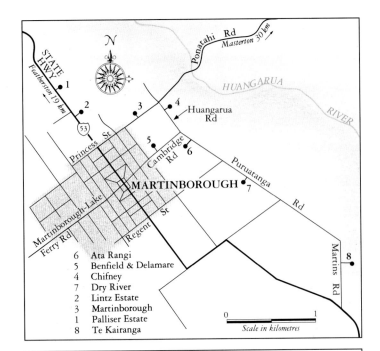

6	Ata Rangi
5	Benfield & Delamare
4	Chifney
7	Dry River
2	Lintz Estate
3	Martinborough
1	Palliser Estate
8	Te Kairanga

PRINCIPAL WINE STYLES

PINOT NOIR

A number of writers and observers seem to have fallen into the trap of assuming that New Zealand's climate simply has to be suited to Pinot Noir, and have not bothered to look closely enough at the wines. Any knowledgeable judge who tasted the Pinot Noir class at the 1990 Auckland Easter Wine Show would know better. Just to underline the point there has not even been a flicker of real style or quality from the Marlborough region, proving again how unpredictable Pinot Noir is. However, Martinborough is clearly an area in which first class Pinot can be produced, combining bell-clear varietal character (cherry/strawberry/plummy) with impressive depth, strength and colour. Again in typical fashion for the grape, the same impressive results do not occur every year, but that is no disgrace. Ata Rangi, Palliser Estate, Martinborough vineyards are clearly the leaders, with Dry River in close attendance.

CHARDONNAY

Once again, the region holds out the utmost promise. Although the growing season is long, and the end extremely cool, the grapes achieve good alcohol levels and the wine has much more richness and weight in the mouth than most Marlborough Chardonnays. The low rainfall also means that the distracting influence of botrytis seldom makes its presence felt.

CABERNET SAUVIGNON

Chifney and Ata Rangi (the latter with a Celebre) have demonstrated that though the region may be better suited to the Burgundian varieties, good Cabernet styles can be made. These do tend to be relatively light-bodied, and are certainly low in tannin, and so need to be judged by the standards of Chinon, France, rather than Coonawarra in South Australia. The earlier ripening Merlot may prove a more logical grape in the long term.

ABOVE: *Limestone rocks show the subsoil of parts of Wairarapa/Martinborough.*

MARTINBOROUGH VINEYARDS — PINOT PACESETTER

In a move reminiscent of that of Dr Andrew Pirie when he selected Pipers Brook, Derek Milne put his money where his research suggested he should in forming the partnership which acquired land in Wairarapa in 1979. His partners were his brother Duncan (an agriculturist), and Russell Schultz (a chemist) and his wife Sue Schultz.

The first vines in the 10 hectare vineyard were planted in 1980, and it now has Chardonnay, Sauvignon Blanc, Gewurztraminer, Pinot Noir and Rhine Riesling in bearing, supplemented by grapes purchased from other growers in the district.

The first few bottles of Pinot Noir and Sauvignon Blanc from the 1984 vintage, followed by the 1500 cases of the 1985 wines, made it obvious for all to see that the vineyard and the area were capable of producing fruit of exceptional quality. It was indeed sufficient for the partners to lure Larry McKenna away from Delegat's to become winemaker prior to the 1986 vintage. McKenna, Australian born and trained, had joined Delegat's in 1980 and became chief winemaker in 1983, a position he held until his departure for Martinborough.

McKenna's arrival was marked in spectacular fashion. Gold medals are far less common in New Zealand than they are in Australia, but each of his '86 Pinot Noir, Chardonnay and Sauvignon Blanc have won at least one gold medal. His 1986 Pinot Noir stands as by far the best New Zealand Pinot Noir I have tasted, magically combining clear cherry/plum varietal flavour with powerful colour and excellent structure. The problem with so many New Zealand Pinot Noirs is that they are pretty when very young but they are exceedingly simple and light, and do not live in bottle. No such criticism could be levelled at the 1986 Martinborough Pinot Noir.

Despite his considerable overall experience, McKenna is the first to admit he is still learning about making Pinot Noir. He attended the 1988 Oregon Pinot Noir winemakers conference (where we first met) and in 1989 and 1990 experimented with some of the techniques and ideas which came from that experience. In the meantime his 1988 Pinot Noir scored an exceedingly rare double, winning gold medals at both the New Zealand and Australian National Wine Shows.

I did not think that the 1988 Pinot Noir was as good as the '86, but I was overwhelmed by the style and quality of his 1988 Chardonnay, a wine which picked up where the very good '86 left off. It was an exceptionally smooth, rich and complex wine with smoky barrel ferment characters augmenting strong peachy fruit. The 1989 Chardonnay was much more subdued as a young wine with pleasant smoky oak, melon/peach fruit, and fairly pronounced acidity. While it did not seem likely to rival the '88, it was clearly destined to grow in bottle.

The 1989 Pinot Noir, by contrast, is a massive wine, deep in colour — freakishly so for a Pinot — and with layers of complexity. In October 1990 it was still to develop the full perfume of mature Pinot Noir, and when I encountered it at the 1990 Air New Zealand Wine Show I indeed wondered whether it was 100 per cent Pinot Noir. Having subsequently learnt its identity, I am certain that it is, and equally certain that it will prove to be exceptionally long-lived.

As the record shows, the skills of the genial but quiet and unassuming McKenna do not end with these two varieties. His gently oaked Fumé Blanc adds yet another chapter to the record of this variety in New Zealand, while the Gewurztraminer rivals the best Matawhero wines in the voluptuous intensity of its flavour. Finally, McKenna exhibits a sure touch with a toasty elegant Rhine Riesling which has an Australian cast to its make-up.

Palliser Estate (the first wines of which McKenna made under contract at Martinborough vineyards) acquired the services of Rob Bowen as winemaker for the 1990 vintage. Bowen, a fellow Australian, made his mark at Plantagenet (in Mount Barker, Western Australia) where he was chief winemaker for a number of years. Bowen then acted as a consultant in 1989 for a number of wineries in or near the Swan Valley (also in Western Australia), and achieved quite miraculous results. Late in 1990 Rob Bowen returned to Western Australia to become winemaker at Capel Vale, and at the time of writing his replacement was not known.

Bowen has left his mark, however, and was the outstanding success of the district in the 1990 Air New Zealand Wine Show.

ABOVE: *Shoot positioning and shoot removal early in the growing season for Pinot Noir at Martinborough Vineyard.*

WINERIES OF THE
WAIRARAPA / MARTINBOROUGH REGION

ATA RANGI   BA-A
Puruatanga Road
Martinborough   (0533) 69 570
Established   1980
Winemakers   Clive Paton, Phyllis Pattie
Production   2000 cases
Principal Wines   Chardonnay, Gewurztraminer, Pinot Noir and Celebre.
Best Vintages   W and R 1986, '89, '90
Ata Rangi seems to have flowered in 1989 and 1990 with a tangy/smoky barrel fermented Chardonnay which has tremendous length of flavour; a powerful, plummy Pinot Noir with silky texture and pronounced oak; and a gloriously fruity and lively Celebre (a blend of Cabernet Sauvignon, Shiraz and Merlot) which had exceptional balance and mouthfeel as a young wine and will probably be drunk long before its due time.

DRY RIVER   BA-BA
Puruatanga Road
Martinborough   (0553) 69 388
Established   1979
Winemaker   Neil McCallum
Production   2500 cases
Principal Wines   Gewurztraminer, Sauvignon Blanc, Pinot Gris, Riesling, Chardonnay, Fumé Blanc and Pinot Noir.
Best Vintages   W and R 1987 '89, '90

Owner/winemaker Neil McCallum, with a Doctor of Philosophy in Chemistry from Oxford, makes remarkably intensely flavoured and tightly structured white wines of quite particular style. Without question one of his most outstanding wines is the Pinot Gris, with rich buttery/toasty/peachy flavours and great mouthfeel, but the fine, bone dry Gewurz-

traminer also shows great varietal definition, while the occasional Botrytis Bunch Selection Riesling can be magnificent.

MARTINBOROUGH   A-A
Princess Street
Martinborough   (0553) 69 955
Established   1980
Winemaker   Larry McKenna
Production   5000 cases

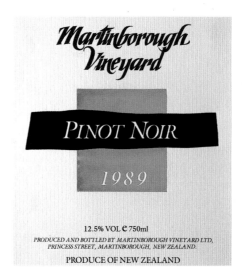

Principal Wines   Chardonnay, Sauvignon Blanc, Riesling, Gewurztraminer, Müller-Thurgau and Pinot Noir.
Best Vintages   W and R 1986, '88, '89
Australian born and trained winemaker Larry McKenna who worked as winemaker and in due course head winemaker at Delegat's for many years, has had outstanding success at Martinborough vineyards since moving there in 1986. He immediately produced what remains the best Pinot Noir I have yet seen from New Zealand (the '86 Martinborough) and in 1988 went close to achieving the same distinction with Chardonnay. These two wines are Martinborough's finest: at its best, the Pinot Noir has intense, sappy/strawberry varietal character and great structure; the Chardonnay is as perfectly modulated and polished as any top Australian example of the variety.

PALLISER ESTATE   NR
Kitchener Street
Martinborough   (0553) 69 839
Established   1989
Winemaker   Robert Bowen
                   (1990 vintage)
Production   Will be 10,000 cases plus.

Principal Wines   Will be headed by Chardonnay and Pinot Noir, but include other premium varietals.
Best Vintages   Not yet rated.
Palliser Estate is by far the largest development to date in the Martinborough area, and the investor/owners have recruited the enormously talented Australian winemaker Robert Bowen for the brand new and lavishly equipped winery. With the combination of Bowen's skills as a winemaker, and the inherent advantages the area has for producing high quality fruit, some spectacular wines should result.

TE KAIRANGA   C-C
Martins Road
Martinborough   (0553) 69 122
Established   1983
Winemaker   Chris Buring
Production   8000 cases
Principal Wines   Chardonnay, Sauvignon Blanc, Fumé Blanc, Gewurztraminer, Chenin Blanc, Pinot Noir and Cabernet Sauvignon.
Best Vintages   Not rated.
Notwithstanding the enthusiasm and knowledge of Tom and Robyn Draper, who head the shareholder group owning Te Kairanga, all of the wines I have tasted (up to and including the 1989 vintage) have had real problems, tending to lack fruit and show some rather bitter/hard flavours. It is possible that bottle age will smooth out some of the rough edges, and the vineyards seem capable of producing high quality fruit, so the future may well be brighter.

OTHER WINERY

CHIFNEY   NR
Huangarua Road
Martinborough (0553) 69 495

ABOVE: *Soil scientist-cum-winemaker Dr Neil McCallum of Dry River showing another aspect of the alluvial gravels of the Wairarapa.*   FACING PAGE: *The tradition comes from Bordeaux, but is no less beautiful at Ata Rangi.*

ADDITIONAL WINERIES OF THE NORTH ISLAND

COOKS   BA-A
Paddy's Road
Te Kauwhata
South Auckland   (0817) 63 840
Established   1968
Winemakers   Kerry Hitchcock (chief winemaker), Tricia Jane, Evan Ward
Production   500,000 cases
Principal Wines   Premium releases are Cook's Winemakers Reserve Chardonnay and Cabernet Sauvignon and Longridge Chardonnay, Fumé Blanc, Gewurztraminer and Cabernet Merlot. Low priced wines are sold under the Chasseur brand.
Best Vintages   W and R 1983, '84, '86, '87, '89

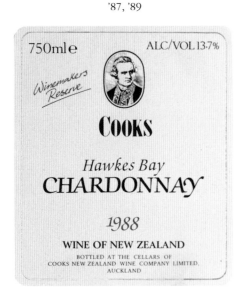

Part of the Corbans/McWilliam/Cooks' empire, having been acquired by Corbans in 1987, Cooks remains an important contributor to quality wine in New Zealand, thanks in no small measure to the skills of chief winemaker Kerry Hitchcock, who is now chief winemaker for the entire group. It sources its grapes from a variety of regions, most importantly Hawke's Bay (for Chardonnay and Cabernet) and Marlborough (Sauvignon Blanc and other varieties). Hitchcock is a believer in the use of American oak, which has tended to 'sweeten up' and enrich the otherwise somewhat tart and leafy flavours of many New Zealand wines.

De REDCLIFFE   B-B
Lyons Road
Mangatawhiri
Pokeno   (09) 779 923
Established   1976
Winemaker   Mark Compton

Production   20,000 cases
Principal Wines   Chardonnay, Semillon Chardonnay, Rhine Riesling, Fumé Blanc and Cabernet Merlot.
Best Vintages   W and R 1988, '89
De Redcliffe's star is growing rapidly in stature. Approximately half its production comes from estate-grown Chardonnay, Semillon, Cabernet Sauvignon and Merlot. The other half comes from Pinot Noir, Chardonnay, Rhine Riesling and Sauvignon Blanc purchased from growers in other regions, principally Hawke's Bay. Quality is a little uneven, but its best wines, typified by its 1989 Semillon Chardonnay and its 1989 Hawke's Bay Chardonnay, are wines of remarkable power and intensity, even if they do not aspire to elegance. In mid-1990 it was acquired by a Japanese company.

MORTON ESTATE   B-B
R D 2, State Highway 2
Aongatete via Katikati (075) 20 795
Established   1979
Winemaker   John Hancock
Production   42,000 cases
Principal Wines   Chardonnay and Sauvignon Blanc released both under the standard White Label and under the Black Label Winery Reserve, also Cabernet Sauvignon, Gewurztraminer, Rhine Riesling and Premium *Méthode Champenoise*.
Best Vintages   W and R 1985, '86, '89

The Chardonnays and Sauvignon Blancs (labelled Fumé Blanc if totally barrel fermented) are wines of absolutely unmistakable style made from Hawke's Bay grapes. They are uncompromising, boots-and-all wines which smother you in a complex web of flavour and structure. I personally find them overpowering and claustrophobic, and in particular do not enjoy the heavy skin contact/botrytis characters which I seem to find in so many of them. Other very good judges rate the wines as New Zealand's

best. The B-B rating is an unashamedly cowardly compromise between the two views.

RONGOPAI   CA-B
71 Waerenga Road
Te Kauwhata   (0817) 63 981
Established   1982
Winemakers   Tom van Dam, Dr Rainer Esenbruch
Production   3000 cases
Principal Wines   Müller-Thurgau, Chardonnay Te Kauwhata (Hawke's Bay) Riesling, Sauvignon Blanc, Cabernet Sauvignon, Gewurztraminer and Botrytised Riesling.
Best Vintages   W and R 1983, '86, '89
A winery which has a deservedly high reputation for its Botrytised Rieslings, which come in various grades from simply Late Harvest to Auslese. Its other wines are variable and idiosyncratic, some reflecting the temperamental climate of Te Kauwhata, some having a surprisingly non-technical approach to winemaking given the extremely high academic qualifications of its two research-scientists/winemaker/owners, while yet others having exemplary flavour and structure.

OTHER WINERIES

THE ANTIPODEAN   C-D
Matakna, Leigh
Northland (09) 444 6064

ASPEN RIDGE   DC-C
Waerenga Road
Te Kauwhata (0817) 63 595

CONTINENTAL   DC-C
Otaika,
Whangarei, Northland (089) 48 7227

GRAPE REPUBLIC   NR
State Highway 1
Te Horo (069) 43 284

KARAMEA   C-C
RD 10, Tuhikaramea Road
Frankton, Waikato

TOTARA   C-B
Main Road
Thames, Waikato (0843) 86 798

VILLAGRAD   NR
Rukuhia Road
Ohaupo, Waikato (071) 292 893

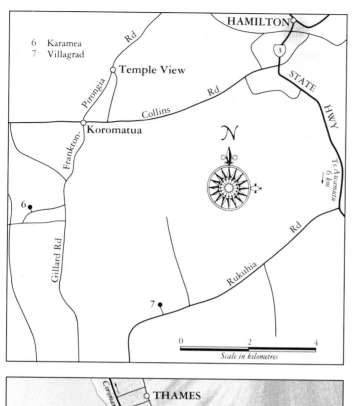

6 Karamea
7 Villagrad

HAMILTON

Temple View

Koromatua

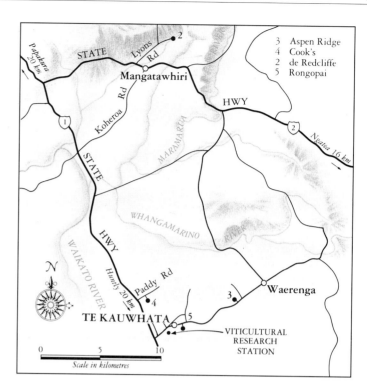

3 Aspen Ridge
4 Cook's
2 de Redcliffe
5 Rongopai

Mangatawhiri

TE KAUWHATA

Waerenga

VITICULTURAL
RESEARCH
STATION

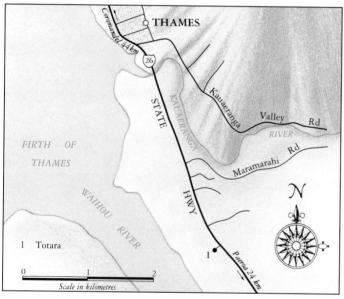

THAMES

FIRTH OF
THAMES

1 Totara

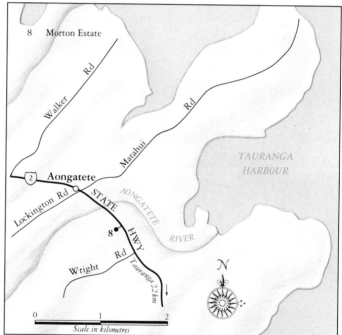

8 Morton Estate

Aongatete

TAURANGA
HARBOUR

ABOVE LEFT: *The gentle touch of infinite experience.*

ABOVE RIGHT: *Half way to harvest.*

NEW ZEALAND

SOUTH ISLAND

Marlborough/Nelson

Canterbury

Central Otago

While most of the viticultural pioneers concentrated their efforts at the top of the North Island, there were a number of attempts to establish vineyards in the South Island from the earliest days. French immigrants planted vines in 1840 at Akaroa on the mountainous Banks Peninsula just south of Christchurch, but in the long term it came to nothing. Romeo Bragato wrote of it, 'The wine industry prospered [there] so long as those by whom it was started remained at the helm, but immediately they began to die off, the vineyards became neglected and in consequence the vines died out'.

Some of the Germans (predominantly Silesians) who were populating the Barossa Valley stopped off at Nelson; a few settled in 1843 and planted vines, but two shiploads took one look at the dense bush before sailing on to South Australia. The Nelson vineyards then succumbed in the same way as those at Akaroa, although F H M Ellis and Sons are said to have made wine near Takaka from grapes and sundry fruits between 1868 and 1939. There is no recorded attempt to grow wine grapes in Marlborough prior to 1973.

There were attempts to grow wine grapes at the southern end of the South Island around Otago — by 1870 Jean-Desire Feraud had established 1700 vines and was making styles as diverse as a prize-winning Constantia through to a Burgundy. The first New Zealand wine tasted by Romeo Bragato on his arrival from Victoria was made by Mrs Hutcheson at Arrowtown, about which Bragato was extremely cryptic; he nonetheless gave Otago his seal of approval.

Despite Bragato's approval, the vineyards faded away as quietly here as they had elsewhere in the South Island, and there was no further attempt to grow wine grapes until the late 1950s, when Robert Duncan planted several thousand cuttings. These succumbed to birds and frost, the latter the greatest viticultural problem in this most marginal climate.

It is hard to predict where the boundaries of viticulture will eventually be drawn in the South Island. It seems probable it will depend upon the suitability of particular sites (of as little as 4 hectares each) in offering protection from frosts and wind, and maximising the available warmth. Wine regions in the conventional sense, such as Marlborough, will not extend south past Canterbury, and even then they will be discontinuous and site-dependent. The Central Otago developments also prove that viticultural conditions and winemaking skills alone will not necessarily determine success or failure. For new wineries everywhere reaching the market is an essential prerequisite. The scenic delights and the already-established tourist industry bring a captive market to Central Otago at almost no cost to the wineries. Provided they in turn understand and service the needs of those tourists (in the manner of Gibbston Valley Wines) they will succeed.

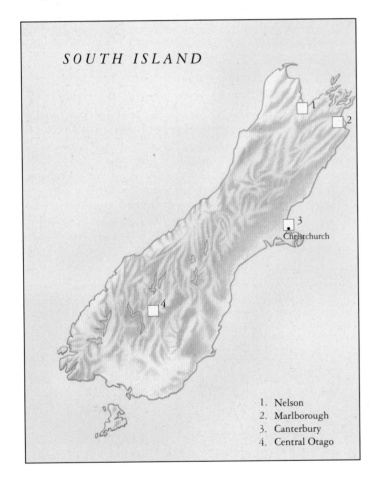

SOUTH ISLAND

1. Nelson
2. Marlborough
3. Canterbury
4. Central Otago

Christchurch

PREVIOUS PAGES: *Montana - Brancott Estate: long days provide abundant sunshine.*

ABOVE: *Pinot Noir in the Ruby Bay Wines vineyard overlooking Tasman Bay.*

ABOVE: *Vavasour Estate with Mt Tapu standing guard.*

MARLBOROUGH/NELSON

If asked to capture the essence of New Zealand wine there is only one possible answer: the crystalline pungency and crisp beauty of Marlborough Sauvignon Blanc. In their different ways, Montana and Cloudy Bay have done more to create awareness of, and credibility for, New Zealand on the world wine stage than any other producers or any other styles. This is in no way to denigrate the achievements of Te Mata, Kumeu River, Martinborough vineyards, Collards, Stonyridge or a host of others: but for all but a handful of wine fanatics, it is through initial exposure to Montana and Cloudy Bay Sauvignon Blanc that the door has been opened.

Yet just as David Wynn ventured into Coonawarra in South Australia on the basis of an extremely sober and cautious report, which pointed out that if all else failed the property could be used for grazing, it was no flash of divine inspiration which led Montana into Marlborough in 1973. Marlborough was chosen partially because Hawke's Bay was considered too expensive (though one is left to speculate how much more Montana had to pay per hectare for its 1990 entry into Hawke's Bay than it would have had to pay in 1973). What is more, Michael Cooper records how the then young DSIR scientist Wayne Thomas was requested by Frank Yukich to obtain second opinions supporting Thomas' suggestion that Marlborough should be planted. 'Confirmation was duly obtained from Professors Winkler, Lider, Berg and Cook', Thomas relates.

The initial plantings were not without their problems. Irrigation was initially regarded as unnecessary, a mistaken view which set back early progress significantly. Nor was the area perceived as a premium wine district. To this day Müller-Thurgau dwarfs all other plantings, and Rhine Riesling and Gewurztraminer were the first premium varieties to be established in any quantity. Sauvignon Blanc and then Chardonnay were planted with initial caution, and the first Montana Marlborough Sauvignon Blanc was not made until 1980.

Marlborough now has 26 per cent of the nation's plantings and 42 per cent of its Sauvignon Blanc, with the latter increasing at a rapid rate. But it is not a single variety region:

Montana's success with its sparkling wine Lindauer led to the 1988 formation of the joint venture with Champagne Deutz and to the release of the first Deutz Cuvée Marlborough in September 1990. Grove Mill and Hunters have achieved

THE REGION IN BRIEF

LOCATION AND ELEVATION
41°31' E 173°57'S Blenheim, Marlborough
41°16' E 173°00'S Upper Moutere, Nelson

25–75 m

SUBREGIONS
Wairau Valley and Awatere Valley (Marlborough).

CLIMATE
The climate is undeniably cool, with an HDD of 1152 and an MJT of 17.7°C. This puts it at the lower end of the spectrum for the major grape growing regions of the world and without doubt the saving grace is the abundant sunshine (7.8 hours per day) of the relatively dry summer. Of the annual rainfall of 740 mm, only 300 mm falls between October and April, making irrigation essential on all except the most favoured sites. Wind is a problem in some years, as it is in most of New Zealand, but birds are not. Until 1990 it was thought that widespread frosts were unlikely between 1 October and 30 April, but the devastating April frost of that year proved otherwise. The climate of Nelson is cooler still over the length of the growing season (997 HDD) with much higher rainfall: 1000 mm overall, and 460 mm falling in the growing season.

SOIL
The soils of the Wairau Valley are extremely variable, from clay to stony gravel, with inconsistent patterns shaped by the meandering course of streams and rivers running down over the ages from the surrounding mountains. The distribution of gravels, stones and fines is laterally and vertically irregular, making vine vigour (and water requirement) difficult to predict. The more stony areas are excessively well drained (and have a very high supplementary water requirement), and are not particularly fertile. While they do not make viticulture easy, the soils are clearly a major contributor to quality. The soils of Nelson are of different origin, having richer loams and being much less stony, leading to greater vine vigour.

HARVEST TIME
From mid to late March for sparkling wine production through to late April/early May for Cabernet Sauvignon. Montana has harvested Sauvignon Blanc as early as 28 March and as late as 3 May.

PRINCIPAL GRAPE VARIETIES
Müller-Thurgau, 378.2 ha   Cabernet Sauvignon, 111.3 ha
Chardonnay, 149 ha
Sauvignon Blanc, 144 ha
Rhine Riesling, 127.8 ha

SHARE OF NEW ZEALAND PLANTINGS, *26.8 per cent*

AUSTRALASIAN WINE REGIONS
1980 – 1990

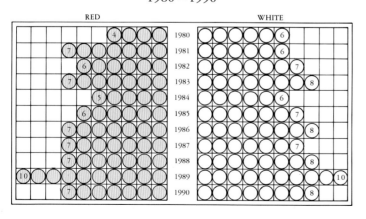

FACING PAGE: *Stoneleigh Vineyard, typical of the alluvial gravel soils of the Marlborough region.*

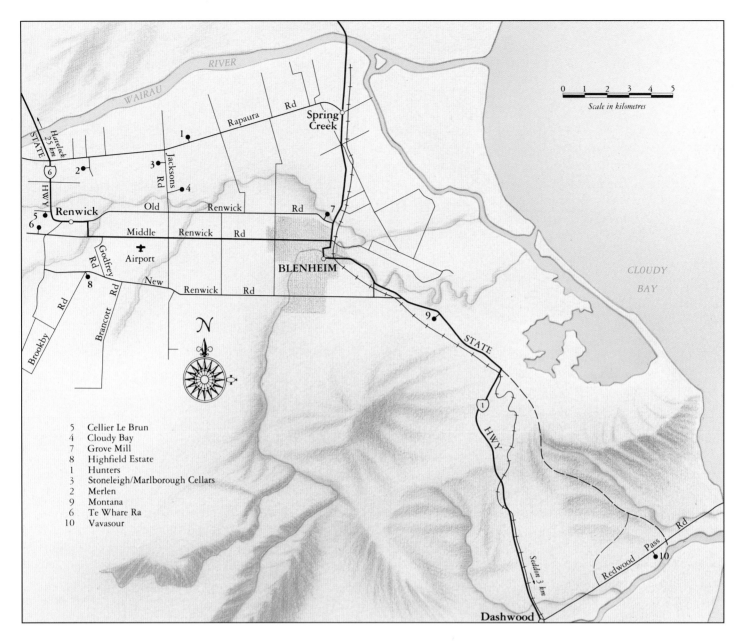

wonderful things with Chardonnay; Cloudy Bay with Cabernet Merlot; Te Whare Ra with botrytis styles; and Vavasour promises much with its red wines. The laser-flat, stony vineyards of Marlborough, framed by the mountains made famous through the Cloudy Bay label, lose nothing in the argument with Hawke's Bay as to which is New Zealand's foremost premium wine district.

Although Nelson (75 kilometres to the east of Marlborough and separated by the Richmond and Bryant Ranges) has less than 1 per cent of the nation's plantings, it has a far longer viticultural history. What is more, those steep hillsides which discouraged most of the would-be German vignerons in the 1840s now contain some of the most beautiful of all the vineyards in New Zealand.

That beauty partially reflects the Achilles heel of the district: while it is much warmer than Marlborough, harvest rainfall (such as occurred in 1990) disrupts the vintage with distressing frequency. Despite that both Neudorf and Weingut Seifried regularly make wines of impressive quality and style, and Nelson's future is assured. Like Central Otago, tourism is a significant source of support and income, a factor which is likely to become more rather than less important as the years go by.

ABOVE: *Women are the backbone of the vineyard force, having the patience and skills which men lack.*

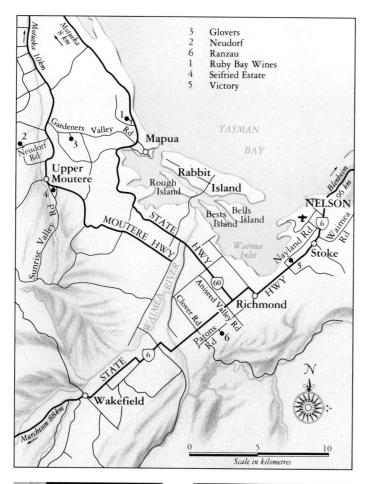

3 Glovers
2 Neudorf
6 Ranzau
1 Ruby Bay Wines
4 Seifried Estate
5 Victory

ABOVE: *George Thompson, travelling cooper, about to recondition barrels at Grove Mill.*

PRINCIPAL WINE STYLES

SAUVIGNON BLANC

Marlborough's most famous wine style is discussed at length on pages 350 and 351 and needs no further comment here, except to say that all the Nelson growers also do well with the variety, producing a slightly fuller and softer style.

CHARDONNAY

One suspects that an ever-growing percentage of this variety is being diverted to sparkling wine use, but Hunters, Grove Mill and Cloudy Bay in particular demonstrate what can be achieved given appropriate winery skills and financial commitment (principally to new oak). In other words, the somewhat bland wines of Montana, while perfectly acceptable within the parameters of their chosen market, do not represent the best the region can offer. The skilled use of barrel fermentation, lees contact and a carefully controlled percentage of malolactic fermentation contribute to the superbly complex and yet beautifully clean wines of the top three producers. Chardonnay is Nelson's leading grape variety (in terms of plantings, at least) with the elegant, barrel fermented wines of Neudorf showing the way.

RHINE RIESLING

While no more in vogue in New Zealand than anywhere else, Rhine Riesling does produce supremely elegant wines in Marlborough — long lived, steely, with delicate Germanic lime juice tones — and a kaleidoscopic range at Nelson, thanks to the skills of Hermann Seifried. Here you find the full range from Reserve Dry to simple Rhine Riesling (albeit of almost Spatlese sweetness) to Late Harvest (of Auslese-weight) to Beerenauslese. The fine, lime juice flavours of Marlborough give way to more lush tropical flavours which attest to Nelson's warmer climate and (one suspects) some botrytis influence even in the dry styles.

MÜLLER-THURGAU

Depending on one's point of view, the same wine can be described as delicately fruity, clean and balanced, or as bland, inoffensive and unremarkable — and likewise for every Müller-Thurgau I have ever tasted.

GEWURZTRAMINER

Gewurztraminer is widely made in both regions, but relatively more important in Nelson than in Marlborough. Overall, the style is excellent, with pronounced spicy/lychee aroma and flavour, yet it avoids oily, tannic heaviness. The market, unfortunately, remains unexcited.

CABERNET SAUVIGNON

Whether the Awatere Valley will be the exception which proves the rule remains to be seen, but all of the Marlborough Cabernet Sauvignon to date has lacked the body and the ripe fruit flavour which consumers are entitled to expect. Rather thin, leafy wines are the order of the day, and age wearies them.

MARLBOROUGH SAUVIGNON BLANC — A FAIRYTALE SUCCESS

Montana did not select the Marlborough region with Sauvignon Blanc uppermost in its mind: if there was a single variety which it hoped would flourish, it was Müller-Thurgau. The decision to plant 23 hectares of Sauvignon Blanc was triggered by a trial wine made by Matua Valley in 1974 from a tiny trial plot at Auckland. Peter Hubscher, who made the decision to plant the 23 hectares, once wrote, 'This represented a huge financial risk; grapes were new to the region and the variety unproven in this part of the world'.

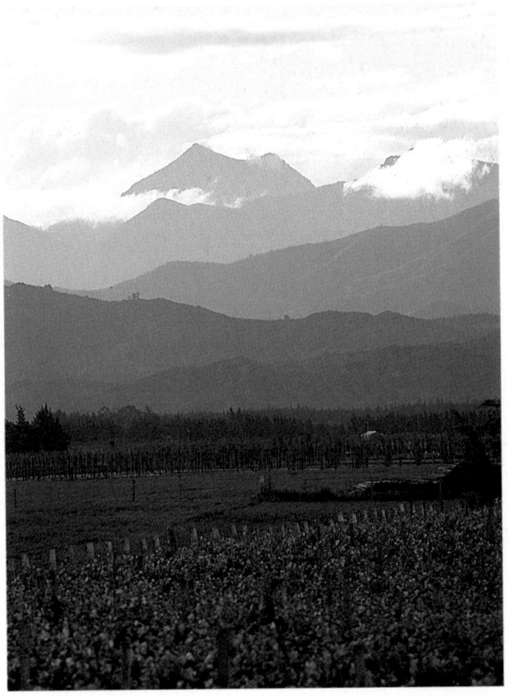

Nothing ventured, nothing gained, as the old adage has it, and it is simply not possible to quantify the ultimate rewards: no amount of money could buy the reputation which Marlborough Sauvignon Blanc has gained. But that success did not come without a struggle, as Hubscher explains: 'Initially the Sauvignon Blanc was planted without irrigation. Vines in areas of low water capacity suffered badly. Premature senescence as a result of water stress in these areas resulted in vines of varying strength. The grapes harvested were of very variable maturity, with some vines producing mature bunches and others gave berries which raisined before ripening.'

The first commercial release was not made until 1980, and it is a wine which nonetheless stands as a landmark, adding its weight to the argument that young vines can produce great wines, or so it may seem. In fact, a 6 year period between planting and first crop is long by French standards, let alone those of the New World. What is more, that first crop was minuscule: 2.3 tonnes per hectare, or 15 hectolitres per hectare. The 1981 crop was not much larger (2.9 tonnes per hectare), but the wine did not have the same luscious intensity. It was not until 1982 that the long term average of around 11.6 tonnes per hectare (or 72 hectolitres per hectare) was reached.

The learning curve continued through the first half of the 1980s. In the vineyard there was an accumulation of knowledge about the timing and quantity of supplementary water: one unsuspected conclusion was that adequate irrigation helped in those exceptional years in which significant summer rains fell. If the vines had had insufficient water, they would eagerly take up the rainfall, causing the berries to swell too rapidly and split, or at the least causing thin skins and bunch congestion ideal for the development of botrytis.

Canopy management also changed and improved immeasurably. New Zealand viticulturists have been among the world's leaders in understanding and promoting the benefits of adequate exposure of the bunches to sunlight, and in developing a mechanical means of leaf plucking around the fruiting zone. Inevitably, many of the early trials were conducted by Montana in its Marlborough vineyards.

Winery and winemaking experience also grew, even though the basic approach to making Montana Sauvignon Blanc has always been very straightforward and simple: fermentation in stainless steel, no oak, and early bottling to retain maximum freshness — simple, but not quite that simple. For a start, skin contact (allowing the crushed grape skins and juice to remain in contact with each other before pressing) has always been practised. But Montana learned it had to reduce the period of contact in years in which deacidification (the latter by a process which Montana regards as one of its trade secrets) is required. While in vintages in which there is significant botrytis not only is the period of skin contact once again shortened, but the juice is pasteurised prior to fermentation.

Nonetheless, for all the learning and fine tuning, the style of Montana Marlborough Sauvignon has remained remarkably consistent since 1980. Some years (such as 1989) produce wines which are a little grassier and crisper than others (such as 1980 and 1987), which are richer and softer, with more gooseberry/passionfruit sweetness to the fruit. But throughout there is an unmistakable common thread of exhilarating, tangy flavour, delicate yet intense, with a lingering but clean, dry finish.

One has to, however, admit that some leading wine critics around the world would strike out that description and substitute 'cat's pee'. It seems to me the latter description may be justified by second-rate wines from the Loire Valley in France but not by those of Marlborough. A less extravagant criticism levelled at Sauvignon Blanc is that it is a second-rate variety producing simple wines which do not age

ABOVE: The Richmond Ranges stand guard over Cloudy Bay's vines; the label doesn't lie.

well. The flavour of Montana's Sauvignon Blanc may be pure (and hence arguably simple) but the wine can age gracefully for 2 to 8 or more years according to vintage. And in any event, why should it have to age: as a young wine, it is a perfect match with almost all seafood and that is no disgrace.

As if to meet the criticism of simplicity, Cloudy Bay burst on the scene in 1985, showing that one could preserve all of the essential ingredients of Marlborough Sauvignon Blanc yet provide an edge of the exotic. It was (and is) a masterly combination of winemaking and winemarketing expertise, spearheaded by Cloudy Bay's immensely evocative label — evocative both in terms of graphic design and the very name of the winery.

The man behind Cloudy Bay is David Hohnen, founder and winemaker of Cape Mentelle winery in the Margaret River region of Western Australia. Veuve Clicquot now has a controlling interest in the combined operation, and the output of both wineries will now increase rapidly, strengthening the already impressive international reputation which Cloudy Bay in particular enjoys. But Veuve Clicquot has no intention of involving itself in production or in winemaking decisions, which in the case of Cloudy Bay rest with David Hohnen and his Australian born and trained winemaker Kevin Judd.

Hohnen got just about everything dead right when he set up Cloudy Bay, and one of his most inspired decisions was to pluck Kevin Judd from Selaks where he had transformed white wine quality and produced (by the standards of the time) startlingly good Sauvignon Blanc. It is a tribute to Hohnen's modesty and no less to his intelligence that he has allowed Kevin Judd to take the lead role — both in real terms and in terms of public perception — at Cloudy Bay, but Hohnen's input should not be underestimated.

Between them they evolved a minutely detailed and precisely determined approach to winemaking style, at once recognising early limitations in the vineyard, the expectations of the market, and the future scope for refinement. Thus up until 1989 all the wines had a subliminal touch of residual sugar, and quite early on they introduced a percentage of barrel fermented wine (now around 15 per cent to 20 per cent).

Cloudy Bay has also worked hard to improve the quality of the fruit coming from the vineyard, and now has 40 hectares of its own, supplementing contract grape growers who work under strict guidelines and with consultancy advice (through Cloudy Bay) from Dr Richard Smart.

As one would expect, the resultant wine is more complex than that of Montana, with a faintly smoky edge to the gooseberry/green melon/grapefruit flavours and aromas, and a more textured palate. For all that, there are a few who will never like the wine, but they cannot legitimately accuse it of being simple or common.

ABOVE: Montana's Brancott Estate at dusk.

WINERIES OF THE MARLBOROUGH/NELSON REGION

MARLBOROUGH

CELLIER LE BRUN   B-B
Terrace Road
Renwick   (057) 28 859
Established   1980
Winemaker   Daniel Le Brun
Production   13,000 cases
Principal Wines   *Méthode Champenoise* specialist offering non vintage, vintage, Rosé and Blanc de Blancs; also Chardonnay and Pinot Noir table wine in small quantities.
Best Vintages   Not relevant.
French born and trained Daniel Le Brun set tongues wagging when he established his close-spaced vineyard and built his cellars into the side of a hill before buying a press which seemed larger than the cellar could possibly need. The early wines had real problems, but in recent years have become a model of consistency, with the Blanc de Blancs showing particularly attractive creamy style. His sparkling wines dominated their classes at the 1990 Royal Easter Wine Show in Auckland.

CLOUDY BAY   A-A
Jacksons Road
Blenheim   (057)28 914
Established   1985
Winemaker   Kevin Judd
Production   25,000 cases
Principal Wines   Sauvignon Blanc, Chardonnay and Cabernet Merlot.

Best Vintages   W and R 1985, '88, '89
The acquisition of a majority interest in Cape Mentelle/Cloudy Bay by Veuve Clicquot was tangible recognition of the phenomenal international brand success of Cloudy Bay. David Hohnen not only recognised the quality of the Marlborough region for Sauvignon Blanc, but also had the foresight to hire Kevin Judd (Australian trained but then winemaker at Selaks) to make the wine. The result was an instant fairytale success, and the gloss has not gone off the Cloudy Bay Sauvignon Blanc. First Chardonnay and then Cabernet Merlot have been added to the range, the 1988 vintage of the latter being an absolutely beautiful red. But to my mind, the smoky, pungent and beautifully balanced Sauvignon Blanc remains one of the outstanding examples of this variety to be found anywhere in the world.

GROVE MILL   BA-BA
1 Dodson Street
Blenheim   (057) 89 199
Established   1988
Winemaker   David Pearce
Production   6000 cases

Principal Wines   Rhine Riesling, Sauvignon Blanc, Chardonnay, Gewurztraminer, Pinotage and Cabernet Sauvignon.
Best Vintages   W and R 1988, '89
If it were not for the lack of track record, I would have been very tempted to give this new winery an absolute top rating. Certainly its wines from the 1989 vintage, spearheaded by the 1989 Lansdowne Chardonnay, were quite outstanding, and strengthened the impact made by the initial releases from 1988. In every respect, a winery to watch.

HUNTERS   A-A
Rapaura Road
Blenheim   (057)28 489
Established   1983
Winemaker   John Belsham
Production   25,000 cases
Principal Wines   Rhine Riesling, Gewurztraminer, Sauvignon Blanc, Sauvignon Blanc oak aged, Chardonnay, Pinot Noir and Cabernet Sauvignon.

Best Vintages   W and R 1986, '87, '88, '89
Hunters, Cloudy Bay and Te Mata must rank as New Zealand's three best small wineries. Consultancy advice from Dr Tony Jordan (of Australia) has transformed wine quality, and also resulted in consistency matched only by the other two wineries I have mentioned. It is hard to choose between the wooded and non-wooded Sauvignon Blanc and Chardonnay as the winery's best: all three have exemplary varietal character, structure and flavour. In particular, there are none of those jungle-like characters which so often appear in New Zealand white wines.

MERLEN   B-B
Rapaura Road
Renwick   (057) 29 151
Established   1987
Winemaker   Almuth Lorenz
Production   4000 cases
Principal Wines   Chardonnay, Fumé Blanc, Rhine Riesling, Gewurztraminer, Müller-Thurgau.
Best Vintages: W and R 1987, '88, '89

TOP: Jane Hunter of Hunters being taken for a walk by Commodore.

German-born Almuth Lorenz spent several years as winemaker at Hunters, establishing a reputation both for that winery and for herself. Energetic and fearless, she made an immediate impact upon setting up Merlen, producing a robust, full flavoured Chardonnay. But she also has a special affinity with Müller-Thurgau and Rhine Riesling, producing excellent wines from these varieties in 1989, together with an extremely good Sauvignon Blanc.

MONTANA   CA-A
Riverlands Winery
State Highway 1
Blenheim
(For further details see pages 314 and 315)

VAVASOUR   NR
Redwood Pass Road
Awatere Valley   (057) 27 481
Established   1986
Winemaker   Glen Thomas
Production   Will exceed 10,000 cases.
Principal Wines   Sauvignon Blanc, Fumé Blanc, Chardonnay, Cabernet Sauvignon and Cabernet Sauvignon Cabernet Franc.
Best Vintages   **W** and **R** 1989
Vavasour is a new but high-profile venture established in the Awatere Valley, separated by a range of hills and some distance east from the Wairau Valley, where most of the Marlborough vineyards are established. The stony ground has been selected as a red wine vineyard, and the triumvirate of owner Peter Vavasour, viticulturist Richard Boling and winemaker Glen Thomas are convinced that great Bordeaux-style wines can be made here. Simply because the winery was not erected until 1988, the only commercial releases as at 1990 were of white wines, the Sauvignon Blanc and Fumé Blanc of that year respectively winning a gold

and a silver medal at the Auckland Easter Wine Show and doing nothing to dampen the high expectations held for the winery.

OTHER WINERY

TE WHARE RA   B-B
Anglesea Street
Renwick
Marlborough (057) 28 581

NELSON

NEUDORF   BA-BA
Neudorf Road
Upper Moutere   (054) 32 643
Established   1977
Winemaker   Tim Finn

NEUDORF VINEYARDS

PINOT
NOIR
1990
PRODUCED AND BOTTLED BY
TIM & JUDY FINN, UPPER MOUTERE, NELSON, NEW ZEALAND
PRODUCT OF NEW ZEALAND
13.0% Alc · 750 ml

Production   3000 cases
Principal Wines   Chardonnay, Sauvignon Blanc, Rhine Riesling, Semillon, Pinot Noir, Young Nick's Red and Cabernet Sauvignon.
Best Vintages   **W** and **R** 1982, '83, '86, '87, '88, '89
Tim Finn is one of those who believes that great wine is made in the vineyard and, not surprisingly, his consistently very good wines attest the wisdom of that belief. Neudorf has always done very well in wine shows, typified by its success at the 1990 Royal Easter Show in Auckland where its 1989 Fumé Blanc, 1988 Pinot Noir and 1989 Nick's Red all topped their respective classes, while the 1988 Chardonnay and 1989 Rhine Riesling both won silver medals. It must be said that overall the style is very much that of New Zealand, with botrytis playing an at times rather obvious role in the dry white wines.

SEIFRIED   B-BA
Cnr Main and Sunrise Roads
Upper Moutere   (054) 32 795
Established   1973
Winemaker   Saralinda MacMillan
Production   20,000 cases
Principal Wines   Sauvignon   Blanc, Chardonnay, Rhine Riesling, Gewurztraminer, Pinot Noir and Cabernet Sauvignon, Gamay.
Best Vintages   **W** and **R** 1985, '86, '88, '89
Austrian born but German trained, Hermann Seifried has built Nelson's largest winemaking enterprise, and one renowned for the consistency of the quality of its wines. Foremost are the aromatic varieties of Müller-Thurgau and Rhine Riesling, the latter presented in almost every guise imaginable from dry to oak aged to Beerenauslese — the latter never less than good and often (as in 1988) quite outstanding with its intensely sweet yet elegant array of tropical fruit flavours.

OTHER WINERIES

GLOVERS   NR
Gardeners Valley Road
Upper Moutere (054) 32 692

RANZAU   NR
PatonsRoad
Richmond
Nelson (054) 23 868

RUBY BAY WINES   C-C
Korepo Road, RD 1
Upper Moutere (054) 22 825

VICTORY   NR
Main Road South
Stoke (054) 76 391

ABOVE: Siefried Estate Vineyard on the road to Rabbit Island.

CANTERBURY

The final verdict on the Canterbury region is still to be delivered. In part this stems from the fact that the industry as we know it today is less than a decade old (the first wines were produced at St Helena in 1981); in part from the small scale of the wineries, some of which are run by owners without formal winemaking qualifications; and in part from the marginal climate which makes the precise matching of site and variety of great importance.

Sporadic attempts at viticulture have been made since the earliest days. I have recounted how French settlers made wine from vineyards planted near Akaroa on Banks Peninsula in the 1840s, although it is not clear how much (if any) was sold commercially. In the 1940s W H Meyers built a small winery called Villa Nova, but gave up after his vines failed to crop adequately.

Interest was rekindled in the 1970s when English-born Dr David Jackson joined the horticulture department of Lincoln College and conducted trial plantings to establish which varieties were most suited to the climate. Not surprisingly, Rhine Riesling, Chardonnay and Pinot Noir stood out, and dominate plantings today. The emergence (since 1986) of Cabernet Sauvignon and Sauvignon Blanc is a little surprising, but presumably reflects the entrepreneurial approach of the Giesen winery.

Lincoln College remains a significant factor in stimulating viticulture, with an ongoing research program covering canopy management (trellising and pruning) and clonal selection trials. Dr David Jackson is also now Managing Director of Torlesse wines, a 21 shareholder group (almost half of them growers spread over West Melton, Rolleston, Lincoln, Kaituna and North Canterbury), which is one of the newest arrivals.

Overall, however, the district owes much of its recognition to the somewhat controversial figure of Australian-born and German-trained Dany Schuster. Schuster arrived at Lincoln College in the early 1980s via South Africa and various parts of Australia and New Zealand. Somewhere along the way he was infected by the Pinot Noir virus, and while his viticulture interests and skills extend across all varieties, his

oenological interest has increasingly been focused on Pinot Noir.

He became winemaker at St Helena, making the 1982 vintage which put the Canterbury district on the map overnight. Until then, great scepticism had prevailed about the potential of the region, and while echoes of that scepticism remain, there is no questioning the role for Pinot Noir.

The 1982 Pinot Noir was the first of three gold medal winning wines from St Helena — 1982, 1984 and 1985 — and when Schuster left St Helena prior to the 1986 vintage, he proved difficult to replace.

He is now owner and winemaker at Omihi Hills Vineyard

AUSTRALASIAN WINE REGIONS
1980 – 1990

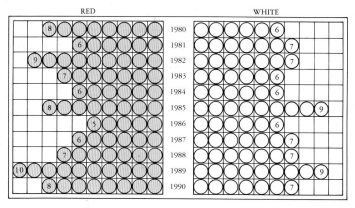

THE REGION IN BRIEF

LOCATION AND ELEVATION
43°01'E 172°51'S Omihi
43°37'E 172°18'S Barnham
25–100 m

SUBREGIONS
Omihi, Waipara, Amberley, Belfast and Burnham.

CLIMATE
This represents the extreme of commercial viticulture in New Zealand: only the early ripening varieties can be expected to perform well, and then only in the warmer years. Christchurch (at the centre of the subregions) has an HDD of 910 and an MJT of 16.4°C, making it substantially cooler than Rheims in Champagne, France. However, some sites claim much higher figures: up to 1140 HDD in the Omihi Valley, for example. Annual rainfall varies between 650 mm and 750 mm, with a very dry (and hence sunny) summer helping to offset the apparent lack of warmth: growing season rainfall is only 280 mm.

SOIL
Because of the varied topography and the geographic spread of the subregions, soils vary greatly. In the central river plain regions, there are alluvial silt loams over gravel subsoils. In the north, on gentle slopes, there are chalky loams rich in limestone, while elsewhere (mainly in the south) there are patches of volcanic and loess soils over rocky subsoils.

HARVEST TIME
From mid-April to mid to late May.

PRINCIPAL GRAPE VARIETIES
Rhine Riesling, 25.5 ha   *Pinot Noir, 14 ha*
Chardonnay, 15.1 ha   *Cabernet Sauvignon, 8 ha*
Müller-Thurgau, 12.3 ha
Sauvignon Blanc, 6.5 ha

SHARE OF NEW ZEALAND PLANTINGS, 2.3 per cent

FACING PAGE: Hand training (removing unwanted shoots) from young Pinot Noir at Omihi Hills.

(previously called Netherwood Farm). The first Pinot Noir vintage (1989) was disappointing, but better things are in store.

In the interim the wineries Larcomb and (in 1989) Amberley Estate have kept the Pinot Noir flag flying. And if the 1989 Omihi Hills Pinot Noir was a disappointment, the Pinot Gris from Omihi Hills of that year was not — it is an outstandingly rich and complex wine.

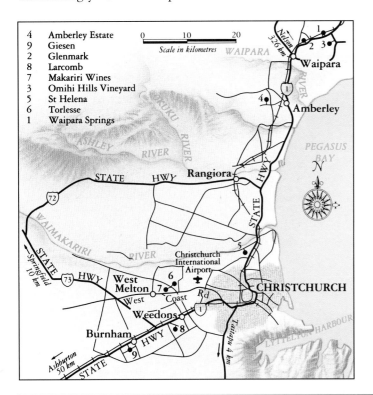

4 Amberley Estate
9 Giesen
2 Glenmark
8 Larcomb
7 Makariri Wines
3 Omihi Hills Vineyard
5 St Helena
6 Torlesse
1 Waipara Springs

PRINCIPAL WINE STYLES

PINOT NOIR
Without question, this is the most important — and most convincing — wine style of the region. For all that, it has fluctuated in weight, intensity and flavour — both with vintage variation and with winemaker experimentation. The saving grace of this style has been authentic varietal flavour, with a combination of cherry, raspberry and plum fruits, allied with a distinctive stemmy/herbaceous cross-cut. Wairarapa has in recent years not only thrown down the gauntlet, but eclipsed the previous claim of Canterbury to be the foremost producer of Pinot Noir in New Zealand, but it is reasonable to assume the fight is not yet over. The Canterbury winegrowers are sure to rise to meet this challenge to their supremacy.

CHARDONNAY
Some surprisingly rich and full bodied wines have been produced in the Canterbury region, particularly by St Helena and Giesen. If these Chardonnays have lacked elegance, they have at least shown that with appropriate levels of chaptalisation (that is the addition of sugar to the fermenting wine), wines with commercially acceptable flavour levels can be made.

RHINE RIESLING
In theory, at least, this should produce wines as good as — if not better than — Pinot Noir. Part of the problem (if there is one) lies with the variety's lack of allure, and part with the fact that ironclad discipline and first rate winery equipment, not great imagination or flair, are required to make great Riesling. For all that, Giesen, St Helena (with one or two lovely botrytised wines) and Torlesse have done well enough to give some support to the theory. The wines tend to be delicate, fine and steely (unless botrytis intervenes), and age well, though not spectacularly.

OTHER WHITE WINES
Pinot Blanc may be a variety for the future: St Helena has produced several rich, mouthfilling wines with that typical slippery texture of the variety at its best. Pinot Gris is produced by several makers (and given various names including Rulander), usually with some residual sugar — and Müller-Thurgau likewise.

OTHER RED WINES
Giesen is the principal contributor with some worthwhile Cabernet Sauvignon dominant blends.

ABOVE: *George Thompson's tools of the trade: barrel making and reconditioning is an art which cannot be allowed to die.*

WINERIES OF THE CANTERBURY REGION

AMBERLEY ESTATE   CB-B
Reserve Road RD 1
Amberley   (0504) 48 409
(PO Box 81, Amberley)
Established   1979
Winemaker   Jeremy Prater
Production   1000 cases
Principal Wines   Müller-Thurgau, Riesling
Sylvaner, Gewurztraminer, Rhine Riesling,
Chardonnay, Sauvignon Blanc and Pinot Noir.
Best Vintages   Not rated.
Owner-winemaker Jeremy Prater learnt
winemaking in Europe, working in Germany,
France and Switzerland (where he gained
diplomas in viticulture and oenology through
the Swiss Federal College) before returning to
New Zealand to work for Montana. The white
wines have been of modest quality, but an
essency, strawberry flavoured Pinot Noir from
1989 gave further support for the potential of
the district for this variety.

GIESEN   CB-CB
Burnham School Road
Burnham, Canterbury (03) 25 6729
Established   1981
Winemaker   Marcel Giesen
Production   2000 cases but increasing.
Principal Wines   Chardonnay, Fumé Blanc,
Riesling Dry, Riesling Medium, Müller-
Thurgau, Pinot Noir, Cabernet Savignon and
Méthode Champenoise Blanc de Blanc.
Best Vintages   Not rated.

Summer by Henry Hope
Canterbury
Gewürztraminer
Alc.   Medium   750 ml
10.3%
by Vol.   1989
GIESEN WINE ESTATE
Christchurch, New Zealand

The brothers Giesen — Theo, Alex and Marcel
— emigrated from Germany at the end of the
1970's to escape overcrowding and to find open
spaces, which they have successfully done in
their large vineyard south of Canterbury. With
no prior experience in viticulture or
winemaking, the early plantings and early wines

had their share of problems, but quality has
become much better and more consistent in
recent years, with Rhine Riesling consistently
showing fine, steely flavour and a 1986 Cabernet
Sauvignon blend surprising with its strength of
flavour. Giesen is also noted for its colourful
labels and aggressive marketing and promotion.

OMIHI HILLS VINEYARD   NR
Reeces Road
Omihi
North Canterbury   (0504) 45 898
Established   1984
Winemaker   Dany Schuster
Production   2000 cases
Principal Wines   Chardonnay and Pinot
Noir.
Best Vintages   Not yet rated.

PINOT NOIR
Daniel Schuster
Alc.13% Vol.   750ml.
Omihi Hills Vineyard Canterbury New Zealand

Dany Schuster is an engaging scarlet pimpernel
of the wine industry. Austrian born and German
trained, with early experience in South Africa,
California, Oregon, France and Australia, he has
now spread his wings to become a significant
viticultural adviser in the Napa Valley of
California while simultaneously establishing
Netherwood Farm. He made his mark in New
Zealand by producing the early St Helena Pinot
Noirs and signalling that this district may
conceivably produce the finest of all New
Zealand wines from this variety. This is
Schuster's personal Holy Grail, and the first
wines from his own vineyard will be watched
with great interest. The limestone soils and
northerly aspect of Omihi Hills Vineyard would
appear to offer excellent growing conditions for
both Chardonnay and Pinot Noir. The first
commercial releases (under the Netherwood
label) were made from grapes purchased in
Marlborough, and are not indicative of future
style.

ST HELENA   CB-CB
Coutts Island RD
Christchurch   (032) 38 202
Established   1978
Winemaker   Mark Rattray
Production   In excess of 5000 cases.

Principal Wines   Chardonnay, Rhine Riesling
and Pinot Noir.
Best Vintages   W and R 1982, '84, '85, '88

1989
CANTERBURY
Pinot Noir
12.5% vol.   *St Helena*   e75cl
Produced & Bottled by ST. HELENA WINE ESTATE
COUTTS ISLAND, CHRISTCHURCH, NEW ZEALAND
PRODUCT OF NEW ZEALAND

Controversy has never been far from St Helena
and its Pinot Noir: first came the extraordinary
(by the standards of their time) Pinot Noirs
made by Dany Schuster in the early 1980s; then
a period of eclipse following his departure; and
more recently something of a return to form
with the 1988 vintage.

TORLESSE   C-CB
Jowers Road
West Melton (034) 26 086
Established   1987
Winemaker   David Moore
Production   3500 cases
Principal Wines   Müller-Thurgau, Rhine
Riesling, Pinot Gris, Gewurztraminer,
Chardonnay, Chello and Pinot Noir.
Best Vintages   W and R 1987, '89
Torlesse has made a solid if unspectacular start,
with Rhine Riesling showing the greatest
consistency, and a 1989 Pinot Noir having good
fruit potential under rather indifferent oak.

OTHER WINERIES

GLENMARK   CB-B
State Highway 1
Waipara 1 (0504) 46 828

LARCOMB   NR
RD 5
Christchurch (034) 78 909

WAIPARA SPRINGS   NR
Waipara Springs Vineyard
RD 3
Amberley (0504) 46 710

SOUTH ISLAND

CENTRAL OTAGO

It is hard to imagine a region which could more comprehensively challenge the usefulness of climatic statistics. If one were to accept at face value the Queenstown HDD summation of 672 and the MJT of 15.6°C, grapegrowing would appear to be impossible. In fact this is by no means the situation.

The reasons why this is the fastest growing wine region in New Zealand are both numerous and complex. First is the tremendous variation in the terrain of this spectacularly beautiful district, roughly centred around Queenstown. There are mezoclimates that lead to heat summations twice that registered in Queenstown: Rippon Vineyard on the shores of Lake Wanaka has its own weather station which shows summations of up to 1350 HDD, although there is yearly variation on that figure.

The second and third reasons are linked: the rainfall is winter/spring dominant, but varies from an exceptionally low 400 millimetres at Gibbston Valley to 625 millimetres at Wanaka (making irrigation essential). So not only is summer cloud a rare phenomenon, but there are very long summer sunshine hours — in this most southerly wine growing region in the world (at a latitude of 44°42'S). The method of compilation of the HDD summation does not allow for this, while sunshine hours do not of themselves indicate temperature. Thus the third reason is the abnormally high number of hours in which the temperature is over 15°C, indeed over 20°C, in the months of December, January and February.

The fourth factor is again linked to the preceding elements: during the summer months this is a very warm area, due in part to its continentality. Daytime temperatures over 30°C are quite common — far removed from the widespread perception of the area as only one step removed from the Antarctic.

The final saving grace is unrelated to climate or topography, it is the tremendous volume of tourist traffic which visits the region year round, attracted by its superb and ever-varied scenery, winter skiing, summer trout fishing and a host of other activities and attractions. Very often it is the wine industry which creates the tourism (the Hunter Valley is a prime example), but for once the newly emerging wineries will be able to benefit from already-existing tourist demand.

For all that, and while it is expected that by 1991 there will be over 60 hectares of vineyards in Central Otago (making it a larger winegrowing region than Nelson), it will be a decade or more before the final potential of the region is likely to be known. Central to this learning process will be the discovery of which varieties are most suited to each vineyard site: the answers may well be different for each individual site.

For while the central 90 days of the growing period is warm, the overall growing season is short. Both spring and autumn frosts mean sites have to be chosen with care, while strong winds — a problem in many parts of New Zealand — can inhibit summer growth and cause havoc during flowering.

The cold nights common even in the height of summer lead to the retention of high acid levels. This phenomenon might be welcome in a longer growing season regime but are a mixed blessing here.

What is known so far is that not all varieties — even varieties such as Rhine Riesling — will fully ripen in the Central Otago climate. In all of the white wines of Gibbston Valley wines there is an underlying chalky/honeysuckle character, which is reminiscent of youthful Chenin Blanc from a medium year in Vouvray (Loire Valley, France), coupled with high acidity suggesting an imperfect taste ripening, whatever the chemical analysis of the wine may be.

Chardonnay and Pinot Noir are obvious choices of grape varieties to grow in such conditions: Chard Farm and Rippon Vineyard have both produced Chardonnays of substance and style. Pinot Noir is a difficult variety anywhere, but the schist rock and silt soils which predominate certainly appear compatible with the variety. The young band of winemakers are still coming to grips with the variety in the winery, but the base is there.

FACING PAGE: *The first bunches appear after budburst almost as quickly as the first leaves.*

ABOVE: *The typically compact bunches of Pinot Noir.*

The Rhine Riesling of the Central Otago region produces an austere wine in its youth, but the 1990 Rippon is a very clean wine with a touch of residual sugar giving balance, while a 1987 Gibbston Valley Rhine Riesling tasted in December 1990 showed excellent bottle-developed characters. Gewurztraminer fares even better than the Rhine Riesling, with Taramea and Rippon both producing wines with strong varietal character.

Sauvignon Blanc presents the usual problems in the vineyard, but Rippon and Gibbston Valley have both produced wines which suggests perseverance with the variety will be worthwhile. Pinot Gris is as yet only sparingly grown, but is certainly a variety to watch, while the ubiquitous Müller-Thurgau performs adequately.

Cabernet Sauvignon and Shiraz have both been grown and have matured to acceptable sugar levels: a wonderfully spicy Cabernet Shiraz blend from Rippon suggests Shiraz could be a dark horse, but Cabernet Sauvignon seems likely to always have a strong herbaceous aspect and is unlikely to stand the test of time.

Dr Richard Smart (see page 332) claimed that Central Otago was one of the country's most exciting wine regions. Romeo Bragato (a hundred years ago) and research oenologist Dr Rainer Eschenbruch (currently) both gave the region their seal of approval. For what it is worth, I now add mine.

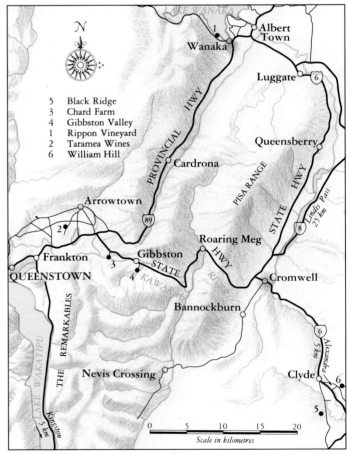

5 Black Ridge
3 Chard Farm
4 Gibbston Valley
1 Rippon Vineyard
2 Taramea Wines
6 William Hill

ABOVE: *Chard Farm challenges the view that New Zealand's viticulturists have an easy time of it.*

WINERIES OF THE CENTRAL OTAGO REGION

CHARD FARM   NR
Gibbston RD2
Queenstown   (03) 442 6110
Established   1987
Winemaker   Rob Hay
Production   300 cases
Principal Wines   Chardonnay and Pinot
Noir, with other wines to be progressively
introduced to the market.
Best Vintages   To early to assess.

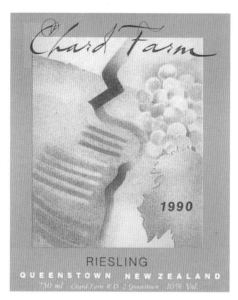

Brothers Robert and Grey Hay come from the
Nelson district. Having obtained his Bachelor of
Science Degree from Otago University, Rob Hay
spent 3 years working in Germany as a
winemaker, before returning to New Zealand.
His research convinced him that Central Otago
could produce wines of great elegance and
intensity, which led to the establishment of their
8 ha vineyards. Rob Hay is currently the winemaker at Gibbston Valley, but the brothers plan
to open their own winery and cellar door sales
area in the near future.

GIBBSTON VALLEY   CB-B
Gibbston RD2
Queenstown   (03) 442 6113
Established   1981
Winemaker   Rob Hay
Production   2500 cases
Principal Wines   Rhine Riesling, Riesling
Traminer, Pinot Gris, Sauvignon Blanc,
Gewurztraminer, Waitiri White, Ryecroft Red
and PinotNoir.
Best Vintages   **W** and **R** 1987, '89
Under the driving force of Irish-born former
television journalist Alan Brady, Gibbston Valley
has become a public company, and the best part
of one million dollars has been invested in the
winery, restaurant and cellar door sales facility.

Production is intended to increase to over 6000
cases in the near future, with grapes being
supplied by growers throughout the Gibbston
Valley subdistrict and elsewhere in Central
Otago. While the facilities are unashamedly
aimed at the tourist trade, Brady is committed
to the production of quality wine from Otago
grapes. The venture will surely succeed, but it
remains to be seen precisely how the sourcing
and marketing of the wine will develop.

RIPPON VINEYARD   BA-B
Mt Aspiring Road
Wanaka   (03) 443 8084
Established   1975
Winemaker   Rudi Bauer
Production   1000 cases
Principal Wines   Rhine Riesling, Chard-
onnay, Fumé Blanc, Osteiner, Müller-Thurgau,
Pinot Gris and Pinot Noir.
Best Vintages   **W** and **R** 1989, '90
Rippon is setting the pace in terms of wine
quality in the Central Otago region. Rudi Bauer,
with winemaking degrees from both Austria and
Germany, is repaying the very substantial
investment which owners Rolfe and Lois Mills
have made in this beautifully situated vineyard
and winery on the shores of Lake Wanaka. The
current 4 ha are about to be trebled, and a second
(new) winery erected for the 1993 vintage. A
winery to watch, and watch with great interest.

TARAMEA WINES   CB-CB
Speargrass Flat Road
RD 1 Queenstown (03) 442 1453
Established   1982
Winemakers   Ann Pinckney,
                   Michael Wolter
Production   300 cases
Principal Wines   Müller-Thurgau, Gewurztraminer and Rhine Riesling.
Best Vintages   **W** and **R** 1987, '88
Taramea Wines is the smallest of the four
wineries, which for a while made the wine under
contract for Gibbston Valley. The limited range
of white wines produced in small quantities is
pleasant, with the Gewurztraminer in particular
showing good varietal character. Frost has,
however, been a problem for the vineyard in
some years.

OTHER WINERIES

BLACK RIDGE   NR
Connroys Gully Road
RD1 Alexandra (03) 449 2059

WILLIAM HILL VINEYARD   NR
Dunstan Road
RD2 Alexandra (03) 448 8436

*ABOVE: Rolfe and Lois Mills of Rippon Vineyard, with winemaker
Rudi Bauer and assistant.*

INDEX

ings

Matawhero Vineyard 329, 333
Matua Valley 20, 312, 316
Maxwell 238
Maxwell, Ken & Mark 238
May, Brother John 211
Mazuran, George 311
Mazuran's 318
McAlister Vineyards 160
McCall, Lindsay 133
McCallum, Dr Neil 338, 338
McClarens on the Lake 241
McDonald, Tom 323
McDonald Winery 20, 315, 323, 327
McGuigan, Brian 55
McGuigan, Neil 51
McIntyre, Dr Richard 133
McIvor Creek 95
McKenna, Larry 337-8
McKenzie, Ian 80, 116, 119, 161, 190, 228
McLaren Vale 233
McLeod, Jim 321
McMahon, Peter 170
McManus Wines 77
McPherson, Rod 293
McRae, Ian 67, 69-70
McRae, Michael 118
McWilliam, B.K. 77
McWilliam, Glen P. 73, 77
McWilliam, L.W. 77
McWilliam, Max 77
McWilliams 14, 35, 42, 73, 77, 79, 323
    Mount Pleasant 21, 51, 51
Meadowbank 303
Melton, Graeme 198
Merlen 352-3
Merrill, Geoff 236, 238, 238
Merrivale 241
Michelton 97-9, 102-3
Middlebrook 241
Middleton, Dr John 169
Mildara 20, 140, 159, 221
Mildura Vineyard 140
Mills, Rolfe & Lois 361
Millstone Wines 55
Millton, James 333
Millton Vineyard 329, 331, 333, 333
Milne, Kim 319, 319
Mintaro Cellars 211
Miramar 67, 70
Miranda 77
Miranda, Lou 77
Mission Vineyards 321, 326
Mitchell 211
Mitchell, David 167
Mitchelton 99, 103
Molloy, Dr Tony 319, 319
Molly Morgan 55
Monbulk Winery 171
Mondavi, Robert 258
Monichino 141

Monichino, Carlo 141
Montana 15, 20, 314-5, 318, 329, 347, 350, 353
    Brancott Estate 351, 342-3
Montara 21, 115, 118, 119
Monten, John 211
Montgomery, Elise 327
Montrose 67, 71
Moody, Robin 240
Moondah Brook Estate 278
Mooney, Paul 326
Moore, David 357
Moorebank Winery 55
Moorilla Estate 21, 296-7, 303
Moorooduc Estate 133
Morlaes, Christian 263, 279
Morris 145, 151
Morris, David 200
Morris, Mick 151
Morrish, Rodney 155
Morrisons 263
Morton Estate 15, 306, 340
Moss Brothers 263
Moss Wood 261
Mount Alexander Vineyard 95
Mount Anakie 105
Mount Avoca 154-5
Mount Chalambar 115, 118-19
Mount Dangar 58
Mount Duneed 110
Mount Helen 103
Mount Horrocks 211
Mount Hurtle 233, 238
Mount Ida 94-5
Mount Ilford 71
Mount Langi Ghiran 115, 119
Mount Magnus 293
Mount Mary 163, 169-70
Mount Ophir 143, 145
Mount Prior 151
Mount View Estate 55
Mount Vincent Meadery 71
Mountadam 21, 175, 175, 177, 179, 183, 183
Mountain Creek Vineyard 155
Mountarrow 62
Mowatt, Reginald 116
Mrs Douglas 233
Mudgee Wines 71
Mugford, Keith 261, 261
Murphy, Tony 79, 83
Murray, Sir Brian 286
Murray Robson Wines 52
Murray Valley Wines 140
Murrindindi Vineyards 158, 160
Murrumbateman Winery 287

Nairn, William 271
Neudorf 348, 353
Newman, Frank 191
Newton, Tom 228, 236, 240
Ngatarawa 322, 326

Niccol, Chris 83
Nicholson River Winery 160
Nioka Ridge Vineyard 79, 83
Nobilo, Nick 316
Nobilo Vintners 316-7
Noon, David 239
Noon's 239
Norman, David 201
Norman's 238
Notley Gorge 302

O

O'Callaghan, Robert 200
O'Keefe, Gregory 236, 239
O'Leary, David 228, 236, 240
O'Shea, Maurice 21, 247
Oakridge Estate 170
Oakvale 52
Oatley, Bob 60, 60
Obst, Stephen 200
Old Barn 203
Old Caves Winery 293
Old Hill Vineyard 51
Old Penola Estate Vineyard 219
Olive Farm 244, 273, 278-9, 279
Omihi Hills Vineyard 22, 354, 355, 357
Omrah Vineyard 244, 249
Orlando 67, 73, 200, 202, 226
    Steingarten 183
Osicka 86, 159
Osicka, Paul 97, 103

P

Pacific 318
Padthaway Estate 226-8, 228
Pallister Estate 338
Pannell, Dr Bill 257
Panorama Vineyard 303
Paringa Estate 133
Parker 333
Parsons, Denis 293
Pask, C J 326-7
Passing Clouds 95
Paton, Clive 338
Patrick, Vic 218, 218
Patritti Wines 190
Pattie, Phyllis 338
Paul, Robert 69, 71
Paul Conti 271
Paul Osicka 103
Paulett, Neil 210
Pauletts 211
Paull, Jane 240
Peace, Andrew 140
Peacock Hill 55
Pearce, David 352
Pearson, James 211
Peel Estate 172
Penfolds 200, 221
    Wybong Winery 60

Peninsula Estate Winery 133, 310
Penley Estate 223
Penowarra 223
Penworthman Cellars 213
Peppers Creek 55
Petaluma 176, 179, 180-1, 184, 185, 211, 221
Peter Lehmann 200
Peterkin, Michael 261
Peterson, Colin 50
Petersons Winery 44, 44, 47, 52
Pewsey Vale 185
Pewsey Valley 13
Pfieffer 151
Pfieffer, Chris 151
Phillips' Goulburn Valley Winery 141
Piccadilly Fields 179
Pierlot, Charles 116
Pierro 261
Piesse Brook 267
Pieter Van Gent 71
Pike, Neil 211
Pikes Polish Hill River Estate 208, 211
Pinckney, Anne 361
Pinelli Wines 279
Pinney, Graham 132
Pipers Brook Vineyard 21, 296, 297, 300-2, 337
Pirie, Dr Andrew 300, 300-3, 337
Pirramimma 233, 239
Plantagenet 253
Platt, Barry 71
Platt's 71
Pleasant Valley 308, 318
Pokolbin Estate 55
Porter, Dominique 155
Pothana Vineyard 55
Potter, Newton 50
Potts, Michael 241
Potts Beasdale 233
Powercourt Vineyards 302
Prater, Jeremy 357
Pratten, Dr Peter 270
Preece, Colin 116
Price, Eddie 151
Price, Phil 83
Pridham, Ursula 238
Primo Estate 189, 190
Prince, Alain le 54
Prince Albert 110
Proud, Chris 210
Purbrick, Alister 100-2
Purbrick, Eric & Reginald 100-1, 101

Q

Quarisa, G. 77
Quealy, Kathleen 132, 170
Queen Adelaide 190
Quelltaler Vineyards 208

R

Randall, Warren 118, 236
Ranzau 353
Rattray, Mark 357
Reads 151
Rebecca Vineyards 303
Redbank 154-5
Redgate 263
Redman 215
Redman, Bruce 221
Redman family 215
Reed, Gary 52
Reed, Stephen 94
Renmano 13, 20, 189
Reynolds Yarraman Vineyard 58, 62-3
Revelry 279
Revington Vineyard 329
Reynell, John 231
Reynella 233-4
Reynolds Yarraman 63
Reynolds, Jon 62, 63
Ribbon Vale Estate 263
Richard Hamilton 239
Richardson, Richard 302
Richmond Grove 52-3
Riddoch, John 221
Ridge Wines 223
Riek, Dr Edgar 286
Riggs, Ben 240
Riggs, Iain 50, 50
Rippon Vineyard 361, 359
Ritchie, Rosalind 160, 160
Riverina Wines 77
Robb, Neill 155
Robert Hamilton & Son 185
Roberto's Winery 83
Roberts, Bob 67, 70
Robertson, David 67, 69, 71, 71
Robertson, Mark 316
Robertson, Peter 79, 326
Robinsons Family Vineyard 291, 293
Robinvale Wines 140
Robson, Murray 52
Rochcombe Vineyard 302-3
Rochford Winery 123, 125
Rockford 195, 195, 200-1
Roe, Tony 279
Romavilla 293
Romsey Vineyards 123, 125
Rongopai 340
Rosemount Estate 37, 43, 56, 59, 57-61, 61, 63, 80, 221
Rosenberg Cellars 213
Rosetto 77
Rosewhite 151
Roseworthy 201
Ross Mclaren Estate 241
Ross, Lindsay 94
Rothbury Estate 14, 48-9, 53, 53, 58, 79
Rotherhythe 302

Rouge Homme 215, 223
Rovalley 203
Rowe, Tony 263
Roxburgh Vineyard 60
Royal, Tony 119
Ruby Bay Wines 344, 353
Rumbalara 293
Ryan, Phillip 51
Ryecroft 233, 239
Rymill Wines 223
Ryrie, Donald 166

S

Sacred Hill 327
Saddlers Creek 55
Salsbury Estate 140
Saltram 195, 201
Samphire Wines 185
San Bernadino 77
Sandalford 244, 263, 274, 279
Sandhills Vineyard 83
Saxon Vale 53
Scapin, Robert 190
Scarborough, Ian 52-3
Scarborough Wines 40-1, 41, 53
Scarp Valley 265, 267
Scarpantoni, Domenico 239
Scarpantoni Estates 239
Schapera, Steven 267
Scholz, Peter 200
Schrapel, Robert & Geoff 198
Schubert, Max 21, 93, 196, 196-7
Schulz, Peter 102
Schuster, Dany 22, 357
Scotchmans Hill 110
Scudamore-Smith, Peter 293
Seaview Vineyard 116, 240, 172-3, 172-3
Sefton, Daryl & Nini 105-6, 110
Seifried Estate Vineyard 353, 353
Selaks 15, 317, 351
Seldom Seen Vineyard 71
Seppelt 13, 43, 80, 86, 113, 115-7, 119, 153, 157, 159, 179, 194, 194,-5, 201-2, 223, 224, 225, 227-8, 231, 233
   Great Western 112, 116-7, 119
   Karl Seppelt Grand Cru Estate 183
   Partalunga 185
Seppelt, J.E. 195
Serenella Estate 58, 63
Settlement Wine Company 241
Settlers Creek 71
Sevenhill 211, 213
Seville Estate 162, 162-3, 170, 170
Shanmugan, Shan & Turid 170
Shantell 170
Shaw, Philip 37, 60, 63, 221
Sheddon, Bill 50
Shemarin 253

Sheppard, Mark 125
Sheridan Wines 63
Shields, Barry 52
Shoreham Vale 133
Shottesbrooke 240
Silkman, Greg 54
Silos 83
Simes, John 315
Simon Whitlam 50, 53
Simons Wine 287
Sissingh, Gerry 223
Skillogalee Wines 213
Smart, Dr Richard 332, 332, 360
Smith, Andrew Sutherland 148
Sobels Winery 55
Soler, Joseph 306
Soljans 318
Springvale 303
Squance, Kevin 263
St Francis 239
St George Estate 327
St Gregory's Vineyard 161
St Hallett 201
St Helena 355, 357
St Huberts 165-7, 170
St Jerome 318
St Leonards 17, 145, 151
St Matthias 302, 302
St Neot's Estate 133
St Nesbit 20, 319
Stafford Ridge 179, 185
Stanley, Lindsay 190
Stanley Leasingham 206-7, 234
Stanton Killeen 151
Steer, Peter 171
Stein, Robert 71
Stein's 71
Stenbens, Wayne 220
Stone Ridge 293
Stonecroft 327
Stoneleigh Vineyard 25, 25, 346
Stoney Vineyard 298, 303
Stoneyridge Vineyard 313
Stoniers Merrick 129, 133
Stonyridge 20, 319, 347
Summerfield 154-5
Summerfield, Ian L. 155
Sunnycliff Estates 140
Sutherland 53
Sutherland, Neil 53
Symes, John 318

T

Tahbilk Vineyard 97-8, 100-1
Talijancich 274, 279
Talijancich, Peter & James 279
Tallara 71
Taltarni 153-4, 154-5, 297
Tamburlaine Vineyard 47, 54
Tanami Red Wines 241
Tanglewood Downs 133
Taradale 321
Taramea Wines 361

Tarchalice 203
Tarcoola 110
Tarrawarra 170
Tatachilla 233
Taylor, Alister 335
Taylors 213
Te Kairanga 335, 338
Te Mata Estate 20, 306, 324-5, 325, 327, 347
Te Whare Ra 348, 353
Terrace Vale 54
Thalgara Estate 55
Thistle Hill 65, 65, 67, 71, 71
Thomas, Gill 271
Thomas, Glen 353
Thomas, Wayne 240
Thomas Fernhill Estate 240
Thomas Hardy 13, 225, 227-8, 234-5, 234-5, 240
Thomas Wines 271
Thompson, George 349, 356
Thompson, John 157
Thompson, Viv 118, 140
Thumm, Hermann 198
Tierney, David 140
Tilba Valley 83
Tim Adams 213
Tim Knappstein Wines 208, 213
Tingle-wood Wines 247, 253
Tinglewood 247
Tinlins Winery 241
Tinson, Harry and Catherine 149
Tisdall 141
Tizzana 83
Toccaciu, Pat 220
Tollana 202
Tolley, Andrew 213
Tolley, Chris 190-1
Tolley Pedare 189, 190-1, 203, 226
Tolpuddle Vineyards 297, 303
Tonkin, Phillip 241
Torlesse 357
Torresan Estate 241
Totara 340
Trentham Estate 79, 83
Trott, Greg 240
Tuerong Estate Vineyard 133
Tulloch 54
Tumbarumba 21
Tuminello, Paul 69
Tunnel Hill 171
Turnbull, Mark 201
Twin Hills 279
Twin Valley Estate 202
Tyrell, Murray 37, 47, 54, 54-5
Tyrells 14, 37, 47, 54-5, 58, 314
Tyrer, Ian 252

U

Ulinger, Bill & Paul 263
Uplands Estate 303

PHOTOGRAPHIC CREDITS

All photographs in this volume were provided by Oliver Strewe, except as detailed below.

l = left; r = right; t = top; b = below; i = inset.

Greg Buchanan/Department of Agriculture: pages 108, 109
Joe Filshie: page 45
Courtesy of James Halliday: pages 217, 360
Houghton: page 277
Phillip Millin: page 332
Courtesy of Jane Mitchell: page 206
Courtesy of Montana: page 315
Courtesy of Rippon Vineyard: page 361
Linda Russo/Orlando Wines: page 150
George Seper: pages 72, 75, 84 i, 84-5, 86, 87, 88 i, 93, 94, 96, 99, 100, 101, 102, 103, 104, 112, 113, 115, 116, 117, 118, 119, 120, 120 i, 122, 123, 125, 129 t, 129 b, 131, 132, 135, 137, 139, 142, 146, 147, 152, 153, 154, 156, 160 l, 160 r, 161, 162, 162 i, 165, 166, 167, 168, 170, 171, 175, 176, 176 i, 180, 181, 183, 184, 186, 186 i, 188, 189, 191, 192, 192 i, 194, 195, 196, 198, 199, 201, 202 t, 202 b, 203, 204, 204 i, 209, 210, 212, 213, 264 i, 294 i, 294-5, 297, 299, 300, 301
Courtesy of St Matthias: page 302
Grenville Turner/Wildlight: page 70 b
Courtesy of Wirra Wirra Vineyards: page 240
Courtesy of Wynns Coonawarra Estate: page 223 r

Illustrations: Jenny Phillips
Diagrams: Mike Gorman/Russell Jeffrey
Maps: Mike Gorman/Cartoscope Pty Ltd